Regions and Powers

The Structure of International Security

This book develops the idea that, since decolonisation, regional patterns of security have become more prominent in international politics. The authors combine an operational theory of regional security with an empirical application across the whole of the international system. Individual chapters cover Africa, the Balkans, CIS-Europe, East Asia, EU-Europe, the Middle East, North America, South America, and South Asia. The main focus is on the post-Cold War period, but the history of each regional security complex is traced back to its beginnings. By relating the regional dynamics of security to current debates about the global power structure, the authors unfold a distinctive interpretation of post-Cold War international security, avoiding both the extreme oversimplifications of the unipolar view, and the extreme deterritorialisations of many globalist visions of a new world disorder. Their framework brings out the radical diversity of security dynamics in different parts of the world.

BARRY BUZAN is Professor of International Relations at the London School of Economics.

OLE WÆVER is Professor of International Relations at the Department of Political Science, University of Copenhagen.

CAMBRIDGE STUDIES IN INTERNATIONAL RELATIONS: 91

Regions and Powers

CAMBRIDGE STUDIES IN INTERNATIONAL RELATIONS

Series list continues after index

Regions and Powers

The Structure of International Security

Barry Buzan and Ole Wæver

CAMBRIDGE UNIVERSITY PRESS
Cambridge, New York, Melbourne, Madrid, Cape Town, Singapore, São Paulo

Cambridge University Press
The Edinburgh Building, Cambridge, CB2 8RU, UK

Published in the United States of America by Cambridge University Press, New York

www.cambridge.org
Information on this title: www.cambridge.org/9780521891110

First published 2003
Fifth printing 2007

Printed in the United Kingdom at the University Press, Cambridge

A catalogue record for this publication is available from the British Library

ISBN 978-0-521-81412-6 hardback
ISBN 978-0-521-89111-0 paperback

To Gerry Segal

Contents

Contents

Contents

Illustrations

Maps

Figure

Table

Boxes

xiv

Preface

Our previous book, *Security: A New Framework for Analysis,* laid the foundations for thinking about regional security in the context of a wider security agenda and a securitisation approach. It is that thread we pick up here. We sought to bring some clarity to the debate about the 'new' security by combining a sectoral approach to the wider security agenda with a constructivist ('securitisation') understanding of what separated 'security' from routine politics. We solved some specific theoretical problems related to the expanded concept of security and to an ensuing rethinking of the 'regional' character of security. We also addressed the tension in the current system between deterritorialising and territorialising processes. Briefly stated, the problem arose because regional security complex theory was developed primarily in relation to the dynamics of the political and military sectors, where, because threats in these sectors travel more easily over short distances than over long ones, distance clearly plays a role in producing regional security complexes. When the concept of security was extended to economic, environmental, and – the part we ourselves have previously contributed most to – identity-related ('societal') threats, doubts arose about whether security interdependence in these non-traditional sectors would take a regional form and, if it did, whether it would generate the same region across the sectors, or different regions according to the sector. It was thus necessary to build a conceptual apparatus able both to handle the extended concept of security and to avoid the 'everything is security' watering-down of the concept. On the basis of this narrower, technical work, we are ready to draw the complete picture in terms of both a general theory of regional security (with explicit links to mainstream theories of International Relations) and an application of it to all regions of the world. Whereas our previous book focused mainly on understanding securitisation by sectors, this one focuses mainly on levels. The two projects were originally conceptualised as one, and only became separated because the Thyssen Stiftung (rightly) thought that the whole was too ambitious.

The idea of regional security complexes was originally Buzan's, but has been much worked on by Wæver and is now part of the Copenhagen School's collective theoretical approach to security. We were attracted by the challenge of operationalising and applying our own theories. We hoped that plunging into empirical work would both provide a demonstration to others of how to use the theory and force us to sharpen up our conceptual thinking. In the latter aim we have not been disappointed. The success or failure of the former aim remains to be seen.

The division of labour was as follows. In part I, chapters 1 and 2 were first-drafted by Buzan. Chapter 3 was first-drafted by Wæver, drawing heavily on our earlier writings, and has been much reworked by both of us. To tackle the empirical work we divided up the world so that each of us got some areas we knew pretty well and some that were, to put it mildly, less familiar. Wæver first-drafted the sections on Europe and the Americas, and Buzan took Asia, and Africa and the Middle East. The conclusion chapters were a joint effort. Both of us have written extensively into the drafts of the other, and we have no hesitation in putting this forward as a single jointly authored text.

Very many people have contributed to this work in numerous ways, and we are grateful to all of them. Particular thanks go to the following. COPRI, and its directors Håkan Wiberg and Tarja Cronberg, provided a congenial environment in which to work and some crucial financial support. The Centre for the Study of Democracy (CSD) and the University of Westminster allowed Buzan the time to take on something as ambitious as this, which would not have been possible under the normal working conditions that now mark academic life in Britain. The Swedish Council for Research in the Humanities and Social Sciences awarded Buzan the Olof Palme visiting professorship for 1997–8, which allowed him to lay some of the foundations for this work, and the Peace and Development Research Institute, Gothenburg University (PADRIGU), was kind enough to act as host, and to share its extensive knowledge about regional security. Some final stages of Buzan's work were supported by the Economic and Social Research Council. The Department of Political Science at the University of Copenhagen – to which Ole Wæver moved during the work on this book – allowed him both to organise parts of his teaching around this project and to be partly 'bought out' to work on the project. The Danish Research Council for the Social Sciences (SSF) funded the project, which not only allowed us to travel to most of our regions for research, but also enabled us to hire consultants and research assistants, without which it is doubtful that we could have completed such a huge task. Our consultants – Kanti Bajpai, Christopher Clapham, Daniel Deudney, Espen Barth Eide, Pierre Hassner, Andrew Hurrell, Robert Jackson, Iver Neumann, James Piscatori, Jaap de Wilde – went through various drafts as well as the whole manuscript, and steered us through what were often for us rather uncharted waters. For most of the project our research assistant was Karen Lund Petersen, but for the last half of 2001 this role was taken by Trine Villumsen. Both were invaluable, and helped out in innumerable ways with unfailing patience and good humour. Morten Hansen handled impeccably the compilation of the final manuscript in the summer of 2002. Many people helped us to organise visits to regions: Amitav Acharya, John Ravenhill, Gowher Rizvi, Gautam Sen, and Ali Tajvidi all did more than the call of duty to assist Buzan. Muthiah Alagappa of the East–West Center in Hawaii, Rosemary Hollis of Chatham House, Christian-Peter Hanelt of the Bertelsmann Foundation, Rut Diamint of the Universidad Torcuato di Tella (Buenos Aires), Lena Jonson of the Swedish Institute for International Affairs, Seyyed Sajjadpour of the Institute for Political and International Studies in Tehran, and Ersel Aydınlı of the Center for Eurasian Strategic Studies (ASAM) in Ankara invited either or both of us to attend workshops or conferences that turned out to be very useful in shaping our ideas. Muthiah Alagappa, Thomas Diez, Rut Diamint Abdelwahab El-Affendi, Lene Hansen, Ulla Holm, David Jacobson, Pertti Joenniemi, Dietrich Jung, Işıl Kazan, Morten Kelstrup, Richard Little, Luis Lobo-Guerrero, William Lume, Arlene B. Tickner, Morten Valbjørn, and the late Gerald Segal read and commented on part, or in some cases all, of the manuscript at one stage or another, as did two anonymous referees for Cambridge University Press. Ole Wæver appreciates numerous helpful comments and suggestions from students who participated in the autumn 1999 seminar on 'regional security' in which an early version of the book was discussed or who did case studies inspired by this seminar and our evolving theory. Thanks for direct assistance from Vibeke Schou Pedersen (North America), Thomas Christensen (theory and ex-Soviet), and Kenneth S. Hansen (Balkans). Thanks also to Steve Smith and John Haslam for welcoming this project into the BISA/CUP series.

In the end, of course, the responsibility for the content of these pages is ours, but the book is also a testament to the spirit of intellectual cooperation and exchange in the academic world, without which it could not have been done, and would not have been worth doing. We dedicate the book to Gerry Segal, and hope it goes some way to meeting his call that theorists should take the real world more seriously.

Abbreviations

ABM	anti-ballistic missile
ACI	Andean Counterdrug Initiative
AIDS	Acquired Immune Deficiency Syndrome
AMU	Arab Maghreb Union
ANC	African National Congress (South Africa)
AOSIS	Alliance of Small Island States
APEC	Asia-Pacific Economic Cooperation
ARF	ASEAN Regional Forum
ARI	Andean Regional Initiative
ASEAN	Association of Southeast Asian Nations
AU	African Union
BJP	Bharatiya Janata Party (India)
BMD	ballistic missile defence
C3I	command, control, communications, and intelligence
CARICOM	Caribbean Common Market (Antigua and Barbuda, the Bahamas, Barbados, Belize, Dominica, Grenada, Guyana, Haiti, Jamaica, Montserrat, St Kitts and Nevis, St Lucia, St Vincent and the Grenadines, Suriname, and Trinidad and Tobago)
CB	chemical and biological (weapons)
CBM	confidence building measure
CCP	Chinese Communist Party
CIA	Central Intelligence Agency
CIS	Commonwealth of Independent States
COMECON	Council for Mutual Economic Aid Economic Union (from 1949 to 1991) of Albania, Bulgaria, Czechoslovakia, German Democratic Republic, Hungary, Poland, Romania, and Soviet Union; later

	without Albania, but with Cuba, Mongolia, and Vietnam
COPRI	Copenhagen Peace Research Institute
CPSU	Communist Party of the Soviet Union
CSA	Collective Security Agreement (of the Tashkent Treaty; members are Armenia, Belarus, Kazakhstan, Kyrgyzstan, Russia, and Tajikistan)
CSCAP	Council for Security Cooperation in Asia Pacific
CSCE	Conference on Security and Cooperation in Europe (OSCE since 1994)
CTBT	Comprehensive Test Ban Treaty
DEA	Drug Enforcement Agency
DOM	*départments d'outre mer* (French overseas departments)
DPP	Democratic Progressive Party (Taiwan)
DR Congo	Democratic Republic of Congo
EAEC	East Asian Economic Cooperation
ECOMOG	ECOWAS's cease-fire monitoring group
ECOWAS	Economic Community of West African States
ELF	Eritrean Liberation Front
ELN	National Liberation Army (Colombia)
EMU	Economic and Monetary Union (EU)
EPLF	Eritrean People's Liberation Front
EPRDF	Ethiopian People's Revolutionary Democratic Front
EU	European Union
FARC	Revolutionary Armed Forces of Colombia
FIS	Islamic Salvation Front (Algeria)
FMLN	Farabundo Martí National Liberation Front (El Salvador)
FNLA	National Front for the Liberation of Angola
FOL	forward operating location (USA)
FRELIMO	Liberation Front for Mozambique
FSB	Federal Security Service (Russia)
FTA	free trade agreement
FTAA	Free Trade Area of the Americas
FYROM	Former Yugoslav Republic of Macedonia
G8	Group of Eight (Canada, France, Germany, Italy, Japan, Russia, UK, USA)
GATT	General Agreement on Tariffs and Trade

GCC	Gulf Cooperation Council
GDP	gross domestic product
GNP	gross national product
GUAM	Alliance of Georgia, Ukraine, Azerbaijan, and Moldova
GUUAM	Alliance of Georgia, Ukraine, Uzbekistan, Azerbaijan, and Moldova
HIV	Human Immunodeficiency Virus
HT	Hizb ut-Tahrir
IAEA	International Atomic Energy Agency
IGAD	Intergovernmental Authority for Development (Horn of Africa)
IGO	intergovernmental organisation
IISS	International Institute for Strategic Studies (London)
IMF	International Monetary Fund
IMU	Islamic Movement of Uzbekistan
INGO	international non-governmental organisation
IR	the academic discipline of International Relations
ISDSC	Inter-State Defence and Security Committee (Southern Africa)
JSDF	Japan Self-Defence Forces
KEDO	Korean Energy Development Organization
LRA	Lord's Resistance Army (Uganda)
LTTE	Liberation Tigers of Tamil Eelam
MD	missile defence
MEK	Interstate Economic Committee (CIS)
Mercosur	the Common Market of the South (Southern Cone in South America)
MNC	multinational corporation
MPLA	Popular Movement for the Liberation of Angola
MQM	Muttahida Quami Movement (Pakistan)
MTCR	missile technology control regime
NAFTA	North American Free Trade Association
NATO	North Atlantic Treaty Organization
NCO	non-commissioned officer
NEPAD	New Partnership for Africa's Development
NGO	non-governmental organisation
NORAD	North American Aerospace Defense Command
NPT	Nonproliferation Treaty
NSC	National Security Council (USA)

NWS	nuclear weapons state
OAS	Organization of American States
OAU	Organization of African Unity
OECD	Organization for Economic Cooperation and Development
OSCE	Organization for Security and Co-operation in Europe
P5	the five permanent members of the UN Security Council (China, France, Russia, UK, USA)
PA	Palestinian Authority
PCW	post-Cold War
PfP	NATO's Partnership for Peace Programme
PKK	Kurdistan Workers' Party
PKO	peacekeeping operation
PLO	Palestine Liberation Organization
PPP	Pakistan People's Party
PRC	People's Republic of China
PRI	Institutional Revolutionary Party (Mexico)
R&D	research and development
RENAMO	Mozambican National Resistance
ROC	Republic of China, Taiwan
RPF	Rwandan Patriotic Front
RSC	regional security complex
RSCT	regional security complex theory
RUF	Revolutionary United Front (Sierra Leone)
SAARC	South Asian Association for Regional Cooperation
SADC	Southern African Development Community
SADCC	Southern African Development Coordination Conference
SAM	surface-to-air missile
SCO	Shanghai Cooperation Organization (China, Kazakhstan, Kyrgyzstan, Russia, Tajikistan, Uzbekistan)
SEA	Single European Act (EU)
SEATO	Southeast Asia Treaty Organization
SPLA	Sudan People's Liberation Army
SSM	surface-to-surface missile
SVR	Foreign Intelligence Service (Russia)
SWAPO	South-West Africa People's Organisation
TAFTA	Trans-Atlantic Free Trade Agreement
TIAR	Inter-American Treaty of Reciprocal Assistance

TMD	theatre missile defence
TPLF	Tigrayan People's Liberation Front (Ethiopia)
UAE	United Arab Emirates
UCK	Kosovan Liberation Army
UNITA	National Union for the Total Independence of Angola
UNOMIG	United Nations Observer Mission in Georgia
UNSC	United Nations Security Council
UNSCOM	United Nations Special Commission on Disarmament (Iraq)
UNTAC	United Nations Transitional Authority in Cambodia
WMD	weapons of mass destruction
WTO	World Trade Organization
ZANU	Zimbabwe African National Union
ZAPU	Zimbabwe African People's Union
ZOPFAN	zone of peace, freedom, and neutrality (in Southeast Asia)

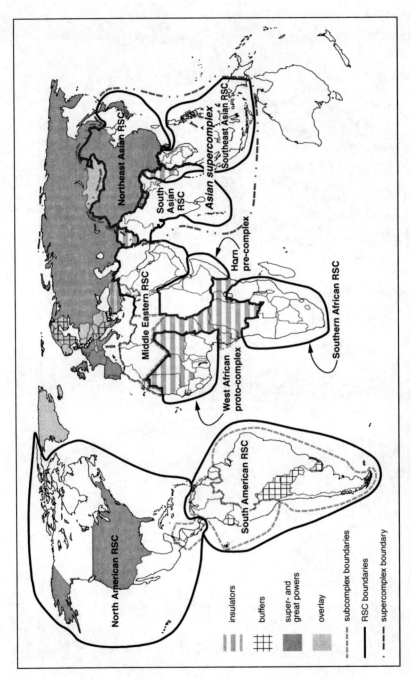

Map 1. Patterns of Regional Security During the Cold War

North American RSC

South American RSC

Northeast Asian RSC

South Asian RSC

Southeast Asian RSC

Asian supercomplex

Middle Eastern RSC

Horn pre-complex

West African proto-complex

Southern African RSC

insulators

buffers

super- and great powers

overlay

subcomplex boundaries

RSC boundaries

supercomplex boundary

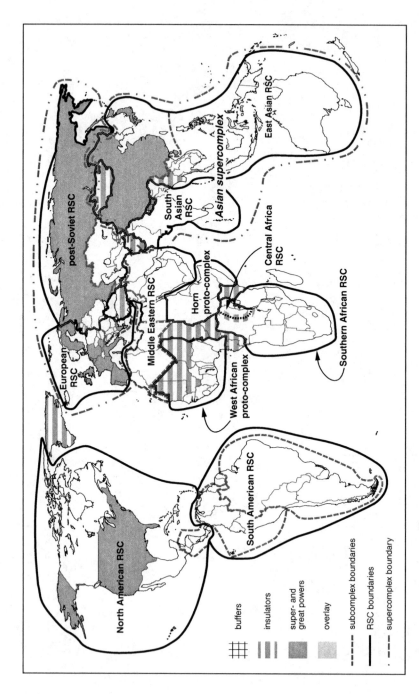

Map 2. Patterns of Regional Security Post-Cold War

Part I

Introduction: developing a regional approach to global security

Introduction

Almost nobody disputes that the end of the Cold War had a profound impact on the whole pattern of international security but, more than a decade after the transition, the character of the post-Cold War security order still remains hotly contested. This book explores the idea that, since decolonisation, the regional level of security has become both more autonomous and more prominent in international politics, and that the ending of the Cold War accelerated this process (Katzenstein 2000). This idea follows naturally from the ending of bipolarity. Without superpower rivalry intruding obsessively into all regions, local powers have more room for manoeuvre. For a decade after the ending of the Cold War, both the remaining superpower and the other great powers (China, EU, Japan, Russia) had less incentive, and displayed less will, to intervene in security affairs outside their own regions. The terrorist attack on the United States in 2001 may well trigger some reassertion of great power interventionism, but this is likely to be for quite narrow and specific purposes, and seems unlikely to recreate the general willingness to intervene abroad that was a feature of Cold War superpower rivalry. The relative autonomy of regional security constitutes a pattern of international security relations radically different from the rigid structure of superpower bipolarity that defined the Cold War. In our view, this pattern is not captured adequately by either 'unipolar' or 'multipolar' designations of the international system structure. Nor is it captured by the idea of 'globalisation' or by the dismal conclusion that the best that IR can do in conceptualising the security order of the post-Cold War world is to call it 'the new world disorder' (Carpenter 1991).

The argument in this book is that *regional security complex theory* (RSCT) enables one to understand this new structure and to evaluate the relative balance of power of, and mutual relationship within it between,

3

regionalising and globalising trends. RSCT distinguishes between the system level interplay of the global powers, whose capabilities enable them to transcend distance, and the subsystem level interplay of lesser powers whose main security environment is their local region. The central idea in RSCT is that, since most threats travel more easily over short distances than over long ones, security interdependence is normally patterned into regionally based clusters: security complexes. As Friedberg (1993–4: 5) puts it (echoing the Federalist Papers Nos. IV and VI; Hamilton et al. 1911): 'most states historically have been concerned primarily with the capabilities and intentions of their neighbours'. Processes of securitisation and thus the degree of security interdependence are more intense between the actors inside such complexes than they are between actors inside the complex and those outside it. Security complexes may well be extensively penetrated by the global powers, but their regional dynamics nonetheless have a substantial degree of autonomy from the patterns set by the global powers. To paint a proper portrait of global security, one needs to understand both of these levels independently, as well as the interaction between them.

RSCT uses a blend of materialist and constructivist approaches. On the materialist side it uses ideas of bounded territoriality and distribution of power that are close to those in neorealism. Its emphasis on the regional level is compatible with, and we think complementary to, neorealism's structural scheme, but it contradicts the tendency of most neorealist analysis to concentrate heavily on the global level structure. On the constructivist side, RSCT builds on the securitisation theory set out in our previous works (Buzan et al. 1998; Wæver 1995c), which focus on the political processes by which security issues get constituted. It thus breaks from neorealism by treating the distribution of power and the patterns of amity and enmity as essentially independent variables. Polarity may affect, but it does not determine, the character of security relations. The processes of securitisation are essentially open, and subject to influence by a host of factors. RSCT offers a conceptual framework that classifies security regions into a set of types, and so provides a basis for comparative studies in regional security. It also offers a theory with some powers of prediction, in the sense of being able to narrow the range of possible outcomes for given types of region. More on this in chapter 3.

In what follows, chapter 1 establishes the plausibility of a regional approach by looking at both the main perspectives on the structure of international security, and the history of regional security. Chapter 2 tackles the question of levels by investigating how we are to understand the structure of security at the global level, seeing this as a precondition for defining the regional one. Chapter 3 lays out a revised and updated version of RSCT, and relates it to system level polarity. This theory sets the frame for the rest of the book.

1 Theories and histories about the structure of contemporary international security

This chapter starts by sketching out the three main perspectives on the structure of international security. The second section gives a short history of regional security, and the third reflects on the legacies of that past for states and regions.

Three theoretical perspectives on the post-Cold War security order

The three principal theoretical perspectives on post-Cold War international security structure are neorealist, globalist, and regionalist. What do we mean by 'structure' in this context? We are using it in broadly Waltzian (1979) terms to mean the principles of arrangement of the parts in a system, and how the parts are differentiated from each other. But our range is wider than the neorealist formulation (though we incorporate it) because we want: (a) to look at structural perspectives other than the neorealist one; and (b) to privilege the regionalist perspective.

The neorealist perspective is widely understood and, since we will have more to say about it in chapter 2, does not need to be explained at length here. It is state-centric, and rests on an argument about power polarity: if not bipolarity, then necessarily either unipolarity or multipolarity (or some hybrid). This debate is about the distribution of material power in the international system, which in neorealism determines the global political (and thereby also security) structure, and the interplay of this with balance-of-power logic. Its interpretation of the post-Cold War structure of international security assumes that there has been a change of power structure at the global level (the end of bipolarity), and its concern is to identify the nature of that change in order to infer the security consequences. Neorealism does not question the primacy of the global level,

6

so its search for change is confined to a narrow range of options within that level: unipolarity or multipolarity.

The globalist perspective (by which we mean acceptance of the view usually labelled 'globalisation') is generally understood to be the antithesis of realism's (and neorealism's) statist, power-political understanding of international system structure. Globalisation is rooted mainly in cultural, transnational, and international political economy approaches. Perhaps its clearest guiding theme is the deterritorialisation of world politics (Held et al. 1999: 7–9; Woods 2000: 6; Scholte 2000: 2–3). In its stronger versions (whether Marxian or liberal), deterritorialisation sweeps all before it, taking the state, and the state system, off the centre stage of world politics (Held et al. 1999: 3–5). Milder versions leave the state and the state system in, but have lots of nonstate actors and systems operating across and outside state boundaries (Held et al. 1999: 7–9; Scholte 2000; Woods 2000; Clark 1999): 'territoriality and supraterritoriality coexist in complex interrelation' (Scholte 2000: 8); and 'Territorialization remains a check on globalization' (Clark 1999: 169). In terms of structure, the globalist position is clearer as an attack on neorealism's state-centric approach than as a statement of an explicit alternative. The global market or capitalism or various forms of world society probably best capture the underlying ideas of system structure in the globalist perspective, and the key point is rejection of the idea that an adequate sense of system structure can be found by privileging states.

Globalisation's hallmark is acknowledgement of the independent role of both transnational entities – corporations, non-governmental social and political organisations of many kinds – and intergovernmental organisations and regimes. Its focus is on how territorial sovereignty as the ordering principle for human activity has been redefined, and in some ways transcended, by networks of interaction that involve actors of many different kinds and at many different levels, and that feed off the huge technological and social improvements in the capacity for transportation and communication of nearly all types of goods, information, and ideas. The state is often a player in these networks, but it does not necessarily, or even usually, control them, and is increasingly enmeshed in and penetrated by them. Marxian and liberal versions of globalisation differ more in their normative perspectives than in their basic understanding of what globalisation means: here, as elsewhere, they are mirror images of the same phenomenon. Both see the macro-structure of the international system as taking a centre–periphery

7

(or 'rich world–poor world' or 'developed–developing') form, with a core of societies (or elites) controlling most of the capital, technology, information, and organisational and ideological resources in the system, and shaping the terms on which the periphery participates. In the Marxian view, this structure is fundamentally exploitative, unequal, unstable, and undesirable, whereas in the liberal one it is fundamentally progressive and developmental, and its tendencies towards instability, though serious, are not without institutional solutions.

It is not in our remit here to go into the entirety of the debate about globalisation or to take on its enormous literature. Our perspective is security, and as Cha (2000: 391, 394) notes there has not been much written about the links between globalisation and security, not least because the security effects of globalisation have been hard to distinguish from the more dramatic effects of the ending of the Cold War. Cha (2000: 397), Clark (1999: 107–26), Guehenno (1998–9), Scholte (2000: 207–33), and Zangl and Zürn (1999) all argue that globalisation is responsible for complicating the security agenda, while at the same time reducing the elements of control that underpin the security strategy options of states. Cha and Guehenno both think that globalisation increases the incentives for states to pursue more cooperative security policies, especially at the regional level, a line of thinking much reinforced by the responses to the attack on the United States in September 2001. Barkawi and Laffey (1999) even want to sweep away state-centric security analysis and replace it with a centre–periphery model. We are less interested in the academic debate about globalisation than in the real world responses to it. From our perspective, what matters most is whether and how either globalisation in general or specific aspects of it (e.g., financial flows, terrorism, migration, trade liberalisation) become securitised by the actors in the international system. If globalisation is seen and acted on as a threat by states and other actors in the system, then it plays alongside, and competes with, more traditional securitisations of neighbours or great powers or internal rivals. Then the global level is directly – not only indirectly – present in a constellation of securitisation.

This quite widespread real world security perspective on globalisation has two sides. The first highlights the dark side of the centre–periphery structure. It is the successor to a long line of ideas going back at least as far as Hobson and Lenin, all emphasising the unequal, exploitative, and coercive aspects of relations between centre and periphery: imperialism, colonialism, neo-colonialism, *dependencia*, cultural imperialism, anti-hegemonism, and suchlike. At the risk of oversimplifying, one can see these ideas as stemming from the perspective of the periphery, and reflecting its resentments about its relative powerlessness, underdevelopment, and vulnerability in relation to the centre. In one sense, they reflect concerns that the practice of economic liberalism is a major key to understanding what generates the wider international security agenda (Buzan and Wæver 1998; Scholte 2000: 207–33). At their most passionate, these ideas carry the accusation that the centre–periphery structure generated and maintains the weak position of the periphery for the benefit of the core, pointing to cases such as Zaire, Angola, and Iraq as evidence. This dark-side securitisation of globalisation is counterpointed by more upbeat liberal interpretations, more strongly rooted in the centre, which acknowledge the inequalities and disparities, but see the process of globalisation as the fastest and most efficient way to overcome them. In this view, globalisation should be a path to the steady erosion and eventual elimination of the traditional international security agenda (and in more radical liberal views also the state). The darlings of this perspective are South Korea, Taiwan, and Singapore, all of which have transformed themselves economically, and up to a point politically, within the embrace of globalisation. Its key great power targets are China and Russia, where the hope is that economic liberalisation (i.e., penetration by globalisation) will eventually generate political liberalisation and a lowering of threat perceptions. But even here there is a security dimension, mostly focused on the potential instabilities in the global trading and financial systems (Buzan et al. 1998: 95–117).

Typical securitisations from the non-liberal perspective on globalisation have been in the 'new' non-military areas of security. They have focused, *inter alia,* on the (in)stability and (in)equity of the liberal economic order, on the contradictions between the pursuit of capitalism and the sustainability of the planetary environment, and on the homogenising pressures of global (read 'Western', or 'American') culture and the threat this poses to other cultures, languages, and identities (Buzan et al. 1998: 71–140; Cable 1995; B. Crawford 1994; Arfi 1998; Stern 1995). During the 1990s, the globalisation perspective generated a more explicitly military-political securitisation, in the process creating an interesting conjuncture between itself and some strands of neorealist thinking. In this view, the periphery is threatened by two linked developments consequent on the collapse of bipolarity:

- The overwhelming military superiority of the West in general and the USA in particular, no longer balanced by a rival superpower.
- The collapse of the political space generated for the third world by superpower rivalry during the Cold War, and its replacement by a much more monolithic domination by the West. Without an ideological challenger within or adjacent to the core, the Western powers can impose much more demanding legal, social, financial, and political conditions on the periphery as the price of access to aid, trade, credit, recognition, and membership in various clubs ranging from NATO and the EU to the WTO. They can also wield increased pressure on states to conform to contested regimes (non-proliferation) or norms (democracy, human rights, anti-terrorism).

Seen in centre–periphery perspective, these developments mean that the centre has become much more cohesive and the international system much more hierarchical. It is hard not to notice how closely parallel this analysis runs to much of the unipolarist thinking within neorealism. In this perspective, globalisation is less an autonomous process and more an expression of US hegemony. The response to this development from those who feel threatened by it has been to take a position against hegemonism and in favour of developing a multipolar global power structure. Such views are prominent in the foreign policy rhetoric of China, India, Russia, Iran, Indonesia, Brazil, and up to a point France to name only the most outspoken exponents. Both the analysis and the cure link globalist and neorealist understandings of the post-Cold War security order.

The regionalist perspective is our chosen approach. We agree with Lake and Morgan (1997b: 6–7) that in the post-Cold War world 'the regional level stands more clearly on its own as the locus of conflict and cooperation for states and as the level of analysis for scholars seeking to explore contemporary security affairs', and we believe this to be true even though we use an understanding of security more open than their rather traditional, military one. This approach can be superficially seen as a post-Cold War focus rooted in two assumptions:

1. that the decline of superpower rivalry reduces the penetrative quality of global power interest in the rest of the world (Stein and Lobell 1997: 119–20; Lake 1997: 61); and

2. that most of the great powers in the post-Cold War international system are now 'lite powers' (Buzan and Segal 1996), meaning that their domestic dynamics pull them away from military engagement and strategic competition in the trouble spots of the world, leaving local states and societies to sort out their military-political relationships with less interference from great powers than before.

Our argument is that the regional level of security was also significant during the Cold War, and that except when global powers are extremely dominant, as they were during the imperial era, regional security dynamics will normally be a significant part of the overall constellation of security in the international system. We accept Lake and Morgan's (1997b: 11) call for security analysis 'to start with regions and employ a comparative approach', and think that this idea should be applied well beyond the immediate circumstances of the post-Cold War period.

The regionalist perspective contains elements of both neorealism and globalism, but gives priority to a lower level of analysis. Because both the neorealist and the regionalist approaches are rooted in territoriality and security, we see RSCT as complementary to the neorealist perspective on system structure, in a sense providing a fourth (regional) tier of structure. But our regional focus and even more our use of a constructivist understanding of security place us outside the neorealist project. Our relationship with the globalist perspective is, on the face of it, necessarily less close. To the extent that globalists start from an assumption of deterritorialisation, their approach is at the opposite end of the spectrum from ours. But this opposition is often more apparent than real. For one thing, globalists have not so far had much concern with security, and therefore are largely addressing a different agenda. For another, the moderate wing of globalists are keen, as are we, to emphasise the interplay between territoriality and deterritorialisation. It is, for example, already widely understood that many aspects of regionalisation, especially the more cooperative ones of regional economic groupings, are responses to globalisation (Buzan et al. 1998: 113–15; Katzenstein 1996b: 126–7; Hurrell 1995b: 53–8). Globalisation constructed as a threat will play a part in our analysis.

So, while we are not dismissive of the force of some of the globalist arguments, we do not see them as yet overriding the continued prominence of territoriality in the domain of security, whether in the form of states, nations, insurgency movements, or regions. Security is a distinctive realm in which the logic of territoriality continues to operate strongly. But non-territorial connections are also possible and some may emerge. Such non-territorial subsystems (see Buzan et al. 1998) are fully compatible with the meta-theory of securitisation and constellations, but they have to override the normal rule underpinning the territorialisation of security relations: that most threats travel more easily over short distances than over long ones. There are two obvious ways for that overriding to happen: (1) by a shift from more territorialised (e.g., military) to less territorialised (e.g., economic) threats; and/or (2) by a rise in levels of absolute power sufficient to enable more and more actors to ignore the constraints of distance. A good case can be made that both of these things are happening – and such arguments are part of the globalist position. But only if these developments become much more common and more evenly distributed than they are now would they begin to question the key element of our theory: that regional security complexes are a principal expected component of international security. We see it as a strength of the theory that it establishes the possibility of its own overturning, i.e., it specifies one of the developments that could annul it. The relevance of territorial versus non-territorial patterns of securitisation is an empirical question, which we leave open to be addressed by the chapters in parts II to V. We have designed our theory so that it can accommodate nonstate actors, and even allow them to be dominant. Although our theory features the regional level, it also incorporates other levels (global, interregional, local), and allows the particular circumstances of time and place to determine which level(s) dominate. The security constellation that we map in each case is one that covers all levels, although to varying degrees as appropriate to the case.

Many securitisation processes around the world (identity concerns in Cairo and Copenhagen, excessive supplies of black market weapons in Albania and Abkhazia, financial fears in Moscow and Malaysia, fears of terrorism in Uzbekistan and the USA, etc.) are in some essential ways caused by the bundle of developments captured in the term globalisation. Both the introversion of the 'lite' powers and the worry about American/Western hegemony are aspects of globalisation, and these can easily trigger regional responses, where the regional level becomes either a bastion against global threats, or a way of obtaining greater power in global level dynamics. Securitisation processes can define threats as coming from the global level (financial instability, global warming, Americanisation), but the referent objects to be made secure may be either at the global level (the global economic regime, the planetary ecosystem, the norm of non-proliferation) or at other levels (community, state, region). Phrases such as 'glocalisation' in the globalist discourse capture the way in which global level causes can trigger consequences and responses on other levels. Global causes can have very different effects in different regions, e.g., a financial collapse leading to disintegration and conflict in some regions and to increased cooperation in others. To understand such outcomes one needs to grasp the regional dynamics.

If global-triggered concerns and resentments cause reactions defined in relation to regional actors and issues, the resulting constellations can easily be regional. The real challenge for a regionalist interpretation is when globalisation as such is securitised as a threat, as it sometimes now is. This has to be a part of the total picture. In many places (e.g., India, Russia, the Islamic world) globalisation is seen as a major threat, and to varying degrees it is seen and treated as more or less synonymous with American unipolarity and (especially cultural) imperialism. However, 'globalisation' has also been securitised in the North American and European core by a diverse coalition of oppositional groups demonstrating against the key institutions of the liberal international economic order, the WTO, the World Bank, and the IMF. In this case, the issue is to a larger extent (as it is also to significant groups in, for example, India) competing visions for the global political economy. To the extent that actors are seen as behind a threat here, they are either the multinationals or the global economic IGOs. In the empirical chapters, such securitisations of 'globalisation' as well as of other global phenomena will be analysed to find out to what extent they make for truly global security dynamics or play a particular local or regional role.

What becomes clear from this consideration of the neorealist, globalist, and regionalist perspectives is that all of them encompass important elements that need to be kept in view when trying to understand the post-Cold War global security order (or any security order). Underlying these three perspectives is a central question about levels of analysis: are the threats that get securitised located primarily at the domestic, the regional, or the system level? This question can be asked about any given time and place in the international system, or about the international system as a whole. In our view, understanding levels is the key to painting a portrait of the global security structure. To show why we favour the regionalist approach to security, it helps at this point to complement the three theoretical approaches with a historical overview. This overview is of course not the only possible reading of the history concerned, but we hope that it shows how an account that emphasises the rising salience of the regional level in the structure of international security can upgrade both neorealist and globalist themes, while also striking a distinctive chord of its own.

A brief modern history of regional security

The modern world history of regional security complexes (RSCs) falls easily into three stages: the modern era from 1500 to 1945; the Cold War and decolonisation from 1945 to 1989; and the post-Cold War period since 1990. The main plot of this story is easily told, and the periodisation is not out of line with most neorealist and globalist accounts. The seeming privileging of the present by giving short modern periods equal weight with longer, older ones reflects the acceleration of history (Hodgson 1993: 44–71, 207–24). During this half-millennium, the first global scale international system comes into being, and the European-style sovereign, territorial state becomes the dominant political form (Bull and Watson 1984; Buzan and Little 2000). These two developments provide the essential framework for the emergence of RSCs: states become the principal players on the security game board and, as the international system reaches global scale, room is created in which distinct regional security subsystems can emerge. A handful of states at the top of the power league play a truly global game, treating each other as a special class, and projecting their power into far-flung regions. But for the great majority of states, the main game of security is defined by their near neighbours. Key to our approach is keeping the security dynamics at the global level analytically distinct from those at the regional level. But a neat pattern of global and regional players does not simply spring into existence fully formed. The binding theme of the story is the emergence of durable RSCs against a background of great power domination. This happens very slowly, and only at the margins, for the first 450 years, and then dramatically and almost universally, in two clear stages since 1945.

Before 1500, premodern security dynamics unfolded in multiple, relatively separate systems, but these were not 'regional' because the global level was not strong enough to generate a global world system, and therefore the separate systems were not regions (subsystems) but really *worlds*.

During the modern era, from 1500 to 1945, the story is heavily tilted in favour of the global level. The European international system expanded until it became global. The new European national states reached out economically, politically, and militarily, creating both formal and informal empires in all quarters of the globe. Sometimes this projection of European power crushed and largely obliterated the indigenous peoples and their political systems, as in the Americas and Australia. Where this happened, European settlers created overseas extensions of European powers, which in turn eventually became entirely new states along European lines. In most of Africa, the Middle East, and Asia, European power eventually dominated and occupied the existing social and international systems, largely stifling indigenous regional security dynamics. There was regional security of a kind, but it was defined much more by global rivalries among the European powers (and towards the end of this period also Japan and the USA) than by security interdependence among local units. Thus one had a variety of regional 'great games' being played out by rival external powers in Central Asia, the Middle East, Southeast Asia, and Africa. For neorealists, this period is one of unbroken multipolarity. For globalists, it is, especially from the nineteenth century, the time during which many of the foundations were laid for the high-intensity global system that took off after 1945.

One could think of Europe during this period as a regional security complex but, being composed largely of great powers, and being in effect the only one, it was of a very special kind. For the European imperial powers, the world *was* their region. Under these circumstances of successful global scale imperialism by great powers, the scope for independent regional security dynamics was small. The main exceptions to imperial dominance were in those areas that either never fully lost their independence to Western overlay, and whose indigenous states retained some capacity for independent action (Japan and China); or those which escaped early from European overlay, and formed independent states of their own (the Americas). The stories of these regions are picked up, respectively, in parts II and IV. Elsewhere, the scattered handful of states that achieved independence during the first half of the twentieth century were not enough to have much impact on regional security dynamics.

During the second stage, 1945 to 1989, the Cold War and decolonisation created contradictory effects. On the one hand, the tidal wave of decolonisation rolled back imperial power, created dozens of new states, and allowed regional security dynamics to start operating among these newly independent actors in most of Africa, the Middle East, and South and Southeast Asia. On the other hand, the bipolar rivalry of the United States and the Soviet Union subordinated most of Europe and Northeast Asia, and penetrated heavily into most of the newly liberated regions. The two superpowers that dominated world politics after 1945 were both, for very different ideological reasons, opposed to the European and Japanese empires. The Soviet Union saw them as extensions of capitalism and therefore as targets for socialist revolution. The United States saw them as extensions of European neomercantilism, and wanted them opened up to free trade and self-determination. Both superpowers quite quickly came to see that the third world was an important arena for their military and ideological rivalry. Decolonisation was in many ways closely enough bound up with the Cold War to be considered part of it. The Cold War assisted the formation of several RSCs in the Middle East, Africa, and Asia. But it was also the mechanism that organised and promoted extensive intervention into the operation of these new RSCs. Neorealists see this period primarily through the lens of the shift from multipolarity to bipolarity after 1945. We more or less accept that premise (see chapter 2), but want to raise decolonisation to equal status in defining the world politics of this era. Globalists rightly focus on the astounding intensification of the global economy despite the obstructions of the Cold War, but for our purposes the territorialising impact of decolonisation is equally significant.

In Asia, Africa, and the Middle East, decolonisation replaced a world of empires and unequal political relations with one of national states, sovereign equality, and at least the legal acceptance of all peoples and races as possessing equal human rights. Some (left-) globalists correctly note that formal political and racial equality was conspicuously not accompanied by any right to economic equality. In effect, decolonisation completed the remaking of the global political system into the European ('Westphalian') form of sovereign territorial states that had begun with the revolutions in the Americas. This wholesale transplant of European political structures was often done badly, particularly in Africa. But in many places it worked well enough to take root, especially where the colonial boundaries bore some resemblance to indigenous patterns of identity, culture, or political history. By the late 1960s, and whether well or badly done, the whole world was politically packaged in the European manner. Territorial states were put into place that drew their legitimacy from the (often contradictory) values of the right to self-determination, and of the ideology of nationalism. They claimed

sovereignty and, even if they could not establish it internally in the relationship between citizens and government, they could almost always
get it accepted externally by the other state members of international society (Jackson 1990). This unprecedented tripling of the membership of
international society was supported by the UN, which not only helped
to legitimise the new members, but also provided the poorer and less
capable of them with a range of diplomatic services without which their
ability to function in international society would have been seriously
circumscribed.

The Cold War decolonisations proceeded in a very uneven manner.
In a few places, most notably South Asia during 1947–8, all of the main
states in one region were decolonised nearly simultaneously, making
the transition from imperial subordination to autonomous RSC in a
single, swift move. Mostly, however, decolonisation happened a few
countries at a time stretched out over a decade or more, as in the Middle
East, Africa, and Southeast Asia. This meant that there was a drawn-out
transition period between widespread colonial control, and the arrival
of conditions in which autonomous regional security dynamics could
begin to operate. The new third world RSCs in South and Southeast Asia,
the Middle East, and Southern Africa were without exception based
on interstate rivalry, and many of them were born in war. Thus even
while the Cold War was defining an intense bipolar security structure
at the global level, much of the so-called third world was structuring
itself into equally intense RSCs. The intersection of these two levels of
security dynamics in Southeast Asia, the Middle East, Afghanistan, and
parts of Africa provided some of the most spectacular, dangerous, and
misunderstood episodes of the Cold War.

The impact of the Cold War on the process of emerging regional security dynamics was pervasive, and the ending of the Cold War therefore
marks the opening of a clear third stage, the post-Cold War period since
1990. The ending of the Cold War had three major impacts on the story
of regional security.

- First, and most obviously, it lifted the superpower overlay from
  Europe, and radically changed the pattern of superpower pen-
  etration in Northeast Asia. With the implosion of the Soviet
  Union in 1991, it also brought fifteen new states, and a new
  RSC, into the game.
- Second, by removing ideological confrontation and Soviet
  power from the equation, it greatly changed both the nature and

17

the intensity of global power penetration into third world RSCs. As we will show in the region chapters, sometimes this was for the better, and sometimes for the worse. Many regional level security dynamics appeared to get more operational autonomy than they had had before because of the increased indifference of the global powers to them. Against this new freedom was the fact that the core was in a more dominant position ideologically and especially economically in relation to the periphery than it had been during the Cold War.

- Third, the ending of the Cold War exposed, and in many ways reinforced, the shift in the nature of the security agenda to include a range of non-military issues and actors, which had been visible since the 1970s.

One way of capturing an overview of the post-Cold War world is through the emerging neorealist consensus that the post-Cold War structure is unipolar (Kapstein and Mastanduno 1999). How this unipolarity is to be understood is still contested. A strong version of US hegemony would in many ways run parallel to a globalist analysis in terms of favouring the dominance of the system level, though of course the two would differ sharply in their understanding of causes. A weaker version of unipolarity leaves room for the regionalist view that the ending of the Cold War created more autonomy for regional level security dynamics.

Another influential interpretation of the post-Cold War world has been the idea that the international system has divided into two worlds: a zone of peace and a zone of conflict (Buzan 1991a: 432; Goldgeier and McFaul 1992; Singer and Wildavsky 1993; and implicitly in earlier versions, Deutsch et al. 1957; Keohane and Nye 1977). For the Western states and their close associates at the core of the global political economy, the big impact was the sudden, and probably long-term, shift out of heavy military security concerns and into a much wider, more diverse, and less clearly understood set of mostly non-military security concerns. The security community that had consolidated itself among the capitalist powers during the Cold War seemed, after all, not to need an external threat in order to survive – or at least, it was still in pretty good shape a decade after the fall of the Soviet Union. These countries therefore no longer faced the worry of military attacks from within their circle, which had for so long been their principal preoccupation. For those in the zone of conflict, the change was less apparent. Military threats were still a part of everyday life, and many of them had been arguing a case for economic security, and a 'new international economic order', since the early years of decolonisation. In the present era, therefore, the story of global security becomes more diversified. A relatively uniform picture of military-political security dynamics dominated by state actors gives way to multisectoral conceptions of security, a wider variety of actors, and sets of conditions and dynamics that differ sharply from one region to another. As we hope to show, the distinction between core and periphery, although a useful simplification, hides some quite sharp regional distinctions. In some places conflictual RSCs, with their predominantly military-political interstate rivalries, remain the order of the day. In others, RSCs have become security regimes or security communities, and the discourses of security have shifted away from both states and military issues. And in yet others, the state framework itself is coming apart at the seams, giving prominence to substate and/or superstate actors.

Whatever the final interpretation of it, the post-Cold War era seems clearly to continue the opening up of scope for regional security dynamics begun with decolonisation. Decolonisation opened the space for regional military-political dynamics, and the ending of the Cold War enabled these dynamics to operate with much more freedom from high levels of rival superpower military-political intrusion. At the same time, the growing power of the global market generated regional security initiatives. The operation of the global market, and its securitising effects both on the environment and on patterns of identity, also took some regional focus. In some regions there was concern about the ways in which the burgeoning forces of globalisation were impacting on local culture. In others, environmental issues took regional forms around such issues as shared river systems, seas, and air quality. Clearly we are looking at a new type of interplay between the much-discussed forces of globalisation on the one hand, and a seemingly paradoxical, but in fact connected, strengthening of territorialised regional dynamics on the other.

Had the premodern multiple systems merged by a parallel, balanced increase in interaction capacity, a global system with multiple regions might have formed during the previous five centuries. Instead, the world became unified by the double move of Europe first expanding to dominate the world and then retracting to leave a world still connected and remodelled into the state format. That second move left room for evolution back towards a global system with multiple regions. This odd route left much confusion about how to think about regional and global levels and many particular legacies. Nevertheless, it is now possible to begin more systematically to conceptualise a global world order of strong regions.

History and diversity: the different state legacies of regional security complexes

The story just given, with its emphasis on the global and regional levels, makes it easy to slip into the assumption that the world has evolved into a fairly uniform system of Westphalian-type states differentiated from each other principally by their degree of power, their geographical location, and their cultural background. But it is all too clear that the state level itself contains variables that play a major role in conditioning the how and why of security dynamics in any given region. The broad-brush account in the previous section already suggests three significant dimensions of differentiation: (a) a few states are great powers while most others are not; (b) many states underwent colonial occupation, while a smaller number of others either did not, or were colonial occupiers themselves; and (c) some states have been established for a long time and have deep roots, while others are recent constructions of decolonisation, sometimes with shallow roots. Each of these dimensions can easily be further broken down. The spectrum of powers from great through middle to small is a well-established convention, if not very well defined. If looked at by age, a few states can trace some sort of coherent ancestry going back several millennia (China, Iran, Egypt, India, Greece), rather more can claim hundreds of years (France, USA, Ethiopia, Japan), many have less than a century (Nigeria, Pakistan, Finland), and some have little more than a decade (Kazakhstan, Macedonia, Eritrea). Ex-colonial countries come in all sorts of conditions. Some are the products of European migrations, which largely displaced the native populations (most of the Americas, Australia, in some ways Russia). Others resulted from the imposition of European state forms on to pre-existing state-like cultures (India, Vietnam, Egypt), or the half-voluntary, half-coerced adoption of European political forms by such cultures in their attempts to stave off colonisation (Japan, Thailand, Turkey, Ethiopia). Yet others resulted from the imposition of European state forms on to previously stateless societies (Central Asia, the Pacific islands, many parts of Africa). To add to the confusion there are hybrids of these models such as South Africa, Ireland, and New Zealand, and variations woven by the slave trade and imperial movements of indentured labour (Brazil, Cuba, Trinidad and Tobago, Fiji). The possibilities for classifying states by their historical legacy multiply endlessly. In this mode, one could also think of different types of government, different levels of industrialisation, different degrees of cultural homogeneity, and so on.

There are no neat correlations among these classifications that would enable a clear simplification of types. Some colonising states were quite small powers (Denmark, Belgium), while some ex-colonial states have become substantial powers (India, USA). Some new states have grown rich and well ordered (Singapore, Taiwan), while others have remained chaotic and poor (Somalia, Pakistan). Some old states are rich and stable (France, Japan), others are not (Russia, Egypt). As demonstrated by the widely accepted hypothesis of democratic peace theory – that democracies rarely if ever go to war with each other – the variety of state types clearly does matter to what sorts of security dynamics are likely to develop. It does not seem unreasonable to think that well-established, democratic, advanced industrial states will tend to have different security concerns from unstable and underdeveloped third world dictatorships. But the number of possible combinations resulting from the existence of so many seemingly important ways of classifying states generates a matrix so huge as to be useless for analytical purposes. And since most of these characteristics do not obviously generate any clear or determined security outcomes, we are not even going to attempt to construct a security theory that hinges on classifications of states into types. Such an approach was tried by Rosenau (1966) and did not prove a viable path for the development of foreign policy analysis.

That said, however, we cannot just ignore this factor and run with the hugely distorting Eurocentric assumption that all states are alike. Part of our purpose in this book is to set out historical overviews of how RSCs have evolved, and there can be no doubt that the ways in which security dynamics have unfolded in different regions are affected by the type(s) of state to be found within particular regions. Yet we also want to leave a good deal of room for political choice and particular circumstance. How else does one explain why states as similar in many ways as Czechoslovakia and Yugoslavia took such different paths to disassembling themselves, or how one group of not very democratic developing countries in Southeast Asia managed to generate a substantial regional security regime (ASEAN), while their neighbours in South Asia did not?

We are already on record with a concept that offers some way forward on how to deal with the interplay between types of states and types of security dynamics: the spectrum of *weak* and *strong* states as a way of thinking about national security (Buzan 1991b: 96–107; see also Krasner 1978: 55–6; Holsti 1996). This spectrum is not about power (weak/strong powers), but about the degree of sociopolitical cohesion between civil society and the institutions of government. In a real sense it is about the degree of stateness (in terms of what Jackson (1990) calls 'empirical sovereignty') that a state possesses. All states can be placed along this spectrum. Those towards the stronger end, being more internally cohesive, will tend to find most of their threats coming from outside their borders. Those towards the weaker end lack much in the way of empirical sovereignty, and so in one sense have less claim to stateness. They are more likely to be forums in which a variety of substate actors compete for their own security, and/or to capture the state. Because they are fragile and internally divided, weak states will, other things being equal, be more vulnerable to most types of outside threat. Extreme weakness results in state failure, which is the collapse of empirical sovereignty. With this idea in mind, it is easy to see that a region composed entirely of strong states is likely to develop quite different security dynamics from one composed entirely of weak states. Reality, of course, is almost never so neatly composed, and the typical region will contain some mixture of state types (Singapore and Cambodia; Angola and South Africa; Albania and France). Nevertheless, this spectrum will give us some explanatory leverage when we come to consider the security history of particular regions.

Running in close parallel to the strong/weak state spectrum is the quite widely used scheme for classifying the contemporary universe of states into three types: *postmodern, modern,* and *premodern* (Holm and Sørensen 1995; Caporoso 1996; Cooper 1996; Buzan and Segal 1996). Although presented as a set of three types, this set can also be seen as positions on a spectrum. Since much of the focus in this book will be on the contemporary international system and its RSCs, we will use this scheme in comparing regions.

The defining central category of this scheme is the modern state, which represents the European classical Westphalian ideal type. Until after the end of the Second World War, modern states were the dominant type. They are defined by strong government control over society and restrictive attitudes towards openness. They see themselves as independent and self-reliant entities, having distinctive national cultures and development policies, and often pursuing mercantilist economic policies. Their borders mark real lines of closure against outside economic, political, and cultural influences, and their sovereignty is sacrosanct. The fascist and communist totalitarian states of the twentieth century represented extreme types of modern state, but pre-Second World War France and the United States show that modern states can also be democracies. In the early part of the twenty-first century, the most conspicuous modern states are mostly outside the core of advanced capitalist states: China, the two Koreas, Iran, India, Burma, Iraq, Saudi Arabia, Turkey, Brazil. Russia has many of the qualities of a modern state, as do, in some ways, the USA and Japan. Modern states can vary quite a lot along the weak/strong spectrum, though they cannot be too close to the failed state end. In some (e.g., Iraq, possibly North Korea), repressive authoritarian regimes may impose modernity without having the consent of many of their citizens. In others (e.g., revolutionary Iran), even quite authoritarian governments may command a high degree of real support. In very different ways, India and Singapore demonstrate the democratic possibilities of modernity. Because of their strong territoriality, modern states tend to securitise very much in inside/outside terms.

Postmodern states are a relatively new phenomenon, mainly concentrated in the capitalist core. All are within the strong state end of the spectrum, and none are much driven by traditional military security concerns about armed invasion or massive bombardment. These states have moved on from the Westphalian model. They still retain the trappings of modernity such as borders, sovereignty, and national identity, but for a wide range of things, especially economic and cultural transactions, do not take them nearly as seriously as before. Postmodern states have a much more open and tolerant attitude towards cultural, economic, and political interaction, and have by and large convinced themselves that opening their economies, and to a lesser extent their societies and politics, to a wider range of interactions is good both for their prosperity and for their security. Necessarily, therefore, they have desecuritised much of the traditional agenda of threats. But at the same time they have acquired a new security agenda, which often focuses on concerns about identity and migration (Wæver et al. 1993) and about the stability of global economic and environmental systems. Postmodern states are pluralist and democratic, and civil society actors from firms to pressure groups are allowed a great deal of liberty to operate both within the state and across its borders. The EU represents the leading edge of this development, with its member states having created a thick layer of institutions among themselves, and being generally embarked on an open-ended experiment to invent a post-Westphalian form of international relations. But the North American states also have some postmodern qualities, as, to a lesser extent, does Japan, and these are reflected in the security community that links these three centres together. Since the postmodern states represent the major centres of power and wealth in the international system, they also project strongly the values of openness into the rest of the international system. Because they pursue elements of openness, postmodern states have less of the inside/outside preoccupation of modern states, and more of a concern with the security of the structures that link them together.

At the opposite end of the spectrum, scattered throughout the third world, but most notably in Africa and Central Asia, are states that can loosely be described as premodern, defined by low levels of socio-political cohesion and poorly developed structures of government. These are all weak states. Some of them are premodern in the sense that they aspire to modernity, and are headed in that direction, but have yet to consolidate themselves sufficiently to qualify. Others are failed states, where the colonial state transplant has broken down, and there is little other than external recognition to sustain the myth of statehood. Premodern states are most numerous in Africa, but can also be found in Asia (Afghanistan, Tajikistan), the Americas (Haiti), and Europe (Albania). Weak states have many vulnerabilities, and securitisation may well begin to move away from the state to substate actors.

All of these state types have their security environment shaped both by the regions within which they sit, and by the international system that contains them. At the regional level, conveniently for our purposes, there is a marked, though by no means perfect, geographical clustering of states according to these three types. Sub-Saharan Africa contains predominantly premodern states. The Middle East, South and East Asia, South America, and Eastern Europe all contain predominantly modern states. North America and, more so, Western Europe are dominated by postmodern states. These clusterings are not pure, and they do not determine the dynamics of security in these regions. But they do predispose them in significant ways, and so provide useful starting points for our comparative analysis.

At the global level, all of these states have to operate in the strong international system that has grown up during the last half-century, but they do so under very different conditions. By 'strong' international system, we mean the globalist package of intensified interaction

24

capacity in transportation and communication; the expanding communities of common fate; the shrinkage of time and space; the interlinkage of production, trade, finance, and environment; and the increasing imposition of the systemic on the local. The strong postmodern states relate to globalisation as its principal generator and beneficiary, though, as sensitivities about things such as migration, terrorism, economic cycles, 'democratic deficits', and sovereignty attest, they can also feel threatened by it.

For modern states, globalisation poses two seemingly contradictory threats: exclusion and inclusion. The threat of exclusion is most strongly felt by modernist states adjacent to the postmodern core, such as Mexico, Turkey, and many Central and East European countries. States that straddle the border line between post-modern and modern statehood often face particularly intense dilemmas and might even become 'torn states' (Aydınlı 2002). For these states, exclusion means relegation to second-class status, and denial of many benefits of membership in the core. The threat of inclusion is general to modernist states and arises from conflicts between their indigenous cultural and development projects on the one hand, and outside influences and penetrations on the other. The longstanding debate in Russia between Westernisers and Slavophiles is a classic example of such tensions (Neumann 1996b). For many modern states, the price of economic and political relations with the postmodern core is exposure to demands for openness and 'standards of civilisation' that amount not just to an assault on sovereignty, but in some cases (most notably Islamic ones) to an assault on identity. Recognition, aid, and trade may be made conditional on legal reforms (particularly for property rights), human rights performance (reflecting liberal values of individual rights), currency reform, adherence to norms of multiparty democracy, and reduction of restrictions on the movement of goods and capital. As Iran, North Korea, Libya, the former Soviet Union, and to a lesser extent Argentina, China, and India can attest, the liberal core is actively hostile to rival modes of development.

For premodern states, the threat from globalisation is broadly defined by an inability to measure up to international standards of good governance. The danger is either that they will be demoted in the ranks of international society to some sort of trusteeship status, no longer recognised as legally equal and capable of self-government, or that they will simply be neglected and allowed to fall into chaos. It may not be possible for some societies quickly or easily to develop modern (let alone postmodern) forms of social and political life when they are exposed to the rigours of a global market and the seductions of a wealthier, more powerful, global culture.

These ideas enable us to take substantial account of unit level factors in thinking about contemporary international security, without getting mired in the hopeless analytical complexity of myriad different types of state. They provide a broad-brush sketch of the main features of the contemporary international security environment, and give us some handles with which both to compare regions and to relate the regional security dynamics to the global ones. But we are not going to go down the road of trying to cast these factors as determinative of security dynamics. Certainly they shove and shape in important ways as 'facilitating conditions'. But as we have argued elsewhere (Buzan et al. 1998), and will continue to argue here, leaders and peoples have considerable freedom to determine what they do and do not define as security threats. Since it is these definitions that underpin security policy and behaviour, they, and the processes by which they are made and unmade, are what must ultimately lie at the heart of security analysis.

Conclusions

This chapter has established the plausibility of taking a regional approach to international security. It has related such an approach to neorealism and globalism, and shown the complementarities among them. It has also set out a historical account, which, by showing the salience of the regional level, validates the task of developing a theory to take it into account. Both neorealism and globalism seek to continue the Cold War IR tradition of finding one dominant story to impose on the whole international system. This is an intellectually attractive strategy, but our argument is that it was a flawed one even during the Cold War, and is increasingly so since. There are distinct stories at several levels with none holding the master key to a full interpretation. The task is to find coherent theoretical tools for keeping these stories in view together, and making sense of the way they interact with each other. A structured approach to regional security can do this. Since a regionalist approach is by definition dependent on an ability to distinguish the regional level from other levels, establishing the grounds on which such a distinction can be made is the task of the next chapter.

2 Levels: distinguishing the regional from the global

The how and why of distinguishing the regional from the global level

Any coherent regionalist approach to security must start by drawing clear distinctions between what constitutes the regional level and what constitutes the levels on either side of it. Lake and Morgan (1997c) draw the distinction between regional and global, but then use definitions of region that effectively conflate these two levels. The fact that the regionalist approach features a *distinct* level of analysis located *between* the global and the local is what gives RSCT its analytical power. Distinguishing the regional from the unit level is not usually controversial. Units (of whatever kind) must have a fairly high degree of independent actor quality. Regions, almost however defined, must be composed of geographically clustered sets of such units, and these clusters must be embedded in a larger system, which has a structure of its own. Regions have analytical, and even ontological, standing, but they do not have actor quality. Only exceptionally does this distinction become problematic, as for example in the case of the European Union (see ch. 11). Mostly, the differentiation of units and regions is fairly straightforward.

Distinguishing the regional from the global is less straightforward. The easy part is that a region must obviously be less than the whole, and usually much less. The tricky bit is actually specifying what falls on which side of the boundary. There would not be much opposition to the proposition that the United States is a global level actor, while the security dynamics amongst the South American states are at the regional level. But the difficulty begins when one tries to position particular actors: should Russia be considered a global power or a regional one? And China? Traditional realism does not help because it tends to think in a global track, positioning states as great, middle, or small powers. This approach bypasses our concern with powers that are structurally significant at the regional level. Public debates show ambivalence, sometimes talking of Russia and China as regional powers (or regional superpowers), sometimes global ones. The problem is that the global level is an abstraction that can be defined in many different ways. It is *not* simply the whole system (Ruggie 1979–80). In security analysis, as also more widely in IR theory, the global level is about macrosystem structures that constrain and shape the behaviour of the units in the system. How these structures are defined thus shapes the nature, and even the possibility, of the regional level. For this reason it is easiest to approach the global–regional boundary by starting from the top down.

Both the neorealist and globalist perspectives centre on a conception of global structure. Neorealism is built around two levels, system and unit, and is principally concerned to define and operationalise the system level. Neorealists either downplay or ignore all levels except the system one, or like Walt (1987) discuss the regional level empirically without considering its theoretical standing or implications. Happily, it is relatively straightforward to slot in a regional level (even as a fourth tier of system structure; see Wæver 1993a, 1994, 1997c, in preparation) without, at least initially, causing too much disturbance to the theoretical architecture (a fourth tier in the sense that, when dynamics from the deeper tiers are actualised, they are mediated by specific regional structures). Neorealism is in some respects strong on territoriality, and the potential harmony and synergy between it and the regionalist perspective are high, especially when states are the main actors. That said, there is room for conflict between neorealism and regionalism when the security agenda moves to issue areas other than military-political, to actors other than the state, and to theories of security other than materialist. Also, the most abstract and theoretically ambitious versions of neorealism (such as Waltz's) tend to conceive 'system' in such abstract terms that territoriality disappears, partly because the theory overemphasises the distance-transgressing superpower level as an effect of the Cold War, partly because maximally abstract concepts of 'system' and 'units' were favoured by the reward structures of American social science. This disregarded many insights of older realisms with closer affinities to geopolitics. In today's IR, neoclassical realism might therefore be a more likely meeting point for the neorealist and regionalist elements (Rose 1998; Schweller 1999; Wivel 2000; Zakaria 1998).

Another potential conflict between neorealism and regionalism is in the latter's contention that the global level has dropped in salience relative to the regional one since the ending of the Cold War. But that is mostly an empirical issue. It does not question the conceptual compatibility between the two except that it requires an open mind about which level is dominant at any given time and place. Hardline neorealists might have trouble accepting the proposition that the system level is not always dominant. But in principle the regionalist perspective should be able to incorporate neorealism's understanding of the global level into its own multilevel scheme (unit, region, inter-regional, global). There is already some linkage in the literature. Lake (1997: 61–2), for example, argues that bipolarity maximises the system level of security dynamics by encouraging worldwide superpower competition penetrating all regions and making the global level exceptionally intense; and Schweller (1999: 41–2) notes the use of polarity analysis at the regional level. Multipolarity and unipolarity are more difficult to assess, with lower competition at the global level, but also fewer constraints on great power behaviour (Miller 2000). These structures could allow either more, or less, scope for the regional level than bipolarity. Wivel (2000) goes further, setting out a whole theory of how variations in global polarity affect the regional level, and B. Hansen (2000: 68, 81) predicts 'high regional activity' under unipolarity.

The fit between regionalist and globalist perspectives is much less obvious, not least because there is no clear and uncontested conception of system structure at the heart of the globalist position (is it capitalism, or the global market, or world society?). As argued in chapter 1 (pp. 7–10), we have no problem with the globalist enthusiasm for interaction capacity as a driving force, though we see it as impacting on the regional level just as powerfully as on the global. Neither do we disagree with arguments that globalisation diversifies and complicates the security agenda, though we prefer to handle this through the device of sectors (Buzan et al. 1998). Aside from the lack of specification concerning system structure, the problem lies in the globalist commitment to deterritorialisation as the key to understanding both world politics and security. As we show in chapter 3, our scheme had state-centric origins, though in its updated versions these become historically contingent. The essential idea in our theory is that security dynamics have a strong territoriality, and on this basis it can accommodate non-state actors without too much difficulty. But it is incompatible with the extreme globalist idea that all levels are dissolving into one. Even if a trend is discernible in this direction, we think it still has a very long way to go before levels cease to be a salient feature in the dynamics of international security. Although some of the new security agenda is deterritorialised, most notably in the economic and environmental sectors, we think that territoriality remains a primary defining feature of many (in)security dynamics. In addition, although we find a core–periphery idea of system structure attractive in some ways, we think it too homogenised for most security analysis. As we hope to show, a regional approach gives both a much clearer empirical picture and a theoretically more coherent understanding of international security dynamics.

From our regionalist perspective, a key weakness of both the neorealist and globalist approaches to security is that they overplay the role of the global level, and underestimate the role of the regional one. Their reasons for doing so are different. Neorealism does not (in principle) have problems with territoriality, but simply chooses not to look much at the levels below the systemic. To the extent that globalism is looking away from territoriality in particular and levels in general, it is not a good approach for picking up things still defined in territorial terms. But the more moderate versions of globalism that allow space for the points of resistance to globalisation do give room for a regionalist perspective. Neorealism provides the better template for differentiating the global and regional levels of our security constellations, yet there remains a problem within the neorealist concept of polarity as the key to the system-level security structure. This problem needs to be clarified before we can proceed.

The task of this chapter is to identify the global level in the post-Cold War international security structure using the neorealist criterion of polarity. The second section picks up the problem of polarity after the Cold War. We know that the system structure is no longer bipolar, but what comes after bipolarity is hotly contested. Our argument is that the global level of security at the outset of the twenty-first century can best be understood as one superpower plus four great powers. It is necessary to differentiate superpowers and great powers even though both are at the global level, and then to differentiate that level from the one defined by regional powers and RSCs.

The problem of polarity post-Cold War

The traditional (neo)realist way of defining the global level for the military-political sector was by identifying the great powers and taking their interactions as the global level. During the Cold War (when most of the theoretical apparatus of International Relations was constructed), the existence of bipolarity made this seem easy to do. There was a big gap between the superpowers and the rest, and their rivalry was openly global in scale. It was during this period that the idea of using *polarity* (defined as the number of great powers in the system) became established as the way of thinking about military-political structure at the system level (Kaplan 1957; Waltz 1979). Superpower bipolarity seemed clear both in theory and in practice, and it was easy to move outward from there to talk about unipolar, multipolar, and diffuse systems. Because Cold War bipolarity was defined by superpowers, and historical multipolarity by great powers, not much thought was given to whether the difference in terminology implied a difference in classification that might matter for polarity theory. Rather, it was treated simply as a shift of language fashion, like that from 'black' to 'African-American'. Leading polarity theorists such as Waltz treated the two terms as virtual synonyms, with 'superpower' simply corresponding to low-number polarities.

The implosion of the USSR unequivocally brought the period of bipolarity to an end. But what was left behind in terms of polarity was less than crystal clear. Enthusiasts for globalisation took this as being not just the end of bipolarity, but the end of polarity *per se,* and the replacement of a Westphalian political order by a more deterritorialised, economy-driven, system structure. Within the realist tradition, debate began about how to define post-Cold War polarity. The problem was a confusingly large range of significant powers, many of which did not easily slot into the categories of the theory. At one end of the spectrum of significant powers the United States was clearly still a superpower by any definition. At the other end were substantial numbers of regional powers such as Israel, Iran, Brazil, Indonesia, India, Pakistan, and Turkey. In between sat a set of second-rank powers that did not come close to measuring up to the USA, but which were significant global players in one way or another, and which clearly transcended regional or middle power status. These included China, Japan, and Russia, and more awkwardly the EU, either as a *sui generis* entity with some state-like qualities, or as united Germany plus France and Britain (or in some renditions a kind of German-led dominion). Initially, the main direction was to see a unipolar 'moment' to be followed inevitably by multipolarity as others caught up with the United States and/or began to balance against it, or as the United States declined, or as it withdrew from global engagement

31

(Krauthammer 1990–1; Layne 1993; Waltz 1993a, 1993b, 2000b; Kegley and Raymond 1994; Kupchan 1998; Calleo 1999). Some attempted mixtures, such as Huntington's (1999: 35–6) idea of 'uni-multipolarity'. Some were simply confused, as for example in Ross's (1999: 83) conflation of the global and regional levels in a discussion of polarity in East Asia. Some sought to exit from polarity back towards classical realism, on the grounds that polarity missed out too much and had failed to achieve any definitional consensus (Schweller 1999: 36–42). For most, the main question arising was how long the 'unipolar moment' might be. Initially, the weight of opinion favoured a fairly short moment but, as the end of the Cold War receded, the unipolar moment began to feel more like an era in its own right. A consensus emerged that a US-centred unipolarity might in fact be stable (notwithstanding the serious difficulties this posed for Waltz's neorealist theory, in which balancing reactions should prevent unipolarity from being a stable option) (Kapstein 1999; Lake 1999; Mastanduno and Kapstein 1999; Walt 2000; Wilkinson 1999; Wohlforth 1999; see also Waltz 2000b).

A full discussion of the problem of polarity is beyond the scope of this book and has been presented elsewhere (Buzan et al. 1993: 51–65; Schweller 1999: 36–42; Buzan forthcoming). Suffice it to say that for the idea of polarity to work as a definition of the system level it requires a single, identifiable concept of great power. Classification of any actor as a great power is not a simple act of measurement. It requires a combination of material capability (Waltz 1979: 131), formal recognition of that status by others (Bull 1977: 200–2), and, from our point of view most importantly, observation of the practical mode of operation of states, particularly which actors are responded to by others on the basis of system level calculations. A power acting at the global level reflects on the balance of power not only in terms of the existing superpower(s) – it has to include in its calculations also the great powers because of the consequences of their coalition behaviour.

If this last behavioural criterion is accepted as the key, then one useful side effect is the elimination of the difficulty that neorealists have created for themselves by accepting Waltz's injunction that a great power, or a system level 'pole', can only be a state. Waltz's argument was (rightly) directed against those who confused system polarity (the number of great powers in the system) with system polarisation (the configuration of alliances in the system). Thus, in 1914, the system was multipolar in terms of powers, but bipolarised in terms of coalitions. However, the idea that a pole must be a state has run into endless difficulties in dealing with the EU, which becomes almost invisible through neorealist lenses despite its steady accumulation of actor quality. But if one accepts the behavioural approach to determining status, this problem disappears. The EU can be judged by how others respond to it. If others treat it as a great power, then it qualifies as such regardless of its ambiguous, *sui generis* political status. The English School understanding that international systems could be seen as 'a group of independent political communities' (Bull and Watson 1984: 1) makes entities such as the EU easier to incorporate.

The problem of what counts as a great power is revealed by the standard list of great powers usually given for 1914 (Austria-Hungary, Britain, France, Germany, Italy, Japan, Ottoman Empire, Russia, USA): there is an enormous difference in role and capability between the top powers on this list (USA, Britain, Germany) and the bottom ones (Italy, Ottoman Empire, Japan). A similar observation could be made about contemporary lists, for example that of Papayoanou (1997: 125). Defining great powers as 'those states which have the capabilities to play a major role in international politics with respect to security related issues', he counts them as the USA, Russia, Germany, Britain, France, China, and Japan.

The idea that great powers constitute a single classification has deep roots. It arises out of the transfer of the great power concept from its classical usage in the essentially regional system of Westphalian Europe, to its current application to a global-scale international system. In the pre-1945 world, still dominated by Europe, a single classification of great power was workable, if misleading. The move from a European-scale to a truly global international system occurred during the twentieth century, and made a single classification of great power so misleading as to be unworkable except in unusual conditions such as those of the Cold War. Size matters: a global-scale international system requires at least a differentiation between those great powers that operate across the whole system (superpowers), or at least a large part of it, and those whose power is mostly confined to their home continent. In the pre-1945 world, Britain and the USA were obvious examples of superpowers; Japan, Italy, and Austria-Hungary (before 1918) obvious examples of 'ordinary' great powers lacking much global reach. The problem is nicely exposed by Lake's (1997: 64) seemingly quite simple and orthodox definition: 'Great powers possess global military reach. They have the ability to project force around the globe, and as a result, they can intervene in any regional security complex whenever it suits their interests.' If one thinks about this definition in relation to the two lists of great powers given in the previous paragraph for 1914 and now, it is perfectly obvious that very few of the states listed meet the criteria. This definition describes superpowers. Kegley and Raymond's (1994: 54, 88, 232) definition of great powers curiously stresses approximate equality of capabilities, which is hard to square with any situation during the last century, or any likely in the near future.

The shift to a planetary scale, and the near quadrupling of the total number of states in the system, generated by decolonisation, requires a more elaborate differentiation among the major powers. Traditional distinctions between 'great' and 'middle' powers will not work in an international system where only a few operate over the whole system, and many are significant, but only in their immediate neighbourhood. The idea of 'middle powers', in any case, reflects a systemic perspective that ignores the significance of RSCs. In a world of nearly 200 states, superpowers (if they exist) occupy one end of the major power spectrum, and regional powers (states such as Brazil, Egypt, Iran, Nigeria, and South Africa, whose power defines the polarity of their local RSC, but does not extend much beyond) occupy the other end. In between are what can only be called great powers, which are clearly more than just regional powers, but do not meet all of the qualifications for superpower. Superpowers and great powers define the global level of polarity, and the line between them and regional powers is the one that defines the difference between global and regional security dynamics. This distinction needs to be asserted. Wilkinson (1999: 141–5), for example, while accepting unipolarity, misses the distinction between great and regional powers by identifying France, Britain, Russia, and China as 'great powers at a regional level'. He makes no attempt to define criteria for inclusion into or exclusion from this category.

Taking these definitional and historical criteria into consideration, we propose the following *definitional criteria for a three-tiered scheme*: superpowers and great powers at the system level, and regional powers at the regional level.

Superpowers – The criteria for superpower status are demanding in that they require broad-spectrum capabilities exercised across the whole of the international system. Superpowers must possess first-class military-political capabilities (as measured by the standards of the day), and the economies to support such capabilities. They must be capable of, and also exercise, global military and political reach. They need to see themselves, *and* be accepted by others in rhetoric and behaviour, as having this rank. Superpowers must be active players in processes of securitisation and desecuritisation in all, or nearly all, of the regions in the system, whether as threats, guarantors, allies, or interveners. Except in extremely conflictual international systems, superpowers will also be fountainheads of 'universal' values of the type necessary to underpin international society. Their legitimacy as superpowers will depend substantially on their success in establishing the legitimacy of such values. Taking all of these factors into account, during the nineteenth century Britain, France, and more arguably Russia had this rank. After the First World War, it was held by Britain, the USA, and the Soviet Union. After the Second World War, it was held by the USA and the Soviet Union. And after the Cold War it was held only by the USA.

Great powers – Achieving great power status is less demanding in terms of both capability and behaviour. Great powers need not necessarily have big capabilities in all sectors, and they need not be actively present in the securitisation processes of all areas of the international system. Great power status rests mainly on a single key: what distinguishes great powers from merely regional ones is that they are responded to by others on the basis of system level calculations about the present and near-future distribution of power. Usually, this implies that a great power is treated in the calculations of other major powers as if it has the clear economic, military, and political potential to bid for superpower status in the short or medium term. This single key is observable in the foreign policy processes and discourses of other powers. It means that actual possession of material and legal attributes is less crucial for great powers than for superpowers. Great powers will usually have appropriate levels of capability, though China has demonstrated an impressive ability over nearly a century to trade on future capabilities that it has yet to fully deliver (Segal 1999). They will generally think of themselves as more than regional powers, and possibly as prospective superpowers, and they will usually be capable of operating in more than one region. But, while these characteristics will be typical of great powers, they are not strictly speaking necessary so long as other powers treat them as potential superpowers. Japan illustrates the case of a country thought of by others as a potential superpower, but which possesses unbalanced capabilities, and is not clearly inclined to think of itself as a superpower candidate. Mostly, great powers will be rising in the hierarchy of international power, but a second route into the category is countries declining from acknowledged superpower status. Declining superpowers will normally have influence in more than one region, and be capable of limited global military operation.

During the later nineteenth century, Germany, the USA, and Japan had great power rank (and Russia if not accepted as a superpower). After the First World War, it was still held by Germany and Japan, and France dropped into it as a declining superpower. During the Cold War it was held by China, Germany, and Japan, with Britain and France coming increasingly into doubt. Here there was the difficult question of how to treat the EU, which as time wore on acquired more and more actor quality in the international system, and which was by the 1970s being treated as an emergent great power, albeit of an unusual kind and with some serious limitations still in place. After the Cold War it was held by Britain/France/Germany-EU, Japan, China, and Russia. India was knocking loudly on the door, but had neither the capability, the formal recognition, nor the place in the calculations of others to qualify.

The justifications for designating these four as great powers in the post-Cold War international system are as follows. Russia qualifies by its recent exit from superpower status, and China, the EU, and Japan all qualify on the basis of being regularly talked about and treated either as potential challengers to the USA, and/or as potential superpowers (Calleo 1999; Kapstein 1999; Mastanduno and Kapstein 1999; Wilkinson 1999; Waltz 2000b). China is currently the most fashionable potential superpower (Roy 1994; Ross 1999: 83–4, 92–4, 97; Wilkinson 1999: 160–3), and the one whose degree of alienation from the dominant international society makes it the most obvious political challenger (Zhang 1998). But its challenge is constrained both by formidable internal problems of development and by the fact that a rise in its power could easily trigger a counter coalition in Asia. Assessment of the EU's status often hangs on its degree of stateness (Galtung 1973; Buchan 1993; Walton 1997; Hodge 1998–9; Wohlforth 1999: 31; Waltz 1993a: 54; 2000b: 30–2; Wilkinson 1999: 157–60; Walker 2000) without it being clear how much state-like quality it has to achieve in order to count as a superpower. The EU clearly has the material capabilities, and could easily claim recognition. But given its political weakness, and its erratic and difficult course of internal political development, particularly as regards a common foreign and defence policy, the EU seems likely to remain a potential superpower for at least some decades. During the early and middle 1990s, there was a strong fashion, especially in the USA, for seeing Japan as the likely challenger for superpower status (Huntington 1991: 8; 1993; Layne 1993: 42–3, 51; Waltz 1993a: 55–70; Spruyt 1998). With Japan's economic stagnation, this fashion has faded, but Japan could bounce back, and its standing as a great power looks relatively firm. Like the EU, Japan is mainly constrained by its political inability to play a superpower role. India, despite its nuclear test, is not talked about or treated as a potential superpower, and so does not qualify.

Regional powers – Regional powers define the polarity of any given RSC: unipolar as in Southern Africa, bipolar as in South Asia, multipolar as in the Middle East, South America, and Southeast Asia. Their capabilities loom large in their regions, but do not register much in a broad-spectrum way at the global level. Higher-level powers respond to them as if their influence and capability were mainly relevant to the securitisation processes of a particular region. They are thus excluded from the higher-level calculations of system polarity whether or not they think of themselves as deserving a higher ranking (as India most obviously does). Regional powers may of course get caught up in global power rivalries, as happened during the Cold War to Vietnam, Egypt, Iraq, and others. In that context, they may get treated as if they mattered to the global balance of power as, for example, during the Cold War when there were fears that escalations from Middle Eastern conflicts would trigger superpower confrontations. But the kind of attention received by an actor that is seen as the spoils in a wider competition is quite different from that received by an actor seen as a global level power in its own right.

These definitions apply across the last few centuries, but they are also historically contingent: before there was a global international system, there were no superpowers and much less scope for regional powers. The three-tier scheme complicates polarity theory by putting two tiers at the system level, but clarifies it by providing a firm demarcation between global and regional powers.

Conclusions

This rethinking of polarity, and its accompanying definitions of superpower, great power, and regional power, enables us to formulate a relatively clear view of the global level structure of international security since the end of the Cold War. What succeeds bipolarity (or in our new terms, the 2 + 3 structure of the Cold War) is a 1 + 4 system structure that has no modern historical precedent, and whose main potential for transformation is into the theoretically uncharted realm of a 0 + x structure. Such a system certainly cannot be adequately captured by simple designation as either unipolar or multipolar. Huntington's (1999: 35–6) idea of uni-multipolarity goes in the right direction, and does capture some of the relevant relational dynamics in the present structure. But it fails to specify criteria for classification, makes no differentiation for the regional level, and locks itself into a single formulation, which limits its scope as a general approach to structural theory. Interestingly, the general idea of a $1 + 4$ world differentiating the 'great power' category into two levels was much more clearly articulated in US policy circles (Joffe 2001: 142–4) and among Chinese academics (Pillsbury 2000) than it could be amongst neorealists still chained to Waltz's dictum of great powers as a single type.

If one follows our suggestion of differentiating the power classifications at the system level into superpowers and great powers, then there does not seem to be much theoretical mileage in hanging on to general hypotheses based on simple numbers. For one thing, the possible combinations are too many. For another, polarity theory depends on the assumption that all great powers operate over the whole international system. With our definition of great power, this assumption has to be abandoned. Given the size of the global system, mere great powers mostly do not operate globally, and only superpowers meet the requirements of polarity theory. One might easily imagine worlds with up to five or six superpowers, at least similar numbers of great powers, and potentially quite large numbers of regional powers. If one confines regional powers to the regional level of analysis, the system level still contains a lot of possible combinations of superpowers and great powers: one superpower and anything between zero and ten great powers; two superpowers and anything between zero and ten great powers; and so on. In practice, the definitions used here mean that the number of superpowers and the number of great powers have a strong effect on each other. The more superpowers there are, the fewer great powers there are likely to be, and vice versa. Thus, a system of six superpowers and ten great powers is rather improbable, as is one with one superpower and no great powers (true unipolarity). In practice this interplay reduces the number of likely combinations, though still leaving it too large to base theory on a handful of categories, as polarity theory has done.

The hypotheses from existing polarity theory would still apply to pure superpower systems (i.e., those composed of x superpowers and zero great powers), but such configurations will be rare. They probably cannot be applied to pure great power systems, because great powers are strongly driven by less than global interests, as well as by their concerns about superpowers (existing or potential). In a $0 + x$ system many of the great powers might be somewhat insulated from each other by distance, and thus interact with each other on a quite different logic from system-spanning superpowers. Thus, defying mathematics, in our extended polarity theory $0 + x \neq x + 0$. In a $x + 0$ system, all the superpowers form a coherent system at the global level and interact accordingly allowing the expected balance-of-power logic to unfold. In a $0 + x$ system the great powers only partly connect, and geography and their regional nesting constrain systemic logic at the global level. Friedberg (1993–4: 5) comes close to this idea with his scenario of great power regions, and a world of 'regional subsystems in which clusters of contiguous states interact mainly with each other'. In the relatively short history of a fully global international system, no pure great power system (i.e., one with no superpowers) has ever existed, and it is not surprising that they have not been the subject of theoretical attention. But a 0 superpower $+ x$ great power system is one of the main potentialities in the present $1 + 4$ structure, and some theoretical attention to it is therefore a matter of urgency. That exercise is beyond the remit of the present book, though we will return to the question in part VI. For all the cases in which there is a mixture of great powers and superpowers, the starting point has to be analysis of how superpowers and great powers relate to each other, how each category relates to the regional level, and also how the nexus between the two categories, constituting the global level as a whole, relates to the regional one. In other words, one needs to take into account the whole security constellation (i.e., all the levels of analysis and their interplay). With these ideas about the global level structure as the backdrop, we can now set out regional security complex theory.

3   Security complexes: a theory of regional security

This chapter presents an operational version of regional security complex theory (RSCT). RSCT provides a conceptual frame that captures the emergent new structure of international security (1 + 4 + regions): hence our title *Regions and Powers*. As we have shown, RSCT has a historical dimension that enables current developments to be linked to both Cold War and pre-Cold War patterns in the international system. It contains a model of regional security that enables one to analyse, and up to a point anticipate and explain, developments within any region. RSCT provides a more nuanced view than strongly simplifying ideas such as unipolarity or centre–periphery. But it remains complementary with them, and provides considerable theoretical leverage of its own. In an anarchically structured international system of sufficient size and geographical complexity, RSCs will be an expected substructure, and one that has important mediating effects on how the global dynamics of great power polarity actually operate across the international system. This makes the theory interoperable with most mainstream realist, and much liberal-based, thinking about the international system. In another sense, the theory has constructivist roots, because the formation and operation of RSCs hinge on patterns of amity and enmity among the units in the system, which makes regional systems dependent on the actions and interpretations of actors, not just a mechanical reflection of the distribution of power. Wendt (1999: 257, 301), for example, makes the connection explicit, pointing out that his social theory can be applied to regional security complexes.

By applying RSCT to the whole of the international system, this book offers both a vision for the emerging 'world order' and a method for studying specific regions. Our view of regions, and therefore our image of the contemporary structure of international security, is almost the

40

reverse of that set out in Huntington's widely read *Clash of Civiliza-tions* (1993). Seemingly we are similar in emphasizing the importance of a distinct middle level between state and global system. Hunting-ton emphasises how large civilisations like Islam, the West, and Asia clash, and how the really dangerous conflicts emerge at the fault lines of these culturally based macro-units. Conversely, we stress that security regions form subsystems in which most of the security interaction is internal; states fear their neighbours and ally with other regional actors, and most often the borders between regions are – often geographically determined – zones of weak interaction, or they are occupied by an *in-sulator* (Turkey, Burma, Afghanistan) that faces both ways, bearing the burden of this difficult position but not strong enough to unify its two worlds into one. The concept of *insulator* is specific to RSCT and defines a location occupied by one or more units where larger regional security dynamics stand back to back. This is not to be confused with the tradi-tional idea of a *buffer state,* whose function is defined by standing at the centre of a strong pattern of securitisation, not at its edge.

Huntington's theory has the polemical advantage of ending up with a struggle that takes place at the system level, thereby putting the United States centre stage. That understandably appeals to an American audi-ence, and was reinforced by the events of 11 September 2001. But seen from most countries of the world, the relevant strategic setting is not primarily at the system level – the first priority is regional. Hunting-ton's delineation of the regions/civilisations differs from ours at several points because his are seen as reflections of underlying cultural affini-ties, whereas our RSCs – though possibly *influenced* by these and other factors – are *defined* (at the more 'superficial' or contingent level) by the actual patterns of security practices. In concrete cases this means that the same conflict (e.g., Bosnia) can be internal to our RSCs and intercivilisa-tional to Huntington. Especially in the book version (Huntington 1996), there are conflicts both within and between civilisations, but the latter are seen as increasingly decisive. In our view, it was a bias of this type, favouring the global over the regional, that led to many of the disasters of Cold War policy from Southeast Asia and the Middle East, to South-ern Africa and South Asia. Since regions matter more in the current era, the costs of underrating them could be even higher.

There are versions of RSCT going back to 1983, as well as a variety of applications of it to particular regions. So far, the most authoritative ver-sion is to be found as one chapter in a more general book (Buzan 1991b: 186–229) and at some points developed further in the context of different

41

applications (notably Buzan et al. 1990; cf. also Buzan, Rizvi et al. 1986; Buzan 1988b; Väyrynen 1988, 1998; Wæver 1989, 1993a, 1993b; Buzan and Wæver 1992; Wriggins 1992; Ayoob 1995; Lose 1995; Coppetiers 1996a, 1996b, 1996c; Lake and Morgan 1997c; Mozaffari 1997; Schlyter 1997; Zanders 1997, 1999; Aves 1998; Engelbrekt 1998; Ohlson 1998; Parmani 1998; Rondeli 1998, 1999; van Wyk 1998; Eide 1999; Haddadi 1999; Kinsella 1999; Muller 1999; Bøs 2000; Cornell and Sultan 2000; Khokhar and Wiberg-Jørgensen 2000; Lobo-Guerrero Sanz 2000; Takahashi 2000; Zha 2000; Jonson and Allison 2001; Kaski 2001; Limaye 2001; Schulz et al. 2001; Turton 2001; Adams 2002; Burnashev 2002; Christensen 2002; Corpora 2002; Hettne 2002; Alagappa forthcoming; Tickner and Mason forthcoming; Rees n.d.; van Schalkwyk n.d.). The purpose of the present book is to integrate the lessons from existing and new case studies, fill in remaining gaps in the theory, produce an operational formulation of the theory, and empirically apply it to all regions of the world. It is an extension of our previous book (Buzan et al. 1998), which was aimed at solving some problems arising from how to integrate the wider agenda of security with a focus on the regional level. Whereas the main focus of that book was on sectors, the main focus of this one is on levels of analysis, the two being linked by the process of securitisation. Although the original theory was largely conceived for third world cases, much of the elaboration of it was made with reference to Europe (our 1990 and 1993 books), and it is therefore important to survey global variations in regional security to expunge Eurocentric elements and produce a general theory of regional security. It is our hope that a book with such a general theory and applications will be of interest not only to security theorists, but perhaps even more for area specialists. Studies of 'regional security' usually take place without any coherent theoretical framework because, other than a few basic notions about balance of power and interdependence borrowed from the system level, none has been available.

The next section explains our approach to understanding security regions, and the second section looks at the main variables within RSCT. The third section sets out RSCT as a descriptive framework for area studies, explains the possible typologies for security complexes, and sets benchmarks for change. The fourth section sets out the predictive possibilities of RSCT through the generation of scenarios. The fifth section reviews the constructivist method of securitisation theory as the way of defining RSCs, and the final section puts all this into the context of the literature on regional security.

Security at the regional level

One of the purposes of inventing the concept of regional security complexes was to advocate the regional level as the appropriate one for a large swath of practical security analysis. Normally, two too extreme levels dominate security analysis: national and global. National security – e.g., the security of France – is not in itself a meaningful level of analysis. Because security dynamics are inherently relational, no nation's security is self-contained. But studies of 'national security' often implicitly place their own state at the centre of an ad hoc 'context' without a grasp of the systemic or subsystemic context in its own right. Global security in any holistic sense refers at best to an aspiration, not a reality. The globe is not tightly integrated in security terms and, except for the special case of superpowers and great powers discussed in chapter 2, only a limited amount can be said at this level of generality that will reflect the real concerns in most countries. The region, in contrast, refers to the level where states or other units link together sufficiently closely that their securities cannot be considered separate from each other. The regional level is where the extremes of national and global security interplay, and where most of the action occurs. The general picture is about the conjunction of two levels: the interplay of the global powers at the system level, and clusters of close security interdependence at the regional level. Each RSC is made up of the fears and aspirations of the separate units (which in turn partly derive from domestic features and fractures). Both the security of the separate units and the process of global power intervention can be grasped only through understanding the regional security dynamics.

One might, then, think that the way to proceed would be to find the cultural or economic or historical sources of regions, and then start to investigate security dynamics in these. This is seen, for instance, in the endless debates about whether Russia *is* part of Europe – with listings of Russian literary achievements versus European intellectual movements that flourished without touching Russia. In a security context such arguments easily become normative-political arguments: security cooperation *should* correspond to the 'natural' or 'true', cultural, geographic, or historical boundaries (see, e.g., the Central European arguments of Milan Kundera and others in the early 1980s; Kundera 1984). This approach might work for securitising actors, but not, in our view, as the starting point for analysts seeking to define regions specifically in the functional terms of security. Security complexes are regions as seen through the lens of security. They may or may not be regions in other senses, but they do not depend on, or start from, other conceptualisations of regionness. We do not rule out the study of causal effects of, for example, cultural or economic patterns on security patterns. Quite the contrary, it is only by *defining* RSCs purely in security terms that this causal relationship is opened up for examination.

If one hypothetically listed all the security concerns of the world, drew a map connecting each referent object for security with whatever is said to threaten it and with the main actors positively and negatively involved in handling the threat, the resulting picture would show varying degrees of intensity. Some clusters of nodes would be intensely connected, while other zones would be crossed by only few lines. Of the clusters that formed, RSCT predicts that most would be territorially based. There will, of course, be some connections across otherwise thinly populated terrain between the RSCs and, in addition, there will be some non-territorially based clusters such as those around 'international terrorism'.

Some clarification of our previous statements of RSCT and security theory in general is called for. The original definition of a security complex (Buzan 1983: 106) was: 'a group of states whose primary security concerns link together sufficiently closely that their national securities cannot reasonably be considered apart from one another'. In our 1998 book (Buzan and Wæver 1998: 201), the definition of RSCs was reformulated to shed the state-centric and military-political focus and to rephrase the same basic conception for the possibility of different actors and several sectors of security: *'a set of units whose major processes of securitisation, desecuritisation, or both are so interlinked that their security problems cannot reasonably be analysed or resolved apart from one another'*. This more complicated formulation does not change the underlying idea or the main properties of the concept. The central idea remains that substantial parts of the securitisation and desecuritisation processes in the international system will manifest themselves in regional clusters. These clusters are both durable and distinct from global level processes of (de)securitisation. Each level needs to be understood both in itself and in how it interplays with the other.

Our 1998 book was aimed at meta-theoretical questions, and its more constructivist – but also more complicated – formulation of the nature of security in terms of practices of securitisation remains our frame of reference. Ultimately, we have an open framework in which it is left for history to decide whether states are the most important referent objects for security or, say, the environment. However, this wider framework does not predefine that states are *not* dominant. It is perfectly possible that the world *is* still largely state-centric, even if our framework is not. The finding is more interesting when the framework does not predetermine the result. Thus, one might see the relationship between the original, state-centric, and partly objectivist formulation of RSCT and the more recent presentation of it within the multisectoral, multi-actor securitisation perspective in parallel to that between Newtonian and Einsteinian physics: the latter is in principle the correct way to phrase things, but for the majority of cases (except extreme border cases) the former reaches the same results and is a much less complicated way of expression. Therefore we will use the terminology of states in the following pages to give the general idea of the normal RSC, and then add the refinements and the implications of the securitisation framework.

Regional security complex theory: main variables

RSCT is useful for three reasons. First it tells us something about the appropriate level of analysis in security studies, second it can organise empirical studies, and, third, theory-based scenarios can be established on the basis of the known possible forms of, and alternatives to, RSCs. These we will turn to in the following two sections, but first we have to clarify the status of RSCs and their main analytical components.

RSCs are defined by durable patterns of amity and enmity taking the form of subglobal, geographically coherent patterns of security interdependence. The particular character of a local RSC will often be affected by historical factors such as long-standing enmities (Greeks and Turks, Arabs and Persians, Khmers and Vietnamese), or the common cultural embrace of a civilisational area (Arabs, Europeans, South Asians, Northeast Asians, South Americans). The formation of RSCs derives from the interplay between, on the one hand, the anarchic structure and its balance-of-power consequences, and on the other the pressures of local geographical proximity. Simple physical adjacency tends to generate more security interaction among neighbours than among states located in different areas, a point also emphasised by Walt (1987: 276–7). Adjacency is potent for security because many threats travel more easily over short distances than over long ones. The impact of geographical proximity on security interaction is strongest and most obvious in the military, political, societal, and environmental sectors. The general rule that adjacency increases security interaction is much less consistent in

45

the economic sector (Buzan et al. 1998: 95–117). All the states in the system are to some extent enmeshed in a global web of security interdependence. But because insecurity is often associated with proximity, this interdependence is far from uniform. Anarchy plus the distance effect plus geographical diversity yields a pattern of regionally based clusters, where security interdependence is markedly more intense between the states inside such complexes than between states inside the complex and those outside it. South Asia provides a clear example, where the wars and rivalries of the subcontinent constitute a distinctive pattern that has been little affected by events in the Gulf or in Southeast Asia (Buzan, Rizvi et al. 1986).

The basic premise that security interdependence tends to be regionally focused is strongly mediated by the power of the units concerned. As shown in chapter 2, superpowers have such wide-ranging interests, and such massive capabilities, that they can conduct their rivalries over the whole planet. Superpowers by definition largely transcend the logic of geography and adjacency in their security relationships. At the other end of the power spectrum are states whose limited capabilities largely confine their security interests and activities to their near neighbours, as in Southeast Asia or Southern Africa. Possession of great power thus tends to override the regional imperative, and small power to reinforce it. Smaller states will usually find themselves locked into an RSC with their neighbours, great powers will typically penetrate several adjacent regions, and superpowers will range over the whole planet. Local states can of course securitise threats seen to come from distant great powers, but this does not necessarily, or even usually, constitute security interdependence.

What links the overarching pattern of distribution of power among the global powers to the regional dynamics of RSCs is the mechanism of penetration. Penetration occurs when outside powers make security alignments with states within an RSC. An indigenous regional rivalry, as between India and Pakistan, provides opportunities or demands for the great powers to penetrate the region. Balance-of-power logic works naturally to encourage the local rivals to call in outside help, and by this mechanism the local patterns of rivalry become linked to the global ones. South Asia during the Cold War gave a clear example, with Pakistan linked to the United States and China, and India linked to the Soviet Union. Such linkage between the local and global security patterns is a natural feature of life in an anarchic system. One of the purposes of RSCT is to combat the tendency to overstress the role of the great powers, and to ensure that the local factors are given their proper weight in security analysis. The standard form for an RSC is a pattern of rivalry, balance-of-power, and alliance patterns among the main powers *within* the region: to this pattern can then be added the effects of penetrating external powers. Normally the pattern of conflict stems from factors indigenous to the region – such as, for instance, in South Asia or in the Middle East – and outside powers cannot (even if heavily involved) usually define, desecuritise, or reorganise the region. Unipolarity might in its extreme form be an exception to this rule; when both sides of a local conflict are dependent on the same power, it is possible for that power to pressure the conflicting parties into peace processes, for example, the Middle East (see B. Hansen 2000) and, in the case of European regional unipolarity, the Stability Pact for Central Europe (Wæver 1996b: 229–31, 1998a: 99–100).

The pattern of amity and enmity is normally best understood by starting the analysis from the regional level, and extending it towards inclusion of the global actors on the one side and domestic factors on the other. The specific pattern of who fears or likes whom is generally not imported from the system level, but generated internally in the region by a mixture of history, politics, and material conditions. For most of the states in the international system, the regional level is the crucial one for security analysis. For the global powers, the regional level is crucial in shaping both the options for, and consequences of, projecting their influences and rivalries into the rest of the system. The regional level matters most for the states within it, but also substantially for the global powers. Security features at the level of regions are durable. They are substantially self-contained not in the sense of being totally free-standing, but rather in possessing a security dynamic that would exist even if other actors did not impinge on it. This relative autonomy was revealed by the ending of the Cold War, when enmities such as that between Israel and Syria, and Iraq and the Gulf Arab states, easily survived the demise of a superpower rivalry that had supported, but not generated, them.

'Regional security complex' is not just a *perspective* that can be applied to any group of countries. One can argue about the correct interpretation of the boundaries formed by patterns of relative security interdependence and indifference, but within the terms of the theory one cannot just use the term RSC for any group of states (Norden, the Warsaw Pact, the Non-Proliferation Treaty members, the GCC states, Africa). In order to qualify as an RSC, a group of states or other entities must possess a degree of security interdependence sufficient both to establish them as a linked set and to differentiate them from surrounding security regions. Regions are not, as some argue, 'necessarily arbitrarily defined' (Khalilzad 1984: preface; B. Hansen 2000: 9). Within the terms of RSCT, RSCs define themselves as substructures of the international system by the relative intensity of security interdependence among a group of units, and security indifference between that set and surrounding units.

Two important questions need to be settled here. First, the existence of an RSC is not in terms of the discursive 'construction of regions'. We are not (in this context) allowing, e.g., 'Europe' to be defined by how actors construct 'Europe' as a way to define its boundaries, or whether 'the Middle East' is an accepted regional definition in the region it applies to (which it is not). *Regional security complex* is an analytical concept defined and applied by us, but these regions (RSCs) are socially constructed in the sense that they are contingent on the *security practice* of the actors. Dependent on what and whom they securitise, the region might reproduce or change. We study the security discourses and security practices of actors, not *primarily* their regional(ist) discourses and practices. The latter is an interesting and important question (see Fawcett and Hurrell 1995; Schulz et al. 2001), and is an *element* of our analysis, but not the basis of it. Our approach is constructed around 'security'. According to our theory 'security' *is* what actors make it, and it is for the analyst to map these practices. Consequently, these two ways of understanding the definition of regions have to be kept separate. The regionalist discourses of actors are part of their political struggle, and how they define the region has to be studied. 'Regional security complex' is our analytical term and therefore something is an RSC when it qualifies according to our criteria, not according to the criteria of practitioners. What we pass judgement on is securitisation practices of practitioners. Their practice in terms of labelling regions is only indirectly related to our criteria as such. RSCs are thus a very specific, functionally defined type of region, which may or may not coincide with more general understandings of region.

A second issue is whether RSCs are exclusive or overlapping. In contrast to the argument made by Lake and Morgan (1997c) that RSCs can have overlapping memberships (which we examine in more detail in the final section of this chapter, pp. 78–82), our position is that they are mutually exclusive. We take as the starting point of the analysis that the whole world has to be divided up on a map producing mutually exclusive RSCs, insulator states, and global actors. RSCs are distinguished from each other by degrees of relative security connectedness and indifference. They are distinguished from global powers by occupying a different level of analysis as defined in chapter 2. If this set-up produces complications, anomalies, and difficulties, these are exactly what should be explained and what the theory has then served to alert us to. External involvement is analysed by the use of 'penetration' and 'overlay'. Difficult border cases between regions may be explained by noticing an insulator state, or a case of asymmetry where a neighbouring great power leans on a weaker neighbouring RSC. Strong instances of interregional dynamics may be indicators of an external transformation (merger) of RSCs.

As argued in our previous book (Buzan et al. 1998: 163–93), it is in the nature of security practice as a prioritising and thus implicitly comparative move that actors themselves integrate and hierarchise security issues. Since one threat is interpreted in the light of other threats, we get an integrated field of security, not separate issues or for that matter separate sectors of say 'economic security' and 'societal security'. Thus, the different issues get tied together, and a world of regions is therefore less unlikely than one might at first think when listing the diversity of security issues each drawing on a particular sector. So if we make the starting assumption that the world can be divided into a definite number of exclusive RSCs, what problems do we then have to solve on the way, which of these are instructive, and which are just artificially self-imposed? We return to these questions in part VI.

Within the structure of anarchy, the essential structure and character of RSCs are defined by two kinds of relations, power relations and patterns of amity and enmity. The idea that power operates on a regional scale is well known from the concept of a regional balance of power, in which powers that are not directly linked to each other still take part in the same network of relations. Thus RSCs, like the international system of which they are substructures, can be analysed in terms of polarity, ranging from unipolar, through bi- and tripolar, to multipolar. This is why it is essential to distinguish regional powers from global level ones.

The second component, patterns of amity and enmity, has been much less featured in IR theory than has power, an early exception being Wolfers (1962: 25–35). Indeed, in the more extreme versions of power theory (maximalist realism), they are simply reflections of power relations: one fears whoever wields greater power. Less dogmatically, they might be seen as 'much stickier than the relatively fluid movement of the distribution of power' (Buzan 1991b: 190; parallel to Krasner's (1983) classical discussion of regimes as intermediary variables and many other modified realisms, see Guzzini 1994). More realistically, these patterns are allocated a historically derived reality of their own as the socially constructed dimension of structure (Buzan and Little 2000: 68–89).

Those of a Wendtian predisposition can see that his social theory can easily be applied as a useful constructivist elaboration of the amity–enmity variable in RSCT, though his scheme is more differentiated than the simple dyad of enemy or friend. Wendt's idea of social structures of anarchy (Hobbesian, Lockean, Kantian) is based on 'what kind of roles – enemy, rival, friend – dominate the system' (Wendt 1999: 247); and how deeply internalised these roles are – by coercion (external force), by interest (calculations of gain and loss), and by belief in legitimacy (understandings of right and wrong, good and bad). All of these ideas work as comfortably at the regional level as they do at the global one. His observation that there is no necessary correlation between type of social structure and degree of internalisation (e.g., warrior cultures, whether tribal or fascist, can believe in the virtue of enemy relations and therefore generate a deeply internalised Hobbesian social structure) is a particularly useful insight into thinking about RSCs. We hope to use our regional cases to assess the viability of Wendt's assumption that one particular role (enemy, rival, friend) dominates sufficiently to assign an overall social structure to a system or subsystem. It is thus not enough to look at the distribution of power in order to predict the patterns of conflict – even if distribution of power might tell us quite a bit about what constellations are impossible and which might be likely. Historical hatreds and friendships, as well as specific issues that trigger conflict or cooperation, take part in the formation of an overall constellation of fears, threats, and friendships that define an RSC. These patterns of amity and enmity are influenced by various background factors such as history, culture, religion, and geography, but to a large extent they are path-dependent and thus become their own best explanation.

RSCs are durable rather than permanent patterns. As substructures, they can have mediating effects on relations between the great powers and the local states as well as on the interactions of states in the regions. The RSC constitutes a social reality, which is more than the sum of its parts, and thus it is able to intervene between intentions and outcomes. Although the RSC does not exist independently of the states and their vulnerabilities, the outcome of their interactions would be different if it were not for the existence of the RSC. It is not a root cause in itself but a structure that modifies and mediates the action and interaction of units.

Descriptive RSCT: a matrix for area studies

The most well-established function for RSCT is as a framework organising empirical studies of regional security. The theory specifies what to look for at four levels of analysis and how to interrelate these. The four levels are:

1. domestically in the states of the region, particularly their domestically generated vulnerabilities (is the state strong or weak due to stability of the domestic order and correspondence between state and nation (Buzan 1991b)? The specific vulnerability of a state defines the kind of security fears it has (Wæver 1989) – and sometimes makes another state or group of states a structural threat even if it or they have no hostile intentions);
2. state-to-state relations (which generate the region as such);
3. the region's interaction with neighbouring regions (this is supposed to be *relatively* limited given that the complex is defined by interaction internally being more important. But if major changes in the patterns of security interdependence that define complexes are underway, this level can become significant, and in situations of gross asymmetries a complex without global powers that neighbours one with a global power can have strong interregional links in one direction); and finally
4. the role of global powers in the region (the interplay between the global and regional security structures).

Taken together, these four levels constitute the *security constellation* (Buzan et al. 1998: 201ff.). Since the earliest development of RSCT we have also allowed the idea of *subcomplexes* as a 'half-level' within the regional one, and we stick with that here. Subcomplexes have essentially the same definition as RSCs, the difference being that a subcomplex is firmly embedded within a larger RSC. Subcomplexes represent distinctive patterns of security interdependence that are nonetheless caught up in a wider pattern that defines the RSC as a whole. The clearest example is in the Middle East, where distinct subcomplexes can be observed in the Levant (Egypt, Israel, Jordan, Lebanon, Syria) and in the Gulf (Iran, Iraq, GCC), but where there is so much overlap and interplay that the two cannot be disentangled (all of the Gulf states are hostile to Israel, rivalry between Syria and Iraq, etc.). Subcomplexes are not a necessary feature of RSCs, but they are not uncommon either, especially where the number of states in an RSC is relatively large. The device of subcomplexes eliminates most of what might otherwise occur as disturbing cases of overlapping membership between RSCs: e.g., if the Gulf and the Levant were seen as separate RSCs, Iraq would be a member of both but, with these as subcomplexes, Iraq can be a member both of the Gulf subcomplex and of the wider Middle Eastern one.

RSCT asserts that the regional level will always be operative, and sometimes dominant. It does *not* say that the regional level *must* always be dominant. We argue that all four levels of a security constellation are simultaneously in play. The question of which level is dominant is not set by the theory, even though particular circumstances (on which more later) might swing the odds one way or another. Determining the balance among the levels rests on empirical observation of particular cases, and in that sense the case studies that compose this book will be a test of our (and others') assumption from chapter 1 that the conditions of the post-Cold War world will enhance the salience of the regional level for security. Just as in the social world individual psychology might be most influential in explaining behaviour in one case, family structures in another, and national society in yet another, so in the international world domestic factors might dominate some security constellations, regional ones others, and global ones yet others. The regional level may or may not dominate, but it will nearly always be in play in some significant sense, and cannot be dropped out of the analysis.

In its descriptive application RSCT is aimed at people working empirically on specific regions. It is mostly a descriptive language, a method for producing order out of complicated data, and for writing structural history. The theory offers the possibility of systematically linking the study of internal conditions, relations among units in the region, relations between regions, and the interplay of regional dynamics with globally acting powers. It also provides some structural logic, most notably the hypothesis that regional patterns of conflict shape the lines of intervention by global level powers. Other things being equal, the expectation is that outside powers will be drawn into a region along the lines of rivalry existing within it. In this way regional patterns of rivalry may line up with, and be reinforced by, global power ones, even though the global power patterns may have had little or nothing to do with the formation of the regional pattern.

One purpose of descriptive RSCT is to establish a benchmark against which to identify and assess changes at the regional level. Because RSCs are durable substructures with an important geographical component, they have both internal structures and external boundaries that can be used to monitor continuity and change and to distinguish significant change from less important events. The *essential structure* of an RSC embodies four variables:

1. boundary, which differentiates the RSC from its neighbours;
2. anarchic structure, which means that the RSC must be composed of two or more autonomous units;
3. polarity, which covers the distribution of power among the units; and
4. social construction, which covers the patterns of amity and enmity among the units.

From its configuration at any given snapshot in time there are thus three possible evolutions open to an RSC:

1. *maintenance of the status quo,* which means that there are no significant changes in its essential structure;
2. *internal transformation,* which means that changes in essential structure occur *within* the context of its existing outer boundary. This could mean changes to the anarchic structure (because of regional integration); to polarity (because of disintegration, merger, conquest, differential growth rates, or suchlike); or to the dominant patterns of amity/enmity (because of ideological shifts, war-weariness, changes of leadership, etc.); and
3. *external transformation,* which means that the outer boundary expands or contracts, changing the membership of the RSC, and most probably transforming its essential structure in other ways. The most obvious way for this to happen is if two RSCs merge, as might happen if Israel became dramatically concerned about Pakistan's 'Islamic' nuclear weapons; or less often two RSCs splitting out from one.

Types of security complex

Within these parameters of structure and evolution, it is possible to identify different types of RSC. In our previous works we have talked about variations in polarity from unipolar to multipolar, and about variations in amity and enmity ranging from *conflict formation* through *security regime* to *security community* (Wæver 1989; Buzan 1991b: 218). Wend-tians should note that conflict formation, security regime, and secur-ity community run in parallel with Wendt's Hobbesian, Lockean, and Kantian social structures. The main differences are that conflict forma-tion is rather wider than Wendt's Hobbesian model, and security regime is probably a rather narrower idea than his Lockean model. The same parallel could be drawn with the English School's three traditions of Hobbes, Grotius, and Kant (Cutler 1991) on which Wendt (1999) draws. We have also sometimes talked about 'centred' regions (Wæver 1993a, 1997b), where centralisation of power in a region reaches a point at which its centre is primarily to be seen as a participant in the global security constellation among the greatest powers, and the regional dynamics can no longer be seen as a subsystem in which the primary fears and con-cerns of a group of states are defined by each other. One example of this is North America. The EU integration process might be thought of as moving towards another, albeit in a rather different way, and we have talked of this in terms of scenarios of 'fragmentation' and 'integration' (Buzan et al. 1990; Wæver et al. 1993). But we have not yet unfolded the whole range of possibilities in sufficient detail, nor have we had the benefit of a clearly worked-out differentiation between the regional and global level such as that set out in chapter 2. Our earlier classifications consequently blur or hide some significant issues.

The presence of several global powers in the international system (as in the present 1 + 4 system) raises questions about how great powers and superpowers interact with regions. The view of polarity cultivated during the Cold War assumed that the superpowers stood outside the regions as well as above them. On that basis, one could construct clear models of global and regional level security dynamics, and ask questions about how the two levels played into each other (Buzan 1991b: 186–229). The global level was distinguished by being unpenetrated by other pow-ers, while the standard condition of RSCs was to be penetrated by out-side powers. This scheme always ignored the regions within which the superpowers sat and, like Cold War polarity theory, fudged awkward questions about which level China occupied. But if there are several global level powers in the system, then it is unlikely that any complete differentiation between the global and regional levels will be possible. Some global level powers will be inside regions, while others, most obviously China at the present time, will have considerable entangle-ments in neighbouring regions, and will be operating at both levels simultaneously. How do we deal with these problems, especially in the light of needing to fill in a map of the whole planet?

The first step is to draw a distinction between *standard* and *centred* RSCs. A standard RSC is broadly Westphalian in form with two or more powers and a predominantly military-political security agenda. All standard complexes are anarchic in structure. In standard RSCs, polarity is defined wholly by regional powers (e.g., Iran, Iraq, and Saudi Arabia in the Gulf, India and Pakistan in South Asia) and may vary from uni- to multipolar. In standard RSCs, unipolarity means that the region contains only one regional power: Southern Africa (where South Africa is a giant compared to its neighbours) provides the clearest example. It is not centred, because the security dynamics of the region are not dominated from the unipolar power at its centre. Although they can be unipolar in this sense, standard RSCs *do not* contain a global level power, and therefore in such regions (currently Africa, the Middle East, South America, and South Asia) clear distinctions can be drawn between inside, regional level dynamics, and outside, intervening, global level ones. In terms of amity and enmity, standard RSCs may be conflict formations, security regimes, or security communities, in which the region is defined by a pattern of rivalries, balances, alliances, and/or concerts and friendships. Within a standard RSC the main element of security politics is the relationship among the regional powers inside the region. Their relations set the terms for the minor powers and for the penetration of the RSC by global powers.

Centred RSCs come in three (potentially four) main forms. The first two forms are the special cases in which an RSC is unipolar, but the power concerned is either a great power (e.g., Russia in the CIS) or a superpower (e.g., the United States in North America), rather than just a regional power. The expectation in these cases is that the global level power will dominate the region (unipolarity), and that what would otherwise count as regional powers (Ukraine, Canada, Mexico) will not have sufficient relative weight to define another regional pole. Part of the reason that India's claim for great power status has not been accepted is that Pakistan still defines a regional pole of power. It is possible that a unipolar standard RSC could also become centred without the unipole thereby elevating itself to global great power status. One can imagine such a scenario developing around regional level unipoles such as South Africa and Nigeria, but in fact we find no cases of this type (more on this in part VI).

One might think of the Cold War relationship between Eastern Europe and the Soviet Union as an extreme case of a superpower-centred region, where Eastern Europe was not just overlaid, but virtually absorbed into a kind of Soviet empire, the whole acting more or less as a single entity at the global level. Less extreme, but comparable, is the situation in North America centred on the United States. The USA projects bases and military interventions into Central America and the Caribbean and, while it certainly cannot be said that this region functions as a unit at the global level, US influence clearly impinges on the indigenous security dynamics in quite major ways. In this rather odd hybrid, the core actor is driven much more by global than by regional security dynamics, and during the Cold War it was primarily global concerns that drove its security impositions on its smaller neighbours. Because the core actor is globally orientated, the security dynamics of the region are hugely distorted and suppressed. But since all other actors in the region have their concerns linked to each other, a general map of global security would still show a clear regional formation of densely knit connections compared to a lack of connections in and out of the region for most units. This therefore can still be treated as an RSC.

The third form of a centred RSC is very different, involving a region integrated by institutions rather than by a single power. The EU provides the example, hanging halfway between being a region in the form of a highly developed security community, and being a great power in its own right with actor quality at the global level. Another, though more problematic, example would be the USA during its 'Philadelphian' era (Deudney 1995). Like one of those drawings that can be either a rabbit or a duck depending how you look at it, the EU can be either a great power or an RSC in security community form. Institutional centredness created by the members of an RSC poses some problems for RSCT. The definition of RSCs (and the general methodology of our security analysis) is based on the security actions and concerns of actors: an RSC must contain dynamics of securitisation. Usually this means that the actors in the region securitise each other. But the development of a security community is marked by processes of desecuritisation, or what Wendt would think of as a Kantian social structure: actors stop treating each other as security problems and start behaving as friends. They still compete and feel challenged now and then, but this is dealt with as are normal political, economic, environmental, and societal problems – not as matters of *security*, i.e., threats to survival that mobilise extreme countermeasures. If a centred region moved into this kind of general desecuritisation, it might eventually leave the world of security altogether and thereby also the map of RSCs (logically, this would also be true of non-centred security communities, though such a development is hard to imagine).

In the real world the extreme case of a region of total desecuritisation is not empirically significant, and the most mature cases of security communities today are not marked by a general forgetting of security concerns but rather by a conscious aggregation of them. As often stated explicitly in Europe, because of the risk of a return to power balancing, rivalry, and thereby eventually war, we Europeans have to do this (integrate) and abstain from that (beggar-thy-neighbour or rival intervention policies). The classical Deutschian definition of a security community (Deutsch et al. 1957: 5–9) states that the actors cannot *imagine* a war among each other. This would imply the complete desecuritisation form of security community and fits nicely with the neofunctionalist strategy of technocratic depoliticisation that marked European integration in the 1950s and 1960s. However, both today and at that time among the elites themselves, the process rested on the generalised security argument that one had to integrate to avoid the wars that thereby *were* imaginable. European integration and cooperation were not fully desecuritised – the historical trajectory itself was highly securitised (see Wæver 1998a; and Hurrell 1998 on Latin America). In a previous empirical study of securitisation in the EU, we found that the most intense and regular threat was Europe itself, the risk of Europe's past becoming also Europe's future (Buzan et al. 1998: 179–89; see also Wæver 1996b). The Southern Cone in South America is close to creating a security community based on securitising primarily an external economic threat, and from this deriving the necessity of regional pacification. The most relevant form of security community contains active and regional securitisation, only it is not actor-to-actor (one state fearing the other and therefore counterthreatening it), but a collective securitisation of the overall development of the region. Therefore, security community is a possible, if uncommon, form for an RSC. It is not a development that necessarily moves beyond the status of RSC.

But the EU case also points to a further difficulty. Not only has the EU moved strongly towards the amity end of the amity–enmity spectrum, it has also created joint institutions that are substantial enough to raise the question of whether it still qualifies as an international anarchy. In principle one could imagine a high level of security community without much in the way of accompanying institutions, but it is easier to imagine that well-developed security communities will normally become increasingly institutionalised and integrated. In the case of the EU, centredness comes not from the domination of a single pole of power, but from the building by a group of states of collective institutions that are beginning to take on actor quality in their own right. It is not unreasonable to ask whether what goes on inside the EU is domestic or international politics, and this question is difficult to answer with any clarity. The situation is *sui generis*, and for our purposes it raises the question of when a process of integration replaces anarchic with hierarchic political structure sufficiently to say that what was an RSC in security community mode has instead become a single actor.

Integration processes may have a variety of impacts. They may, as would be the case with an EU actor, transform virtually a whole RSC into a great power, and thus transform the structure of polarity in the international system as a whole. But integration processes can also occur within RSCs, as happened with the unifications of the USA in North America, Germany and Italy in Europe, and as might happen in Korea, changing the local but not the global polarity. There may of course still be security dynamics in a centred region – cultural units will still be concerned about their societal security (the European nations in a future unified Europe, the 'races' of today's United States), and environmental security obviously is still at stake, but as centredness becomes the making of a new unit, the political consequences of these securitisations are constrained by the disappearance of balancing options and the increasing salience of a centre–periphery constellation.

What links these three types of centred RSC together is the idea that the security dynamics of a region are dominated from a centre located within it. This is partly a question of how dominant the centre is (i.e., the degree of power asymmetry), but equally of the form of hegemony established. A centred RSC is more likely to be stable if the centre establishes a kind of open or penetrated hegemony, where dominated states are given access to the policy process of the 'imperial centre' (see Deudney and Ikenberry 1999; Kupchan 1998; Ikenberry 2001). Even stronger is the case where the centre is a construct of the units such as the EU and the early USA, when still anarchically structured (Deudney 1995). Wholly imperial centred regions retain their form mainly as a result of power, and are less likely to survive changes in the distribution of power (viz. the break-up of the Soviet empire). These considerations run parallel to Kratochwil's (1989) and Wendt's (1999) ideas about how social structures get internalised: superficially if coercion is the mechanism, deeply if they get accepted as legitimate. We will use Adam Watson's (1992) term *legitimacy* in this context as the general designation of the degree of acceptance (also among the peripheral units) of centredness as natural and correct, not imposed against some timeless standard of maximum independence.

Having sorted out the distinction between standard and centred RSCs, the second step is to deal with the cases that do not fit into either category and in a sense fall between them. These cases arise from having a number of global level powers scattered throughout the system. The more such powers there are in a system, the less room there will be for standard RSCs; the fewer, the more room. Having great powers scattered through the international system creates two possibilities other than centred complexes: *great power regional security complexes*, and *supercomplexes*. In the present 1 + 4 system, both possibilities are most clearly visible in Asia.

In a great power RSC, the polarity of a region is defined by more than one global level power being contained within it. This was traditionally the case in Europe, and is now the case in East Asia, where China and Japan form the core of a bipolar great power RSC. Great power RSCs have to be treated differently from ordinary RSCs for two reasons. First, their dynamics directly affect balancing calculations at the global level in ways that one would not expect from a standard RSC. Second, because great powers are involved, one would expect wider spillover into adjacent regions, in other words, a higher intensity of interregional interaction than would normally be the case. Great power RSCs are hybrids of the global and regional levels. In some ways they can be analysed in the same way as standard RSCs in terms of polarity, amity–enmity, boundaries, and suchlike. But because their dynamics involve global level powers, they affect, are indeed part of, the global level security dynamics. In a 1 + 4 system, or anything like it, the existence of a great power RSC as a subset of the global polarity shapes the options available both to the powers involved and to the other powers in the system. Where two or more great powers share a regional RSC, then the internal dynamics of that RSC, whether of amity or enmity, will be a significant factor in global level security dynamics. If the great powers are all in centred RSCs, then the regional level does not directly affect how they interact with each other, except inasmuch as trouble *within* a centred RSC might weaken its great power in relation to its peers (Russia's problem).

The second difference from standard RSCs arises from the spillover effects consequent upon the presence of great powers. Great powers will normally be capable of projecting their power into adjacent regions and, other things being equal, can be expected to do so. The presence of global level powers in an area is thus likely to violate the rule that interregional security dynamics will usually be weak, by allowing an adjacent great power to play strongly into one or more neighbouring regions in a sustained way. The clearest example here is China, which during the Cold War played not only into the great power RSC in Northeast Asia, but also into the standard RSCs in Southeast Asia and South Asia. China plays into South Asia as an ally of Pakistan and an opponent of India, meaning that India has to divert substantial energies to balancing China. Similarly, in Southeast Asia during the Cold War, China fought a war with Vietnam. A weaker version of the same story can be found in US engagement with South America. The fact of adjacency makes this relationship qualitatively different from a normal global power intervention into an RSC because the option of disengagement is not really available in the same way. The USA or Russia can decide whether or not to be in Southeast Asia in a way China cannot (or cannot without endangering its status as a great power).

Put more formally, the rule violation attendant on the presence of great powers is that, in contrast to standard RSCs, we should expect them to generate a sustained and substantial level of interregional security dynamics. Rather than expecting the security dynamics of the interregional level to be weak in relation to those of the global and regional levels, we expect them to be strong. This spillover might result from the actions of a single great power, as in the case of China. Or it might result from the dynamics of a great power RSC, as might be imagined if China and Japan became serious rivals or friends in Asia. Either way, such intense spillover may well bind together what would otherwise be separate RSCs into *supercomplexes* with one or more great powers at their core. In such cases the security constellation becomes more elaborate than usual. Instead of there being just three main levels (domestic, regional, and global) to take into account, one may have to add a fourth, superregional, level to replace the normally weak interregional one. In a supercomplex, the interregional level is strong and sustained, as it has been between Northeast Asia and South Asia, but not so strong as to override the regional dynamics in the penetrated RSC (in this case, South Asia). If the interregional dynamics do override the regional ones, as happened during the 1990s between Northeast and Southeast Asia, the spillover subordinates the previous patterns of regional security dynamics, and the component RSCs within the supercomplex undergo external transformation, merging to form a new and larger RSC (in this case, East Asia). More on this in part II. As with the idea of subcomplexes, supercomplexes pick up cases of what would otherwise seem to be dual memberships.

Analysing cases of this sort requires paying close attention to the whole spectrum of levels making up the security constellation: domestic, regional, superregional, and global. In the Asian case, all the levels are in play at the same time, confronting all of the states concerned with an extremely difficult hand to play: China and Japan cannot disentangle their regional and superregional roles from their global ones. In supercomplexes, as in standard ones, weaker powers may well seek superpower and/or great power support against the regional power (Huntington 1999: 45–7). In a standard RSC, the consequences of such alignments will resonate mostly at the regional level, and only indirectly at the global one (if, for example, there are rival superpower engagements in a region, as in the Middle East during the Cold War). But in a great power RSC, or a supercomplex, such alignments will resonate directly at the global level, as well as at the regional one. As the United States discovered in Vietnam, and the Soviet Union in Afghanistan, misunderstanding the interplay of the different levels can come at a high price.

Explaining the absence of RSCs

So far we have talked only about the nature and definition of RSCs, and the theory has implied that, in principle, the map of any international system meeting the conditions of the theory could and should be completely filled in by a set of RSCs. But this is not the case. There is also the possibility that the regional level fails to function because the local actors do not generate their own patterns of security interdependence. RSCT presupposes that the units concerned are normal members of an international system: 'normal' in the sense that they possess autonomy to make their own policy and the power capabilities to engage the other units in the system. There are two general sets of conditions in which RSCs do not, or cannot, form: *overlay* and *unstructured*.

> *Overlay* is when great power interests transcend mere penetration, and come to dominate a region so heavily that the local pattern of security relations virtually ceases to operate. It usually results in the long-term stationing of great power armed forces in the region, and in the alignment of the local states according to the patterns of great power rivalry. The strongest examples of overlay are European colonisation of Africa, Asia, and the Americas, and the situation of Europe itself during the

Table 1 *Summary of types of security complex*

Type	Key features	Example(s)
Standard	Polarity determined by regional powers	Middle East, South America, Southeast Asia, Horn, Southern Africa
Centred		
Superpower	Unipolar centred on a superpower	North America
Great power	Unipolar centred on a great power	CIS, potentially South Asia
[Regional power]	Unipolar centred on a regional power	none
Institutional	Region acquires actor quality through institutions	EU
Great power	Bi- or multipolar with great powers as the regional poles	Pre-1945 Europe, East Asia
Supercomplexes	Strong interregional level of security dynamics arising from great power spillover into adjacent regions	East and South Asia

Cold War, when the classical European security dynamic was overlaid by the superpower rivalry. Northeast and Southeast Asia during the Cold War were heavily penetrated but not overlaid because their regional level dynamics remained significant. The term overlay will not be applied to dynamics *within* regions although the pattern in a centred RSC in some ways can be seen as analogous because a great (or super) power dominates a region. But since it is a power *of* the region, the region has not succumbed to extra-regional dynamics and therefore the situation is not designated overlay. Even situations where a distinct subcomplex is secondary to the core of an RSC (Central America in North America, the Balkans in EU-Europe) should not be designated overlay, because the subcomplex is part of what constitutes the RSC.

Unstructured security regions occur for either or both of two reasons: first, where local states have such low capability that their power does not project much, if at all, beyond their own boundaries; and, second, where geographical insulation makes interaction difficult (for example, islands separated by large expanses of ocean). Either condition can result in insufficient generation of security interdependence to form the structures of an RSC. Low capability of course amplifies the

effect of geographical insulators, and high capability reduces it. But
even for capable actors it makes a difference whether one's borders are
defined by seas (Britain, New Zealand) or high mountains (Spain), or
by open plains (Poland). Parts of sub-Saharan Africa and the Pacific
after decolonisation illustrate this condition.

In the case of overlay, the security region is defined by outside powers.
In the case of unstructured regions, it is defined in part by the absence
of regional dynamics, and in part by the negative space left over on the
map when all of the other security regions have been filled in.

Our previous presentations have not looked in much detail at these
options, but moving to predictive RSCT requires that we do so. Attention
must also be paid to the boundaries of these concepts, which like most
things in social science are matters of definition and degree rather than
sharp lines of discontinuity.

The main problem with overlay is to determine the boundary between
it and mere heavy penetration of an RSC by great powers. The key
to the distinction is that outside powers, rather than the interests and
interactions of the local states, must shape the main security dynamics of
the region. Normally this will mean that great powers have substantial
military forces based in the region. Overlay is easiest to see when it has
been imposed by force, by the invasion and occupation of a region by
outside powers. Thus when Britain took over South Asia, it overlaid the
local system, imposing on it both a strategic unity and a set of security
dynamics driven by the 'great game' of colonial rivalry with Russia.
More problematic is the semi-voluntary acceptance of overlay, when
local states agree to subordinate themselves to a significant degree to an
outside hegemon, and accept the stationing of its forces on their territory.
This describes the situation of much of Western Europe during the Cold
War (though less so of Germany where overlay extended from defeat in
war and subsequent occupation). Even so, Europe during the Cold War
counts as a case of overlay: clearly so in the east, but also in the west
on the grounds of more or less complete suppression of local security
dynamics plus extensive stationing of outside military forces. East Asia
was heavily penetrated rather than overlaid.

While overlay is clear enough in snapshot, it is more problematic when
looked at in historical perspective (Buzan 1989; Wæver 1990a). It might,
for example, seem possible to conceptualise Cold War Europe as 'an RSC
that is overlaid', in other words seeing overlay as a temporary phase in a
longer history where an RSC exists on either side of the overlay period.
However, this is rather dangerous, because when overlay is imposed on

what was an RSC, the region can easily be transformed, as happened in much of the third world during colonialism, and to Europe during the Cold War. What emerges after overlay might be a different RSC or no RSC. Therefore, overlay is in principle a non-RSC form that describes an area, although in practice it will often be a former and future RSC that is overlaid.

The simplest model of an unstructured security region is one in which the units are too weak as powers to generate security interdependence on a regional level. No regional RSC exists because the units do not become each other's main security concern. The image is of a security constellation dominated by the domestic level, and perhaps also the interregional and global levels. Reality, however, is rarely that simple, and a pristine unstructured region containing largely inward-looking units is hard to find. The South Pacific islands probably come closest to this model. The question is when security interaction becomes sufficient to start generating a regional security substructure. Unstructured regions thus must in one sense be seen as RSCs in the making, and where such conditions exist it is useful to employ some intermediate concepts. We will talk of *pre-complexes* when a set of bilateral security relations seems to have the potential to bind together into an RSC, but has not yet achieved sufficient cross-linkage among the units to do so. The Horn of Africa is a good example. And we will talk of *proto-complexes* when there is sufficient manifest security interdependence to delineate a region and differentiate it from its neighbours, but when the regional dynamics are still too thin and weak to think of the region as a fully fledged RSC. West Africa is the clearest example of this condition.

At this point, recall from chapter 1 the distinction (Buzan 1991b: 96–107) between weak/strong states and weak/strong powers. Obviously, security independence can very well be the product of the weakness of units, not only of their strength. In Africa weak states create more room for mercenaries, insurgencies, etc. When the states are weak and nonstate actors take on a relatively larger role, the question of the power of units (weak/strong powers) should logically be asked equally of all units, state and nonstate. If some of the 'other' units were strong and formed stable constellations of threat and vulnerability – e.g., transnational tribal groups – this could very well qualify as an RSC (and not only a pre- or proto-complex). Low interaction capacity in a region makes it difficult for RSCs to form.

Given that our aim in this book is to fill in the world map according to RSCT, we now have to hand the whole descriptive apparatus that we need. First we fill in the global level powers. Next we fill in the various types of RSC (standard, centred, great power), and any insulators between them. The internal character of the RSCs will range along a spectrum from conflict formation through security regime to security community, though institutionally centred RSCs will necessarily be towards the security community end of the spectrum. We expect that all of the global level powers will fit within either centred complexes or great power ones, though it is just about possible to imagine a political geography that would allow a global level power to stand alone. Then we fill in any supercomplexes, which would be superimposed on the pattern of complexes. Finally we add in any areas that are either unstructured (noting any pre- or proto-complexes) or overlaid. The proportions of these options will vary from one era to another. At the beginning of the twenty-first century, the bulk of the international system is filled with one or other type of RSC. But during the nineteenth century much of it was overlaid, and in earlier periods there large swaths were unstructured.

Predictive RSCT: scenarios

The descriptive framework set out in the previous section is useful not only for structuring empirical studies of particular areas. It also sets out the full range of possible conditions for a security region as a basis for generating scenarios. Using RSCT to generate predictive scenarios is a more demanding and more controversial role for the theory than providing an analytical framework for area studies. Ontologically, the scenarios are soft limits. One can make negative predictions on the basis of a scenario analysis (Wæver in preparation). It can be specified which options are relevant under which conditions. For instance we previously presented three scenarios for European security (Buzan et al. 1990) – we have since stated that history has now narrowed them down to two: fragmentation (a reassertion of balance-of-power logic within Europe and thus a return to some form of standard RSC) or integration (the replacement of the RSC by a single, global level actor) (Wæver 1991, 1993a, 1993b; Wæver et al. 1993). The scenarios are deduced logically from the range of possible conditions in which a security region can exist. We claim that they constitute actual *possibilities* – in contrast to those scenarios devised as ideal types, which are therefore so extreme that they are *less* likely to exist than the in-between situations. The question of what is possible is always a question of probabilities. Anything is possible. It is just a matter of how many other elements of our world have to change in order to make it so. Thus, the scenario analysis says: given the structure of the international system as it is, there are these possible forms the area can take. Which one becomes realised depends ultimately on politics, and structurally on the compatibility with other conditions – for instance, the dominant discursive structures regarding foreign policy orientation in the main powers (Holm 1992; Wæver 1994).

The scenarios cover the whole range of possible forms and, until the situation has reached one of these forms, the scenarios as realistic possibilities influence the situation as structural pressures pushing towards resolution in one direction or another. An example of such structural pressures is the role that integration and fragmentation options play in the EU (ch. 11). In general terms, the options are as follows:

> An unstructured region has the possibility of becoming an RSC or getting overlaid. It is hard to imagine an unstructured region leaping straight to integration without passing through one condition or the other.
> A standard RSC can undergo internal or external transformation or get overlaid. It is more difficult to imagine it unravelling back to an unstructured region, though not impossible (as, for example, if plague or environmental disaster greatly weakened all of the units), or moving directly to integration. An RSC in security community form has the possibility of building itself into a centred RSC, and possibly a new actor, by creating institutions. A centred great or superpower RSC, or a unipolar standard one, might do the same, probably more coercively, by becoming an empire. Conversely, either form could unravel back to standard multipolar mode, as happened to the Soviet empire. If an RSC contains subcomplexes, then these serve as markers for a possible split if the overarching issues tying the subcomplexes together fade away.
> An overlaid security region could transform into any of the other forms, depending on the depth and character of the changes induced in it by the experience of overlay.
> An integrated actor can disintegrate, as happened to the Soviet Union, Yugoslavia, Czechoslovakia, and Pakistan. If the actor is a large one, the most likely outcome is the creation of new RSCs and/or the internal or external transformation of existing ones. The disintegration of smaller actors is most likely either to define an internal transformation in the complex (Yugoslavia) or to have no effect on the essential structure of the complex (Pakistan, Czechoslovakia). The secession of Bangladesh from Pakistan is an interesting case of a major (in the sense of regional polarity-defining) actor disintegrating *without* affecting

the essential structure of the RSC: West Pakistan remained powerful enough to hold its position as a regional pole. It is rather unlikely that such disintegrations would move towards unstructured regions, though not at all impossible that elements of overlay or annexation might result.

The potential for internal transformation can be monitored by checking material conditions for possible changes (or not) of polarity, and discursive ones for possible changes (or not) of amity/enmity relations. The potential for external transformation can be monitored by looking at the intensity of interregional security dynamics, which should act as precursors to change. Where these are sparse and of low intensity, no change in the boundaries of RSCs is likely. Where interregional security dynamics are fairly thick, intense, and increasing, external transformations become more likely. Applying these general observations to specific cases allows one to focus more precisely on what are the likely, and unlikely, options for transformation. Here one can deploy additional variables such as interaction capacity, power differentials, and system polarity to fine-tune the general assessment.

Interaction capacity (technological and social infrastructure for transportation and communication: Buzan and Little 2000) plays quite strongly into the basic forms of security region. Low interaction capacity within the region is probably a necessary condition for unstructured security regions. It is safe to predict that Europe will not move towards being an unstructured security region because its internal interaction capacity is much too high to permit such an option. As we argued before, the real options for Europe seem to be two: either it continues to integrate, at some point becoming a new unit on the international stage, or it falls back towards one of the versions of a standard RSC. Since the Europeans have hung their security community so firmly on joint institutions, and since the present phase of these institutions does not look like a stable resting point (the degree of institutionalisation having created a democratic deficit and its accompanying legitimacy crisis, and more democratisation requiring more integration), and more generally because of the structural pressure of regional security, only these two options look possible (Wæver in preparation). Standard RSCs require quite high levels of interaction capacity within the region, and it is hard to imagine integration without high interaction capacity. Overlay, of course, can occur when interaction capacity in the region is low, but higher in the wider system.

The relative levels of power between the region and global actors is important primarily because overlay emerges as a relevant option at high degrees of disparity (to the advantage of the global actors). The prospects for overlay depend also on discursive structures (within both sides) on questions of imperialism and national interest. At the beginning of the twenty-first century, it is safe to predict on both grounds that Europe is not in danger of overlay. Africa might be vulnerable to it in power terms, but is protected by the unfashionable standing of imperialism worldwide, which restrains the powers that might otherwise have the capability and the interest to impose it. For an RSC to operate it must not be overlaid by the global level. Because many regions now meet this criterion (unlike during the nineteenth century) we are confident in supporting the view that the regional level will be more important in the post-Cold War world. In the particular situation where none of the regional actors is a global power, but a joint regional centre would be of first global rank (as the EU potentially could be), a specific dynamic is instigated, because unification serves the dual purpose of intra-regional pacification and extra-regional power status. The classical Realpolitik argument against integration, that states do not give up their status as powers, is partly turned upside down because only by integration do they become or remain global powers. In this situation global and regional polarity are mutually defining – one is not given as a precondition for the other.

Global polarity has a difficult role because on the one hand it is a very strong factor but on the other hand it is not possible to formulate in strong terms because geography intervenes – a region which is located close to one of the parties to a bipolar rivalry (Central America) is likely to be overlaid by one of the parties, a region that is posed between can be overlaid in the form of division (Europe), and a strategically peripheral region might be left largely on its own (South America).

Those options that are evidently possible operate as structural pressures on the units. They translate structural dynamics into the regional context, and thereby operate as the fourth tier of structure in a Waltzian universe. Thus, when the region has fallen into one scenario as a clear trend, the structural forces of the international system tend to reinforce this trend – the way Waltzian structure generally contains reproductive rather than transformative logic (Waltz 1979; Ruggie 1983; Dessler 1989) – making it in this way self-reinforcing until some major shock hits it from either inside or outside. This can be seen in the way that the demand pull from outside for the EU to act as a great power often seems stronger than the push towards a common foreign and security policy from inside, or by the attempts of the international community to stop the disintegration of the USSR and Yugoslavia. The three forms of security region (RSC, unstructured, overlaid), plus the main options within them, plus the possibility of exit to another level by regional integration, are all relevant as predictions because they are the only long-term stable forms. Since some of their conditions can be specified, it is possible in any given situation to say which ones are relevant if the situation is to change. To characterise an area in terms of which of the forms it is in is furthermore relevant at any given time – without change – because the different structures generate distinctly different security dynamics.

Orthodox Waltzians often make the error of explaining developments in a given region directly from the global power distribution (e.g., Mearsheimer (1990) in his famous 'Back to the Future' analysis of post-Cold War Europe), but the relevant power structure for the main actors in a region is the regional one. The main reasons for this oversight in mainstream neorealism are probably two. One is a general American bias towards thinking globally and seeing regions from above, as parts of a larger strategic, superpower setting, not bottom-up as the relevant context for regional actors. The other is a product of the scientific (and scientistic) preferences of American social sciences for general, abstract, and natural science-like theories (see Ross 1991; Wæver 1998b). Realist theory has therefore evolved away from geopolitical and historical specificity towards abstract 'systemic' theory which operates with 'units' that are defined as alike and non-located, i.e., the basic, simple premise of international politics that states are non-mobile is ignored (Mouritzen 1998). In classical geopolitics – and in RSCT – states (and other units) are located in concrete places and distance is mediated by terrain (Wæver 1997b). Global polarity is among the conditions that enable or constrain various possible polarities regionally, but within the regional level, whether the region is bipolar, multipolar, or unipolar generally tells one more about regional security than does the global polarity in which it is embedded (Wæver 1993a).

Our approach is akin to a security version of much political geography. However, this is much less common in the study of international security than one should expect. Within the discipline of IR, the mainstream lost geography in its search for abstract theory, and the critics usually reacted against the reactionary connotations of geopolitics. Academic geopolitics seem to have become polarised. Traditional geopolitics are too materialist and mechanical (Mackinder 1904; Cohen 1994), while 'critical geopolitics' on the other hand seem too absolutist in studying only the social construction of space (Ó Tuathail 1996). We believe that geography as such matters but that it has to be analysed in a political framework. In the policy literature, titles with 'The Geopolitics of...' are common (of Caspian oil, of the Yugoslav wars, etc.) but this usually means an atheoretical survey of some power politics. RSCT is a theory of security in which geographical variables are central.

Predictive SCT is *not* offered as a causal model in which each situation automatically produces one and only one scenario – a necessity if one is to be able to test the theory as a traditional causal model. The aim is to narrow down the range of relevant scenarios in any specific case. That there is often more than one possibility is the analytical point of establishing scenarios: i.e., that one points towards the space for political choice in shaping the outcome. For much of history, only one scenario appears as relevant, not necessarily because of these causal conditions, but because development has turned on to one of the tracks that then becomes self-reinforcing. At crucial moments of historical change, the situation is open and several scenarios become possible, though, as we have seen, rarely all. We will follow through these ideas about scenarios and structural conditions in each of the regional chapters.

Revised RSCT: constructivist method and the wider agenda of securitisation studies

Along with many others we have in recent years found it increasingly necessary to include in security studies more than military-political security. At first, one might expand the concept of security to new sectors while keeping the state as the focus, as the only 'referent object'. Especially when working on 'societal security', we realised that this was problematic. If security is always for the state, it implies that 'societal security' means the security of the state *against* society, i.e., society itself might be insecure and societal security high. This was too perverse, and in our 1993 book (Wæver et al. 1993) we eventually opened up the option of another referent object: in the societal sector, the referent object is any collectivity that defines its survival as threatened in terms of identity (typically, but not only, nations).

Once we had made this decisive move, it became clear that, although empirically most security action might be concentrated around states and nations, one could not analytically defend the exclusion of the possibility that other units or levels might establish themselves as referent objects for security. Also, the case of societal security underlined the importance of distinguishing between referent objects (that which is to be secured) and securitising actors (those who make claims about this security). The distinction has typically been ignored in the classical security literature because the state has an official system for 'who speaks security', and even the 'alternative' literature, because written up against the traditional one, mixed up the two issues as a general (rhetorical) question about who security was for.

When distinguishing between referent objects and securitising actors, it becomes possible to formulate a general theory of the conditions under which an actor successfully 'securitises' some threat on behalf of a specific 'referent object'. For contingent, empirical reasons this is more easily done on behalf of limited collectivities (states, nations, religions, clans, etc.) than on behalf of individuals or humankind, but there is no absolute necessity to this, and 'universal' principles are now beginning to take on some importance as referent objects in the political and the economic sectors (free trade, human rights, non-proliferation). Thus, it is possible to formulate a theory that is not dogmatically state-centric in its premises, but that is often somewhat state-centric in its findings.

To set up such an open, analytical framework able to catch security in its increasing variation – across sectors, levels, and diverse units – and to be able to judge when an instance qualifies as security, it is necessary to focus on the characteristic quality of a security issue, i.e., to have criteria by which to avoid the slippery slope of 'everything is security'. A security issue is posited (by a securitising actor) as a threat to the survival of some referent object (nation, state, the liberal international economic order, the rain forests), which is claimed to have a right to survive. Since a question of survival necessarily involves a point of no return at which it will be too late to act, it is not defensible to leave this issue to normal politics. The securitising actor therefore claims a right to use extraordinary means or break normal rules, for reasons of security (Wæver 1995c, 1997a; Buzan et al. 1998). With this definition of security, the approach has clearly turned constructivist in the sense that we do not ask whether a certain issue is in and of itself a 'threat', but focus on the questions of when and under what conditions who securitises what issue. The very act of labelling something a security issue – or a threat – transforms this issue and it is therefore in the political process of securitisation that distinct security dynamics originate. Although the theory specifies 'facilitating conditions' that make securitisation more or less likely (Buzan et al. 1998: 32–3, 46–7), the theory is not causal in a traditional sense, because securitisation is conceptualised as a performative act never exhaustively explained by its conditions. It not only realises already given potentials, but also produces genuine novelty; in what Bourdieu (1991) calls an act of 'social magic', something happens at this exact point and therefore the act can never be reduced to a transmission belt in causal chains (Derrida 1977, 1992; Weber 1995; Butler 1997; Campbell 1998: 25–8; Wæver 2000b).

Traditionally, RSCs were usually generated by bottom-up (or inside-out) processes in which the fears and concerns generated within the region produced the RSC. However, the new definition intentionally opens the possibility of another kind of construction of RSCs that is increasingly relevant especially in the 'new' sectors: regions can be created as patterns within system level processes (Buzan et al. 1998: 198–200). A group of countries that find themselves sharing the local effects of a climate change is a case of collective responses to shared fates arising from outside systemic pressure. However, the RSC is still constituted by the regional actors because they are the ones defining the problem in such terms and interacting to produce a regional formation over the issue. RSCs are ultimately defined by the interaction among their units – the causes behind their action might be bottom-up (and thus internal to the region) or top-down (and thus external/global), but these causes never fully explain the outcome. It is in the nature of politics – and thus security too – that some autonomy is left for the acts of securitisation by actors in the region. The pattern formed by these acts defines the RSC. If it were purely a product of global processes, it would obviously not be a regional level phenomenon.

As implied in this discussion, the new formulation also entails that the network of interconnecting security worries is no longer necessarily symmetrical. What one actor sees as a threat is not necessarily in itself an actor and thus not necessarily the subject of a counter-securitisation. The chain reactions are more complicated because A might securitise B as a threat with the effect that C becomes worried and securitises A as a threat. For instance, if Japan securitises foreign rice as a threat to Japanese national identity, and thereby legitimises protectionist measures in violation of WTO regulations, the United States might securitise this as a threat to the liberal international economic order (and to US economic interests), and the United States thereupon takes measures that, e.g., the EU/France and Russia see as symptoms of unipolar arrogance, and therefore they securitise ... and so forth. The complication is that it is really the relationships (the moves) that tie together, not the particular referent objects (Buzan et al. 1998: 21–47, 163–93; see Rosenau 1984 on relationships of relationships).

To trace RSCs empirically, one needs to look at the pattern of security connectedness in three steps:

(1)   is the issue securitised successfully by any actors?;
(2)   if yes, track the links and interactions from this instance – how does the security action in this case impinge on the security of who/what else, and where does this then echo significantly?, etc.;
(3)   these chains can then be collected as a cluster of interconnected security concerns.

When this case together with the patterns from all the other cases are aggregated, we can see on what level the processes of securitisation and the patterns of interaction are concentrated.

The main task in this book is to survey the cases that are established as major security issues today – for whatever reason and through whatever measures. A detailed tracing of each process of securitisation is mandatory in a study of a single case, but in large-scale, aggregate analyses like the ones that follow in this book, we cannot report on the process behind each securitisation. Size matters here too. Because we want to produce a global overview, we have had to operate on a high level of generalisation. To do that we need to use broad indicators of securitisation rather than investigating each instance in detail. In most cases we will therefore use visible outcomes such as war, mass expulsions, arms races, large-scale refugee movements, and other emergency measures as indicators of securitisation. If people are killing each other in organised ways, or spending large and/or escalating sums on armaments, or being driven from their homes in large numbers, or resorting to unilateral actions contrary in major ways to international undertakings, then it is virtually certain that successful securitisations have taken place. In practice, the use of such events as indicators is not much different from the analysis generated by a traditional perspective since it operates from the security issues that are on the agenda. This means that the immediate indicators used to establish security issues cannot except in the most crucial or tricky cases be the ideal ones of discourse itself; they will most often be phenomena that register in the media and traditional literature and that are systematically associated with securitisation. Only in the cases where the securitisation perspective makes an explicit difference to traditional perspectives will its terminology and apparatus be exploited to the full (i.e., cases that are only beginning to become security issues, or being desecuritised, or are contested as to whether they 'really' are security issues).

In practice this use of general indicators for securitisation means the chapters mainly unfold a relatively traditional story at the surface, so to say, of securitisations, without probing into their origins. It differs from traditional, objectivist security studies in taking securitisations rather than objective security problems as the basic dynamic of RSCs, i.e., the problems that are articulated as security problems, not those we project on to the region. However, a full-blown securitisation analysis would have to study more carefully how successfully different issues are securitised, by whom, and who contests this securitisation. Mostly we do not go into the single instances to clarify the nature of specific securitisations, because the nature of the present study as an integrative, synthesising, large-scale work prohibits this. With the maturing of securitisation studies, a synergy is emerging between micro-studies drawing on macro-studies and vice versa, but so far we have only a limited number of case studies to draw on, and these are mostly for Europe and North and South America, and to some extent the Middle East, Southern Africa, and South Asia. However, in each chapter we try to identify the defining or decisive issues on which developments hang – the questions that the large-scale analysis shows to be what the situation hangs on – and for each chapter one case is studied in more detail allowing for a little more of the refinements of securitisation analysis. Our case studies should thus be seen as preliminary sketches offering a template, or a target, for more detailed securitisation analyses.

These 'deep looks' in each chapter will not be identical in form. This is both because the needs are different from chapter to chapter and because we want to explore different forms of analysis. In some cases, the task is mainly to map what is securitised or check if some particular securitisation is powerful or not (in contrast to using indicators). In other instances, we want to explore the depth and solidity of some specific securitisation. When the focus is on a single country, this can be done by looking at the way securitisation draws on national identity and thereby which securitisations are easy or difficult to articulate. In several regions, the focus is naturally on the security debate of the central state: India in South Asia, Russia in the CIS, the USA in North America, and – with a more specific question – China in East Asia and South Africa in Southern Africa. Especially in centred RSCs, it will very often be the domestic struggle over security in the central state that determines major developments. In the case of the EU, it would be interesting to explore securitisation in relation to national identities in each of the major states, but given the number of states this would be impossible within the limited space available for each 'deep look', and has to some extent been done elsewhere (Holm 1992; Larsen 1997; Malmborg and Stråth 2002; Wæver 1990b; Wæver et al. 1989, 1990). Instead, we explore the emerging security discourse at the European level and how it constructs time and identity. In South America, one of the major open questions is the future of Mercosur, both economically as an integration project and as a pillar of security. Some light can be thrown on both questions by looking at the security arguments in relation to Mercosur: do leading politicians in the two key countries, Brazil and Argentina, securitise (anything) in ways that serve to produce a security argument for Mercosur which in turn will make it more likely that the regional scheme will, in critical situations, eventually be given the priority necessary for it to survive? In the Middle East chapter, the case is terror groups like bin Laden's and the question of whether they are non-regional in taking aim directly at a global level actor, the USA, or whether their struggle is still rooted in the region.

The regions differ between those driven predominantly by military-political security (all of Asia, Middle East, to some extent CIS) and those dominated by other sectors (the Americas, EU-Europe). Africa, as ever the odd man out, hangs in a complicated way between these two positions. To some extent the regions can be organised along an axis from 'traditional' realist regions to 'postmodern' ones, but with some complications such as Africa being pre- and post-traditional as well as in other respects exhibiting hyper-traditional realist dynamics. Latin America is also difficult because in terms of underlying societal development it is not postmodern but its regional security order raises some questions atypical for a traditional region.

Another more serious problem is raised by having an open ontology allowing for post-sovereign, non-state focused situations, but largely telling state-centric stories. In principle, the 'unit' of securitisation and security dynamics can be of any kind, and thus it would seem natural to say that 'internal' is internal vis-à-vis the units of the regional security dynamics whatever they may be, with international correspondingly

translated into inter-unit. This would, however, make a constantly fluctuating analytical scheme out of the four-level model. Instead, we keep
the state as the defining unit for locating things in this scheme – one
might call it the 'measure' – but this should not be taken to prejudice the
analysis in favour of states necessarily being the main units (cf. Buzan
et al. 1998: 7; Wæver 1997a: 347–72).

Our general assumption is that the post-Cold War security order will
exhibit substantially higher levels of regional security autonomy than
was the case during the Cold War. With the new agenda of the wider
concept of security, one might try to produce sector-specific (homogeneous) complexes and thus generate different maps for each sector. This
will show both some variation in the degree of regionalisation (versus localisation and globalisation) but also sometimes only partly converging maps (same 'Europes' but different 'Middle Easts' in different
sectors). However, a strong case can be made for 'heterogeneous complexes' where all security actions are linked across sectors (Buzan et al.
1998: 16–17, 166–70). The key is the synthesising done by actors. The
actors, not only the analysts, have to make up their mind about how
the different kinds of security concerns add up. Importantly, because
of the prioritising nature of securitisation, the different cases cannot be
disconnected: a securitisation of an economic threat will tend either to
push down a competing military threat construction or to link to it and
draw energy from the same threat appearing in several sectors. The integrated approach has two important advantages. First, it captures all
those loops, security dilemmas, and spillovers that occur across sectors –
Latvia being concerned about both demography and the Russian military and, on the basis of this securitisation, taking steps that Russian
minorities construct as threats to economic, political, and societal security. Second, it often explains why an issue is treated not only as an
environmental problem but as an environmental *security* problem. This
often happens when the actor deemed responsible is one that is already
seen as a security problem in another sector.

This clarifies one important issue. This book does not try to map
the formation and development of regions in general. This could be the
impression given by the inclusion of the new sectors: economy, environment, identity. It should be remembered: we are interested in economic
security, not economy *per se*, environmental *security*, not everything that
happens in the environmental sector. Otherwise, we would be suggesting an integrated theory of everything. Instead, this is a reading of the
world political development through the perspective of *security*.

76

Place in the literature

Before we move to the case studies, it may be helpful to some readers to set the nature and explanatory structure of this book into the context of the existing literature on regions.

Towards the end of the 1960s, a literature emerged on regional subsystems (Russett 1967; Cantori and Spiegel 1970, 1973; Kaiser 1968–9; Haas 1970). Although it did not usually define the regions as 'security regions' (it was partly stimulated by the literature on regional integration), it often operated within the traditional quasi-realist image of the state system and thus produced theories of regional subsystems that were clearly security-relevant and in some ways precursors for the concept of RSCs. However, this attempt to theorise international regions has generally been seen as a failure and has often served to keep others from attempting any theory of regional subsystems (Thompson 1973). One reason for this was the complexity of the models, which began to make theory look more Byzantine than reality. Another was the comparative success of global level neorealist and neoliberal theories that arose during the 1970s, eclipsing the regional approach (Lake and Morgan 1997b: 6) and seeming to give a more accurate portrait of the Cold War. A third, subtler explanation arises from the behavioural scientific fashions of the day, which also affected small-state theory, comparative foreign policy, and to some extent foreign policy analysis at large. The attempt at theorising regional subsystems in a behaviouralist mode meant that a lot of effort was put into producing precise, operational definitions and finding generally valid correlations about the subject. Therefore, when, for example, small states could not be defined with sufficient clarity and when few generalisations were valid for all small states, the theory was said to have failed. In the case of foreign policy analysis and regional subsystems, the problem was rather that the approach developed into an ever-expanding net of relevant factors that increasingly put a question mark on the functionality and relevance of the theory. In all these cases, the problem was to a large extent the expectations. Much good work was done, important questions were raised and sometimes answered, and mechanisms were even uncovered but, due to the prevailing view of 'science', this was deemed unsuccessful and helped to keep others away from these areas. Post-Cold War, however, a new wave of books has emerged that study regionalism and regional security orders (Daase et al. 1993; Fawcett and Hurrell 1995; Holm and Sørensen 1995; Lake and Morgan 1997c; Adler and Barnett 1998; Schulz et al. 2001).

Fawcett and Hurrell (1995) and Schulz et al. (2001) really have region-alism as their dependent variable: are regions becoming more or less 'regionalised' (coherent and separate, maybe integrated)? In both volumes, but most explicitly Schulz et al., something close to RSCs enter the picture because the degree of regionalisation is explained by two kinds of factors: security and economics. Schulz et al. have tried to structure this by using RSC analysis as theory on the security side and globali-sation for economics. Schulz et al. in particular have turned this into a teleological project in which regionalisation is an aim in itself, though the social consequences of globalisation and the maximisation of security are also part of the normative agenda of the book. Fawcett and Hurrell (1995) is more of a general overview of the problematique of regionalism with perceptive theory overviews and rather basic, solid, but not very theory-informed case studies. Daase et al. (1993) is a loose collection of theoretical and empirical articles on regional security with a number of case chapters on most of the regions of the world. It is not organised by a particular theory. By contrast Adler and Barnett (1998) and to some extent Holm and Sørensen (1995) are explicitly theory-based. Adler and Barnett is more coherently organised by a single theory than perhaps any other book, but the theory is that of security communities, which is highly relevant for some regions but hardly at all for others (see Kacowicz et al. 2000 on 'stable peace'). Holm and Sørensen is not pri-marily about security but uses the lens of globalisation and in particular uneven globalisation to survey regional variation.

More recently, a number of single-authored studies have come for-ward proposing distinct theories about regional security but applying the theory only to one or a few case studies (Mares 2001; Kacowicz 1998; Solingen 1998; Lemke 2002).

Lake and Morgan is in many ways the book that comes closest to ours: it takes RSCT (as developed by Buzan) as its starting point and tries to study specifically security-defined regions. The book argues nicely why regional security is likely to become more salient after the end of the Cold War (Lake and Morgan 1997b: 6ff.). It spells out that only a comparative approach does justice to regions. On the one hand there is a strong IR perspective according to which international relations is always and everywhere the same, which if true means that regions are not very important. On the other hand, many area studies specialists claim that their case is unique, and thus that a general theory of regions is impossible. Only with a comparative approach is it possible to say both that regions differ, and that it is possible to generalise about them (Lake and Morgan 1997b: 8ff.). Finally, theorising regions is made necessary by the argument that regions are not just micro-versions of the global system in which case the same theory could be used (ignoring the fact that it would have a dynamic of regional–global added even if each level followed classical neorealist systemic logic). Lake and Morgan (1997b: 9) argue that global and regional systems differ because the former are closed systems and the latter inherently open. These and many other points are shared between Lake and Morgan and the present volume.

But there are some differences. The first is that we (and also Schulz et al. 2001) attempt a full global picture of all the regions that exist. This holism is necessary both in order to see how well (or badly) our theory works, and to get the full benefit of the comparative approach. Selecting cases that fit too easily allows the ones that might embarrass the theory to be sidelined, especially if there are no explicit criteria for their selection.

The second difference between this book and Lake and Morgan's concerns what the whole effort is intended to explain. Their ultimate research question is the emergence and variation of regional security orders – i.e., who solves security problems how? This links nicely to the traditional, policy-orientated security literature with its focus on different security orders or systems or models. Their analytical set-up is then (in principle) that the structure of RSCs is to explain the regional outcomes in terms of conflict management and the shape of the regional security orders. But their concept of the structure of the RSC includes many different causal variables beyond security and thus recreates the problem that marred the old subsystem literature: too many causal connections and a lack of focus. They know how to solve this in principle, by a model of three-level games, but they acknowledge that in practice such theory has not been sufficiently developed and thus this part is indeterminate (Lake and Morgan 1997b: 14). Our set-up, in contrast, stays more narrowly with security and security-defined activities, and uses RSCT as a general instrument for telling a structured version of world history, past, present, and future. The possible forms that regions can take are derived from the concept of the RSC, not from the existing debate, and the various domestic and global causal factors are those that are directly part of security, such as domestic vulnerabilities, not domestic politics and society in all its complexity. The concept of the RSC plays a stronger role in our construction, and is allowed to define the possible orders on the outcome side and to select the relevant parameters on the input side. This approach forfeits the possibility of loose, ad hoc inclusion of additional variables in order to push as far as possible with one integrated theoretical scheme, thereby showing both its virtues and limitations.

The third difference involves the fundamental understanding of what an RSC is. Since both our book and Lake and Morgan's start from this concept, this difference matters a lot to how the respective analyses unfold. This is a basic methodological question that must affect any attempt to construct regional theory, and so it is worth examining in some detail. The essential difference is that we see the whole regionalist approach as hanging on the necessity of keeping and the ability to keep analytically separate the global and regional levels, whereas Lake and Morgan are happy to conflate the two levels into one. Their key move (Lake and Morgan 1997b: 12; Morgan 1997: 29–30; Lake 1997: 50–1; Lake and Morgan 1997a: 349) is to dissolve levels of analysis with the argument that 'geographical proximity is not a necessary condition for a state to be a member of a complex', and that great powers particularly should be counted as members of even remote regions into which they project force in a sustained way. In our view, this not only destroys the meaning of levels, but also voids the concept of region, which if it does not mean geographical proximity does not mean anything. They say that, if, for example, the USA is a consistent participant in European security, it is as much a member of the European security complex as Italy. Likewise in East Asia, they see the main *regional* powers as China, Japan, Russia, and the USA. We, in contrast, insist that regions are defined exclusively, and that external powers are treated in terms of penetration or overlay, not as members of the RSC as such. In our scheme, China and Japan are members of the East Asian complex, but Russia and the USA are not. In the light of Lake and Morgan's move, we are puzzled by the accusation (Lake 1997: 48) that 'Buzan's conception... fails to distinguish adequately how regional interactions differ from global interactions', when by conflating the two levels in this way they make such a differentiation almost impossible. Our approach in this book, as should already be clear from these first three chapters, is to improve our ability to draw this distinction.

At first, readers may side with Lake and Morgan. Our position of forcing a distinction between countries of the region and outsiders even though they are equally consistent participants in the security dynamics of the region, as the United States is in NATO and the OSCE, may seem excessively territorial. In conducting any particular regional security analysis it seems useful to be able to include the relevant powers in each regional case irrespective of the question of whether these states are located in the region, or appear in another RSC or at the global level. However, in practice, their seemingly more pragmatic approach has some serious analytical problems. Ultimately, this is not a question of what concept produces the easiest snapshot, but which concept produces the best theory. With the Lake and Morgan definition, one ultimately generates an RSC for each security problem. This is actually also what is said in their theory chapter which sets out a definition of RSCs defined in terms of 'security externalities': 'I define such a complex as the states affected by at least one transborder but local security externality' (Lake 1997: 46). 'If the local externality poses an actual or potential threat to the physical safety of individuals or governments in other states, it produces a regional security system or complex' (Lake 1997: 48–9). Many readers probably find this quite economistic formulation a bit extreme, and will take the different elements of the Lake and Morgan approach as separate, e.g., accepting the revision of RSCT on delineation but not the definition in terms of externalities. However, the two are closely connected logically, because the security externality definition fills the hole left by the removal of the geographical criteria.

This approach must lead to an unmanageable multiplication of issues (and thereby security complexes), which can be contained only by taking a narrow (military) definition of security. It would be a tall order to structure a security complex and a full analysis around each single issue and, in practice, this is done by none of the empirical chapters of their book. Furthermore, by including external great powers as members of an RSC, the Lake and Morgan approach throws away all of the analytical leverage generated by levels of analysis. If remote great powers are 'in' the regions, how can one differentiate between global and regional level security dynamics in order to investigate their interplay? Although the United States may be 'in' Europe and East Asia and the Middle East in a seemingly durable way, it makes a big difference that it always has the option to withdraw from (or be thrown out of) these regions. China and Japan are in East Asia whether they want to be or not. The USA has a choice, and this choice underpins a whole range of policy options not possessed by actors that are really 'in' their regions. A major point of RSCT is to separate the global and regional security dynamics in order to see what each looks like separately, and then to see how they interact with each other. By collapsing this distinction, Lake and Morgan risk repeating the analytical and policy errors of the Cold War in which superpower dynamics were given far too much weight, and regional ones far too little, in evaluating events in the Middle East, Southeast Asia, and elsewhere.

In terms of prediction and policy advice, the 'exclusive' approach has some advantages because it contains a picture of what the RSCs of the world, their borders, and their insulators are. Thereby, it can for instance judge which cooperative schemes are more or less likely to work depending on how they fit the structure.

As explained above, our operationalisation of RSCT is founded on a disciplined separation not only of the global level from the regional one, but also of each RSC from all the others. The reason for doing this is to cast maximum light on the distinctiveness of security dynamics at each level and within each RSC, so that the interplay between levels and among regions can itself be investigated as a distinct subject. If this approach generates anomalies or difficulties, then those are what should be explained and what the theory has served to alert us to.

Conclusions

Throughout these three chapters we have referred to regional security complex *theory* as a theory, and this claim needs to be explained. Indeed, for the study of regions, RSCT might be the only existing theory of regional security. Some typologies, matrixes, and checklists exist, but hardly anything that qualifies as theory. In the field of security/strategic studies, theories exist for specific problems: deterrence, alliances, not of (regional) security as such. Finally, theories have been developed for security orders – security community (Deutsch et al. 1957; Adler and Barnett 1998), zones of peace/stable peace (Kacowicz 1998; Kacowicz et al. 2000), collective security (Claude 1984; Morgenthau 1978: 417–29; Finlayson and Zacher 1983), security regimes (Jervis 1982; Inbar 1995), and concerts (Kupchan and Kupchan 1991) – but these are, in the nature of things, valid only for some situations. The only candidates for theories of regional security are those that deny the issue any specificity and therefore unproblematically integrate it into general theories such as neorealism.

The nature of (this) theory

The answer to the question of whether or not something qualifies as theory often depends on where it is asked. Many Europeans use the term theory for anything that organises a field systematically, structures questions, and establishes a coherent and rigorous set of interrelated concepts and categories. Americans, however, often demand that a theory strictly *explains* and that it contains – or is able to generate – testable hypotheses of a causal nature. RSCT clearly qualifies on the first (European) account. In American terms, it probably does too:

1. It predicts when RSCs are expected to emerge and when not (basically whenever anarchy and diverse geography are combined *unless* low interaction capacity or overlay offsets this).
2. Specific hypotheses are attached to the different situations: e.g., conflict formations draw in outside powers along the lines of the initial conflict.
3. The theory enables construction of a restricted set of scenarios and thus narrows down the zone of predictions. Much of the explanatory power stems from neorealism and other existing IR theories but, since the regional component is missing from the existing general theories, the addition of this component generates a number of new insights and explanations. This should reasonably be seen as a distinct theory.

Some readers might still be puzzled that we do not put forward more ambitious general explanations about why security takes a particular form in this region or that, or what causes major changes like the end of the Cold War or the rise and demise of particular regional conflicts. However, this would be against the basic aspiration of allowing for a more regional understanding of the world. The agenda of allowing for regional diversity speaks for a more minimalist conception of theory. The overall plot of the book is that it is not possible to tell one, coherent, neat, and homogeneous story about the world – regional variation goes deeper than filling out different boxes in one overarching global scheme. Regions develop in different directions and this makes increasingly difficult the task of understanding each on its own terms while keeping up a language allowing for comparison. Typically, the IR theorist will generalise in ways not accepted by the area specialist, while area specialists claim that the uniqueness of 'their' region prevents the application of any general theory. Both have a point, and therefore we want to create a framework that is sufficiently open and abstract that it allows for far-reaching differentiation to develop among regions, while maintaining a general set of categories with which to describe this. A 'strong' theory would be improper because it would impose identical concepts and mechanisms on regions, and override the important fact that security means something different in East Asia, in Central Africa, and in Western Europe.

Almost all other conceptions of world order after the end of the Cold War are too top-down in either (or both) of two main ways: in most IR theory the system level is allocated far too much power, thus continuing the Cold War error of seeing regional systems as mainly shaped by and relating to the global level. Most sociological theories (such as much globalisation theory) universalise key categories and apply them homogeneously across the world and thus assume an excessive sameness (even if fitted into, e.g., two contrasting types). Even two-world theory is top-down in the sense that its categories (core and periphery) are generated at the global level and the regions then fitted into them. Our approach, in contrast, is bottom-up in attempting – in a way that comes closer to the aspiration of area specialists – to capture the particularities of regions and then assemble the global picture from these components. To do this in a systematic way we need some categories and dimensions on which to sort regions, and this probably at times creates the impression of an excessively taxonomical enterprise: regions are fitted into typologies and described as to their location on various axes. This, however, is the natural procedure of such a minimalist theory that does not want to have large, central machinery operating that from the start keeps regions in their proper place and animates them to play their part in a global game.

Despite its minimalism, the effort is a theoretical one. The regions of the world cannot be compared without formulating theoretical concepts. These concepts generate observable connections and mechanisms that could not be specified without the theoretical frame being in place. The concept of RSC itself has a number of structuring effects:

> It separates regional and global in a systematic way and thereby allows this relationship to be studied. More generally, the theory puts forward levels as a structuring device.
>
> It separates one RSC from the next and this makes it possible both to understand the nature of each and to register the main cases where the division is difficult: i.e., crucial insulators, sub- and supercomplexes, and dense interregional dynamics that might signal possible transformation.
>
> Through the notions of what constitute the internal structure of an RSC, the theory proposes benchmarks for the study of change. Thus, the theory is by no means static, even though the focus on typologies and structure can create this impression. However, a picture of general flux is actually less able to designate important changes than a more structural analysis that points out the underlying continuity of some seeming change while thereby focusing attention on the cases of real structural change.

> The concept of RSC is the basis for the general typology of the forms a region can take and thus enables the predictive element of what change is more or less likely given various scope conditions.

In addition, the concept of securitisation is a main theoretical tool for mapping regional variation. An objectivist theory of security uses its own view of things and thus fits regional events more easily into its general theory of what drives the behaviour of actors. A securitisation-based theory will accept that the security agenda is about different things in different regions: the actors differ, as does the relative importance of different sectors. It avoids prejudices about how people 'should' react.

As explained above, the whole apparatus of securitisation studies plays two different roles in the present study – roles that would come together more seamlessly in a 'full' multi-volume, encyclopaedic version of this enterprise. Here these roles stand at either end of the theory. At one end, securitisation has a meta-theoretical function in insisting that one can never infer mechanically from objective factors to ensuing security dynamics because 'security' is a political battlefield on which is fought out what counts as security issues and thereby what is acted on in a security mode. Thus, securitisation protects us from objective security including its blindness to regional variation. The second function of securitisation is to be mobilised on key issues. In most regions, one or a few questions are drawn out to be exposed to the direct light of securitisation analysis. Turning points are studied, and actors, politics, and decisions enter the stage where they have otherwise been less visible due to the grand scope of the analysis. In relation to the past, the present, and (not least) the future, we analyse a few such constellations of crucial political decisions and thus enable an understanding that goes against materialist generalisation.

Causal mechanisms can generally enter the theory in two ways. One is in terms of 'facilitating conditions' (Buzan et al. 1998: 31–3). Certain conditions make certain types of securitisation more likely. For example, the ability of a securitising actor to securitise the neighbouring country in military terms depends on the length and ferocity of historical enmity, the balance of material capabilities, and various signs of hostility (rhetorical as well as behavioural). Also, the vulnerability of the referent object shapes the likelihood of different forms of securitisation. The material world often matters. This is a crucial part of the theory because, if this were not the case, there would be no room for the basic assumption that adjacency matters, and there would be no RSCs. Securitisation is not arbitrary – it is influenced by various facilitating conditions and it is mostly here that geography enters. However, if causes were introduced only as facilitating conditions, we would both create meta-theoretical problems and miss out on a lot of mechanisms. The result would be not a thoroughly constructivist theory but a materialist theory with added noise: securitisation would only be a marginal space allowing for some deviation from an underlying pattern that could be predicted solely and ideally from material factors alone. This would be deeply unsatisfactory as well as incomplete. The dynamics of securitisation as such explain a lot as well. Patterns emerge from the fact that different actors securitise differently; different political and cultural situations enable securitisation in different sectors and they have different dynamics (e.g., the peculiarities of societal security caused by the inherent paradoxes of securing identity). Thus, generalisations of causal patterns should equally be thought of as existing at the level of securitisation as such, not only in terms of facilitating conditions.

In both cases, we prefer not to put forward an elaborate scheme of causal mechanisms, but take the minimalist route of setting up our framework and theoretically generated conceptual apparatus, applying it to all the RSCs of the world, and then drawing together an aggregate picture. There are thus two key theoretical investments that structure the book, and up to a point our project stands or falls with them. If they fall, the value of the theory is diminished. The first is our choice of mutually exclusive regions, the logic and consequences of which were outlined in the discussion above contrasting our scheme with Lake and Morgan's. The second is the importance of the regional level as such and more generally of levels. This is far from uncontroversial, but we put it forward and construct the book around this format. The regional is not necessarily the most important level, but we suggest that it is consistently significant. We focus much attention on studying the countercase: the role of the global level, of the transregional and of non-territorial subsystems, but we assume originally that this is not strong enough to invalidate a regional set-up. If the regional level fades or levels generally fuse, our chosen set-up will ultimately be less helpful. If we are wrong about the ongoing salience of territoriality for security, then RSCT will become less relevant for the future. It would still be necessary for analysing history up to the late twentieth century, but thereafter would serve mainly to provide benchmarks against which to track the emergence of a deterritorialised structure of global security politics.

The structure of the book

Since the main purpose of this book is to explore the question of levels in the post-Cold War global security order, its design comes out of the regionalist perspective. The chapters that follow are structured to start at the regional level and work up to the interregional and global levels and down to the domestic one. But the theory underlying it does not predetermine which level is dominant, leaving that as an empirical question to be investigated. The next ten chapters are divided into four groups: Asia, the Middle East and Africa, the Americas, and Europe. The sequencing of these takes us from the modernist, largely military-political, security agendas still dominant in Asia, the Middle East, and (in a different, more premodern sense) Africa to the increasingly post-modern, and often non-military, security agendas in the Americas and Europe. This can also be seen as generally moving from the periphery to the core, though the fit is not perfect. The regionalist perspective, for example, puts Japan in Asia despite its individual standing as a post-modern core state. These ten chapters take a narrative approach. Each of them will look at the formative process, operation, transformation (if any), current condition, and prospects of the RSCs within the part of the world under discussion. The main emphasis in each case will be on the period since 1990. The RSCs will be investigated in terms of the following points:

1. the historical legacy of the units in the RSC and the way this conditions the principal security actors and the agenda that they generate;
2. the principal security actors, issues, and referent objects defining the RSC, and the nature of the processes that created and sustain it as a process formation;
3. the essential structure (anarchy or integration, power distribution, and patterns of amity–enmity, securitisation–desecuritisation);
4. the interregional dynamics between the RSC and its neighbours;
5. the global dynamics between the RSC and forces and actors from the global level;
6. the relative weights of the domestic, regional, interregional, and global levels, and of securitising versus desecuritising trends;
7. the most likely scenario(s) for the future given the current condition and dynamics of the RSC.

The final two chapters will sum up in two different ways. Chapter 14 will draw together the empirical story, and speculate about the future of international security given the structures, potentialities, and dynamics of the international system at the beginning of the twenty-first century. It focuses particularly on the interplay between regions and powers and on isolating the most important points of potential change in the current global order. Chapter 15 spells out the comparative results from the regional studies and reflects on the problems of conceptualising international security and re-examines our most important starting assumptions: the continued explanatory power of territoriality and regionality.

Part II

Asia

Introduction

South Asia was the foundational case study around which regional security complex theory first developed. But we start our *tour du monde* with Asia because it is still an exemplar of traditional regional security dynamics found largely in military-political mode. The popularity of 'comprehensive' and 'cooperative' security rhetorics in many Asian states is a significant development, most notably in Southeast Asia where ASEAN constructed a noteworthy third world security regime. But in Asia old-fashioned concerns about power still dominate the security agendas of most of the regional powers, and war remains a distinct, if constrained, possibility. The realist quality of Asian regional security enables us to start our story on familiar ground, easing our way into the complexities of how the wider security agenda affects the regionality of security dynamics overall.

While this simplifies things a bit, the Asian case nonetheless has some striking features that set it apart. Asia contains two great powers (China and Japan) and a third state (India) that is the leading aspirant to elevation from regional to great power standing. It also contains three nuclear weapon states (NWS – China, India, Pakistan) and a possible fourth (North Korea), plus three nuclear threshold states (Japan, South Korea, Taiwan) practising 'recessed deterrence' – the capability to move quickly to NWS status should their local environment become more threatening militarily, or the promise of US support lose its credibility. A co-location of adjacent great and regional powers on such a scale has only one other precedent, Europe, and the most apt comparison is not with today's Europe, embedded in a thick weave of regional institutions, but with the balance-of-power Europe of the nineteenth century. Asia now, like Europe then, contains a range of substantial powers in varying degrees of industrialisation. Japan, like Britain, is an advanced industrial society, well ahead of the others in wealth and development, and located offshore from a turbulent continent. China, like Germany, is big, centrally located, rapidly increasing in its absolute and relative power, has border problems and historical enmities with several of its neighbours, has an authoritarian government, backs on to Russia, and is in nationalist mood. Many in the region fear rising Chinese military power and assertiveness (especially Vietnam and Taiwan, and to a lesser extent India). Some fear the migration threat that might unfold if China fell into political turmoil, and the environmental threat from its rampant industrialisation. Nationalism is widespread and strong throughout Asia, and has plenty of cultural, ethnic, historical, status, and territorial issues to feed on. As in nineteenth-century Europe, liberal democracy is deeply rooted in only a few places, thinly present in others, and completely absent in many. Industrialisation means that both absolute and relative power levels are in flux. It also means, as it did in Europe, that there is sustained tension between the desire to seek national economic advantage and the pressure to get entangled in economic interdependence. Sovereignty and independence are highly valued, not least because it is still within living memory for many that these were denied by Western and/or Asian imperialists.

There are limits to this analogy. Europe was also obsessed with sovereignty, nationalism, and social Darwinism, but it did not suffer from the political and social traumas of recent colonisation and decolonisation by outsiders. By contrast, the contemporary great powers in Asia are boxed in by a superpower and two other great powers. Also unlike nineteenth-century Europe, Asia has no regional parallel to the European concert of powers, finding itself instead embedded in a global international society largely created by the Western powers. Asia's weak regional institutional development is, however, offset by two constraints not available to nineteenth-century Europe: the deterrence effect provided by nuclear weapons, and an outside superpower prepared, up to a point, to hold the ring for Asian security (in the sense of having specific commitments to the security of several Asian states, and a general role as external balancer and referee). Asia is also much bigger than Europe, and the geographical barriers to interaction within it are much more formidable than those in Europe. The Himalayas, for example, are a rather more significant insulator than the Alps, with the unsurprising consequence that Asia is much more culturally and ethnically diverse than Europe. These differences matter, as does the fact that the liberal global Zeitgeist of international relations in the late twentieth and early twenty-first centuries is quite different from the imperial one of the nineteenth.

Therefore nothing in this analogy suggests that Asia is inevitably heading into its own version of Europe's calamitous civil war of 1914–45, or that Asia, like Europe before 1945, will inevitably form a single RSC. What it does suggest is the high probability of fairly classic power-politics behaviour as the Asian standard over the next few decades. Military-political security has priority, and the use of force, even all-out war, is understood as a possibility in many places. Economic development is a priority not just for welfare objectives and maintaining military strength, but also for moving up the ranks of military power.

Asia carries its own distinctive historical baggage. With the exception of Japan, China, and Thailand, all Asian states are postcolonial constructions, and even those three were heavily penetrated and influenced by Western imperialism (Gong 1984). But in Asia, unlike in the Americas and Africa, the process of decolonisation left behind a state system that by and large reflected patterns established by precolonial political history. This meant that, with the exceptions of a few *de novo* creations such as the Philippines and Indonesia, the postcolonial states in Asia had the advantage of being able to anchor their legitimacy in their own history. While this synergy helped a system of modern states to take root in Asia, it also carried precolonial history forward into postcolonial international relations. Before Asia was incorporated into the European-made global international system, it had its own security dynamics. For much of East Asia, the main reality was the waxing and waning of Chinese imperial power, though for China the main strategic problem was barbarian invasions from the north. South Asia was largely separate from this Sino-centric system. It had its own internal cycle of empire and fragmentation, and worried about barbarian invasions from the northwest. Indian empires never expanded militarily beyond the subcontinent, but at various times South Asia's commercial and cultural influence extended throughout Asia. In Southeast Asia there are long histories of wars among Burmese, Cambodian, Thai, and Vietnamese kingdoms, and also a long history of Vietnamese resistance to Chinese power. During the late nineteenth century, there were substantial migrations of Chinese into many Southeast Asian states, and the consequences still play a big role in the domestic politics of these states and in their relations with China. Asia also had its own colonial history, with Japan's imperial venture between 1895 and 1945 leaving deep scars throughout East Asia, and particularly in China and Korea.

This linkage between the new states and indigenous history underpins the idea of the state, and thus resonates in the security dynamics of Asia on all levels. In some cases it feeds into contemporary securitisations between states (India and Pakistan, two Koreas, China and Vietnam), and in some within them (China, Indonesia, India, Pakistan). It also conditions how Asia relates to the global level, particularly to the great power claims of India, China, and Japan.

In terms of the framework set out in part I, Asia is strongly shaped both by the insulating qualities of its geographical size and diversity, and by the presence of great powers within it. The impact of geography is expressed in the formation of three distinct RSCs in postcolonial Asia: first, a great power one in Northeast Asia emerging during the late nineteenth century; and, after the Second World War, two standard RSCs respectively in Southeast and South Asia. The fact that Asia contains great powers means two things: first that the interregional level of security dynamics has been much stronger than would be expected among a set of standard RSCs; and, second, that Asian regional security dynamics have stronger links to the global level in both directions than one would expect in the global–regional links of a standard region (where the global level might well penetrate strongly into the regional, but the reverse is much less common). These features set the framework within which the Asian security story has unfolded over the last half-century. Because of its links to the global level, Asia, and especially East Asia, was a major area of superpower rivalry during the Cold War, second only to Europe. As a consequence, the transition from Cold War to post-Cold War matters a lot in Asia. The subdivision of Asia into three distinct RSCs was a product of intervening geography and low interaction capacity. But as the level of absolute power available within Asia rose, geography mattered less. As a result, a second theme in this story is the steady knitting together of the three regional security dynamics, especially between Northeast and Southeast Asia and, to a lesser extent, between both and South Asia.

In a nutshell, the story to be detailed below looks like this. During the Cold War, two out of the three great powers were located in Asia. Asia consisted of three RSCs, all heavily penetrated by the superpower rivalry, with Northeast and Southeast Asia so embroiled in the Cold War as to have their local security dynamics severely affected by it. With the communist victory in China's civil war in 1950, China became steadily more influential in the security dynamics of both South and Southeast Asia. The resultant interregional security dynamics were both strong enough and sustained enough to generate an Asian supercomplex centred on China, but with only weak links between South and Southeast Asia. The ending of the Cold War shifted the global structure to 1 + 4, with two of the four great powers in Asia. Soviet/Russian penetration into the region largely evaporated. US military engagement remained strong in Northeast Asia and, after weakening considerably in Southeast Asia during the 1990s, began to be rebuilt. Japan chose to stay largely subordinate to the United States, albeit on somewhat altered terms. China's relative power was the major beneficiary of greatly reduced superpower penetration, and this strengthened the interregional dynamics of the Asian supercomplex. Southeast Asia also benefited from superpower withdrawal, and moved away from being a conflict formation shaped substantially by outside ideological rivalries, and towards an ASEAN-based regional security regime. At the same time as this internal transformation, Southeast Asia underwent an external transformation, effectively merging its security dynamics with Northeast Asia to form a single East Asian RSC. South Asia retained its status as an independent RSC, but still remained tied into the China-centred Asian supercomplex. India further inched its way towards great power standing by creating a complex centred on itself, but at the time of writing had not yet succeeded in breaking the bipolar pattern with Pakistan in South Asia.

In addition to its interest as a part of the world where the 'old rules' of international relations are still substantially in play, and where great powers are a part of the local picture, Asia has three further points of interest as a case study for RSCT. First, it is a place where one can observe processes of both internal and external transformation. In South Asia one witnesses a slow shift from bipolarity towards unipolarity. In Southeast Asia, one can follow a virtually complete shift from conflict formation to security regime, and at the same time the dissolving of the boundary defining Southeast and Northeast Asia as distinct RSCs. Second, Asia is the place where one can see most clearly the phenomenon of a supercomplex in operation over a long period of time. Because China and Japan (and potentially India) are global level great powers, these developments not only define the conditions for security of the states and peoples of Asia, but also shape the context within which the Asian great powers play their global role. Whether the Asian supercomplex develops more as a conflict formation or more as a security regime will make a huge difference to China's potentiality (or not) to bid for superpower status. Third, Asia contains three insulators, Mongolia, Burma,

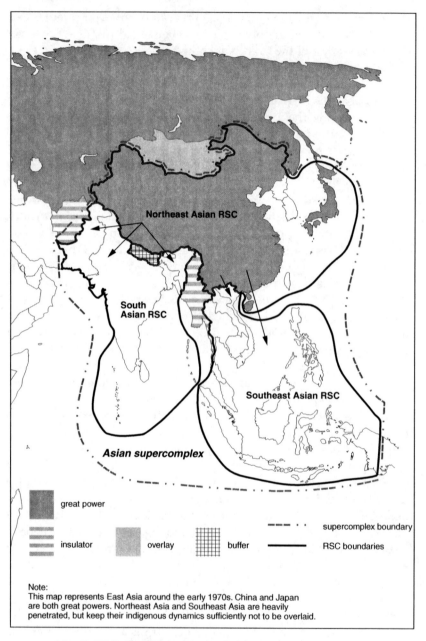

Map 3. RSCs in Asia during the Cold War

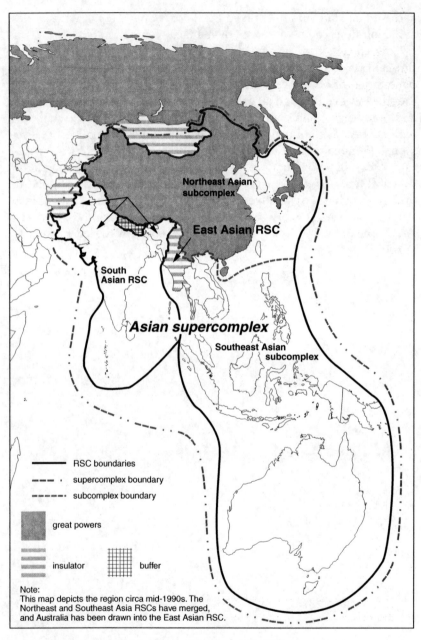

Map 4. RSCs in Asia Post-Cold War

and Afghanistan, and one mixed insulator/buffer, Nepal, whose roles and evolutions can be observed over a fairly long period.

How can we best present the Asian story when all four levels of (in)security dynamics are strongly in play simultaneously? Given the penetration of both local and external great powers, many threads of the story weave through all of the RSCs. The merging of the Northeast and Southeast Asian complexes means that levels change: what was regional becomes subregional, and what was interregional becomes regional. Organising the story from the bottom up as that of three separate RSCs will tend to underplay what connects them. Organising it top down in terms of global level and superregional patterns will tend to underplay what is distinctive in the regions. The best compromise is to tell the South Asian story separately, and the Southeast and Northeast Asian ones together, tying the threads together in the conclusion to part II.

4   South Asia: inching towards internal and external transformation

The argument in this chapter is that the security dynamics on the domestic, regional, and global levels show a lot of continuity. But the strengthening of the Asian supercomplex means that the interregional level is rising in importance relative to the others, and the bipolar structure at the regional level is weakening as Pakistan loses ground in relation to India. The first section briefly summarises the development, structure, and operation of the South Asian conflict formation during the Cold War. The next section looks at how the complex has evolved since the ending of the Cold War, asking whether it has remained essentially stable in form, or is showing signs of transformation. The third section concludes by considering the outlook for the South Asian RSC.

The South Asian RSC during the Cold War: decolonisation to conflict formation

South Asia has been examined in depth using RSCT (Buzan, Rizvi et al. 1986), so here we focus on bringing the study and the interpretation up to date, and locating the South Asian story more systematically in an all-Asia context.

The South Asian RSC, like most other postcolonial security regions, came into being as a conflict formation. India and Pakistan were born fighting each other in 1947 when what had been a societal security problem of religious conflict between the Muslim League and the Congress Party was transformed into an interstate, military-political one between an Islamic Pakistan and a secular, multicultural, but dominantly Hindu India. Political rivalry based on religion was long-running in South Asia and in that sense represented continuity. But the particular form of the postcolonial state system was unique. Pakistan was a new state with no particular historical roots. Sri Lanka did have its own historical tradition. India could most easily be thought of as the successor to the empires (Mauryan, Gupta, Mughal) that occasionally held sway over most of South Asia when it was not a fluid system of warring states. Societal elements thus continued to play a role in security dynamics both at the regional level, where the interstate conflict between the two biggest powers formed the core of the RSC, and at the domestic level. Before independence, the process of securitisation was based on Muslim claims for politico-cultural autonomy. Afterwards, it was partly based on rival claims to territory (especially Kashmir) by the two new states, partly on status and balance-of-power issues, partly on claims of mutual interference in domestic instabilities, and partly on the rival principles of legitimacy embedded in their constitutions. India's secular, federal constitution, and its imperial legacy, motivated many in Pakistan to suspect India of wishing to reunite the subcontinent. The principle of Pakistan's ideology as a homeland for Muslims fuelled Indian fears that its own fractious patchwork of ethnic groups and religions would break apart. This constitutional tension provided fruitful ground for securitisation of national identities on both sides: governments found it convenient to cultivate threat perceptions of the other for their own domestic political purposes. The rivalry generated three wars (1947–8, 1965, 1971), several serious crises in which war looked a possibility (1984, 1987, 1990, 1999, 2002), and numerous lesser military incidents (Gupta 1995: 51–2). Overspill of domestic conflicts also helped fuel the India–Pakistan rivalry: Hindu–Muslim generally, and particularly in Kashmir; and Sikh separatism in the Punjab. It was common practice for both governments to accuse the other of fomenting domestic political violence across the border. All of this sustained military competition, which from the mid-1970s onwards, and explicitly after 1998, acquired a nuclear dimension.

Like Pakistan, the secondary and minor states in the region (Nepal, Bhutan, Sri Lanka, Maldives, Bangladesh) were all in one way or another tied into the RSC because of their economic and societal entanglements with India. Partly because of their isolation from each other, and partly because even their collective weight could not begin to match India's, there was never a tendency for the whole RSC to polarise around an anti-Indian alliance centred on Pakistan. Neither was there much sign of the smaller states bandwagoning with India, though at times Bangladesh and Sri Lanka had bilateral security agreements with India (not relating to Pakistan), and Nepal has been in India's security zone since 1950.

Neither Pakistan nor India attracted any South Asian regional allies, which meant that India succeeded in keeping the high politics of the region on a bilateral basis. The South Asian Association for Regional Cooperation (SAARC) never amounted to much and has not affected the security politics of the region. Nepal and Bhutan were both dependent on India for trade and transit, and Bhutan was a formal dependency. Sri Lanka was broadly neutral between India and Pakistan, but was tied to India by the long-festering problem of its Tamil minority, which linked what became a civil war to the large Tamil population in southern India. There was a major Indian intervention from 1987 to 1990, which failed to resolve the issue. The Maldives gained independence in 1965, and its turbulent domestic politics moved it to request an Indian intervention in 1989. Bangladesh was born in 1971 as a combined result of civil war in Pakistan and the third major war between India and Pakistan, and is tied to India by shared Bengali culture, by river water, and by migration problems. As a rule, economic relations among the South Asian states remained sparse during the Cold War. Economic relations were not significantly securitised at the regional level, and economic interdependence was much too limited to constrain the region's military-political antagonisms. India's continental scale and mercantilist economic policy have, until recently, kept it relatively unpenetrated by the global economy.

The South Asian RSC was also quite well insulated from those around it by Burma (from Southeast Asia) and Afghanistan (from the Gulf) – see map 3, p. 98. Major wars within these three RSCs tended not to spill over into neighbouring complexes. Had Nehru been able to maintain Tibet as an insulator between South Asia and China, the South Asian RSC would also have been well insulated from the north. But the annexation of Tibet by China put Chinese borders close to India's heartland and during the later 1950s created increasing friction over the disputed border. This resulted in a border war between India and China in 1962, a mini-crisis in 1987 (Gupta 1995: 57), and an enduring sense of insecurity in India about China. In parallel with this, a durable military partnership, though not an alliance, developed between China and Pakistan from the early 1960s. Significant security dynamics between South Asia and China posed a problem for early attempts to formulate South Asia as a model for RSCT. This problem was handled by putting China wholly at the global level. In the light of a more fully formulated theory, the Sino-Indian security dynamics arising during the later 1950s can better be seen as part of the wider process by which an Asian supercomplex was forming at that time. Although Chinese involvement in South Asia did in some ways link upwards to the Cold War, it was primarily located at the interregional level, making it no surprise that it was not much affected by the ending of the Cold War.

At the global level, the South Asian RSC was marginal to the main theatres of the Cold War, but nonetheless became penetrated by it. As RSCT predicts, when there is rivalry among the global powers, an RSC in conflict formation mode will draw in outside intervention along the lines of its own internal split. Thus Pakistan sought from an early stage to associate itself with the United States and, a bit later, China. By the early 1950s it had succeeded in becoming part of the US network of containment alliances. Although its relationship with the USA was often troubled, especially from the 1970s onward over nuclear proliferation issues, Pakistan regained US support during the 1980s as an ally against the Soviet occupation of Afghanistan. This linkage between the USA and Pakistan, and especially US arms supplies to Pakistan and US naval manoeuvres in the Bay of Bengal during the 1971 Indo-Pakistan war, fed a durable securitisation of the USA in India. An Indo-Soviet association began to form from the early 1960s, initially on the basis of Soviet arms supplies, and then in 1971 as an alliance. The Sino-Indian war in 1962 both reinforced India's drift towards the Soviet Union and cemented the China–Pakistan relationship. In this way, the local split in South Asia became tied into, and reinforced by, the global level patterns of the US–Soviet and Chinese–Soviet rivalries.

For this period, one can sum up the South Asian complex in terms of RSCT as follows. It was a standard complex with a bipolar essential structure rooted in mutual securitisations between India and Pakistan. Because Bangladesh was so weak as both a state and a power, this bipolar structure was hardly affected by its secession from Pakistan. Bipolarity was bolstered by the nuclearisation of the military rivalry between India and Pakistan from the mid-1970s onwards. All of the states in the region can be classified to some degree as weak states, though India's robust democracy pushed it towards the middle of the weak–strong state spectrum (Buzan 1991b: 96–107). They had turbulent and often violent domestic politics fuelled by ethnic and religious differences and, since ethnic and religious affiliations often crossed national borders, there was strong interplay between the domestic and regional levels in South Asian insecurity. This pattern of domestic–regional linkage remained stable throughout the Cold War, as did the pattern of linkage upward to the three-cornered Sino-Soviet-US rivalry.

Despite the impressive stability of structure, three possibilities for change were always discernible during this period:

- Internal transformation, with Pakistan being unable to sustain bipolarity either because of its own political disintegration, or because India's natural weight advantage eventually became overwhelming. Pakistan's enthusiasm for alliances with outside powers and the nuclear option were its trump cards in attempting to forestall any such development.
- External transformation by an escalation of the India–China rivalry to a point where it pushed the South Asian regional level into the background. This possibility also was affected by the growth of nuclear weapons capabilities in South Asia, and by India's potential to achieve great power standing beyond the regional level.
- External transformation linking South Asian and Middle Eastern security dynamics. Although the Middle Eastern and South Asian security dynamics generally stood back to back, there were two mechanisms that might fuse them together. One was Pakistan's attempt to balance India by seeking ties first with Iran, and later with Saudi Arabia (especially in regard to the anti-Soviet war in Afghanistan, but also in the hiring of Pakistani troops for internal duty in Saudi Arabia). The other mechanism was Israeli concern over Pakistan's rhetoric about an 'Islamic' nuclear bomb, and the possibility, mooted during the 1970s, that Israel and India might therefore find a pressing common cause. In the event, neither of these mechanisms became strong enough during the Cold War to threaten the essential separateness of South Asian and Middle Eastern security dynamics, though they did make for an active interregional level.

South Asia was never more than a sideshow to the main events of the Cold War. Its regional dynamics were strongly autonomous and, although exacerbated by the military inputs from the global level, were neither created nor reshaped by them in any fundamental way.

Post-Cold War: continuity or transformation?

Since the Cold War imposition was never that great in South Asia, simply reinforcing what were already strong domestic and regional patterns, it is not surprising that the ending of the Cold War created no dramatic transformations in the security dynamics of South Asia. But neither can one simply say that the South Asian case has been 'more of the same' since 1990. There is a substantial case for continuity, but there are also signs that the South Asian RSC is moving towards a quite radical transformation.

The case for continuity

The case for continuity can be made across all four levels. On the domestic, regional, and interregional levels this is not particularly surprising given the deep roots of the dynamics at these levels. It is more surprising at the global level, which has undergone a big change.

Domestic level – The general pattern of violent internal politics in most of the countries in the region remained much the same, as did the pattern of spillover from this level to the regional, interstate one. Progress towards democratisation in most of the South Asian states did little to mitigate this pattern. In Sri Lanka, the civil war rooted in frictions between the Sinhala and Tamil populations dragged on into its third decade. Despite over 60,000 deaths (Gunaratna 1995: 80), and some extension of the conflict into India, neither side could defeat the other. The war remained largely contained within a still functioning Sri Lankan state, and the Liberation Tigers of Tamil Eelam (LTTE) became a more or less permanent nonstate player in South Asian security dynamics. By 2002 there were once again hopes that a truce might pave the way for a political deal, with the incentives for the LTTE increased by post-11 September antagonism to terrorism. In Bangladesh, fractious and sometimes violent domestic politics avoided civil war but kept the country weak and marginal. Equally incompetent government in Nepal seemed, by 2002, to be drifting towards civil war. None of these developments threatened the bipolar structure of the RSC.

Because of its defining position in the South Asian RSC, similar domestic turbulence in Pakistan raised more concern even though it was not discontinuous with earlier practice. The whole machinery of state remained distorted by a passionate commitment to a lopsided military rivalry with India that Pakistan could not win, but which inflicted on it a large, expensive, and politically active military establishment. Spectacularly corrupt and chaotic government combined with internal violence to raise questions about the long-term viability of the state. There was serious speculation that Pakistan was drifting towards the sort of semi-permanent political chaos achieved by Afghanistan and

Somalia. Pakistan's political elites were 'more concerned with looting the economy than developing it', and often pursued their bitter personal rivalries more in the street than in the parliament (Bray 1997: 322, 330). Its army dominated political life whether in or out of government, in the process contributing to the degradation of democracy, and becoming a quasi-autonomous actor in its own right (Ahmed 1998; Rais 1995). In 1999, the military once again seized political power. Pakistan's quasi-autonomous military and intelligence services had engaged the country deeply in the Afghan war against the Soviet Union and, after the Soviet withdrawal, in the civil war that followed among the varied religious and ethnic factions in Afghanistan. Among other things this allowed large numbers of Afghan refugees to train and arm inside Pakistan, and Pakistani-sponsored Islamic militants increasingly penetrated the life of Pakistan itself, bringing with them a lively trade in arms and drugs, with their associated warlords and mafias (*Strategic Survey* 1994–5: 198–9). The enforced recruitment of Pakistan into the US war against terrorism forced the government to abandon its Taleban allies. But after the fall of the Taleban, many of them and their al-Qaeda allies retreated into Pakistan and linked up with their supporters there (Ayoob 2002: 55–60), creating further prospects for domestic instability. In addition, there were ongoing instabilities in the southern provinces of Baluchistan and Sind that sometimes looked like civil wars, and a growing securitisation of religious identity accompanied by open violence between Pakistan's dominant Sunni Muslims and its Shi'a and Christian minorities (Saikal 1998: 123–4; Roy 1998; Stern 2000).

On the surface, India might seem to present a similar picture, with corruption scandals and unstable governments serving as a backdrop to ethnic and religious domestic political violence. Given India's size, it was not unreasonable to think that the South Asian RSC was shaped just as much by India's relations with its neighbours as by India's internal military-political relations. The long-running insurgency in the Punjab, which was costing several hundred lives per year, peaked in 1992 but subsided into quiescence thereafter. The violence in Kashmir, which was more closely tied into Indo-Pakistan relations, rumbled on with high casualties, periodic crises, and no sign of solution. Also worrying was the flaring up of communal violence between Hindus and Muslims, and its association with the rise during the 1990s of so-called Hindu nationalist parties, particularly the BJP. How significant is the decline of the secular, modernist Congress Party that dominated India from independence to the early 1990s (Corbridge 1998) and its apparent replacement by the BJP? Does the BJP's 'Hindu nationalism' suggest that India is undergoing a shift in its national identity towards a narrower cultural self-identity more akin to that of its Islamic neighbours? There are grounds for doubt about this (not least in the continued regional fragmentation of Indian politics), but if it is the case, the implications for securitisation both domestically and regionally would be substantial. Yet the military remained clearly subordinate to political authority, democracy had robust roots, and for all the seeming unsteadiness there was no sense, as there was with Pakistan, that the country was in danger of tipping into the ranks of failed states or lurching into political extremism. After the serious economic crunch of the early 1990s (Corbridge 1998: 8–10), measures of liberalisation generated a respectable rate of economic growth that was not too much disrupted by the economic crisis of the late 1990s in East Asia.

Regional level – Security politics in the region, and their linkages to domestic insecurities, continued in the Cold War pattern, with on-again/off-again tensions between India on the one hand, and Nepal (borders, trade and transit agreements, migrants, water), Bangladesh (water allocations, migrants, insurgency spillovers), and Sri Lanka (Tamil politics) on the other. In relations between India and Pakistan, however, the traditional pattern of sustained hostility was not only maintained, but considerably escalated.

The India–Pakistan rivalry continued to burn around three long-standing issues: border questions, particularly Kashmir; communal issues, exacerbated by the rise of the BJP; and military rivalry, escalated by the increasing nuclear weapon and missile capabilities of both sides. Border skirmishes between the two armies continued over the Siachen glacier and in Kashmir, and insurgent groups in Kashmir continued to find both official and unofficial support in Pakistan, linking them across to its Afghan engagements. India's defence of its claim to Kashmir occupied over half a million of its troops, and its attempts to suppress local rebels blurred into numerous border incidents and cross-border exchanges of fire with Pakistan. Politically, the intense domestic rivalry during the 1990s between Benazir Bhutto and Nawaz Sharif fuelled competitive anti-Indian rhetoric over Kashmir, escalating the two states' mutual accusations of interference in each other's domestic affairs. Pakistan also made much political mileage out of the various Hindu–Muslim clashes within India. All of this contributed to a virtual breakdown of diplomatic relations between the two states lasting from 1994 to 1997. Despite India's diplomatic initiative under the more liberal

'Gujral doctrine' (Sen Gupta 1997), the two fought a small border war in the Kargil area of Kashmir during the summer of 1999, and in the spring of 2002 were again in heavy military confrontation as India responded to a series of terrorist attacks which it blamed on Pakistan. Short of all-out war, there was no end in sight to the longstanding pattern of alternating hostility and dialogue between the two states on high politics issues, accompanied by a steadier ability to cooperate on issues such as the sharing of the Indus waters (Abraham 1995: 26–30).

On top of all this was an intensifying nuclear and missile rivalry, though in 1991 the two countries did manage to agree on nuclear installations and in 1992 on the non-use of chemical weapons (Krepon and Sewak 1995). India, with some Russian technical assistance, is steadily pursuing a whole family of SSMs (PPNN 1998a: 16). Pakistan has almost certainly had substantial assistance from North Korea and China for several short-range and one intermediate-range SSMs, and has for some years possessed Chinese M-11 SSMs (*Strategic Survey* 1992–3: 135; 1996–7: 208; Chellany 1998–9; Heisbourg 1998–9). Both states have long-standing military nuclear programmes. Pakistan received substantial assistance from China, and India possibly from Israel (Walker 1998: 518; PPNN 1998a: 19, insert pp. 3, 6; Kumaraswamy 1998: 45–6). Since the 1980s the general assumption was that both either possessed, or could very quickly possess, operational nuclear weapons. Their nuclear tests in May 1998 confirmed these suspicions, with both claiming weaponised nuclear capability (Walker 1998: 518). Many observers of this process are worried that poor C3I, underdeveloped strategic doctrines, and vulnerability to crisis instability could all override restraints on nuclear use (Joeck 1997; Walker 1998: 506; Heisbourg 1998–9: 82–6; Quinlan 2000–1). This concern was reinforced by reports that the Pakistani military had begun readying its nuclear missiles during the 1999 Kargil crisis (*International Herald Tribune* 16 May 2002: 8).

Interregional level – At this level, continuity is partly about the Asian supercomplex, and partly about the security interplay between South Asia and the Middle East. Continuity in the Asian supercomplex hinges on the pattern of relations between China, and India and Pakistan. South Asia continued to be a fairly minor front for China, and China's strategy for keeping it that way was to sustain support for Pakistan's effort to maintain the bipolar conflict formation in the subcontinent. This thoroughly realist strategy meant that, if India could be distracted by Pakistan's challenge, it would be diverted from making trouble for China. China's game in South Asia was helped by the demise of the

Soviet Union and India's consequent loss of a compensating coun-
terthreat against China. China continued to back Pakistan's attempt to
match India's achievements in nuclear and missile technology, and India
continued to cite the threat from China, more than Pakistan, as the justification for its nuclear and missile programmes. Although an important
element of continuity, this pattern should not be overinterpreted. There
were limits to China's support for Pakistan, and Sino-Indian relations
were in some ways cooperative. China did not want to be drawn into an
Indo-Pakistani war, and did not have an alliance with Pakistan in that
sense. It was concerned about Pakistan's instability, and even more so
about the Islamisation of Pakistani politics, which had implications for
China's own problems with its Muslim minorities. And despite India's
use of China as the rationale for its own nuclear developments, India's
actual military deployment is against Pakistan. Indeed, India and China
have maintained a stable diplomatic relationship since the 1980s. There
are regular high-level visits, and sustained talks on border issues. In the
immediate aftermath of the Cold War there were some border agreements in 1993, and some prospect of demilitarising the border (Gupta
1995: 56–7). But no major shift has taken place in what essentially
remains a correct but cool relationship.

Continuity across the South Asia–Middle East boundary prevails despite the upheavals caused by the wars in Afghanistan and their repercussions in both regions. This boundary remains active, as during the
Cold War, and is in principle therefore still a candidate for external transformation. But that activity has not linked, and does not look likely to
link, together the security dynamics of the two regions. If anything, the
war against the Taleban looks likely to reinforce Afghanistan's role as
an insulator, whose fragmented warrior clans engage all the neighbours
locally without causing the major regional security dynamics to merge
(more on this below). In the past, interest in this boundary was over
whether there would be some direct integration of security dynamics resulting either from Israel's engagement with Pakistan's 'Islamic' bomb,
or from Pakistan's perennial seeking for support in the Islamic world.
These concerns remained active, but never took on sufficient importance
to bring the basic separateness of South Asian and Middle Eastern security dynamics into question (Kumaraswamy 1998: 7; PPNN 1998a: 19,
insert p. 6). Between South Asian and Middle Eastern regional security
dynamics, Afghanistan was always an insulator that faced simultaneously north, east, and west, engaging its neighbours on all fronts, but
keeping them apart much more than pulling them together. Even if a

more sustained Western engagement in Afghanistan results from the war of 2001, this basic characteristic seems unlikely to change.

Afghanistan remains the key to the boundary between the South Asian and Middle Eastern (as well as ex-Soviet) RSCs. The civil war that followed the ending of the Soviet intervention created a mini-complex, reflecting political fragmentation at the substate level, but nonetheless generating a conflict formation that possesses most of the qualities of a state level complex. In particular, the conflict formation serves to channel external interventions along the lines of the internal rivalries. This mini-complex is comparable to that in the Caucasus, where a not wholly dissimilar ethno-political fragmentation sustains another mini-complex. Both of these mini-complexes act as insulating zones between larger patterns of regional security dynamics: Russia and the Middle East in the case of the Caucasus; South Asia, the Middle East, and Central Asia/Russia in the case of Afghanistan. In both cases the mini-complex draws in neighbouring states, but its internal dynamics are strong enough to keep the larger dynamics separate. The mini-complexes do not generate enough power or concern to become themselves the centre of a new larger regional formation, and they are less important to most of the states around them than security concerns that pull in other directions.

The basic forces that have been in play in the Afghan mini-complex are roughly as follows:

- mostly Pashtun, Sunni Islamic forces, initially organised as the Hizb-e-Islami under Gulbuddin Hekmatyar, but from 1993/4 to 2001 organised as the Taleban, and supported by Pakistan and for a time Saudi Arabia;
- Hazara Shi'as, supported by Iran;
- Uzbeks, supported by Russia and Uzbekistan;
- Tajiks, mostly organised under Ahmad Shah Masoud, and with some support from Tajikistan.

Pakistan was a major player in this game, from 1991 putting its considerable weight behind the Pashtun–Sunni forces, and helping to create the Taleban by making use of the three million refugees from the Afghan civil war camped in its territory (Saikal 1998: 116). With Pakistani and Saudi support, the Taleban were able to capture the south and centre of the country between 1994 and 1996. The Taleban's strength polarised the conflict into a Pashtun/non-Pashtun affair, so forcing the other groups to join forces in the Northern Coalition. This polarisation extended to the outside players as well, effectively putting Pakistan and Saudi Arabia on one side, and Russia, Uzbekistan, Tajikistan, Iran, India, and even Pakistan's partner China on the other. The United States, initially supportive of the Taleban, turned against them in 1997 because of their Islamic extremism and many violations of human rights in general and women's rights in particular (Saikal 1998: 118–22; Roy 1998). That hostility turned to war after the terrorist attacks on the United States in September 2001 linked the Taleban to al-Qaeda, and made the Uzbeks and Tajiks into allies of the United States.

It seems a fairly safe prediction that political turbulence and instability in Afghanistan will be a durable feature, sometimes muted by a weak central government, sometimes not. The divisions within the country run deep, and its warrior culture makes internal conflict frequent and easy to instigate. The various factions all have outside supporters in neighbouring territories, where kin and substantial refugee populations are to be found. During the 1990s all of Afghanistan's neighbours developed an interest in containing spillovers of religious extremism, drugs trade, and terrorism. Those interests will remain, now joined by a wider Western one of preventing the country from being used as a base for terrorists. Taking rival positions in Afghanistan has been part of the more general Gulf rivalry between Saudi Arabia and Iran, and that may well continue. All of this, plus the transnational character of radical Islam, might seem to point to a serious breakdown of the boundary between South Asia and the Middle East (not to mention Central Asia), as exemplified by the involvement of Afghan fighters in Kashmir. Yet that does not seem to be the correct way to interpret what is unfolding.

The key points are four. First, none of the neighbouring countries is either interested in, or capable of, establishing its hegemony over, let alone occupying, Afghanistan. The resistance power of Afghanistan against outsider occupiers was conclusively demonstrated by the Soviet invasion. Second, all of the neighbouring states have more pressing security concerns in other directions. Third, Afghanistan itself lacks the power to force any knitting together of wider security dynamics. Its power is mostly chaos power. It can neither project much power abroad (except terrorism) nor become the central focus of a new complex by drawing its neighbours in. Fourth, with the exit of the Taleban, Afghanistan has lost much of its utility as a safe haven for Islamic radicals. Taken together, these points mean that Afghanistan will continue to fulfil its function as an insulator, at best with a weak central government trying to balance among both the local warlords and the outside powers. On some of the gloomier assessments about the 'Talebanisation' of Pakistan, all or part of that country might get absorbed into Afghan-like instability (*Strategic Survey* 1996–7: 208; Saikal 1998: 123–4; Ayoob 2002). Some might think this a fitting irony given Pakistan's hand in promoting the Taleban in the first place. Neither Iran nor India has any interest in expanding into what might be called 'the Afpakistan area'. Both have more pressing concerns in other directions, and share a durable interest in containing the chaos without getting too involved in it. The long-term interests of both of these key players are in maintaining the back-to-back tradition of the security dynamics in the Gulf and South Asia. Here the Sunni–Shi'a split in Islam serves India well, by denying Pakistan the strategic depth of serving as the frontier of Islam against India. By committing itself to the Saudi-backed Sunni cause in Afghanistan, and by tolerating violence against its own Shi'a minority, Pakistan has made a strategic error of potentially the same gravity as that which lost it Bangladesh. Its key ally, Saudi Arabia, is itself a conspicuously weak state, with an anachronistic and inefficient ruling elite sustained only by huge oil revenues. Pakistan's heavy involvement in Afghanistan, and its alliance with Saudi Arabia for this purpose, might be thought to raise the prospect of breaking down the border between the South Asian and Middle Eastern complexes. But more likely is that it will further weaken Pakistan, and encourage all of the other neighbouring states to pursue containment.

Global level – Given the general upheavals in the global power structure since 1990, it is noteworthy how much continuity at the global level there was in South Asia. During the later decades of the Cold War, the Soviet Union was an ally of India; the United States generally supported Pakistan over the Soviet invasion of Afghanistan during the 1980s, but opposed its nuclear programme, and did not politically support its rivalry with India even though its military supplies *de facto* strengthened Pakistan against India. In the initial fluidity following the collapse of the Soviet Union it seemed as if the Cold War pattern of external great power penetration into South Asia might change. India, Pakistan, and Bangladesh all supported the United States during the Gulf War, despite internal dissension on the issue. The implosion of the Soviet Union in 1991 removed India's ally, and disrupted its lines of military supply, already in some chaos because of the financial squeeze following India's extravagant military buying spree during the late 1980s (Gupta 1995: 3–6, 34–43). The confusion of post-Soviet politics made it difficult for

India to re-establish relations. With the disappearance of the Soviet threat in Afghanistan, United States–Pakistan relations swung into the negative. The United States invoked the Pressler amendment in 1990, cutting Pakistan off from military and economic aid because of its nuclear programme. For a year or two there seemed a prospect that the United States would swing to India, and that Sino-Indian relations might warm up.

But within a short time much of the old pattern fell back into place. India began to rebuild its relationship with Russia both as its main source of arms, and for transfer of military technology. United States–India relations cooled as Washington put more emphasis on non-proliferation and human rights goals than on building ties with India. In 1995, the United States seemed to tilt back towards Pakistan, lifting the Pressler amendment for one year after successful lobbying by Benazir Bhutto, and thus allowing some significant arms supplies to be delivered to Pakistan. The United States also began to find some common cause with Pakistan in supporting anti-Iranian forces in the Afghan civil war. Both India and Pakistan experienced severe US pressure over the negotiations on the renewal of the NPT and on a CTBT during 1995–6. During the late 1990s, it was not difficult to find either political rhetoric or academic analysis in Delhi that unhesitatingly identified the United States as the key threat to India (interviews; Bajpai 1998: 174–7). Thus, at least for the first decade, the ending of the Cold War left a surprising amount of the global pattern in South Asia more or less in place.

But, although the pieces from the Cold War alignments slotted into the same pattern during the 1990s, they did not have the same significance. India and Russia did rebuild some aspects of their military relationship, but these were largely confined to arms supply, and no longer contained the element of strategic alliance. The ongoing political and economic weakness in Russia largely put it outside the balance-of-power game in South Asia. The US role in the subcontinent remained as inconsistent as ever and not very deeply or continuously engaged. Until September 2001, nuclear proliferation remained the dominant US concern in the region. This meant that its relationship with India remained cool and prickly, and with Pakistan fluctuating between warm (mostly over intervention in Afghanistan) and cool (on nuclear proliferation). At least for the 1990s, the ending of the Cold War weakened what was in any case a fairly marginal American engagement in South Asia, and this worked most strongly against Pakistan. US responses to the nuclear tests in 1998 clearly hurt Pakistan more than India, and by 1997 the United States had lost its interest in making common cause with Pakistan in the Afghan affray.

All of this was pushed aside by the US war against Afghanistan in 2001, which forced Pakistan to be on-side with the coalition, and interrupted a warming phase in US relations with India that had reflected the new US administration's concerns about Chinese power. The sharp deterioration in Indo-Pakistan relations that ran alongside the war in Afghanistan left the United States in an awkward position in South Asia, with India, like many other states, attempting to link its own struggle against insurgents to the US war on terrorism. The United States seemed to be stuck with an engagement with Pakistan in order to prevent chaos within the country bringing its Islamic extremists and its nuclear weapons together. Indeed, Pakistan could be forcibly deprived of its nuclear weapons if the United States thought there was a real danger that they might fall into the hands of Islamic extremists. Like India, the United States could not afford to let Pakistan fall apart, because the consequences of its disintegration would be worse than the costs of its continuation. Potentially, this situation tied the United States into South Asia as a ring-holder between India and Pakistan for the long term. But the US commitment to the subcontinent remained as ambivalent as ever, with both the durability and the direction of its commitment in doubt.

At first glance, therefore, there is much to be said for the view that the RSC in South Asia was not much affected by the ending of the Cold War. Its essential structure remained unaltered, as did the local forces driving it, and, at least up to 2002, the patterns of interregional and global penetration into the region, never anyway the dominant factor, did not change much. But 'more of the same' would nevertheless be a premature conclusion to draw about this RSC.

The case for transformation

The case for transformation does not rest on any immediate or dramatic effect from the ending of the Cold War. Rather, it comes about as a result of slower-moving forces, some generated within the region and others mostly happening at the interregional and global levels. The case for transformation can almost be interpreted as a kind of continuity, because the two main paths down which the evidence points are the same as those sketched above that were already being discussed during the Cold War: (1) internal transformation caused by the decay of the regional bipolar power structure; and (2) external transformation caused by the intensification of India's rivalry with China.

Internal transformation – The difficulty of Pakistan's task in maintaining bipolarity against India means that the possibility of an internal transformation has always been present in South Asia. But in the absence of some transformative event, such as wholesale defeat in war or the collapse of the state, the problem is to determine whether or not a set of incremental developments have undermined Pakistan's claim to be a regional pole of power. This question is almost wholly about power, for there seems little prospect that Pakistan will abandon its securitisation of India (Ahmed 1998: 361). Indeed, the whole socially constructed aspect of India–Pakistan relations seems locked into hostility (Rajmaira 1997). On the face of it, the evidence about bipolarity pulls in opposing directions. On the one hand, the achievement of nuclear parity equips Pakistan with the great equaliser, and therefore confirms the bipolar power structure in South Asia. But, on the other hand, there is much suggesting that Pakistan is steadily fading away as a plausible rival to, or balancer of, India. In other words, it is in danger of losing its status as a distinct number two to India and sinking down towards being more of a nuisance than a challenger.

In simple material terms, India's population is seven times and its land area four times that of Pakistan. India's GNP is more than six times that of Pakistan, and its current growth rate slightly ahead, though its GNP per capita is still only two-thirds that of Pakistan. But India's military expenditure is well over three times Pakistan's, and its military manpower twice as great (*Strategic Survey* 1998–9: 295–9).

These statistics have not prevented Pakistan from holding a plausible 'number two' position in South Asia over several decades. The main problem is Pakistan's apparent slide from being a weak state towards being a failed one, and the contrast with India's relatively robust democracy. The dismaying spectacle of Pakistan's political elites looting the state's coffers while at the same time indulging in highly personalised rivalries – and as the country spirals into economic and political chaos – is comparable to some of the worst performances from African kleptocracies. Venal, incompetent, and imperious leadership has already caused Pakistan to experience fission once, in 1971, and many of the same forces of ethnic resentment that generated that result are still present within what remains of the country. Although its leaders make much of the threat from India, 'the external threat is less severe than the country's internal fault lines' (Bray 1997: 330). Indeed, it is the chaotic state of politics within Pakistan that fuels its need to exaggerate the threat from India (Ahmed 1998: 361). The illusory stability of yet another military government since 1999 does not hide the fact that Pakistan is 'in the middle of a deep crisis' (Ayoob 2002: 59).

Even a sympathetic observer of Pakistan's politics (Rizvi 1998: 110) writes (before the 1999 coup) that:

> Pakistan's civil order and domestic political economy is in turmoil. Widening ethnic, regional and religious-sectarian cleavages, the after-effects of the Afghan War, and weapons proliferation all pose serious challenges to the government. Pakistani society is now so fractured, inundated with sophisticated weapons, brutalised by civic violence and overwhelmed by the spread of narcotics that it is no longer possible for any civilian government to operate effectively without the Army's support...Competing political forces tend to be intolerant towards each other, thereby undermining political institutions and processes. There is no consensus among them as to how to keep the military out of politics.

Although securitisation rhetoric is still strong at the interstate level, Pakistani society seemed increasingly to be fragmenting into substate referent objects for security based mainly on ethnic and religious identity. The army and intelligence services both have a quasi-autonomous character, but it is far from clear that their interests are the same or that either is immune from internal fragmentation. And there is no sense that this internal incoherence is a temporary or recently developed situation. It is of a piece with Pakistan's entire political history since independence, and this deepens the suspicion that there is scant hope for any major change of direction. Pakistan has been steadily dissipating the political resources that gained it independence in 1947, and it is not clear how long the state can soldier on before it either disintegrates or sinks into sustained incoherence within its existing borders. The prospect of political fission thus stands to undo the strategic gains that Pakistan made with nuclear fission.

With the loss of US support during the 1990s, the army became no longer the match for India that it once was. It is far from clear that the renewed US support since 2001 will address any of these problems, and it could easily make many of them worse. As Manor and Segal (1998: 64) note, India is now basically secure on the subcontinent: 'Pakistan is an inferior power and will remain so with a minimum of Indian effort.' Evidence for this was clear in the rhetoric and behaviour surrounding the 1998 nuclear tests. India studiously downplayed Pakistan's nuclear tests, conspicuously not taking up the opportunity to follow Pakistan's tit-for-tat behaviour, and referencing its own behaviour mostly against that of China and the other nuclear weapon states (PPNN 1998a: insert p. 4).

The line of argument for internal transformation is that Pakistan is losing the capacity to stand as a pole of power against India, and that the South Asian RSC is thus easing towards unipolarity.

External transformation – Transformation across the frontier with the Middle Eastern complex having been ruled out above, the remaining possibility is that the South Asian RSC will undergo an external transformation on the basis of developments in relations between India and China. The traditional form of this scenario was an increase in Sino-Indian tensions to the point where they transcended India–Pakistan ones. As India's nuclear rhetoric and China's continued arms supply to Pakistan indicate, this line of thinking still has some relevance. But the escalation of Sino-Indian military rivalry is not the only way that external transformation along this axis can occur. The other path is for India to transcend its region by rising to the status of a third Asian great power. India's reach for great power status does not require all-out rivalry between India and China, and could occur in a context of improving Sino-Indian relations. But it does give China a substantial and increasingly widely recognised role as the benchmark for India's status (Chellaney 1998–9; Delpech 1998–9). Before and after the May 1998 nuclear tests, India's defence minister George Fernandez repeatedly identified China as the main threat to India (*Economist* 9 May 1998: 86; PPNN 1998a: insert p. 4), even though in general terms Sino-Indian relations have been relatively cordial since their 1993 border agreement.

It might be objected that this is nothing new. Since independence India has measured itself against China, and has always thought of itself as a great power. Among the post-test rhetoric was an Indian government statement that: 'Our strengthened capability adds to our sense of responsibility, the responsibility and obligation of power' (Walker 1998: 520). India's nuclear tests were clearly intended to reinforce its claim to great power standing. In RSCT terms, there are two problems for India's claim: first, India's actual military deployment has remained mostly focused on Pakistan and, second, neither China nor the rest of the world has acknowledged its claim. There is evidence of some continuity in this posture. China condemned India's tests in general terms, but refused to take up the Indian defence minister's challenge to pose itself as a threat to India, and avoided making any overt countermove such as resuming its own nuclear tests (PPNN 1998b: 4, insert p. 3; *Economist* 9 May 1998: 86). China's response to India's test and India's response to

Pakistan's are strikingly parallel: the smaller power sought to measure itself against its larger neighbour, with the bigger power doing its best to ignore or downplay the challenge. But, like the decay of Pakistan, the rise of India is an incremental event lacking much in the way of dramatic points of transformation. Again, as with Pakistan, the question is whether enough has changed, or is on the brink of changing, to warrant a re-evaluation of the regional security structures.

India's assertion of nuclear weapons state (NWS) status notwithstanding, the material statistics do not strongly favour its claim to great power status. Globally, it ranks alongside Mexico and the Netherlands in terms of GNP, and Brazil and Israel in terms of military expenditure. Its GNP per capita lies alongside that of Senegal and Nigeria, at around 7 per cent of the level of the main Western states. Even within Asia, India is not unquestionably in the front rank. Its GNP and military expenditure compare with those of South Korea, Taiwan, and Australia, rather than Japan or China. There is not much doubt that its leaders and peoples conceive of India as having special rights and duties in the management of international society based on its status as one of the world's major civilisations, and on population size. The doubt lies in whether other leading members of international society are willing to accord India that right formally, and whether they treat it *de facto* as a great power in their own foreign policy calculations.

The West still tends to answer this question negatively. Washington has not treated Delhi with the same respect, either formal or informal, that it accords other great powers. There is also the obstacle that the legal framework of the Nonproliferation Treaty (NPT) makes it almost impossible to grant India formal status as a NWS, and that this status denial is one of India's main grievances (Walker 1998: 511–12). Until President Clinton's visit in March 2000, the United States seemed to classify India along with Brazil as a regional power located in an area of marginal interest. Clinton's visit may have marked some movement, and there are signs that the Bush administration's more assertive attitude towards China could help India's cause. There is some prospect of the United States giving more sustained acknowledgement not only to India's status as a longstanding democracy, but also to its economic potential and to its possible utility as a counterweight to China. As Manor and Segal (1998) note, India's economic performance since 1994 has been quite impressive, and it looks well placed to continue down this path (*Economist* 29 April 2000: 69–70). Renewed US interest demonstrated the borderline quality of India's global level status as lying between the biggest of the regional powers and the smallest of the great powers, but India does not seem to be a beneficiary of the US engagement in the region in 'the war against terrorism'.

Regardless of whether or not India succeeds in convincing the West of its credentials, it may well find a more responsive audience in Asia. To the governments and peoples still resident in the 'zone of conflict' India's nuclear tests will be seen as significant and impressive. Right across Asia from Iraq and Iran, through Russia and China, to Korea and Taiwan, there are governments and peoples who will have no difficulty empathising with India's position regardless of whether they regret or support its action. India may well be close to a position from which it can play China's old trick (Segal 1999) of trading on its future as an up-and-coming power. The prospect of economic growth and rising military capability may put India in a position where both China and the United States have to take it seriously. India could be an ally or an opponent of both. If China and the United States begin to compete for India's favour, then it will be well on its way to achieving great power status. From this perspective it becomes clearer that substantial changes may well be underway in the standing and relevance of the South Asian RSC itself. As we have seen, the domestic and regional security dynamics within South Asia have largely preserved their traditional form. But saying that is not necessarily to say that their overall significance in the larger pattern of things remains the same. Despite the ongoing confrontation with Pakistan, there is evidence both that the South Asian regional level is diminishing in importance to India and that India's significance within the Asian supercomplex is increasing.

The case to consider here is that India is steadily transcending its long-standing confinement to South Asia, and beginning to carve out a wider role as an Asian great power. This is certainly the hope of those advocating a nuclear weapons policy more openly focused against China (Chellaney 1998–9). It was also the aim of what came to be called the Gujral doctrine (Sen Gupta 1997), by which India has, since the early 1990s, sought to pacify its smaller neighbours, make accommodative agreements with them, and increase intra-regional trade. This policy was based on the understanding that India had no hope of being taken seriously outside the region until it could stabilise its own local environment. Although not without its frictions (common to any regional community), this policy has generally been considered quite successful. Pakistan is the most resistant to it, but, even there, informal trade is said to be much larger than the official figures would suggest. And the political decay of Pakistan, despite its nuclear arsenal, reinforces this development. It opens the way for thinking of the South Asian RSC as transforming from being a vigorous bipolar conflict formation towards a kind of unipolar hegemony. By labelling this a 'unipolar hegemony' we are not saying that India has successfully dominated or overawed its neighbours in a classical imperial sense. That might be true of its relations with Bhutan and Sikkim, but it is clearly not the case with Sri Lanka and Bangladesh, and certainly not with Pakistan, whose sense of rivalry with India remains acute. Rather, we mean that India no longer feels strategically threatened from within South Asia, at least not severely so, and that it has the resources and the will to carve out a wider great power role on the Asian stage. This does not suggest that the South Asian regional level ceases to operate. It will not be easy for India to stabilise or contain the potentially very dangerous relationship with Pakistan. But unless Pakistan, or factions within it, succeeds in keeping alive the threat of head-to-head war with India, India will steadily get more room to develop roles outside the region.

Perhaps the most significant move in this respect was India's acceptance of the invitation to join the ASEAN Regional Forum (ARF) in 1996, an invitation that was pointedly not given to Pakistan despite its earlier links to the region as a member of the now defunct SEATO alliance. No matter how toothless one might think the ARF to be, it is nonetheless a substantial piece in the security architecture of the Asian supercomplex (see ch. 6). There can be little doubt that the Southeast Asian states wanted India to join as a counterweight to China, and that both India and China understood the significance of that move. India's membership also complemented its 'look east' economic policy from the early 1990s, which sought to link the country to the East Asian boom. The military complement to this – and also India's response to China's cultivation of Burma – was a greater Indian naval presence in Southeast Asian waters and plans to build up a naval base in the Andaman Islands. All of this was much battered by the economic storm in East Asia during the late 1990s, and it is still too soon to tell what will become of it, though India has recently expressed interest in the former Russian naval base in Vietnam (*Strategic Survey* 2001–2: 302). Although not having any immediate military significance, India's joining of the ARF broke its traditional security insulation from Southeast Asia, and thereby consolidated its place in the Asian supercomplex. A similar, though less significant, indicator of India's move upwards from regional power is its role in the Indian Ocean Rim Initiative, which aims to strengthen local control over that ocean.

National identity and security discourse in India

India's choice of securitisation is crucial to the development of the RSC. Indian security policy is unusual not only for vacillating between different countries as primary threat, but also for these being at three different levels: Pakistan at the regional, China at the superregional, and the United States at the global level. In addition, domestic security plays an important role, not so much as competitor for external security (as in South Africa), but as implicated in each of the external threats.

A survey or mapping of actual securitisation will in this case not tell us much that is new because these different threats – and especially the relationship between the United States and India – have been quite volatile without any trend standing out clearly. Instead, we will look at deeper factors that might condition or constrain securitisation and therefore help to predict the likely dominant future pattern. Two historical patterns will be presented: what kind of security concerns have traditionally shaped Indian conceptions, and the nature and effects of national identity.

Historically, security concerns in India have typically been about internal/external combinations. Kanti Bajpai concludes from a historical survey that across the different strategic threats, partly inherited from British India, an important 'lesson' was that 'invasions succeeded because Indians were internally disunited and because they were backward' (1998: 160). India's own stability is the key to security. Internal weakness and disunity are exploited – and/or caused – by outside threats. This understanding of India's history and its consequences for security is an important line of reasoning for nationalists, because any division is thereby potentially a security risk. It also serves to elevate development as a security issue.

National identity would at first seem to be fully occupied by the split between secularism and Hinduism in Indian politics. The BJP 'revolution' has altered the relationship between ethno-religious identity, state identity, and security. And in the presentation of secular Indians (who are the ones most often heard outside India), this is almost a security risk in itself, because it threatens the raison d'être of India. The Hindu-nationalists, in return, think about the Congress Party and the other seculars as a threat to 'India'. However, both have a Hindu background: the secularists' slogan of 'unity in diversity' is an ideal that developed within Hinduism as a way to reconcile the many forms of worship within it (Banerjee 1997: 36–7). Both draw from the idea that India is an ancient civilisation and should be recognised as such. Exactly how this civilisation is defined is not a point of agreement, but they both pursue a policy aimed at global recognition that India is a *world civilisation*. It is an important aspect of security discourse that 'for India survival means survival as a great power and security has become synonymous with the safety that enables India to develop, maintain and prosper in its political eminence' (Ashley Tellis quoted by Kak 1998). Obviously, the Hindu-nationalist wave and its clash with secular visions is very important. But we should not necessarily accept the self-presentation of the parties according to which they share almost nothing with each other. The general challenge to any discourse in this area is to link security and identity, threat and nationalism.

The three main external threats should be assessed against this background.

Pakistan as a threat clearly fulfils the internal/external criteria very well – it is about an external power that is mainly a problem because it supports a revolt within India. The other dimension is more tricky. Does a conflict with Pakistan help to get India its sought-after recognition as a great power and/or a world civilisation? As a smaller state, Pakistan cannot be the mirror in which India becomes a great power. However, the civilisational question is at stake, both because seeing the Pakistan challenge off is crucial to lifting India above the region, and because the conflict itself is a threat to the civilisational vision. To secularists, Pakistan is a threat because the religiously based self-definition of Pakistan pushes India in the direction of a similar self-conception which would mean a 'smaller' India, an ethnic nation, not a large world civilisation. To Hindu-nationalists, Pakistan's Islamism represents the great invader that dominated India's Hindu civilisation for many centuries. The conundrum is that Pakistan threatens India's identity in basic ways, but that conflict with Pakistan defines the principal obstacle to India's culture-aspiration to be recognised as a great power.

China performs relatively weakly on the internal threat dimension. A few remote border areas remain contested, but China's impact on India's domestic affairs is limited and does not threaten identity. China, however, performs strongly as a means for producing an Indian great power. China is the most obvious choice here because, if India wants to ascend the ladder of power status, the Asian supercomplex seems to be the next step after it transcends Pakistan.

The United States would at first seem unlikely to connect to the internal/external factor. However, as argued by Bajpai (1998: 174–9), the major threat in New Delhi since 1991 has been a concert of the United States and the other leading industrial countries. It dominates world politics to an extent that limits India's autonomy, and 'one of the greatest fears' is that powerful outsiders will intervene regionally to constrain India. The fear is that external actors might get involved in the main regional conflicts such as Afghanistan and Kashmir, or support the smaller states in disturbing ways. In terms of recognition, the US strategy seems the most promising. In a good Hegelian way, it is important to mirror oneself in as powerful an entity as possible to become recognised as that which one strives for.

The most likely outcome is a continued vacillation among the three levels. In addition to the practical problems associated with eliminating Pakistan, taking on China, or challenging the United States, each securitisation only partially fulfils the needs in relation to national identity and tradition.

Conclusions

Much of this region's story still fits within the state-centric, military-political terms of 'classical' RSCT. India–Pakistan is still largely a story of securitisations about military power, weapons, and political status. The more open attitude of revised RSCT towards non-traditional sectors and referent objects does draw more attention to the domestic level, but using a securitisation approach does not significantly change the profile of what was observed using more traditional methods. In terms of sectors, societal insecurity is a big part of the domestic story, and draws more attention to the internal goings-on in the states of the region, particularly Afghanistan, Pakistan, and Sri Lanka, but also India. It helps one to see a variety of substate actors and entities with standing as security actors and referent objects within states, and sometimes on a regional scale. But even this non-traditional sector is substantially integrated into the interstate rivalries, and much of it is readily visible through military-political lenses. So far the economic and environmental sectors make a relatively minor appearance on the balance sheet of securitisation within the region. Water sharing is the key environmental concern on the subcontinent and, up to a point, has been successfully handled politically. To the extent that the economy has been securitised, this is with reference to the impacts of globalisation (Mahendra 2002), though that could change if intra-regional trade continues to expand. The fact that so much of security in this region can be comprehended in the old style reinforces the idea put forward in part I that the post-Cold War international system divides into 'two worlds' for purposes of security analysis. Within that model, South Asia is clearly in the zone of conflict, where the traditional power-politics rules of international relations still prevail.

A second observation is that there is evidence of a considerable disjuncture between the picture that would emerge from traditional strategic analysis and the one that results from a securitisation approach. Traditional strategic analysis focuses on the India–Pakistan and India–China rivalries, with their associated wars, tensions, military deployments, and material capabilities. But, in a wide range of interviews conducted by Buzan in Delhi early in 1999, Pakistan was mentioned mostly as an irritant, and not even its nuclear threat was taken seriously. China was not seen as an immediate threat, despite its support for Pakistan, and even as a future threat was largely seen as a problem for the United States to handle, not India. The overwhelming weight of rhetorical concern was on the United States as the main threat to India. One heard repeatedly the (what seemed to an outsider highly exaggerated) idea that the United States 'threatened India with nuclear weapons' during the 1971 war. And given US hegemony post-Cold War as the last superpower and as the leader of global capitalism, there was not much sympathy for the idea that the global level had become less important relative to the regional one as a result of the ending of the Cold War. The image was one of an increasingly coordinated core pressuring a periphery made weaker by the demise of the Soviet Union – thus a stronger global level, not a weaker one, when viewed from a third world perspective. Both its preoccupation with the United States and its dismissal of Pakistan make sense in the light of India's self-perception as a great power. Its relatively calm and detached attitude towards China is harder to explain, and could be crucial in how the Asian supercomplex unfolds.

To sum up, we can make the following points about how the South Asian complex and the wider security constellation within which it sits have evolved since the ending of the Cold War.

- At the domestic level the general pattern in the region shows a great deal of continuity across the transition from the Cold War to the post-Cold War era. Within this pattern, domestic political life in Afghanistan and Pakistan became conspicuously more fragmented, chaotic, and violent.
- At the regional level, the pattern of amity and enmity remained broadly similar, with some intensification of the hostility between India and Pakistan. But Pakistan's seeming slide towards failure as a state looked increasingly to be bringing the power bipolarity of the South Asian RSC into question. Despite Pakistan's nuclear equaliser, India looked more hegemonic in the region. Thus, although the regional level retained its traditional form, it was becoming less important to India, and allowing it more latitude to define wider security horizons. If the honeymoon between the United States and India opened by Clinton's visit survives the turbulence unleashed by the 2001 war against Afghanistan, this could reinforce India's status within the Asian supercomplex.
- At the interregional level, one finds mainly continuity in the patterns between South Asia and the Middle East and between China and South Asia. The South Asian RSC underwent no external transformation, but its position in the Asian supercomplex was strengthened by India's membership in the ARF. The boundaries between the South Asian complex and its neighbours were *not* breaking down and forming new configurations of amity/enmity and polarity. Instead, something quite different seemed to be unfolding. The regional boundaries remained broadly stable, while the whole South Asian regional level diminished in relative importance for India. In effect, India was beginning to establish its great power credentials at the interregional level in Asia, though it was still at best only in the early stages of doing so at the global level.
- At the global level there was a high degree of continuity in the overall pattern of outside intervention in South Asia. Although India lost its support from the Soviet Union, Pakistan seemingly retained its on-again/off-again relationship with the United

States, developments which left China in an improved position vis-à-vis influence in South Asia. The main option for change was the possibility that as a consequence of its 11 September engagements in South Asia, the United States would find itself more durably drawn into the region as a ring-holder between India and Pakistan.

5 Northeast and Southeast Asian RSCs during the Cold War

An RSC covering all of East Asia is a recurrent pattern. Before and during the Second World War, Japanese power and imperial ambition linked Northeast and Southeast Asia together into a single security region. Earlier still, periodic waxings of Chinese power also brought these two regions into the same security sphere. But before the rise of imperial Japan in the late nineteenth century, and during waning periods of Chinese power, Northeast and Southeast Asia sometimes had largely separate regional security dynamics. During the Cold War, the patterns of regional security in East Asia were heavily penetrated by, but not completely subordinate to, the two superpowers. Although somewhat masked by Cold War patterns, this chapter will tell their story as separate Northeast and Southeast Asian RSCs, albeit with some interregional crossover by China (Buzan 1988a, 1988b, 1994). After the Cold War, penetration from the global level diminished substantially and altered in form, and the regional level story is best told on an East Asian scale. That will be the approach of chapter 6.

In Southeast Asia, decolonisation produced a fairly typical postcolonial conflict formation. It was almost entirely composed of weak states, but since most of these had solid historical roots, a set of relatively durable modern states eventually emerged. Like that in the Middle East, this RSC quickly became heavily penetrated by outside powers. In Northeast Asia, only the secondary states (Korea and Taiwan) were postcolonial. China and Japan had never fully lost their independence to the colonial powers, and both came out of a great power past. The Cold War situation in East Asia (especially Northeast Asia) was parallel to that in Europe inasmuch as the region was a main frontline in the superpower rivalry, with stationing of superpower forces in several countries. But it was different in that Europe was overlaid (the regional dynamic subordinated to the global one) and therefore ceased to function as an RSC, whereas in Asia China only briefly, if at all, lined up with the superpower securitisation, and indigenous regional dynamics remained active under the Cold War cloak. The East Asian RSCs were heavily penetrated by the global level, but not overlaid by it.

Cold War logic divided Korea, China, and Vietnam, so generating the local hot wars that also differentiated Asia from Europe. It tied Taiwan, South Korea, and Japan firmly into the pattern of Cold War alliances constructed by the United States to contain the communist powers. Except as a historical shadow (Buzan 1988a, 1996), Japan was almost completely out of the picture as an independent strategic player in the region, featuring mainly as a US ally and dependant. After 1960, an independent China played mainly at the global level in a three-cornered game with the United States and the Soviet Union. But China also played a significant role in Southeast Asia, pursuing a rivalry with Vietnam that had roots independent of the Cold War. Thus, although we will present Northeast and Southeast Asia as distinct RSCs for this period, there were already strong signs of the linkages to China that would later draw the two regions together into a single East Asian regional security dynamic.

The domestic level

In the immediate aftermath of the Second World War, domestic level security dynamics were prominent throughout the region. In particular, China's huge civil war did not end until 1950, and nearly all of the Southeast Asian states suffered serious post-independence internal conflicts. These were usually along communist/anti-communist lines, paralleling the logic that split China, Korea, and Vietnam into competing states. The change of government in Indonesia in 1965 came at a cost of well over half a million lives in a massive purge against communists and Chinese. Indonesia's occupation of East Timor in 1975 cost at least 100,000 lives. Burma, the Philippines, and Cambodia, and in a different way South Vietnam, had long-running civil wars, but in many countries the domestic level eventually stabilised, and security priority moved to the interstate level. The China–Taiwan dispute, confusingly, can be read both as an unresolved civil war and as an interstate rivalry. The host of domestic troubles in the region that pitched communists against anti-communists (or sometimes one communist faction against another) all attracted extensive outside intervention, and are hard to disentangle from the heavy penetration of global level powers into East Asian politics. This was true of China, Vietnam, Cambodia, Malaysia, Indonesia, the Philippines, and Korea. Burma was less affected in this way, though China gave some support to the military government. Thus, although dominant at the beginning and chronic in a few countries (Philippines, Burma, Cambodia), the domestic level fairly rapidly moved into the background, giving way to regional and global security dynamics. As in South Asia, relatively high levels of domestic political violence were mostly contained within the state structures, though also offering possible access for intervention by outsiders.

The regional level

Northeast Asia

The Northeast Asian case provides a rare example (other than Europe) of an RSC emerging naturally rather than out of decolonisation. The Western powers failed fully to subordinate China, Japan, and Korea. All three managed to resist Western penetration until well into the nineteenth century (by which time the United States was among the imperial powers besieging their gates). The easy defeat of China by Britain in the Opium Wars of the early 1840s opened the way for Western penetration into the region, but did not involve overriding the formal political independence of either China or Japan. Japan in particular embarked on a rapid and uniquely successful programme of turning itself not only into a European-style state, but also into a European-style imperial great power. By the early years of the twentieth century it had achieved recognition as a great power. In 1895 it defeated China, in 1902 it became an ally of Britain, and in 1904–5 it defeated Russia's Far Eastern forces, in the process carving out an empire incorporating Taiwan and Korea. With a fully independent Japan engaging a quasi-independent China, the makings of an RSC in Northeast Asia were in place, and continued to unfold during the 1920s and 1930s. This emergent complex was, however, operating within a local environment still heavily under Western control. Britain, France, the United States, and the Netherlands all had major colonies in East Asia, and Russia/the Soviet Union was a geographically adjacent superpower. Nevertheless, here too we see the logic of regional security emerging as soon as the necessary conditions are met: the global international system is in place, local actors are independent, and Western overlay is weak.

In the immediate aftermath of the Second World War, the regional level in Northeast Asia was almost inert, and the main security dynamics were on the domestic level (China's civil war) and the global level (US occupation of Japan, and joint Soviet and US occupation of Korea). Not until the communists had won the civil war in China (1949), the superpowers had withdrawn from the two Koreas they had created (1948–9), and Japan had been released from occupation government (1951) was there real potential for indigenous regional security dynamics to develop. Up to 1960, superpower penetration remained heavy, and could almost have passed for overlay. US military forces were strongly present in Japan (where the US–Japan Security Treaty of 1951 gave them substantial basing rights) and South Korea (as a result of the Korean War). North Korea and China were seemingly firm allies of the Soviet Union. The Korean War had cemented into place an East–West split in the region, which was further reinforced by the renewed intervention of the United States in China's unfinished civil war, effectively preserving the independence of Taiwan. The main fault lines and flashpoints in the region all fell along the boundary of containment that cut through the Taiwan Strait, Korea, and the Sea of Japan. But, although China and North Korea were allies of the Soviet Union, and under its nuclear umbrella, they did not allow the stationing of Soviet forces on their territory.

After 1960, China cut free from the Soviet alliance and pursued an independent course as a great power in opposition to both superpowers. Much of its behaviour is best understood in the context of its triangle with the two superpowers, though it still retained some substantial regional roles. Even though it could not nearly match the military power of the United States and the Soviet Union, China succeeded in being taken seriously as an ideological and strategic threat by both. From 1971 onwards, once the United States recognised China's value as an ally against the Soviet Union, it also succeeded in playing a kind of balancer role between them.

But underneath all of this global level action and imposition, and largely masked by the extremely similar position of its fault lines, was an active set of regional security dynamics. One subset of these was unresolved leftovers from the Second World War and earlier, most notably the quite public fear and dislike of Japan in China and the two Koreas. All three countries took care to keep their worst memories of Japan alive, and their diplomatic rhetoric escalated at the slightest provocation into securitisation of the possible (or suspected actual) remilitarisation of Japan, or its intention to revive the hegemonic structure of its pre-1945

'Greater East Asia Co-Prosperity Sphere'. An additional irritant was the existence of territorial disputes over small islands between Japan and South Korea on the one hand, and Japan and both Chinas on the other (Buzan 1978: 37–9). Although in the case of China and North Korea this securitisation of Japan could be, and often was, read as part of the Cold War rivalry, it contained a strong regional thread that was independent of the Cold War. The fact that South Korea indulged in it almost as much as the other two while being on the same side as Japan in the Cold War suggests just how strong this indigenous regional element of securitisation really was. In the case of China, the underlying fear was of a rival great power that had attacked it twice within the past century, and might once again dominate the region in the future. In the case of the two Koreas, the underlying fear was of again becoming vassals to an overmighty neighbour. Parallels might be drawn between Japan's position as an object of fear and hatred in Northeast Asia and Germany's position in Europe. But this parallel was of diminishing relevance. The division of Germany, its internal and external coming to terms with its own past, and the steady integration of its Western part into the European Community all served to weaken and erode the historical pattern of insecurity in Europe. No such change took place in Northeast Asia. The Japanese largely refused to confront the question of war guilt, and their neighbours remained suspicious of Japan's conversion to pacifism. Although the old pattern was submerged under, and/or incorporated into, the Cold War, it remained politically vital and alive, and much more available as a resource for securitisation than was the case in Europe (Buzan 1988b, 1996).

The other subset of indigenous security dynamics in Northeast Asia was created by the Cold War, but took on a life independent of it. This was the conflict created by the making of two Koreas and two Chinas. Unlike in Southeast Asia, where the postwar division of Vietnam was overcome in a protracted and bloody struggle, in Northeast Asia the postwar divisions took root. The military option for reuniting the two Koreas was tried in 1950 by the North, but failed, producing a stalemate that has endured since 1953. The military option was not tried in the case of China, partly because of the military difficulty of mounting an invasion across the Taiwan Strait, and partly because of US involvement. In both cases the result has been the steady de facto consolidation of separate states. But this consolidation was not recognised de jure by either side in both pairs, with the consequence that both pairs of states grew up locked into military confrontation and still committed to reunification (but in deep disagreement about how the unified state should be governed). Although products of the Cold War, these two divided states quickly became a regional level fact, whose mutually linked securitisations were independent of the Cold War, and could (and did) survive their creator.

During the Cold War, Northeast Asia was subjected to heavy penetration by global level security dynamics, but still retained an autonomous regional security dynamic. Once they had recovered from the Second World War, two of its four states resumed their role as great powers: first China, taking up the role vigorously; and later Japan, not by self-assertion, but by the response of others to its spectacular economic recovery. Regional level dynamics remained in the form of strong local securitisations that were reinforced by, and in many ways incorporated into, the global level security dynamics of the Cold War.

Southeast Asia

The Southeast Asian RSC emerged in a protracted and often conflictual process of decolonisation. Thailand had never been a colony. The Philippines gained independence in 1946, Burma in 1948, Indonesia in 1949, Cambodia in 1953, Laos and Vietnam (in two parts) in 1954, Malaya in 1957 (and then as the wider Malaysia in 1963), and Singapore in 1965. From the very beginning this process was heavily penetrated by Cold War ideological alignments of communist versus anti-communist, setting a pattern that was to last right through the Cold War. European colonial involvement was lingering, with the French engaged in major conflict in Vietnam until their defeat in 1954, and the Dutch in confrontation with Indonesia until 1962. The struggle to reunite Vietnam, which was tragically caught up in superpower rivalry, went on until 1975.

In Southeast Asia the new RSC was shaped by a mixture of the characteristics of the Middle Eastern and South Asian ones. Like South Asia, its conflict came in bipolarised form, and thus attracted a relatively clear pattern of superpower intervention. But, like the Middle East, it had diverse geography and a multipolar power structure, being composed of several medium-sized powers and a few small ones. Although Southeast Asia, like the other new third world RSCs, contained a wealth of interstate conflicts and rivalries, these dominated neither its operation nor its formation. Unlike either South Asia or the Middle East, Southeast Asia became so heavily penetrated by superpower (and Chinese) rivalry that its essential structure largely followed Cold War alignments

(Buzan 1988b; Khong 1997). For a time, it seemed in danger of over-lay, with massive US troop deployments between 1962 and 1973, and superpower military bases in Vietnam (variously US and Soviet), the Philippines (US), and Thailand (US). The domestic level was significant for most states, but only in the case of Cambodia did this have serious spillover consequences into the regional level.

Because penetration from the global level was so strong, the indigenous regional security dynamics in Southeast Asia are difficult to differentiate, but nonetheless are present and significant. As the process of decolonisation came to an end, there were some signs that a complicated pattern of local rivalries analogous to that in the Middle East might develop. The postcolonial states bore enough similarity to the precolonial political structures to pick up resonances of historical securitisations among them. Thailand and (North) Vietnam drifted into rivalry in Cambodia and Laos, and Cambodia resisted Vietnamese hegemonism. Between 1963 and 1966 Indonesia threatened to extinguish the new Malaysian federation, and had frictions with Singapore. There was also a territorial dispute between Malaysia and the Philippines over claims to Sabah. What looked like a drift towards a typical postcolonial conflict formation was, however, reversed by the change of government in Indonesia starting in 1965 (Khong 1997: 321–7). Indonesia shifted from *confrontasi* with its neighbours to a policy of promoting regional political stability in order to underpin region-wide (but nationally controlled) economic development projects. Rather than sharpening their national identities against each other, Malaysia, Singapore, the Philippines, Indonesia, and Thailand set up ASEAN in 1967, within which they began to construct a subregional security regime.

This development was powerfully reinforced by alignment imperatives deriving from the Cold War. Particularly influential was the US intervention in Vietnam from the early 1960s until its defeat in 1973, and the subsequent reunification of Vietnam in 1975. ASEAN was always Western-leaning, and the Philippines and Thailand were key US allies. It was thus not long before Southeast Asia consolidated into two groups: a communist-led, Soviet-aligned, and Vietnamese-dominated group of three (Vietnam, Laos, Cambodia); and the anti-communist, Western-orientated ASEAN group (becoming six in 1984, adding Brunei). Vietnam's victory over the United States weakened the latter's role in the region, forcing ASEAN into a more active role against Vietnamese expansionism (Khong 1997: 332–5). As Samudavanija and Paribatra (1987:

22–4) note, this pattern represented a transformation from an earlier situation in which most of the Southeast Asian states contained severe ideological divisions *within* themselves, to one in which the ideological polarisation was constructed along regional, interstate lines. There are parallels here with the way in which South Asia's domestic religious divisions turned into interstate ones with decolonisation. Burma, which remained inward-looking and isolated throughout the Cold War, served as an insulator between the RSCs in South and Southeast Asia.

The ASEAN states managed to shelve the disputes among themselves, effectively forming a weak subregional security regime whose members agreed not to pursue their disagreements by force. But the same was not true in Indochina. Thailand was in the front line against the communist trio along its borders with Laos and Cambodia, a role that combined both traditional elements of Thai–Vietnamese rivalry and strong inputs from Cold War alignments. Small-scale military clashes were a regular feature on these borders, as was Thai provision of sanctuary for anti-Vietnamese forces. Thailand, with the support of its ASEAN partners, was unsettled by the prospect of immediate adjacency to Vietnamese communist power that resulted from Vietnam's domination of Laos and Cambodia (Simon 1983: 306, 310–11; Gordon 1986). Laos had been largely under Vietnamese control since its days as a supply corridor to the south during the war against the United States. But the acutely fragmented and conflictual domestic politics of Cambodia meant that it, or at times parts of it, was sometimes at war with Vietnam. After the reunification of Vietnam, and the Khmer Rouge takeover in Cambodia in 1975, the two communist regimes fell into severe rivalry, escalating to major fighting in 1977. In late 1978 Vietnam invaded and occupied Cambodia, installing a puppet government and pushing the Khmer Rouge into guerrilla warfare. The Vietnamese remained in occupation of Cambodia until 1989. With 140,000 troops in Cambodia and 50,000 in Laos, Vietnam was, until the end of the Cold War, effectively in control of an Indochinese empire. Thailand opposed this by providing support and sanctuary to the Khmer Rouge and other anti-Vietnamese rebel groups, actions that resulted in Vietnamese military incursions into, and sometimes occupation of, Thai border territory. At least one major battle resulted, when Thai troops expelled well-entrenched Vietnamese forces in 1987.

In Southeast Asia, therefore, the regional level was neither fully autonomous nor subordinated to the point of overlay. Cold War penetration was exceptionally heavy, and played a major role in shaping the regional bipolarisation of conflict. But woven through this were substantial elements of still active regional level securitisation.

The interregional level

There are five elements to consider at this level. First are the linkages between Southeast Asia and the South Pacific. These mostly comprised defence treaties linking Australia and New Zealand to states in Southeast Asia. The Southeast Asia Collective Defence Treaty of 1954 tied them (as well as other Western powers and Pakistan) to Thailand and the Philippines, though it largely ceased to be active after its organisation (SEATO) was dissolved in 1977. The five-nation defence agreement of 1971 linked them (and Britain) to Singapore and Malaysia. Both of these arrangements can be considered mostly as offshoots of global level dynamics, respectively US containment alliances and British postcolonial arrangements. But they did provide specific, albeit modest, interregional links that otherwise would not have existed. It was notable in defining the regional boundary between Southeast Asia and the South Pacific that neither Australia and New Zealand nor Papua-New Guinea (which gained independence in 1975) joined ASEAN. The South Pacific states did develop some loose regional forums, but distance and water enabled this part of the world to remain unstructured in regional security terms.

Second is the unresolved territorial dispute between Japan and the Soviet Union over four small islands off the northern coast of Hokkaido. This dispute was much amplified by the Cold War alignments, but not dependent on them. It meant that there was no formal treaty ending the Second World War between Japan and the Soviet Union.

Third is the residual fear and dislike of Japan shared by all of the countries that experienced Japanese occupation before and during the Second World War. This was much stronger in Northeast than in Southeast Asia, the latter having suffered such occupation for only a few years during the Second World War. But it was a standing reminder of how easily the region could become a strategic whole in the presence of a local great power, and this memory played a significant role in keeping Japan neutralised as an independent strategic player in East Asia.

Fourth are the linkages to South Asia comprising China's border disputes with India and its alliance with Pakistan. These have been covered in chapter 4.

Fifth, and most central to RSCT analysis, are the linkages between Northeast and Southeast Asia. As would be expected from the different levels of power, there was almost no spillover from south to north in East Asia, but quite a lot from north to south, almost wholly in the form of China's direct engagement in Southeast Asia (though also including Taiwan's territorial claims and bases in the South China Sea, and Japan's historical shadow). This linkage bears striking resemblance to China's role in South Asia, and like it posed some classification questions for RSCT. In part, China's role in these neighbouring regions can be read at the global level in the context of China's role as an independently minded great power. But in part it reflected genuine interregional dynamics that would have existed regardless of the Cold War. In both cases the security linkage between China and the adjacent region was lopsided, with some of the local states placing China high on their list of threats to national security, but with China placing them relatively low in priority compared to its worries about the two superpowers and Japan.

Although similar in form to China's involvement in South Asia, the pattern in Southeast Asia represented a considerably stronger interregional link. As in the South Asian case, there was a Chinese dispute with a local state (Vietnam), and consequent alliances with other local actors (Thailand, Khmer Rouge). The rivalry between Vietnam and China traces back to a very long history of Chinese attempts (often successful) to impose its suzerainty on Vietnam, and Vietnamese resistance to this. During North Vietnam's struggle to overcome the US attempt to keep Vietnam divided, communist solidarity and the logic of Cold War anti-Americanism overrode local differences, and cast China as an ally of North Vietnam. But once Vietnam achieved unity, and began to consolidate its grip on Laos and Cambodia, the regional level became active again (thus, *inter alia*, making a nonsense of the US rationale for its intervention in Vietnam that it was to prevent Chinese hegemony in the region). China vigorously opposed Vietnam's takeover of Cambodia. Along with ASEAN and the West, it supported the Khmer Rouge throughout the decade of Vietnam's occupation with a substantial flow of arms supplies, and made common cause with Thailand in this venture. During 1978 heavy fighting broke out along the Sino-Vietnamese border and, in 1979, in response to Vietnam's invasion of Cambodia, China launched a month-long punitive war against Vietnam.

In addition to Vietnam, several other states in Southeast Asia had strong historical reasons for seeing China as a threat. China's many centuries of suzerainty over, and sometime occupation of, Indochina is felt particularly strongly by Vietnam. But most Southeast Asian states contain significant populations of Chinese, which during the Cold War gave rise to fears of fifth-column treason, particularly in Malaysia and Indonesia (Girling 1973: 127–9; Simon 1983: 304, 312–13; 1984: 526–7; Tajima 1981: 9–10, 21–6). These fears were amplified by the history of post-independence links between local Chinese populations on the one hand and communist parties supported, and/or inspired, by Beijing on the other (Simon 1984: 523–5, 527–30; Tajima 1981: 17–21).

A final parallel with South Asia is the presence of direct Chinese (and Taiwanese) territorial claims in the region. But, whereas Chinese claims in South Asia concerned only remote border territories in the Himalayas, its claims in Southeast Asia concerned islands, reefs (the Paracels and Spratlys), and seabed rights in the South China Sea. These claims plant Chinese sovereignty right in the heart of Southeast Asia. The principal conflicts were with Vietnam and the Philippines, and the former could not be disentangled from the wider dispute between China and Vietnam. Chinese forces expelled Vietnamese ones from the Paracel Islands in 1974, taking advantage of the confusion arising from the dying days of the reunification war in Vietnam. Further military conflicts took place between China and Vietnam in the Spratly Islands during 1988, and Chinese claims prompted both Vietnam and the Philippines to strengthen their military positions in the Spratlys.

This story can be told as a strong interregional linkage involving a great power and territorial rivalry though, as with the regional level, its dynamics were greatly affected by those of the Cold War.

The global level and East Asia

Once the struggle for decolonisation was over, the European powers ceased to matter much as players in East Asian security. The principal outside powers active in the region were the United States and the Soviet Union, and much of China's security policy, especially after 1960, has also to be understood in the context of global power rivalries. For the global powers, calculating mainly in terms of their relationships with each other, the distinction between Northeast and Southeast Asia, or indeed regional and global, mattered little, and their failure to make these distinctions explains some of their policy disasters.

For the United States, the main game was the military and political containment of communism in general and the Soviet sphere of influence in particular. Until 1971 the USA lumped China in as part of the Soviet bloc. It played the containment game of forward defence vigorously throughout East Asia, in the process engaging itself in two major wars: Korea (1950–3) and Indochina (1961–75). After the US diplomatic opening to China in 1971, China became a possible counterweight to the Soviet Union, but remained a threat to US allies in East Asia, particularly Taiwan. US actions and engagements in East Asia – from its extensive network of bilateral and multilateral alliances, through its maintenance of forward military bases in Japan, South Korea, and the Philippines, to its military actions in Korea, the Taiwan Strait, and Indochina – can all be broadly understood within the containment framework. After its defeat in Vietnam, the United States reverted to a more stand-off policy, based on naval power and support for local allies rather than direct engagement. Although the US position in Northeast Asia remained firm, from the 1970s onward Sino-Soviet rivalry was more important in both South and Southeast Asia than was US–Soviet or Chinese–US rivalry.

Soviet strategic policy in East Asia started as a simple game of countercontainment, seeking to strengthen and widen the communist bloc, and to challenge or breach containment wherever possible. But once the Sino-Soviet split became public around 1960, the Soviet Union had to add a second game, which was its own policy of military-political containment of China. Once China had been lost as an ally, the Soviet game against the United States was pursued by building up its military forces in the Far East, and by supporting its allies in North Korea and (North) Vietnam. These policies also served in the containment move against China. Although both China and the Soviet Union supported (North) Vietnam during its struggle against the United States, Chinese support dropped away sharply after the US withdrawal. Soviet support continued on a large scale, and was instrumental in sustaining Vietnam's military capability both against China and for its costly ten-year occupation of Cambodia. In return the Soviet Union acquired ex-US naval bases on Vietnam's coast, which greatly improved its power projection against both the USA and China (Ross 1986: 92–5). It was not without significance that Vietnam sought and obtained a military security treaty with the Soviet Union just one month before launching its invasion of Cambodia in 1978. Like India in 1971, Vietnam needed the Soviet link as a guarantee against a massive Chinese response to an attack against one of its local allies. Indeed, the Soviet relationship with India, cultivated since the early 1960s, was another part of Moscow's containment policy against China. In addition to cultivating allies on China's borders, the

Soviet Union also pursued containment by strengthening its military deployments along the Sino-Soviet border. Doing this increased its overall military burden, and was costly in terms of the Soviet–US rivalry.

If a single theme can encompass China's security policy during the Cold War, it probably hinges on an obsessive concern with the completion and consolidation of the communist revolution. This project was necessarily linked to consolidating the sovereignty of the Chinese state and endowing it with enough power to prevent any repetition of the foreign intrusions and invasions that had humiliated China since the middle of the nineteenth century. In some ways this project resembled that of many newly independent states, but it was conducted on a far vaster scale and at a much higher pitch of intensity. Among the prime objectives were: (1) to complete the unification of the country by taking Tibet and Taiwan, (2) where possible to construct or maintain sympathetic buffer states against the West along its borders (North Korea and North Vietnam), and (3) by a combination of territorial defence and nuclear deterrence to make the country secure against invasion or attack. China had good reasons to fear the United States. Washington had supported the Nationalist side in China's civil war, and from 1950 stood in the way of China retaking Taiwan. China had had to wage a costly war against the United States to prevent the Americans from overthrowing North Korea after they had thwarted the North's invasion of the South. It also had to endure US nuclear threats in the context of the Korean War and the various crises in the Taiwan Strait during the 1950s.

Although the Soviet Union was a crucial ally against the United States during the first decade after the revolution, relations between Moscow and Beijing were never close. Moscow's highly penetrative and controlling attitude towards its allies, as demonstrated in Eastern Europe, was in contradiction with China's goal of strong national independence, and this clash was amplified by widening ideological differences. The apparent folly of China moving itself into a position of open hostility to both superpowers during the 1960s is inexplicable in both balance-of-power and bandwagon terms, and by the late 1960s there were serious military clashes on the Sino-Soviet border. Except for the low probability of a US–Soviet coalition against it, China was protected against the two most powerful military states on the planet only by its fledgling independent nuclear deterrent and the reputation of guerrilla warfare as a means of inflicting high costs on invading forces. Once the Sino-Soviet split opened up, China found itself playing a double game of counter-containment against both the United States and the Soviet Union. Only during the 1970s did China's strategic policy begin to make sense in balance-of-power terms.

Its policies in the regions bordering it have to be read as a mixture of global and interregional. Its support for North Vietnam was almost wholly in the global context of China's countercontainment against the United States. China was perhaps never keen to see its historic rival Vietnam reunified (Keylor 1984: 390), and certainly opposed the extension of Vietnamese hegemony over Laos and Cambodia (Gordon 1986: 68–9). Its opposition to Vietnam and India, and support for the Khmer Rouge and Pakistan, was a mixture of playing local balances against potential Asian rivals and running a countercontainment policy against Soviet allies. Vietnam confronted China with particularly difficult choices about the tradeoffs among its interregional objectives in Southeast Asia, and its global ones vis-à-vis the United States and the Soviet Union. After 1971, China's link to Pakistan became a useful complementarity in its relations with the United States, for whom Pakistan was also a containment ally. China also had to struggle against the fact that most of its potential allies in the region viewed it as a threat. From the late 1970s, after the consolidation of the Soviet–Vietnamese alliance and the Vietnamese occupation of Cambodia, China's natural security interest was to identify itself with ASEAN's fears of both Vietnam and the Soviet Union. But the complicated interplay of local and great power security dynamics, not to mention China's territorial claims in the South China Sea, made this logic far from straightforward. Thailand was the most amenable of the ASEAN states to China's position, because it was by far the most exposed of the ASEAN states to the threat from Vietnam, and welcomed the Chinese counterweight. Malaysia and Indonesia, by contrast, focused more on the longer-term threat of Chinese hegemonism to the region than on the more immediate, but in the long run much smaller, threat from Vietnam (Simon 1983: 310–11; 1984: 526–33; Calvocoressi 1982: 19–20; Tajima 1981: 15). Because opinion in ASEAN was divided, Vietnam could portray itself and the Soviet Union as serving regional interests by resisting the reassertion of Chinese hegemony over Southeast Asia (Simon 1983: 312–13).

This interaction between local and great power security dynamics explains the failure of all attempts during the Cold War to create a security regime covering the whole of Southeast Asia. ASEAN's promotion of a 'zone of peace, freedom, and neutrality' (ZOPFAN) confronted two difficulties. First, it created divisions within ASEAN about the meanings of the terms in relation to the trade and security links that individual members already had with outside powers. Second, it was paralysed by the acute division between the ASEAN group and Vietnam (Simon 1983: 309–10; Kim 1977: 755, 766; Weatherbee 1978: 411–13; Simon 1975: 53–7; Girling 1973: 125–6). The Soviet proposal for Asian Collective Security, first floated in 1969, attempted to approach the problem from a different angle. As in South Asia, the Soviet Union wished to dampen down the local security rivalries in order to highlight the common threat to the region posed by China, and wanted local conflict resolution in order to strengthen its containment programme against China (Tajima 1981: 30). The Chinese, in turn, favoured an ASEAN-style ZOPFAN as a means of excluding the Soviet Union from the region.

In Northeast Asia the picture is more about contradictions in policies among the great powers. Despite their split, China and the Soviet Union both supported North Korea as a communist ally and strategic buffer against the West. They also had similar policies towards Japan, seeking to weaken its ties to the United States, but also to keep it militarily and politically weak and pacifistic in attitude. The reverse was the case regarding Taiwan, where, after the Sino-Soviet split, the Soviet Union was more in line with US policy, though for different reasons. Moscow was probably quite happy to see the division of China maintained, both as a distraction to Beijing and as an irritant in US–China strategic relations.

Conclusions

Using the levels-of-analysis scheme from RSCT to think about East Asian security dynamics during the Cold War produces the following picture. From a global perspective, the triangular game of containment and countercontainment among the United States, the USSR, and China spanned not only East Asia but also South Asia. This global power game penetrated deeply into domestic and regional security politics throughout the region. At the interregional level, the geostrategic position of China and, to a lesser extent, historical memories of Japanese imperialism spanned the Asian area sufficiently to think of it as a supercomplex: three regions loosely linked by great power-driven interregional security dynamics. But at the regional level, South, Northeast, and Southeast Asian security dynamics were largely separate. In Northeast Asia an older conflict formation was heavily penetrated by superpower rivalry, though it remained visible in the local securitisation rhetoric. In Southeast Asia there was a more active regional bipolarisation, albeit one heavily shaped by Cold War impositions. The United States, in stark contrast to its policy in Europe, cultivated mainly bilateral alliances, and did nothing to encourage the formation of regional alliances or institutions either within or between the two halves of East Asia (Katzenstein 1996b: 141). It was that pattern of relative mutual indifference that was to change after 1990, when the relinking of Northeast and Southeast Asian security dynamics at the regional level (and not just in Chinese, Japanese, US, and Soviet perspectives) began to unfold.

6 The 1990s and beyond: an emergent East Asian complex

Unlike in South Asia, where the ending of the Cold War did not make much difference to the regional security dynamics, in East Asia it made a big difference. In Southeast Asia the withdrawal of Soviet power and the pulling back of US forces facilitated the shift away from a conflictual bipolarisation and towards a security regime. In Northeast Asia, the confrontation on the Korean peninsula continued, and Japan chose to remain a subordinate partner of the United States. The military confrontation of the Cold War dropped away, but only to give more freedom of action to China, whose weight in the region was increasing rapidly. This encouraged the local states to begin relinking their security affairs on an East Asian scale. The main argument in this chapter is that, by giving more weight to China, the ending of the Cold War opened the way for an external transformation in the regional security architecture of East Asia. From the 1980s economically, and during the 1990s also in a military-political sense, the states of Northeast and Southeast Asia increasingly began to merge into a single RSC. A benchmark date to signal the before and after points of this merger could be 1994–5, when the ASEAN Regional Forum (ARF) was set up, and Vietnam joined ASEAN. This merger had both historical precedents and Cold War precursors as sketched above. As well as being driven by classical military-political security dynamics, the making of an East Asian complex was also driven by the Japan-centred economic integration of the region, which added a strong economic dimension to its securitisation processes. As in Europe, the key US alliance structures stayed in place, but in East Asia the US role as ring-holder in the regional security dynamics remained considerably stronger than it was on the other side of Eurasia.

Within the framework of RSCT, the process of external transformation involved in the merger of Northeast and Southeast Asia changes the content of some levels. What had been regional becomes subregional, and what had been interregional between Northeast and Southeast Asia becomes an East Asian regional level.

The domestic level

With the ending of the Cold War the domestic level of security became more prominent in two ways: instability in some countries, and big questions about the direction of evolution in others. Cases of direct instability were most prominent in Burma, Cambodia, and Indonesia.

Burma remained locked under a repressive military dictatorship in longstanding tension with more democratic parties, and in civil war with some minorities. But with Chinese support, the military remained successful in both suppressing the democratic opposition and defeating the main ethnic rebel groups along its borders.

The long-running civil war in Cambodia, which had continued after the withdrawal of Vietnamese troops in 1989, was temporarily capped by an expensive UN military and political operation (UNTAC 1991–3) to try to get Cambodian politics back on to a civil basis. Despite some success in staging a national election in the face of violent opposition by the Khmer Rouge, this operation largely failed to overcome the militarisation of Cambodian politics, and violence resumed in 1994. But, by the later 1990s, domestic political violence was no longer on a large scale, and during the 1990s Cambodia ceased to be a hotly contested issue among either regional or global powers, and therefore ceased to have the wider impact it had had during the Cold War.

After the East Asian economic crisis in 1997, the succession crisis facing Indonesia became critical, and at the time of writing it was far from clear whether the muddled shift to electoral politics would be able to handle the turbulent mix of economic disaster, secessionism (East Timor, Aceh, Irian Jaya), and recurrent bouts of communal violence in various places. Indonesia had all the appearance of a crumbling empire, and its internal disarray and weak leadership contributed to the paralysis of ASEAN, which was already burdened by both overambitious expansion and the impact of the regional economic crisis.

The question of domestic evolution affected many states in the region. For most, the force driving the uncertainty was the acute tension between the authoritarian, mercantilist inclinations of the region's postcolonial states, and the more liberal economic and political pressures coming from the global level. Some countries, such as South Korea,

Taiwan, and Singapore, handled it fairly well. But others, notably the Philippines, Malaysia, and Thailand, all had ongoing difficulties finding a workable mix of legitimate government and stable economic development. After 11 September, there was also heightened concern about radical Islamism in Indonesia, the Philippines, and Malaysia. The really big questions, however, focused on three countries: North Korea, China, and Japan. North Korea was crucial because of its position at the heart of one of East Asia's flashpoints; China and Japan were crucial because how they evolved domestically would determine how they behaved as great powers.

North Korea was one of several authoritarian states experiencing prolonged succession crises during the 1990s, but in this case accompanied by severe economic collapse and famine. Despite regular expectations of its imminent demise, the North Korean regime seemed to manage a smooth transfer of power to Kim Jong-il after Kim Il-sung's death in 1994, reinforcing its bizarre system of dynastic communism. It also retained a tight grip on the country despite the disastrous state of the economy. At first, the question was whether the North's regime would collapse or not. When it survived, the question became whether or not it would make some sort of peace with the South. Either way, the prospect of a reunified Korea raised awkward questions not only for Japan and China, but also for the USA.

Japan did not face the same liberal–authoritarian dilemmas as most of its neighbours. For Japan, the main question was whether it would retain the curiously introverted and dependent military-political posture that it had adopted after its crushing defeat in the Second World War, or whether, as some hoped and some feared, it would become in realist terms a more 'normal' country. To do that it would have, *inter alia*, to replace the weak foreign and security policy-making machinery that had sufficed throughout the Cold War (van Wolferen 1989). The deeper question was whether Japan was pioneering a new type of state – 'civilian power' (Maull 1990–1) or 'trading state' (Rosecrance 1986) – in which case its transformation would be permanent, or whether it was simply suffering a long hangover from defeat, and would at some point follow realist logic by resuming the normal great power role it had played up to 1945. The ending of the Cold War undermined the existing rationale for the US–Japanese Security Treaty, and seemed to offer an opportunity in which this question might get a decisive answer. Would Japan once again undergo a major, externally driven, internal transformation like those of the Meiji restoration and the late 1940s? Or

146

would its conservative domestic structures (Katzenstein and Okawara 1993) and/or deeply institutionalised norms and conceptions of security (Berger 1993) mean just more of the same?

But no such answer was forthcoming. No major political reform took place, and the economy remained mired in recession. Opinion remained divided about whether Japan was about to bounce back, or whether it still faced a long haul of reform. Inertia on the domestic level meant a *de facto* continuation of Japan's subordinate role to the United States in East Asia. The only notable change was the passing in 1992 of a law enabling the Self Defence Forces to participate in UN PKOs, albeit in limited numbers and only in non-combatant roles. This paved the way for a leading Japanese role in the UN's rescue operation for Cambodia, and for some slightly more adventurous military commitments in the war against the Taleban. Although not without symbolic significance, these hardly amounted to restoring Japan as a 'normal' power.

China was by far the biggest and most important case of the liberal–authoritarian dilemma. How was it to sustain its engagement with the global economy without destabilising its already shaky political structures? China was experiencing sustained and unprecedentedly rapid economic growth, and, although this generated new resources, it also unleashed its own domestic instabilities. Could such growth be sustained, and if so how would China use the newfound wealth and power under its command? Could China reconcile the mounting contradiction between its authoritarian government and its rapidly marketising economy? It was ironic that a profoundly anti-liberal state such as China, which embraced traditional realist Machtpolitik in much of its international thought and behaviour (Hughes 1997: 116–19; Li 1999: 6, 18), should so firmly embrace the quintessentially liberal doctrine of separating economics from politics. 'Market communism' looked like an oxymoron whose historical run would be short. In addition, there was some open, and growing, resistance to Beijing's control in Tibet, Xinjiang, and Inner Mongolia, the latter two taking inspiration, and sometimes support, from the newly independent successor states in Central Asia and Mongolia respectively.

For China's neighbours, the question resulting from all this was whether China would grow strong (and aggressive) or become more internally fragmented by uneven development, penetration of foreign capital and ideas, and a weakening political centre. The combined impact of marketisation (which stimulated mass internal migration,

147

decentralisation of power, challenge to authority, corruption, crime, environmental problems, and dangers of structural instability and over-heated economic growth) and political uncertainty (succession struggles, loss of ideological authority, rise of nationalism) meant that the outcome of China's rapid development during the 1980s and 1990s was very hard to read. Impressive rates of economic growth, a willingness to increase military expenditure, and occasional forays into aggressive foreign policy all pointed towards China as a potential world-class power in the foreseeable future. But the profound internal contradictions of market communism, the tensions of uneven development between the coast and the interior, the uncertain state of the ruling CCP and its problems of leadership transition, and the widening gap between central and provincial political authority all pointed towards a potentially much more erratic future. The government's somewhat hysterical securitisation of the Falun Gong was suggestive of a deep insecurity about the political future. The chance of China fragmenting, or undergoing prolonged political and economic turbulence, seemed just as great as the chance of its emerging as an Asian or global great power (Roy 1994; Segal 1994; Shambaugh 1994; Van Ness 2002: 139–43).

As with Japan, no decisive answer has emerged. By 2002 it was still possible to speculate on a whole range of possible futures for China. China seemed to escape the economic turbulence in East Asia, but it was far from clear whether this could be sustained, and if so whether China's economic success would come at the expense of its neighbours' export markets. There was concern that Chinese politics were developing in a more nationalist direction. Fear of China's disintegration and collapse was counterpointed by fear that its success would generate an overbearing power. These twin fears posed sharp dilemmas for those outside as to whether their priority should be to engage or contain China. The worst outcome would be a China strengthened by trade and investment, but still authoritarian, nationalistic, and alienated from Western-led international society. However China's great experiment turned out, it would have a big impact on the Chinese people, China's neighbours, and the global power structure.

These open questions about the future of the political economies of East Asia's two main powers had huge significance for all other levels of security dynamics. In principle, one could imagine sharply different scenarios for these two great powers within the next couple of decades. At worst, both could be militarily powerful and nationalistic. At best, both could be rich, democratic, and (up to a point) liberal. Or both could remain in something like their present positions. How they would behave, not only towards each other, but also towards their region and the world, hung on how their domestic political economies would develop. There was no way of predicting this, and not much consensus on the most likely outcome.

China's securitisation of words from Taiwan

A secret report from the State Council's Policy Research Center in China, leaked in 1997, deemed war between China and the United States possible in the future: 'With the return of Hong Kong and Macao to Chinese rule, the Taiwan issue will inevitably become China's major event around 2010. If the United States uses force to meddle in China's sovereignty and internal affairs, China will certainly fight a war against aggression, thus leading to a limited Sino-US war' (Li 1997).

The Taiwan question has a special status among all security concerns in China (Harrison 2001). This could be seen from the way it played in the background throughout the process leading to the return of Hong Kong and how it influences relations with the United States and, for example, the Chinese stand on the US plans about missile defence (Van Ness 2002: 144–5). Often to the surprise of foreigners, who think China could achieve economic and political aims more rationally by focusing on other questions, Taiwan remains the fulcrum of politics (see Li 2001: 6, 25). This could be given a purely cultural explanation in terms of the importance of national identity as a frame of reference (see L. Katzenstein 1997), but also – partly as a specification of the former more general option – it can be explained in terms of securitisation along somewhat peculiar patterns involving an unusual centrality of dangerous words.

In the 1990s there were two major crises between Beijing and Taipei, in 1995–6 and 1999. The first was in the run-up to the first presidential elections in Taiwan and culminated in large-scale military exercises and missile tests by the PRC near Taiwan, and the United States deploying two aircraft carriers to the area. The triggering event was President Lee Teng-hui of Taiwan's 'private' visit to the United States (Li 1996). This was seen in Beijing as an intensification of a general attempt by Taipei to promote its political profile and international status through 'pragmatic diplomacy', which meant giving up the all-or-nothing line regarding diplomatic recognition and improving relations also with countries that had diplomatic relations with the PRC. Also, membership in international organisations was accepted under all kinds of awkward names including 'China (Taipei)', 'China (Taiwan)', 'China-Taipei', 'China-Taiwan', 'Taipei China', 'Taiwan-Republic of China', 'Chinese Taipei', 'Taiwan-Penghu-Jinmen-Mazu', and 'Taipei' (P. Yu 1996: 477; deLisle 2000: 37). 'Beijing's leaders repeatedly claimed that China would resort to force if Taiwan declared independence ' (Jian 1996: 459).

The 1999 crisis erupted when Lee Teng-hui in a German radio interview said that PRC–ROC relations were 'state-to-state or at least nation-to-nation' (deLisle 2000: 35). 'China's reaction was swift, warning that the rhetorical shift could jeopardize any future talks between it and Taiwan...Beijing also reiterated that it reserves the right to use force if Taiwan, which it considers a renegade province, declares formal independence' (CNN.com 13 July 1999). Naturally, this has to be understood on the basis of the legal and political struggle between Beijing and Taipei, where originally both competed for the mandate of the heaven, i.e., legitimacy to represent all of China. Mao Zedong and Chiang Kai-shek were in total agreement on this much: there was only one China. It was the same historical 'China' that both claimed. This meant that, for Beijing, Taiwan was a threat only if it managed to achieve this representation, which it basically lost in the 1970s, or at the opposite extreme if Taipei changed its policy towards declaring independence as favoured by the opposition party DPP.

While never taking the DPP line, the official Taiwanese position started to change under Lee. In 1991, Taipei abandoned its claim to represent all of China internationally. In May 1992 the ROC started to recognise the PRC as a political entity, and since June 1994 it has not competed with the PRC for representation as the only China. Taiwan is part of China but not part of the PRC (P. Yu 1996: 477). Interestingly, this position does not in itself or by any logical necessity imply a claim for independence or sovereignty for the ROC, but paradoxically the decrease of challenge to the PRC implied a threat by undermining the 'one China' dogma. The PRC policy of 'one country, two systems' is challenged by the ROC increasingly pursuing the view of 'two essentially equal political entities', which separately rule parts of a temporarily divided China (deLisle 2000: 51). It was within this meaning that the formulation about 'state-to-state relations' led to the 1999 crisis.

The security logic of this has to be stressed, because this whole political struggle is not necessarily so much about approaching actual unification – the Chinese conception of political and historical time usually implies more patience than the Western one (L. Katzenstein 1997). To understand the issue's intensity (including threats of use of force), it is necessary to see how much is negatively driven by the risk implied in alterations of linguistic and/or legal status quo.

States are generally extremely careful and cautious about conceding any principles in drawn-out battles where legal principles are bastions – as seen for instance in the Cold War case of divided Germany. However, there *is* a particular Chinese twist to this because of a specific conception of sovereignty. In Chinese eyes, there simply is a historically given China including its borders, an unalterable 'China'. And it is necessarily one. Since both sides took this position, the surrounding world had the option simply to 'acknowledge' that this was the Chinese position, however awkward and unconventional the result was (deLisle 2000: 36).

To cede anything of this China, even in a hypothetical or principled form, would be very risky. This should be understood against the dominant Chinese view of the history of the last few centuries. After the 'century of shame', it is paramount now to restore prior greatness and therefore it would symbolise a reversal of this cause to accept any infringement on the unity of China. Taiwan is particularly symbolic due to its history of being ceded to Japan as a result of defeat in the 1894 Sino-Japanese war and recovered in 1945 at the moment when China started on its road back to international status (Jian 1996: 460).

Therefore, the issue ultimately impacts the legitimacy of the communist regime. Creating a communist society and restoring China to a powerful position internationally were its two main missions – with increasing emphasis on the second (Jian 1996: 460–1; Li 2001; Zhao 1999: 341; Roy 1996: 440). A Chinese leader who presided over a loss of territory like this would be labelled by historians as *qianguzuiren*, eternally guilty man (P. Yu 1996: 478).

A further intensification of the threat follows from a fear that any concessions over Taiwan would lead to falling dominos in relation to 'other separatists' – Tibetan, Mongolian, Islamic (Li 2001: 6, 25; Jian 1996: 461; Roy 1996: 441). This must be seen on the basis of a historically conditioned sense of vulnerability, where domestic threats are central because China's history is viewed as a cycle of break-ups and re-unifications (Roy 1996: 440). The central finding here is that the sensitivity of the Taiwan question is not due to an urgency about achieving unification – it is about defending a legal principle and a political fiction of huge importance. Therefore, the front line becomes one of words.

The subcomplex level

Although the overall argument is that East Asia was coalescing into a single RSC during the 1990s, Northeast and Southeast Asia still retained some locally based security dynamics. Like the Middle Eastern RSC, East Asia had two main subcomplexes. This section will look at continuities within these. The next section will make the case for integration of security dynamics on an East Asian scale.

Northeast Asia

Unlike in Southeast Asia, the ending of the Cold War had surprisingly little effect on local security affairs in Northeast Asia. Since the indigenous regional issues had largely run in geostrategic parallel with the Cold War ones, all that was revealed by the removal of the Soviet factor was how important the underlying regional level had been all along. As before, the regional security dynamics revolved around three issues: Japan's troubled relations with its neighbours, the tense relationship between China and Taiwan, and the unresolved war between the two Koreas.

Japan continued to fail to come to terms with its neighbours over pre-1945 history, and its mixture of limited apology, intransigence, and unwillingness to confront the questions of history in its domestic life did not foster much sense of progress. A substantial gulf remained, on the one hand, between what it was domestically possible for Japanese politicians to do about this and, on the other, what kind of coming to terms would satisfy the neighbours. Japan's relations with both China and the two Koreas remained cool, and subject to periodic flare-ups over Japanese military policy, territorial disputes over various islands, and Japanese behaviour during the Second World War. One longtime observer of the region even argued that South Korea's military development, particularly its acquisition of naval forces, should be read as preparation for a post-unification rivalry with Japan (Simon 1994: 1055). In contrast to the securitisation of Japan by its neighbours, Japan remained relatively relaxed. North Korea, especially after its missile tests over Japan in 1993–4, was viewed as a threat, but China by and large was not (Twomey 2000) or, at least, not much (Soeya 1998; Clermont 2002: 25–8; Sansoucy 2002: 11–14). Japan did move towards collaboration with the United States in developing theatre missile defences (TMD), and Goldstein (2000: 25) observed that 'Japan is in the distinctive position of being able to piggyback its balancing efforts geared towards the anticipation of increased Chinese capabilities on its short-term effort to counter the dangerous capabilities North Korea may be deploying.'

Relations between China and Taiwan unfolded in a curious twin-track manner, and against the backdrop of the countdown to China's reabsorption of Hong Kong. On the economic track Beijing encouraged extensive manufacturing investment by Taiwan, as well as by Hong Kong and South Korea, and this meant that the Taiwanese and mainland economies were increasingly tied together in a shared boom (Tucker 1998–9: 159–61). Politically and militarily, however, things got worse. In 1994, a steadily democratising Taiwan renounced its claim to be the government of all of China, and Beijing reciprocated with repeated pronouncements that moves towards Taiwanese independence would be treated as a *casus belli*. Beijing responded with hostility to elections in Taiwan both in 1995–6, when it mounted a military demonstration, including provocative missile testing just off Taiwan's coast, and in 2000 when it confined itself to raising the level of verbal threat. It also built up its missile capability against Taiwan, and worked towards an ability to mount an amphibious invasion (*Strategic Survey* 1999–2000: 201).

Finally, the strange dance among the two Koreas, their three big neighbours, and the United States continued almost unchanged as a microcosmic leftover of the Cold War (Polomka 1986). By the early 1990s, new variables were the visible decline of North Korea's economy and rising concern over its apparent progress towards nuclear weapons capability. Economic decay and the loss of support from Russia, and up to a point China, put pressure on the North to come to terms with the OECD states. In March 1994 things reached crisis point when the IAEA declared North Korea to be in non-compliance with its NPT obligations, and North Korea withdrew from the IAEA. North Korea threatened war in response to sanctions, and the USA reinforced its military presence in South Korea. An intervention by Jimmy Carter broke the move towards confrontation, and initiated the negotiations that led to the formation of the Korean Energy Development Organization (KEDO) and to a deal in which North Korea traded suspension of its nuclear programme, and re-opening to international inspection, in return for oil supplies, two light water reactors, and normal diplomatic relations with the United States.

While it diverted the immediate crisis, this deal quickly became simply a new framework within which North Korea could pursue its obstructionism. Uncertainties caused by the prolonged transfer of power in North Korea, and by evidence of mounting famine, made that country's future difficult to read. Its generally erratic and periodically bellicose behaviour continued to keep tensions with the South high, and to raise awkward questions about both food aid and fulfilment of the KEDO programme. Periodic military clashes disrupted the relationship, and South Korea's dropping into economic crisis during 1997 raised questions about the financing of the much-delayed KEDO deal. Increased hostility to North Korea from the Bush administration, mounting problems with both the KEDO deal and North Korea's compliance over fissile material and missile moratorium, and the apparent failure of the South's 'sunshine' policy of being nice to the North all suggested a continuation of the up-and-down, crisis-prone set of relations surrounding North Korea. Even before the economic crunch, the South's enthusiasm for a quick reunification had been diminished by the costly lessons of the German experience. The acute liberal–realist dilemma of whether to support a North that remained an active military threat, or cut it off and risk nuclear proliferation and war, remained as awkward as ever to solve. At the time of writing, North Korea's restarting of its nuclear weapons programme posed this dilemma in a particularly stark form.

Behind all of these disputes sat the issue of the region's nuclear capabilities. As noted above, all five of the states in the region were in some sense nuclear-capable. With the exception of North Korea, fear of nuclear proliferation restrained the behaviour of the Northeast Asian states towards each other, restrained China's options towards Japan, and kept the United States engaged in the region.

Southeast Asia

In Southeast Asia the ending of the Cold War triggered two transformations: from conflict formation to security regime, and from RSC to subcomplex. As Soviet power drained out of Southeast Asia at the end of the 1980s, the main impact was to weaken Vietnam with respect to both China and ASEAN. Vietnam withdrew its troops from Laos in 1988 and Cambodia in 1989. While having to give up its overt confrontation with China, Vietnam turned increasingly towards ASEAN as its best bet in the long term for dealing with China. This move effectively ended the bipolarised conflict in Southeast Asia, and opened the way for ASEAN to unite the subregion in a security regime based on Westphalian principles of sovereignty and non-intervention, though not a military alliance (Acharya 1993: 76–7). Vietnam joined in 1995, and with the subsequent membership of Cambodia, Laos, and Burma ASEAN fulfilled its goal of encompassing all of the subregion's states by 2000. A Southeast Asian Nuclear Weapon Free Zone treaty was concluded in December 1995. With the influence of the Cold War out of the way, and rising concern about China looming on the horizon, the conflictual regional dynamics largely faded away. Burma seems to have gained admission, despite its near-pariah status globally, because of awareness in ASEAN that isolation of Burma simply pushed its military government into closer relations with China.

ASEAN's general progress in the region was severely disrupted by the economic collapse of the late 1990s, which it was not able to handle, and which both destabilised its biggest member, Indonesia, and degraded the association's consensus. All of Indonesia's neighbours were caught in the dilemma of how to deal with its possible fragmentation should East Timor prove to be only the first of several successful secessions. In addition, the economic turbulence weakened the ASEAN security regime, allowing old local securitisations to resurface between Singapore and Malaysia (Goldstein 2000: 36–7), and new ones between Thailand and Burma. But there was no general unravelling of ASEAN and, except for wider concerns about the possible implosion of Indonesia, the main security focus shifted towards the emergence of a larger East Asian RSC. As the IISS stated bluntly: 'since the end of the Cold War, South-east Asia has lost its utility as a strategic concept' (*Strategic Survey* 1994–5: 183).

The regional level

During the 1990s, the patterns of regional security interdependence in Asia underwent an external transformation because of the knitting together of Northeast and Southeast Asia into a single RSC. What had been the strong interregional links of the Asian supercomplex became sufficiently dominant to meld the two eastern components of the supercomplex into a single East Asian RSC. The supercomplex continued on as the relationship between East and South Asia. This knitting together of an East Asian RSC involved two main stories. The first was China-centred, and grew out of the Cold War and earlier security links between China and Southeast Asia. With Soviet power out of the picture, the longstanding military-political links between China and Southeast Asia became more important, triggering the growth of links in the military-political security dynamics of Northeast and Southeast Asia. The second was Japan-centred, and stemmed from patterns of East Asian economic linkage that had been growing strongly during the 1980s. These economic patterns became increasingly linked to regional security relations during the 1990s, providing an additional sector of security interdependence across the whole of East Asia.

The military-political story hinges on both the actual and expected rise of China's power in a regional context that during the 1990s was less constrained by outside powers than at any time during the twentieth century. Partly this was simply a matter of China's relative regional weight being increased by the almost total withdrawal of Soviet, and the partial withdrawal of American, power from the region. In both the Soviet/Russian and US cases, this withdrawal was much more conspicuous in Southeast than in Northeast Asia. Partly it was to do with the juxtaposition of China's strong economic growth during the 1980s and 1990s, with the faltering of Japan's economy during the 1990s (Alvstam 2001) combined with its continued political weakness. In combination, these two developments left China freer to act without the constraint of either a fully fledged regional balancer or heavy competitive engagement in the region by outside superpowers.

The resulting enhancement of China's weight and freedom of action in East Asia focused attention on its domestic developments, and what kind of state – and neighbour – it was likely to become. As argued above, finding a firm answer to that question remained an elusive goal. If China remained centralised and grew strong, then the question was whether it would be aggressive or benign. Some argued that it would be militarily incapable of serious aggression (Kang 1995: 12–13; Dibb 1995: 87–8); and/or that it would be restrained from such adventures by its interest in development (Kang 1995:12; Mahbubani 1995) and its adaptation to international society (Zhang 1998; Foot 2001). Concern about a possible 'China threat' nevertheless became widespread in East Asia, not helped either by China's sometimes bellicose behaviour or by its lack of transparency (To 1997: 252, 261; Soeya 1998: 204–6). Those wanting to take a more malign view had plenty to draw on. There was the general idea that rising powers seek to assert their influence (Segal 1988; Shambaugh

1994). Attached to this were two ideas that seemed to amplify it. First was the idea of China as a revisionist power, not closely wedded to the existing international order, and with many territorial, cultural, and status grievances against it (especially over Taiwan). Second was the idea that China was a classic model of authoritarian modernisation (Bracken 1994: 103–9), unrestrained by democracy and vulnerable to nationalism and militarism. Reinforcing these views was China's continued willingness to resort to aggressive behaviour and to the threat or use of force against its neighbours – India, Philippines, Taiwan – and its continued cultivation of historical hatred of Japan. Some saw China and Japan as 'natural rivals' (Roy 1994: 163). In support of these malign views were China's cavalier attitude towards nuclear testing and the export of missile and nuclear technology to Pakistan and Iran, and the gathering reaction against its unfair and inhumane economic and political practices (prison labour, piracy). Its behaviour in the South China Sea, and towards Taiwan, offered a distinctly mixed prospect to those hoping that China could somehow be brought into the regional process of dialogue and diplomacy.

Throughout the 1990s uncertainty about China's domestic developments made it difficult to fix an image of how it would relate to the wider Asian region. This uncertainty affected both the US and ASEAN responses to what the IISS called China's 'creeping assertiveness' (*Strategic Survey* 1994–5: 191). As the 1990s unfolded, China's relations with the region settled into a mix of unilateral bellicosity (over Taiwan and the South China Sea), and increasingly comfortable and skilled use of multilateral forums such as the ARF to support those regional voices still concerned about excessive US influence. China also came out well from the economic crisis, both because of its contributions to rescue funds and because of its ability to avoid the devaluation of its own currency. This strengthened its position against Japan, which continued to be unable to assert leadership.

By the early 1990s, loss of external support had largely forced Vietnam to abandon its direct military confrontation with China, and to seek a place within an expanding ASEAN. This shifted the strategic focus away from Cambodia and the Sino-Vietnamese land border, and towards the South China Sea in particular and the wider East Asian pattern in general. During the Cold War, China's territorial assertiveness in the South China Sea had been mainly against Vietnam, but also affected Brunei, Malaysia, the Philippines, and later Indonesia. The Chinese military extended their occupations to the more southerly Spratly Islands in 1992, occupying atolls and asserting claims to continental shelf resources, and in 1994 occupied the Mischief Reef, long claimed by the Philippines though not occupied by it. ASEAN failed to take a strong stand against these Chinese moves. China ignored various agreements not to use force and continued with its policy of incremental occupations.

The shift to a wider regional strategic focus with China at its centre began soon after the collapse of the Soviet Union changed the global and regional distribution of military power. As Leifer (1996: 26, 46) argues, post-Cold War ASEAN has been forced to see itself as part of a bigger security picture, no longer confined just to Southeast Asia. Its not-so-hidden agenda is to engage China, which ASEAN does not want to do by itself or only in East Asia, but in a Pacific and even global context. The main vehicle for this reorientation has been the ARF, which came into being in 1994. Japan played a significant role in this development, though eschewing leadership for itself (Foot 1995: 242) or having its bids turned down (Okawara and Katzenstein 2001: 176–82). The ARF usefully binds both Japan and China into a regional institutional framework, allowing Japan to address its historical problem (Sansoucy 2002: 15–16), China to address the fears of its neighbours, and both to avoid conspicuous balancing behaviour towards each other. The result, however, is the rather anomalous situation of a regional security body created and run by the minor powers in a region. An attempt by Japan in 1996 to bolster the security dimension of its relationship with ASEAN got a cool response, as ASEAN proved unwilling to provoke China with any hint of an anti-China alliance (*Strategic Survey* 1996–7: 180–2). This episode underlines the tension within ASEAN between the preferred option of trying to engage China diplomatically by building a regional international society, maximising the engagement of outside powers in the region, and trying to extend an ASEAN-style security regime to East Asia; and the fallback option of putting in place the means to resist China should engagement fail.

The ARF was helped into being by the fact that the United States, with less strategically and more economically at stake in East Asia, ended its longstanding opposition to multilateral security dialogue in the region. The ARF linked together the middle and small powers of ASEAN with their 'dialogue partners' the United States, Japan, China, Russia, South Korea, Australia, New Zealand, Papua-New Guinea, Cambodia, and the EU. Initially, North Korea and Taiwan were not included but, after the summit of the two Kims in 2000, North Korea was invited to participate. On the basis of its membership, the ARF had some standing as a loose

Asia-Pacific security regime. As Leifer put it (1996: 55), 'The undeclared aim of the ARF is to defuse and control regional tensions by generating and sustaining a network of dialogues within the over-arching framework of its annual meetings, while the nexus of economic incentive works on governments irrevocably committed to market-based economic development.'

One way of understanding the setting up of the ARF is to see it as a response to ASEAN's inability to construct itself as a counterweight to China, and the need therefore to try to socialise China into being a good citizen. In addition to concerns about China's interventions in Cambodia, its disputes with Vietnam, and its expansion in the South China Sea, there was also concern about its growing influence in Burma. Chinese support for the military junta in Burma not only strengthened the junta against its domestic rebels and the civil opposition, but also allowed China to deploy intelligence facilities in the Indian Ocean. Given China's role in Pakistan, this excited concerns in India about Chinese military encirclement of India. The diplomatic isolation of Burma facilitated Chinese penetration. China was thus a key to explaining why ASEAN, pushed mainly by Singapore and Indonesia, invited both India and Burma to join the ARF, hoping thereby to counter Chinese influence as well as acknowledging a shared interregional strategic concern between ASEAN and India in containing China (*Strategic Survey* 1996–7: 193).

After initially being uncomfortable with multilateralism, China quickly adjusted to the ARF, seeing advantage in using its soft procedures to fudge conflicts (Cossa and Khanna 1997: 222). The diplomatic level of the ARF is accompanied by the 'track two' arrangements of CSCAP (the Council for Security Cooperation in Asia Pacific), which brings together academics and policy analysts from the various countries. China upgraded its participation in the ARF and CSCAP in 1996 in response to deteriorating relations in Northeast Asia and with the United States. ASEAN had to struggle hard to maintain its leadership within an ARF containing several large powers. Japan and the United States wanted more influence for themselves, and could threaten to use APEC as an alternative forum. China and India found ASEAN's leadership a good mechanism for limiting US domination of the ARF. There was a tension between, on the one hand, the desire of many East Asian states (especially Japan) to keep the United States engaged in the region to provide the balancer to China that they were unwilling to provide themselves and, on the other hand, the tendency of ASEAN to appease

China, or not to resist its encroachments, while at the same time resisting, or not supporting, the maintenance of a US military presence. Whatever its operational feebleness as a security regime, the ARF was a symbolically important move in tying together Northeast and Southeast Asia. But because of ASEAN's central role, the ARF was much more effective in tying the northern powers, especially China and Japan, to Southeast Asia, than it was in tying Southeast Asia to the security dynamics of Northeast Asia. Taiwan was not a member of the ARF, and this excluded one of the key disputes in Northeast Asia from the ARF's agenda. The ARF made no response to the Taiwan Strait crisis in 1995–6. Given the post-1997 disarray in ASEAN, the dominance of Northeast Asia in the East Asian region was increasingly symbolised by the 'ASEAN plus 3' (the 3 being China, Japan, and South Korea) meetings, in which ASEAN was no longer in the leading role.

In the military-political sector, it was thus a combination of factors during the 1990s that tied Northeast and Southeast Asia together into an East Asian RSC. One key was a rising shared background of concern about China, reinforced by a set of active disputes and weaker balancing of China at the global level. Another was the expansion of ASEAN's security regime to cover all of Southeast Asia, which both brought relations with China into greater prominence and provided the platform from which to launch the ARF. Some Asian security problems remained largely disconnected from this move, most obviously the dispute on the Korean peninsula. The China–Taiwan dispute was also not linked into the ARF, though Taiwan's huge investments in Southeast Asia certainly gave the ASEAN countries an interest in the issue. It is easy to be dismissive about the ARF's incessant 'dialoguing' and apparent inability to confront conflicts directly, especially in the wake of the East Asian economic crisis, which weakened ASEAN and the ARF. But if viewed as the opening stages of an attempt to build a regional security regime in an area notable for the absence of regional institutions, it looks more impressive. Cultivation of ideas such as 'cooperative security' (nicely captured in the phrase often heard from Australian diplomats that they 'seek security with Asia, not from it') is beginning to develop a shared rhetoric of desecuritisation across East Asia. This is reinforced by the promotion of norms regarding peaceful settlement of disputes, regular multilateral dialogue at several levels, and adherence to some international arms control agreements such as those on nuclear non-proliferation. Although doing so slowly and unevenly, such cultivation does lay the foundations for elements of an East Asian security regime. These elements may not yet look very impressive when compared either with those in Europe or with the depth and extent of security problems in East Asia. But they look more impressive when the network of bilateralism that underlies and complements them is taken into account (Okawara and Katzenstein 2001), and also when compared either with the absence of them before or with the situation in South Asia or the Middle East.

Viewed in a more realist perspective as a response to concerns about rising Chinese power, the ARF could be read in two seemingly contradictory, but in fact complementary, ways. On the surface, it was a collective East Asian attempt to socialise China into being a good neighbour by entangling it in the dialogue networks. Given the ARF's lack of dispute settlement or enforcement mechanisms, this aspect of it could, and often did, run close to being institutionalised appeasement of China. But under the surface the ARF could also be read as laying the collective foundations for balancing against China if the socialisation attempt failed and the more malign interpretations of China's development turned out to be true. The fear was that too conspicuous a pursuit of the resistance option would derail the preferred engagement one, and this reinforced a tendency within ASEAN, and indeed all of Asia, to see the balancing of China as first of all a US responsibility and only in the last resort a local one.

The second element in the merger of Northeast and Southeast Asia was the Japan-centred East Asian economic interdependence, which had already developed during the last decades of the Cold War. Often referred to as the 'flying geese' model, this took the form of a hierarchy of finance, production, and technology spreading out from Japan into the countries of East Asia (Helleiner 1994). As Japan exported many of its lower-tech industries under the pressure of high wages and the strong yen, it created concentric circles of investment in its neighbours, with Korea and Taiwan in the first circle, and Southeast Asia and China further out. During the 1970s and 1980s, this created a unique form of regionalism largely based on private capital and with virtually no international political institutionalisation. It rested on strong commitment to shared pursuit of economic development goals. In many ways it was also based on shared adherence to the Japanese model of political economy. Alongside this Japan-centred economic system was the phenomenon known as 'Greater China', in which Chinese communities in Hong Kong, Taiwan, Singapore, and elsewhere played a leading role in promoting trade with, and investment in, China (C. Yu 1996), so adding to the economic interdependence between Northeast and Southeast Asia.

These arrangements delivered unprecedented rates of growth during the 1980s and first half of the 1990s, and this growth plus the shared commitment to development goals came to assume an important role in the region's self-understanding and self-presentation of its security (Cossa and Khanna 1997). Using arguments close to those associated with liberal thinking about interdependence, the line was developed that East Asia's many political rivalries, territorial disputes, and historical antagonisms could all be overcome, or at least shelved, by subordinating them to the common economic enterprise. Sustaining economic growth thus acquired an important security dimension in both the domestic and the international politics of East Asia. Domestically, growth supported the legitimacy of authoritarian regimes that might otherwise have come under pressure to democratise. Internationally, the 'flying geese' model linked the region's growth aspirations together, thereby providing a strong and immediate common interest among states that might otherwise have let their political antagonisms drift to the fore. In parallel to ASEAN's earlier achievement, much of East Asia came to accept that military-political stability was a necessary foundation for the successful economic development that would underpin regime legitimacy.

Signs of economic downturn in the region as a whole were appearing by 1996, and in 1997 this turned into a financial and then an economic catastrophe. Huge drops in the value of many of the region's currencies were followed by credit collapse, widespread bankruptcy, and sharp economic shrinkage. The intense economic pain was a major problem in its own right, but it also became a security problem in three ways. First, it threatened political stability in some authoritarian states, most notably Indonesia where it coincided with an already unstable succession problem. Second, it threatened the region's economic model, so raising major questions about its ability to sustain growth into the future. And, third, it stripped away the economic blanket that had been used to cover the region's unresolved political and territorial disputes, leaving exposed a threatening combination of weakened governments and a classical agenda of military-political security problems (Dibb et al. 1998: 9; Cossa and Khanna 1997: 225–7).

The more democratic governments seemed to weather the crisis quite well, but the difficult transition in Indonesia and increased authoritarianism in Malaysia undermined the political cohesion of ASEAN, weakening it as a regional stabiliser. Doubts about the Asian development model undermined confidence in the future, and these doubts were re-inforced by the prolonged failure of the region's economic leader, and the source of its model, Japan to find its own way out. Did the fault lie in the Asian model of capitalism, with its cronyism, lack of investment in longer-term development, unsound investments, and overcapacity; or was it to be found in the wider practices of Western financial liberalism, reinforcing credit bubbles, empowering currency speculators, and cre-ating unstable collective irrationalities in the global financial markets? The latter interpretation fed a strong line of securitisation against glob-alisation, and strengthened demands for a regional response (Bergsten 2000). In part, this securitisation can be interpreted as a direct response to the crisis, but in part it also reflected fear of the potential securitising dynamics that the crisis opened up in the region itself, and can be seen as a (successful) attempt to divert attention away from those. It seemed clear that blame lay in both places, and that the Asian model of high debt-to-equity ratios was particularly vulnerable to liquidity shrinkage and currency collapse. This opened up a contradiction between pursuit of the model and pursuit of the global financial liberalisation that cre-ated the possibility of such destabilisations in the future. More broadly, there was a contradiction between domestic political legitimacy and global economic rules and norms that undermined distinctive national development projects. At the time of writing, recovery from this crisis remained very uneven and the economic underpinnings of East Asian security were still shaky.

Whatever the balance of fault, this crisis can be seen as a normal part of capitalist development, which has always proceeded by alternating bouts of success and failure. Like the other societies that have mastered this type of development, the Asians will have to undergo a learning process in which the cycles of success and failure teach them how best to adapt their political economies and societies to marketisation and mod-ernisation. This process has never been smooth anywhere, and there is no reason to expect that it will be so in Asia. If the past is a guide to the future, cyclical recessions, occasional depressions, domestic politi-cal upheavals, and dangers of extreme nationalism will all be part of the process, albeit within the context of a considerably more globalised international political economy than was the case for the first and sec-ond waves of modernisers. The question is how this almost inevitably turbulent process of development will impact on regional security in East Asia. The problem is a set of circumstances in which the main-tenance of both domestic and international political-military security is strongly tied into an ability to sustain growth. The presence of only nascent regional institutions and a thin veneer of cooperative security, combined with a rather daunting agenda of traditional securitisations, means that in East Asia nothing except prosperity, a thin commitment to desecuritising dialogues, fear of nuclear weapons, and the presence of the United States acts to moderate the regional (in)security dynamic.

In sum, the case for an emergent East Asian security complex rests on three parallel developments.

- First, a shared concern throughout Northeast and Southeast Asia about the implications of growing Chinese power.
- Second, the creation, albeit partial and fragile, of institutional security connections linking Northeast and Southeast Asian states.
- Third, the build-up of an East Asian regional economy, which is widely thought within the region to have strong links to politico-military stability.

The interregional level: an expanding supercomplex

The set of military-political dynamics that pushed towards the formation of a China-centred East Asian RSC was strong enough to extend beyond the confines of Northeast and Southeast Asia. As we have seen, security concerns about China impinged strongly on South Asia, and had underpinned an Asian supercomplex since the 1950s. During the 1990s, this supercomplex extended also to Australia. The South Asian part of the story has been told in chapter 4. In this chapter, we have also seen that Burma's longstanding role as an insulator between the South and Southeast Asian RSCs began to erode. Interestingly, this erosion was not to do with any change in the linkage between South and Southeast Asian regional security dynamics. Instead, it came from China's cultivation of Burma's pariah military government, which drew both India and ASEAN to engage with Burma, and India to look to naval balancing of China's military presence in Burma. The interregional influence of China thus began to override what remained an insulator between South and Southeast Asian regional security dynamics. China's influence also began to be felt in Central Asia (see ch. 13). So far China has mostly acted defensively due to concerns about Islamic unrest in Xinjiang and narrowly in relation to oil interest. But in Central Asia, especially prior to the 2001 US involvement via the war in Afghanistan, China was widely viewed as a strong contender for long-term power due to economic trends. Formally, China's link to the region was most clearly expressed in the Shanghai group where Russia, China, and Central Asian states met, in actuality mostly to deal with Islamic radicalism.

During the 1990s, Australia, previously part of the unstructured South Pacific, also began to be drawn into the China-centred Asian supercomplex. During the Cold War, Australia's links to Southeast Asia had come mostly in the form of its attachment to global level alliances constructed by the United States and Britain. During the 1990s this changed. Australia remained as keen as ever to retain its global level links, and was a leading player in the making of APEC, the central function of which was to keep the United States engaged in East Asia (Buzan 1998). But from the mid-1990s Australia began to take independent steps that increased its security linkage to Asia. The Australian defence white paper of 1994 pointed to China as the source of concern (*Strategic Survey* 1994–5: 168), and in December 1995 Australia and Indonesia entered into a defence accord. This was widely taken as a signal to China, and represented a notable departure for both countries (*Strategic Survey* 1995–6: 179, 195–6), though how much of it survived the turbulence in Indonesia, and Australia's role in the intervention in East Timor, remains unclear.

There are thus clear signs of an integrated, Asia-wide set of interregional security dynamics focused on China. These dynamics were primarily military-political, and it was not difficult to imagine that they might strengthen markedly given either or both of two developments:

1. China develops towards the scenario of being an aggressive regional power; or
2. the United States pulls away from its security engagement in Asia.

The economic links connecting South Asia and Australia to this wider circle were much weaker than those binding East Asia. Although Australia did get caught up in the backwash of the regional economic crisis, and both it and India were negatively affected by the downturn in the region, neither could be described as part of the group of Asian model economies. Both were, however, increasingly seeing their economic and security interests in all-Asian terms, and by doing so strengthening the reality of an Asian supercomplex.

The global level

In many ways it is fair to see the transformation of the regional level in Asia during the 1990s as a mirror image of the equally big changes at the global level. Within a few years around the ending of the Cold War, the major games of containment and countercontainment between the United States and the Soviet Union, and between the Soviet Union and China, had disappeared. All that was retained of the extensive Cold War structure of great power intrusion into East Asia was the US position of local containment against China in support of US allies in Northeast Asia. Superpower disengagement raised 'the prospect that East Asians will be left to come to terms with their own long-standing rivalries that were often suppressed under the blanket of the Cold War' (*Strategic Survey* 1991–2: 117). These effects were most dramatic in Southeast Asia. By 1992, Soviet/Russian forces were largely out of Cam Ranh Bay, and US ones were out of the Philippines; the United States normalised relations with Vietnam during 1994–5. The United States retained a generalised engagement with East Asia through its membership in APEC and the ARF, but this rested on an explicit underlying linkage between the economic and military relations in the Asia-Pacific. American statements at APEC summits in 1993 and 1994 made it clear that the United States linked the costs of its regional leadership role and military presence in Asia to continued access to the Asian economy (Stuart and Tow 1995: 48; Simon 1994: 1051). Public connections of military and economic relations in this way were not just a means of bringing American pressure to bear against the East Asian enthusiasts for a more specifically East Asian bloc. They were also a way of underlining the unequal quality of trans-Pacific relations, and the continued dependence of the East Asians' political and military security on the US presence. The US seizure of the leading role during the East Asian economic crisis underlined its dominance, and by the late 1990s the United States was even re-establishing some of its military presence in Southeast Asia, a process reinforced after the terrorist attacks on 11 September 2001.

The virtual removal of the Soviet Union/Russia from East Asia as an intervening outside power had quite mixed effects. It certainly improved China's military position and increased its leverage against India and Vietnam. But it also weakened China's bargaining power vis-à-vis the United States, meaning that China had to make more concessions on things like adherence to the NPT and MTCR, and on trade and human rights issues. China had to balance among three not always complementary goals: not wanting to submit to US hegemony or to allow the United States to dominate Asia; not wanting to be drawn into a direct confrontation with, or be constructed as a rival to, the United States; and wanting to increase its standing in international society generally, and its integration into the world economy in particular. In response to its new position, China cultivated relations with both Japan and ASEAN states, and its relations with South Korea, both economic and diplomatic, continued to blossom. It placed greater emphasis on its relations with East Asian and OECD states and less on those with the third world. Russia was a dwindling military force even where its territory abutted East Asia. Sino-Russian relations were good, with China becoming a major purchaser of sophisticated weapons and defence industrial goods from Russia, and the two countries sharing an anti-hegemonic line against the USA as sole superpower. They concluded a series of border agreements and CBMs to desecuritise their relations, and both supported the continued existence of North Korea. In some eyes, this was a kind of strategic partnership, aimed at offering some balance against US hegemony. But it was also a limited and shallow partnership, and was weakened by Russia's tilt towards the United States after 11 September. By contrast, Russo-Japanese relations remained cool, and the basic problems between them unresolved.

As already noted, the pattern of US engagement in Northeast Asia was remarkably little disturbed by the ending of the Cold War. Indeed, after a period of uncertainty in the early 1990s, these US ties grew somewhat stronger. The US role in Korea became more central with the actions taken to stem North Korean nuclear proliferation. Its engagement with Taiwan deepened as a consequence of the major US military role in the Taiwan Strait crisis during 1995–6 (Tucker 1998–9). Most complicated were United States–Japan relations, with the ending of the Cold War throwing the US–Japanese alliance into some disarray by taking the immediate rationale out of defence cooperation. Japan remained committed to keeping the United States active in the East Asian security equation, and did not challenge US leadership. Japan began reforming its defence guidelines towards allowing a wider role for the JSDF and closer coordination with US forces in the region. But despite some formal revision of the US–Japanese defence cooperation guidelines, doubts remained about whether, and to what extent, Japan would support the United States in a crisis (Twomey 2000).

The removal of the Soviet factor brought US–Chinese strategic relations into sharper focus, not least by stripping away any ambiguity about the reasons for continued US military engagements in Northeast Asia. Within this context, United States–China relations nonetheless continued to fluctuate much as they had done during the last decade of the Cold War. Expectations of China's rapid rise to the status of a great power, or at least of a regional challenger in Asia (Christensen 2001), remained strong, and were underlined by the harder line of the Bush administration on China. The 11th of September temporarily eclipsed this concern, but did not remove it from the administration's longer-term priorities. China and the United States no longer shared a common concern about the Soviet Union, and there were tensions between them, *inter alia*, over trade; copyright violations; Chinese arms and nuclear and missile sales to Iran, Pakistan, and others; US arms sales to and political support for Taiwan; US plans for missile defences; nuclear weapons testing in the run-up to the 1995 NPT renewal conference and the CTBT negotiations; and navigation rights. The high point of US–Chinese tensions occurred over Taiwan during 1995–6, first over the US granting of a visa to Taiwan's president, Lee Teng-hui, and then over robust US naval responses to China's military manoeuvres against Taiwan. Despite Chinese blustering, the United States successfully demonstrated its military superiority over China even in the latter's home waters (*Strategic Survey* 1995–6: 176–9; 1996–7: 167). Following this, the United States staged joint naval exercises with India in the Indian Ocean early in 1996, thus underlining the emerging all-Asia scale of security concerns about China. The Taiwan Strait crisis left the impression that China's military bellicosity had been restrained only by a strong US response, and not by the still weak bonds of economic interdependence.

The post-Cold War pattern at the global level thus continued to run in close parallel to those at the regional and interregional levels in Asia. The dominant sector of security is the traditional military-political one, albeit with linkages to the economic sector, and China sits at the centre of all these patterns. The pattern of US engagement in the region both backs up the regional and interregional Sino-centric security dynamics and shares their ambivalence and uncertainty about the nature of the threat from China (if any) and the types of relationship with China that are both possible and desirable. The only substantial exception to this pattern is Korea, where the USA supports the South and Japan against military threats from North Korea. In part, US–Chinese relations have to be interpreted as part of the 1 + 4 global level dynamic, and the weight of this level could easily increase if China's power grows sufficiently to make it a challenger for superpower status, or if the United States again focuses on it as the most likely challenger. But, as during the Cold War, this global pattern remains entangled with the regional and interregional ones, in which China is the central indigenous player, and the United States is an outside power intervening in that RSC.

The problem for both the United States and China's neighbours of how to deal with it can be seen as one example of the more general liberal–realist dilemma. Given that industrialisation inevitably carries with it increasing capabilities for military production, how are other states to deal with unliberal, revisionist, modernist states such as Iran, Iraq, and China? To pursue trade and investment with them is to gamble that the liberal logic of interdependence and domestic transformation (from market to democracy) will work more quickly and powerfully than the realist logic of strengthening an opponent that one day you may have to fight. There is no easy escape from this dilemma. Traders and investors are competing with each other, making coordinated action difficult. If Japan, for example, began to securitise Chinese power, it could not easily switch from liberal to realist behaviour. Doing so would simply turn the profits from the Chinese market over to other players, weakening Japan and antagonising China. Taiwan already faces this dilemma in acute form. So long as the liberal logic remains strong, China will be able to feed on the resources of those it may later wish to confront. Only if its behaviour managed to frighten all of its neighbours, as well as the West, would there be any possibility of coordinated action to restrain China's power.

Assessing the weight of the global level in the East Asian RSC is not as straightforward as might at first appear. A simple regionalist approach sees a big drop in the impact of the global level because of the withdrawal of the Soviet Union, the ending of its containment and countercontainment games with the United States and China, and the weakening of the rationales for the United States to remain in East Asia. All of this works to increase the weight of China within the region. But the removal of the Soviet factor has also strengthened the position of the United States, both globally and in Asia. Asians concerned about China have nowhere else to turn except to the United States, and their economic dependency on it was revealed by the crisis of the late 1990s. There is therefore a question as to whether the global level has *dropped* in significance compared with the regional one or merely *changed in character*, from bipolar to unipolar superpower intervention, without changing in relative weight. The United States remains as, or more, important to the security of Japan, China, and India, not to mention to the Koreas, Taiwan, and ASEAN, than any of them are to each other.

Conclusions

As should by now be obvious, we reject the view that international relations in East Asia are somehow unique, and that general theories of the international system therefore cannot be applied to it (Richardson 1994; Mahbubani 1995; Kang 1995). As the history sketched above shows all too depressingly, East Asian international relations are quite amenable to analysis in terms of securitisation, power politics, and RSCT. Much of the securitisation and desecuritisation is of a fairly traditional sort, and the levels framework reveals a useful story of continuities and changes. The main features of that story up to the end of the twentieth century can be summarised as follows:

- At the domestic level, the main question is not – with some significant local exceptions – about internal instability. It is about how the political economies of the two big powers in the region will evolve.
- At the regional level, one sees strong continuities from Cold War to post-Cold War in Northeast Asia, and a dramatic shift from highly penetrated conflict formation to security regime in Southeast Asia.
- At the interregional level, the big development is the merger of Northeast and Southeast Asian RSCs into an East Asian one, contingent on concerns about China, on institutional developments, most notably the ARF, and on acceptance of a strong linkage between security and economic interdependence. This development changes the structure of levels through the process of an external transformation merging two RSCs into one. South Asia remains in much the same position within the supercomplex despite this merger, though India's membership of the ARF and its concerns over Chinese penetration of Burma strengthen the supercomplex pattern, as does the drawing in of Australia.

- At the global level, superpower rivalry and Soviet power are withdrawing from the region, and while this weakens US engagement in some ways, it strengthens it in others.

In order to consider the outlook for Asia, and bring the scenarios element of RSCT into play, we need now to reintegrate the East and South Asian stories.

Conclusions: scenarios for the Asian supercomplex

Which SCT scenarios are possible and which are not in Asia? Given the level of development of the region, the unstructured scenario is ruled out for all parts of it. Overlay is also ruled out other than existing US commitments in Japan and South Korea. No outside state, not even the USA, now has the capacity to overlay the region, and no state within the region has the capacity to establish suzerainty over it. China would be the only possible candidate for that role and, whatever traditional inclinations to seek regional suzerainty might still live within its political instincts, it lacks both the coercive capability and the civilisational attractiveness that it once possessed. As Van Ness (2002: 143) notes, China has no real soft power resources, and its communist government is now mostly a liability in terms of international image and attractiveness. Like Europe before it, Asia now has too many substantial powers within it to allow any one of them to take over the whole, and it has collectively become too big a centre of power for any one country to dominate it without that domination having major repercussions at the global level. Asia's future is thus as some form of RSC, which leads to questions about its shape, and about its essential structure in terms of polarity and amity–enmity.

Asia has already seen one internal transformation (Southeast Asia) and one external one (the merger of the Northeast and Southeast Asian complexes). A second internal transformation looks close in South Asia, as it moves from bipolarity to unipolarity. There are no conspicuous interregional dynamics suggesting that external transformations between Asia and either the Middle East or Russia/CIS look at all likely. What remains a distinct, though uncertain, possibility is that the interregional dynamics linking South and East Asia will strengthen, transforming the supercomplex into a fully fledged Asian RSC (more on this below).

In terms of polarity, the prospects look fairly clear. In South Asia, unipolarity is a distinct, though not certain, possibility. Slowly but probably surely, India seems destined to outgrow its South Asian challenger and lift itself into prominence as an all-Asian regional power, if not a global great power. In East Asia, bipolarity looks durable, since no other state comes close to matching China and Japan. The Asian supercomplex is tripolar with little prospect of change.

In terms of amity–enmity the possibilities run from conflict formation through security regime to security community. South Asia remains a conflict formation and nothing points towards any prospect of it becoming a security community. Nuclear rivalry, water sharing, migration, and environmental stress could all amplify the traditional sources of hostile securitisation in South Asia. So too could India's increasing hegemony, though there is little that India's mostly feeble and internally divided neighbours will be able to do about it short of Pakistan initiating a nuclear war. But in general South Asia has proved resilient against major changes, and a good case can be made that India cultivates moderation by being an essentially balanced and slow-moving actor (Bajpai 1998: 193–7). Thus incremental change in the same direction as during the 1990s seems the likely path.

In East Asia the picture is more nuanced. Southeast Asia has moved from conflict formation to security regime, whereas Northeast Asia largely remains a conflict formation. There seems little prospect that either East Asia, or Asia as a whole, will be able to form a security community in the foreseeable future. To achieve a security community requires a strong shared view of the status quo, allied to a shared culture and/or well-developed institutions. Democracy may not be a necessary condition but, as suggested by the democracy and peace literature (and by the empirical cases to date), it is a huge asset (Lake 1992). East Asia seems a long way from meeting these conditions. Although ASEAN might count as a security regime, many other states in Asia are prepared to use force and to have it used against them, spectacularly so in the case of India and Pakistan, the two Koreas, and China and Taiwan, but also true between India and China, Vietnam and China, Singapore and Malaysia, and quite a few others. Border clashes remain a possibility in many places, but there is not much chance of one country invading and occupying another. There is not much shared culture, and there are still only the beginnings of solidly rooted institutions, though there is some shared interest in economic development.

Two plausible scenarios remain: East Asia could unfold into a classical conflict formation, or it could become a security regime. Either of these scenarios seems likely to strengthen the links between East and South Asian security dynamics, and thus to expand the process of external transformation that began with the merger of Northeast and Southeast Asia. As East Asia goes, so will go the Asian supercomplex.

Conflict formation

The East Asian RSC, and therefore the Asian supercomplex, could easily become a conflict formation. History has left numerous territorial disputes, status rivalries, fears, and hatreds among the successor states and their peoples. It is hard to think of two adjacent countries within the region that do not have either serious unresolved issues between them or active processes of securitisation, or both. The region has no shared cultural legacy, few traditions of international cooperation, and a worrying number of strong nationalisms. The Cold War has left it with two divided countries, Korea and China, a number of nuclear and near nuclear states, and a still weak and mostly recently established framework of regional organisations. Berger (1993: 130) notes that none of the Western arguments for the decline of war (democracy, interdependence, institutions) applies in East Asia, and whether nuclear weapons will stabilise or exacerbate otherwise securitised relations is a matter of hotly contested debate. Segal (1997: 236–43) argues not only that China looks increasingly like a national socialist regime, but also that the process of democratisation, especially where combined with nationalism, can inflame rather than ameliorate relations with neighbours.

As already argued, Asia is not unlike nineteenth-century Europe. It is dominated by powerful modern states that are the successful inheritors of the postcolonial legacy. Asia contains some very weak and even failed states, and for the people within those states the domestic level of security is very much to the fore. But overall there is a robust set of Asian regional powers whose interplay creates a strong regional security dynamic. These conditions may enable, but they certainly do not make inevitable, a slide into conflict formation. The key to the outcome lies in what happens with China and the United States. If China remains unified and adopts an aggressive posture, *and* if the United States reduces its security engagement in East Asia, then a conflict formation becomes the most likely outcome. It is hard to say how these two developments might interact. A US disengagement might well encourage

174

Chinese hegemonism. Pugnacious Chinese behaviour could either draw the United States in (constructing China as a global rival) or push it out (fear of engagement in Asian wars). Movements on the Korean peninsula (war, reconciliation, or a triumphalist takeover by the South) are unlikely in themselves to determine the direction of the region, but in conjunction with US and Chinese developments could help to push the region towards conflict formation mode. As suggested by talk during 2000 of a 'global partnership' between Tokyo and Delhi (*Strategic Survey* 2000–1: 184), a more assertive China could also draw India into the RSC as part of an anti-hegemonic coalition against China. Fear of China resonates in the domestic politics of the several Southeast Asian states with significant Chinese minorities, especially Malaysia, Vietnam, and Indonesia. It could encourage the open acquisition of nuclear weapons by Taiwan, and possibly Korea and Japan. In this scenario, China would certainly keep Pakistan as an ally, and perhaps Burma as well (depending on its domestic politics). A unified Korea still hanging on to its dislike of Japan might well try to stay neutral or bandwagon with China.

An East Asian conflict formation would be unlikely to end in war among its great powers, not only because of the fear of nuclear weapons, but also because of fear of jeopardising economic achievements. More localised conflicts in Korea, over Taiwan, and in the South China Sea would be a distinct possibility.

Security regime

A security regime does not imply that relations among its members are harmonious and without conflict. Rather, conflict exists, but the actors agree to cooperate to deal with it. There has to be some agreement on the status quo among the great powers, a desire to avoid war, and an expectation that states will act with restraint when disputes arise (Jervis 1982: 360–2).

It is possible to imagine East Asia developing into this mode despite its difficult historical legacy. Those who hope for the triumph of economic rationalism and the effectiveness of Asia's informal, transnational diplomatic style (Mahbubani 1995; Richardson 1994; Higgott 1994) support this scenario. The key conditions for it are: (1) that China either fails to develop into the dominant power in the region, or that it evolves into a great power that is perceived by its neighbours as relatively benign; and (2) that the United States remains significantly engaged in

East Asian security as the ring-holder. Korea is again unlikely to shape the outcome by itself, though unification could complicate the maintenance of a US military presence. Since this scenario is contingent on the desecuritising logic of economic rationalism being a stronger force than the securitisation logic of power politics, it is dependent on a reasonable recovery from the economic crisis of the late 1990s. It is also dependent on the relative successes and failures in the various attempts at institution-building around the region, particularly the ARF, but also the moves towards economic regionalisation noted by Bergsten (2000).

The economic uncertainty in East Asia and the relative fragility of its institutions suggest that, if a successful regional security regime is to develop, it will be able to do so only in the context of a supportive global international environment. In one sense, this is simply another way of stating that the necessary condition for this scenario is that the United States must stay engaged in East Asia. Many of the existing organisations in the region can be seen as designed primarily to help bind the United States to East Asia by creating at least a rhetoric of an Asia-Pacific superregion. But as some of the more astute observers in the region understand (Mahbubani 1995), the USA is not an East Asian state. It looks also to the Atlantic and to Latin America, and Asia is only one of its spheres of operation. It can choose to be engaged in Asia to a greater or lesser extent, but it is external to the region in either case (Buzan 1998).

These transregional organisations and economic relations are also more than just ways to ensnare the United States into a role in East Asia. However feeble they appear, they do represent a willingness on the part of states in the region to begin talking formally and regularly (however superficially) about their regional security relations. It seems unlikely that this development could go forward without US participation. For better or worse, many of the East Asian states trust the United States more than they trust each other. Symbolic of this is the leading role played by the USA in trying to defuse the nuclear crisis in Korea. Regardless of whether one approves of the KEDO deal or not, it is hard to imagine that anything would have been done within the region to stop escalation if the USA had not taken the lead. It might even be argued that such an externally supported arrangement is not a true regional security regime at all. In reality it lies somewhere between a conflict formation and a security regime, with the states of the region in effect allowing their security to be managed by an outside player.

RSCT-based scenarios suggest that the security options for East Asia can be reduced to a surprisingly narrow band. The East Asian RSC seems almost certain to end up either towards the milder end of the conflict formation scenario or somewhere near the weak end of the regional security regime. Only very extreme Chinese aggressiveness and a complete transformation of Japan (both hard to imagine) could push the region into a real warring conflict formation such as Europe was before 1945 (and South Asia and the Middle East still are). Equally hard to imagine, at least for many decades, is anything that could make East Asia into a strong security regime, let alone a security community with a confederal structure like the EU with actor qualities. Only if China becomes democratic and liberal do moves in that direction become a possibility.

But although RSCT enables us to confine the scenarios for Asia to a fairly narrow range of possibilities, it remains the case that the two crucial variables on which the future of Asian security depends – China and the USA – are fundamentally indeterminate (Buzan 1996). Developments in Korea could have a big local impact, but are unlikely to determine the course of the region as a whole. Japan could in principle reshape the region, but seems so mired in structural and historical problems that its most likely role is to adhere to the status quo, not changing much unless severely pressured by external events. Acquisition of nuclear weapons by Japan would almost certainly trigger securitisation in China, but such a move by Japan is almost inconceivable without major prior changes in US and Chinese behaviour. Huntington (1996: 234–8) notes Japan's historic tendency to align with the dominant power in the system and, if still true, this could raise interesting questions if it eventually has to choose between the United States and China. Russia could re-emerge as a major player in East Asia, but given the depth of its domestic disarray this seems unlikely for the foreseeable future. India is unlikely to change Asia by itself, and much of its potentiality in the supercomplex hangs on how China and the United States choose to relate to it. Indeed, it is a disturbing thought that India's best chance of achieving the global status recognition it craves is if China and the USA fall into rivalry and the latter recruits India into a containment alliance.

That leaves China, which is already central to the security dynamics of the Asian supercomplex, and the United States, which almost alone carries the burden of how much or little the global level impinges on the regional one in Asia. With China, the question is how quickly (or slowly) its power grows, and how much (or little) its postures and policies arouse fear in its neighbours. With the United States, the question is how much (or little) it will remain engaged as an outside player in East Asia's regional security dynamics, and whether or not Chinese–US rivalry will grow to take on a major global level dimension. In both cases the answers to these questions will be found largely within the domestic political economies of these two countries.

The China variable is quite straightforward and easy to understand. Part of it is a simple realist story about how China's increasing power impinges on its neighbours and triggers securitisations. The other part is a more liberal story about the political character of China, and the likelihood and timing that its evolution from dictatorship to democracy will shift perceptions of its power from malign to benign, and thus trigger desecuritisations. In this context, it is worth noting the striking similarities between India and China in their general outlook (Bajpai 1998; Wu 1998). Both hold strongly realist perspectives towards their regions and the wider world. Both locate themselves in a historical self-perspective as great and ancient civilisational centres to which other peoples traditionally came for trade and enlightenment, but which were not themselves usually militarily expansive outside their region. Both have been sensitised by colonial experience, and consequently display a high concern with national cohesion (as an issue of power, and to prevent repeats of disunity allowing in foreign penetration). Both give high value to autonomy in economy, foreign policy, and military capability, but both are also moving towards more liberalised economy despite strong anticapitalist traditions. Both perceive the United States as a key threat, but are nonetheless pragmatic enough to align with it on some matters. Both favour a multipolar international system, mostly understanding this in the same way as US advocates of a less global US security engagement, as a 0 + x system of great powers with no superpowers. Such a structure gives greater autonomy to regional level dynamics, and to great powers within their localities. These deeply rooted and shared features make both India and China likely to be essentially Westphalian great power players in Asian security. They will be changed, if at all, only by thoroughgoing internal liberalisations of a type not in prospect for many decades.

The US variable is, by contrast, surprisingly difficult to understand. The easy part to see is that a US withdrawal from Asia is unlikely because of US economic interests there, and because it would mean the end of US superpower status. Withdrawal would have huge consequences because of the large role the USA plays in Asian security. The US presence enables Japan to remain a civilian power, suspends the question of what Sino-Japanese relations would become if left to the two governments to handle by themselves, and provides leadership for local fire-fighting over issues such as Korea and Taiwan. Neither China nor Japan (nor India) has the standing to take up the role of Asian regional leader, and none of them looks likely to acquire it soon. ASEAN cannot by itself provide adequate regional leadership, though its ARF is better than nothing. How long it will take the Asians to grow out of this dependence on the United States is hard to say. As in Europe, many find it comfortable (and cheap) and, despite some inflated rhetoric, few oppose it absolutely. One consequence of this dependence is that US withdrawal could only really come about as a result of a domestic triumph of neo-isolationism in US politics that made it indifferent to Eurasian security, and content to set aside most of its global engagements. Such a development is not unimaginable, but neither does there seem to be any very strong move in that direction, and there is a host of powerful military and commercial interests likely to oppose it.

What is more difficult to see is the effect of the United States being, and staying, engaged in Asia's security. A simple realist reading would be the ending of the Cold War meaning that the United States shifted from playing the more committed Cold War role of *protector* of the region to playing the rather less committed one of *balancer*. A protector has to make sacrifices to preserve and strengthen its allies against a larger outside threat. A balancer can expect its allies to make sacrifices to court its favour. It is not for nothing that Britain was known as 'perfidious Albion' when it played the balancer role in Europe. Any state so placed will be tempted to manipulate the local divisions to its own economic and political advantage. Waltz (1993b) goes so far as to argue that the United States itself will come to be seen as a threat by other powers as is already visible in some of the behaviour of India and China. In the absence of a superpower rivalry to constrain its behaviour, the United States still remains deterred from excesses of self-interest both by its economic interests in East Asia, and by the desire to preserve the legitimacy aspects of its superpower status. But idiosyncratic US projects such as national missile defence, largely driven by its domestic dynamics, could still have major impacts on Asian security, as could the much commented-upon US drift towards increasingly unilateral behaviour. The claim that US deployment of missile defences would trigger a proliferation chain in Asia, causing China, India, and Pakistan to increase and upgrade their nuclear arsenals, is entirely plausible.

179

This realist view offers important insights into the US role in Asia. But a reading through RSCT requires one to focus more closely on how the regional (and in the Asian case also interregional) security dynamics interplay with the global level ones. The puzzle to be solved here is why there is much less balancing behaviour against China than its rising power, increasingly nationalist government, and behaviour in Pakistan, Burma, the South China Sea, and Taiwan would suggest is appropriate. There are four possible explanations for this apparent underperformance of the balancing mechanism.

First is that the traditional sort of strategic analysis that sees threats emanating from China to its neighbours is simply wrong. Either China does not represent a serious threat to its neighbours, and they are therefore correct in keeping their securitisations of it at a rather low level; or it does, but its neighbours are somehow blind to the facts. Given the sustained, and overtly military, pressure that China has put on India (by seizing territory and nuclearising Pakistan), on ASEAN (by occupations and claims in the Paracel and Spratly Islands), and on Taiwan (by frequent threats and military demonstrations), it is hardly plausible that its neighbours would not have noticed, or not have correctly evaluated, the threat.

Second is that Chinese diplomacy has somehow been so effective that it has been able to intimidate its neighbours into a form of appeasement that restrains them from publicly responding to its provocations. The mechanism here is the threat that any balancing responses will cause an immediate worsening of relations and escalation of threats. This could be plausible given China's ability to deal with the separate regions of Asia more or less in isolation from each other, and the formidable difficulties of constructing an anti-China coalition stretching from India through ASEAN to Japan. There is also the fact that China's behaviour towards Taiwan is (rightly) seen as a special case, and its similarity to China's behaviour in Southeast and South Asia therefore gets underplayed, making the whole pattern less visible.

Third is the possibility that the Asian international subsystem is dressed in Westphalian clothes, but is not performing according to a Westphalian script. This line of thinking (Fairbank 1968; Huntington 1996: 229–38; Kang 1995, 2000) projects Asia's past into its future. It assumes that what Fairbank labelled the 'Chinese World Order' – a Sino-centric and hierarchical form of international relations – has survived within the cultures of East Asia despite the superficial remaking of the Asian subsystem into a Western-style set of sovereign states. Its principal effect is to subvert the expectation of balancing as the normal response to threat and power imbalance in a Westphalian system, and to replace it with a propensity among the weaker powers to bandwagon. The idea is that hierarchical behaviour remains so deeply ingrained in Asian cultures that it makes their international relations not conform to the realist models of IR (see the argument by Watson (1992) about 'legitimacy' in chapter 3). This intriguing, and potentially extremely important, proposition cannot really be tested unless the USA pulls out of Asia, leaving the Asian supercomplex to sort itself out entirely on its own terms. Its prediction does explain the observed underperformance of balancing, though it is hard put to explain India's conformity with it given that India was never part of the Chinese world order.

Fourth is that the impact of the US engagement in Asia explains the underperformance of balancing: in other words, that there is a strong interplay between the security dynamics of the Asian supercomplex and those at the global level concerning US–Chinese relations within the context of a 1 + 4 system. The argument is that the US presence as security ring-holder in Asia allows Asian governments to see the job of balancing China as falling to the United States. As a consequence, India, Japan, and most members of ASEAN underperform locally in balancing China. The United States encourages such underperformance in several ways. It projects nuclear non-proliferation norms strongly on to the two Koreas, Japan, Taiwan, India, and Pakistan; it cultivates Japan as a military dependant; and it has traditionally opposed Asian multilateral security initiatives. This behaviour is not simply a local application of US global policy, since the USA has made little attempt to restrain Israel's nuclear deterrent or, earlier, those of Britain and France. Only Vietnam has tried to balance China, and did so in the face of US hostility to Hanoi. Since the United States has to worry about China at the global level, and since China's global prospects are heavily conditioned by its position in the Asian supercomplex, this underperformance of balancing locks the United States in. It potentially stimulates US–Chinese rivalry by putting the United States into the front line against China. This logic has unsettling links to that of the Chinese world order sketched above. Westphalian logic suggests that, if the USA drew back from its ring-holding position, other Asian states would be forced to balance, thus doing the USA's job for it at the global level. But, while that interpretation creates incentives for the United States to disengage, the Chinese world order explanation makes disengagement much more hazardous. If Asian international behaviour is to bandwagon with threateners, then

US disengagement would hand China a regional suzerainty in Asia, which would greatly enhance its global position.

On this reading, and barring extreme behaviour by either China or the United States, something like the existing configuration in Asia is potentially quite stable over a timespan of a few decades. The USA cannot risk withdrawing, and so has to preserve its sole superpower status by keeping Japan bound to it, and by pursuing with China what Segal (1999: 35) called 'constrainment': containing China militarily and politically, while at the same time engaging with it economically in the hope of liberalising its internal development over the medium and longer term. China has a different incentive to play the waiting game, hoping that its growing material capabilities will eventually deliver more of an ability to balance internally against the USA, and not wanting to provoke Japan to shift from recessed to deployed nuclear deterrence. None of the Asian powers wants to become an overt rival to China or a frontline outpost for the United States in some kind of mark two superpower rivalry. If one thus brings the global and regional level dynamics together in assessing Asian security, a quite powerful case can be made that the main scenario is a slow working-out of the existing patterns. The eventual outcome will turn on which happens first: either China becomes more internally liberalised, and therefore less threatening; or it becomes powerful while still nationalistic and authoritarian. The main threat to this scenario is a serious escalation in the Taiwan Strait. The problem is that China sees this as an internal question, whereas most others see it as an international one (albeit recognising the special character of the case). If China feels compelled to deliver on its rhetoric against Taiwan, and proceeds against Taiwanese independence by force, then huge questions will be put on the table. Will the United States prevent a Chinese takeover of Taiwan? Will Japan help it to do so? A 'no' answer to the first question would break the credibility of US engagement in Asia. A 'no' answer to the second would break the United States–Japan alliance, and thus throw open the whole pattern of security dynamics in the Asian supercomplex.

Part III
The Middle East and Africa

Introduction

Africa and the Middle East are traditionally linked by trade (including the slave trade) and religion (the spread of Islam) stretching back to the seventh century AD (Deegan 1996: 7–27). More relevant to our theme of regional security is that they share a long and ambiguous boundary through the Sahara across which there is significant security interaction. Both share the experience of decolonisation, with the consequence that many of them are shallow-rooted weak states. But this simply makes them part of a wider third world. A more interesting parallel is that both started their post-independence life equipped with pan-regional identity movements: pan-Africanism in Africa and pan-Arabism and pan-Islamism in the Middle East. There was substantial geographical overlap in these movements, most obviously in North Africa. But their main importance was the challenge they raised to the viability of a post-colonial state system based on national identity and sovereignty.

Into this brew of an imposed Westphalian system and pan-regional identities one has to add Krause's (1996: 324–7, 335–42) idea that many postcolonial states escaped from the European process of state development sketched out by Tilly (1990; also Howard 1976) in which the demands of military competition and war fed back into the creation of bureaucratic, then national, and finally democratic states. In this model, the state needed to raise revenue by taxing its population, which gave it an interest in economic development and required it to develop ways of relating to its population in a long-term and stable manner. In both Africa and the Middle East this link between military challenge and state development has not functioned. It has been broken by the presence of a strong international society which supports postcolonial states with a system of juridical sovereignty (more on this in the Africa chapter), and enables regimes, and even nonstate actors, to finance military power

185

by direct control of internationally marketable resources, especially oil and diamonds (Malaquias 2001). The creation of durable direct links between economic resources and military power enables state regimes and nonstate warlords to bypass, and often suppress, their populations.

Despite these parallels and connections, the stories of regional security in these two areas follow very different trajectories. In both cases, pan-regional identity movements failed to override the Westphalian transplant. In Africa, pan-Africanism never developed much beyond background symbolics. Unlike pan-Arabism and pan-Islamism, pan-Africanism was a recent political construction with no historical roots. It never threatened the postcolonial state system, and was largely sustained as a unity of negatives against South Africa's apartheid regime rather than as any positive development of identity politics. The African state mostly did not consolidate itself either, often having little empirical reality, and sharing the political, military, territorial, and economic stage with a wide variety of insurgency movements and other substate actors. In the Middle East, by contrast, the system of sovereign states did steadily consolidate itself, forcing both pan-Arab and pan-Islamic sentiments to accommodate themselves to its political reality. Only in a few patches, most notably Lebanon after 1976 and northern Iraq, did African-style state disintegration take place. In some ways the Middle East can be seen as the EU story in reverse. While Europe struggled to create a collective identity to counterbalance its strong nation-states, the Arabs tried to create strong states and national identities in the face of pan-Arab and pan-Islamic sentiments. Paradoxically, both developments, despite their opposite directions, seem to lead to increased predictability and improved conditions for diplomacy, thus testifying to the methodological principle of respecting regional particularity in spite of the temptation to make causal generalisations about an isolated variable. Helped by oil resources and lavish Cold War aid, its ruling regimes created a functioning system of authoritarian, but not national, states. As a consequence, the Middle Eastern story can largely be told in terms of state and interstate security dynamics, with some admixture of nonstate actors, but the African story is a complicated mixture of states, regimes, and insurgency movements, in which interstate security dynamics feature much less.

7   The Middle East: a perennial conflict formation

Introduction

The Middle East is a place where an autonomous regional level of security has operated strongly for several decades, despite continuous and heavy impositions from the global level. Its RSC is a clear example of a conflict formation, if one that is unusually large and complicated, and that also possesses some distinctive cultural features. As in many other places in the third world, the insecurity of ruling elites within their domestic sphere plays a significant role in shaping the dynamics of (in)security overall. On the surface, this is a region composed largely of postcolonial modern states, albeit mostly weak ones. But this structure is riddled with still powerful premodern elements of clan, tribe, and religion. Definitions of the Middle East vary, but we see a pattern of security interdependence that covers a region stretching from Morocco to Iran, including all of the Arab states plus Israel and Iran. Cyprus, Sudan, and the Horn are not part of it. Afghanistan is an insulator between it and South Asia, and Turkey between it and Europe. Turkey's insulating function was enhanced by the fact that, although it had once ruled much of the Arab world (as the heartland of the Ottoman Empire), from the 1920s onwards it largely turned its back on this past in order to pursue Ataturk's Westernistic vision of its future.

The Middle Eastern RSC: 1948–1990

The regional level

Putting an exact date on the emergence of the Middle Eastern RSC is problematic because there was no clear point of shift from colonial status to independence. Turkey, Iran, and Saudi Arabia were never colonised.

The distinction between colonial status and independence was often murky, as in Egypt, Iraq, Jordan, and Oman, where colonial powers retained a strong presence in formally independent states. In addition, the process of decolonisation was protracted, stretching from Egypt, Iraq, and Yemen during the interwar period to Bahrain, Qatar, and the UAE in 1971. When did this process achieve a sufficient critical mass of independent actors to start operating as an RSC?

Many of the present conflict dynamics of the region have roots reaching back into the interwar years. Inter-Arab rivalries (between Hashemite and Saudi monarchies, between Iraq and Egypt for leadership of the Arabs) and conflict between Palestinians and Zionist immigrants were visible during the 1930s, as were territorial disputes (Lebanon versus Greater Syria) and the emergence of Arab nationalism (Yapp 1991: 49–208; Barnett 1998: 55–83; Podeh 1998). Podeh (1998) argues that such interaction was sufficient to constitute an Arab state system, and in our terms it looks like a proto-RSC. But right through to the end of the Second World War, British and French colonial presence was also strong, and their military-political overlay dominated the region. For this reason, the best date for the beginning of the Middle Eastern RSC comes after the wave of decolonisations between 1945 and 1948, which generated a critical mass of independent states.

Like South Asia, the Middle Eastern RSC was born fighting. The independence of Israel moved the earlier conflict between Palestinians and Zionist immigrants to the state level, and triggered the first of many interstate wars. Unlike South Asia, whose regional insecurity dynamics centred around a single rivalry between two big powers, the Middle East presents a much more complicated picture. At its peak, more than twenty states, many relatively equal in weight, formed the RSC. These numbers, plus dispersed geography, meant that this RSC developed three subcomplexes: two main ones centred respectively in the Levant and the Gulf, and a considerably weaker one in the Maghreb. Divisions of distance were, however, partly offset by extensive labour migration among the Arab states, driven by oil money. A case might be made that the Horn of Africa constitutes a fourth weak subcomplex in this set. Somalia, Djibouti, and Sudan are all members of the Arab League, and there is a clear and persistent pattern of conflict and hostile intervention connecting them with Ethiopia, Eritrea, and sometimes Egypt. But we concur with the firm consensus among the experts (e.g., Clapham 1996: 128–9; Tibi 1993: 52, 59) that the Horn subcomplex is part of Africa, and should *not* be considered part of the Middle East.

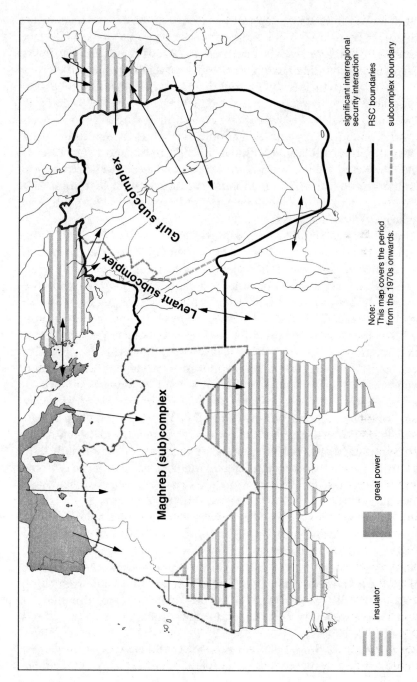

Map 5. The Middle Eastern RSC

It is tempting to try to capture the security interdependence of the Middle East in terms of some simple ethnic or religious formula. The fact that the two main cores can be interpreted as Arabs versus 'others' (Jews, Iranians), and that there is an earlier legacy of Arabs versus Turks from Ottoman days (which is still present in a variety of Kurdish problems), suggests an ethnic explanation of the region's insecurities. Religion gets woven into this. Israel represents religious differentiation from its Arab (mostly Islamic or Christian) neighbours, while Iran represents the Shi'a side of the Sunni–Shi'a split within Islam. As Chubin and Tripp (1996: 4) note: 'For Iran, a dispute with any Arab neighbour risks becoming a dispute with all its Arab neighbours', an observation that applies to Israel with even more force. Arabism and Islamism are competitive as well as closely interlinked ideas (Dawisha 2000).

But while this simplification captures an important element of the truth, it does not cover the whole. As Barnett (1998) has demonstrated, the construction of Arab nationalism has generated considerably more inter-Arab rivalry and conflict than cooperation and harmony, and the same could be said about inter-Islamic relations. The region thus also contains strong and distinct inter-Arab and inter-Islamic agendas. Inter-Arab rivalries concern competition for leadership of the Arab world and interpretations of Arabism, as well as more traditional types of rivalry over territory, water, and ideology, not to mention clan interests and issues of royal succession. Islamists are often the domestic opposition in Arab states, and Islamic states (Iran) are easily seen as a threat by many of their neighbours (Karawan 1997). There has been quite a bit of interplay between the Arab versus non-Arab dynamics on the one hand, and the Arab versus Arab ones on the other. A case could be made that, as a rule, the Arab versus non-Arab disputes take precedence over the Arab versus Arab ones, but there are important exceptions to this. Arab Syria aligned with non-Arab Iran when Iran was at war with Arab Iraq. Both Jordan and Syria have attacked the Palestinians despite their collective Arab stand against Israel. Syria occupies a substantial chunk of Lebanon, and has on various occasions threatened force against Jordan. The patterns of amity and enmity in the Middle East are remarkable for their convoluted and crosscutting character. But while overarching explanations for conflict may not be possible, the regional pattern of security interdependencies shaped by three subcomplexes can be described quite clearly.

The first, and defining, core subcomplex was that centred in the Levant between Israel and its Arab neighbours. This was a local struggle between Israel and the Palestinians, which set up and sustained a much wider hostility between Israel and both its immediate neighbours and the wider Arab world (Tibi 1993: 183–4). To a lesser extent, this was shadowed by a conflict between Israel and the even wider Islamic world (particularly, after 1979, Iran). The Arab-Palestinian conflict focused, amplified, and in some ways defined (Barnett 1998: 121–3; Dervis and Shafik 1998: 508) the transnational qualities of Arab nationalism that gave the Middle East as a whole its overall coherence as an RSC. From Morocco to Iraq, a robust rhetorical stand in support of the Palestinians was often integral to the legitimacy of governments among their own peoples. Without common cultural bonds, it is quite unlikely that the national security concerns of a collection of small and medium-sized powers with members as geographically far apart as Morocco and Oman would ever have cohered into a single pattern of security interdependence. It was the shared symbols of Arabism and Islam, and their focus on the conflict with Israel, that enabled the security dynamics of the Middle East to link up across such large distances. Without them, there would almost certainly have been no single Middle Eastern RSC. Instead, distance would have dictated two or possibly three smaller RSCs formed around the Gulf, the Maghreb, and the Levant.

The Arab–Israeli conflict gave rise to a well-known string of substantial wars (1948–9, 1956, 1967, 1969–70, 1973, 1982) as well as an endless sequence of lesser military clashes within and around Israel. This subcomplex involves principally Israel and its immediate neighbours, and is a mixture of states (Egypt, Syria, Lebanon, Jordan) and nonstate actors (PLO, Hamas, Hizbollah). Several countries further afield have been directly engaged against Israel in significant ways (Iraq, Iran, Saudi Arabia, Kuwait, Libya, Tunisia), giving rhetorical, financial, and sometimes military support. Nearly all Arab countries were engaged to some degree, even if only rhetorically, and the effects of the wars had a major impact on inter-Arab politics, particularly on the waxing and waning of Egypt's fortunes as the leader of the Arab world, and the consequent opportunities for Saudi Arabia, Iraq, and others to bid for that role (Tibi 1993).

The Gulf subcomplex formed after Britain's withdrawal from the area in 1971. It centred on a triangular rivalry among Iran, Iraq, and the Gulf Arab states led by Saudi Arabia. There is also a peripheral rivalry between Saudi Arabia and Yemen (and within Yemen), which has generated a lot of local wars, and has at times drawn in wider Arab participation along rival royalist versus radical lines. The Gulf Arabs (Saudi

Arabia, Kuwait, Bahrain, Qatar, the United Arab Emirates, and Oman) have since 1981 been grouped together in the Gulf Cooperation Council (GCC), a weak subregional strategic partnership that formed in response to the Iraq–Iran war, conspicuously excludes those two, and is generally understood as being a response to fear of them (Tibi 1993: 171). The 1979 revolution in Iran added a sharp ideological element to its rivalry with Saudi Arabia, since both states claimed leadership of competing Islamic universalisms (Chubin and Tripp 1996: 15, 71). The hostility between Iran and Iraq stems from a variety of border disputes, the rival power ambitions of leaders in both states, overlapping problems with Kurdish minorities, and the fate of a large Shi'ite population in the south of Iraq. It can also be understood as an extension of a very much older rivalry between Arabs and Persians and between the Shi'a and Sunni variants of Islam that goes back to the seventh century AD. Westerners tend to forget that the Ottoman Empire, which controlled the Eastern Mediterranean littoral and most of the Arab world from the sixteenth century to 1918, was regularly at war not only with Europe, but also with the Persian Safavid Empire to its east. The Ottoman Empire was mostly of Sunni persuasion, while the Safavids espoused Shi'a Islam (McNeill 1963: 618–28; Hodgson 1993: 194–5). These ethnic and sectarian factors played a similarly significant role in modern tensions between Iran and Iraq, and between Iran and the Gulf Arabs. The inter-Arab tensions between the Gulf Arabs and Iraq are more particular, having to do with disputes over the price of oil, a general fear among the Gulf Arabs of the hegemonic ambitions of Saddam Hussein and, in the case of Kuwait, the specific fear created by disputes over crossborder oil resources and by Iraq's repeated rejection of its claim to independence.

An early move in the formation of this subcomplex was Iran's seizure of some disputed islands from the UAE in 1971. After the British departure, there was a substantial arms build-up in the region, and the Iranian revolution in 1979 led to both meddling in the domestic politics of the Arab states along Sunni–Shi'a lines and the First Gulf, or Iran–Iraq, War, a bloody affair lasting from 1980 to 1988, which ended in a draw. The Second Gulf War opened in 1990 with Iraq's annexation of Kuwait following a dispute over oil pricing. This resulted in a war against Iraq early in 1991 by a US-led coalition, which restored Kuwait's independence and put Iraq under heavy international sanctions.

Although the Gulf added a second core to the Middle Eastern RSC, the nature of its internal security dynamics did not generate anything like the same symbolic intensity that enabled the Arab–Israeli one to tie together a wide geographical spread of Arab and Islamic states. But the close geographical proximity of these two cores means that, despite their independent local dynamics, there is a lot of crossover between them, and this helps to knit the whole RSC together. For example, Syria is a main rival to Israel, but also to Iraq, and took sides against Iraq during both Gulf Wars. In both of these rivalries Syria is an ally of Iran. Iraq and Syria are allies against Israel, but otherwise have been hostile to each other. The Gulf Arabs play a financial role in the conflict against Israel, having contributed perhaps $10 billion to the PLO during the 1980s (Legrain 1991: 79), and, by their funding of Islamic groups, also in the domestic politics of many Arab states. Egypt, although a central player in the Arab–Israeli conflict, is also prominent in the Gulf. It intervened extensively in Yemen during the 1960s, and during the Second Gulf War sided with the Gulf Arab states and Syria against Iraq.

The third, weaker, subcomplex in the Middle East during this period was in the Maghreb. It was basically about a shifting and uneasy set of relationships among Libya, Tunisia, Algeria, and Morocco (and Western Sahara). But for the Maghreb, as also further east, the border with Africa was blurred: Maghreb security dynamics pushed into Chad, Western Sahara, and Mauritania; and Libya and Morocco (and Israel) played politics in several sub-Saharan states. The main regional security problem in the Maghreb was the Moroccan annexation of Western Sahara starting in 1975, which led to a twelve-year tension with Algeria and Libya, who backed the Polisario fighters against Morocco. Morocco in turn backed Libya's opponents in Chad. Libya had been involved in the Chadian civil war since 1980, and also had a territorial dispute with Chad over the Aouzou strip, occupied by Libya in 1973. The Maghreb states had enough involvement in the Arab–Israel dispute, and also in the Gulf conflicts, that their membership in the Middle Eastern RSC was not in doubt. Libya took a strong political stand against Israel, and sided with radical – and opposed traditionalist – regimes in the Gulf. Algeria often played a mediating role in Arab politics. Tunisia (somewhat reluctantly) hosted the PLO offices for many years, and Morocco provided troops for several Gulf Arab regimes. In the other direction, Egypt aided the Algerians during their war of liberation against France, but in general the rest of the Arab world was not much involved in the disputes of the Maghreb subcomplex.

All of this defines a strong set of rather Westphalian-looking interstate (in)security dynamics at the regional level. The Middle Eastern conflict formation was driven by a traditional agenda of territorial disputes, ideological competitions, power and status rivalries, and ethnic and cultural divisions. Into these were mixed disputes about oil, water, and religion. How did this level relate to those above and below it? Or, in other words, what did the security constellation as a whole look like? Broadly put, both the regional and the global levels were independently very strong. The domestic level was also significant, displaying the typical postcolonial pattern of insecure regimes with obsessive concerns about making themselves secure within their states (Ayoob 1995: 188–96; Barnett 1998: 9). But, with few exceptions, domestic insecurities were largely contained within the framework of the state system. The interregional level was of only marginal importance.

The domestic level

As in Southeast Asia, most of the states in the Middle East are towards the weak end of the spectrum of sociopolitical cohesion. Democracy is rare, dictatorship common, and the use of force and repression in domestic political life endemic. Strong links among authoritarian regimes, oil resources, international capital, and great power allies have allowed rentier states to deploy extensive internal security forces to suppress their populations and delink their regimes from civil society (Krause 1996: 339–42). Oil state regimes, most notably the members of the GCC and Libya, have been able to buy off their populations, though this makes them politically vulnerable to oil price fluctuations (Kemp 1998–9: 136–7, 140–1). Islamists constitute the opposition in many Arab states, but they are not a plausible alternative to the regional state system, and in most cases are too fragmented or too weak to be likely alternatives to existing state regimes. Islam and its symbols have become interwoven with nationalism and the state. Although Islam itself has strong transnational qualities (including funding links to the Gulf Arab states), Islamists have been poor at building wide political coalitions either within or between states, and good at fragmenting themselves into rival factions. State repression, often supported from outside, has effectively broken Islamist military strength in most places (Karawan 1997; Eickelman and Piscatori 1996: 138, 150–1).

With some notable exceptions, and in contrast to Africa, domestic turbulence in the Middle East mostly does not determine the international security agenda. Governments in Iraq and Syria have slaughtered tens of thousands of their citizens; Lebanon, Sudan, Algeria, Israel, and Yemen have experienced prolonged civil wars; Iran underwent a major revolution, which generated a radical and often repressive Islamic state;

and government crackdowns on militant dissidents are a regular occurrence in Egypt and most of the Gulf Arab states. But all of this took place within a framework of states that proved much more robust than often predicted. Authors such as Tibi (1993: 181) argue that the European state form 'has never really been able to establish stable internal foundations in the Middle East'. That view is supported by the many cases of civil war and repression, and by the effects of pan-Arab and pan-Islamic ideologies, both of which offer transnational identities and authorities that can be mobilised against the project to construct national states. It is easy to demonstrate the many deficiencies of the Arab state (in terms of democracy, justice, development). But the fact remains that the Arab state system, unlike the African one, *has* consolidated itself sufficiently both to contain domestic violence and to dominate regional international relations. Hurst (1999: 8) notes the remarkably long tenure of many leaders and political systems in the Middle East. Yapp (1991: 35–46, 411–18, 432) argues that, despite the decades of war and turbulence, the state structures left behind by decolonisation have nearly all survived. Iran and Iraq outlived their long war with each other, and Iraq even survived its catastrophic defeat in the Second Gulf War. Barnett (1998) also argues that the norms and values of sovereignty and national identity have steadily gained ground over pan-Arab alternatives, notwithstanding the sustained use of pan-Arab rhetoric by many Arab leaders to undermine each other's domestic legitimacy by appealing to the Arab 'street'.

Nevertheless, while the state framework is dominant in the Middle East, it does not go unchallenged from the domestic level, where a number of substate entities have played significantly on the regional and global levels as securitising actors. Most notable among these have been Palestinian and Kurdish organisations. Of the two main exceptions to the general rule of state primacy, the Israeli–Palestinian conflict is the main one. It is a domestic conflict that is in some ways the key to the whole Middle Eastern RSC. In that sense, the Israeli–Palestinian conflict is comparable to that within apartheid South Africa, where a domestic level security conflict within a regional power projected its influence into a whole region and became the defining dynamic for an RSC. Palestinian refugees became a domestic problem in Lebanon and Jordan, and the Israeli–Palestinian struggle became the main driving force of the antagonism between Israel and the wider Arab and Islamic worlds. The fact that Jerusalem, the third holiest site of Islam, was ensnared in the Israeli–Palestinian conflict gave Palestinian organisations wider and deeper support then they would have received just for being a symbol of the oppression of the Arabs (Piscatori 1991b: 5–6). The other exception is the Kurds, a substantial non-Arab population of more than 25 million divided among Turkey, Syria, Iran, and Iraq, and also internally divided into frequently feuding clans and insurgency movements. All four states ruthlessly suppressed their Kurds, and during the Cold War the main room for manoeuvre that remained to the latter was created by interstate rivalries. Thus Iran and Iraq supported each other's Kurds, and Syria supported Kurds in Turkey.

As Piscatori (1991b) argues, the cross-currents of Arab nationalism, Islamism, anti-Zionism, and anti-Westernism blur across the domestic and regional levels in complicated, contradictory, and often potent ways, affecting attitude and opinion both in the streets and among the ruling elites. During the Second Gulf War, for example, Saddam Hussein managed to cast himself quite successfully as an Islamic (and Arab) hero for the whole Middle East by playing to anti-Israel and anti-Western sentiments. This was despite the long anti-Islamic record of his regime, his attack on an Arab neighbour, and the transparently instrumental nature of his rapid conversion to Islamic rhetoric. While Saddam may have been stunningly inept at playing the global media, at the regional level his exploitation of symbols and his ability to link his cause to the Palestinian one were skilful. By contrast, the Gulf Arabs were unable to translate their large financial subsidies for Islamist movements into popular support, and instead were tainted by their dependence on Western military power, and their allowing forces seen as anti-Islamic, anti-Arab, and pro-Israel into the heartland of Islam. Thus while pan-Islam and pan-Arab ideas failed to supplant or threaten the state system in the Middle East, they nonetheless powerfully affected how that state system operated.

The domestic and regional levels also played into each other as governments supporting domestic factions in other states: Libya, and after 1979 Iran, supporting radical movements, and Saudi Arabia conservative and Islamic ones. The activities of quite a few substate organisations such as Hamas, Islamic Jihad, Hizbollah, elements of the Jewish religious right, and of course the PLO have been an important element in the security dynamics surrounding Israel. In Lebanon, various factions and militias have found outside sponsors. In the Gulf, local Shi'a groups have had links with Iran. Some aspects of regional (and indeed global) politics became domestic, most notably in the problem of 'Afghani' returnees, who brought US-funded military training, Islamic militancy, and combat experience from the war against the Soviet Union back to their own countries. The Afghanis formed a transnational network of militant Arabs, alienated from both their own states and the West and available for recruitment into al-Qaeda and other radical Islamist organisations (Asaria et al. 2001). More generally, the insecurity of most regimes in the Middle East spills over into regional security politics. The GCC, for example, is as much a means of reinforcing the domestic security of a set of anachronistic monarchical regimes as an alliance against external threats (Acharya 1992). Of wider application is the importance of the struggle against Israel for the domestic legitimacy of many regimes in the region. This issue reinforces the pan-regional identities in linking the domestic and regional levels of security dynamics. Arab nationalist, Islamist, and Zionist sentiments at the level of the 'street' have generated serious domestic resistance in many states to Arab–Israeli deals. It is questionable, for example, whether Sadat and King Hussein would have been able to make deals with Israel if their countries had been democracies, and not a few regimes in the region fear that a resolution of the conflict with Israel will leave their domestic security problems at the top of the agenda. Such fears affect the whole peace process, and thus connect the domestic, regional, and global levels.

The global level

The global level operated strongly in the Middle East during this period. In effect, the region became a third front in the Cold War, after Europe and Asia, and its oil resources tied it powerfully into the global economy. After the break-up of the Ottoman Empire, the dominant penetrating powers became Britain and France and, to a lesser extent, Italy, the Soviet Union, and Germany. Britain and in some places France remained the dominant outside powers up until the mid-1950s. But the exposure of their weakness in the Suez fiasco in 1956, plus the gathering pace of decolonisation and the French defeat in Algeria, had by the early 1960s reduced them to marginal players.

Given the crosscutting complexities of internal alignments in the Middle East, it is difficult to trace a clear Cold War pattern of great power intervention. The British and French roles in the creation of Israel (widely seen in the Arab and Islamic worlds as an extension of Western colonialism), and the desire of some Arab governments (notably the Hashemite monarchies in Jordan and Iraq) to maintain close security relations with Britain and France, did play a role in defining the anti-Western elements of Arabism (Barnett 1998: 108–29). The fact that the state system was largely a creation of disliked colonial powers, and could be understood as a conscious breaking-up of Arab unity, exacerbated the difficulty of making the new states legitimate in the eyes of their citizens. And, although the metropolitan powers withdrew, Western oil companies remained closely tied into the local political economies.

The United States and the Soviet Union were latecomers as major players in Middle Eastern regional security, though the former had long-standing oil interests there. The two superpowers were drawn into a pattern of regional turbulence that was already strongly active. Their interest in the region was heightened by the fact that, like Europe, the Middle East sat on the boundary between the spheres of the communist and 'free' worlds. Stalin's aggressive policy after 1945 had pushed Turkey and Iran into the arms of the West. Turkey became a member of NATO, and was thus fixed into the main European front of the Cold War. Until the Islamic revolution in 1979, Iran fell increasingly under American sway, not only through corporate oil interests, but also as part of the loose alliance arrangements that connected American containment clients in Turkey, Iran, and Pakistan. To counter this US success right on its borders, the Soviet Union tried to play in the Arab world behind this front line, by establishing political and military links to the radical regimes and movements that sprang up in the Middle East during the 1950s and 1960s (Syria, PLO, Iraq, Egypt, Libya, Algeria, Yemen) (Yapp 1991: 411–18).

Although drawn into the Gulf by its oil investments, and into Turkey and Iran by containment policy, the USA was a reluctant entrant into the wider Middle East. It had no real interest in the numerous local disputes, but the nature of its economic (oil) and political (anti-communist) engagements inevitably entangled it closely in the domestic politics of its clients. The United States could not ignore Soviet successes during the 1950s and 1960s in arming the radical Arabs behind the containment front line. Having itself exposed the weakness of Britain and France in 1956, thus hastening their departure from the region, the United States was drawn into the vacuum. To the extent that Soviet successes had linked communism and Arab radicalism in US thinking, Israel's resounding success in the 1967 war established its usefulness to the USA as a local ally capable of defeating Soviet clients (Yapp 1991: 411–18). Thereafter, and despite the waning of Soviet influence in the region after 1967, and even more so after 1973, the United States became increasingly tied into the fate of Israel, not least through the influence of the Jewish lobby in Washington. Since being allied to Israel tended to put it at odds with the Arab and Islamic states, the United States found itself in a bind in relation to the pursuit of its oil interests, which required good relations with the Gulf Arabs, Iran, Iraq, Libya, and Algeria. The oil crisis of the 1970s, with its implications for the stability of the whole Western political economy, also consolidated American engagement in the region. These contradictory commitments, plus a basic lack of interest in the local conflicts, made it almost impossible for the United States to have a coherent Middle East policy, even though it was increasingly the main outside player in the region. Only its huge power and wealth enabled it to sustain these contradictions.

Although both superpowers poured a lot of resources into the Middle East, neither ever established much control over the behaviour of its clients. Both frequently found themselves at the mercy of domestic and/or regional dynamics. One example is when they lost control of the events leading up to the 1973 war, the Soviets even being expelled (in 1972) from an Egypt they had just rearmed. Others are the chronic inability of the United States to control either Israeli policy towards the Palestinians, or Arab and Iranian policies towards the price of oil, and the inability of either superpower to do much about the war between Iran and Iraq. Both superpowers were at the mercy of the often-fractious domestic politics of the Middle Eastern states, finding themselves either invited in or thrown out as a result of changes in regime. The coming of radical secular governments favoured the Soviet Union. The maintenance of traditional monarchies favoured the USA. Neither superpower was particularly scrupulous about the ideological rectitude of its allies in the region. The arrival of Islamic fundamentalists, as most spectacularly in Iran in 1979, favoured neither, even though the Soviets had the pleasure of seeing the United States lose one of its key allies in the Gulf. Both superpowers tried to meddle in the domestic politics of the region, but neither achieved anything approaching durable control over either the domestic or the regional security dynamics of the Middle East.

It is difficult to discern clear patterns of relationship between superpower penetration and regional dynamics, although Miller (2000) claims to see regional dynamics as being more determinative of hot war and warm peace, and global dynamics as being more determinative of cold war and cold peace. There was some clarity in the peripheral subcomplex in the Maghreb, where the Soviets armed Libya and Algeria, while the United States supported Morocco. But in the two central subcomplexes, with their crosscutting alignments and enmities, coherence was almost impossible. In the earlier years of the Arab–Israeli conflict, the Soviet Union backed most of the Arab frontline states, and the United States (after 1967) backed Israel (and also Jordan). But this picture blurred after 1973, with Egypt shifting to the United States. Egypt then joined Israel as a regular recipient of US aid: some $2 billion a year since the late 1970s (Gerges 1999: 113). This Egyptian shift effectively prevented the formation of an Arab coalition against Israel. In the Gulf, only the US position among the Gulf Arab states has remained at all stable. Its position in Iran crashed in 1979. The interplay with Iraq has been the most convoluted of all. Iraq was a Western client under the monarchy, but then shifted more towards the Soviet Union after the military coup in 1958. Thereafter it oscillated, sometimes drawing support from both superpowers, as in the First Gulf War, and sometimes from neither, as in the Second. Soviet support for Iraq was useful inasmuch as Baghdad challenged American clients in the Middle East, but problematic in the context of its rivalry with another Soviet client, Syria. The USA faced the same problem in supporting Iraq against Iran, but opposing it vis-à-vis the Gulf Arabs and Israel. Soviet attitudes towards post-1979 Iran faced similarly twisted choices. On the one hand Iran should be supported because of its anti-US stand. On the other, Iran's own power ambitions and its Islamic propaganda were in themselves a threat to the Soviet empire and, after 1992, to Russia's interests in the Caucasus and Central Asia.

There can be no doubt that massive influxes of oil money, armaments, and aid to key regional players from the global level impacted strongly on the Middle Eastern RSC. The superpowers raised the overall level of military capability in the region, mostly by arms transfers, occasionally by putting their own forces into play. They changed the distribution of power (most obviously in favour of Israel). They enabled rapid rearmaments after wars. They sustained authoritarian regimes in many countries, and sometimes produced shifts of alignment. Yet, despite all this, superpower intervention neither controlled the Middle East nor played more than a marginal role in shaping the powerful military-political security dynamics at the regional level.

The interregional level

In contrast with the other levels, and in line with the expectations of RSCT, the interregional level for the Middle East is quite marginal to the overall configuration of the security constellation. There was quite a lot of activity across the frontier zone between the Middle East and Africa, but this was a largely one-way relationship with influence flowing from the Middle East into Africa, and not much coming the other way. There were also some security links between Pakistan and both Iran and Saudi Arabia, reinforced by shared linkages to the United States at the global level. But these links were never of such an extent even to begin to blur the boundary between the essentially distinct security dynamics of these two regions. The one relationship that might have merged the security dynamics of the Middle East and South Asia, an alliance between India and Israel against Pakistan's project for an 'Islamic bomb', never amounted to more than rumour.

In sum, the regional security dynamics of the Middle Eastern RSC were exceptionally strong, and deeply rooted in the character of local politics and history. The impact of the global level was also strong, but the superpowers and their ideological rivalry did not, as in Southeast Asia, strongly shape the regional patterns. Since most of the conflicts within the region were not primarily about Cold War issues, it is no surprise that they survived the ending of the Cold War largely unchanged, albeit within a regional structure that was significantly affected by the outcome of the Second Gulf War.

The post-Cold War peace process and its failure

The post-Cold War era in the Middle East can be conveniently dated from the Second Gulf War in 1990–1. This war, and its long historical shadow, changed some of the basic structures of the Middle Eastern RSC and its component subcomplexes. Its main consequences were:

- It weakened Iraq militarily in relation to its neighbours, thus changing the distribution of power in the Gulf subcomplex, though not altering the basic triangular structure of the rivalry in the Gulf.
- It strengthened the position of the Western powers, and especially the United States, in the GCC states, making them more explicitly into protectorates. The replacement of a failed US policy of balancing in the Gulf with one of 'dual containment' of Iran and Iraq increased the relative weight of global factors in the security dynamics of the Gulf.
- It opened the way for the beginning of the peace process between Israel on the one hand and the Palestinians, Jordan, and

Syria, as well as some of the more peripheral Arab states, on the other.

- By opening the possibility of a resolution to the Israeli–Palestinian problem, the peace process weakened the link between the five Maghreb states and the rest of the Middle Eastern RSC. The Maghreb states were not strongly engaged in Gulf security, and supported neither Iraq nor the intervention against it.

- Finally, by using Arabist rhetoric to justify annexing another Arab country, Saddam's venture struck another heavy blow to pan-Arabism. This helped both to strengthen the consolidation of the Westphalian state system and to hand the high ground of radical politics to the Islamists.

These effects of the Second Gulf War were reinforced by the demise of Soviet military and political support for its former clients in the region. The level of global intervention into the Middle Eastern RSC did not decline, but its character changed radically. Instead of projecting a bipolar superpower rivalry into the region, reinforcing its internal lines of conflict, global intervention took a unipolar form, with a dominant United States using its influence to dampen the interstate (but not intra-state) conflictual security dynamics of both core subcomplexes.

The question for the 1990s was whether the peace process was going to change the whole security constellation of the Middle East permanently. By mid-2002, the peace process looked much more like a temporary phase, with the regional conflict dynamics reasserting themselves strongly. US efforts at peacemaking (Levant) and conflict suppression (Gulf) did not succeed in transforming the regional level dynamics for the long term. During the 1990s, global level intervention in the region largely ceased to amplify local interstate conflict, while playing a considerably stronger role in repressing and moderating the indigenous regional conflict formation. It created a possibility that the Middle East might move towards a less intense type of conflict formation. This was not overlay in the classic sense, though in the Gulf it had some of the military presence, and alignment effects, of overlay. It was an impressive display of hegemonic global level leverage on a strong set of regional conflict dynamics (B. Hansen 2000).

Yet while dampening interstate conflict, the US intervention increased the stresses within many states, most obviously Saudi Arabia and Egypt. Most Arab states were, in any case, under internal pressure from weak economies, burgeoning populations, dysfunctional education systems, and political disaffection from the regimes (Sayigh 2002). Those associated with the United States could not avoid being tainted by its bad image in the Arab street and, unlike the United States, they did not have the resources to cope with the contradictions that oil and Israel embedded in US policy. It did not seem unreasonable to argue that contempt for and frustration with the failures and sellouts of the Arab governing elites played a significant role in legitimising the purveyors of international terrorism among the Arab peoples. For its part, the United States was burdened by an unenviable collection of 'assets': Israel, with a seemingly bottomless talent for making enemies of its neighbours; Saudi Arabia, a corrupt autocracy with a long record of supporting Islamic militants; and Egypt, likewise corrupt and undemocratic, and riddled with political tensions.

The Gulf

Because it changed both the nature of global level intervention and the local distribution of power, the defeat of Iraq in 1991 was probably more important than the demise of the Soviet Union in shaping subsequent developments in the Gulf. It set in train four sequences of events that largely defined the security dynamics in the Gulf throughout the 1990s and to some extent into the twenty-first century.

First, it put sustained internal and external pressure on the domestic security of Saddam Hussein's regime. The war was followed by uprisings in Kurdistan and the south, both ruthlessly suppressed by Saddam Hussein's forces. Iran, Turkey, and the USA all played militarily and politically into the ever-fractious politics of the Kurds and, although a quasi-autonomous Kurdish enclave was sustained in the north, this has not so far showed any sign of threatening Saddam's hold over the rest of the country. The war precipitated an ongoing string of bloody but unsuccessful coup and assassination attempts against Saddam and his family, often encouraged by the United States, and even bloodier reprisals by Saddam.

Second, the indecisive outcome of the war, caused by the unwillingness of the coalition to do much more than liberate Kuwait and degrade Saddam's military strength, resulted in the United States shifting from its frustrating and failed policy of balancing to so-called dual containment of Iraq and Iran. Dual containment has become deeply embedded in US domestic politics and, given the mutual hostility of Iran and Iraq on the one side, and Israel on the other, has helped tie together the two core subcomplexes in the Middle East (Sick 1998: 6–10, 22). So long as oil makes the Gulf a prize for decades to come, the domestic consensus in the United States on maintaining a strong military presence there is likely to remain firm (Kemp 1998–9).

Third, the war weakened Iraq in relation to its neighbours, and strengthened the position of Iran. It initiated a sustained process of UN hunting-down and dismantling of Iraq's weapons of mass destruction (WMD), and a cat-and-mouse game between Iraq and the UN Security Council. This process achieved substantial but not total success before it broke down in 1998, followed by the USA and Britain resuming their controversial air patrols and bombardments. Although far from disarmed, Iraq no longer possessed the military capability to mount invasions of its larger neighbours, and its military movements were closely watched. It might have retained some retaliatory capability in the form of hidden missiles and CB weapons, and was widely thought to be rebuilding its capabilities for WMD.

Iran played a studiously neutral role during the war, and was a main beneficiary of the weakening of Iraq. In 1993 Iran made several air strikes into Iraq against mujahiddin forces based there, but diplomatic relations between Tehran and Baghdad nonetheless improved. Both opposed the peace process between Israel and the PLO and the intrusive US role in the Gulf, and from 1993 both were the objects of US 'dual containment'. Iran got to keep the 100-plus warplanes flown there by Iraq during the war, and took the opportunity to strengthen its military position by making major arms purchases from China and the Soviet Union/Russia, and working on its own missile and WMD programmes. Freed from the Iraqi threat, Iran could allow itself to get diplomatically drawn into Central Asia by the break-up of the Soviet Union in 1992. In that year it also got involved in the revival of an old dispute with the UAE dating from 1971 over the sovereignty of the Tumb Islands and Abu Musa. This raised tensions between Iran and the UAE (and the GCC), and undermined Iran's objective of placing itself at the centre of an anti-Western regional security regime (*Strategic Survey* 1992–3: 121–2). The lines of tension between Iran and the GCC remained active throughout much of the decade (Chubin and Tripp 1996), though diminishingly so. Adding to the regional tensions were the facts of the GCC's more overt dependence on US military support and Iran's continued hostility to all things American. Another factor was the rival Iranian and Saudi positions in Afghanistan, where they supported different factions in the ongoing Afghan civil war. But, towards the end of the 1990s, Iran's domestic politics began to mellow, and the country had some success in desecuritising its relations with the Gulf Arabs. By 1998 it had explicitly withdrawn its support for the Shi'a opposition in Bahrain, and generally abandoned overt policies of exporting its revolution. Iran continued to oppose the US presence in the Gulf even though it was primarily the United States that kept Iraq weak to Iran's advantage.

Fourth, the Second Gulf War pushed the GCC states into something like protectorate status vis-à-vis the West and particularly the United States. The Gulf states flirted briefly with Egypt and Syria (the major Arab participants in the anti-Iraq coalition) but quickly concluded that bilateral linkages with the Western powers plus rearmament provided a 'less intrusive form of security arrangement than anything offered by their Arab allies'(*Strategic Survey* 1991–2: 101). Ongoing fear of Iran and Iraq meant that the GCC leaders stuck as close to their Western allies as domestic opinion would allow. Following the war, many of the Gulf Arab states, but particularly Saudi Arabia and Kuwait, placed very substantial orders for military equipment from the United States, Britain, and France (Cordesman 1997: 26–9). Saudi Arabia and the United States agreed closely on the policy of dual containment against both Iran and Iraq (Chubin and Tripp 1996: 21–2), and many of the GCC states were prepared to lower their previous sensitivities to overt military collaboration with the West, such as prepositioning of equipment. But Saudia Arabia's qualified support of the USA during the 2001 war in Afghanistan demonstrated that a direct threat like Iraq's was necessary for the regime to pay the price of open alignment with the USA, whereas even a political threat like bin Laden's who aimed as much at Saudi Arabia as the USA was dealt with by domestic repression rather than international action (Gause 2001). And while the GCC retained its dependence on the West, its internal cohesion, never strong, deteriorated. There were disagreements over attitude towards Iraq, over old territorial disputes, over clan politics and meddling in each other's sometimes turbulent internal affairs, and over liberalising moves in some of the sheikhdoms. The September 2001 terror and a possible US attack on Iraq spurred a debate in the West about the viability of Western alignment with thoroughly undemocratic regimes in the Gulf and the relationship between democratisation and stability in the long and the short term respectively.

In the light of 11 September, it now seems clear that a fifth, less visible sequence of events was embedded in this fourth one: the construction of the al-Qaeda network in response particularly to the US military presence in Saudi Arabia, but more generally in reaction to the enhanced US role in Middle Eastern politics as a whole (see box).

Islamic terrorism and the USA

The terrorist attacks against US cities on 11 September 2001 raised a number of questions for RSCT. In chapter 10, we discuss the implications for the US security outlook, and in chapters 2, 10, and 14 the impact on global patterns. A major question, however, is whether the action as such is a case – then a major one – of deterritorialised security transcending and thus questioning the regional structure. Can the activities of bin Laden's al-Qaeda and related organisations be located within a regional context, or is it a global level phenomenon qua direct interaction with the United States?

How do the terrorists securitise: exactly what is presented as an existential threat to what and how does that set the parameters for meaningful action? One can reach two different conclusions dependent on approaching the question by tracing the theological and philosophical roots of bin Laden's worldview, or reading his statements. This tension is the key to understanding Islamist terror. Islamism as such is characterised by its reaction to the modern trauma of Islam's fall from centuries of superiority to defeat and encroachment by the West (Lewis 1982: 39–57; Hodgson 1993: 224; Pipes 2000; Mozaffari 2002). Western ways have to be replaced by life fully in accordance with the Shari'a, the sacred law. Despite this rejection of Western influence, Islamic fundamentalists appropriate much from the West. They defend their religion 'by crafting new methods, formulating new ideologies, and adopting the latest processes and organizational structures' (Almond et al. 1995: 402). This is because fundamentalism is securitisation: fundamentalists are defensive and present true faith as seriously threatened. Consequently, it is not enough to be a conservative or a traditionalist, because effective defence demands much more radical measures, more innovative ways of fighting back (Almond et al. 1995; Juergensmeyer 1993; Laustsen and Wæver 2000).

This first step is generally valid for a wide variety of groups. To find the terrorists of 2001, we have to focus on a specific 'track' within this larger group of fundamentalists. Mawlana Mawdudi (founder of Pakistan's Jamaat-i-Islami party) started in the 1930s to advocate jihad against al-Jahiliyyah (those in ignorance). In the Quran this term referred to the ignorance of the Arabs before Islam, but Mawdudi extended it to all non-Muslims, and Sayyid Qutb of the Muslim Brotherhood in Egypt included Muslim societies and rulers who had strayed from the right course (Jansen 1997: 49–74; Euben 1999: 49–92; Bahadur 2000; Juergensmeyer 2000: 79–83). The errors by the elite in the Islamic world were so severe that the few acting in truth had to rebuild Islam from a small core, just like the prophet himself (Kepel 2002: 16–17, 318).

According to this analysis Islamic societies have been the target of a military, economic, and cultural onslaught from the West. Qutb presented 'a warning alarm about the fate of humankind in the thrall of a materialist civilization, devoid of faith and human spirit – the white man's civilization' (quoted in Euben 1999: 49). This appeal fulfils the criteria outlined in chapter 1 (p. 8) for being a direct securitisation of global level phenomena, of globalisation of Western civilisation as such. Accordingly, it is possible to aim violent action at any expression of the West without demanding any specific link to a particular cause. In theory, being already at war with the West/United States legitimises more or less any action. However, in practice most activists offer a more specific explanation why, e.g., the United States is co-responsible for the issue this particular group is attending to in, say, Egypt, Lebanon, or India (Juergensmeyer 2000: 178–82).

If we turn to bin Laden's few but in some cases elaborate (pre-2001) statements and appeals (bin Laden 1996a, 1996b, 1998; bin Laden et al. 1998), we see that these are directed against 'the Zionist–Crusader alliance under the leadership of the USA', who occupy Jerusalem and especially 'the land of the two holy places', i.e., Saudi Arabia with Mecca and Medina. As a consequence, the Saudi regime has lost legitimacy and Saudi Arabia is 'a huge volcano at the verge of eruption'. A second track that underpins this analysis is the way the 'Zionist–Crusader alliance' has silenced 'the scholars (Ulama) and callers (Da'ees) of Islam': i.e., those speaking the truth have been kept from explaining things, and thus even the failings on the side of the Muslim world are not solely of their own making but due to US manipulations. 'All these crimes and sins committed by the Americans are a clear declaration of war on God, his messenger, and

Muslims...Nothing is more sacred than belief except repulsing an enemy who is attacking religion and life.' The most important duty is to push American troops out of Saudi Arabia. Due to the actual correlation of forces, one has to pick 'suitable means of fighting', i.e., guerrilla warfare (women's contribution is to boycott American goods).

In contrast to the widespread assumption that bin Laden's act is desperate or 'irrational', he presents a rational strategic vision: he explains that the Americans are sufficiently cowardly that they actually can be terrorised away, as seen e.g. in Lebanon and Somalia.

Thus, the 1998 joint fatwa with other radicals (in what they call the 'World Islamic Front') declares that 'to kill the Americans and their allies – civilians and military – is an individual duty for every Muslim who can do it in any country in which it is possible to do it'. It is legitimate to terrorise the United States – to 'kill the Americans and plunder their money wherever and whenever they find it' – *as long as the United States is in Saudi Arabia*. But bin Laden's vision reaches beyond liberating the sanctities of Islam, because he believes that doing this will lead towards a unification of the Umma (the whole community of the Muslim faithful).

Thus, within the broader tradition of ultra-radical Islamism, there are modes of securitising that could make the relationship to the United States a direct one. Globalisation and the very existence of the West and the United States would be the threat. On the other hand, the actors that so far seem to have gone furthest in actually attacking the United States 'at home' do not base their actions directly on this logic. They have primarily securitised the US presence in Saudi Arabia and, secondarily, the alliance between the United States and certain Arab regimes. If the relationship is seen as one primarily between the United States and bin Laden and his closest colleagues (such as the 'World Islamic Front'), it is a part of the Middle Eastern RSC – it is about the US penetration of the region. However, as a confrontation develops between these two nodes in the RSC, it is possible that other groups will mobilise who take the former way of securitisation and thus target the United States (and the West) for its very being and what it represents in the world.

Strategically, these two securitisations could have different implications, because the bin Laden type could in principle at least be dealt with by adjusting US policy towards the region, whereas the abstract one is impossible to handle short of closing down capitalism, global-isation, and the whole global, 'Westernistic' civilisation (Buzan and Segal 1998).

The actions of bin Laden are not closely linked to the faltering peace process between Israelis and Palestinians. However, as expressed by bin Laden's authorised biographer, Hamad Mir, Osama bin Laden is 'the main beneficiary' of Muslim fury over what some perceive to be the United States' blind support for Israel against the Palestini-ans, transforming him into a cult hero (Lakshmanan 2001). He has previously attacked Americans at times of progress in Palestine, and he mentions it only a few times in his declarations (after September 2001, however, he opportunistically emphasised Palestine). Thus, a harsher Western policy on Israel is unlikely to influence bin Laden (see Ajami 2001: 15–16, 27; Berger and Sutphen 2001), but it might determine how many new terrorists will be recruited in a new spiral of escalation between the USA and Islamic fundamentalists. Some other groups like Hamas and Hizbollah are obviously focused more on the Palestine question, but their actions, too, are so far directed at the local actors.

These three distinct focal points of securitisation can be tied to-gether in chains of interacting securitisations with the United States and other external actors. However, the most radical actions so far and those that on the face of it seemed most anti-regionalist are very strictly linked to a regional issue: US troops in Saudi Arabia. The cosmic securitisation that links the United States and Middle Eastern radicals directly is attractive to theorists but, for practitioners like bin Laden, securitisation is easier with a concrete object. Such specific se-curitisation draws on the deeper layer of general securitisation, but it will most likely continue to be mobilised around concrete referents. In practice, this means that Islamic terrorism is likely to reappear reg-ularly. It is equally misleading to represent Islam as such as pointing towards such actions (Armstrong 2001) and to imagine that the prob-lem is over once bin Laden's network is crushed. There is widespread support in the region (and beyond, in the non-Middle Eastern Islamic countries) for a way of thinking that leads to a sense of existential threat and a justification for radical action. Rather than erupting into total and indiscriminate war against the West, this forms a platform from which new terrorist movements are likely to emerge – some as a reaction to the reaction to bin Laden.

In RSCT terms, the bin Laden attack is mostly a product of an interplay between regional–global dynamics (the US penetration of the Middle Eastern RSC) and an insulator (the availability of a base because Afghanistan had previously – as long as the interaction capacity of nonstate actors was lower – served most purposes well as an insulating zone of chaos; more on this in chapter 15). Thus, key categories of RSCT explain the phenomenon better than a globalised interpretation in which Bush and bin Laden are seen as meeting directly in a global arena.

Arab–Israel

In the Arab–Israel subcomplex, the demise of the Soviet Union carried more weight than in the Gulf because it took the Soviet Union out of the game of lavish arms supply to Israel's enemies, particularly Syria. It increased US influence in the subcomplex and weakened Syria's military position vis-à-vis Israel, though consolidating Syria's grip on Lebanon. The combination of Soviet withdrawal plus the Second Gulf War paved the way for the peace process, which dominated the security dynamics in this subcomplex through the rest of the 1990s. As part of the inducement to form the anti-Iraq coalition, the United States promised its Arab allies that it would work harder on solving the Arab–Israeli problem, and the administration of the first President Bush was prepared to take a tougher line with Israel on the settlements issue (*Strategic Survey* 1991–2: 85; Barnett 1998: 221). As in the Gulf, only more so because of the diplomatic entanglements of the peace process, heightened US influence in the region served to temporarily suppress most of the interstate conflict dynamics. It had much less restraining effect on substate actors, particularly Hamas and Hizbollah, and also on the domestic level, where, as in the Gulf, it worsened domestic tensions.

A detailed account of many ups and downs of the peace process is beyond the scope of this chapter. Key highlights were:

- the 1993 Oslo Accords, which put Israel–PLO relations on a more direct footing, and opened the way for a Palestinian statelet;
- the 1994 Israel–Jordan Peace Treaty, which protected both Jordan and the Palestinians against domestically destabilising forced exoduses of Palestinians caused by Israeli expulsions;
- the 2000 Israeli withdrawal from Southern Lebanon;

- ongoing cycles of violence between the Palestinian *intifadas* and the Israelis, and Israel's refusal to curtail expansion of its settlements;
- the inability of Israel and Syria to agree a settlement on the Golan Heights;
- the wrecking of the Palestinian economy, and eventually of the Palestinian Authority itself, by Israeli measures;
- the failure of various US-sponsored Israeli–Palestinian negotiations.

The pattern of successes and failures was intimately tied to shifts in domestic politics, particularly in Israel and the USA. For a while, the peace process made some significant, if slow and difficult, progress (Jentleson and Kaye 1998). But by 2002 it looked to be in terminal failure, with conflict resumed, hopes dashed, and attitudes of extreme hostility entrenching themselves for the long term (Hollis 2002). As confrontation between Israel and the Palestinians heated up again, so also did the cold war between Israel and the wider circle of Arab and Islamic states. The unfolding of events after 11 September added a further layer of problems to all this. Not only did the Palestine question complicate the USA's task in putting together and maintaining a supporting coalition for the 'war against terrorism', but the events also raised in a particularly difficult way the question of overall US support for Israel in the context of a catastrophic breakdown of the peace process. Israel's attempts to identify its own situation with the 'war against terrorism' exposed all of the most awkward aspects of the 'terrorist/freedom fighter' dilemma. The Bush administration's acceptance of Israel's interpretation hugely amplified the hatred and frustration felt towards the United States on the Arab street. The United States found itself in an almost impossible political position, where it could not be seen to be meeting any of al-Qaeda's demands, but was under strong pressure to do something to invalidate the terrorists' charges against it. It was all too easy for radicals to blame the United States for everything, and the highly charged atmosphere made it difficult for the Americans to reflect on their own position and objectives. The USA got little credit for being the only agency attempting to control the region's conflicts, and many brickbats (some deserved) for its way of handling matters. It got even less help from the disputing parties in trying to put the peace process back on track.

Adding to the difficulty of the military-political issues, but not determining them, lay the large, long-term problem of water. Unlike in the Gulf, where water issues affected only a secondary relationship (Turkey-Syria-Iraq), in the Levant they were at the heart not only of Israel–Palestine relations (mostly about sharing aquifers) but also of Israel's relations with Jordan, Syria, and Lebanon, and Jordan's with Syria (*Strategic Survey* 1998–9: 270–1). In February 1996, Israel, Jordan, and the Palestinians agreed a Declaration of Principles for Cooperation on Water-Related Matters. Whether this would solve the very difficult long-term problems about sharing the region's limited supplies of river and ground water remained to be seen. Water rights issues complicated both Israel's withdrawal from Lebanon and its negotiations with Syria over returning the Golan Heights (both significant sources of Israel's current water supply), not to mention the creation of a separate Palestinian state. Particularly for Israel, the Palestinians, and Jordan, water rights could easily be constructed as an existential issue.

Despite its failure, the 1990s peace process changed the political landscape of this subcomplex, perhaps permanently. The creation of a Palestinian statelet and the peace with Jordan put in place two necessary elements for building a security regime in the future. Whether either of these would survive Israel's demolition of the Palestinian Authority during 2002 remained an open question. With both Israel (settlements, state terrorism) and the Palestinians (political incoherence, transnational terrorism) busily sowing dragon's teeth, the prospect for a Westphalian solution to their problem looked bleak. The events since 1991 increased the cross linkages between the Gulf and Arab–Israel subcomplexes, a process almost certainly given further impetus by the 'war against terrorism'. This was not only because of the increased prominence of the United States in both, but also because of increased Iranian and Iraqi involvement in the confrontation against Israel as well as the networks woven by al-Qaeda.

A further (and also US-related) development in this subcomplex was the re-engagement of Turkey in the Middle East. This perhaps began with Turkey's participation in the US-led war against Iraq, but the main development has been a 'strategic partnership' between Israel and Turkey with Jordan as a shadow partner (Buzan and Diez 1999; Nachmani 1999: 19–29; Jung and Piccoli 2000; Piccoli 1999; Inbar 2001; Kazan 2002). This is not an alliance: neither state has taken on obligations to defend the other. But it is certainly a significant alignment, and is seen as such by the Arab states and Iran, who take it as aimed against them. Israel and Turkey have no historical difficulties between them, and share opposition to both Islamic fundamentalism and the proliferation of WMD. They share antagonisms against Syria, Iraq, and Iran. They are also both Westernistic states with problematic relations with the EU, but which have close ties to the United States. Since 1996 they have developed a wide range of overt military cooperations including intelligence exchanges, joint training, and quite extensive arms trade. Their military needs and capabilities are complementary across a wide range. They have moved closer on questions of counterterrorism and Greek–Turkish disputes. Each relieves the other's isolation, and together they make a stronger presence in Washington. This partnership almost certainly played a role in Turkey's threats to resort to force against Syria in 1998, which got Syrian compliance in downgrading support for Turkey's Kurds and expelling the PKK leader Abdulla Öcalan. Turkey's extensive dam-building projects on the Tigris and Euphrates are also increasing its leverage on Syria and Iraq, and its water riches may yet play a part in solving (or exacerbating) the region's water problems. Turkey's re-engagement with the Middle East during the 1990s raised questions about the shape of the Middle Eastern RSC, on which more below.

Maghreb

During the 1990s the subcomplexes in the Gulf and the Levant became more closely entangled with each other. By contrast, the Maghreb subcomplex drifted away from the core, relating less to Arab issues, and becoming more like an independent RSC in its own right. It also came more under the sway of the EU, recreating pre-Cold War patterns of alignment, albeit in new forms (Joffe 2000; Haddadi 1999). The Maghreb countries were more or less neutral during the Second Gulf War. Mostly, they were marginal players in the Arab–Israeli peace process, though Morocco did play a significant role in making the opening to Israel. Confrontation with Israel gave them a role, and bound them into the wider Middle Eastern RSC, but a drift towards peace had the opposite effect. Libya's mercurial leader even declared openly his disillusion with Arab causes, ostentatiously turning his foreign policy towards Africa (Huliaris 2001). Cultural and religious ties to the Middle East of course remained, but security interdependence, never as strong as between the two core subcomplexes, largely dropped away (Gause 1999: 25). The Maghreb countries became more preoccupied with their own domestic security affairs, and more concerned about their economic relations with an EU whose deepening and widening moves threatened their principal trade ties. Domestically there was rising concern about

Islamist insurgencies, particularly in Algeria, where a vicious civil war caused perhaps 100,000 deaths, demonstrating again the ability of Middle Eastern regimes to defeat Islamic insurgents militarily, while they still failed to integrate state and civil society. There was also heavy repression against Islamists in Tunisia and Egypt. Under this pressure, the Islamists divided into conflicting factions and degenerated into terrorism within their own communities (Gerges 1999).

One parallel between the Maghreb subcomplex and those in the core was the muting of its interstate conflict dynamics under outside pressure. Since independence, the Maghreb subsystem had been a conflict formation, albeit at low levels of interstate violence. But the EU's Single European Act (SEA) of 1986, and the economic threat that this was seen to pose to the Maghreb states' heavy economic dependence on Europe, forced a general shift from balance-of-power relations towards a collective focus on Europe (Cammett 1999). In 1988, Libya and Tunisia, and Algeria and Morocco improved their previously troubled bilateral relations, which paved the way in 1989 for the formation of the Arab Maghreb Union (AMU). The AMU was a specific response to the EU's SEA, and was intended to increase intra-Maghreb economic cooperation, and to enable it to act as a dialogue partner with the EU's southern four (Portugal, Spain, France, Italy). The AMU has not removed political tensions from intra-Maghreb relations, and has not become a strong organisation. But it nevertheless indicates a detachment from the Middle East, and a rise in the EU's influence as an outside power. During the 1990s the Arab–Israeli peace process allowed the Maghreb to move towards becoming a separate RSC strongly influenced by a neighbouring great power. The breakdown of the peace process reasserted the pull of Arab and Islamic symbolism, and thus of the Middle Eastern RSC, but probably not sufficiently to override the increasing attraction from the EU.

Looked at from a European perspective, the strategy is clearly one of interregional boundary management. The EU has made it clear that North Africa is not eligible for membership, but that it is eligible for degrees of economic partnership and aid aimed at stabilising the region so as to prevent it from generating threats of migration, crime, terrorism, and disruptions to oil supply (Hollis 1997: 24–5; 1999). Population in the Middle East has increased fivefold between 1945 and 1995 and rapid growth continues, threatening economic development (Maoz 1997: 27–30; Dervis and Shafik 1998: 507). This animates fears of mass migration, which feed a rhetoric of securitisation in Europe. This rhetoric has perhaps been most explicit in NATO, which has on occasions constructed the South in general and the Middle East in particular as an area of potential threat to which the alliance needs to pay attention (Behnke 1999). This can be interpreted largely as a reflection of US policy which takes a more global angle in contrast to a European regional one (Wæver and Buzan 1999), and a distinction drawn between US engagement in the Eastern Mediterranean and EU dominance in the Western Mediterranean.

Overall, the EU's economic engagement with the Middle East is much larger than that of the United States, but US military-political engagement in the two core subcomplexes gives it the dominant position there. There are policy disagreements between the USA and the EU, most notably over Iran and the Israel–Palestinian issue, with the EU as the main economic supporter of the Palestinians, and generally thought to be pro-Arab in the context of Arab–Israeli conflicts (Hollis 1997: 15). A Euro-Mediterranean Partnership scheme was launched in 1995 at Barcelona, which plans to create a free trade area by 2010. This was an explicit attempt by the EU to address a range of 'soft' security threats from its southern periphery by assuming that liberalising economic measures will not only reduce incentives for migration, but also foster democracy and democratic peace. The rhetoric of 'partnership' conceals both huge economic and political inequality, and a desire by the EU to hold its southern periphery at arm's length (Hollis 1999). This scheme gives the EU only a minor role in the core Middle Eastern subcomplexes, but a major one in the Maghreb. Since the EU's principal concern is to avoid the build-up of problems on its southern border, it is the natural friend of any regime that promises to keep order and promote development in the Maghreb.

Conclusions

Although the Arab–Israeli conflict still remains politically and symbolically central, it is no longer the epicentre of the region's violence. Maoz (1997: 10–15) notes the significant drop in the centrality of the Arab–Israeli conflict to Middle East security in terms of both military and civilian fatalities since the 1980s. This method of measurement ignores the crucial symbolic importance of Israel in Arab and Islamic eyes. But the overall regional fatality figures from 1945 to 1995 (74,000 military and 18,000 civilian fatalities in Arab–Israeli conflicts, 345,000 military and 561,000 civilian in other Middle Eastern conflicts) suggest that other conflicts, both interstate and civil, would carry the RSC even without the Arab–Israeli enmity. So also does the history of inter-Arab rivalry. Indigenous reasons ranging from religious and ideological differences, and disputes over status and leadership, to ethnic, territorial and water rights disputes, provided powerful and durable local sources of conflict and insecurity.

Superimposed on the regional level, and penetrating into it, is a powerful global level. The superpowers were not responsible for generating the local patterns of amity and enmity that drove the Middle Eastern RSC. There would undoubtedly have been a vigorous conflict formation in the Middle East even without interventions from the global level. But they did play into the regional level in three ways. First, and mostly through arms supplies, they shaped the distribution of power and the absolute levels of force available, so tending to sustain, and at times to amplify, the regional dynamics. Second, superpower interventions sometimes significantly suppressed or moderated the regional interstate conflict dynamics, though not the domestic ones. This has been especially true of the USA since the end of the Cold War.

Third, the global level was widely seen within the region as a powerful source of threat in its own right, as well as a source of support in local rivalries. This was not simply a replay of the securitisation of the global political economy common in much of the third world, though elements of that could also be found in the Middle East. In addition, specific elements concerning Islamic culture and Israel were in play. In Arab and Islamic eyes the close linkage of the United States to Israel was a major part of the threat, and there was also a more general cultural fear of, and antagonism towards, the West (or in some cases to communism) vis-à-vis Islamic values. Arab nationalists and Islamists could securitise a Western threat to cultural referent objects more easily than to economic ones.

Lustick (1997) puts a more statist twist on the region's problematic relationship with the West, arguing that one can read the history of this region as a sustained attempt by the Western powers to prevent the reemergence of a Middle Eastern great power. Since the break-up of the Ottoman Empire, the global powers have preserved the fragmentation of the postcolonial state system in the Middle East, and prevented countries such as Iraq and Egypt from becoming the cores of a new imperial aggregation. In this view, the war against Iraq in 1991 was merely the latest example of this policy.

The Middle East fits clearly into the typical pattern of a decolonisation process turning into a conflict formation. As in Africa, many of the postcolonial states had arbitrary boundaries and shallow cultural and political roots, but in the Middle East this condition was exacerbated by the potential of pan-Arab and pan-Islamic ideologies to drain legitimacy away from the new states. Their leadership elites were insecure, and state-building was a major preoccupation. Although its domestic politics have generally been turbulent and non-democratic, they have for the most part been successfully contained within the state system. Of course, in all three subcomplexes, there have been major spillovers from the domestic to the interstate level, carrying with them African-style developments of insurgency movements playing significant security roles. But, except for Lebanon, these have not succeeded, as they often have in Africa, in undermining the state system itself. In general, it has been the political and military dynamics of interstate relations, shaped in some ways by pan-regional identities, that have shaped international (in)security in the Middle East. Other issues are clearly present in the region, most obviously water rights, especially in the Levant and Mesopotamia; and societal (a host of identity issues, both religious and ethnic, affecting minorities, refugees, and migrant workers). As Barnett (1998) argues, political disputes (over the definition and leadership of Arab nationalism) were often more important security issues in Arab states than military threats from other Arab states. But purely military dynamics were to the forefront in relations between Arab and non-Arab states (particularly Israel and Iran), and especially in the Gulf also between Arab states. As a rule, non-traditional security issues have simply been absorbed into the existing framework of interstate rivalries and conflicts. Iraq, Syria, and Turkey, or Israel, Syria, and Jordan, for example, do not attempt to separate their squabbles about water from the ideological and power rivalries that already make their relations hostile.

Overall, the record suggests that a consolidating, if still primitive, Westphalian state system has steadily pulled most other issues into its framework. Arab and Islamic identities have largely made their accommodation with the state, with Islamists focusing more on opposition to their local governing elites than on wider crusades. Water disputes are locked into existing interstate politics. The Sunni–Shi'a split is substantially defined by Iran's relations with the Arabs. The main failures of this process so far have been the Palestinians and the Kurds.

The perennially conflictual character of the Middle East makes it a near perfect example of a classical, state-centric, military-political type RSC. In many ways it is similar in structure and behaviour to early modern Europe, but with two big differences. First, early modern Europe

217

did not have a strong global level intervening in its security dynamics. Second, the crosscutting and mixing of Arab nationalist, Islamic, anti-Zionist, and anti-Western sentiments in the Middle East, not to mention statist concerns and regime interests, have meant that balance-of-power policies for both the local states and intervening powers have been extraordinarily difficult to operate. In the Middle East it is difficult for any actor, whether local or global, to support another against a shared enemy without at the same time threatening a friendly third party. The USA, for example, could not support Iraq against Iran without strengthening Iraq against Israel. Neither could it destroy Iraq without advancing the cause of its enemy Iran against its Gulf Arab allies: a problem that dogs the plans of the second Bush administration to get rid of Saddam. Saudi Arabia and Kuwait could not accept Western help against threats from Iraq and Iran without exposing themselves to charges within the region of betraying Islam. To understand this unusually convoluted RSC one has to see its full constellation as an interplay across the domestic, regional, and global levels. The early 1990s shift of the United States from a failed policy of balancing to one of dual containment becomes more understandable in this light. Containment may be more demanding of great power resources, but it looked far simpler and more reliable than trying to balance in Middle Eastern conditions.

8 Sub-Saharan Africa: security dynamics in a setting of weak and failed states

Introduction

Sub-Saharan Africa (hereafter, Africa) has always been a challenge for IR theory, and this is also true for RSCT. The problem is certainly not a lack of security dynamics. A snapshot of Africa during almost any of the previous forty years would show a catalogue of wars, famines, plagues, mass population displacements, ruinous and barbaric political practices, and environmental despoliations. Africa is a pessimist's paradise, a place where the Hobbesian hypothesis that in the absence of a political Leviathan life for individuals will be nasty, brutish, and short seems to be widely manifest in everyday life.

At the centre of the problem lies the postcolonial state, which was the price to be paid for rapid decolonisation. Transplanting European-style states, modes of economic development, and forms of Westphalian international relations to non-European peoples was not easy anywhere. But, while in much of Asia the new states and their system of political economy eventually took root, in most of Africa the transplant has to varying degrees failed. Consequently Africa has retained some of the superficial diplomatic appearance of a Westphalian-style state system over the past forty years, mainly in the continued diplomatic recognition of its states, but it has had rather little of the political, social, or economic reality of functioning states. The African state has been for the most part weak both as a state (i.e., low levels of sociopolitical cohesion) and as a power (i.e., commanding small economic, political, and military resources, both in absolute terms and relative to non-African states). Rather than consolidating the empirical reality of a modern bureaucratic state, the trend since decolonisation has been more in the opposite direction, towards highly personalised, kleptocratic, 'neo-patrimonial' regimes with no interest in developing the state as such, or even outright warlordism (Reno 1998). Because of these weaknesses, a variety of nonstate actors and entities, particularly family, clan, and tribe, now more fashionably referred to as 'ethnic groups', of which by one estimate there are more than 1,500 in Africa (Mazrui 1997: 3), have remained vitally in play as sources of social and political authority and economic activity. In one sense, these ethnic and kin-based entities are carryovers from the indigenous social arrangements of the precolonial period. But, because the traditional arrangements were so extensively changed and disrupted by both the colonial and postcolonial experiences (Oliver and Atmore 1994), they are more aptly referred to as *post-traditional*. The precolonial past is not recoverable in Africa, but its institutions and processes have not been eliminated.

The central theme of this chapter is that most of the security problems of Africa largely hang on the failure of the postcolonial state. The analysis thus privileges the military-political sector as a way of telling what is otherwise an almost impossibly complicated story. It does not say that securitisations in other sectors are absent or unimportant, but it does argue that state failure underlies most of them. It thus rejects both the view that the main problem is economic underdevelopment and the view that the political and the economic can be separated. Africa's economic and political failures are tightly linked, and economic improvement alone, even if it could be achieved, will not break the cycle. Strong (or at least strongish) states (or other political structures) are not a sufficient condition for economic development, but they are a necessary one. Most of Africa has failed to solve this problem, and it is that failure and its causes that define the nature, extent, and intensity of its insecurity.

The extent of state failure in Africa is indicated by the fashion for constructing 'back to the future' scenarios. Bach, for example, argues that the weakening of the African state, by *inter alia* its own poor performance and loss of resources, has promoted a shift of wealth, authority, and trade to nonstate actors, many with traditional roots, some criminal, transnational, and/or international. This shift is steadily eroding the position of the state on the map of Africa, raising the prospect of a return to 'stateless configurations articulated on the basis of primordial and patronage attachments' (Bach 1995: 16; see also Bayart et al. 1999). Clapham (1998c: 269) gives a more specific vision, suggesting that 'the new Africa is likely to owe...much to its precolonial origins, with zones of reasonably effective government interspersed with ones in which anything readily identifiable as a "state" is hard to discern'. The image is one of some remaining islands of state-like structures mostly in the traditional areas of dense population and developed trade routes, surrounded by areas in which little or no Westphalian political structure exists. He wonders (Clapham 1998a: 154–6), as does Kaplan (1994), whether some parts of Africa might not revert to precolonial patterns of relationship with the West. This line of reasoning suggests that the period of colonisation and decolonisation might, in the long view, appear as something of an interlude, a period with its own distinctive characteristics, rather than a point of permanent transformation from premodern to modern. If back-to-the-future pessimism is right, then what we are looking at now is some phase in the terminal collapse of the Westphalian experiment in Africa.

Even so, there can be no doubt that the Europeans made a huge impact. Africa's political economy was so extensively remade during the period of colonial overlay that, at least for the first several decades after independence, there is not much to be gained by trying to relate the indigenous post-independence dynamics of security to those that preceded the European impositions. Trade, slavery, and colonisation drastically changed the balance of power among ethnic groups in Africa, often reversing the traditional dominance of the interior peoples by empowering the coastal ones. The colonial powers overrode traditional political frameworks and imposed their own system of boundaries and administration, and it was these impositions that defined the political framework for the postcolonial regional order. The pattern of decolonisation in Africa resembled that of the Middle East in being quite protracted, and having two clear waves: the larger one from the late 1950s to the mid-1960s, and the smaller one during the mid-1970s.

But, unlike in the Middle East and elsewhere, the process of decolonisation in Africa did not immediately begin to generate a set of regional conflict formations. Jackson and Rosberg (1982, 1984, 1985) capture what was unique about post-independence Africa with their distinction between *empirical* sovereignty (the Weberian understanding of the state as an organisation having the real capacity to govern a territory and people) and *juridical* sovereignty (the recognition of a state's legitimacy by other states in the system). Traditionally, empirical sovereignty was the first requirement of statehood and the basis for recognition by others. But, much more than in any other part of the postcolonial world, Africa turned this formula on its head. African states were for the most part created by international society, and supported by it. They had firm juridical sovereignty long before most of them acquired (if they ever acquired) the capacity for empirical sovereignty.

What resulted was a unique construction mixing post-traditional, modern, and some almost postmodern features. The post-traditional element mostly comprised ethnic groups, which retained a strong position as sources of identity, legitimacy, economy, and obligation. The structures of these groups generally bore little relation to the colonial political boundaries, often either spreading across them or being contained, along with others, inside them. As Jackson and Rosberg (1982: 5) note: 'the social and political boundaries between these ethnic entities may well be more significant in terms of public attitudes and behaviour than are the boundaries between the countries'. The modern element consisted of the new state system, much of which quickly descended into personalised authoritarian, and often military, rule. Despite this development, the African state system mostly did not follow the Westphalian model into military rivalry and interstate war. Instead, it developed three almost postmodern features: (1) a loose ideology of pan-Africanism; (2) a continental institution, the OAU, which at an early stage pre-empted what could have been a drift towards rival territorial claims by institutionalising the rule that there would be no forceful changing of the postcolonial boundaries (Jackson and Rosberg 1984); and (3) a willingness to experiment with a variety of regional institutions. This combination of weak states and a quite strong regional international society, supported in many ways from outside by the UN, produced relative stability in interstate security relations. Even as late as the decade 1988–98, twenty-one of the twenty-five conflicts in Africa were internal rather than interstate (Goulding 1999: 158). But, as these figures imply, by imposing arbitrary and ill-fitting political boundaries on to Africa's complicated social structure, juridical sovereignty did little to constrain, and may well have encouraged, a widespread and dismal record of violence *within* the political life of the new African states (Jackson 1992).

The framework of juridical sovereignty protected the new African states during their early decades. In neorealist terms, it largely removed them from the pressures of competition that are supposed to shape states living under anarchy. One consequence of this (as well as of the intrinsic weakness of most African states) was that regional security dynamics did not develop as quickly, clearly, or strongly as they did elsewhere. Another consequence was the stagnation and decay of many African states, and the steady replacement of the illusion of a Westphalian system by something much more complicated and chaotic, which is not readily reducible to a levels-of-analysis scheme rooted in Westphalian assumptions.

It is impossible to cover this vast subject in any detail in one chapter, and our aim will be to present a general overview of the security landscape in Africa. Because political violence has been such an endemic feature of the African landscape, and because the crisis of the African state is so central to the pervasive insecurity on the continent, we will take the existence of systematic political violence to indicate the presence of a dominant securitisation without being able to explore in detail the innumerable specific processes of securitisation that underlie the whole pattern (see ch. 3, pp. 70–76). There are no doubt also major stories to be told about economic, societal, and environmental security in Africa, but they will take a back seat here. Most of the securitising actors on the environmental front are located outside Africa, and much of the story of underdevelopment, famine, and denial of basic human needs arises directly out of widespread failures in the political sector.

The story we tell here almost certainly has more of a state-centric bias than it should. We have had to depend on a secondary literature, much of which presents history in that frame, that is focused on the crisis of the African state, and that is primarily concerned with how to get the African state back on its feet (e.g., Zartman 1995; Keller 1997). But, as implied in the remarks about the increasing significance of nonstate actors above, there is almost certainly another important story to be told, one that is becoming stronger as time goes on. This would be about 'regional' security in Africa in which much of the imprint of the Westphalian state system, with its assumption of meaningful boundaries and central governments in control of territories and peoples, faded into the background, bringing into view networks of nonstate actors and their systems of security interaction. In understanding post-Cold War security in Africa, this emergent pattern of nonstate actors may well hold more of the future than the decaying state system.

What follows should thus be read with some circumspection. It is partly the story of the transitional period of juridical sovereignty, and what Jackson (1990) labels quasi-states. In that mode it is structured to reflect the conventional levels in the security constellation: domestic (meaning inside states), regional, interregional, and global. But we hope it also reflects something of the nonstate realities of African security dynamics, and for that reason the domestic level features as the most important in the constellation.

The domestic level

The prevalence of weak and failed states in Africa means that domestic level security dynamics are usually dominant, though of course the very form of this statement brings into question the relevance of thinking of these security dynamics as 'domestic'. As Shaw (1998: 2) notes: 'the prevailing assumption remains that "Angola", "Liberia", "Somalia", etc. constitute short-term domestic "crises" bounded and contained by effective national borders. Instead, the converse is much closer to the truth: no civil conflict/peace-keeping "emergency" in contemporary Africa is contained within one territory and the majority are really long-term.' The 'domestic', in this sense, *is often as much about the alternative story to the state system* as about what goes on *within* particular states. Perhaps nothing illustrates this categorical blurriness so strikingly as the term 'sobels', coined in Sierra Leone, and applied when the supposed soldiers of the state become rebels against it.

It is easy to find arguments that during the 1990s the African state system has been collapsing (Clapham 1998c; Reno 1998). The 'neopatrimonial' state and its support system of juridical sovereignty were both under attack by the early 1980s. A decade of Western-led attempts at reform (structural adjustment programmes, pressures for democratisation, heavy engagement of NGOs, use of UN peacekeeping operations) had largely run its course by the early 1990s without achieving significant breakthroughs. Reno (1998) argues that much of this external economic engagement further weakened the African state by reinforcing the already rampant privatisation of the local economies by neopatrimonial leaders and warlords who had no interest in developing either the state or society. By the mid-1990s hope was pinned on a new group of African leaders – Yoweri Museveni in Uganda, Meles Zenawi in Ethiopia, and Issias Afeworki in Eritrea – who had claims to empirical sovereignty forged in successful insurrections (Connell and Smyth 1998). But by the late 1990s most of these 'African Renaissance' leaders were engaged in heavy wars with their neighbours (Uganda in Sudan and DR Congo, Rwanda in DR Congo, Eritrea and Ethiopia against each other), suggesting that even moves towards Westphalian standards of empirical sovereignty were not a short-term solution to Africa's military, political, and economic chaos. For better or for worse Africa was increasingly left to its own devices, and to those of a range of transnational actors ranging from firms and NGOs to mercenaries and mafias. To take an indicative snapshot, the IISS notes that in 1994 there was war or violent rebellion in twenty-six of Africa's forty-nine mainland states (*Strategic Survey* 1994–5: 206–7). Many states seem locked into civil war: Liberia, Sierra Leone, Sudan, Chad, Angola, Somalia, Rwanda, Burundi, DR Congo. A few have recently emerged from such wars into a shaky peace (Mozambique, Ethiopia, Uganda, maybe Sierra Leone), but many more are so badly governed (Nigeria, Gabon, Kenya, Zimbabwe) that it is not difficult to imagine them joining the ranks of failed states. The ethnic and religious resources for generating conflict are plentiful, complementing many traditional rivalries between herdsmen and farmers.

While the elements of this picture are not in question, the overall impression it gives of a state system in crisis may mislead as much as it informs. There are two good reasons to hesitate before putting the state at the centre of security analysis in Africa: the nonstatist nature of the African state itself, and the nonstate rivals to it.

The nonstatist African state

What is meant by 'the state' in Africa? The clothing of juridical sovereignty encourages outsiders to see some version of modern state, albeit a weak and enfeebled one. But this may be mostly illusion. Often it is more important to look at the regime rather than the state. Neo-patrimonial and/or warlord regimes 'govern' very largely in their own interests, with little or no concern to develop bureaucratic states that function in the interests of the citizens. Such regimes, just like nonstate political entities, 'rule through control of commerce rather than by mobilising bureaucracies', and 'political authority and command over resources come mainly through the decisions of specific individuals who act to serve their private interests, largely without regard for formal government institutions, rules or processes' (Reno 1998: 79–80, ix). Nowhere was this divorce between regime and citizens more clearly demonstrated than in Mobutu's Zaire. The 'government' of Zaire did nothing other than defend its own security of tenure and extract resources for the use of the elite (McNulty 1999). So little did the state mean that even its name changed when the regime did: Zaire/Democratic Republic of Congo. Angola similarly enjoys high GDP growth based on oil, combined with a devastated and impoverished citizenry. Political leaderships in much of Africa effectively own the state (Clapham 1996: 3–27). Yet they are detached from both it and their populations, dependent on outside allies and resources to stay in power, and highly insecure as regards both their tenure and their lives. Even military leaders (as they often are) have always to worry about coups from rival generals, disaffected junior officers, or sometimes even NCOs. The personalisation of politics in Africa often goes so far as to void concepts such as 'national security' or 'national interest' of any meaning.

This focus on regimes puts into a different light many standard observations about the African state. Throup (1995), for example, notes that the African state is too weak to govern effectively, to penetrate society more than superficially, or to deliver social services; but it is strong enough to grab scarce resources, to become the key target for rivals in the process of resource allocation, to push much economic activity into the black market, and to crush other institutions. The regime perspective suggests that the important thing is not so much that the African state is *unable* to govern effectively (though that may well be true), but that in many instances it *does not want or try* to do so, because it is not actually functioning as a state in the modern sense.

The explanation for this malaise seems to lie in a deep combination of elements of African society with the impact of colonialism. Berman argues that the patron–client relationships of precolonial African politics were selectively reinforced by colonial practice. This may explain why many Africans 'expect and mostly get incompetence, bias, venality, and corruption' (1998: 341) in dealing with 'their' state, which in turn explains why patron–client relations dominate politics and the state fails to develop as any sort of 'neutral container' for its people. Ekeh (1975) formalises this in his 'two publics' argument, saying that the civic side of African public life is systematically exploited and degraded in order to maintain 'primordial' networks within which reside the traits of morality, loyalty, obligation, and commitment that are denied to the state. Clapham (1998d) sees this as the key to the general failure to transplant a Westphalian-style state system into Africa. He does not blame this on the arbitrary character of colonial boundaries, noting that even African countries with fairly sensible ethno-political boundaries (Somalia, Rwanda, Burundi) failed to develop coherent civic states. Both Clapham (1998b: 147) and Jackson and Rosberg (1984, 1985) agree that the whole framework of juridical sovereignty created by decolonisation, and quite effectively reinforced by the OAU Charter, has not worked to promote either economic or political development in Africa. It may indeed have reinforced the personalised, kleptocratic politics, and the dominance of loyalty to kin, clan, and patron–client relations over that to civil society or the state.

Under these conditions, it is hardly surprising that the promotion of democracy in Africa failed to work any miracles during the 1990s.

The IISS puts this down to a 'lack of a political culture of compromise', 'the failure of most states to develop a sense of national community or consciousness', and the prevalence of a deeply rooted 'winner takes all' mentality in the political classes, in which losers expect winners to abuse both their office and the rights of the opposition, and would do so themselves if the positions were reversed (*Strategic Survey* 1993–4: 202–13). As Throup (1995: 245) argues, in Africa 'everything of value is at stake in an election'. That Western-style democracy does not easily fit into the weak states of Africa remains true despite the self-interest of various dictators in saying so. As the *Economist* (24 January 1998: 50) noted of the situation in Rwanda: 'for Tutsis, democracy means death'. Criticising the state for its many shortcomings may be of less relevance to understanding security in Africa than seeing through the image of the state to nonstate realities behind it.

Nonstate rivals to the African state

There are plenty of formidable nonstate actors on the African political scene, often constructed on similar lines to the notionally state-possessing regimes. Juridical sovereignty is unquestionably a useful asset because of the access it gives to international recognition and support, and this often makes the state a valued prize fought over by rival claimants. But as durable entities such as Somaliland, Taylorland, and UNITA demonstrate, in Africa possession of the state is not a necessary condition for the creation and maintenance of successful political, military, and economic actors that may last for decades. During the whole decolonisation period, and in many places still, substate, often transnational insurgency movements have also been prominent security actors on the African scene. One study lists ninety-eight such entities (more than double the number of sub-Saharan states), some short-lived but others as old as, or even older than, their associated states (Turner 1998: 252–62; see also Clapham 1998a). These insurgencies often claim strong ties to post-traditional structures: UNITA to the Ovambo people, SPLA to the Dinka, LRA to the Acholi. Sometimes they capture the state (often meaning not much more than the capital city), and sometimes not.

Clapham (1995, 1998b) sees the prominence of these insurgency groups as symptomatic of the decay of the African state in favour of other actors. He focuses on the many insurgency groups that claim and exercise control over territory, population, and trade, sometimes with elements of external recognition, sometimes without. Such groups often have support from other African states, and are key points of contact for NGOs and corporations wanting to work in the areas they control. Like the neo-patrimonial regimes, these insurgencies are often about establishing control over local resources: diamonds in Angola and Sierra Leone, timber in Liberia, minerals in Zaire, oil in several places. To do this they usually need (and get) partnerships with outside business interests who show little shyness about the legitimacy or morality of their partners if good profits can be made (Reno 1998: 24–8; Jung 2003). The same logic applies to African regimes, as in the longstanding partnership between Mobutu and UNITA in the trade in diamonds and arms. The character and style of these insurgencies vary hugely. Some, such as Savimbi's UNITA and Charles Taylor's operation in Liberia (before he became president), were warlord political economies with state-like features (Reno 1998: 79–111). At the other extreme are insurgencies such as the LRA, which had its roots in a particular tribal history, and evolved under a string of bizarre charismatic spiritualist leaders into an opportunistic terrorist gang (Doom and Vlassenroot 1999).

The delinking of 'citizens' and 'state' is reinforced by the subsistence economy. 'Citizens' can and often do drop into subsistence farming or local trade/smuggling (Throup 1995: 243). What Hyden (1983: 8–29) calls 'the economy of affection' ('a network of support, communication, and interaction among structurally defined groups connected by blood, kin, community, or other affinities, for example religion') also inhibits the development of stronger states, though at the local level it may also be for most Africans the key to their well-being or even survival. Because it stands in the way of the impersonal, contractual relationships of a modern economy, the economy of affection is 'a non-starter as far as development of the nation-state goes'. The relative autonomy of the subsistence economy insulates regimes and warlords on the one side, and people on the other, from each other. This separation is often reinforced by external economic support which plays 'a pivotal role in insulating rulers from societal demands' and which may be supported by transnational mercenary companies (Reno 1998: 219; Howe 1998).

Given these conditions, it is not surprising that the main focus of security in Africa is domestic – or more accurately substate. Unstable leaderships, mismanaged economies, coups, civil wars, famines, refugee migrations, crime, disease, and communal conflict dominate the security agenda. Civil society is fragmented and localised, and so therefore are many of the discourses of securitisation. The local players are a mixture of weak states, personalised regimes often internationally accepted as states, and a variety of nonstate actors in control of significant territorial, economic, and military assets. Interleaved among these are NGOs, UN humanitarian and peacekeeping operations (PKOs) of various sorts, mafias, firms, mercenary companies, and even a few postcolonial garrisons. Because African states are so weak, and because there are so many other actors in play within and alongside the state, intervention by outside actors mostly occurs at the substate rather than at the interstate level. There is a conjuncture between the need of national political actors for outside economic and military resources, and the fact that highly personalised leadership means that big shifts in policy can follow a change in leadership. This structure gives outsiders strong incentives to meddle in local politics. As a host of cases from Angola to Sudan demonstrate, the rule from RSCT about global and local patterns of alignment lining up in conflict formations applies in Africa, but happens much more at the substate level than at the interstate one.

The regional level

An RSC depends on there being significant levels of security interdependence among a group of states or other actors. Security interdependence, like other types of interdependence, requires substantial interaction among the units concerned. In much of Africa, the main lines of security interaction take place either within states or across state borders by nonstate actors. Westphalian-style security interaction between states has been constrained not only by the quasi-security regime of postcolonial juridical sovereignty, but also by the weakness of African states as both states and powers. Even the constraint of a shared leadership interest in boundary maintenance and a desire to avoid postcolonial territorial disputes may now be weakening as leaders with more empirically based claims to sovereignty, based on successful insurgencies, come to power in some countries.

These constraints mean that interstate security dynamics in Africa are often simply spillovers of domestic dynamics, particularly refugee flows, expulsions of foreigners, and civil wars. In a sense, security interaction in Africa is generated more by weakness than by strength, as when imploding states inflict spillover on their neighbours. Intervention by neighbours in domestic turbulence is fairly common, but until recently there has been relatively little of the state-to-state rivalry, war, and alliance that marks international relations in the Middle East and most of Asia. The more typical form has been patterns of conflict and

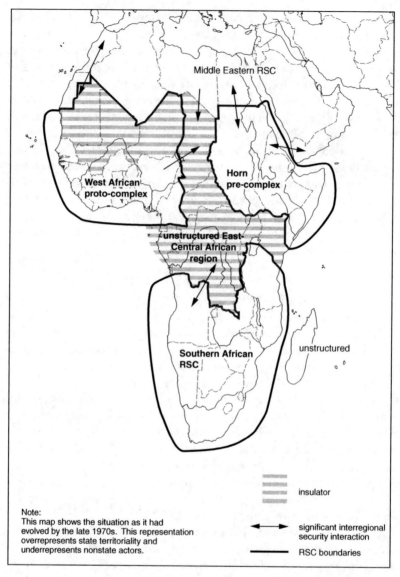

Map 6. Patterns of Regional Security in Africa During the Cold War

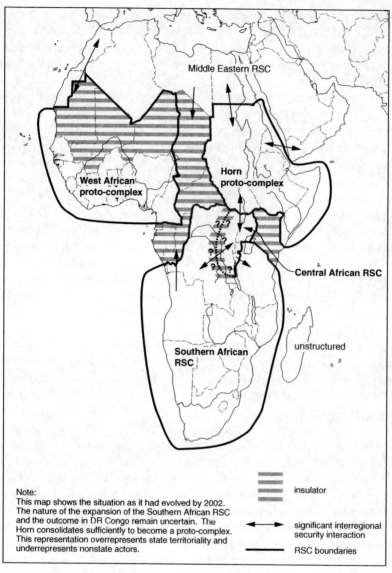

Map 7. Patters of Regional Security in Africa Post-Cold War

alliance with a state or regime on one side and an insurgency movement on the other. It has been relatively rare to find African states,
other than the local giants Nigeria and South Africa, engaging in substantial security interactions with actors other than their immediate
neighbours.

This localist tendency, combined with the general agreement not to
contest borders, goes a long way towards explaining why it is difficult to find clearly demarcated patterns of regional security in Africa.
Spillover interactions between neighbours can create what might look
like regional patterns, but these patterns have no obvious boundaries,
and they are more often chains of discrete events rather than coordinated
patterns of alliance and rivalry. Thus, for example, Somalia and Ethiopia,
Ethiopia and Sudan, Sudan and Uganda, Uganda and Rwanda, Rwanda
and Zaire/DR Congo, and Zaire/DR Congo and Angola have all played
into each other's civil wars, creating a potential chain stretching from the
Arabian Sea to the South Atlantic. But little if anything makes this chain
more than the sum of its parts. There is not much interplay between
Somalia and Sudan, or Sudan and Rwanda, or Rwanda and Angola,
let alone between Somalia and Angola. The general pattern is that each
country sits at the centre of a set of security interactions connecting it to
its immediate neighbours, but with limits of power meaning that these
individual patterns have not as a rule linked significantly into wider
patterns of security interdependence. The main exception to this rule
has been when a local great power such as Nigeria or South Africa does
have the resources to create wider linkages. In the 1990s, however, there
were signs that this pattern was changing. Both in the Horn and in Central Africa more classical types of joined-up interstate security dynamics
began to emerge.

For most of the postcolonial period, our argument is that the level of
security interaction in Africa has been too low and too local to sustain
well-developed interstate regional RSCs of the type commonly found
elsewhere in the international system after decolonisation. Had we the
resources, it might well be possible to map out large numbers of micro-
RSCs based on nonstate actors, though also enmeshed to varying degrees in the state system. In an extremely loose sense one might attribute
the absence of typical postcolonial regional conflict formations in part
to the existence of the OAU, which could therefore be seen as a kind of
thin security regime. Contra Keller (1997: 296–301) up to 2002 we see
no strong case for thinking of Africa as a whole as an RSC. This could

change if the new African Union (AU) fulfils the conflict management hopes of its charter, though there are scant grounds for optimism about such a development anytime soon.

If we stay within the interstate frame, there are a number of nodes where the first outlines of pre- or proto-RSCs can be traced on the basis of local patterns of interaction (Clapham 1996: 117–25; Keller 1997: 296–301; Kacowicz 1998: 125–75). Up until the 1990s, only Southern Africa looked like a fully developed RSC. West Africa is best defined as a proto-RSC (i.e., clearly formed, but with rather weak security interdependence). Both of these are centred on a local great power and have defining regional organisations. Regional organisations do not always, or even usually, line up with RSCs, and so have to be treated with caution as evidence for them. They may, like the OAU, be bigger than an RSC or, like the GCC, be contained within a larger RSC. A case might be made for the Horn of Africa as a pre-RSC (a set of bilateral security relations that has the potential to bind together into an RSC, but has not yet achieved sufficient crosslinkage among the units to do so), though locating its boundaries is difficult. This is a case where it is far from clear whether the regional organisation, IGAD, lines up with an emergent RSC or not. The problem of local security dynamics blurring one into another in a more or less seamless web is even bigger in Eastern and Central Africa. Here, until the late 1990s, it was virtually impossible to identify even pre-RSCs. Uganda illustrates the difficulty, seeming to be a kind of regional hub, yet without providing much connection between the different security dynamics in which it was engaged. Uganda plays into the Horn because of its interaction with Sudan, into Central Africa because of its interactions with Rwanda and DR Congo (Clark 2001), and into Eastern Africa because of its interactions with Kenya and Tanzania. Where regional security is so weakly structured all states are in some senses insulators, and their region is unstructured.

It is worth looking in more detail at these cases, first at the two where regional security dynamics are most clearly visible, Southern Africa and West Africa; then at the pre-RSC in the Horn; and finally at Eastern and Central Africa, where a quite new and dramatic set of interactions is reshaping the previous picture.

Southern Africa

The relative clarity of the regional level in Southern Africa hinges on the central role played by South Africa as the regional great power.

This is a standard, unipolar RSC with South Africa at its core, and this centre–periphery structure is mirrored in South Africa's longstanding economic dominance of its neighbours (Odén 2001: 85). South Africa achieved independence several decades before its neighbours and, as elsewhere, the RSC formed as decolonisation created a subsystem of independent states. In Southern Africa, decolonisation started in the mid-1960s, but South Africa was insulated from regional security dynamics by the survival of the Portuguese empire in Angola and Mozambique until 1975 and of white rule in Rhodesia up to 1980 and Namibia up to 1990. The new black-ruled states could not but fall into a relationship of mutual threat and antagonism with apartheid South Africa, and so the postcolonial RSC first developed, as elsewhere, into a conflict formation. The principal binding mechanism defining the RSC was mutual interference in each other's domestic politics, with the white-ruled states on one side and the black-ruled 'frontline' states on the other playing mutual games of destabilisation by supporting armed insurgencies in each other's territories. As elsewhere in Africa, spillovers of domestic instability were the driving force for wider security interactions. All of the countries experienced civil war to some degree, Angola and Mozambique in a prolonged and intense manner, and these generally spilled over into, and/or attracted intervention by, neighbouring states. Angola's war, for example, spilled into and drew in Zaire/DR Congo, Namibia, and Zambia. But given the dominant position of South Africa, it was that country's projection of its internal difficulties into the region that did most to structure the RSC.

The history of this RSC divides into two clear periods hinged around the achievement of majority rule in South Africa. During the apartheid years, South Africa projected its domestic instability (constructed as a 'total onslaught' against it) throughout the region in a kind of forward defence of its own domestic political arrangements. It eventually became the only white-rule state confronting all the others, and conducted some substantial crossborder military interventions, most notably against Angola between 1975 and the late 1980s, and into Mozambique, Botswana, Lesotho, and Zimbabwe. Since the frontline states were not powerful enough to confront South Africa in direct military fashion, they had to confine themselves to supporting South African opposition groups, most notably the ANC. In 1979 the frontline states (Angola, Botswana, Lesotho, Malawi, Mozambique, Swaziland, Tanzania, Zambia, Zimbabwe) set up the Southern African Development Coordination Conference (SADCC) to try to decrease their collective economic

234

dependency on South Africa and extract more aid from the West. This form of the Southern African RSC remained quite stable from the early 1960s to the end of the 1980s.

With the ending of apartheid, the Southern African RSC began a fairly rapid shift from conflict formation to security regime. SADCC transformed itself into SADC (the Southern African Development Community) in 1992, and South Africa joined in 1994 after elections had established majority rule. Negotiations starting in 1993 (Cawthra 1997b: 6–10) resulted in 1996 in the formation of the SADC Organ on Politics, Security, and Defence, including the already active Inter-state Defence and Security Committee (ISDSC). All of this amounted to the construction of a fairly ambitious security regime, with potential not only for joint action and collective security against outside threats or for peacekeeping in Africa, but also for internal cooperation on policing, human rights, and democratisation. Early action was in police and intelligence work to meet joint concerns about migration, arms traffic, and crime (all of which problems extended well outside the SADC area). SADC acted in Lesotho in 1995 and Mozambique in 1996 when pressure was put on RENAMO to cooperate in elections (Odén 2001: 87–8).

But this promising start quickly unravelled. A bungled South African intervention in Lesotho in 1998 under SADC auspices generated high casualties. By the later 1990s, the security regime was looking frayed, and the boundaries of the RSC were expanding northward. The main cause was SADC's 1997 decision to admit Kabila's DR Congo. This tied SADC into that country's unfolding crisis, adding Namibia and Zimbabwe to Angola's longstanding involvement in Zaire/DR Congo (more on this below). Serious splits began to unravel the sense of security community, especially between Mugabe's increasingly authoritarian regime in Zimbabwe and South Africa. The promising security regime developments of a few years earlier were paralysed. Mbeki's South Africa became inward-looking, involved with its own problems of crime, AIDS, and unemployment, and failed to provide regional leadership.

Internal and external securitisation in South Africa

The Southern African RSC is unipolar. South Africa is dominant to an unusual degree compared with other standard regions. Dominance shows in the high percentage of resources of the region held by South Africa (Møller 2000), and in the readiness of the other states in the region – at least originally, after the 1994 change in South Africa to majority rule – to accept South African leadership. Probably, the neighbours were mainly driven by a hope of South Africa becoming the locomotive for regional growth, but with some willingness to consider a possible stabilisation around a security centre, i.e., a legitimate, centred order. This has not happened for several reasons. Some are mistakes in South Africa's handling of its leadership role (such as the 1998 PKO in Lesotho), and others the difficulty of agreeing in practice on how to divide roles and responsibilities, notably South Africa versus Zimbabwe. However, the theoretically interesting question, which will be the focus here, is whether a major cause – underlying both the mishandled cases and the actions not taken – is the magnitude of domestic securitisation and the ensuing shift of relative weight of levels.

In 1994, South Africa had to start almost from scratch in devising a new security strategy and conception. The discourses of 'total onslaught' and ensuing 'total strategy' (Coleman 1990; Møller 2001: 1) were prime cases of extremely wide-ranging securitisations beating even Cold War doctrines in East and West in terms of how much could be put into one mega-securitisation with total implications (see Buzan and Wæver 1998).

The new doctrine drew – probably to an internationally unprecedented degree – on the academic writings on security and was constructed around the two main pillars: sectoral widening and 'human security' (Cawthra 2000). This, however, raised the classical securitisation dilemma that a wide concept of security could easily reinstall the military and not least intelligence in far-reaching (domestic) roles. The new regime and its intellectuals attempted to use the wider concept of security to elevate new tasks to importance while reducing the relative weight of the military (Cawthra 2000). Notably, the 1998 Defence Review specified that the military should support the police and other domestic services only in 'extreme situations' (quoted by Cawthra 2000: 10), which means that each case for military involvement in domestic affairs has to be securitised in its own right; the military has not been admitted with a general ticket. The resulting 'security sector' (Cawthra 2000; Møller 2001) – a term used more systematically as a generic category in South Africa than most other places – encompasses armed forces, police, intelligence, and more.

236

Widening security, then, meant that a number of domestic and transnational problems were approached in terms of security. Even at the regional level, concern has focused on the 'new' security threats: 'population growth; the environment and the competition for scarce natural resources; mass migration; food shortage; drugs; disease and AIDS; ethnocentric nationalism; crime and small arms proliferation; the crisis of liberal democracy; the role of the armed forces; poverty and economic marginalisation' (Söderbaum 1998: 79). Key among these is the extremely high level of violence in South African society. The spread of weapons and especially crime are systematically securitised. The most common usage of the terms 'safety and security' in South Africa's politics is in relation to crime (see e.g. Mbeki 1999a, 2001a, 2001c; Mufamadi 1997). The minister responsible for police is called the 'minister for safety and security', and the use of secrecy is legitimised in the fight against crime in much the same way that this securitisation is usually employed in relation to external security (Maduna 1999).

More specifically, the problem of domestic order has been formulated in terms of the development of gang warfare 'from urban street gangs to criminal empires' (Kinnes 2000), the number of lethal weapons available in society, transnational organised crime (Gastrow 2001), and international disaster relief (Schoeman 2000). The latter two are examples of new security tasks that are not traditionally state-to-state but can still lead either to domestic orientations or into regional schemes. Another example where domestic meets regional is the question of border control in the light of regionalisation (Minnaar 2001; Hennop et al. 2001).

To the list of domestic security problems, it would seem natural to add AIDS. It is certainly a major challenge to society (likely to have caused 7 million deaths by 2010; Dorrington et al. 2001), but it is rarely securitised by the state and equally, in society, attempts to securitise AIDS have been widely contested. This seems to be an important case of an issue for which it is worth tracing and explaining the processes whereby something is *not* securitised (L. Hansen 2000), because there are strong a priori reasons to expect it to be, and it is actually possible to point to some specific mechanisms driving the non-securitisation. One is economic: that especially if the state securitises something, it has to act on it. Another factor is denial of the link between HIV and AIDS, which in turn reflects culturally rooted problems of accepting social occurrences that are otherwise not tolerated as part of the self-conception of society, notably homosexuality (Dorrington et al. 2001: 3; cf. Mbeki 2001b).

The key is, however, the rise to primacy of the issue of crime, partly crystallised by vigilante groups transforming the public agenda. The organising discourse of the post-apartheid ANC regime was originally one of development, but around 1996 this was replaced by one of security (Jensen 2001).

Is it then possible to conclude that it is 'South Africa's own internal challenges which have detracted from coherent foreign policy formulation and engagement' (Cilliers 1999)? In contrast to the original expectations for the 'new' South Africa, its actual role has been limited. Its general African policy has become increasingly symbolic, as represented by the discourse on 'African renaissance' (Mbeki 1999b), although Mbeki played a leading role in the 2002 initiative for NEPAD (a new partnership for Africa's development) presented with some limited result to the G8 (BBC News 28 June 2002). More importantly, a thorough regional policy never materialised. The concrete link between prioritising the domestic and downgrading the regional is the essentially relative quality of security. Security is about prioritising issues on the political agenda and, especially where resources are limited, such prioritising is a zero-sum game. It is possible to legitimise this reorientation towards domestic problems as being for the general (regional) good: 'Regional security cannot be divorced from domestic security. Basic stability and law and order must be provided within a country that wishes to provide the same in its neighbourhood' (Cilliers 2000: 6). This does not detract from the fact that, if the country at the centre of a unipolar region securitises domestic security far more than regional or international and it has severely limited resources, this will weaken the possibility of constructing a legitimate, centred region around it.

West Africa

Although Liberia became independent in 1847, Ghana in 1957, and Guinea in 1958, most of West Africa was decolonised in 1960–1. Until the mid-1970s this group of countries was an unstructured security region. Most of the big security issues were internal: as Kacowicz (1998: 125) notes, during its first forty years after independence, West Africa 'can be characterized by relative international peace and by domestic war'. The ex-metropolitan states, particularly France, retained a strong presence; and there was nothing of the conflictual security interdependence that emerged quickly in Southern Africa. The main event was the Nigerian civil war of 1967–70, but this did not much involve the other states in the region. Except for Ivory Coast, which (along with its backer France) supported and helped arm Biafra, all of the external support for Biafra came from outside states: South Africa, Rhodesia, Portugal, France, Gabon, Tanzania, and Zambia (Clapham 1996: 112).

Until the formation of the Economic Community of West African States (ECOWAS) in 1975, there was insufficient security interaction to call this even a pre-complex. ECOWAS linked together the whole block of coastal states from Nigeria to Mauritania, and the three interior landlocked states Mali, Niger, and Burkina Faso, sixteen in all. This development would almost certainly not have occurred without the oil wealth that allowed Nigeria to act as its core and leader. As in Southern Africa, the main West African regional security dynamic was unipolar. As observed above, the existence of a regional organisation does not necessarily, or even probably, indicate the existence of a matching RSC. But the key here is ECOWAS's explicit move into military-political security shortly after its formation, which looked significant enough to justify labelling West Africa as a proto-complex. In 1978 ECOWAS agreed a Nonaggression Protocol, and in 1981 a Protocol on Mutual Assistance and Defence. In 1990 a Standing Mediation Committee was established, which generated ECOMOG, the Nigerian-led peacekeeping force that intervened in the Liberian and Sierra Leonean civil wars (Söderbaum 2001; Aning 1999). One can nevertheless ask questions about whether or not ECOWAS is the proper measure of the West African RSC. Nigeria was involved in the civil war in Chad from 1979, and has a perennial border dispute with Cameroon that has generated military skirmishes on several occasions. At the very least these two countries would have to be counted as insulating boundary states to the RSC, and there is a case for placing Cameroon within it.

The existence of ECOWAS, in parallel with that of SADC in Southern Africa, would seem to qualify the West African RSC as a security regime, albeit a fairly weak one. Whatever their faults, the ECOMOG interventions in Liberia and Sierra Leone are unusual examples of regional level peacekeeping/making operations in the third world. They also reflect the primarily domestic nature of the security problems within the region. Interstate clashes have been infrequent and small-scale. But ECOWAS has not stopped either a certain amount of interstate meddling in domestic politics (typically through support of insurgency movements) or interstate spillovers of refugees and migrants. There have been several instances of large-scale movements of refugees from civil wars, particularly from Guinea, Sierra Leone, and Liberia, and mass labour migration has resulted in periodic bouts of expulsions of foreigners, especially from Ghana and Nigeria. Since the late 1980s, the main focus of ECOWAS has been attempts at peacekeeping in the interlinked civil wars of Liberia and Sierra Leone. This violent and sorry tale is still ongoing, and has unleashed banditry and warlordism of the most horrifying kind. It has produced tens of thousands of dead and hundreds of thousands of refugees, and has displayed the dynamics of states playing into each other's domestic conflicts at their most ruthless and rampant. It shows how links to outside commercial interests can sustain any armed group that can capture and hold a valuable resource (in this case diamonds and timber), and it has exposed all the weaknesses and difficulties of peacekeeping in failed states.

The paradox of this proto-complex is that Nigeria is both its mainstay (as the sponsor of ECOWAS) and itself hanging on the brink of failure as a state. During the 1990s the worry grew that sustained misgovernment in Nigeria would cause the country to fall apart, in the process destabilising the whole region (*Strategic Survey* 1995–6: 228–35; 1999–2000: 47–8; Maier 2001). These worries were fed by serious clashes between rival ethnic and religious groups in various parts of the country. Escalating societal securitisations between Muslims and Christians were particularly worrying for the long-term cohesion of the country.

Thus the West African RSC, like the Southern African one, is an unusual mixture. Both comprise a set of weak states, most of which are also weak powers, dominated by a regional power that is also a weak state (though Nigeria is a considerably weaker state than South Africa). In West Africa direct interstate security interaction other than PKOs is mostly at fairly low levels, but there is a lot of spillover from and meddling in the domestic level, and quite a lot of transnational interaction arising from the post-traditional networks and the interplay between regimes and insurgency movements. Substate rather than interstate security issues dominate the agenda, and as a consequence the proto-RSC has formed more as a weak security regime than as the conflict formation that would be the normal consequence of decolonisation. The outlook is highly uncertain, depending crucially on the fate of Nigeria. If Nigeria implodes, then the 'back to the future' scenarios could easily describe the region's destiny.

Horn

Decolonisation in the Horn of Africa was a prolonged affair. Ethiopia was colonised only briefly by Italy during the Second World War. It was a rare case of an African state having a longstanding indigenous state tradition as an empire. Sudan gained its independence in 1956, and Somalia in 1960. Eritrea gained its independence in 1993 after a long civil war in Ethiopia, and the small territory of Djibouti, independent in 1977, is still under strong French influence. For most of the period up to the early 1990s, there were two main stories of security interaction in the Horn: the linked civil wars in Sudan and Ethiopia, and an interstate conflict between Ethiopia and Somalia over possession of the Ogaden region. Interwoven with these was a much older tradition of conflict between sedentary highland Christian agriculturalists and nomadic lowland Muslim pastoralists. For the period under review here, the Horn of Africa looks mostly like a pre-complex, having many elements of strong bilateral security interdependence, but failing to link these together into an integrated pattern.

The main elements in this story are:

- Three prolonged civil wars, driven mainly by secessionist agendas. The first was in Sudan, starting in 1956, but more active after 1982, and still ongoing, pitching a mostly Arab, Islamic north against a mostly black, non-Islamic south (Deng 1995; Sloth 2001). The second was in Ethiopia, starting in 1961, but intensifying from the early 1970s, and ending with a rebel victory in 1991 and the secession of Eritrea in 1993 (Plaut and Gilkes 1999; Abbink 1998). The third was in Somalia, starting in 1991 after the failed dictatorship of Siad Barre, and still ongoing in 2002, with two autonomous entities, Puntland and Somaliland, having emerged in the north, and a set of unstable clan fiefdoms in the south.
- A pair of substantial interstate wars about borders and territory. The first was between Ethiopia and Somalia in 1977–8, but which sputters on still in 2002, in which Somalia failed to detach the Ogaden from Ethiopia. The second was between Ethiopia and Eritrea in 1998–2000, in which Ethiopia defeated Eritrea in a

post-secession dispute over border demarcation and economic relations, with a UN PKO subsequently holding an uneasy border. The Horn is unusual in Africa in having real interstate wars, which give this region a more Westphalian feel than elsewhere in the continent.

- A host of usually mutual crossborder interventions in which the government in each state supports insurgencies in the other: Somalia and Ethiopia, Eritrea and Ethiopia, Sudan and Uganda, Sudan and Eritrea, Sudan and Ethiopia. As elsewhere in Africa, these were the main instruments of most governments against each other.

- Some substantial outside partisan interventions, particularly Soviet and Cuban support for Ethiopia in 1977, which turned the war against Somalia in Ethiopia's favour, and US support during the 1990s for insurgents against the radical government in Khartoum, and for backers of those insurgents in Ethiopia, Eritrea, and Uganda.

- Some international interventions: a failed humanitarian one in Somalia in the early 1990s, and a peacekeeping one on the Eritrean–Ethiopian border starting in 2000.

The combination of war and famine arising from these conflicts, and the interplay between them, killed and displaced huge numbers of people. In Somalia, perhaps half a million died during the 1990s. The long civil war and associated famines in Sudan have killed upwards of 2 million and displaced around 5 million more. The short war between Eritrea and Ethiopia killed tens of thousands and displaced more than a million. Unlike in West, East, and Central Africa, most of the displaced persons remained within their state of origin rather than crossing a border.

The case against seeing this history as evidence for anything more than a pre-complex is the lack of much significant linkage between the Ethiopia–Somalia dynamics on the one side, and the Ethiopia–Sudan ones on the other. The two security dynamics intersected inasmuch as rebel groups in Ethiopia were supported by both Somalia and Sudan, but other than that there seemed to be neither direct nor indirect contact between the Sudanese and Somalian sides of the equation. This therefore appeared to be a chain of localisms without any clearly defined regional pattern of security interdependence. Some increase in regional linkage emerged with the Eritrean–Ethiopian rivalry in the late 1990s, which reached into both the Sudan–Ethiopia and Ethiopia–Somalia dynamics, connecting up the previously rather delinked conflicts in the Horn sufficiently to move it to proto-complex status.

Another problem for RSCT is that there is no really clear southern boundary to the Horn region. Although the border between Ethiopia and Kenya might count as a place where security dynamics stand back to back, Somalia has had territorial disputes with Kenya, and the Sudanese civil war spills over the boundaries with Uganda and DR Congo, pulling the region into Central Africa (Doom and Vlassenroot 1999). There is a weak regional organisation, the Intergovernmental Authority on Development (IGAD), which comprises Djibouti, Eritrea, Ethiopia, Kenya, Somalia, Sudan, and Uganda, and again this links the Horn and East/Central Africa. As yet, IGAD has no comparable standing to ECOWAS or SADC as a regional security body. Despite its ostensible role as an environmental and economic organisation, IGAD has functioned mostly as a security forum, and by 1998 was involved in conflict resolution attempts for both Sudan and Somalia (El-Affendi 2000, 2001).

These moves have run into an increasingly activist Egyptian policy in the region, raising the specific possibility of an Egyptian–Ethiopian rivalry, and the general one of an enhanced Arab–African divide. Although Egypt has its own longstanding colonial history along the southern Nile, it was a peripheral player in the events sketched above. But its position was consistently anti-Ethiopian, supporting Somalia in 1977 and Sudan in 1976. Despite the many frictions between Cairo and Khartoum, not least over the 1995 assassination attempt against Mubarak, the two governments are now moving closer together. Egypt worries about control of the Nile waters, and thus opposes both the secession of southern Sudan (through which flows the White Nile), and (in a situation with many parallels to that between Turkey and Iraq) also worries about Ethiopian plans to build dams on the headwaters of the Blue Nile. In both the development of IGAD into security roles and the possible emergence of a long-term rivalry between Egypt and Ethiopia, there is potential for the making of an even wider RSC in the Horn (more on this in the conclusion to part III).

East and Central Africa

For most of the period since decolonisation it was hard to see any coherent state level regional security patterning at all in this part of Africa. Not even pre-complexes suggested themselves. Each state seemed to sit at the centre of its own pattern of security interactions, often

243

stemming from its own domestic turbulence. Spillovers were common, but until recently very little linked together the various local events in any sustained or systematic way, and there were (and are) no regional organisations to speak of. Until the late 1990s, this area was a kind of insulating zone, containing some individual stories of its own, but not itself structured at the regional level. It served as the broad frontier in which the Horn, Southern African, and West African security dynamics both faded out and were kept apart from each other. Within this zone, the main security dynamic has been that of weak postcolonial states oscillating between dictatorship and civil war, and having their internal instabilities spill over into, and be played into by, their neighbours. Even more so than in the Horn, these various bilateral links failed to connect into a regional pattern.

The principal elements were:

- Four major civil wars in Zaire/DR Congo (1960–5, 1996 on-going in 2002), Rwanda (on and off since the late 1950s, with a huge outbreak in 1994), Burundi (continuous, with periodic peaks), Uganda (1980–6). Most other states in this area (Congo-Brazzaville, Central African Republic, Gabon, Equatorial Guinea) have had unstable or violent internal regimes, but apart from some refugee flows there has not been extensive spillover from them.
- Two interstate wars. The first was between Tanzania and Uganda during 1978–80, in which Tanzania ousted Idi Amin but failed to install a stable replacement, precipitating six years of civil war. The second, still ongoing as of 2002 but at a much lower intensity, grew out of crossborder interventions between Zaire on the one side and Rwanda and Uganda on the other. It blended into the civil war in DR Congo, and by 1998 had drawn in Rwanda and Uganda (and to a lesser extent Burundi) on one side, and Angola, Zimbabwe, and Namibia on the other.
- The usual array of mutual crossborder interventions, some within the region: Uganda and Rwanda, Uganda and Zaire/DR Congo, Rwanda and Zaire/DR Congo, Burundi and Zaire/DR Congo. Befitting its unstructured character, there were also mutual crossborder interventions between states within East-Central Africa and states in other security regions: Uganda and Sudan, Zaire/DRC and Angola, Angola and Congo-Brazzaville, Tanzania and South Africa.

244

- Some international interventions: a big one into DR Congo in the early 1960s; small ones by France and Belgium into Rwanda in 1990, and by France, Belgium, and Morocco into Zaire in 1977–8, plus sustained US support for Mobutu in Zaire from 1965 to the early 1990s.
- Some small regional and international attempts at mediation and peacekeeping in Rwanda and Burundi, and DR Congo.

In this part of Africa, war and dictatorship have been a bigger generator of casualties and migration than famine: perhaps 800,000 dead and 2 million refugees in Rwanda during the mid-1990s; a cumulative total of perhaps 500,000 dead and well over a million refugees in various outbreaks of violence in Burundi since the early 1970s; perhaps 200,000 killed in Uganda during the dictatorship of Idi Amin; some 250,000 refugees pushed from Zaire's Shaba province into Angola during 1977–8; and perhaps 2 million people displaced and as many dead in the civil war in DR Congo since the 1990s. Major spillovers of refugees have occurred from Rwanda into Burundi, Uganda, Tanzania, and Zaire/DR Congo; and from Burundi into Tanzania, Rwanda, and Zaire/DR Congo.

Until the early 1990s, this region remained fairly unstructured, with its various lines of security interdependence largely disconnected from each other. But during the mid-1990s, the post-Mobutu upheavals in Zaire/DR Congo caused many of these stories to link together much more tightly around a core comprising DR Congo, Rwanda, and Burundi. Uganda also seemed to become a kind of regional power, with Museveni playing a significant role not only in Sudan, by backing the southern rebels, but also in Rwanda (backing the Tutsi RPF) and in Zaire/DR Congo (first backing the takeover by Laurent Kabila, then trying to oust him). At this time it became common to refer to the 'Tutsification' of Central Africa, with Tutsi governments in Rwanda and Burundi, and substantial Tutsi roles in Uganda and DR Congo (*Strategic Survey* 1996–7: 212–19).

The war that broke out in 1996 reflected the interlocking domestic insecurities of Uganda, Rwanda, and Burundi on the one side, and DR Congo on the other, with the former three countries plagued by insurgencies based in DR Congo. The admission of DR Congo to SADC in 1997 reflected the longstanding linkage between the seemingly endless civil war in Angola and the government of Zaire, Mobutu (with US help) having long supported UNITA's insurgency in Angola (McNulty 1999: 77). An audacious airlifted attack by Uganda and Rwanda on

Kinshasa in 1998 triggered intervention under SADC defence agreements by Angola, Namibia, and Zimbabwe. As in Rwanda and Uganda, Angola's motives were strongly linked to its own domestic conflict: in this case the desire to cut off the diamond trade lifelines that sustained UNITA. The war eventually involved substantial numbers of troops from several countries as well as a variety of local rebel groups. Zimbabwe, physically remote from DR Congo, but heavily engaged, seemed to be hoping for economic profits and a status boost to Mugabe's rivalry with South Africa within SADC. Sudan supported Kabila as part of its rivalry with Uganda, and even Chad and Libya joined in supporting Kabila (Shearer 1999). It would be a mistake to see this whole affair as primarily the interplay of states. It was partly that, but the main reality was a complicated interplay of alliance and conflict among a set of regimes (few wholly in control of their notional territories) and an array of insurgency movements. As McNulty (1999: 80) notes: 'the region's internal dynamic is key to understanding conflict there, and much of the failure of the external response to these conflicts may be explained by the failure to understand this dynamic'. Part of that dynamic, especially in DR Congo and Angola, was the ready cash available from the global economy in exchange for the rich mineral resources of the region. The Congo war was partly about political issues, but part of it was simply about attempts to control lucrative resources.

At the time of writing, the war had deteriorated into a messy stalemate and a shaky negotiated truce. Rwanda, Uganda, and their local allies controlled the east of the country, but had fallen out seriously enough between themselves to trigger several substantial battles. The DR Congo government, now under Joseph Kabila, and his allies controlled the west, but the whole situation was becoming diffuse. None of the participants wanted the break-up of Zaire and several feared it (Shearer 1999; McNulty 1999: 53–4), though de facto partition was the reality and neither side had the strength to achieve victory. Zimbabwe's engagement looked secure only so long as Mugabe's discredited government could stay in power, and Angola's interest had been reduced by the apparent victory of the government in the long-running civil war. Nevertheless, DR Congo was inside SADC, and there seemed little doubt that the Southern African complex had extended its boundary northward.

At the same time, there were increasing grounds for seeing Uganda, Rwanda, Burundi, and northeastern Zaire as an RSC centred on the Great Lakes. The disintegration of the state in Zaire/DR Congo temporarily pulled the security dynamics of East-Central Africa into contact with those of Southern Africa. Restoration of a functioning state in DR Congo might restore the insulator, but this seems unlikely in the near future. Continued partition would divide the two RSCs, but leave a direct, and perhaps unstable, border between them. A full integration of the two regions into one RSC is unlikely. Weak states with low interaction capacity have already shown their inability to sustain an RSC on this scale and the Zaire/DR Congo centred conflict pattern has begun to disintegrate.

Conclusions on the regional level

Given the shallow roots and parlous condition of the Westphalian state system in Africa, one would hardly expect to find robust postcolonial interstate conflict formations of the type common elsewhere in the third world. Yet, despite the dominance of domestic insecurity, the regional level is not empty. There *are* distinctive regional patterns to be found, including state and nonstate elements, though seldom do they have the relatively clear boundaries and differentiated security dynamics that one finds elsewhere. We have used a language of 'pre' and 'proto' RSCs to some effect on these phenomena, and this of course carries the implication that things will develop along Westphalian lines into 'proper' RSCs. But if the 'back to the future' view of the African state is correct, this may not be the direction in which things go. A further disintegration of the state system in Africa would bring to the fore a quite different set of relationships among a wide variety of units. The existing regional patterns in Africa already show this tendency, for much that defines African security regions is driven by domestic spillovers of one sort or another, and insurgencies are often as important as states in the patterns of security interdependence. In the nonstate/less-state scenario of back-to-the-future, RSCs are still likely to form; however, they will be made up of a more complex constellation of types of units (as seen to some extent in EU-Europe).

Serious interstate wars are still rare, though the Horn is something of an exception to this rule. And it is noteworthy how many of the alliances that operate in Africa are between a state and an insurgency group in another country. Interstate alliances are almost nonexistent, and the one recent example (Uganda and Rwanda in DR Congo) proved short-lived. By contrast, alliances between governments and insurgencies are common (e.g., Zaire and UNITA, Sudan and LRA, Uganda and SPLA, South Africa and RENAMO, Uganda and RPF, Rwanda and Banyamulenge), as are alliances between insurgencies (e.g., EPLF and the TPLF, MPLA and SWAPO, ANC and SWAPO, ANC and ZAPU, Charles Taylor and RUF). Such alliances might be shaped by common ethnicity (e.g., Tutsi), shared ideology (e.g., Marxism), or common cause (opposition to white rule). Alliances (or oppositions) between insurgencies can move up to the state level when one or more of the parties succeed in gaining control of the government. Charles Taylor, the ANC, the MPLA, the EPLF, the RUF, the TPLF, and others have all made the transition to state leadership. This transition can carry historical baggage: when the ANC took power in South Africa, part of its problem with neighbouring Zimbabwe was that the ANC had supported ZAPU, whereas it was Mugabe's ZANU that was in power in Harare. Regional security in Africa is thus substantially defined by the substate level. It is less about states threatening each other in the traditional way, and more about spillovers from domestic instabilities. Nonstate actors are as big a part of this picture as are states, and the framework of notional interstate boundaries may be more misleading than helpful as a way of understanding the security actors and dynamics in play.

The interregional level

Given the weakness of the regional level in Africa, and the general propensity of African security politics towards vague frontiers rather than hard borders, it comes as no surprise that the interregional level is not particularly easy to delineate. It has two elements distinct enough to be worth considering separately. First is the frontier zone between the Middle Eastern RSC and Africa, which we will look at in the conclusions to part III. Second is longer-range security interactions between African states. The OAU and its successor the AU exist as overarching bodies including all of the African states. But the OAU has been too weak to define a security region, though it has occasionally tried to play a role in conflict resolution, as in Chad during 1981–2. Up to 1994, the OAU served as a forum in which the weight of African opinion could be focused against the white minority regime in South Africa, and which helped to support and legitimise the struggle against apartheid. But, although symbolically and rhetorically important, the OAU did not constitute a dominant security framework for any of its members except in the sense of helping to bolster juridical norms of non-intervention and acceptance of boundaries. Whether the AU will improve on this record remains to be seen.

Most of the security interaction in Africa has been on the domestic level, whether transborder or not. Sometimes local powers, notably South Africa and Nigeria, have been able to project their influence beyond their immediate neighbours. These moves have laid the foundations for two of the RSCs that one finds in Africa. Occasionally, these two states have reached outside their regions, with Nigeria playing some role against apartheid South Africa, and South Africa's armed forces defining their zone of strategic interest as stretching up to the northern borders of Kenya, Uganda, Zaire, Congo-Brazzaville, and Gabon, and including Madagascar (Cawthra 1997a: 135). Occasional examples can also be found where other distant states play some local role: for example, Kenya allowed RENAMO to have diplomatic offices in Nairobi (Clapham 1996: 224) and gave some support to Inkatha; Ivory Coast, Burkina Faso, Togo, Gabon, and Rwanda all helped UNITA to trade diamonds for weapons (Hurst 1999: 28); Mengistu of Ethiopia took refuge in Harare after being overthrown (cashing in on his earlier support for ZANU in Rhodesia). Some of these incidents represent personal contacts among leadership elites, sometimes going back to pre-independence life in Europe, and such elite contacts remain an important element in African politics. At the opposite end of the social spectrum is the phenomenon of long-distance migrants, which has partly historical roots. Like most other security interactions in Africa, migrants and refugees often move locally. But one can find refugee Hutus in northern Mozambique, and a steady flow of Africans towards South Africa from as far away as West and East Africa.

Given the vagueness of regional security formations in Africa, it is somewhat problematic even to talk about an interregional level. But the security picture could not be fully painted without this level, even though it is conspicuously thinner than the regional level, which is itself thinner than the substate one.

The global level

Given the general weakness of African states, both as states and as powers, it does not require much in the way of resources for outside actors to make a significant impact on local security relations – though it would require very major commitments to attempt any repeat of colonial overlay. Aside from some interest in bases and strategic raw materials, Africa was mostly marginal to the main concerns of the Cold War protagonists, though, given the huge resource disparities, the Cold

War rivalries nevertheless had a big impact on Africa. The main points of superpower intervention were areas where postcolonial ties with the former metropole had not been sustained: the Horn and Southern Africa. Both superpowers, as well as China and the ex-colonial powers, all pursued their rivalries there. The United States was most active in Angola, Ethiopia, Kenya, Liberia, Somalia, Sudan (up to 1985), and Zaire, and the USSR in Angola, Mozambique, Somalia, Ethiopia, and Guinea. Mostly this was in the form of aid, arms, and military training, though Cuba made quite substantial commitments of its own troops in Angola and Ethiopia. Cold War-inspired external military assistance had the biggest impact in the Horn and in Southern Africa, where the quantities of arms supplied were large, and sometimes included heavy equipment such as tanks, armour, and artillery, and sophisticated items such as SAM systems and military jets. Cuban forces and Soviet equipment (along with the UN arms embargo on South Africa) were crucial in denying air superiority to South Africa in Angola, thus blocking South Africa's interventions aimed at helping UNITA to overthrow the MPLA government. One estimate suggests that between 1977 and 1987 the USSR sank some $4 billion into aiding the MPLA (O'Neill and Munslow 1995: 182–90). With the ending of the Cold War, outside interest in Africa's security issues has declined. Russian and Chinese military influence has more or less disappeared. The USA remains generally at arm's length, though it does support Uganda and Ethiopia against the militant Islamic regime in Khartoum, and played a role in the coming to power of Kabila in Zaire/DR Congo (*Strategic Survey* 1996–7: 212, 223).

Of the ex-colonial powers, France retained the strongest presence, not infrequently including small, but locally weighty, military forces. It has intervened in Chad, the Central African Republic, Gabon, Rwanda, and Nigeria, and engaged in a territorial dispute with Madagascar over some Indian Ocean islands. French troops were directly involved in the civil war in Chad on various occasions, and the extent of French presence and engagement in West Africa has made it in some ways the main 'local' rival to Nigeria. France supported Biafra during the Nigerian civil war, rivalled Nigerian interventions in Chad, and backed Francophone support for Charles Taylor against the Nigerian-led ECOMOG force in Liberia (Clapham 1996: 121–5). With the ending of the Cold War, even France has reduced its presence in Africa. But its record there shows how even quite small outside resources can rival those available locally in Africa, and so make a disproportionate impact, a fact illustrated during 2000 by the ability of a few hundred British troops to shift the military balance in Sierra Leone. The same logic applies to mercenary forces. Mercenary companies such as Executive Outcomes have worked for MPLA in Angola, and in civil conflicts in Uganda and Sierra Leone. Mercenary interventions have taken place in the Comoros, the Seychelles, and Sierra Leone.

Superpower security dynamics thus made a substantial impact on Africa even though the resources committed were relatively small. Like almost everything else in African security, the global level had its main impact locally, and was itself largely shaped by local events. As in the Middle East, it is hard to find cases where outside powers generated conflicts, and easy to find cases where outside interventions added fuel to (or sometimes poured water on) fires already burning for local reasons. By the end of the 1990s, there was a clear sense that outside powers had no strong political interests in Africa and were reluctant to entangle themselves in its seemingly endless cycles of crisis and war. The 11th of September provoked some US interest in al-Qaeda connections in Sudan and Somalia, and to the West African diamond trade. But these developments did not change the essentially marginal place of Africa in global power concerns, and the meagre results of the G8's 'Africa summit' in June 2002 looked unlikely to break this pattern. During, and more so after, the Cold War, the global level political impact in Africa was perhaps most strongly carried by the UN. In a general sense, the UN sustained and legitimised the system of juridical sovereignty, which served Africa so badly. In a specific sense the UN and its agencies provided much of the aid and the PKOs that in the event largely failed to solve Africa's political, military, and economic problems.

Two further aspects of the global level need to be mentioned. First is that many African elites publicly embraced a negative view of globalisation, and took the view that their weak position in the global periphery was a major explanation for their difficulties. This led to a convenient rhetoric of 'neo-colonial' securitisation that sought, often successfully, to divert attention from the indigenous causes of Africa's difficulties. Ironically, many of those elites drew the financial support for their power from the availability of global markets for diamonds, hardwood, oil, tantalum, and a variety of other mineral resources, and it was the ease of this relationship that fuelled many of Africa's dictators, warlords, and insurgency movements.

Second is the noteworthy extent to which outside actors securitise events in Africa, which are not (or much less so) securitised in Africa itself. The most obvious current example of this is AIDS, which has attracted securitisation moves in both the UN and the United States, but which until recently seemed to be a taboo topic across large sections of African elites and masses. Given the horrendous levels of HIV infection in many African states (e.g., over 4 million in South Africa), and the already large social and economic impact of the disease, this local reticence seems an outstanding example of undersecuritisation in the face of a palpable existential threat. Outside actors also seem much more minded than African ones to securitise other elements of African life, whether wildlife and rainforest preservation, other aspects of public health, or migrations. Perhaps this imbalance between securitisations made inside and outside Africa can also be laid at the door of the failed postcolonial state. With such a poorly developed political apparatus, and with such fragmented civil societies, Africa is incapable of giving adequate voice to its own security agenda. The extreme scenario on this external/internal split is Kaplan's (1994: 52) prediction of an 'Atlantic wall of disease' constructed by the United States following from a securitisation of Africa's development as one grand slide into anarchy, producing transnational security threats to itself and others and therefore to be isolated, i.e., Africa securitised as such.

Conclusions

The security problem in Africa since decolonisation has been dominated by the widespread failure of postcolonial weak states. Such states are not unique to Africa, but nowhere else are they clustered together in large numbers unmixed with stronger neighbours. It is this clustering, plus the extremeness of state weakness, that gives Africa its unique security qualities. The theme of this chapter has been the dominance of the domestic level, which with only a few exceptions frames the great bulk of security dynamics in Africa. Paralleling that has been our persistent discomfort with the designation of these dynamics as 'domestic', with its implicit overprivileging of the state. Rather than being domestic, this level is better seen as substate, involving a quasi-autonomous pattern of actors and security dynamics that is only partly attached to, and only partly dependent on, the ragged framework of the Westphalian state system in Africa. In some places, the state framework is fairly robust, in others it is enfeebled to the point of disappearance, leaving the field open to other players, whether ones with traditional roots or simply warlordist gangs. A more detailed exploration of the security dynamics among these actors has been beyond our resources. But it may be the key to knowing how 'regional' security dynamics in Africa really work, and research along these lines looks like becoming increasingly necessary for understanding African security during the coming decades.

Conclusions

One comparative insight comes from Krause's (1996) argument about how most of the third world has failed to benefit from the developmental interplay between war and state-making that eventually generated the strong states of Europe. Given the accounts just presented, Krause's argument would seem to hold true for both Africa and the Middle East, though its effects have been quite different between the two. In Africa, the ability of military-political elites to obtain economic resources to fight wars without engaging in the economic or political development of their societies has largely wrecked the process of state formation. On the other hand, in the Middle East it has resulted in the consolidation of a regional state system populated largely by authoritarian regimes, and full of interstate wars and rivalries. Consequently, in neither place is there much prospect of democratisation, and therefore not much hope of democratic peace. In both areas, pan-ideologies remain influential, but subordinate to more fragmented political structures. Both areas are also subject to strong patterns of securitisation by the West that are in some respects markedly different from the patterns of securitisation generated within the regions. The West (especially Europe) fears migration from both, and securitises oil, WMD, and radical Islam in the Middle East, and public health and the environment in Africa.

The political disintegration of Africa and the interstate conflict formation in the Middle East respectively underpin the prognoses that RSCT allows us to project for them.

Africa

In Africa, the ending of the Cold War mattered, but not as much as elsewhere. It made a specific difference in Southern Africa, where the delegitimation of anti-communism as a securitising rhetoric in South Africa helped to pave the way for the winding down of apartheid. More generally, it helped stimulate the slow but steady disengagement of outside powers from Africa's military-political troubles. The increasing tendency to leave Africans to their own devices reflected Africa's marginality to the post-Cold War global political economy. Unlike in the Middle East, where the end of the Cold War produced a shift from bipolar to unipolar intervention, in Africa the shift was from bipolar intervention to a near absence of any sustained great power interest or engagement. Africa may not have much in the way of power resources to resist external intervention or overlay, but neither does it have much in the way of attractions, especially not when overlay itself is unfashionable.

More salient than the ending of the Cold War has been the ending of the decolonisation era, which ran in parallel with the Cold War and was partly linked to it. The decolonisation era in Africa was largely defined by the belief that the transplant of a Westphalian state system would eventually take root, and by the attempt on the part of the international community to hold that system in place. Running in parallel with it was the Cold War ideological rivalry, which served both to stimulate outside engagement in Africa and to define it as an arena for ideological competition. During the 1990s, all of that disappeared. Belief that the African state system can be made to work (or at least that this can be done on a timescale of decades rather than centuries) has declined, as has the will of outside states to hold the system in place. This has occurred without any alternative vision arising to take the place of the failed Westphalian project, of how Africa could and should be politically structured. If it has been the crisis of the African state that has defined the security problem in Africa during the decolonisation era, it may well be the absence of the state, or any other form of political order higher than warlordism, that defines it for much of the continent in the coming decades.

Despite the low levels of power in Africa, there is no chance of renewal of colonial overlay either by recolonisation or as some new form of UN mandate. With the possible exception of Southern Africa, there is also little chance of any of Africa's RSCs becoming centred, either around a single dominant power or through the development of security communities (although the West African one clearly is unipolar, a Nigeria-centred order would have limited legitimacy). If the more pessimistic scenarios of state failure dominate, then much of Africa will move back towards unstructured status, or at least a status structured only on a micro-scale. If the more optimistic scenarios about state development prevail, then the likely outcome is a consolidation of the pattern of conflict formations and weak security regimes already in place. Because Africa's RSCs are still quite weakly formed and often lack very clear boundaries, the potential for external transformations is quite high. This is most obviously so in relation to the fluid situation in Central Africa. Because many of Africa's states are so unstable, the possibilities for internal transformation are legion. Given the high degree of political fragmentation in Africa, changes in individual actors may not matter all that much to the essential structures of its RSCs. But in some cases it would matter: the disintegration of Nigeria, for example, would effectively kill the weak security regime in West Africa.

The Middle East

In the Middle Eastern RSC, conflict is overdetermined, and it is not clear that *any* likely development in the region would change its character as a classic conflict formation. The failure of the peace process cements Arab–Israel hostility into place for many more years, now with the additional burdens and complications created by the 'war against terrorism'. But even if, at some future point, Israel was not acting on the assumption of being existentially threatened, but merely one (strong) player in a more fluid balance-of-power system, its much higher level of development would still imbue its neighbours with fear. As already apparent during the peace process, Arab and Islamic rejection of the right of the Jewish state to exist could be replaced by fears of becoming an economic periphery to an Israeli core. Also indicative of the embeddedness of the conflict formation in the Middle East is the effect of Turkey. The addition of a more active Turkey strengthens Israel by giving it a powerful local partner, and reinforces the US position in the region. It also adds new conflict and alignment possibilities especially with Syria, Iraq, and Iran. Democratisation in the Arab states would, at least initially, almost certainly exacerbate conflict by giving voice to the opinion of the Arab 'street', and is unlikely to happen soon anyway. The region is too well developed to fall back into an unstructured position, and given the high degree of enmity and rivalry within it, the chance of a serious security regime or security community coming about during the next two decades seems virtually nil.

The probability of overlay is also low, both because of the powers of resistance within the region and because (with the possible exception of

US ambitions towards Iraq) of a lack of will to undertake such a project among the great powers. The currently quite high levels of US penetration into the region will be sustained so long as the United States defines itself as a superpower and retains its concerns about oil, Israel, and global terrorism, but seem more likely to decrease than increase as time wears on. A diminution in the economic importance of oil would almost certainly reduce global level interest in the region. The US position is not secure. Revolutions or big political shifts within the GCC states could easily sweep away its positions in the Gulf, as happened earlier in Iran, and to the Soviet Union in Egypt. As Saddam Hussein knows too well, the territorial boundaries of Iraq, Syria, Jordan, and the states of the Arabian peninsula have only shallow roots. These states are held in place as much (or more) by international society's framework of juridical sovereignty as by their own history or legitimacy. Among other things, this is what makes the consequences of another major US intervention into Iraq so laced with potentially extensive and destabilising side effects. A greater EU role in the core subcomplexes is too far away to be worth thinking about, though not in the Maghreb.

There are quite a few possibilities for internal transformation, whether by changes in the power structure or changes in patterns of amity and enmity. Some of these might make a substantial difference, as if the Arab–Israel hostility died down, or if several of the Gulf Arab states imploded, or were captured by Islamic extremists. Because many of the players in this RSC are weak states, changes of leadership can make a big difference, and many new leaderships are in the offing as an older generation passes. But given the singular complexity of crosscutting alignments and enmities among the many members of this RSC, changes would have to be dramatic in order to make much difference to the functioning or character of the RSC overall. In this sense, the dominant level of security in the Middle East is the regional one. The regional level has so far outlasted and overridden superpower interventions of whatever sort. It also seems to be the case that the security dynamics of the Levant and Gulf subcomplexes are becoming increasingly interlinked, strengthening the dynamics of the RSC as a whole over those of its core subcomplexes.

External transformation by northward expansion of the RSC into Central Asia or the Caucasus does not look likely. Iran, Turkey, and Saudi Arabia all have economic and cultural interests in those regions, but no clear-cut interest in a security engagement where other big powers are also in play (see ch. 13). Nothing obvious seems likely either to draw these new states into the Middle East's security dynamics, or to draw Middle Eastern states into these areas to such an extent as to turn them away from their more immediate and traditional security preoccupations. Turkey seems likely to remain an insulator between the Middle East and European RSCs, but probably a considerably more engaged one than during the Cold War. It may become more like Afghanistan, not in the sense of being internally chaotic, but in the sense of engaging in several different directions without knitting their security dynamics together. As argued in part II, Afghanistan seems likely to remain an effective insulator between the Middle East, Central Asia, and South Asia despite the intrusion of Arab politics into its domestic life with the alliance between al-Qaeda and the Taleban, and the consequent US-led assault on the country. Southward, however, when one considers the interplay between the Middle East and Africa, the picture is not so clear.

Interplay between the Middle East and Africa

It is not controversial to consider the Middle East and Africa as politically and culturally distinct. Yet in some ways to talk of a border between the Middle East and Africa is to misrepresent the reality. What exists is a frontier zone running from Mauritania in the west to Sudan in the east, within which the Middle Eastern RSC on the one hand, and the West African and Horn RSCs on the other, blend into each other (as do the peoples, races, cultures, and religions). Notwithstanding the insulating effects of the Sahara desert, there has been quite a lot of security interaction within and even across this zone. As Clapham (1996: 117, 128–9) notes, because of the disparities in wealth and weapons, 'for Arab states Africa was a hinterland into which they could seek to extend their own power and influence'. This inequality is the key to the frontier. Although they intervene regularly in Africa, the Arab world's primary security concerns have been with Israel, each other, and the West. With the exception of mostly Europe-bound migrants, very little of African security dynamics penetrates back into the Middle East, so the flow is largely one-way. Although they are in part the northern tier of the West Africa proto-complex, Mauritania, Mali, Niger, Chad, and perhaps the Central African Republic have a loose enough association with it that they can also constitute an insulator zone between the Maghreb and West Africa. Mauritania, for example, is a member of both ECOWAS and the AMU. Sudan is pulled in several directions: north towards the

Arabs, east towards the Horn, south towards the Great Lakes, and west towards the Sahel (Clapham 1996: 118).

Several of the Middle Eastern states have penetrated regularly into the boundary zone, and some of them have reached deep into tropical Africa. Libya has intervened with money, arms, and sometimes its own troops, in Benin, Chad, Burkina Faso, the Central African Republic, DR Congo, Ethiopia, Gambia, Liberia, Niger, Sudan, and Uganda, sometimes operating as part of a Soviet-sponsored grouping, such as the 'Aden Axis' of Libya, Ethiopia, and South Yemen during the early 1980s. Morocco, sometimes operating as an ally of the United States, has intervened in Angola, Benin, Equatorial Guinea, and Zaire. Saudi Arabia, Iraq, and Syria have occasionally intervened in the Horn, as has Israel. There have been interregional territorial disputes between Libya and Chad, Eritrea and Yemen, and Morocco and Mauritania (over Western Sahara).

Two tricky questions arise about the regional security structure along the Middle East–Africa frontier: what is happening to the Maghreb? And, how is Egypt to be positioned?

We have argued that, during the 1990s, the Maghreb (Libya, Tunisia, Algeria, Morocco, Western Sahara) seemed to be drifting away from the Middle Eastern core. The link between the two was never particularly strong. Some regional experts do not even count the Maghreb as part of the Middle East (Gause 1999: 25). What linked them was the Arab/Islamic mobilisation against Israel, which declined during the peace process. The breakdown of that process makes the drift away more difficult, though the Maghreb remains exposed to the influence of its neighbouring great power, the EU, which will strongly shape its internal dynamics. But unless migration becomes a leading feature of securitisation within the EU, the Maghreb will *not* become a subcomplex of Europe. For the EU, the Mediterranean is an interregional boundary, and the relationship with North Africa is to be managed in that context.

Within the frame of RSCT, Egypt poses a challenge. We have positioned it as a major player in the core complex of the Middle East, and for the period under consideration that seems accurate. Egypt has not much involved itself in the affairs of either the Maghreb or the Horn, and has been largely focused on Israel and the balance of power and influence in the Arab heartlands. But, in the past, Egypt has projected its power south into Sudan, and west into the Maghreb, as well as north and east. Should that pattern recur, Egypt could be a member of three RSCs at once, which the theory does not allow. There are some historical and structural parallels between Egypt's position and that of Turkey. According to RSCT, Egypt would either have to unite all of the complexes of which it was a part, or act as an insulator between them. Given Egypt's strong links to the Middle East, a disengagement sufficient to allow an insulator role seems unlikely. Given that Egypt is a leading regional power, the theory predicts merger. A more active interplay between Egypt and the Maghreb would not be troublesome given that the Maghreb is still within the wider Middle Eastern RSC. That would simply strengthen connections that already exist. But a more active interplay between Egypt and the Horn would require a merger of two currently separate RSCs. Egypt has significant ties to Sudan (sometimes hostile, sometimes friendly) and a persistent low-level rivalry with Ethiopia. Given the strong link created by the Nile River system, and Egypt's total dependence on its waters, it is possible to imagine the emergence of a regional security dynamic across the present divide. Sudan has Arab and Islamic ties, and Israel, Yemen, and Saudi Arabia already play into the Horn. For the time being, Egypt is an outside player in the Horn, but in the future the Horn could become a subcomplex within the Middle Eastern conflict formation.

Part IV
The Americas

Introduction

In contrast to what happened later in Africa and Asia, the Americas were not just occupied, but largely repeopled, by Europe. With the exceptions of Canada and a few Caribbean colonies, the European settler-states in the Americas broke free from Britain, Spain, and Portugal during the late eighteenth and early nineteenth centuries. As happened later in Africa and Asia, this first wave of decolonisation was achieved by taking on the form of the European state and, as this was done, the conditions for standard RSCs came into being.

Despite recurrent hemispheric projects, the Americas are not one RSC. North and South America have different security dynamics and connections are highly asymmetrical. US engagement in Latin America is a classical case of a complex containing a great power impinging on a neighbouring one without great powers. South America has only infrequently been the primary security concern of the United States, and in South America the driving security dynamics are mostly regional, not US-orientated. So even recurring US involvement does not justify seeing the Americas as one RSC. The USA is an (important) external actor in South America, and South America has some spillover security effects in North America, but most issues that upset Canada will be of minor relevance to Brazil and vice versa.

It is clear that North America is one RSC, and equally clear how to delineate it towards north, east, and west, but it is less clear where it ends to the south. Traditionally the concept of North America did not include Mexico, which was grouped on cultural and linguistic grounds with Latin and/or Central America. Today it is much more common to see Mexico counted as North America. This is not only because of NAFTA – rather NAFTA reflects a change in larger patterns.

South America also forms one RSC. Subregions within South America are quite distinct and – the analysis will show – increasingly differentiated. This could motivate treating the Southern Cone and the Andean North as separate RSCs, but security concerns for all of South America still connect too much for that. State level chains of interconnecting dyads and triangles that were the traditional type of connector have gradually declined in intensity and saliency. But significant transnational spillover does cross the boundary, and Brazilian concern about Latin America as such, and therefore about issues such as US military involvement in Colombia as well as the competing integration schemes (Southern Cone, Andean, NAFTA, and all-American FTAA), plays a key part in tying the South American RSC together.

How to designate Central America and the Caribbean is less self-evident. The Caribbean has many distinct features, and regularly links up to Central or South America. If left to itself, the combination of weak powers and insulating water would make the Caribbean an unstructured region. Central America has strong enough indigenous security dynamics to count as a subcomplex, and its links to Latin America are strong. But whatever their original form, during the last decades of the nineteenth century both areas were drawn into North America by expanding US power and in some cases sovereignty. The United States ejected Spain from Cuba, overtook Mexican and British influence, acquired several Caribbean island territories, and created Panama to host a canal that would greatly facilitate its own shipping and naval movements. Despite their southward ties (which we signal by using the term 'Latin America') these areas were absorbed into the North American RSC. This case is a useful example of where the pattern of *regional security* does not line up with other patterns of regionality.

In North America, the USA gradually became by far the most powerful state, and by the late nineteenth century was extending its own formal and informal empire into Central America and the Caribbean. South America too was penetrated by US power, but not so heavily as to constitute overlay. The new South American states fell into a classical conflict formation with arms competitions, territorial disputes, power rivalries, security dilemmas, and a few substantial wars and crises (Paraguay vs Argentina, Brazil, and Uruguay, 1865–70; Chile vs Bolivia and Peru, 1879–84; Paraguay vs Bolivia, 1928–35; Colombia vs Peru, 1932–3). The operation of this regional security dynamic was muted by low interaction capacity: the limited capabilities of the local states concerned, plus the formidable geographical barriers that separated many of the main areas of population from each other. Nevertheless, it constituted a clear and early example of a 'third world' RSC, complete with penetration by outside rival powers looking for both political influence and access to resources and markets.

The Cold War allowed the United States to maintain its hegemony over North America and, up to a point, to increase its penetration of the South American RSC. Canada became closely bound to the United States in both NATO and NORAD, though it managed to avoid any significant stationing of US forces on its territory. The already heavy US penetration into the Caribbean and Central America was highlighted by US bases in Panama and Cuba, and a regular pattern of political and military intervention (Guatemala, Dominican Republic, Grenada, Panama). Castro's revolution in Cuba and his subsequent alignment with the Soviet Union created a defiant exception to this rule, and provided a reason for the USA to draw South America more closely into its Cold War policy network. Although falling far short of overlay, and not involving any significant basing of US military forces, the anti-communist policy shared by Washington and most South American governments did bring the South American RSC more closely within the US sphere of influence. Membership in the OAS gave the United States a legitimate role in South American regional politics. Perhaps most significant was that shared Cold War security logics reduced the prominence, and possibly even the intensity, of indigenous security dynamics. South America was neither overlaid like Europe, nor subject to heavy military penetration like East Asia, but its autonomy as an RSC was quite seriously constrained. Similar to the pattern in Cold War Southeast Asia, its former indigenous regional security dynamic of interstate rivalries was downgraded in favour of domestic conflicts that most often posed military governments against leftist rebels, mirroring Cold War alignments.

The end of the Cold War has had some limited and largely indirect effects in South America and potentially huge but unsettled effects in North America. Regional relations generally improved, especially in the southern part of South America, though this was at least as much a consequence of democratisation and pressures from globalisation as of the ending of the Cold War. In North America, a more radical but hypothetical possibility is that the nature and cohesion of the US state will change because of diminished external challenge, although the terrorist attacks of September 2001 temporarily pushed this scenario into the background. The overall global policy of the United States certainly is at stake. US military presence in the Caribbean and Central America

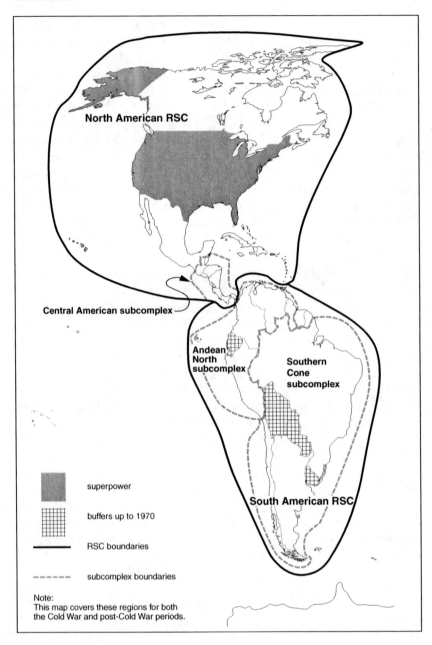

Map 8. RSCs in the Americas

diminishes with the removal of Cold War concerns about extra-hemispheric intrusion, i.e., global dynamics, but the increasing centrality of a securitised drugs issue might very well uphold the general US involvement. In the case of a decreasingly global orientation of the USA, hemispheric security would be likely to increase its salience in US security.

Similarities between North and South America include: European settlers, an indigenous population that has been relegated to a marginal role, and colonies gaining independence more than a century before the rest of the third world and therefore being among the first non-European states in international society. The Americas set much of the precedent for later decolonisation. Among the differences is that North American independence came some decades earlier than South America's, and that the United States and Canada have been economically more successful. North America also became a centred RSC and, in contrast to the conflict formation and balance-of-power system of South America, developed the first modern security community on this basis. 'But had the Portuguese gained Pacific and Caribbean footholds, or had the Spanish left a united Spanish America, how differently might local and strategic geopolitics have evolved' (Kelly 1997: 169). North America contains a great power; South America is a standard RSC, although with a twentieth-century history that has an unusually low number of wars. This raises the question about the existence of one or more security regimes, or even a security community. Since North America includes the leading power of the twentieth and the early twenty-first century, the regional development in North America has been closely connected to global developments. North America is the classical case of a centred RSC. It is therefore an interesting place to explore the nature of such a complex where the traditional interstate dynamics are weak. Finally, the relationship between the two RSCs is interesting because the longevity of asymmetrical relations in relative isolation from other external involvement makes the Americas an ideal case for exploring an interregional constellation.

9   North America: the sole superpower and its surroundings

Introduction

Most books on regional security omit a chapter on North America. This might reflect American intellectual hegemony whereby 'regional security' comes to mean 'all the other regions as an element in American global policy'. If regional security means 'the rest of the world as seen from here', 'here' is not a region. Furthermore, with a traditional concept of security it is not evident what should be covered under the heading of regional security in North America. Already before the Cold War it was well established that the states in the region did not fear or threaten each other in a military sense; during the Cold War their enemy was the Soviet Union, and since the end of the Cold War the most lively security debate has been in the USA, where the concerns of the official debate are located outside the region. In the field of security as elsewhere, the USA is 'utopia achieved' (Baudrillard 1988: 77) in the sense that the dominant IR vision in the USA right from the start has been to leave the world of security, to create in America a New World freed from the anxiety and corrupting dynamics among the states familiar from Europe. Judging from most books on regional security, this has been a success: there seem to be no such things as regional security problems in North America. We will show here what the securitisation-based story of North America looks like.

North America is among the settler-regions where mainly European immigration replaced indigenous polities with new states. Continuity with pre-settler history is sufficiently thin that a history of the RSC (orientated towards the present as ours is) need not go back to the interplay between 'Indian' tribes. The United States was the first settler-nation to gain independence, and compared to that of most other regions the history of North America as an independent RSC is long. It is theoretically important to RSCT because it is the textbook case of a 'centred' region. In EU-Europe and the CIS, and possibly Southern Africa, West Africa, and South Asia, we are watching efforts to structure a centred RSC, but the one long-established case is North America.

The first part of North America's history follows the relatively common pattern in which an RSC is born by decolonisation and becomes a conflict formation. The less common part and thus what should be looked at more in detail is the process whereby the region became both centred and a security community.

In relation to future 'scenarios' and 'transformations', the North American case has a number of givens. The unipolar structure is not an issue (unless one believes in real disintegration of the USA as an option). The boundaries of the region also look relatively stable for the future, not least with the more definitive inclusion of Mexico – now also in self-perceptions, not only from an observer's perspective – in North America since the 1980s. In addition to North America proper, the RSC has absorbed the Caribbean and Central America. As explained in the South American chapter, one possible change in the future is an extension of overlay south into the northern, Andean part of South America (due to the anti-drugs involvement). This, however, would hardly affect the central dynamics of the North American RSC. Deep transformation of the region is not on the agenda in terms of boundaries or the basic structural form of the RSC. The main current issues are transformations in the nature and hierarchy of security issues and a changing relationship among the levels.

The second section of this chapter, covering the pre-Cold War period, opens with early American security history (1585–1870). The United States is at the centre of this section, as it is, to some extent, of the chapter, because it achieved independence first, because its characteristics have shaped the region, and because it is the central power. To this core is then added the basic pattern of North American interstate relations, that is US–Mexican and US–Canadian relations (1848–c. 1990) plus Central America and the Caribbean. Finally, this section briefly describes how the USA became a global power and what this meant to regional security. The Cold War period is covered in the third section and the post-Cold War RSC in the fourth.

During the twentieth century North America was an atypical RSC. In other centred regions the key powers consciously shaped their region as a way to manage security. In the case of North America the paradox has been that the United States was the key power shaping the region, but it did not think much in regional terms, and acted mainly on global concerns (with strong domestic colouring). Its shaping of the region was therefore an indirect byproduct of its global concerns. The other countries of the region by contrast are much more interested in the regional situation. Traditionally, Mexico has guarded carefully against the negative effects of this US dominance, while Canada has maintained a more open regime but has still been watchful.

The formation of an RSC in North America

Early American security history (1585–1870)

From the 1520s, 'New Spain' gradually extended northwards through Central America into what is today the United States. Half a century later, small colonies of British, French, and Dutch settlers started to grow along the East Coast. Increasingly, both the colonists (and even more so strategists in the mother countries) started to think about the long-term position and control of the region. As a result, regional security first coalesced in the middle of the eighteenth century in the form of triangular politics of British, French, and Indians (especially the Iroquois Confederacy; Richter 1983; N. Crawford 1994). This exerted pressure on the British settlers to unite or at least cooperate. By 1763, all of North America east of the Mississippi was in the hands of the British. Demographically, the French grew very slowly compared to the British community, and the Amerindian populations were stagnating and soon to enter rapid decline.

Already at this point, local factors in the New World played a surprisingly large role in a game involving two of the leading powers of the day. This general pattern emerges even more clearly towards the beginning of the nineteenth century: the Americans benefited from conflicts in Europe which tied down the great powers, preventing them from devoting many resources to faraway places like North America (Bemis 1957; Perkins 1993: 230–1).

So far North America behaved largely like a normal balance-of-power system: with one threat gone, new rivalries took over – the colonies gained independence and the next balance was the one between them and the British with occasional French involvement. At another level, North America did not develop according to the classical European model. As argued by Deudney (1995), 'the Philadelphian system' within the United States differed fundamentally from the Westphalian one. It was not based on the concentration of power in states that led to anarchy externally and hierarchy internally, but on a states-union, a 'compound republic' made up of semi-autonomous republics. From independence to the Civil War, this construction tried to stave off the dual threat of anarchy and hierarchy, to secure against external threats as well as internal tyranny (a 'negarchy' according to Deudney). After the Civil War, much of this uniqueness was lost because the latterday United States could more easily be fitted into the classical category of the state and the story therefore more neatly divided into foreign and domestic. Important for our purpose is the higher status of the internal threat of tyranny as a 'Philadelphian' security concern equally important to foreign attack – and the close connection of the two. Notably, the fear of a tyrant using (alleged) external threats to consolidate power domestically (e.g., through the use of 'standing armies') became a permanent element in American politics.

In terms of securitisation, the fight for independence was not motivated by 'national security', since the colonists began the war thinking of themselves as British. It was partly a fight for principles, against what they saw as a tyrannical conspiracy against liberty (e.g., Bailyn 1992; Perkins 1993: 17ff.); partly for a 'quasi-nation', an emerging 'we'. However, the latter was rarely defined in terms of existential threat, but rather interests – economic or political, for example, 'no taxation without representation'. The survival issue was interestingly mainly to do with the former, i.e., political principles relevant for all the king's subjects.

When deciding afterwards how to structure the newly independent polity, the decisive arguments of the *Federalist Papers* (Hamilton et al. 1911) were phrased very much in terms similar to our scenarios. An independent RSC had to decide whether it should be a decentralised balance-of-power system or centralised enough both to restrain internal security threats and to deter external ones. Notably, the external part was not formulated in terms of threats from other North American parties (neither the loyalists to the north, Spanish or French colonies to the south, nor native Indians). The arguments were phrased as if the United States was already alone on the continent, threatened only by extra-regional powers (Europeans). The other North American actors were treated solely as manifestations of their European masters, implying that only the United States was truly American. The threats were therefore either internal among the thirteen former colonies (discord or dictatorship depending on the side one took in the federalist/anti-federalist

271

struggle) or region-external. This probably reflects the largely implicit assumption, which became much more important in the middle to late nineteenth century, that the US-Americans were destined to overspread the continent and establish like-minded republics or – as became increasingly the view – expanding the one republic.

The specific steps of US expansion need not interest us here. Important milestones were the Louisiana purchase (1803) by which the French were totally removed and the continent opened towards the west; acquisition of the Floridas (1819) and Texas (1845); the 1846 war with Mexico producing the current border to the south; and the 1867 purchase of Alaska from Russia. Indian resistance remained active until late in the nineteenth century.

To the north, the expectation was clearly continental, i.e., the 'Canadians' would join sooner or later. But after the failed 1812 attack, this expansion was expected to come peacefully by way of the attraction of US dynamism ('the gravitational theory'; see Shore 1998). This optimism seemed particularly obvious in the case of what became Canada, because it was seen as constituting what the United States had been – British colonies – and thus, given the inevitability of the US development, the same had to apply to Canada even if it were delayed. This logic did not apply to Mexico because of racism – one did not want to bring 'inferior' races into the United States (Perkins 1993: 173). To be born out of British political institutions, in contrast to having Latin roots, was also seen as the reason for successful democracy; in addition, strong anti-Catholicism in the United States made southern expansion unattractive. Consequently, the policy towards the south concentrated on shifting the boundary towards the 'natural border', the Rio Grande (Perkins 1993: 177). The belief in 'manifest destiny' at first mostly applied to western expansion.

Although the phrase 'manifest destiny' was coined only in 1845, John Quincy Adams already in 1816 wrote that the United States was destined to be 'coextensive with the North American Continent, destined by God and by nature to be the most populous and powerful people ever combined under one social contract' (Perkins 1993: 4, 177). 'A continental empire' and de facto dominance of North America was achieved, but not a single republic. The formal pattern was eventually made up of three states: Mexico (independent 1821), Canada (from 1867 dominion, independent 1926), and the United States.

The US Civil War reintroduced international relations in every sense of the term to the heart of the continent. The pattern of limited global

272

level interference continued because the British did not more fully support the Confederacy (Adams 1973: 110–27; Jones 1992; LaFeber 1989: 140–5). Primarily, the Civil War is important for the RSC through its *effects on the USA* – not only the immediate effect of maintaining one state, but equally the effect on the degree of stateness. The Civil War was a turning point in American state-building, triggering both a new kind of nationalism, and an expansion and strengthening of the state apparatus (see Skowronek 1982; LaFeber 1989: 148ff.; Bensel 1990; Zakaria 1998). Of course, the accelerating industrialisation of the North contributed both to the outcome of the war and to the transformation of the state afterwards, but much of the 'Philadelphian' system with its constraints on stateness collapsed during the Civil War and the period of reconstruction.

Both the growing industrial output of the United States and the show of military might during the war contributed to the general acceptance in the world that the country had become a great power. Its ambitions were mostly regional, concentrated within the hemisphere (and with colonial forays into the Pacific) until the First World War and more importantly the Second. The British attempt to balance in the region was given up (Bourne 1967), and the region at this point became a centred RSC.

This shape of the region explains the asymmetrical treatment of the states in this chapter. US domestic developments have structural implications for the region in a way that those of the other states do not. For instance, the US way of thinking about foreign policy is important for understanding the relations that emerge. A dominant power will always have more leeway to follow its internally generated preferences – and thus project domestic dilemmas or ideational peculiarities on to the system, whereas a weaker power to a larger extent will let the domestic situation adapt to the internationally possible (see Rosenau 1981).

If summarised, the explanation for regional centralisation includes at least three factors. First are power and dynamism, i.e., the overwhelming growth in the population and economy of the United States compared to all other powers. Second is a 'philosophical' component, according to which the United States did not strive for creation of a balance-of-power system, but aimed to transcend such Europeanness and create a 'negarchy' which implicitly pointed towards internalisation of the relevant world, i.e., a universalist, regional vision for a system originally in between domestic and international, and eventually conducive to a legitimate centralised system. Third is a global–regional relationship in which global powers did not penetrate the region as much as they could have done and in which, at crucial points, external powers even helped the emerging regional great power (i.e., French support for the American revolutionaries).

Establishing the basic pattern of North American interstate relations (US–Mexican and US–Canadian relations 1848–1990)

One important background for the emergence of US–Mexican and US–Canadian relations is the US self-conception and understanding of IR, *not* conceived in terms of *balance*. The US tradition of international thought is predominantly universalist and based on principles rather than reciprocity (see e.g. Bercovitch 1978; Brands 1998; Campbell 1992; Greene 1993; McDougall 1997). None of the relations therefore developed on the basis of a presumption that they ought to approach some kind of equality norm. The Canadians and especially the Mexicans, in contrast, have therefore vigorously pushed the basic sovereignty principles of international law.

The US–Mexican relationship had to develop out of the shadows of a war (1846) that was a national disaster for Mexico. The boundary was broadly settled by the peace treaty after the war mostly along the Rio Grande, but continued to raise minor controversies because of asymmetrical interests in what and how the border divides and because the river itself was unstable (Prescott 1987: 81–92).

From 1876 to 1911 the relationship was defined by the relative stability and liberalisation of the Profirio Díaz presidency, which allowed American investments to significantly influence Mexico's economy and society. The Mexican revolution (1911–17) defined the basic conditions for the policy until 1982: strong nationalism and close monitoring of American influence in Mexico. Issues of nationalisation – especially of oil – were a source of tension and potential American intervention, until accepted by Roosevelt in 1938 as part of the 'good neighbour' policy (see ch. 10). Both world wars helped relations, because the United States worried more about the otherwise unlikely scenario that Mexico would bolster its position by an alignment with an extra-regional enemy of the United States. The Cold War partly had this effect too, but it contributed to tensions as well because of disagreement about US interventions in Central America and tough policy towards Cuba.

Until the 1980s, Mexico was in many ways in the same situation as the Central American states only more so. The general pattern of security concerns between the United States and Central America is a highly asymmetrical one, in which as argued by Gonzalez and Haggard the United States worries about (1) 'the willingness and capacity of the smaller power to protect the property rights and economic interests of the larger', i.e., conflicts over expropriation, debt repayment, and the general climate for American firms (Gonzalez and Haggard 1998: 299); (2) crossborder externalities – previously banditry, now immigration, drugs flows, and environmental problems; and (3) concerns about 'the underlying political stability, and thus reliability, of the smaller one'. To this should be added that the weaker states in turn are worried about (1) cultural and economic dominance by the United States, and (2) direct interventions. Military interventions have been increasingly unlikely in relation to Mexico – whereas they have remained relevant in US–Central American relations – and the threat to Mexico is, instead, US unilateralism, i.e., one-sided decisions about the operation of US drugs police across the border and similar infringements on Mexican sovereignty. This was the general pattern for US–Mexican relations for almost all of the twentieth century.

The US–Canadian relationship is the core of the centred, non-balancing, and security community features of the North American RSC. Had this remained tense and conflictual, the RSC would have had to go through some form of major test – probably a war – to settle whether the USA should be counterbalanced on the continent or Canada absorbed. Instead a mutual acceptance developed of a situation in which Canada remained independent and (unofficially) the USA pre-eminent on the continent. Thus, the centred formation gained the 'legitimacy' that Watson (1992) deems crucial for centred formations.

This outcome was in no way predetermined. The border was originally militarised and much territory was contested. Annexation was widely desired in the United States and generally seen as inevitable. In 1812, the USA failed to conquer Canada, but the assumption of inevitable annexation actually helped to stabilise the relationship, because the USA could afford to stabilise a border that would one day disappear. Eventually, demilitarisation and mutual recognition of that border served to desecuritise the relationship. As argued by Shore (1998), the border became a trust-generating mechanism, and in his view it became a second core process leading to the security community: the emergence since the First World War of a shared North American identity. The North American peace ('the world's longest undefended border') became part of an understanding of the American self as contrasted to a

European other. Building identity (partly) on the specific peacefulness of North America made it politically more difficult for groups arguing for a defence build-up to get a hearing. Thus the security community became self-reinforcing.

In terms of military security, the United States and Canada not only shut off mutual concerns, they also became involved on the same side in wars, although not always with exactly identical intensity or motivations: the First and Second World Wars, the Cold War, and Korea, but not Vietnam. During the twentieth century, the hostility between the United States and Britain turned into the 'special relationship' of the Anglo-Saxon democracies, thus taking Canada out of the role of forward base for a foreign enemy. This did not mean an end to security concerns in the wider sense. The unbalanced relationship generated constant Canadian worries about cultural and economic 'Americanisation', especially during periods like the 1990s in which economic growth and dynamism was markedly higher in the United States than in Canada (*Economist*, 'Survey of Canada', 24 July 1999). Such worries became more existential because linked to the societal, domestic vulnerabilities of Canada. Even if there was no big neighbour, the question of Canadian identity and coherence would be posed. Only with the 1867 Confederation was a unified Canada created and not until 1926 was it independent. Interaction and a sense of commonality were not strong along the East–West axis, and the split between Francophones and Anglophones remained deep. Canadian identity has always been fragile and ambivalent about its element of shared North Americanness versus the widespread tendency to define Canada as not-the-USA. In an international context this generated Canadian ambivalence whether to define itself as hemispheric American, North American, or European.

In sum, the US–Canadian relationship was demilitarised and partly desecuritised, and the centred regional formation gradually met legitimacy from both sides. But security concerns remained on the Canadian side, primarily in the societal and economic sectors where they were directly focused on a threat from the USA. However, due to the French/English division, political security was also an issue and one only indirectly linked to the USA.

Central America and the Caribbean

As discussed in the introduction to part IV, Central America and the Caribbean pose some special problems. Central America is grouped with South America as Latin America in most studies of regions and regionalism, mostly for cultural reasons. From a security perspective, however, the intense penetration of both subregions from the North constitutes for most of the periods de facto US control and constantly enough influence to move these subcomplexes into the North American RSC. Standard regionalist terminology is not helpful to security analysis because the term 'Latin America' is a cultural rather than a geographical one, and does not even include the English-speaking countries in the Caribbean; and, although regional processes in areas other than security follow these cultural lines, security patterns are different, and these define the RSCs. Still, Central America and the Caribbean are distinct enough that they cannot be dealt with simply as ordinary components of the North American RSC. We use a restrictive definition of Caribbean, including only the islands. The northern coast of South America is more closely tied into South American than Caribbean security dynamics. Central America has previously had a history closely linked to the Caribbean, but during and after the Cold War it developed distinct dynamics and became a subcomplex in its own right.

As Munro (1964: 3) notes, 'The Caribbean was a theatre of conflict between rival imperialisms long before the United States became independent. By the end of the sixteenth century, foreign smugglers and pirates, frequently supported by their own governments, were challenging Spain's claim to exclusive possession of America.' Spain had not effectively occupied all of the islands, and the British, French, Dutch, and others settled on some of them. The West Indies were much coveted as plantation colonies, and seen as much more valuable than major portions of the North American mainland. Independence began as early as Haiti's successful slave revolt in 1804, but the main moves came later with the decline of the Spanish empire, which let the United States into the region.

Cuba was widely believed in the United States to be destined for annexation sooner or later – and to be a valuable addition both for economic and strategic reasons. However, the attempts to buy or otherwise acquire Cuba in the 1850s and 1860s failed and, when Cuba returned to the agenda in the 1890s, the general US strategy had changed towards informal control. After a direct involvement in freeing Cuba from Spain, the United States ensured in 1901 through the Platt Amendment to Cuba's constitution a continued right to intervene, and Cuba was for all practical purposes a protectorate of the United States (LaFeber 1989: 196ff.; Smith 1996: 25–36; Schoultz 1998: 125–51). Puerto Rico, in contrast, was annexed as an 'unincorporated territory', meaning the

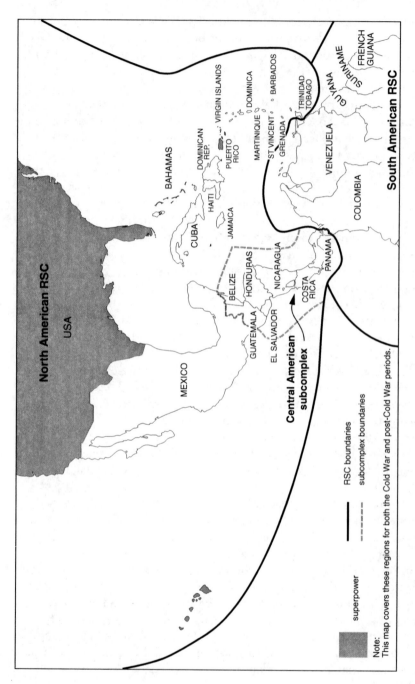

Map 9. Central America and the Caribbean

inhabitants are not US citizens (LaFeber 1989: 198–200). The Caribbean has been the part of the hemisphere where the United States has intervened most systematically and unapologetically both before and during the Cold War.

Later rounds of decolonisation produced a number of island states of very limited size and population. Martinique and Guadeloupe are French *départements d'outre mer* (DOM) and thus a direct part of France; Puerto Rico is a 'dependent territory' of the United States without being (or wanting to be) a separate state, and the American Virgin Islands are American possessions too.

The Caribbean is unusually fragmented as a product of the early competition of European colonial powers, in contrast to, e.g., Indonesia where numerous islands ended up as one colony. Furthermore, their economic, political, and cultural ties linked them to their mother countries in Europe, not to each other (Widfeldt 2001: 212–13). Most of the states are extremely weak as powers and therefore generate few interstate security threats. Security has predominantly been domestic and increasingly (as we will see in the next two sections) transnational. For most of the states the only interstate security question was the United States.

Delineation of the (sub)region is controversial. One definition is in terms of an archipelago including the islands of the greater West Indies, the mainland states of Guyana, Belize, Suriname, and French Guiana as well as parts of the coasts of Central America and northern South America (Levine 1989). An alternative, more geopolitical definition (common especially in the United States) sees a wider Caribbean basin or 'Circum-Caribbean' (Atkins 1999: 34). In addition to the archipelago, it includes Mexico, the five Central American republics, Panama, Colombia, and Venezuela. (For instance, the 1994 Association of Caribbean States includes Cuba, the Dominican Republic, Haiti, the fifteen independent CARICOM countries, Costa Rica, El Salvador, Guatemala, Honduras, Nicaragua, Panama, Colombia, Mexico, and Venezuela.)

Central America became independent of Spain during the 1820s as part of the larger republics of Mexico and (in the case of Panama) Colombia. The formerly Mexican part became the Central American Union, and then in 1838 the separate states of Guatemala, El Salvador, Honduras, Nicaragua, and Costa Rica were formed. Belize had been British since 1776 and did not become independent until 1981. The boundaries in Central America are today essentially where they were in 1870 (McEvedy 1988: 104).

London shaped the region for half a century after independence, but increasingly 'US companies and military power became overwhelming. By 1900, the United Fruit Company of Boston dominated Costa Rica's and Guatemala's economies. Soon, United Fruit's control of Central American affairs reached a point where the company was called "The Octopus". Sam "The Banana Man" Zamurry of New Orleans gained control of Honduras's economy after 1900, until that country became known as a banana republic' (LaFeber 1989: 167). Before 1914, US investments in Latin America went predominantly to the Caribbean and Central America (LaFeber 1989: 340). Several Central American states became almost directly ruled by either American economic actors or by the American military. The American involvement was not much driven by security concerns. The motivation was mostly economic, and the legitimation often quasi-racist and paternalist (Schoultz 1998; Kenworthy 1995). One case, however, was securitised: the need for a trans-isthmian canal. The US State Department in 1856 declared that 'it would be difficult to suggest a single object of interest, external or internal, more important to the United States than the maintenance of the communication, by land and sea, between the Atlantic and Pacific States and Territories of the Union. It is a material element of the national integrity and sovereignty' (Schoultz 1998: 65). After much manoeuvring against British and French as well as Central American actors, the solution was found which involved 'helping' to create an independent Panama and having this new state cede a ten-mile-wide strip with full rights to the United States as well as generally broad rights for it to interfere in Panamanian domestic life as deemed necessary in order to protect the canal (Schoultz 1998: 152–75).

The early twentieth century saw regular interventions in Central America; e.g., 'the Wilson administration supervised the most active period of military intervention in the history of US–Latin American relations: in Nicaragua, the Dominican Republic, Haiti, Cuba, Honduras – even Panama was twice obliged to cede domestic police powers to US armed forces' (Schoultz 1998: 234). However, the United States increasingly shifted away from direct intervention towards 'dollar diplomacy' and, from 1933, the 'good neighbour' policy of Franklin D. Roosevelt. The Marines were pulled out of Haiti, the Platt Amendment ended, Panama was given the right to help operate the canal, and so forth (LaFeber 1989: 356). The result was largely that, by removing those political and military elements that angered the Latin Americans, it became possible to increase US economic influence. In some places, like

Nicaragua, the new policy involved cooperating with corrupt and brutal leaders like Somoza. This policy shift was to a large extent driven by the securitisation of developments in Japan and Germany and therefore a need to free resources and make Latin American policies more self-reliant. However, it also turned out to be in many cases a better way to ensure the same kind of hegemony as previously pursued with a 'big stick'.

Security among and within the states was in the shadow of the USA. All Central American states were relatively weak, with regular political violence and rare cases of democracy. However, at the height of American informal empire, domestic political struggles would never be purely domestic because the United States was concerned about maintaining friendly regimes. Conflicts among the states were often spillovers either from domestic revolts or from controversies over relations to the United States (e.g., military bases).

A pattern of conflicts existed among the Central American states themselves, with especially a struggle for leadership between Guatemala and Nicaragua. Both wanted to recreate by force – and to head – the Central American Federation (Mares 2001: 61). During the nineteenth century, this led to repeated invasions of El Salvador, Honduras, and Costa Rica by one of the two and rescue operations by the other. Mexico had conflicts with Guatemala (including boundary problems and Guatemalan aid to a revolt in Chiapas) and feared a strong southern neighbour if Guatemala managed to become the leader of a reunited Central America. Mexico tried to play the Nicaragua card, while the United States supported Guatemala. However, Mexico was unable to sustain this form of competitive penetration of the subregion and from around 1910 the USA became clearly dominant. With one dominant external power, penetration intensified.

A global power emerges – continental expansion, Pacific imperialism, and European world wars

The idea of the United States playing in global politics as a great power was alien to most of the Founding Fathers. The United States was to be a great force in the world but mostly by the power of its example, including the example of a republic *not* engaging in power politics. Nevertheless, during the nineteenth century and especially around the turn of the twentieth century, it expanded across the Pacific and into the Caribbean, and became recognised as a great power in world politics. This familiar story is important to our analysis because of the relationship between global, interregional, regional, subregional, and domestic levels. The changing US position in global politics is a major factor explaining its changing views of the different parts of Latin America.

Whether this change of policy was triggered by the end of western expansion inside North America and the need to replace this outlet for energy and dynamism with other missions (Turner 1993) or by more traditional economic and political 'imperialist' aims is not vital here. Security arguments played a decreasing role as expansion moved further away from the mainland. Policies towards Central America and the Caribbean were originally motivated by strategic reasoning about keeping extra-regional powers out. Increasingly, this was not an issue, and expansion here took on its own momentum. In the Pacific, competitive logic certainly played a large role, especially in relation to the big Chinese market. Some element of relative gains logic vis-à-vis Germany and later Japan was therefore in play. But the USA did not enter this in a 'top-down' way, i.e., seeing itself as a global power that needed to concern itself about the global balance; it rather came in a 'bottom-up' fashion where each gain was justified in its own terms. This shows that the United States at this time – when in the middle of its transformation to great power – did not think in the form characteristic of a great power (see ch. 2). Step by step, and more as a continuation of continental expansion – i.e. almost 'domestic', but certainly more regional than global – the USA created an empire in the Pacific (Midway 1867, Hawaii 1898, Samoa 1899, Philippines 1899, Guam, and so forth). Beginning in 1886 and even more clearly in 1890, the United States started to build 'the Great White Fleet' which became decisive in the 1898 war and was the basis for the notable US Navy of the twentieth century.

The conventional date for the birth of the US as a great power is 1898. 'America's resounding victory in the Spanish–American War crystallized the perception of increasing American power both at home and abroad' (Zakaria 1998: 11; see e.g. LaFeber 1989: 181). Before this time, the USA had been a great power if measured in production and energy consumption, but, with its tiny army and navy and a minor diplomatic apparatus, 'America was treated like a second-rank power, on par with countries that possessed a fraction of its material resources. When in 1880 the Sultan of Turkey [sic] decided to pare down his diplomatic corps, he eliminated his missions to Sweden, Belgium, the Netherlands, and the United States' (Zakaria 1998: 47). That the United States still did not pursue policies driven by the global level and great power calculus is clearly illustrated by the well-known American ambivalence about entering the First World War and Congress's refusal after the war to accept US entrance into the League of Nations.

In terms of the Americas as a whole, the dominant actor, the United States, saw itself mostly in a hemispheric context with global forays during world wars. Given the asymmetry of relations, the whole constellation can therefore almost be boiled down to the equation: hemispheric considerations by the US = domestic and regional security problems for most of the others.

The structure of the Cold War RSC

The Cold War was present in North America in two ways. Most importantly this was because the United States, as a key actor in the Cold War, became shaped by it. Second, politics in Latin America were polarised along ideological East–West lines. The American interpretation overemphasised this and often categorised conflicts in Cold War terms more than local conditions merited, but, given the power of the United States, such categories often became real. The case of Cuba, however, meant that the Cold War was present in the region in ways other than through US (mis-)interpretation.

Global level

The referent object for securitisation was both geopolitical and, to a large extent, values and principles. Initially the Soviet Union was a security problem mostly as a challenge to American values, way of life, and world leadership. Only in the 1960s did it become a direct military threat. However, even early on, a part of the challenge was that the effort to meet the threat could demand a mobilisation and militarisation that in itself threatened American liberty (Lasswell 1950; Leffler 1992; Buzan and Wæver 1998) – and therefore it was necessary to have an ambitious geopolitical approach that faced the Soviet Union in a forward defence and mobilised allies.

The concept of security as generally used is greatly shaped by the Cold War. The usage of (national) 'security' as a key concept was an early 1940s invention in the USA, but the institutionalisation of it (National Security Act, National Security Council) occurred in the early Cold War, as did its export first to allies and then to more or less everybody in the international system (Buzan and Wæver 1998; Wæver 2002). A major purpose of elevating 'national security' to such unprecedented prominence was to justify – and coordinate – a multisectoral, long-term mobilisation contradicting the US tradition of suspicion against the political implications of both systemic political engagements and 'large standing military forces'.

In most other chapters, the global level is discussed in terms of global level actors penetrating the region. This happened in North America only in the form of the Soviet involvement with Cuba and in much more limited form in Nicaragua, Grenada, and a few other short-lived attempts. However, the global level also covers the global role of the United States. Its transformation into a global actor during the Second World War, and the entrenchment thereof by the Cold War, had major repercussions on both regional and domestic politics.

Regional, subregional, and interregional levels

The Cold War affected regional, subregional, and interregional (hemispheric) security dynamics. The United States became more cooperative in the hemisphere because of a fear of states aligning with an external power. It is in the nature of bipolarity that the superpowers as well as weaker powers have an interest in alliances (Snyder 1984). But the USA became also more interventionist in some phases due to the fear of communism. Thus, the effect of the Cold War was to further deregionalise the American approach to foreign policy. The driving concern of the United States was now clearly global and all regional questions derived from this. There was no risk of Central America, the Caribbean, or, for that matter, South America being ignored or forgotten. The hemisphere had a special status because – in continuation of the Monroe Doctrine (see p. 307) – it was seen as a particularly intense and unacceptable risk that the Soviet Union might get more of a foothold than Cuba.

At first, in 1945, the United States approached its relations with Latin America from the principle of support for democracy. American policy was formulated mostly in terms of 'Latin America' and did not distinguish systematically between a region, which we see as an RSC in its own right, and regions that were incorporated into North America. Dictators who had been supported because of the Second World War fell into disfavour (Schoultz 1998: 316ff.). In terms of economic relations, the United States did not deliver much of what the Latin Americans expected (see ch. 10), and thus US political influence in the region, and especially its ability to construct pan-American organisations with real clout, was limited. Economic influence remained large, especially in Central America. The threat from communism was not deemed imminent in Latin

America, and security motivations could not drive the United States into more 'costly' policies. The interventions that the United States did carry out in the early Cold War period – most famously Guatemala in 1954 – were largely driven by commercial interests, but a justification was developed that introduced communism as a threat. Even if communists could not really be blamed for the reform government of Guatemala, it could be claimed that they were exploiting the situation, and the metaphor of falling dominos made its entrance (Schoultz 1998: 343). Increasingly, friendly dictators came back into focus, and the more idealistic element was taken care of by programmes for economic development. The latter were much reinforced after 1959 to forestall more Castros, but the grandiose 'Alliance for Progress' launched in 1961 failed, and US focus swung back from democracy and development to pragmatic anti-communism (Ladd Hollist and Nielson 1998: 260). Covert and indirect operations through threats or backing of coup-makers, especially by the CIA, outnumbered the direct military interventions (Rosenfelder 1996; Blum 1995).

Under the Reagan presidency in the 1980s, the United States got involved in Central American civil wars in a more systematic and drawn-out way. El Salvador and Nicaragua were embroiled in civil war from opposite sides. In El Salvador, Reagan fully supported a repressive, conservative regime, to which President Carter had ceased assistance, against a revolutionary movement, FMLN. In Nicaragua, the radical Sandinistas had overthrown the Somoza dynasty in 1979, and the United States supported and to a large extent organised the counterrevolutionary Contra guerrillas. In contrast to the fast and usually effective coups of the past, the United States was now involved in a continuous struggle. The Reagan administration elevated this to a symbolic expression of the newly intensified Cold War, and in 1981 the US ambassador to the UN, Jeane J. Kirkpatrick, even made what Smith calls 'the absolutely remarkable statement' that 'Central America is the most important place in the world for the United States today' (Smith 1996: 180). Had this been true, it would be a striking revision of the relationship between the levels in North America, but in reality it probably meant rather the complete dominance of the global level and its colouring of Central American policies. The USA approached the region according to the new strategy of 'low-intensity conflict', and thus tolerated the drawn-out battle because, in contrast to previous involvements in the region, this was seen as an integral part of the cosmic struggle against the 'evil empire'. These civil wars were not finished until after the end of the Cold War.

The core of the Cold War Caribbean is the 1959 Cuban revolution. Having for almost a century kept any realistic extra-hemispheric challenger out of Latin America and all unacceptable ideologies away from power in Central America and the Caribbean, the United States was unprepared for a radical challenge so close to home. The Soviets were surprised too. They had not been very active in the region and local communist parties were never close to power. But the economic crisis of the region led to a radicalisation. And in Cuba, where the USA had been the real power behind the government for so long, radical reform would necessarily also take an anti-American form.

The size and location of Cuba makes it naturally the key to US–Caribbean relations, more so in the intense global conflict of the Cold War. After the failed US intervention in 1961, confrontation reached an apex with the Cuban missile crisis in 1962. The outcome stabilised a situation in which Cuba remained closely allied to the Soviet Union and in deep conflict with the United States but with limited chances of becoming used offensively against it. The United States created various subversive programmes against the Castro regime, and a large exile Cuban community, especially in Florida, made sure that a confrontational policy would not be relaxed. The American base at Guantánamo Bay in Cuba was retained despite Cuban protests. Castro on his side followed consistently anti-American policies in international organisations and among third world countries. Furthermore, US policy towards the rest of the Caribbean became interpreted through the Cuban case, most notably the interventions in the Dominican Republic in 1965 and Grenada in 1983. The Johnson doctrine said that the president could use military force whenever he thought communism threatened the hemisphere. Most of the other islands in the Caribbean received US military assistance, including education and training programmes. These were a major source of US influence: recruiting useful local political figures and creating a military-to-military structure that lived a life of its own. To the local ruling elites, in turn, this cooperation was important to domestic security, i.e., against insurrection and increasingly also against transnational challenges that they were not strong enough to handle.

During the 1980s, the increased US military presence numbered more than twenty military installations, Puerto Rico, Panama, and Guantánamo forming a strategic triangle at the core. The US security motivation was a combination of strategic resources, sea lines of communication (related to the Panama Canal), and the internal/external threat from communism/the Soviet Union. Meanwhile, the sense of vulnerability of the local states grew as the pressures from the global economy increased at the same time as did transnational threats from drugs and crime (Griffith 1995: 4–7).

The North American region in the narrow sense was surprisingly little influenced by the Cold War except by its relative decline of importance (to the United States) compared to the global level. Mexico's security concerns were continuous with those of the pre-Cold War period with the addition of controversies over policy towards the Caribbean and Central America, where Mexico was often unwilling to follow US anti-communist policies. This was in no way an expression of a communist orientation of Mexico and its constantly ruling party, but it was a way for Mexico to mark its distance from the big neighbour.

Canadian–US relations were further desecuritised through the joint alliance against communism. Canada could use NATO to create more distance from the USA and sometimes to multilateralise relations (e.g., in the UN). In the 1960s in particular, Canada cultivated a coalition of like-minded, especially North European, countries. At the same time, Canada became more closely tied in a military-strategic sense to the United States, especially through joint air defences and warning systems.

Domestic level

Security became a US domestic concern during the McCarthy era when a communist threat was projected as substantial within the country. Also more generally, the political climate of the United States was shaped by the Cold War. Liberalism was transformed into a more apologetic Cold War liberalism (Arblaster 1984), and the state, which traditionally had a very circumscribed and vulnerable legitimacy in the USA, was able to consolidate its growth from the New Deal and the Second World War with the ideological support generated by the Cold War.

In the Caribbean, vulnerability increased as more and smaller states became independent, and the Cold War was projected into the region, mostly via Cuba. Transnational challenges grew, especially towards the end of the period, and internal instability was recurrent, even increasing, due to the economic difficulties of the region.

Central America was the most politically polarised subregion of North America. During the 1980s it came to be totally dominated by an amalgamation of domestic conflict and globally driven US regional intervention.

Cold War security in North America

Striking about the North American, centred RSC during the Cold War is the dominance of the global level. Despite the near absence of external global level actors in the region, the fact that its dominant power became one of the poles of the bipolar Cold War redefined security at all levels in the region. In some cases, it can be argued that the regional level is important, in others that it is the domestic level, but it was always closely shaped by the overall dominant global level.

Security in North America after the Cold War

The end of the Cold War has had potentially far-reaching but so far quite ambiguous effects on security in North America. Via the agency of the USA, the Cold War moved the global level to an unprecedented pre-eminence in North America, where it coloured almost all security issues at other levels. There are secondary elements of continuity from Quebec in the north to drugs trafficking in the south, but the main ongoing element is the inevitability that US grand strategy remains decisive in shaping the region's security. The main discontinuity is the dropping of the Cold War agenda, but this carries the ambiguity that nothing so clear-cut as the war against communism has emerged to define the US securitisations (despite attempts after September 2001 to define the war on terrorism as fully equivalent). Therefore, this section maps the emerging agendas by subregion and at the core, country by country. The levels format will be reserved for the final summing up of the results of this survey. The 'deep look' of this chapter will address the US debate about concepts of security, and the section ends on the issue of US global 'grand strategy'. The question of how to balance and link domestic, regional, interregional, and global security in North America remains largely a US decision.

Central America

In Central America, the security situation changed radically during the 1990s as several interconnected peace processes ended the civil wars of the 1980s. The main initiatives came from different levels:

- Interregional (Latin American): the 1984 Act for Peace and Cooperation in Central America proposed by the Contadora Group (the main Latin American states bordering the Caribbean

Basin, Colombia, Mexico, Panama, and Venezuela, later supported by Argentina, Brazil, Peru, and Uruguay).
- Subcomplex: the 1987 Esquipulas II Agreement among the five Central American heads of state defining a process towards peace.
- Domestic: agreements were reached between governments and guerrillas in Nicaragua (in 1989, leading to free presidential elections in 1990), El Salvador (1991–2), and Guatemala (1996).

The original initiative was a clear disapproval of the Reagan administration's definition of the Central American problem in terms of US–Soviet competition and as one to be solved by military aid and covert operations (Hey and Kuzma 1993: 30–1; Eguizábal 1998: 70). Later, after the end of the Cold War, Washington, Moscow, and the UN would occasionally assist with mediation, monitoring, and pressure on parties (Eguizábal 1998: 78), and the change of international context certainly helped to make the processes possible.

During this process, Belize and Panama came to be accepted as 'Central American' by the traditional five Central American states and as formal members of subregional organisations (Atkins 1999: 36). In an RSCT perspective, both had been members of the subcomplex since their independence.

Partly as a result of the successes with the peace process, partly reflecting the general turn to regionalism in the Americas and the world, Central American regionalism was surrounded by much optimism in the early 1990s. However, progress slowed as the political agenda shifted from the original goals of ending the civil wars and achieving democracy and development, towards a more narrow agenda defined by the challenge from globalisation, i.e., the task of securing a place for Central America in the global economy. As part of this shift, Benedicte Bull (1999: 967) notices that the issues that are securitised 'changed from being first military threats, then a wide range of threats to human survival and, in the end, primarily globalisation'.

Political and economic challenges are tough for all countries that have been through war or civil war, and the countries of Central America – where a country like Guatemala might be said to have emerged from a 36-year civil war (McNulty 2000) – are no exception (Pearce 1998; Ruthrauff 1998; Faulkner and Pettiford 1998; Eguizábal 1998). Adding to their difficulties, the transnational security challenges from the drugs trade and its ensuing crime and violence have been growing steadily during the 1990s (Pearce 1999; Fishel 1997). The US invasion of Panama in December 1989 signalled the priority of the anti-drugs issue to the United States (Smith 1996: 273). Panama became symbolic of the changed security pattern in another respect as well. The canal (and Canal Zone) was handed over to Panama at the Millennium New Year. Although some worry remained in the United States (e.g., about Chinese companies gaining influence over the canal; *Economist* 16 December 1999), this was generally an expression of a downscaling of US control and military attention to the region, as expressed also in the closing of bases in Panama and moving of most assets to Puerto Rico. Since the late 1990s, much US assistance has been in terms of disaster relief due to earthquakes and hurricanes.

The Caribbean

Even more than in Central America, transnational security issues have taken over in the Caribbean: drugs trafficking (and related crimes like money-laundering), arms-trafficking, illegal migration, and HIV/AIDS. In addition, the Cuba question continues as a Cold War hangover (Tulchin 1994; Griffith 1993a, 1993b, 1995, 1998a, 1998b, 2000; Serbin 1998; Clissold 1998; Sutton 1993; CFR 2000).

As part of Cold War policy in the region, the United States worked closely with local military and police forces. Reagan's 1982 Caribbean Basin Initiative continues mainly in the area of trade, while the security component has been decreased. But in relation to the island mini-states of the Eastern Caribbean, the US-promoted Regional Security System continues and is geared more to the new security issues. Since most of the states in the region (except Cuba) pursue outward-looking trade and development policies, they have become more and more closely connected to the United States. This is true for drugs and migration too, whether this is seen as cause or effect of the closeness in other areas, or as part of a general trend. As for drugs, the Caribbean states are mainly relevant in terms of transit and of related activities such as money-laundering through 'offshore' banks. Military cooperation is increasingly about surveillance and interdiction of drugs transportation. US attempts to deal with these issues are almost inevitably intrusive in relation to the sovereignty of the local states. The reach of US policy 'echoes the Caribbean's historical position as both an internal and external region of the United States'. The 'Caribbean peoples themselves seem undecided as to whether the United States is a foreign power to be negotiated with at arm's length or the "home country"' (Muñiz and Beruff 1994: 121). Payne (2000) has gone even further in seeing the emerging relationship as 'a new mode of transterritorial governance'. Seen from the Caribbean states, especially the very small ones, the core of the problem is that their vulnerability is so limitless that they are on the one hand unable to deal with the illegal transnational actors (see newspaper articles like 'Colombian Drug Lords Bring Terror to Caribbean Paradise', *LA Times/Washington Post* 27 April 1997, and book titles like *Drugs and Security in the Caribbean: Sovereignty Under Siege*; Griffith 1997), but on the other hand US policy countering such actors is often even more intrusive and uncontrollable. One response to this has been to emphasise membership in regional groupings such as CARICOM and the Association of Caribbean States.

Haiti has been the core of the US concern about instability fuelling illegal migration – as witnessed by the 1994 intervention, about which Margaret Thatcher (1996) said, it 'was defended as an exercise in restoring a Haitian democracy that had never existed; but it might be better described in the language of Clausewitz as the continuation of American immigration control by other means'. A scenario looms in which developments in Cuba could cause much larger migration. The public political struggles over Cuba policy are most often fought in surprisingly unchanged Cold War terminology, but in administrative and military circles thinking about Cuba is being integrated into the new agenda that otherwise has taken over fully in relation to the Caribbean.

In conclusion, the PCW security issues are very much contained in the vulnerability dilemma of the Caribbean states: the transnational challenges especially from the drugs trade can be securitised, but if securitised they must also be handled (Wæver 1995c: n. 24; 1997a: 219 and n. 21), and this in turn means close cooperation with the USA. This creates other problems. US infringements on national sovereignty could be securitised instead, and one could tolerate some of the illegal business and try to keep more of a distance from the United States. The centrality of this dilemma supports the continued location of the Caribbean within the North American RSC.

Canada and Mexico

Mexico has two and a half focal points for security, which are only weakly connected. One is the insurgency in southern Mexico (in Chiapas and other states). The other is the relationship to the United States – the problems of handling US insistence on unilateral or joint handling of transnational issues ranging from migration to drugs. The half is the drugs issue if perceived as a problem in itself and not a problem only because the US securitises it (see Nunez 1999; Schulz 1997; Rochlin 1997).

Insurgency especially in Chiapas has a long history in Mexico, and Indians there and elsewhere have repeatedly rebelled against landholding elites. From 2000, the Fox presidency attempted to end the rebellion, but encountered opposition in Mexico City to far-reaching concessions. The tensions over US intrusions are certainly not new either, but they have gained a new quality with NAFTA and more generally with globalisation. It has led to North American transnational security policy on drugs, the environment, and to some extent migration. In various fields that traditionally were protected by national sovereignty, not least in a strict Mexican interpretation, NAFTA allows international monitoring and intervention. Although attention in the first post-NAFTA years was caught by the erection of something close to a new Berlin Wall, and a militarisation of the border was alleged (e.g., Dunn 1996), the trend is towards a deterritorialised form of security – executed less at the border and more through regional redefinition of threats and international and transnational implementation.

Mexico has partly refocused security and delinked border and security in the way characteristic of the postmodern North (Europe and North America). Coming from a very strong version of national(ist) security with particular emphasis on sovereignty and non-intervention (often meant as a counterweight to US interventionism), the shift away from state security is not complete, but is highly significant nevertheless. President Salinas said in 1991: 'Historically, nationalism has responded to an external threat. Today that threat has become the prospect of remaining outside, at the margins of the worldwide integrationist trend ... To fail in that challenge would be to weaken oneself and succumb' (quoted in Gonzalez and Haggard 1998: 314). After some ambivalence, the Fox presidency seems to have put Mexico back on this track. The end of seventy-one years of rule by the Institutional Revolutionary Party (PRI) and the arrival of a president who is not only a former Coca-Cola executive but a strong free-trader created a general optimism in the United States (Johnson 2000; Bailey and Godson 2001).

However, the basic constellation of the dilemmas remain: Mexico has become more important to the United States (it is now the United States' second-largest trading partner after Canada), and a strong US pressure for transnationalisation of various issues remains. This can easily touch national sensitivities in Mexico, and only in the case of cooperation to clear mutual benefit, i.e., general good times in Mexico, will this be

possible. Although not directly linked to the United States–Mexico relationship, Chiapas aggravates the tension by making the political system
in Mexico more vulnerable.

The ending of the Cold War has had even less of an influence on
Canada; NAFTA, for example, may have a larger potential impact on
the main internal security question: Quebec. A stronger regional level
puts the Quebec question in a new light. An independent Quebec would
not be fully on its own but a constituent component of 'North America'.
(The Quebecois are naturally strongly pro-NAFTA, as Scottish nationalists support the EU.) It might be questioned whether the secession of
Quebec is a security issue at all, or is rather, now, a part of normal politics. However, it is still common to see speculation that the survival of
Canada is at stake – especially after NAFTA and a decade of American
high growth (*Economist*, 'A Survey of Canada', 24 July 1999). If Quebec
seceded, would this then trigger a process in which each province went
its own way, probably all ultimately converging on the United States?
The Quebecois securitise less than previously – independence is rarely
phrased in existential terms the way it is today in Europe by many
secessionists, who claim to be able to become themselves only in an independent Croatia/Kosovo/etc. A 1995 referendum confirmed Quebec
within Canada by an ultra-thin margin.

The second longstanding security issue in Canada is the general one
of US cultural dominance. Even if the 1990s might be claimed to have
been a particularly tough period, the basic nature of this is unchanged,
and so is the probable outcome. In the end, Canada does not stop being
Canada. Nor does it seem that securitisation of this issue is escalating
beyond the normal level. Joining the OAS in 1990 and pursuing an active
Caribbean diplomacy imply elements of 'balancing' the USA.

In the military field Canada has less of a NATO (and probably also
less UN) multilateral context for balancing the United States. On the
other hand, the military relations are less sensitive and less crucial for
either party (despite missile defence). Canada's main concern in the
military sector relates to the US reordering of command structure after
11 September. To fully accommodate homeland defence and missile defence, StratCom and SpaceCom have been merged and a new
Northern Command created. To Canada this poses the dual challenge of getting too distant from the USA as NORAD is marginalised
and Canada thereby loses privileged access notably to intelligence,
and getting too closely involved with the USA as homeland defence
points towards 'perimeter defence' and Canada becomes enrolled in

US internal security. In the final analysis, Canada is likely to get more of a hemispheric context for balancing and multilateralising the USA.

The United States

We have previously (Buzan et al. 1998: 130ff.) pointed to an increasing securitisation with new referent objects in the post-Cold War United States. Arguments are made in society about 'threats' that are not necessarily put forward as candidates for official security, but rather as signs of postmodern fragmentation or devolution.

It is not new to the United States that societal groups securitise directly on their own behalf and take security action themselves. Many eighteenth- and nineteenth-century Americans had no state to turn to for local protection. As the United States became more of a normal state in the twentieth century, security increasingly concentrated in foreign affairs, and other forms of security retreated.

From the 1970s, cultural divisions in US society deepened and were occasionally securitised. The ending of the Cold War removed the one issue that had trumped all others, and the state as arbiter of domestic conflicts was delegitimised in many quarters. This allowed new issues to move to top rank and to be treated as existential.

Race/culture is probably the most important example. Ethno-racial identity is the primary attachment for large groups who insist on the United States being defined in truly multicultural terms to leave room for this identity. African-, Hispanic-, Asian-, and Native Americans ('first nations'), and other ethno-racial groups want to protect a self-defined culture against a dominant US universalism seen as reflecting a hegemonic Anglo-white elite (see Taylor 1992). The securitising actors are small activist groups but the referent objects are large collectivities of 10–15 per cent in the case of Hispanics and African-Americans. Although most often part of ordinary politics, these issues regularly get intensified to the point of securitisation, and they clearly hold this potential due to emotional power and the assumption that such units exist and should survive.

Equally serious is the countersecuritisation by which radical whites act, self-appointed, on behalf of the majority. The new particularism has been seen by some mainstream intellectuals as a threat to the integrative, universalist culture on which American stability rests (Schlesinger 1992; Hughes 1993; Huntington 1999–2000). As the Oklahoma City bombing in 1995 and the growth of militias in the 1990s showed, a defence of the 'true' (white) America against the liberal state and its constituent minorities can lead to serious violent action (Wills 1995; Bennett 1995).

Other domestic issues can be mentioned more briefly: gender is mostly only politicised but radical groups securitise it. Religious fundamentalists and secularists are structurally poised to see each other as existential threats (see Marty and Appleby 1995; Laustsen and Wæver 2000). Migration intensifies much of the ethno-racial confrontation and is occasionally a hot issue locally, but it is much less of a mobilising issue in its own right in North America than in Europe. Finally, the separate states were originally the main referent for security action. With the consolidation of the North American federal states, only a few cases were securitised (Quebec, Chiapas), and in the USA not even Texas is the referent object of securitisation to any significant degree.

If the state does not generate a powerful new external securitisation, the possibility emerges of a United States and North America increasingly driven by domestic – and thereby region-internal – security concerns. This would be a dramatic reversal of the Cold War constellation. However, it seems more likely that the state will continue to place external security issues above these fragmentary ones.

Widening security in official US security policy

The academic debate on wide vs narrow concepts of security had an important American side (see Florini and Simmons 1998a, 1998b). 'New security issues' have entered official planning to different degrees. We will here assess how far they have been officially acknowledged in policy statements and intelligence assessments, and reflected in departmental structure (a 'deputy under secretary for environmental security' is relevant both as a sign that specific action is likely to be taken with reference to this kind of justification, and in itself as proof that a certain degree of securitisation has already succeeded), and ultimately how high they have made it on the security agenda. Within the policy world, securitisations of new threats have had two trajectories.

1: The first category is made up of threats that have been accepted as security issues, but that, instead of conquering the top of the list, have only gained a niche position.

Environmental security was the primary example in academic rethinking of security, and was picked up by the policy side. The

US Defense Department got a 'deputy under secretary for environmental security' and similar changes were made on the intelligence side and in the NSC (Florini and Simmons 1998b: 39). Numerous times the top people of the Clinton administration recognised the security status of the environment (see also Moriarty 1997; Goodman 1996), mostly as a global level threat.

Epidemics/global infectious diseases are the object of separate intelligence assessments (e.g., NIC 2000) but have not yet been widely accepted as very high ranking. They have a regional dimension but are mostly defined in global terms. Seemingly, the department for homeland security is not to include unintentional threats in this category, only terrorism-related ones like the anthrax attacks. Paradoxically, the 2001 scare led to less concern about natural epidemics, because the image of wilful use of epidemics has come to dominate threat images. The Clinton administration – and Clinton after the end of his presidency – regularly pronounced HIV/AIDS in Africa an international security issue, but the implications of this were never made clear.

Organised crime is a threat (e.g., Albini 2000; US Government Interagency Working Group 2000), but mostly to vulnerable, developing countries and only indirectly to countries like the United States or Canada (Castle 1997). Serious security urgency is usually reserved for drugs-related organised crime.

Drugs were declared a national security threat in 1974 by President Ford, but the Reagan administration lifted the issue to prominence and started to organise a 'war on drugs' (Campbell 1992: 198). Much of this 'war' is a domestic – moral and police – effort. Internationally the war focuses on Latin America (see ch. 10). Drugs constitute one of the few issues to be securitised in the otherwise notoriously upbeat annual 'state of the union' message by the president (see years 1994, 1996, 1998, 1999), and a large institutional apparatus is geared to dealing with different dimensions of the problem, often in a militarised form. Still, it is the ideal type example of a niche security issue. It is intensely and consistently securitised, but it is not a serious candidate for taking top rank and defining overall policy.

2: The second category comprises issues for top-rank securitisation.

The first of these, *geo-economics*, looked strong during the early 1990s, but eventually faded. In the first post-Cold War years academics and pundits presented economic competition especially with

Japan as *the* new test of power that was to replace the Cold War (Luttwak 1993; and discussions in Mastanduno 1991 and Campbell 1992: 223–44). The early policies of President Clinton (around 1992–3) phrased the priority of economic policy with an urgency bordering on securitisation. As Japan weakened and the US 'new economy' boomed, geo-economic 'strategic trade policy' was replaced by more classical American policies of free trade and active usage of the multilateral trade regime. Geo-economic considerations have shifted mainly towards China where they are part of a more traditional power calculus. The economic threat did not become the one dominant matrix for post-Cold War security.

Terrorism was widely agreed, already before the attacks on New York and Washington in September 2001, to be on the list of new threats – with many claims that it ought to be given even more attention (*Economist* 15 August 1998: 15–17; Phillips and Anderson 2000; Bremer 2000; United States, Department of State 2000; Hoffman 2001; Lee and Perl 2002). In 1998, President Clinton announced the establishment of the post of 'national coordinator for security, infrastructure, and counter-terrorism' (Lipschutz 1999: 423) and, after the September 2001 attack, President Bush created a cabinet-level post (and later department) for homeland security. Until September 2001, terrorism had primarily found high-politics expression by being packaged together with 'rogue states' and nuclear proliferation leading into the discussion of missile defence. As a separate issue, terrorism had been securitised, but had not led to dramatic specific measures prior to the September attacks. After the attacks it did – domestically, in the form of investigations and prosecution beyond constitutional and legal normality. Internationally, 'the war on terrorism' became the organising principle for overall foreign policy and was obviously very much securitised, since it justified foreign policy shifts overruling former principles, by which, for example, states became allies that previously were criticised or even under sanctions, such as Uzbekistan and Pakistan. More concretely, in order to make the concept discriminatory enough to matter (and not just a blank cheque to be used by all states against all political dissidents), the war on terrorism was operationalised as two phases (Bush 2002), one during which all networks connected to bin Laden were to be traced and destroyed, and one aimed at states procuring weapons of mass destruction (WMD).

Proliferation, 'rogue states', and WMD are general security concerns and various anti-proliferation policies have long existed. However, the public debate has increasingly focused on the question of a distinct group of threatening states that both are outside international society and try to obtain WMD and the means of delivery. Increasingly during the 1990s, this threat moved up to where it might be claimed to have become the most focused candidate for organising a new US image of global threat. '[T]he "Rogues" have supplanted the "Reds"' (Hoyt 2000: 297; see Klare 1995; Tanter 1999; Bonde 2001). A quantitative analysis of American policy statements shows that the mention of 'rogue states' grew from zero in 1993 to a peak in 1997 (Hoyt 2000). From June 2000 to early 2001 the term itself was replaced by 'states of concern'. With or without the rogue term itself, the move is to construct certain states as irrational, irresponsible, and undeterrable. They raise questions of three kinds: they cause concern about regional balances of power, they stimulate thinking about asymmetrical warfare because they are particularly likely to be completely unscrupulous in using unconventional strategies; but, not least, they raise a need for new forms of defence of the United States itself. Therefore, the rogue state argument has been at the core of the debate over missile defence. Missile defence is a clear example of securitisation because extraordinary measures like revoking a key arms control treaty have been justified by existential threats.

A combined institutional expression of the last two threats is the elevation in the *Quadrennial Defense Review* (United States, Department of Defense 2001) of homeland defence to top priority for US defence (see below).

This examination of new US securitisations shows that all major 'new' threats are cast as military ones. The final stage of securitisation is therefore defence planning. Until 2001, the debate could roughly be seen in terms of how to balance three kinds of threats: the rise of 'a global peer competitor', the scenario of two simultaneous regional wars, and asymmetric warfare (including information warfare, WMD, and terrorism). A new superpower rival is realistically decades away and thus this threat is best met by optimising technology in a long perspective. Similarly, the asymmetric threats are probably best met by technological change and reorientation. Therefore, the key question has been whether it was possible to downgrade the demands for here-and-now large-scale capability (i.e., measured as the capacity to fight two major regional conflicts at the same time), and even to spend less on the next generation of weapons, and jump to the following generation. This would maximise preparation both for a peer competitor far down the line and for adjustment to new, asymmetric threats (Hillen and Korb 1998; Thompson 1999; Metz 2000; Carter 1999–2000; Shelton 2000; US Commission on National Security 2001). Donald Rumsfeld arrived as secretary of defence in 2001 with an ambition to push such a development. By August, when the Quadrennial Defense Review (QDR) was getting ready, very little had seemed to come of this adjustment. Winning two major regional conflicts would be changed to winning decisively in one war and repelling aggression in another simultaneously (Rumsfeld 2001; Wolfowitz 2001). The 11th of September and the terrorist attacks are likely to speed up the new investments by overcoming bureaucratic inertia and by allowing for larger defence budgets. The reduction side of reform, however, was at first postponed because of the profusion of funds (*Strategic Survey* 2001–2: 69–79).

US security still has military threats at the top – some conventional and some unconventional. The most conventional is the concern about potential peer competitors, i.e., how to preserve unipolarity (Posen and Ross 1996–7; Gholz et al. 1997; Mastanduno 1997; Layne 1997; Art 1998–9; Wohlforth 1999; Walt 2000). Its most explicit securitisation is found in relation to China. The unconventional military threats are terrorism and ballistic missiles. In contrast with Europe where security does not have to be military to count, and increasingly political-economic dynamics have become core, major security threats in the USA are by definition military (Wæver 2001b).

In the US case, homeland defence can hardly be imagined in relation to conventional state-to-state war and invasion, so it testifies to the centrality of non-conventional, military threats that the major departure from the previous QDR is the 'primacy' (United States, Department of Defense 2001: 17) of homeland security – 'to be effective abroad, America must be safe at home' (United States, Department of Defense 2001: iii). In practice, two threats dominate this area: terrorism (responsibility of the Department of Homeland Security) and missile defence.

A strict neorealist analysis might well claim that there really is no threat to the United States, and that perhaps the greatest threat is the difficulty of handling the absence of any serious security threat (Waltz 2000a, 2000b, 2002). As Colin Powell, then chairman of the Joint Chiefs of Staff, said in 1991 'I'm running out of demons. I'm down to Kim Il Sung and Castro' (quoted in Conetta and Knight 1998: 32). Have external threats become a necessary tool of governance for the US polity to which its state and industrial structures became addicted during the Cold War and now need in order to stave off internal fragmentation? Since September 2001, the scenario with internal fragmentation and absence of external securitisation has become less likely.

Debates on grand strategy in the United States might testify to this difficulty, because the dominant doctrine is increasingly independent of specific threats. Strategy has a paradoxical relationship to securitisation wherein direct security threats count less, but this move away from specific threats rests on some underlying general securitisation. In addition to the rationale for overall policy this is reflected in the procedure that guides defence planning. It has moved from being scenarios-based (depicting a credible threat) to capabilities-based (what we can do) (Conetta and Knight 1998 and, more specifically in relation to missile defence, Kadish 2002). The overall strategy is produced by making the amount of US preponderance the main guarantee not only for handling challenges but also for forestalling them.

In academic analyses this is known from the debate about what can explain the persistence of unipolarity against basic balance-of-power logic. The liberal version (Ikenberry 2001) that stresses institutionalisation, self-binding, and openness is not the basis for current policy; instead, it is the (totally contrary) argument that unipolarity is stable, because the United States is *so* dominant that no one will dream of trying to counterbalance (Wohlforth 1999). Therefore, the best security strategy is to maximise US military power and freedom of manoeuvre (read: no binding treaties). In punditry, a more extreme version makes the case for a US empire (Krauthammer 1999, 2001a, 2001b; Boot 2001) – since globalisation makes invulnerability impossible, the United States must use its power actively to run the world in a way that forestalls risks. The official policy of pre-emption fits here (as does the fact that a bestseller argues the relevance of ancient warrior cultures to US global strategy: Kaplan 2002). The net result is a narrowly conceived equation between US military power and world order (with no room for security dilemmas or any other complications). Therefore it is possible to handle security problems without knowing them – without measuring specific threats. Whatever the problem, the answer is always the same: maximise US military power. This demands a generalised securitisation, and this was partly in Bush's policy already as a presidential candidate, but it has become much easier after 11 September: it is a basic, realist case for the world being a dangerous place, for enemies lurking out there, and that today, when they have WMD, the United States is under fundamental threat and needs to act accordingly. The deficit of specified precise threats is therefore no puzzle – the general worldview points to a universal reply. Paradoxically, 11 September may therefore lead to less clear and distinct securitisation, but the whole political climate is marked by an underlying tone of insecurity.

Conclusions

For most of the twentieth century and especially the Cold War period, the levels of securitisation in North America followed a concentric circles pattern in which the United States at the centre was dominated by the global issue (although often strongly coloured by domestic dynamics); the first-row neighbours had a strong component of regional security dynamics mostly defined by US dominance; and the smaller, more distant states in Central America and the Caribbean were to a larger extent driven by domestic security but with the United States as intermittent intervener. To understand possible shifts it is not enough to 'weigh' the levels against each other – it is more important to capture their inner connections.

The constellation of domestic, regional, and global security has gone through four phases:

1. In its early history, North America was strongly penetrated by global powers but wars in Europe often meant fewer resources for those powers to spend on North America (although, on occasions, the opposite happened, and North America became indeed the very place to attack the opponent). This global/regional interplay made way for the emerging power, the USA.
2. Circa 1800 to the late 1930s: US foreign and security policy had a regional, hemispheric focus (with imperialism in the Pacific added).
3. Global involvement in two world wars and the Cold War had a deep impact on the United States, due to the strengthening of the state ('standing armies', secret service, etc.) and shaped the region in the concentric circles form described above.

4. Post-Cold War and globalisation: the changing strategic perception of most actors in the region led to NAFTA and more regionalism. But the two big questions relate to the United States. Will it continue to see global threats and therefore define itself globally, or will it become regional? How will the end of the Cold War and the absence of credible rivals influence the position of the state in the USA (see Friedberg 2000)? And, conversely, how will internal developments – including a possible decreasing legitimacy of state security and the increasing presence of multiple securitisations – influence the US global commitment? Will the terrorist attacks on 11 September 2001 have long-term effects on this, and perhaps as the *Economist* suggests: 'These things could halt – or at least slow – the erosion of faith in the federal government that has marked American politics for a generation' (Economist.com 28 September 2001; for the beginning of a reversal of this effect according to polls, see *Economist* 10 January 2002).

Again in this chapter we meet the importance of Watson's pendulum: the legitimacy of regional centralisation vs decentralisation. However, in this case, where one state is such a big part of the region, the pendulum operates within a state: a crucial variable is the legitimacy of centralisation/decentralisation *inside* the United States.

The trend of the 1990s pointed towards declining internationalism, which did not lead to isolationism but to unilateralism. The United States maintained its military pre-eminence but was reluctant to use it. In the words of Moïsi (2000): 'In world history, the US is the first empire that has ever combined so much comparative power and so little interest in the affairs of a world it *de facto* controls.' With a decreasing sense of direct threat to the USA, policies become shaped more by immediate interest than by long-term strategies for international order. In Julian Lindley-French's succinct summary: 'unilateralism is in many ways the result of a complex deal between an élite who recognises the need for some engagement and an American people, many of whom would prefer to have little to do with the world beyond. In effect, unilateralism represents the terms on which the American people permit the American élite to engage the wider world – "OK, if you must but only on our terms"' (2002: 19). On a range of issues – UN payments, CTBT, international war crimes tribunals, land mines, the Kyoto agreement, NATO enlargement, many details in the Balkan operations, the war in Afghanistan, dislike of peacekeeping, and not least missile defence – the United States has acted in ways that are seen even by close allies as extremely unilateralist and idiosyncratic (see Huntington 1999; Heisbourg 2000; Waltz 2002). In the US domestic discussion, this dilemma does not exist because the source of world order *is* maximum power and freedom of action for the United States. This is hardly the dominant view outside that country.

The result could become not an isolationist but a more isolated United States, increasingly unwilling (or unable) to build coalitions, and therefore leaving behind what has been the most distinctive and effective characteristic of its foreign policy over the previous half-century. For this book, the crucial question is whether the United States will continue to be a superpower – and the global polarity structure therefore what we call $1 + 4$. It is basically an American decision if the world should change to $0 + x$.

During the Cold War, securitisation justified unpopular policies. The United States had an economic interest in protecting the liberal international economic order, and it could be given the added security rationale that the liberal economic order was necessary to the fight against communism. This also justified a need to take into account the interests of allies and other crucial states. With the end of the Cold War, the United States became much less attentive to the interests of even major allies. Even if some of the unpopular American policies were argued on the basis of securitisation (e.g., BMD), the explanation for the reduced ability to form stable coalitions is equally about the weakening of securitisation. There were no pressing security threats able to justify policies that were not immediately popular in the United States.

The major question after September 2001 is whether this is a long-term trend, or whether the new fight against terrorism can domestically justify similar accommodation to international 'necessity'. So far, the United States has handled the 'war' in ways that point to continuation of the trend away from leadership, towards narrow engagement. This unilateralist behaviour poses a long-term question about the social sustainability of US leadership, and therefore over its continued status as the sole superpower.

10 South America: an under-conflictual anomaly?

Why are there relatively few interstate wars in South America? Interstate security dynamics have mostly been secondary to domestic issues, and the 'unstructured' explanation that works for such a situation in Africa does not hold for the much more developed South America. The possibility of war certainly has not been absent from the continent: military force has been threatened or used more than two hundred times in the twentieth century (Mares 1997: 195; 2001: 38). South America has not been a security community or anything close to it. Still there have been relatively few wars, and those that have occurred in the twentieth century have been markedly more limited and less destructive than those of the nineteenth century. In the nineteenth century, wars 'were long, spread beyond two parties, and entailed great loss of life and exchange of territory. Twentieth century wars have been more limited affairs' (Mares 1997: 196). Yet political violence is not low, quite the contrary. In one sense, the wars of independence continued into wars of state formation that then became civil wars. The civil wars of the Americas are among the bloodiest conflicts: the American Civil War, the Mexican revolution, the *violencia* in Colombia, the Central American wars of the 1980s.

Other issues to be given special attention (partly because of their particular interest for RSCT) are: (1) the relationship to a dominant great power neighbour; and (2) the process of a possible division of an RSC as the northern and southern parts of South America seemingly part ways – and the factors that restrain such a process. However, the questions of most profound importance for the future of the region are the ones at the core of each of the subcomplexes: the war on drugs in Colombia and the future of Mercosur in the Southern Cone.

304

The origins and character of the RSC

The existing states and main patterns of relations in South America are a reflection neither of precolonial nor directly of colonial patterns. Before it was conquered by the Europeans, South America contained empires – Maya and Aztec in Mexico and Inca in Peru – but these were eradicated and had only a very marginal, mythical importance for later state formations. Nor, except for the Spanish–Portuguese division, did the colonial pattern directly produce current relations. The larger pattern of states does not follow a colonial map and, with independence as far back as 1810–25, the local powers have had time to develop an independent history. Also given the distance to Europe and the hemispheric dominance of the United States, the influence of the ex-colonial powers has been limited. Thus, post-independence history is the key to understanding the present shape of South America.

Although the South American RSC is today something of a puzzle, it started in the familiar postcolonial way. Most regions that formed out of decolonisation started as conflict formations. This one was not born fighting to the extent we have seen in South Asia and the Levant: independence did not immediately trigger major wars. But independence led to many unstable or contested borders and consequently to wars among the new units about their exact number and delineation. Some of the most important interstate wars in Latin America have been: the Cisplatine War (Brazil vs Argentina, 1825–8 – eventually producing Uruguay); the Triple Alliance War (Brazil, Argentina, and Uruguay against Paraguay, 1865–70); the War of the Pacific (Chile gained territory at the expense of Peru and Bolivia, 1879–83); the Chaco War (Bolivia vs Paraguay, 1932–5 – Paraguay gained territory from Bolivia); the Leticia War (Colombia vs Peru, 1932–3); the Zarumilla War (Peru vs Ecuador, 1941 – and in 1981 and 1995); the Falklands/Malvinas War between Argentina and Britain (1982). Some civil wars were more bloody than most of the interstate wars: '*la violencia*' in Colombia (1949–62); the repression of dissidents in Chile (1973–7); 'the Dirty War' in Argentina (1976–80); the fight against the *Sendero Luminoso* in Peru (1982–c. 2000); and now the ongoing armed conflict in Colombia. Most interstate wars were fought over boundaries – some resulting in new states, most about contested areas. As noted by Kelly (1997: 138), five of the seven major wars directly engaged the buffer states, and often the outcome was loss of territory by the buffer state (Polandisation). No state ceased to exist because of defeat in these wars.

305

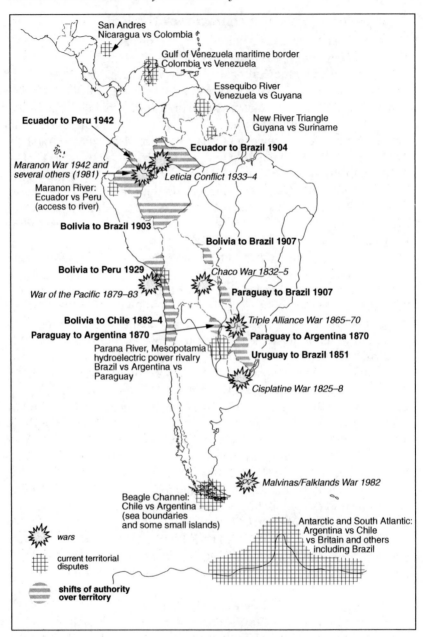

Map 10. Wars and Territorial Disputes in South America

The reason for this pattern is to be found in the historical origin of the states. Latin America created the precedents for later decolonisations of *uti possidetis juris* – that new states should take over the previous administrative or colonial boundaries. This principle was extended and thereby became central again in the case of the dissolution of the Soviet Union and Yugoslavia, where it came to mean more generally that internal borders should be the new state borders. However, because Latin American independence happened much earlier than in Africa and Asia, the borders were less clearly delineated. Bolívar's dream of one big republic failed. Also the attempt to move to the 'next level down', the units of the viceroyalties, did not last, and most of these broke into smaller units with even less clear boundaries (Prescott 1987: 199ff.; Shumway 1991: 1–80). Including the intense fragmentation of Central America, the result became that a 'century after the end of Spanish colonial rule, its four viceroyalties had become eighteen sovereign states' (Winn 1999: 83). In contrast, the Portuguese colony remained one Brazil. Many borders were unclear – and there were many boundaries: in contrast to the three long international boundaries in nineteenth-century North America, Central and South America had thirty-five long and short boundary segments (Prescott 1987: 195).

A major issue right from the beginning was the role of the United States. The ritual reference to 1823 and President Monroe's declaration against European attempts to extend their political presence in the Americas is misleading. Latin America was actually not a major interest at the time, and the United States did not have the naval power necessary to protect the Americas against the conservative European countries of the Holy Alliance (to whom the message was directed) – the British did this in practice (Mace 1999: 21; Atkins 1999: 44). The message was turned into a doctrine more by later policy-makers and should therefore be seen in the context of *their* policy (Smith 1994).

Seen in the context of European imperialism, into which the newborn United States soon entered to play its part, there was no doubt that the latter approached South America as its natural sphere. Outright annexation was applied to the remaining French and Spanish possessions in North America, and to much of Mexico when it gained independence (see ch. 9). In the nineteenth century, Cuba was widely seen as a proper target for US territorial expansion. John Quincy Adams in 1823 stated that Cuba and Puerto Rico comprised 'natural appendages to the North American continent' (Smith 1996: 25). In contrast, Latin America further south was not to be annexed. Partly this was a matter of space, of differentiating the close from the distant, and partly of time in the sense that, by the time these areas entered the agenda, the strategy had shifted 'from the acquisition of territory to the creation of a sphere of interest' (Smith 1996: 27). US strategy became more focused on economic expansion and competition. In many ways, what is otherwise seen as a change of policy under Franklin Roosevelt (the 'good neighbour' policy) can equally be seen as a culmination of a successful policy in which economic leverage became more and more central, and heavy-handed interventions were downplayed (Smith 1996: 66, 87).

Already during the age of empire (c. 1880s to 1910s) the United States started to act as regional policeman (Theodore Roosevelt's 'big stick') (Mace 1999: 21–2). The policy was not driven, however, by an urge to produce a regional security system, but primarily by economic interests (LaFeber 1993: 60) and by geopolitical concerns about the threat to the United States should the most threatening European powers of the day acquire positions in the hemisphere (Smith 1996; Schoultz 1998).

US visions for a regional system were regularly rejected by Latin American governments. Since the United States was willing neither to submit its own policy to multilateralism, nor to seriously engage itself in the economic development of the region, the Latin American countries did not have a strong interest in a very elaborate system. The institutions created (the International Union of American Republics, the Pan-American Union, in 1947 TIAR, the Inter-American Treaty of Reciprocal Assistance, and in 1948 the OAS) served as frameworks to legitimise US interventions, and as an arena for Latin American countries to push their demands and to try to gain some influence on US policy. US policy regarding interventions was irregular and continued into the Cold War (when the anti-communist element was added).

Should the United States be treated as part of the RSC, as interregional, or as global? In an approach like that of Lake and Morgan (1997c) and others who include all major actors into a region, the United States obviously would be a member of the South American RSC. Since we operate with mutually exclusive regions (see ch. 3), the United States would be a member only if there were a western hemisphere RSC (and there is not). So it is an external actor. This raises two questions: should it be seen as global or interregional, and does the US role amount to overlay or not?

It is useful to make a distinction and say US intervention is global when it is driven by concerns about global affairs, i.e., communism, but interregional when it follows only from the two regions being neighbours. And since the United States has for the last century been the only major external actor (with apologies to Britain, the Soviet Union, Spain, Portugal, and the EU), the categories of interregional and global can be collapsed into one level for South America.

The relationship is marked by penetration, not overlay. US preponderance makes the relationship highly asymmetrical and the United States a major factor in security calculations in the region – for good and for bad. But the US engagement is not constant and the United States neither 'rules' the region nor even generally shapes it. South America basically has its own dynamics into which the USA intervenes irregularly. During the twentieth century, US military intervention became focused on Central America and the Caribbean, where the United States openly intervened some forty times, compared to zero such overt interventions in South America. Covert operations such as in Chile in 1972 come to mind, but the contrast to the overt ones in the Caribbean and Central America is nevertheless important because it shows a US assumption about the legitimacy of its penetration into the Caribbean and Central America which is absent in South America.

Much of the basic pattern in South America predates, continued during, and still exists after the Cold War. This is a standard RSC marked by domestic social tensions and political instability, regional rivalries and transnational spillovers, and great power, mainly American, interventionism. The main security dynamics before the Cold War can be summarised as follows:

□ As indicated by the main wars, there are a number of dyads and triangles, mostly over *territorial issues*. Often these resulted in wider geopolitical patterns of alignment according to a checkerboard pattern or the old maxim of 'my enemy's enemy is my friend'. Most of the states aligned against their immediate neighbour – and then sought more or less systematic alignment with the other enemies of their enemy (Kelly 1997; Kacowicz 1998: fig. 3.2, 93).

□ *The cultural dimension* – Spanish versus Portuguese – did not lead to an overall patterning. A potential general alignment along these lines was usually weaker than the dynamics of the normal checkerboard pattern (i.e., Chile would support Brazil rather than Argentina, with which it had territorial conflicts). Culture acted only as an undercurrent to the potentially most important

rivalry: Brazil vs Argentina. Possible Brazilian regional hegemony was partly offset by the ambivalence in Brazil's policy:
whether to see itself as a member of the region; leader of it; or
non-regional, as a global power or closer to Europe and/or the
USA. The main security implication of the cultural factor has
been Brazilian fear of encirclement (McCann 1983).

☐ *Transnational politics*: domestic politics have regularly spilled
over from one country to another – be it in the form of radicals,
conservatives, populists, and/or military coup-makers. Direct
interference has been relatively rare, and parallel histories are
more often caused by ideational spillover.

☐ *External powers*: already before independence, Latin America
had been the object of sporadic competition between external powers other than Spain and Portugal (Newton 1991).
Britain had scored economic and the USA political gains. Mid-
century, the latter achieved naval parity with the former in the
Caribbean, but Britain still dominated trade and investment in
the Caribbean and especially Latin America (Winn 1999: 451).
American economic growth during the second half of the nineteenth century demonstrated that the USA would eventually be
the main external power in the Caribbean and Central America
(see ch. 9). In South America, Britain in the 1890s deferred to the
United States in some defining crises (Smith 1996: 33–5; Schoultz
1998: 91–124). Already before the 1920s when the United States
replaced Britain as the principal banker, foreign investor, and
trading partner in Latin America (Winn 1999: 452), it was US
power that caused most alarm in Latin America. Cultural and
intellectual anti-Americanism mixed with a geopolitical image
of a threat from the north. Through international law and multilateral diplomacy, the Latin American states worked to restrain
US unilateral interventionism. In the 1920s–30s American policy
changed to 'dollar diplomacy'. American economic dominance
became constantly bigger – and culminated in the early Cold
War years to which we now turn. The USA remained concerned
about extra-regional influence in the region throughout the pre-
Cold War period (e.g., Germany's overtures to Mexico during
the First World War, and Argentine 'neutrality' and openness to
Nazi activities during the Second World War; USIS 1998). The
nature of the extra-regional threat was the major change with
the advent of the Cold War.

The Cold War

In this case, we modify our four-level scheme by merging interregional and global: because the only relevant neighbouring region is North America, all main interregional connections go via the United States, which is also a global power.

Domestic level

Many states in Latin America were vulnerable, primarily because of social tensions and a particular pattern of domestic politics, which went through constant swings between different forms of extremism. A characteristic cycle went from conservative to populist to radical and back (Ward 1997: 6ff.). Rulers were therefore often concerned about domestic security, but rarely because of secessionism or minorities. The states were weak because of lack of effective government, social tensions, and political polarisation. The amount of political violence in society – a primary indicator of the weakness of a state (Buzan 1991b: 100–1) – was generally high. This violence was about the control of government in existing states, not about dismantling or merging states. The political systems moved in partly synchronised regional patterns between degrees of democracy, military rule, and other undemocratic forms.

Although individual countries exhibit much variation, a pendulum pattern can be seen in which, e.g., Peron-style populism was powerful in many but not all countries in the late 1940s–early 1950s; military coups between 1948 and 1954 left only four democracies in all of Latin America ('even by generous standards for classification', Smith 1996: 130); several dictators were ejected in the second half of the 1950s, but six popularly elected presidents were ousted by the military during the Kennedy years alone (Dunbabin 1994: 400). In the 1960s and early 1970s, the USA helped depose several elected politicians who it feared would fall into the arms of the Soviets: British Guiana in 1963, Brazil in 1964, Chile in 1972–3. Consequently, the pendulum swung to military dictatorships during the 1970s. Especially in the Southern Cone countries, this became a period of ruthless military regimes engaged in a cycle of escalation with leftist urban terrorists. Brazil after 1964, Pinochet's Chile after 1973, and most intensely Argentina's 'dirty war' between the post-1976 military regime and ex-Peronist guerrillas left thousands killed or 'disappeared'. Although originally helping these regimes, the United States was increasingly worried – and criticised – over their behaviour.

Military and other aid was diminished, and the dictators were followed by a turn to democracy in the 1980s.

The major domestic level change consequent on the Cold War was that right-wing actors could exploit the constant US fear about leftist movements in the region. The domestic polarisation which already existed in many places became aligned to Cold War patterns, and the more peculiar Latin American forms of populism, progressivism, and radicalism were squeezed into Cold War categories as either Marxist stooges of the Soviet Union or Christian, capitalist, and 'democratic' allies of the free world. It was tempting for elites in Latin America to formulate doctrines of 'national security' drawing on anti-communist litanies and to sign up to the anti-communist crusade (Kacowicz 1998: 78–81; Buchanan 1999). Internal subversion and revolutionary warfare were heavily securitised (Smith 1996: 199). This securitisation also stimulated that which it depicted as a threat, because close regime alignment with the USA fed into the threat images of the left according to which the main security problem was the USA. Revolutionary movements increasingly took the form of guerrillas. The option of a third way, however, remained attractive and explained the involvement of several Latin American regimes in the third world campaigns for nonalignment, development, and a 'new international economic order' (Smith 1996: 204ff.). Violent societies in Latin America were carried over from the pre-Cold War period. The Cold War novelty was that violence was politicised consistently in a specific configuration and not least that it was usually internationalised.

In line with general militarisation during the Cold War, the United States wanted to strengthen the armed forces of the region as a bulwark against insurgents, and Latin American militaries were increasingly cultivated as political allies (Smith 1996: 130). The US Army 'School of the Americas' opened in 1946 in Panama as a hemisphere-wide military academy working from a doctrine of national security, in which the chief threat was defined as internal subversion.

State form plays a major role in shaping the nature of security in a region (ch. 1). As argued by Kacowicz (1998: 107, following Hurrell 1998: 239), 'the state in South America seems to occupy a middle way in the weak/strong state continuum: it has been strong enough not to fall apart as in other postcolonial situations (like those in Africa). At the same time, it has been weak enough to find it hard to mobilise its society for war and conquest.' The liberalist 1990s have seen a retreat of interventionist states that were historically at the centre of politics and economics. This further weakens the propensity for classical interstate conflict, while it might stimulate many of the 'new security problems' (Serrano 1998).

Regional level – and subcomplexes

The region has many interstate controversies. The nineteenth century saw major wars, but conflicts continued into the twentieth century and, as late as the 1980s and 1990s, tensions were very high between Peru and Ecuador (with a brief war in 1995), Venezuela and Colombia, and Argentina and Chile, and until around 1980 the crucial Argentine–Brazilian relationship pointed towards escalating rivalry (including nuclearisation). An important question about this RSC in the twentieth century is why various latent conflicts have not become manifest, or if they have why they did not escalate into large-scale war, especially in a region filled with geopolitical thinking and suspicion, and with a record of forcible boundary changes.

One explanation often given is the huge, impenetrable, thinly populated tracts of land with poor or no infrastructure. This explanation caused much worry especially in the 1970s, because the states gradually conquered the wilderness and spread their transportation infrastructure so that the barrier was eroding. Would predictions about increasing interaction capacity leading to increasing violence then hold? In the northern part of the region, there has been a tendency for some of the longstanding border disputes to become more manifest, while the Southern Cone moves the opposite way. This might fit the geopolitical explanation since some of the major changes regarding penetration of previous barriers have happened in the north and middle part of the RSC; this is less so among Argentina, Brazil, and Chile.

Geopolitical factors explain the seeming paradox between the region having more boundary questions than almost any other yet looking comparatively peaceful in a global perspective. Vast, thinly populated tracts make for weak control by the states at the edges, which are more easily contested than the core. Therefore the region has had little existential state-threatens-state security, but a lot of 'flexibility' at the outer reaches of the states. This explanation cannot be constructed in a mechanical way whereby expectations for the future become necessarily defined by the geopolitical factor.

Another explanation is Brazil as hegemonic stabiliser (more important than the often-made reference to the United States as regional hegemon; see Kacowicz 1998: 89–90; Mares 2001: 55–83). Following Brazil's territorial gains during the last part of the nineteenth century and the beginning of the twentieth, it became essentially a status quo power preferring a 'diplomatic way' and with a strong vested interest in regional stability. The turn to regional cooperation can be seen as a gradual realisation by especially Argentina of the advantages of recognising and reinforcing the Brazilian choice of this regional role (Kacowicz 1998: 90–1).

The interstate conflicts can be grouped into three categories according to the regional position of the states.

1. *The central one was Brazil–Argentina.* It mixed questions of status (leadership in the region) with direct balance of power and competition for influence in the three buffer states between them. They did not go directly to war with each other after 1870, but continued their rivalry over the east bank of the Rio de la Plata, over the control of the river system, and over the territory that became the buffer states. Already by the middle of the nineteenth century, 'the language of power balancing had become well established as the dominant frame of reference for understanding the relationship' (Hurrell 1998: 230–1). Explicitly geopolitical thinking was widespread (Kelly 1997), and mutual threat perceptions were high for most of the twentieth century. Brazil feared encirclement by Spanish America led by Argentina; Argentina feared Brazilian expansionism and domination. Both countries for a period pursued nuclear programmes, and originally both refused to ratify the Treaty of Tlatelolco (1967) establishing a Latin American Nuclear Weapon Free Zone (Serrano 1992).

   In terms of external allies, the United States often gave Brazil preferential treatment epitomised in the 'key nation' strategy of Nixon/Kissinger. Spanish America saw Brazil as acting in league with the USA, enforcing American schemes and using American assistance to become dominant in the region. Generally, the question of Brazilian hegemony is a key to South American regional affairs. Brazil has certainly had visions of 'manifest destiny' and schemes for how to reach the Pacific (and the Caribbean) which was traditionally seen as the key to becoming regionally dominant the US way. Brazil – and Portugal before independence – was successful in gradually expanding, although the aim of reaching the Pacific was never achieved.

Often expansion followed a pattern of illegal colonisation of uninhabited lands across frontiers, followed by arbitration and annexation (Kelly 1997: 73, 177). It is therefore a source of suspicion, especially in Uruguay, Paraguay, and Peru, that Brazil continues to develop its hinterland more efficiently than they do. The spectre of Brazil again overflowing borders to settle on the other side continued to haunt these countries and thereby the regional considerations of Argentina.

2. *Relations between the other significant states.* The major and medium-sized states Chile, Argentina, Bolivia, Peru, Colombia, and Venezuela had a number of remaining disagreements mostly over boundaries.

- Argentina–Chile: the two have struggled over the southern tip of the continent, the surrounding seas, parts of Antarctica, and thereby the status of the two countries as powers in one or two oceans. They almost went to war in 1978 over three islands off Tierra del Fuego, but negotiations in 1984 solved most questions.

- Chile–Bolivia: in the 1879–83 War of the Pacific, Bolivia lost its coastal provinces and thereby its access to the sea. In addition to the difficulty of accepting significant territorial losses, the practical question of access to the sea and thus a route for trade has led to Bolivia keeping this issue alive. Increasingly, the question has been less about territorial revisionism and more about finding an arrangement for securing Bolivian transit and possibly leasing land for a port terminal.

- Chile–Peru: the scars left from the War of the Pacific are not as deep as for Bolivia.

- Peru–Ecuador: the Marañón border conflict led to incidents in 1980 and 1995. Ecuador wants to be linked to the Amazon area – and Brazil supports this. The 1998 agreement produced by the four guarantor powers of the 1942 Rio Protocol (USA, Brazil, Argentina, and Chile) included Ecuadorian navigation rights on the Amazon (*Economist* 31 October 1998: 57–8).

- Colombia–Venezuela: they have a maritime boundary dispute over the Gulf of Coquivacoa/Gulf of Venezuela and the Monjes Islands.

- Five-eighths of Guyana's territory is claimed by Venezuela.

- ☐ Argentina vs Great Britain over the Malvinas/Falkland Islands, which culminated in the 1982 war whereby Great Britain fortified its control; negotiations since have been difficult, although relations are slowly improving.
- ☐ Finally, the Antarctic conflict is in principle resolved, in that national claims are locked in by the 1961 Antarctic Treaty System, but competing proposals continue, including Brazilian schemes to get in, and conflicts between Argentina and Chile (linked to their territorial disputes) as well as Chile vs Great Britain (Kelly 1997: 144ff.). Potentially, the stakes here are higher than in most of the local conflicts and it could thus become important in the future.

3. *The buffer states (and their territorial losses).* The widespread use of geopolitical ways of thinking about the region shows in the general acceptance of Ecuador, Bolivia, Uruguay, and Paraguay as buffer states. As mentioned above, they have all lost significant percentages of their territory. All four have had question marks attached to their survival, but they have also – exactly due to the general acceptance that they function as buffers – been kept alive to avoid escalation among the major states.

Finally, there are some minor questions such as Guyana's border problems with Suriname, and other questions around the minor states – often with Brazil as guarantor of the status quo.

In RSCT perspective, an important question is to what extent the different conflicts add up. They do not align on any central pattern. In many cases, one conflict links up to the next. For instance, Chile's conflict with Argentina has been seen as part of the balance-of-power system in the Southern Cone. Alliances have mostly been rather informal ententes. Chile has historically acted to prevent a possible Peru–Bolivia–Argentina axis; Argentina worried about a Brazil–Chile alliance. Also, interconnected conflicts show simply in the worry that a third state would be able to exploit the weakening of one part of a conflict: Peru feared that if it got into a war with either Ecuador or Chile, the other would exploit the situation (a fear not supported by recent events) (Mares 1997: 210).

Even the most consistent pattern of alignments – Brazil–Chile and Argentina–Peru – never consolidated into a kind of European-style bipolarisation and fixation of alliances, because the conflicts were too many and interests therefore crosscutting. In this respect, the RSC is moderately integrated. It is not integrated as much as if it had one overriding conflict or integrative project, but the different conflicts and securitisations have independent roots that tie together as they develop.

Another question important to the region is to what extent it falls into distinct subcomplexes. Although, historically categorisations have operated with four, five, or even more subregions (such as the Rio de la Plata valley, the Southern Cone, the Andean, the Amazonian, and the Caribbean sectors), the relevant security map has been in terms of two subcomplexes: Southern Cone and Andean North. The Southern Cone subcomplex contains the major powers of the region and was traditionally defined by the interconnected rivalries among Argentina, Brazil, and Chile with the buffer states Paraguay, Uruguay, and Bolivia (plus traditionally Peru which we do not include here anymore). Later the same countries became formal or informal members of Mercosur and constitute a gradually maturing security regime pointing towards a security community. In the Andean North, the subcomplex consists of Peru, Ecuador, Colombia, Venezuela, and Guyana. This too was traditionally structured by interconnecting rivalries – dyads and triangles – but in contrast to the Southern Cone, conflicts have not been overcome and have instead been aggravated by adding transnational security problems primarily related to drugs and the war on drugs.

How cohesive the RSC is also depends on joint action at the regional level. One approach is to look at formal organisations; another, perhaps more realistic, one looks at the reaction of other Latin American countries to aggression in the region and more generally the (non-)role of regional conflict management. Mares (1997) sarcastically calls this a division of labour: the Latin Americans uphold the principle of non-intervention while the United States does the intervening. Collective security never unfolded in a South American framework but instead as the OAS, i.e. pan-American and usually with US policy at the centre, a situation somewhat parallel to the current US one in East Asia. On the other hand, external involvement commonly increased Latin American coherence as a reaction (Atkins 1999: 31).

Finally, a form of connectedness would be transnational solidarity. There has been spillover in which some political move inspires repetition elsewhere (and the pendulum movements thus formed partly out of parallel socioeconomic developments, partly by imitation), but outright support for ideological allies has not been a major factor. From Che

Guevara's ill-fated export of guerrilla warfare to Bolivia in the 1960s to the attempted solidarity of the Southern Cone military dictatorships of the 1970s, the differences of conditions and interests proved a formidable barrier for such transnationalism. The region has been transnationally unified more at the level of ideas and ideals, where symbolic figures are often shared, whereas the level of interests and actions has remained more fragmented.

Interregional and global levels

This is almost exclusively a question of the USA. Spain and the EU attempted some involvement in Latin America but mostly in Central America and by way of EU–Mercosur relations, to which we return below. Venezuela has extra-regional relations through OPEC. Brazil has some interest in Africa and the vision of a South Atlantic role, but it has little chance of playing a role in relation to Europe or Asia; thus interregional usually means inter-American. Whereas US policy was defined by an alleged Soviet threat, actual Soviet action always remained limited in South America, and episodic in Central America and the Caribbean even if one episode was exceptionally dramatic (Cuban missile crisis in 1962).

Whereas Latin America had been a central policy concern for Washington prior to the Cold War, it now became only one among many arenas, and not a primary one. However, with the intensification of rivalry with the Soviet Union, concern about extra-hemispheric powers was heightened, and initiative in formulating Latin America policy shifted from business elites to state policy (Smith 1996: 322–8). The resulting level of attention to Latin America was at least as high as before the Cold War but now as part of a much more consistent policy. This in combination with the general strength of the US position in 1945 meant that the two decades from 1945 became the high point of US influence in the whole region, i.e., reaching even to the Southern Cone (Atkins 1999: 47–9).

During the Cold War period, the main security problem that could trigger intervention was the presumed communist threat – much intensified after Castro took power in Cuba (1959). Before the Cold War, the United States had been more open about acting often in relation to economic interests and, during the Cold War, much of the debate over US interventionism was about whether the United States was actually still driven primarily by economic motives. Whether this was so or not, the actions were usually legitimised by security arguments (and the defence of 'democracy' if just vaguely plausible), and usually the one about communism and the risk of a Soviet foothold in the western hemisphere. 'The Cold War altered the basis of inter-American relations, elevating the concept of "national security" to the top of the US agenda and turning Latin America (and other third world areas) into both a battleground and a prize in the conflict' (Smith 1996: 6). Dominguez (1999) has argued that the Cold War has to be recognised as ideological reality in order to explain US interventionist behaviour. If interpreted as just another phase in the pursuit of economic self-interest (fear of economic losses from hostile regimes) or as Monroe policy (fear of alignment with the Soviet Union), it cannot explain the actual record of interventions and non-interventions.

Was the USA a stabiliser and/or threat? It has been a constant potential intervenor since the 1880s. This has occasionally meant leadership in establishing joint American action and thus strengthened, e.g., OAS ability to act and handle conflicts. However, the US engagement – predominantly defined unilaterally – has also been a source of insecurity for Latin American states. Furthermore, the USA is seen not only as 'a state' (with a policy), it is also seen as MNCs and 'cultural imperialism'. The general policy towards the United States has been one of 'constrained balancing' (Hurrell 1995a: 254, 273): the Latin American states have tried to diversify away from the USA though it was clearly impossible to establish direct alignment against it. Strategies of Bolivarian unity or extra-hemispheric protection were tried only occasionally. More consistent was the use of international law and international organisation, of social revolution, of third world solidarity, and finally (as practised by the authoritarian right) of direct alignment with the United States (Smith 1996: tab. 5, 331). As argued by Peter H. Smith, it is important to realise that Latin American policy is not, as often claimed, driven by a schizophrenic love–hate relationship to the United States or other culturalist irrationalism. 'Latin America's reactions to the United States reflected just as much logic and regularity as did US policies' (Smith 1996: 330) – only the available options were not always many or attractive. 'Latin American politicians, pundits, and intellectuals developed . . . cultures of resistance' and even cultural 'anti-Americanism' as part of strategic efforts to handle the difficult relationship with 'the colossus of the North' (see Smith 1996: 329ff. and tab. 5; Kelly 1997: 198ff.). Based on quantitative data, Mares finds that US hegemony correlates clearly with neither war-avoidance nor war, and concludes 'that both those who favour and those who oppose hegemonic management dramatically overstate US influence on conflict dynamics in the security complex' (Mares 2001: 56).

Composite picture

The main factors at play in Cold War South American security were four: (1) domestic instability, (2) contested borders and bi- or trilateral geopolitical speculation, (3) considerations about regional balance/hegemony mostly involving Brazil and Argentina, and (4) US involvement. The four factors have interacted, but each had its independent status and they combined only in each individual, unique case. The RSC was a conflict formation, not centred and not a great power complex. It was not overlaid but there was significant penetration from the USA.

Post-Cold War changes

Latin America is probably the region where the end of the Cold War as such meant the least. But several changes happened around this time or a bit earlier in the 1980s, so we can still usefully divide Cold War from post-Cold War dynamics.

Domestic level

On the domestic level, three interlinked developments mark the 'post-Cold War' period, though both began during the 1980s: democratisation, a reduction in the influence of the military on politics, and neoliberal reform with internationalisation of economies and restructuring of states. Democratisation as such is not new, but the characteristic swings between radicalism, populism, and military coups seem to have ended. The systems seem to have become more stable and all sorts of radicalism have declined. Possibly, democratisation in some places exacerbated interstate conflicts by opening them to popular pressure. On the other hand democracy has created an increased ability to act predictably internationally, and has thereby bettered chances of regional cooperation. This latter dynamic is more pronounced in the Southern Cone, where regional cooperation was initiated by the military dictatorships but qualitatively deepened after democratisation. Although civil–military relations are far from uncomplicated (Diamint 1999), the process of integrating the previously ruling militaries into the new democratic structures is progressing, if slowly.

Military spending has been going down markedly, but the political influence of the military profession still remains an issue, including questions about independent control over defence policy. Changes of military policy and developments in domestic politics are often linked. A weakened role for the military in society enables changes of foreign and security policy (for example, the shift from defence circles to foreign ministries in Argentina and Brazil during the rapprochement); and lower levels of tension tend to marginalise the military politically. Despite the general move from military to civilian rule, in several countries the militaries are still a significant power factor (see Pion-Berlin and Arceneaux 2000; Fitch 1998; Loveman and Davies 1997; Zagorski 1992; Schulz 1998; Diamint 2000). They retain some of their US connections related to counterinsurgency, intelligence, and covert operations even when somewhat out of tune with official US foreign policy. Often, counter-drugs policy helps sustain old practices (Zagorski 1992; Curry 1995).

In the Southern Cone the three main countries have taken different routes, but in none does a military return to power seem realistic. Yet to actually establish a functioning civilian ministry of defence, and generate civilian expertise on military matters, is not easy (Beltran 2000; Diamint 1999, 2000). The three countries are located on an axis with Chile and Argentina at either end and Brazil in between. In Chile, transfer of power was negotiated so that the military secured its position. In Argentina, the military lost all credibility due to economic and military failure (Malvinas/Falklands war) and had little influence after the change of power. In Brazil, military and political elites largely unified in a joint vision for the country (Beltran 2000).

A redefinition of military roles interacts with a new US policy for the militaries. After decades of teaching them about internal security, the project is now – under the label of cooperative security – to think about external security (but not in the sense of fearing the neighbour). This to some extent goes against the US 'war on drugs' which pushes some South American militaries back towards dealing with (new) internal threats (Buchanan 1999).

Two other elements of securitisation are also present in some places. First, indigenous peoples' movements are politically influential in Ecuador, and race is potentially important in Peru, Bolivia, Colombia, and Brazil. The indigenous peoples 'consider themselves to be nations, and their conception of national security is intimately connected to their survival as nations' (Van Cott 1996; cf. Mares n.d.: 2) and therefore societal security is for them often the first priority. An escalation of securitisations is always possible in these places. Second, 'the securitisation of social development' means that 'spatial and social marginalisation is presented as "existential threats"', says Herz (2000) – who also quotes the Brazilian foreign minister: 'social development is the condition for economic development and constitutes the first line of national defence and of maintenance of sovereignty'. While security rhetoric is clearly present, it is less clear that such rhetoric leads to any dramatic counter-measures. However, the developments in the late 1990s and especially early 2000s with Argentina's collapse, bizarre coups and countercoups in Venezuela, and swings towards the left in several countries, including possibly Brazil, might point to an increasingly consistent constellation, in which globalised elites see the public as a security risk because it prevents the necessary adjustments to demands from the market/the North/international economic institutions, while the public sees these very elites and their globalisation as the threat to their own livelihood. 'Economic security' has begun to appear more often in debates, pointing in contradictory ways to either or both sides of this tension (Tulchin and Espach 2001b: 13–14).

Experiences with the doctrine of national security legitimising military intervention in domestic affairs has meant that, in South America, the idea of a wider concept of security has been received with hesitation, because it is feared to empower military and other 'security' agencies (Atkins 1999: 103; Diamint 2001).

Regional level and subcomplexes

At this level, the most interesting trend was the increasing differentiation of the two subcomplexes, with the possibility of an internal transformation, by splitting into two, of the South American RSC. There was also slow reorganisation of the military forces towards more defensive postures (Beltran 2000), more conspicuously in the Southern Cone than the Andean North. As the economic sector assumed more prominence in the region's security dynamics, regional integration projects came into tension with hemispheric ones.

The most dramatic changes in the South American RSC have been in the Southern Cone subcomplex, where three key developments have transformed a longstanding conflict formation into something approaching a security community.

☐ *A rapprochement between Argentina and Brazil*: Economic cooperation led to a major shift in trade patterns and became institutionalised in Mercosur. In the military sphere, the nuclear programmes were stopped, confidence-building measures instigated, military postures redefined, and geopolitical modes of thinking generally ended. The process started around 1976–7 with Brazil's proposal for an Amazon Pact for joint development of the Amazon Basin and, more spectacularly, resolution of the longstanding struggle over the waters of the Paraná River. This energy policy coordination between Brazil, Argentina, and Paraguay was paralleled by a shift from military competition to civilian cooperation in the nuclear field (see Hurrell 1998; Kacowicz 2000; Banega et al. 2001; Petersen 2001). Economic cooperation was then added by the newly elected democratic presidents in the mid-1980s. Because it transformed the pattern of amity and enmity in the region this rapprochement is, in RSCT, a structural change in the Southern Cone subcomplex.

□ *Regional integration in Mercosur*: Argentina and Brazil started creating a common market in 1986. They signed the Treaty of Asunción in 1991 and initiated Mercosur (Mercosul in Portuguese) – the world's third largest trading bloc – on 1 January 1995, with Paraguay and Uruguay bringing the numbers of members up to four. Most important is the internal common market and a common external tariff, but the scheme is relatively broad and ambitious (and clearly inspired by the EU) with common ID card, special queues in airports, and dispute settlement mechanisms, and aiming at free movement for goods, capital, labour, and services.

□ *Resolution of border questions*: From Peru south, all but one of the major internal and external conflicts have ended. Peru has signed permanent peace treaties with Ecuador and Chile, Chile and Argentina have solved their remaining problems, and Peru has practically ended the war with the 'Shining Path' Marxist guerrillas (*Strategic Survey* 1999–2000: 80; Contreras Q. 1999) The remaining conflict is Bolivia's search for access to the sea, which involves Chile and Peru. An agreement has been close on several occasions and it is likely that a solution will be found. Regional conflict resolution mechanisms started to appear in relation to the Peru–Ecuador conflict in 1995 (Sethi 2000; Marcella and Downes 1999), and democracy monitoring in OAS (and other forums) in relation to Peru in 2000 in what was a striking departure from South America's traditional hardline non-intervention (*Strategic Survey* 2000–1: 76–7).

Latin America is infamous for grandiose, non-realised plans for regional integration, and Mercosur has emerged as an apparent exception to that rule. Regional integration returned to Latin America in the mid-1980s/early 1990s in the form of two competing processes: local (Mercosur, plus some revival of the Central American Common Market, CARICOM, the Andean Pact, and a number of bi- and trilateral free trade agreements; Hurrell 1992: 122–3) and hemispheric (NAFTA enlargement and/or a Free Trade Area of the Americas, FTAA).

Mercosur had an immediate impact on intra-regional trade, which grew as a proportion of total trade from 28 per cent in 1985 to 43 per cent in 1994 but fell to 20.7 per cent in crisis-ridden 1999 (Banega et al. 2001: 242; *Economist* 31 March 2001; compare *Economist* 22 November 1997: 69). Chile, Bolivia, Venezuela, Colombia, and Peru have shown an interest in joining or linking up to Mercosur, and in 1996 Chile joined Mercosur's free trade zone without adopting the common external tariff system. Mercosur will be much influenced by its success in eventually attracting new members, most importantly Chile. Rivalry between Mercosur and all-hemispheric and/or 'NAFTA+' schemes is very direct in the competition for new members. In the light of recent European experiences, Mercosur attempted to organise the region not by creating an unwieldy all-regional organisation, but instead starting out with the hard core and letting it expand as the power of attraction begins to work (see Peña 1995; Hurrell 1998: 248). After striking initial success, Mercosur met difficulties towards the end of the 1990s – both internally with actually implementing and deepening plans, and externally as notably the East Asian crisis of 1997–9 hit Brazil, and later Argentina plunged into a cascading crisis. The crisis could, however, also be taken as a proof of the strength of regional reorientation and cooperation, because the region did not return to old ways. The IISS concluded on the Argentinian crisis that 'Mercosur has, if anything, been strengthened politically' (*Strategic Survey* 2001–2: 120) as demonstrated by Brazilian expressions of solidarity. The crisis taught everybody about their mutual, regional dependence. Neither, however, has Mercosur settled some major questions about its own structure. Will it be essentially a projection of Brazilian power (*Economist* 16 December 2000: 64), or a Brazil/Argentine joint hegemony (Pedersen 1998), or some kind of EU-model multilateral arrangement able to handle countries of different weight? It is a classical pattern that the leading power prefers less structure, but Brazil might find that it is able to pursue hegemony only at the price of self-binding and institutionalisation (Ikenberry 2001; Deudney and Ikenberry 1999;

Kupchan 1998; Ikenberry and Kupchan 1990). So far, 'Brazil has often seemed to see Mercosur as just a large visiting card to show in its dealings with the outside world' (*Economist* 16 December 2000: 64).

The other regional organisations in Latin America have been economically successful too, even if not as influential in terms of reshaping political and security relations as Mercosur (*Economist* 11 April 1998). Beyond economy, Mercosur diplomacy towards the other regional groupings is part of the larger pan-American political manoeuvring, i.e., as counterweight to US-centred pan-Americanism. The Andean Community and Mercosur occasionally floated ambitious plans for a South American free trade area (Andean Community 2002).

Security and integration in the Southern Cone

Mercosur has been in crisis for a while and is likely to face more crises in the coming years. Brazil and Argentina especially will have to implement some unpopular measures if Mercosur is to be defended. They face strong temptation to use security reasoning to enhance the importance of Mercosur in order to justify such measures.

The original launch of Mercosur was partly driven by two security arguments. One was the fear of marginalisation in a globalising and regionalising economy – it 'instilled a sense of urgency' in Brazilian policy-makers (da Costa 2000: 8). This was much reinforced with the end of the Cold War. The second argument was a defence of democracy. Argentina and Brazil after the military dictatorships saw their democracies as vulnerable. Mercosur stabilised democracy both by economic prosperity and by weakening the militaries by taking the heat out of Argentina–Brazil confrontation. Thus, the security community in the Southern Cone can hardly be seen as an instance of 'democratic peace'. It was not solid democracies that generated peace. It was the potential loss of democracy that motivated security measures. This in turn means that, with the widespread assumption now in both countries that democracy is firm, this security argument for Mercosur has lost force.

However, in recent speeches it is a constant theme that Mercosur is (in a formulation often used in Argentina) 'strategic'. Mercosur, and the alliance with Brazil, is 'strategic' meaning it is basic and long-term, not to be compromised by short-term manoeuvring, and it is the basis on which other things are built (Giavarini 2000; Argentina, White Paper on National Defense 2000). A lot of controversy was created in 2001 when the Argentine economics minister Cavallo allegedly hinted at a lesser role for Mercosur, more bilateral negotiations with the United States and negotiating FTAA without Mercosur, but the president was very active denying that this had ever been said. An economics minister – bent on a very difficult economic salvation mission – might try to manoeuvre, but a president responsible for the overall project had to avoid at all costs the impression that the relationship with Brazil or the priority of Mercosur was still open for discussion. There is no explicit securitisation in the sense of spelling out threats, but there is an implicit sense of extraordinary policy, of danger and a no-go area. The European-style argument about the threat of Europe's past becoming its future (see ch. 11) does not exist here in its full form. But the Mercosur case does carry the same strategic sense that regional institutions must not be threatened because they are the key to a future that is more desirable in several profound respects than the past.

In Brazil, a similar 'strategic' logic was involved when President Cardoso argued that Mercosur is 'our destiny' whereas the FTAA was a mere 'policy option' (*Economist* 31 March 2001: 14). In the context of Brazilian defence and foreign policy it is a dogma always to list Argentina and Mercosur as first on any list of strategic directions, partners, or projects (e.g. Corrêa 1999): first comes 'The importance of relations with Argentina. In a Brazilian diplomat's sphere of action there is no more important issue than this. In view of what it has historically represented and of what it has come to represent since integration, Argentina poses the highest priority challenge, which requires from Brazilian foreign policy persistence, creativity, and a vision of the future. The institutional stability and the economic and social development of South America are today closely linked to the Brazil–Argentina binomial.' Second is 'Mercosur and regional integration', 'without any doubt the most powerful, distinctive feature of Brazilian–Argentine relations and the keystone of our strategic alliance' and, third, the 'political Mercosur'.

In the analysis of Thomaz Guedes da Costa (2000: 7), 'No single factor more clearly shapes Brazil's foreign policy agenda than the effort within . . . [Mercosur] to manage the economic integration and political co-ordination with Argentina.' Regional stability is closely identified with the transformation of the Argentine–Brazilian relationship but this in turn is the basis for Brazil achieving the position internationally which is to some an almost existential matter, i.e., defending Brazil's vision of itself. Even to those who do not take this ambitious line on what is necessary internationally for Brazil to be Brazil, the 'platform' argument can take on a security quality because, as spelled out below, the USA can be a threat to Brazil, not least with its environmental and its anti-drugs policies, and therefore it is crucial that Brazil is in a position to counter such efforts. This requires a strong Mercosur and partnership with Argentina.

In these speeches, Mercosur is given a security rationale. In one part it avoids conflict and defends the invaluable gain in local stability that an improved Argentine–Brazilian relationship creates. And in the other part it creates an interregional and global security argument for South America: only with a desecuritised relationship between Argentina and Brazil and a credible Mercosur can they (and not least Brazil) act vis-à-vis others (read: the United States) with the power of a region.

In the Andean North, a more traditional conflict formation picture still prevailed, albeit with some new twists. With the 1995 Peru–Ecuador conflict, direct war returned after a regional pause. Venezuela returned to its claims for a majority of Guyana's territory. Democracy has been under pressure in all of the Andean states (Whitehead 2001; Naím 2001; Hoskin and Murillo 2001; Calderón 2001; Lucero 2001). And, not least, the dynamics related to drugs – farming, production, smuggling, and countermeasures against these – have accelerated and intermingled with a general destabilisation and fragmentation of especially Colombia, as well as increasing US involvement. Drugs are not a new post-Cold War challenge, but the issue has come more into focus. It was less of an issue during the Cold War because the communist threat dominated the US agenda, and domestic politics in Latin America were more shaped by the radical swings. Now the situation in countries like Colombia and Bolivia is close to the original nineteenth-century situation (before centralised states took hold): significant amounts of power rest with *caudillos*, individual strongmen with control of local territory and armed men.

Much of this problem is focused on Colombia – 'the most troubled country in the hemisphere'. 'Every day, 10 Colombians perish in politically related strife. Over 35,000 people have been killed over the past decade... In the process, some 1.3 million people in Colombia have been displaced or turned into refugees' (Marcella and Schulz 1999: 213). The violence is a complicated four-sided war between left-wing guerrillas, drugs businesses, paramilitary 'self-defence' groups, and the state. The picture is complicated by the involvement of all sides with drugs money, resulting in the blurring of the categories ('narcoguerrilla' etc.), as in parts of Africa. Seen from within Colombia, these different problems merge in a general weakening of the state and privatisation of violence. From the outside, it is drugs that mainly mobilise resources for the US engagement. However, to complicate things, some of the US agencies entrusted with operations seem in practice to be in line with some Colombian forces in seeing it as a counterinsurgency affair rather than anti-drugs. The central element has been the training and equipping of three counternarcotics battalions in Colombia to support fumigation of illicit crops and dismantling of laboratories, thereby depriving the guerrillas of income. After 11 September, the USA has openly and officially redefined its involvement as aimed against 'terrorists' which de facto means supporting the government against left-wing guerrillas (LaFranchi 2002; *Washington Post* 21 June 2002; *Strategic Survey* 2001–2: 89, 101–12; Storrs and Serafino 2002; Serafino 2002). The Bush administration has requested permission to broaden the authority of the Defense and State Departments to support the Colombian government's 'unified campaign against narcotics trafficking, terrorist activities, and other threats to its national security' (quoted from Storrs et al. 2002: 15). This support against 'other threats' includes defence of an oil pipeline with sizable US investments.

The attacks of 11 September have raised an analytical question in this region too. Does the link become more global than interregional with a potential redefinition of the US effort in and around Colombia as part of 'the war on terrorism' (a global effort) rather than 'the war on drugs' (de facto hemispheric)? So far this has not been the case, because the activities are not tightly integrated into a coherent 'war' that structures in any systematic way. It is mostly a relabelling and a legitimisation of conducting the war on drugs as a counterinsurgency operation, as several actors had wanted for a while. The guerrillas have been linked to the IRA but not to Middle Eastern Islamists, and they are therefore fought partly because of the drugs issue, partly qua Marxists – in both cases very much with the classical hemispheric optic.

The main coca fields traditionally were in Bolivia and Peru, and the cocaine refineries and drugs barons in Colombia and Mexico. The US 'air bridge strategy' has been successful in hindering deliveries from Peru and Bolivia to Colombia, and coca production in Peru has fallen by 56 per cent since 1995 and similarly in Bolivia (*Strategic Survey* 1999–2000: 86). However, the main result of this has been a massive increase in production in Colombia. The whole problem increasingly concentrates on already troubled Colombia, where, among other things, it triggers regional concerns about migration (Mares 2001: 44; n.d.: 3).

The Colombian government for several years pursued a somewhat confusing dual policy of on the one hand negotiating with the guerrillas (FARC and ELN) – even granting de facto control over a Switzerland-sized 'de-militarised zone' to FARC from 1998 to 2002 – and on the other hand setting up an ambitious anti-guerrilla plan with a major military component and campaigning for US investment in it. Eventually, in 2000 the United States went in on a large scale allocating its $1.3 billion share of the intended $7.5 billion 'Plan Colombia', which involved a major military effort against the left-wing guerrillas but not against the right-wing paramilitaries. US policy came to include major sums for Colombia's neighbours and thus points towards general US involvement in the Northern Andean region. Since 2001 this has been known as the Andean Regional Initiative (ARI) with a 2003 budget request of almost $1 billion, of which around three-quarters is counternarcotics assistance (ACI, Andean Counterdrug Initiative). Colombia gets more than half (in addition to unspent Plan Colombia money) and the rest goes to Peru, Bolivia, Ecuador, Brazil, Panama, and Venezuela (in descending order of size) (Storrs and Serafino 2002). The plan has been much criticised for focusing solely on drugs producers rather than consumers as the problem, for its militarised approach (despite its link to the Andean Trade Preferences Act), and for its one-sided involvement in the Colombian armed conflict. The strategy of the CIA and Pentagon deviates from that recommended by the Drug Enforcement Agency, DEA. But the conflict has taken on enough of a momentum that military calculations seem to follow their own logic. This is exactly what worries many in both North and South America.

Given the disintegration of Colombian society, the USA is not likely to find easy victory (not even with the more hardline President Uribe elected in May 2002). Coca cultivation in Colombia increased by 25 per cent in 2001 (Storrs and Serafino 2002: 9). A long-term, large-scale presence in the region seems likely. Policy-makers have been encouraged by the successes in Peru and Bolivia, but the market mechanism works against the United States here. Driving down production in one place increases the price and the business becomes more attractive to others. As long as demand is high, not only will individual producers continue to come forth; some country will prefer the political economy of a drugs-based economy to US alignment unless the USA enforces an extremely consistent and ambitious policy in terms of both development assistance and military interventions.

This multidimensional crisis is regional to the whole Andean North partly due to parallel economic and political difficulties, partly due to spillover from the Colombian conflict. With differing emphasis all neighbours worry about refugees, about the possibility that elements of the coca business are pushed across the border by Plan Colombia, and about combatants crossing the borders. Although President Chavez of Venezuela has probably had the closest ties to guerrillas in Colombia, other neighbours have also had some degree of sympathy and up-held various forms of 'neutrality' towards the conflict. Chavez and his peculiar form of oil-based, leftist revolutionism – inspired by Bolivar and Castro – add an element of unpredictability to the area with his rapid shifts between threats and alliances with neighbours, his Cuba connection, and his application for membership of Mercosur; he is in-creasingly the object of separate US concern (and in 2002 the United States was accused of having a hand in the attempted coup against Chavez). However, in relation to Colombia, during 2001 he came in-creasingly into line with the other Andean states and even the United States and Colombia at least in terms of diplomacy, though not necessar-ily on the ground. Among the neighbours, Peru and especially Ecuador are most likely to import instability and coca-growing from Colombia. Bolivia, also, is part of the 'balloon effect' whereby suppression of pro-duction in one country leads to more in another, and the rather direct US involvement in Bolivia's successful coca eradication has begun to draw criticism in both countries (Faiola 2002; *Strategic Survey* 2001–2: 105). Peru and Ecuador have implemented military redeployment away from their mutual border and towards their borders to Colom-bia (Storrs and Serafino 2002: 13, 15) and the USA established one of its Forward Operating Locations (FOLs) in Manta (Ecuador) (in addition to Aruba and Curaçao, Netherland Antilles, and Comalapa, El Salvador). Bolivia is probably the weakest link in the chain because coca grow-ers are well organised, have their own political party, and, with refer-ence to both the indigenous population and postwar social orientation of Bolivia, securitise counternarcotics efforts as both an economic and an identity threat, drawing support from the general scepticism about globalisation in the region (Gentleman 2001: 6–7, 23–5; Storrs and Serafino 2002: 13–14).

Panama raises the question of the border between North and South America and the possibility that Panama has been – at least at times – an insulator between the two. For long periods, Panama was among the most heavily penetrated elements of Central America. It was de facto controlled by the USA. In recent years, the American presence has wound down, with bases being closed and the canal handed over (1999). Panama is sometimes not counted as part of Central America because the other countries were all spun out of the original Central American Federation, while Panama was detached from Colombia (by the United States). Are the connections between Panama and Colombia then close enough to tie Panama into the South American RSC? No. There have been periods where actual fighting from Colombia moved into Panama, possibly connected to domestic issues, including the future relationship to the United States (*Economist* 8 January 1998). Otherwise, the direct military link has not been strong. Refugees are feared, but the main connection has been that both the guerrillas and the paramilitaries used Panama to hide, to rest, to receive supplies (including arms), as a transit route for drugs, and for money laundering (*Economist* 5 October 2000; Gentleman 2001: 25–7). Panama has probably profited from the conflict in Colombia as much as it has felt threatened by it, although its position is vulnerable given that Panama has no military. The PCW security interaction between Panama and Colombia is not alarmingly high for a boundary between two RSCs. Should violence in the future spill over the uncontrollable border to a much larger extent, Panama could be transformed into an insulator between North and South America.

The Andean subcomplex is not easily understood in terms of state-to-state security relations, but the complicated 'transregional' security dynamics that tie together domestic and international (intermestic) issues do not produce total deterritorialisation. They tie together at a relatively consistent Andean subregional level (Tickner and Mason 2003, forthcoming; compare Manwaring 2002).

Are we then witnessing an increasing split between a Southern Cone subcomplex marked by desecuritisation and integration, and a Northern subcomplex with a weakening of states, increasing external involvement, and much violence at all levels of society? Could one speculate that North America is extending further south? The situation of Central America and the Caribbean increasingly goes for Colombia and some of its neighbours. Simultaneously, the Southern Cone emerges as more and more coherent and distinct. Thus, the amount of US penetration might be constant – only it is more and more concentrated in the northern part, and South American regionalism finally happens, but only because it is first attempted for only part of the region. To optimists, this could be seen as somewhat parallel to Europe, where head-on all-continental schemes proved impossible, but six countries started a cooperation that has grown step by step until today it shapes the whole region. Pessimists would focus instead on the challenge posed by the split and the possibility of spilldown from north to south.

Although the differences between the Southern Cone and the Andean North are striking enough to justify seeing them as distinct subcomplexes, Brazil remains the linchpin that holds the South American RSC together. Brazil is obviously central to the Southern Cone, but it also has both direct and indirect interests in the Andean North. It is concerned about spillovers from both the drugs problems and increasing US involvement. The Brazilian view is that the USA is excessively dominant and unilateralist in its global policy, and a major question for the future is how Brazil is going to react to the spiral of violence in the north. Will Brazil get involved in the war on drugs, formulate an alternative approach and have it multilateralised in South America, or try a more geopolitical engagement with selected countries in the subcomplex?

Brazil has been worried about the Colombian situation and especially a number of violations of the border (Mendel 1999). Consequently, Brazil has strengthened its police and military presence in the relevant districts, moving towards the possibility that it could start to offer services to other countries in the north. Brazil could become the core of regional campaigns against drugs traffickers as an alternative to the US-sponsored Plan Colombia with its emphasis on coca eradication. However, Brazil might become hampered in this by its increasing domestic problems with drugs consumption and smuggling, which tends to produce silence on the issue.

Brazil's relocation of the thrust of its military effort towards the north (Beltran 2000; Gentleman 2001: 27–31) has much to do with the Colombia-centred drugs and guerrilla crisis. However, there is a second rationale to Brazilian policy, which is crucial to the total configuration of regional and interregional securitisation. Especially in military circles a threat – which others occasionally call paranoid – is imagined whereby states and NGOs of the north seek 'to transform the Amazon region into an area of global interest' (Filho and Zirker 2000: 106). This 'internationalisation of Amazonia' is seen as more likely when the United States and allies talk about 'new threats', when they modify the concepts of sovereignty and non-intervention as in Iraq and Kosovo, and especially when they talk about the rainforest as an issue of global concern or elevate the issue of native rights. Criticism of Brazilian environmental policy is seen in this light and, in the most spectacular scenarios, Brazil could be threatened by intervention on environmentalist grounds (Filho and Zirker 2000, n.d.; Herz 2000; Dreifuss 1999; Perruci 1999). These different securitisations of threats to and in Amazonia produce an increased Brazilian presence there, and this eventually becomes the main obstacle to South America breaking apart into an Andean North that drifts off to North American overlay or internal disintegration, and an integrating Southern Cone. Geography makes Brazil the potential connector as long as Brazil defines serious security problems in its sparsely populated north. So too, in the longer run, does the potential for Mercosur to expand into the north.

That it is unsustainable to see the Andean region as currently forming a separate RSC shows in the attempt by Luis Lobo-Guerrero Sanz (2000) to analyse it in these terms, because, in addition to giving the USA a very central place, he includes Brazil. Similarly, the ARI includes Brazil and Panama. That the Andean subcomplex is indeed made up of Colombia, Venezuela, Bolivia, Ecuador, and Peru corresponds to the US thinking around the ARI, whereby Panama and Brazil are defined as more marginal than the others.

Interregional and global level

Several issues linked across the regional and hemispheric levels, most notably drugs, economic liberalisation, and regional integration, and all of these reshaped South America's relations with the USA. Both Argentina and Brazil reached the conclusion that their main policy could be neither close alliance with the United States, nor a confrontational policy against it (Hurrell 1995a: 255). The alternative was subregionalism within an American context. Whereas previously one of them was almost always in harsh opposition to the United States, and Brazil sometimes in close cooperation, they now both moved into relatively normal relations with it. Brazil is, however, increasingly wary of US universalistic interventionism as witnessed by humanitarian interventions, notably in Kosovo, and the risk of similar action against Brazil on the basis of environmental securitisation. Also, Brazil sees itself as the key counterweight to the USA in the negotiations on the FTAA. At the same time, Argentina has moved towards relations with the United States so close as to warrant since 1998 the rare label of 'major non-NATO ally' – and dubbed 'carnal relations' by Foreign Minister di Tella. Although reminiscent of the classical polarisation between Argentina and Brazil (though opposite to the most common pattern) and US divide-and-rule policy, the policies of the two South American countries were still sufficiently compatible not to be a source of destabilisation. The lack of US support during the 2001–2 financial collapse drove Argentina away from this policy of 'automatic alignment' and 'further into bed with Brazil via the Mercosur trade bloc' (BusinessWeek Online 14 January 2002; see Rohter 2002; *Strategic Survey* 2001–2: 91, 121).

The changing relationship with the USA is partly a product of changing US priorities. After the Cold War, Latin America regained some of its geographically motivated priority. However, at the same time the threat of extra-hemispheric intrusion was lower than ever, and the general definition of US interests shifted from security to more social and economic issues, more influenced by interest groups (Smith 1996: 325–9). Because the Cold War was not replaced by any similarly dominating global security priority, Latin America became relatively more important to the United States as an adjacent region, but in a much more selective way. Concern about drugs and migration naturally focused on the nearest parts of Latin America: Central America, the Caribbean, and the Andean North of South America. The US factor thereby became less directly relevant to the Southern Cone countries, and the 'divide and rule' factor diminished as the United States became an external motive for Southern Cone cooperation.

In a general sense, the challenge from globalisation, the success of East Asia, and the lessons from the debt crisis led to a change of economic strategy (from import substitution to export-oriented neoliberalism) and to an increased interest in regionalism for economic reasons. Especially the threat of a three-bloc world and a marginalisation of South America spurred regional cooperation (see Mace and Bélanger 1999). Thus, regionalism was less caused by economic logic than driven by 'economic security'. But the question was which cooperation: subregional, regional, or hemispheric?

Hemispheric cooperation has a long but far from glorious history. From Bolivar's 1826 'Congress of Panama' through the 1890 'International Union of American Republics' (after 1910 'Pan American Union') to the 1948 formation of the OAS, the aims of the USA and the major Southern Cone states have differed strongly. The former wanted a regional organisation for security and conflict management but was willing neither to deliver the parallel economic structure demanded by the Latin Americans nor to submit its own decisions about interventions to multilateralism. The OAS has therefore functioned as an organisation not for the western hemisphere but for Latin America including US activities in that region. With Canada joining (in 1990), it is possible that the organisation will actually become more hemispheric. Hemispheric economic cooperation was revived in the first President Bush's 'Enterprise of the Americas' speech in June 1990, which launched NAFTA but also included hemispheric promises for what became the project for a Free Trade Area of the Americas. The US primarily works on the plan for a FTAA, but has realised that the key will be to negotiate with Mercosur/Brazil. The hemispheric format is unlikely to win out: US interest in far-reaching regionalisation is limited. The rationale is more like those for Asia (APEC) and the Trans-Atlantic (TAFTA), i.e., to weaken regional attempts that do not include the United States and replace them by thin meta-regionalisations that do (Buzan 1998; see also pp. 455–7 below). Getting approval for NAFTA expansion will be domestically difficult in the USA, and business circles are ultimately not interested in a protective bloc in the Americas, but in global free trade. Hemispheric cooperation – especially in the NAFTA format – is not necessarily attractive to Latin Americans. Due to compensation measures demanded in the United States, NAFTA is quite intrusive on Mexico and would be equally so on any Latin American entrants.

As often noticed, NAFTA and Mercosur are 'two competing models' (Bernier and Roy 1999) for regionalisation, but in the end the result is probably not strict competition. Thin hemispheric integration could be compatible with a process in which the real impetus is in a parallel evolution of concentric circles around NAFTA and Mercosur. Another possible scenario – which Brazil in particular is conscious of – is that a more consequential FTAA is actually realised but then Mercosur functions as a way to increase Brazil's influence on this process (da Costa 2001).

The question of hemispheric/regional/subregional integration (rather than, as in the past, military doctrine) is a privileged issue through which to read 'grand strategy'. But it is also important because Mercosur is at the core of the emerging security community in the Southern Cone. Thus, the fate of Mercosur determines the stability of this subregional peace. Whether Mercosur eventually becomes the core of an all-regional concentric circles scheme as in Europe is probably more doubtful. Thus, South America will remain, for a long time, an RSC with two distinct centres, each with its characteristic dynamic. Mace and Bélanger have shown that trade patterns in the western hemisphere already coalesced around two groups of countries, a US and a Brazil–Argentina pole (1999: 51ff.). In economic terms, it is thus likely that Andean integration will eventually be subsumed in larger schemes, and the open question is how the 'boundary zone' will turn out between the systems formed around each of the two centres of attraction.

Hemispheric cooperation is strengthened in other areas as well, including counterterrorism after 11 September and an inter-American democratic charter that opens at least the interpretation that it allows for a right to interfere if democracy is threatened (Habel 2002). TIAR, the collective security mechanism, was saved by 11 September. Mexico cancelled an announced withdrawal from the treaty, and reflections about its obsolescence were replaced by an activation – like NATO's, although more reluctantly – of its article about an attack on any American state being an attack on all.

Another linkage point between the regional and the hemispheric is the problem of drugs. American anti-drugs strategy has required a controversial yearly 'certification' of states regarding their participation in the war on drugs. It has created major embarrassments, such as when Mexico ought to have been decertified, which was impossible, or when Colombia was embarrassing whether certified or not (*Economist* 7 February 1998: 63–4; *Economist* 20 February 1999: 59–61). The Latin American countries thoroughly resent the whole idea of the United States unilaterally certifying nations. They complain that, if the USA is serious about pan-Americanism, it could at least multilateralise certification. In Latin America it is widely assumed that drugs are not the problem – prohibition is. And the US fight against drugs creates many more problems than the coca leaf ever did. However, because the United States is the United States, the countries of the region have to have a policy on the issue – otherwise they will end up just accommodating Washington's policy. Thus, the drugs issue might eventually become part of what ties all of South America (and in some respects all of the Americas) together, whereas now it mostly divides the two halves of South America. Latin American pressure has paid off: since 2000, attempts have been made to get a softening of the certification procedure through Congress, and it was temporarily modified for 2002.

All of the 'new' security threats the United States sees from Latin America – drugs, migration, the environment, and insurgents (Hurrell

1995a: 271; Dunbabin 1994: 422ff.; Payne 1999: 509; Chace 2000) – reinforce the US concentration on Mexico, Central America, the Caribbean, and increasingly the northern tier of the Andean countries (Hurrell 1995a: 280) where problems are most intense and closest to the United States.

Conclusions

South America has traditionally been an RSC, not overlaid (although penetrated) and not unstructured (although, compared to all the other regions except Africa, it is the one where the relationship between interaction capacity and distance/geography has had the most limiting impact). It was a conflict formation for most of its history. But recently there have been some notable changes in the South American security constellation. The pre-Cold War and Cold War constellation contained domestic vulnerability; weak interstate dynamics (i.e., restrained interstate conflict and little cooperation); and regular interregional or rather global interventions (from the USA). The post-Cold War one contains for most states less domestic vulnerability of the classical political kind; more interstate dynamics (i.e., both more conflict and increasing regionalism, which in turn imply competing regional schemes as a new object of rivalry); and the relationship with the United States changing from being more driven by global dynamics to being mostly interregional. This in turn means that the US relationship with different countries and subregions within South America becomes more shaped by distance, and the northern part the main object of attention. Increasing interaction – driven partly by increasing interaction capacity, partly by domestic political change – creates more cooperation in the Southern Cone, but in the Andean North it has reactivated some interstate conflicts, found transnational expression in crossborder security problems, and drawn in the USA.

Most other RSCs have one or two levels that dominate (the domestic in Africa, the regional and the global in the Middle East, etc.). But in South America the four levels are unusually balanced. The linkages across the levels are sometimes strong, sometimes weak. Some domestic conflicts have spilled over (and been exploited) both regionally and in external interventions, and domestic democratisation has helped shift regional relations away from conflict formation. But the regional dynamic has not been strong enough to shape domestic developments in any significant way, in part because the region never became firmly polarised – neither along an internal axis such as Argentina–Brazil, nor by penetration from outside. Linkages across the regional and interregional levels have been quite strong.

In a world where integration schemes and strong regional organisations seem invariably to fail outside Europe, South America has for long been an interesting case. A security regime has been strengthening for at least twenty years, and it is now asked whether it approaches a security community. How solid is the foreign policy reorientation of Argentina and Brazil, and how stable is Mercosur? Mercosur has experienced a lot of difficulties but, even when the Asian financial crisis hit Brazil and Argentina tumbled into a devastating crisis, the countries resisted the temptation to return to old patterns. The reorientation is begining to be embedded in a restructuring of defence forces. Finally, the pattern of securitisation seems to reinforce cooperation. The old geopolitical thinking that created threatening scenarios among the South American states has been largely abandoned, and the main threats today are global economic competition and – especially to Brazil but with some resonance in most other countries – the need to stand up to the USA, albeit in a cooperative way. Exactly because the relationship with the USA is relatively good it is necessary to be strong enough to influence it, i.e., to get a better scheme for the war on drugs than the American approach and to be influential in the negotiations on the FTAA.

The end of the Cold War has in itself not been very significant in this region. Globalisation and regionalisation had more of an impact on the Southern Cone, and the end of the Cold War had at best an indirect effect to the extent that the drugs and terror issues moved up the US hierarchy of security issues. The two focal issues after the Cold War are narcoterror/USA in the north of the region and the difficulties and potentials of Mercosur in the south. The question is what kind of total picture emerges. The two developments are different on many dimensions. What unifies all this? What is to become of South America?

Is South America close to an external transformation: breaking into two? In the most extreme scenario, the northern part becomes so shaped by the United States (Plan Colombia etc.) that it comes closer to Central America and the Caribbean, i.e., North America expands southwards. Two main links inside South America prevent this for now: (1) Brazil, the key to the Southern Cone but also a regional power in the north, guarantor of some of the small coastal states, and a potential threat to some of the others; (2) the interrelationship between the different integrationist schemes: Mercosur, the Andean Pact, NAFTA, and the pan-American FTAA. The fate of the South American RSC hangs on how these factors unfold.

Conclusions: scenario for the RSCs of the Americas

Unlike in Asia, there is no American supercomplex that can form the basis of a joint scenario discussion for all of part IV. The main scenarios are regional and in some cases sub-regional, and the separate chapter conclusions therefore stand.

South America is increasingly developing as two subcomplexes with contradictory trends. The Southern Cone is on what is locally taken to be a quite robust, irreversible route to integration. With Argentine–Brazilian rapprochement firmly in place and all border questions solved, the subregion is beyond being a security regime, approaching a security community. It is in the grey zone between the two kinds of RSC, normal and centred. In the northern (Andean) part of the continent, on the other hand, security is increasingly structured by the drugs issue, US involvement, and domestic instability that keeps the border conflicts alive in that part.

North America is and remains one RSC. It became centred early (by the 1860s) and centredness supported a great power (and later superpower) role for the United States. The region has been a security community and largely desecuritised internally under this centred/global regime. With the end of the Cold War, the region is (with some parallels to EU-Europe) resecuritising but along non-state lines, i.e., in post-sovereign format. Due to the historical anti-statism in the USA, such a development can have more far-reaching effects than it would elsewhere in the developed world. The big question is whether this, together with the changing nature of the international system, creates pressure for changing the global role of the United States and thus the structure of the international system. If, on the other hand, the USA stays globally engaged, the exact nature of this choice will have implications at the regional level in the Americas, as well as elsewhere in the world.

Part V
The Europes

Introduction

Throughout its history, Europe has experienced a limited number of decisive structural changes. In various periods the continent has tried out most of the forms a region can take: centralised, fragmented, overlaid, and itself overlayer of most of the world. Furthermore, it has been through processes of mergers of and redifferentiation into several RSCs. During the Cold War the Soviet Union moved up to the global level becoming co-constitutive of the 2 + 3 world. Thus Russia was lifted out of Europe, and had no RSC around itself (due to its direct dominance of potential members). In the current 1 + 4 world, Europe has two of the four great powers, but in contrast to Asia they are members of separate RSCs. After the end of the Cold War, Europe has wavered between a formation as one, two, or three complexes. In the first post-Cold War years, a large 'OSCE' Europe began to form which included Russia, but the latter increasingly drifted off to become the centre of its own RSC. The Balkans for a while looked as if it formed a distinct RSC. This development ultimately did not materialise, and Europe now consists of two centred RSCs which have decisively curbed its traditional power balancing and friction. The geographical closeness of Europe's two great powers (EU and Russia) makes a reunification of the two complexes a possibility and today they form a loose supercomplex. The Baltic states are the most important zone of contact, but generally the EU and Russia are not enough involved in each other's security issues to turn 'Europe' into one large RSC. Because of these post-Cold War vacillations, this part of the book will be divided into three chapters (EU-Europe, Balkans, post-Soviet space) focused mainly on the post-Cold War period. Because Europe has had a partly joint history, and because early history is more relevant here than in the parts of the world remade during colonisation and decolonisation, the historical development of Europe prior to 1989 will be dealt with as a whole and presented in this introduction.

If one understands West and Central Europe as now arranged around an EU great power which gradually replaces the existing powers, Europe is unique for having *only* global level great powers and *no* regional powers. In simple polarity terms this follows from the nature of both RSCs as centred and unipolar, which implies that dropping down to regional polarity adds no new powers in addition to those at the global level. However, four complications make this an inexcusable simplification. In EU-Europe, the 'old' great powers – notably France, the UK, and Germany – are still regional great powers for some purposes and even act at the global level in some fields. Germany is an economic world power; France and the UK are permanent members of the UN Security Council and nuclear powers. This first complication is the deepest: West-Central Europe cannot unequivocally be categorised as a system with one great power, the EU. These two realities are like two different pictures that each capture much of the situation, but that occasionally have to give way to the other picture for a situation to be meaningfully represented. EU-Europe is primarily shaped by the simultaneous existence of powers at two levels, and the tension between these two realities makes up a central security dynamic of the current situation.

Second, there have been signs in the CIS area of attempts at a countercoalition to Russia – the so-called GUUAM cooperation (Georgia, Ukraine, Uzbekistan, Azerbaijan, Moldova) which if successful might lift at least Ukraine to the status of regional power as part of a regional polarity structure. This might also drag Russia down from the level of great power to that of regional power (similar to the way rivalry with Pakistan prevents India from rising above the South Asian RSC). Third, Turkey is an insulator and therefore not part of the polarity of any RSC. It is a strong and active insulator with ambitions of playing a role as 'regional' great power within the loose European supercomplex formed by EU-Europe and the CIS (and to the extent that it includes also the Middle East: an interregional constellation). Fourth, the world's only superpower, the United States, is not only present the way it is everywhere in the world, it is deeply involved in European institutions (NATO, OSCE) in ways that often make analysts define the United States as a European power. In our categories, the USA is not a member of the European RSC, but it is certainly involved in a more consistent and systematic way than in most other regions of the post-Cold War world.

344

Formation of the European RSC

A unified European security order on a large scale was first formed by the Roman Empire, and the long story can therefore be told as one of first a gradual loosening of central control towards a decentralised balance-of-power order, and then the beginnings of a swing back towards a more centralised order founded on the EU project (appropriately based on a 'treaty of Rome'). In RSCT terms, the development in Europe since the fall of Rome has roughly gone from many mini-complexes, through two large ones (Southwest and Northeast), to one (1700–1945), with a new split into two since 1989. In most other parts of the world, the RSC was born by decolonisation, whereby new actors emerged out of hierarchy and into (regional) anarchy. While Europe is obviously the great exception to this, being the source of colonisation rather than the object of it, there is some similarity to what happened after Rome: a former hierarchy gave way to a regional anarchy.

The system experienced regular external pressure from barbarians, but these rarely formed into enduring conflicts and mostly functioned as shake-ups and compressions of the West European system itself. Throughout all of this, the Eastern Roman/Byzantine Empire continued, mostly defending itself against waves of migrating peoples coming in from the northeast and southeast, until finally it was replaced by the Ottoman Empire. The Byzantine Empire first tried to reconquer Italy, then for a long time was mainly engaged in (defensive) power struggles in directions other than west, whereas the Ottoman Empire from the start was on the offensive, not least in relation to Europe.

The big intriguing exception to this pattern is the Crusades (1096–1291). The connection surely was by way of securitisation: the occupation of the Holy Land by infidels was very much a security issue (a threat to faith; Laustsen and Wæver 2000; Riley-Smith 1997; Jensen 2000). A strong, temporary but also narrow link was forged between Europe and the Middle East. The two sides did not become *general* threats to each other as they were in Roman times. The Christians were not powerful enough to pose a threat to the main Muslim power centres – only to one of their belongings, Jerusalem.

From the early sixteenth to the late seventeenth century, a more consistent and regular pressure operated in the opposite direction: an 'Islamic' challenge to Europe. Arabs no longer held the Iberian peninsula. But the Ottoman Empire covered what became later the Balkans, and for a long period held around a quarter of Europe's territory, pushing forward

345

to Vienna in 1529 and 1683. This contributed to making the period c. 1500–1700 in one respect the most important precedent to the present, because it is the only period when Europe contained one or more RSCs participating as equals in a wider international system. As argued in chapter 1, the connections had previously not been strong enough to form international systems beyond the regional scale, and Europe eventually became so dominant that its position was not that of a region in the world but as the power centre of the world. This was by no means an obvious outcome in the sixteenth and seventeenth centuries. Around the sixteenth century, the regional systems of the European state system, the Ottoman Empire, the Aztecs and Incas, and more tentatively India and China began to be connected in a larger international system in which European primacy was initially far from assured.

In addition to the powers one usually focuses on in Western Europe, another RSC formed in Northern Europe as states emerged there. Scandinavia, Poland-Lithuania, and Russia formed from at least 1523 an RSC centred on the Baltic Sea with a continuous power struggle, a series of wars, and patterns of shifting alliances (Kirby 1990). Despite Dutch and British interventions in the local struggles to secure access to the Baltic, the separate RSCs lasted until the Swedish intervention in the Thirty Years War (Watson 1984a: 17) or even to c. 1700 (the Great Northern War, 1700–21). The two RSCs merged conclusively, as the powers of the Western/Southern RSC became so concerned about outcomes in the North/East that they intervened systematically, and Russia started to be seen as a general player on the European scene (Kirby 1990: 323–4). From 1700, Europe became a single RSC covering more or less the entire space of EU-Europe and the former Soviet Union, and with the same ambiguities as today about Turkey.

Operation of the RSC until 1989

The operation of the single European RSC from the seventeenth century has been defined by two main processes. One is the 'pendulum' movement described by Adam Watson (1992) in which all regions move back and forth between centredness and multi-unit independence. The *legitimacy* dimension of this is the shifts over time in the relative power of thinking that is generally *European* versus narrowly conceived national self-interest. The other process is the external relations of the continent: external threats and Europe's own expansion. A third dynamic is normally given more or less all the attention: the rise and fall of *particular* powers, the various bids for hegemony. This third dynamic, however, is cyclical and thus less important for understanding the development over time than the other two. If different states take turns in being quasi-hegemonic, the shifts between these make a lot of difference politically, but from an analytical perspective it is more important whether the continent moves towards more centralisation, i.e., whether it is unipolar and hegemonic, or less, i.e., a multipolar balance-of-power system (the first process) rather than who precisely holds the dominant position (third process).

The balance between particularity and universalism changes in one long gradual process that can (despite fluctuations and reversals) be summarised as universalism decreasing from the fall of Rome to the early twentieth century and then a reverse trend. Medieval struggles were much shaped by universalistic assumptions produced partly by the memory of Rome, partly by shared religion. Struggles were conducted in the name of the same universal values and principles, and thus largely seen as competing claims for representation of the uncontested whole (Grewe 1988: 55–162; Hall 1999; Ullman 1974). Early modern Europe with its system of independent sovereigns is all too often presented as the end of the universalism from Rome and the Christian Middle Ages. However, the operation of interstate politics can hardly be understood without including the continued power of more general loyalties and assumptions. During the classical era of the European state system (1650–1900), the system was clearly state-based but states' rationality was deeply shaped by assumptions about the whole they formed (as emphasised within IR by the international society tradition of the English School). The balance of power was not the inadvertent result of decentralised self-interest but a self-conscious concern about systemic conditions (Little 1989). Similarly, to act according to 'interest' and 'reason of state' meant to follow the 'rules of the international game' including taking the concerns of others into account (Kratochwil 1982; see also Kissinger 1957; Jervis 1982; Wæver 1995b). This order gradually broke down from 1870 as states started to conceive of their interests in gradually more narrow (and social Darwinist) ways (Kissinger 1968; Kratochwil 1982). Thus, it is misleading when twentieth-century interwar and postwar arguments for wider responsibilities are seen as an uncharacteristic 'idealism' deviating from some kind of 'natural', narrow state-centredness of previous centuries. The pendulum had been swinging all along and there were many philosophical and political traditions to draw upon – not in order to replace states by other communities, but to redefine the meaning of statehood and the nature of state interest in a more Europeanised way.

The second dimension is the interregional position of Europe. Since Roman times this displays a relatively steady, long-term cycle of expansion and external pressure, the last round of which was European global expansion 1500–1945, and the dramatic overlay of Europe during the Cold War.

An enduring complication in this whole story is whether the Roman/ Byzantine legacy most represented by the Ottoman Empire should be dealt with as external threat or as a member of the European RSC (Bull 1984a: 117; Neumann and Welsh 1991; Watson 1987, 1990, 1992; cf. Jung 1999: 216–19). Europe was not the main security concern for the Ottomans. They engaged in wars in several directions, and the partial conquest of today's Iran, Iraq, and Egypt was most important, for both economic and religious reasons (Goodwin 1999: 78). The Ottoman Empire is thus hard to count as an ordinary member of the European RSC, nor does it tie together a larger Euro-Asian RSC, nor place itself as insulator. Rather it was a great power in a complex of its own and, during the period in which it was much stronger than the European powers, it performed the familiar interregional spillover from a great power containing complex to a weaker neighbouring one (Europe). Ambiguity still marks Europe's relations with Turkey.

Europe's expansion after 1600 had important repercussions for intra-European dynamics. Some hoped and others feared that revenues from overseas empires would shift the balance of power in Europe, which they never fully did. In the nineteenth century a relatively peaceful, cooperative concert of European powers rested on the possibility of expanding and compensating beyond Europe (Jervis 1982; Mackinder 1904; Lenin 1961; Dehio 1963). When the concert unravelled, rivalry over colonies and control of the seas started to feed negatively into relations among the powers at the centre. At the height of its influence, Europe had created a global international system with all the major actors being European powers. Gradually, this gave way to a more truly global system with non-European states first being admitted as members (Bull and Watson 1984; Gong 1984) and some later becoming great powers. The globalisation of Europe did not fundamentally change the nature of the European RSC, nor the patterns of amity and enmity, but it changed the boundaries dramatically as they moved from encircling this minor continent to being close to global – and back. In an even more

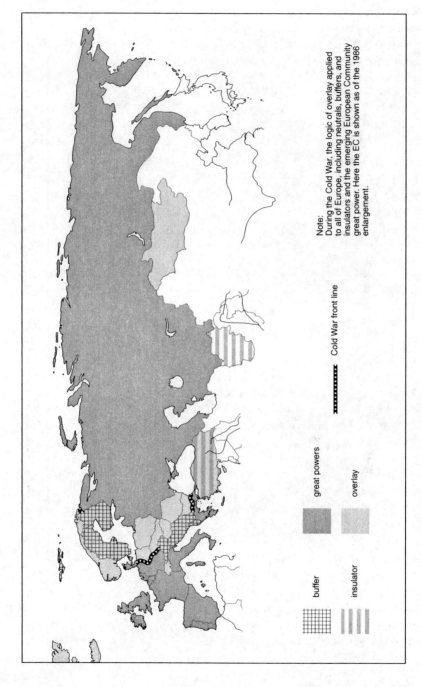

great powers

Cold War front line

overlay

buffer

insulator

Map 11. Cold War Europes: Bipolar Overlay

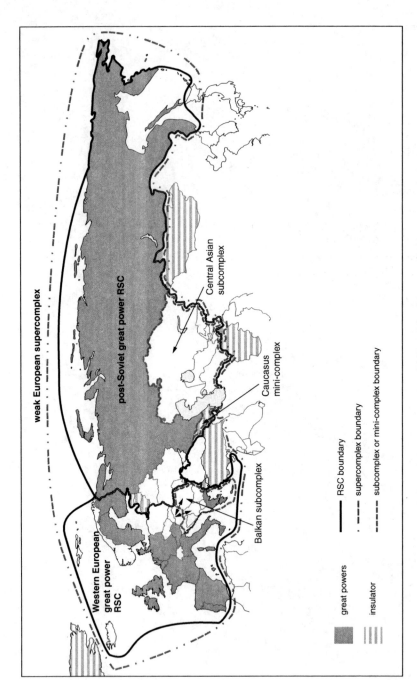

Map 12. European Great Power Centred Regional Complexes Post-Cold War

Legend (within figure):

weak European supercomplex

Western European great power RSC

post-Soviet great power RSC

Central Asian subcomplex

Caucasus mini-complex

Balkan subcomplex

RSC boundary

supercomplex boundary

subcomplex or mini-complex boundary

great powers

insulator

abrupt turnaround, a shrunken Europe after 1945 became overlaid by global powers and had its own internal dynamics suppressed.

The end of overlay raised the question of what kind of Europe would re-emerge. Overlay has the potential for transforming a region so that what reappears has very little resemblance to what was overlaid. This happened in much of the world colonised by Europe. However, Europe reappeared with much the same powers and in the same basic form – states – although with the USA deeply involved, with the state format supplemented by the EU, and with structural change in the form of completely changed patterns of amity and enmity (but with the old ones never totally forgotten). The big question after 1989 was what structure of RSCs would emerge from the lifting of overlay in Western and Central Europe and the retreat of a diminished Russia from global superpower status. The interesting context for this was that the RSCs in Europe now operated alongside many others, no longer in any sense either acting as the core of the global system, or so isolated as to be a world of its own.

11 EU-Europe: the European Union and its 'near abroad'

EU-Europe is the most institutionalised part of the world. Although the exact nature of the EU is hotly debated, its experiment in post-sovereign politics undoubtedly pushes peaceful, regional integration to new limits. Europe is developing unique forms of political organisation neither by replicating the state form at a higher level, nor by annulling the old order, but by mixing a continuity of sovereignty with new forms (Rosenau 1990; Ruggie 1993; Wæver 1995a). Consequently the European *security* landscape is becoming distinctive. The traditional near-monopoly of the state on security status and security action is challenged in Europe, where numerous other referent objects from mini-region to the EU itself, from environment to 'universal' political values, are acted upon in a security mode. Securitisation theory enables one to see this picture different from the one of only states (while allowing also for *that* possibility).

During the Cold War, the area that would become EU-Europe was overlaid and the dominant security concerns in the region were defined externally. Security politics during the Cold War mostly consisted of struggles over how intensely to securitise superpower rivalry versus desecuritise it through détente or deterrence. Post-Cold War EU-Europe was 'set free' – despite continued US involvement in one of the leading organisations, NATO – and the security agenda at first fragmented into numerous loosely connected concerns raising serious questions about both the spatial interconnectedness of 'Europe' and the thematic coherence of 'security'. A decade into the post-Cold War era, security concerns are still diverse but they have become sufficiently coherent that a new picture has emerged.

Among the EU members a security community has formed based on the integration project. This project is built on a meta-securitisation: a fear of Europe's future becoming like Europe's past if fragmentation and power balancing are allowed to return. The integration project itself, however, generates securitisation, which is largely 'societal security', i.e., fear for (national) identity. Traditional interstate security concerns exist only beneath the surface. Their effects are most often in the form of the generalised fear of 'back to the future', rather than the concrete fear of a specific Other.

EU-Europe has a centre–periphery structure: 'Central' Europe organises itself as concentric circles around the western core. Because these countries are included in the EU-centred order, security issues in this part of the continent partly follow the same pattern as in Western Europe but have additional complications, e.g., because the dependence on Western Europe is both anchor of stability and line of intrusion. 'Central' refers to the Cold War's 'Eastern Europe'. The security agenda is today very different in those countries that were market democracies during the Cold War (and that had formed nation-states early on) and those now engaged in 'transition' economically and politically (that were until the twentieth century mostly contained within the Austro-Hungarian, Russian, and Ottoman Empires).

European security during the Cold War

During the Cold War, by definition the main threat was seen to be the East–West conflict. The most thorough securitisation on either side was the other side as threat. Western oppositional forces securitised the nuclear confrontation itself either because it could run out of control and lead to nuclear war, or because the East–West conflict dominated Europe and repressed other possible identities (Thompson 1982). The division was felt most intensely in divided Germany and the 'East' European countries which felt misplaced in the Soviet sphere and had the communist system imposed on them. Overlay was complete with alliances, stationing of foreign troops, and a suppression of older intra-European conflicts.

The intensity of the Cold War in Europe welded together military and political fears with elements of economic and societal security. It is fair to say that all levels became organised by the Cold War so that it was reproduced by practices from the domestic through the regional to the global level.

There is not space here to recount the familiar history of the Cold War, though it is worth noting on the Western side that international cooperation took a unique form as the North Atlantic alliance developed into an *organisation* (NATO) uncharacteristic for alliances. Much Cold War politics became a question of deviation from the official line on either side: were 'dissidents' really agents of the other side? Or was there a third way, which eventually could lead Europe out of the tight grip of the Cold War? Examples of this were the debate in the 1970s on Euro-communism in especially Spain, Italy, and France (Tökés 1979), on some of the peace movement and social democratic proposals of the 1980s (Kodama and Vesa 1990; Schlaga 1991), and not least the attempts in Eastern Europe to create 'reform communist' and often 'national' ways (Il Manifesto 1979; Davies 1997: 1099–1109). The latter tried increasingly to be both within a socioeconomic commitment to socialism and securitywise compatible with Soviet interests. Nevertheless, the Soviet Union each time eventually chose to securitise and crack down on them. Partly for this reason, some of the reform attempts ended in uprisings against the Soviet Union, triggering military repression: 1956 in Hungary, 1968 in Czechoslovakia, and 1980 in Poland.

These failed reforms showed the stability of the East–West structure and the impossibility of any quick, 'smart' outmanoeuvring of the other side. Hassner (1976) has argued convincingly that especially Prague/Paris 1968 led to a change in the nature of détente: the period of 1961–8 was one of 'selective détente' where one tried to lure allies out of the grip of the other side and use détente for immediate gains in the East–West conflict. The events of 1968 created the definite shift towards 'status quo détente', i.e., one that accepted the basic East–West pattern of alignments and socioeconomic orders. Still, détente on both sides involved calculations of long-term relative gains too (see Jahn 1981, 1982; Galtung 1984). The détente that started in Europe in the late 1960s and culminated in the early to mid-1970s (with Germany's Eastern Agreements and the CSCE) aimed at improving life during the Cold War, softening the effects of division without trying to overcome it right away.

Much of the specificity of European security during the second half of the Cold War followed from different détentes. Superpower détente was mostly about arms control and without much broader vision. In Europe, in contrast, détente was combined with competing political visions – primarily for change on the other side, but often with implications for domestic development on one's own side (see Hassner 1968a, 1968b; Jahn 1981, 1982). In West Germany, questions about détente and the German question about how to overcome division became almost two sides of the same coin. A pattern of mutual suspicion followed: Europeans worried about superpower relations both when they were too bad (risk of confrontation) and too good (condominium), and the superpowers worried that European détente might become a pretext for nationalism. The United States supported the development of the EU as part of its own forward defence against the Soviet Union, but also worried that the EU might become a challenger to US dominance of NATO.

During the Cold War, Western Europe went through periods of insecurity (i.e., threat and a sense of insufficient defence) in the 1940s and 1950s, security (i.e., a threat but also a reliable defence) in the 1960s, and desecuritisation in the 1970s to reach a situation in the 1980s and especially 1990s of resecuritisation (Wæver 1998a).

Desecuritisation was a result both of the success of the neofunctionalist strategy of solving security problems by focusing on something else and of the paradoxical stability of the nuclear 'balance of terror'. Security arguments underpinned both the integration project and the military mobilisation of the Cold War, but it all became stabilised as a kind of normality. Integration was not on the surface about security, and deterrence was, outside the circle of worried specialists and protesters, perceived as an order, which 'solved' the security problem. Thus a paradoxical desecuritisation happened in the middle of the Cold War. Debates on a new and wider concept of security began to emerge in the 1970s, partly exploiting the 'opening' created by lessened urgency of the old security issues. From the early 1980s, securitisation started to return to mainstream politics: through the so-called second Cold War (new nuclear missiles, peace movements, and Ronald Reagan) and through Europe's position in the global economic order. The military threat led to probings into unified European action in the area of foreign and security policy. The threat of Europe decisively and irreparably falling behind Japan and the USA in a way which would threaten both the living standards of Europeans and the standing of 'Europe' drove the internal market and the whole mobilisation around '1992' (Zysman and Sandholtz 1989). The process was not linear and the end of the Cold War gave a sense of threats disappearing and led to some very high hopes for a desecuritised future. However, a sense of uncertainty accompanied this change and resecuritisation continued.

In addition to the marks left by division, the Cold War gifts to EU-Europe were desecuritisation and reconciliation internally in Western

Europe, dense institutionalisation including far-reaching multilateralisation of the military sector (NATO), and a consolidation of the EU to the point at which it became a great power, from somewhere in the 1970s.

Securitisations in post-Wall Europe: the EU core

What kinds of security problems do actors in the EU part of Europe articulate? After 1989, several new elements were added to the security discourse in Europe: environment, immigrants, ethnic conflict, organised crime, and terrorism. The list in Europe achieved maximum breadth covering all sectors and almost all levels. The issues were mostly not new, but with the end of the Cold War they became articulated as *security* problems. At first, increased diversity was easy to see, though a new pattern was not. The atmosphere was one of 'insecurity' again, contrasting strongly with the asecurity of the 1970s but also with the security of the 1960s. Of the ten securitisations listed below, the first two increasingly came to organise the whole field.

1. The strongest security discourse in post-Wall Europe has been the argument that Europe has to avoid a return to its own notorious past of wars and power balancing, and therefore integration is a necessity. This argument qualifies as a security argument because it posits an existential threat and a possible point of no return: 'Europe' is the referent object, and will be lost in a fragmentation scenario. If developments turn on to the track of power balancing and internal great power rivalry (Mearsheimer 1990), they will be self-reinforcing and thereby at a certain point too late to change. It is therefore necessary to act in time if peace and 'Europe' are to be saved (Wæver 1995a, 1996a, 1998a; Buzan et al. 1998: 179ff., 188–9). Integration is thereby invested with a security quality, which is typically mobilised (not least in Germany but also to some extent in France) whenever a change of overall foreign and Europe policy is considered. In this discourse, Europe's Other is neither Russia nor Islamic fundamentalism: Europe's Other is Europe's past. The term 'European security' more and more often refers exactly to this argument, and underpins the security of individual states (see box, pp. 361–4).

2. The other main security argument is the reverse of the first. European integration itself is presented as a threat, primarily to national identity. Various – mostly nonstate – actors have mobilised a resistance against EU integration based on the security claim that integration threatens national identity. Often, this converges with 'nationalist' or 'xenophobic' reactions against 'foreigners' (immigrants and refugees),

but also in some cases against globalisation/Americanisation (especially in France). The two scenarios produce an overarching conflict not so much between *different* particularisms as between the universalism of internationalising elites on the one hand and particularism in general, i.e., the reaction of 'mass politics' on behalf of different cultures against cosmopolitanism (Hassner 1993; Reich 1991).

The security argument about Europe's past has experienced and will experience various developments that respectively strengthen and challenge it. First, the wars in the Balkans have generally served to strengthen this discourse. They reintroduce the idea that war in Europe is possible, and 'one of the main clichés about the Balkans [is] that they are the part of Europe which is haunted by the notorious "ghosts of the past", forgetting nothing and learning nothing, still fighting centuries-old battles, while the rest of Europe is engaged in a rapid process of globalization' (Žižek 2000: 3). The Balkans has served as Europe's ghost, reminding it of the risks of war, and defining Europe's own identity in terms of no longer being susceptible to internecine war. Second, Eastern enlargement has more ambiguous effects. On the one hand, the growing of the EU is likely to mean that the Franco-German tandem, which has been the main home of this discourse, becomes less dominant simply because it becomes a smaller fraction of the whole. On the other hand, the project of enlargement reinforces the historic sense of the EU project, of what it has done to Western Europe and now is to do in Eastern Europe. How these two will balance out is hard to predict.

The total European security landscape is extremely complicated, exhibiting almost all imaginable forms of insecurity except the classical military one. In addition to these two dominant and reciprocally opposed ones, we can list others more briefly, though most of these increasingly tie back into the two basic ones. Economic security is mostly articulated at the regional and global level – for Europe or in relation to the principles of the liberal international economic order. Because European states have accepted far-reaching integration, they have to accept desecuritisation of specific vulnerabilities. Political security is surprisingly little articulated in relation to the sovereignty of the states especially in the continental EU countries (see Wæver 1995a), but the EU is highly securitised. In several countries, issues of regionalism and minorities constitute political security problems, for both state and region/minority, but none of these threaten to have regionwide implications. Much of the state security has been displaced to the societal sector and is articulated in terms of identity, i.e., threats to national identity. In some countries the opposition to EU integration is articulated primarily with reference to national identity (societal security), in others to state sovereignty (political security). Notable is that state security is articulated almost only in the context of the EU issue (pro and con) and other *vertical* conflicts (regionalism, state vs minority), and not *the* classical security issue: horizontal threats to one state by another.

3. Some local conflicts are intense without tying much into the European whole: Northern Ireland, the Basque region in Spain, Corsica, and (more peacefully) South Tyrol. Although not enacted as state-to-state conflicts, these are quite traditional conflicts in being territorial and in some sense state-centred ('we want to be one', or 'we belong to the wrong state'). Cyprus (and thereby the general Greek–Turkish conflict) also has a domestic conflict at the core, but here the antagonistic involvement of the states is much more direct and unrestrained (see pp. 368–9). With the exception of Greece-Turkey-Cyprus, these local conflicts do not threaten to have repercussions beyond the local setting. A European dimension to these conflicts emerged in the 1980s when it was widely expected among the leaders of some of the regionalist movements (Scotland, South Tyrol, Catalonia) that European integration would solve the conflict with the central state. Sovereignty would soon become an irrelevant goal as the old states lost it too. However, the 1990s disconfirmed this view.

Although major security issues locally, it is striking that these conflicts are rarely even mentioned in general rankings of security issues in Western Europe. In contrast, more often Western Europe is seen as threatened by the following.

4. 'Ethnic conflict' in Eastern Europe was one of the most talked about security issues in Western Europe in the early 1990s (sometimes referred to as 'regional stability'). Increasingly, it merged with securitisation-1. Ethnic conflict is bad enough in itself, but it is primarily a *security* threat to Western Europe if an ethnic conflict drags those powers in on opposing sides and thus triggers the return to power politics among the EU core states. (Sometimes, the threat of refugees functions similarly as accelerator of the threat, making it directly relevant to the member states in a way in which the conflict itself is not.) Thus, the reflections on conflicts e.g. in the Balkans are overpowered by the calculation of effects on EU integration/fragmentation dynamics.

5. Instability in Russia and the Mediterranean has a different status from that in Eastern Europe, because Eastern Europe is supposed to become part of the EU very soon and thus threats are both more

problematic (if they block enlargement and send the EU into crisis) and less likely (because those countries are not perceived as being radically different from Western Europe) (Hansen 1995; Larsen 2000: 225). Russia and the Mediterranean are usually not presented as military threats or radical Others either, but they are more unreliable than Eastern Europe (see p. 369).

6. Globalisation and immigrants, securitised as threats to national identity, increasingly merge with securitisation-2; and integration becomes the scapegoat for all effects of globalisation, but 'the foreigners' themselves are also defined as the root problem and real threat by political actors in many countries.

Increasingly, globalisation appears in a second function in European politics. Whether this has reached the point of securitisation is more doubtful, but flirtations have certainly appeared: the argument is that the European welfare state model, more than many other societies, is threatened by globalisation. This becomes a threat to identity – national and European – as well as welfare and independence. In this version, the argument is used strongly pro-EU integration to argue the necessity of paying a price to defend themselves against globalisation. What appears to the ordinary citizen as sovereignty losses due to the EU are rephrased in this discourse as countergains of sovereignty via the EU against the onslaught from globalisation. Since welfare issues are generally hard to securitise because they are gradualistic and therefore lack a clear breaking point ('existential threat') (Buzan et al. 1998: 95–117), this argument holds most potential as a security discourse when related to identity and independence. On the countermeasure side, it is used to justify integration one otherwise would not tolerate.

7. Terrorism, international organised crime, drug trafficking, and illegal migration are often presented as security problems especially in sources specifically related to EU policy making (Larsen 2000: 226; Politi 1998: 122–5). Notably, these questions have become a standard package which implies that immigrants are at the root of these problems and that the solution is to tighten the regime of 'policing in depth' and other mechanisms that allegedly compensate for the removal of internal borders in the EU (Bigo 1996). Thus, securitisation-7 partly channels back into the package with ethno-national fear of foreigners, and partly it supports practices of 'internal security'. (More on terrorism in securitisation-9. Prior to 11 September 2001, terrorism was mostly placed as part of this package. Whether it stays here or moves towards item 9 is not yet clear.)

8. Environmental security is high on the agenda in many places, partly because the high density and small size of units in Europe make many environmental issues border-crossing: e.g., the Danube dam, nuclear power plants in the former east, air pollution mostly blowing eastwards, and upstream pollution (such as that of Swiss medical giants) threatening downstream areas along the Rhine. This issue does not so far tie much into the two master discourses, although the EU has made some attempts to merge integration and environmentalism (Jachtenfuchs and Huber 1993; Jachtenfuchs 1994; Buzan et al. 1998: 186–7).

The continued multiplication of security concerns with diverse referent objects and in all sectors testifies to the post-sovereign trends in Europe. The state has lost its (always partial or fragile) monopoly on being the securitising actor and being the referent object. Whereas one could imagine that these complicated tendencies would tend to erode the spatial solidity of the European RSC, the cross-sectoral linkages between different kinds of security and the interlocking chains of security concerns, as well as concerns over principles linking different conflicts, have so far been sufficient to tie together the different securitisations into a network that is ultimately a European RSC. This is reinforced by the fact that the two dominant and generalised discourses are explicitly European.

9. Global terrorism, regional conflicts, extra-European environment, and infectious diseases are security issues originating further away from Europe. When approaching regional conflicts in all other regions, including even the Gulf, and 'new' global threats such as the environment and AIDS, it is striking that Europeans are inclined to define these in two characteristic modes that are distinct from the American approach (Wæver 2001b). One is a developmentalist discourse in which all conflicts from intra-state to major regional wars are ultimately caused by problems of resources and lack of development. Thus, while Europe participates in American-led efforts such as the Gulf War, the characteristic profile of its own efforts is not military but constitutes attempts at redefinition. The other characteristic European angle is to export its own regionalism, i.e., emphasise (against American attempts to see all conflicts in a global perspective) the necessity of allowing indigenous dynamics to evolve in the particular region.

Even in the reaction to the terrorist attacks on the USA in September 2001, the debate in Europe showed clear signs of the inclination towards developmentalism. The argument was heard in the USA too, but in Europe public debate has to a much larger extent established almost as common sense that terrorism is attributable to socioeconomic causes, and official statements hint in this direction.

Other global threats such as AIDS are also largely defined as problems of development.

10. Traditional state-to-state securitisations play a surprisingly marginal role on the European security agenda. The most important presence is in the form of a worry about Germany, which is then politely rephrased as securitisation-1 (worry about Europe's past tendencies).

Security in Western Europe is a uniquely complicated constellation (probably rivalled only by sub-Saharan Africa), but it does have a core dynamic and a discernible pattern.

The meaning of history, national identity, and European security

The main security discourse at the European level has been the argument that Europe's past should not be allowed to become Europe's future (Buzan et al. 1998: 179–89). Integration therefore takes on a security quality and has to be defended at almost any cost. During the years 2000 and 2001, European statesmen delivered a series of 'big' speeches on the future of the EU, which we will use as a source for investigating whether the basic narrative remains the one about the negative European identity defined by wars and balance of power which is dialectically turned into an obligation to integrate.

In the major German speeches, this argument is clearly present. Foreign Minister Fischer opens with it: 'Fifty years ago almost to the day, Robert Schuman presented his vision of a "European Federation" for the preservation of peace. This heralded a completely new era in the history of Europe. European integration was the response to centuries of a precarious balance of powers on this continent, which again and again resulted in terrible hegemonic wars culminating in the two World Wars between 1914 and 1945. The core of the concept of Europe after 1945 was and still is a rejection of the European balance-of-power principle and the hegemonic ambitions of individual states that had emerged following the Peace of Westphalia in 1648, a rejection which took the form of closer meshing of vital interests and the transfer of nation-state sovereign rights to supranational European institutions' (Fischer 2000). He returns to it again and again: 'A step backwards, even just standstill or contentment with what has been achieved, would demand a fatal price of all EU member states and of all those who want to become members; it would demand a fatal price above all of our people. This is particularly true for Germany and the Germans.' Enlargement follows from this, because if Eastern Europe is left forever in the old 'system of balance', this will spill back on Western Europe. Chancellor Schröder uses the argument, but less consistently. It comes as no surprise that the construction is most stable and operative in its classical form in Germany. As argued by Martin Marcussen et al. (1999: 622ff.), German national identity is based on the same argument. Modern Germany and European integration are part of the same grand historical trajectory that points away from Europe's past.

France has witnessed some recent change in argumentation, which might indicate a weakening of this rhetorical structure. But the new argument draws on the old figure. Today, the core of European identity and security for French leaders is the formation of a unit capable of acting. The lesson of Bosnia and especially Kosovo is that it is time for Europe (and France) to show its identity by proving that it cares for the destiny of humanity. Military action is *so* necessary that it must be undertaken even if this demands moving closer to the Americans. Now that war *is* here, the anti-war policy has to be heroic civilisational war practice (e.g. Chirac 1999; *Le Monde* 11 March 1999). Ulla Holm (2000: 179) argues that this is a shift in the construction of history and identity for two reasons: civilisation as the core of European identity essentialises certain positive values as the 'soul' of Europe. This challenges the representation of a negative past. Second, the past that has to be fought is no longer the internal European one of Franco-German conflict, but the outward one of Munich-like cowardice (Chirac 2000; *Le Monde* 11 March 1999).

In the big speeches of 2000–1, the French president and prime minister made the obligatory references to the Franco-German relationship – 'Germany, our neighbour, our adversary yesterday, our companion today' (Chirac 2000), but although the general history argument did not carry the speeches the way it did for especially Fischer, this particular Franco-German dimension has become if anything *more central* with the alleged crisis of the relationship. When searching for the argument about 'the meaning' of Europe, the openings and endings of speeches are usually most revealing. Chirac ends like this: 'What France and Germany have experienced and undergone in history is unlike anything else. Better than any other nation, they grasp the deep meaning of peace and of the European enterprise. They alone, by forcing the pace of things, could give the signal for a great coming together in Europe... Long live Germany! Long live France! And long live the European Union' (Chirac 2000). The Franco-German couple remains privileged because it is their experience, their past, that defines the story, but the future is not about them, it is about strengthening the capacity of the EU to act internationally. The war/peace = past/future formula is thus still the foundation, only it is not necessary to play with the – somewhat unconvincing – image of Western Europe at war because the French shift the battleground to the outside.

In Britain, the 'classical' version of 'integration is necessary for us to avoid our past of wars' is not found for several obvious reasons (there were fewer wars on British territory in recent centuries, and super-integrationism is not in high standing). However, both Prime Minister Blair and then-foreign secretary Cook used a closely related dichotomy. During the Kosovo war, Cook (1999) wrote: 'There are now two Europes competing for the soul of our continent. One still follows the race ideology that blighted our continent under the fascists. The other emerged fifty years ago out from behind the shadow of the Second World War. The conflict between the international community and Yugoslavia is the struggle between these two Europes. Which side prevails will determine what sort of continent we live in. That is why we must win.' But it should be noticed that the nature of the Western/good side of the equation is tied clearly to European integration, not to NATO or just our societies in general: 'The other Europe is the Modern Europe. It was founded fifty years ago, in the rubble that was left after the Second World War. We surveyed what was left of our continent. We saw the extermination camps, the piled bodies of the victims and the pathetic masses of survivors. And we made a promise. We vowed Never Again. It was on that pledge that we built the Modern Europe.' Blair in a November 2000 Zagreb speech refers to the EU in the context of a similar dichotomy: 'The 15 member states of the EU – countries that in the lifetime of my father were at war with one another – are now working in union, with 50 years of peace and prosperity behind us. And now, holding out the prospect of bringing the same peace and prosperity to the Eastern and Central European nations and even to the Balkan countries' (Blair 2000b). In his more famous October 2000 Warsaw speech (the 'superpower, but not a superstate' speech), Blair's main message is for Europe to become a power on the world scene (Blair 2000a).

The straightforward version is in place only in Germany, but France and surprisingly also the UK still construct their argument about the current phase of European politics by securitising the past.

Securitisation in the eastern circles

The overall pattern of European post-Wall politics is of a centre–periphery nature. Almost all non-members aspire to membership of the EU, and with a few more exceptions in NATO too. Western ways are widely seen as *the* winning model, and the former 'Eastern' countries want to 'return to Europe' (or in the case of Russia even phrased for a while in terms of a return to 'civilisation'; Williams and Neumann 2001). This attempt to join reinforces a dominance that would be strong anyway due to the sheer size of the EU bloc compared to any individual non-member. The standards of the EU tend also to be the standards for non-EU Europe whether one speaks of technical, industrial standards or human rights. This dependence has become a central security mechanism because it makes East Central European countries abstain from securitising questions of minorities and state borders, and reinforces their adherence to democracy, the market economy, and rule of law (Keohane 1990; Wæver 1993a, 2000a). From the side of the EU it is partly an implicit, unintended mechanism, and partly explicit and formalised in stability pacts in which minority and border problems around Hungary and in the Baltic states had to be solved in order for the relevant states to be accepted as applicants. From the applicant side it is in the first phase a question of rational strategy – of for instance Hungary downplaying minority issues in order to become a member (in some versions even becoming a member in order to be stronger when finally raising the minority issue in relation to non-members Slovakia and Romania). But when playing the EU game of focusing on welfare, the old Monnet strategy works, identities change, and the old issues suddenly are non-issues. However, since the mechanism starts as rational policy, it works only for those who see themselves as realistic future members, and therefore it works most strongly for the geographically nearest. In an ideal scenario, the mechanism rolls eastwards – as the first countries join, the second echelon becomes first, the third becomes second, etc. A pattern of concentric circles has formed by countries being more or less close to membership and thereby more or less likely to change behaviour to obtain EU recognition.

To non-members the relationship with the EU (and to some extent NATO) is both a solution to security concerns and a source of insecurity in itself. The West is their anchor of stability – the source of 'security guarantees' as well as prosperity. However, the relationship is also a source of security concerns, especially with far-reaching intrusions of Western organisations into domestic decision-making in the applicant countries. This is particularly problematic in countries that combine economic and political reform with a national revival. The countries which became independent with the end of the Cold War, but also to some extent the former Warsaw Pact allies, have had a dual agenda of 'returning to Europe' and of returning to themselves, i.e., rediscovering their allegedly repressed nationality. The two seemed perfectly compatible in the immediate liberation perspective: both Europe and the nation were opposites of Soviet oppression. But as adaptation to the new realities becomes concrete, the two conflict more often. Europeanisation implies opening and internationalisation, which is often resisted by nationalist politicians. (This tension has been particularly thoroughly explored in the case of Lithuania: Jurgaitiené 1993; Jurgaitiené and Wæver 1996; Miniotaite 2000; Pavlovaite 2000.)

The eastern half of the RSC articulates most of the same security issues as do EU members (pp. 356–61), but some are either added or accentuated (and one downplayed). Classical interstate fears are relevant in the Baltic states, sometimes between Hungary and its neighbours, in the Balkans (see ch. 12), and between Greece and Turkey. Societal security problems and political security link up in the classical way because in many cases (the above plus e.g. Polish and Czech relations to Germany) it is a matter of debate within 'host' countries to what extent the striving for 'regionalism' among minorities should be seen as an alternative or a prologue to secessionism. In Western Europe, it is generally assumed that no country will exploit its neighbour's minorities to expand its own territory. With the 1998 Anglo-Irish agreement, the last question mark of this type was probably removed and we see increasingly state-to-state cooperation against nonstate (UK and Spain over Gibraltar, France and Spain over the Basques, UK and Ireland in Northern Ireland). The dilemma for 'host states' in Western Europe is how devolved and Europeanised they are willing to become, not whether someone is plotting to move the border. In Eastern Europe, this worry about borders remains for Hungary vis-à-vis almost all of its neighbours, Poland and the Czech Republic towards Germany, in relation to nearly all minorities in the Balkans, and further east for all hosts to Russian minorities.

Economic, broadly 'social' and 'law and order' issues sometimes come close to constituting a security threat to 'society', not in the identity sense of our societal sector but to the coherence and functioning of society as social order.

One case of *less* intense securitisation than in the West is the environment. Only in a few, more local instances, such as the areas in Poland and the Czech Republic where air and soil pollution are most acute, do local actors dramatise the issue. Economics probably explain much of this non-securitisation, but the change is striking in countries where environmentalism was important to the struggle for independence. Environmental degradation was presented as a Soviet threat to national identity and survival whereby 'they' ruined 'our' national landscape or even the genes of the people. After independence, suddenly the same installation – mining in Estonia or the Ignalina power plant in Lithuania – is seen as 'ours,' 'we' need it economically, and 'we' defend it against criticism from mainly the West.

One of the primary security questions in Hungary and Romania regards the Roma population – the extreme Other who refuses to be territorial. Increasingly, traditional local racism mixes with concern about chain effects as the West starts to react to Roma migration and e.g. blacklist all people from Romania. This is likely to unfold differently from other ethnic conflicts in East Central Europe – potentially very vicious locally, but not likely to influence international dynamics significantly (Matras 2000; Braham and Braham 2000; Goldston 2002).

In some of the easternmost countries, Russia is presented as a threat. When it was played up in order to gain Western attention, as by the Baltic states, they learned that the West did not want trouble spots; therefore it was better to downplay the threat and become 'normal' (Joenniemi and Wæver 1997). The Russian threat seems unlikely to become directed towards anybody in the RSC in any reasonable future (see ch. 13). Due to historical experiences and the domestic usefulness of a Russian threat, it will probably continue to be invoked for a while, and, like all securitisation, it can have an effect even if the threat is implausible. However, given the decreasing power of Russia and its preoccupation with its own RSC and the global level, this is unlikely to become a driving issue in East Central Europe.

When enlargement eventually takes place, the category of East Central Europe (to the extent that this means 'to the east of the EU') will move eastwards as e.g. the Visegrad countries become members while Ukraine, Moldova, and perhaps Georgia become serious about seeking membership. However, this group will probably become gradually smaller as countries at the one end of the group join the EU and the new members joining 'East Central Europe' from the east become less and less realistic as members (culminating with the impossibility of Russia joining). Those who leave the group and join the EU will retain some of their differences and particular problems compared to other members, but in most respects they will increasingly become part of the same security agenda as Western Europe (Croft et al. 1999; Friis 1999).

A result of the interventions in the Balkans was heavy EU involvement which has activated the question of eventual membership even for these countries otherwise not in the enlargement limelight. A crucial question is whether the EU finds the right balance of avoiding both enlarging so fast as to dilute the EU and being so slow as to make applicants give up.

NATO enlargement got off the ground faster and under heavy American steering, and the first round of enlargement included Poland, Hungary, and the Czech Republic only (Goldgeier 1999). Russian opposition increasingly concentrated on avoiding membership for former Soviet republics but, with the improved atmosphere after September 2001 and the upgrading of Russia–NATO cooperation in early 2002, Russian opposition to the second eastern enlargement became relatively mild.

To sum up, East Central Europe has local security issues related to minorities and other historical and ethnic issues, but the overriding pattern is structured by EU integration. Still it is not identical to the dilemma in the western part of the continent. It is a dilemma of dilemmas: in Western Europe, EU integration generates two contradictory security issues, a fear of fragmentation and a fear of integration. As participants in the EU-based security order – formal members or not – the East Central Europeans join this dilemma. But they add another to it: due to their asymmetrical relationship to the EU, the latter is a source of both security and insecurity, a disciplining force that dampens local security problems but also an intruding and demanding *external* threat to national independence and sovereignty. However, this image is an important corrective to the image often given in the media and to some extent the security literature of Central Europe. Due not least to the Balkan events, Central Europe is often presented as an area of potential ethnic conflicts, nationalism, and intense security risks: this threat is then used to distance

EU-Europe from Central Europe, or more often to justify enlargement of the EU and NATO. In the worst cases, Central Europe is presented as one big Yugoslavia waiting to blow up. This is a misleading image since most of Central Europe – although equipped with minorities and contested borders – is on a completely different trajectory. The leading applicants are on a basically promising course towards stable democracies, market economies, and EU membership – three having already joined NATO. The classical security issues are fading from all but a few increasingly isolated states. Europe's traditional security problems are increasingly concentrated in the Balkans with the Baltic as a not yet fully assured second area. And the most classical problems of great power balance of power, alliances, and great power wars are to be found nowhere.

The outer circles of EU-Europe

Most of the attention regarding the EU-dominated parts of Europe goes to East Central Europe. However, the RSC of which the EU is the centre is larger than this. In the southeastern part of the continent, there are countries not usually discussed as 'Central Europe', but involved in the enlargement process nevertheless: Cyprus and Turkey. One member country, Greece, is involved in a conflictual relationship with Turkey – partly over Cyprus – which has many features uncharacteristic of the rest of the RSC and therefore deserves special attention. The other – often forgotten – periphery is the southern one, the Maghreb. Because they are less fully shaped by the processes of the EU core, these cases require more detailed examination.

Greece and Turkey have been in a general state of confrontation since the Second World War. The most serious issue has been the territorial division in the Aegean Sea with its implications for oil and gas resources, but they have generally defined each other as threats and securitised various other issues including the conditions for the Turkish minority in Greece (Karakasidou 1995). Increasingly, the conflict over Cyprus has moved to the centre of the relationship. After various low-level controversies including remonstrations over intimidation and atrocities, the postcolonial constitution guaranteed by Greece, Turkey, and Britain broke down in 1974. The military junta in Greece supported a political coup by the majority Greek-Cypriot leadership, and Turkey reacted by invading the northern, Turkish-minority, part of the island. An independent 'Turkish Republic of Northern Cyprus' has been recognised only by Turkey.

Populations were exchanged and the island de facto divided with UN troops keeping the two sides apart. The Greek-Cypriots claim to represent the whole island and refuse the Turk-Cypriot state any legitimacy, while the Turk-Cypriots claim equality of the two sides. This has made all negotiations difficult. Since Cyprus is officially high on the list of applicants to the EU, and since the EU refuses to import border and minority problems, finding a solution has become urgent. The EU has gambled that opening negotiations would function as some kind of catalyst. But how exactly this was to work given its entanglement with the difficult question of Turkish membership remained unclear (Diez 2002). The Cyprus question and the EU question (for Cyprus and for Turkey) have become more and more totally entangled. The overall Greek–Turkish relationship worsened in the 1990s due partly to the conflicts in the Balkans, but earthquakes in both countries in 1999 triggered mutual solidarity and assistance, and there is a desire on both sides to get out of a paralysed conflict that has trapped them for so long (*Economist* 18 September 1999: 39). This part of Europe is influenced very strongly by the relationship to the EU, but here the dynamics of a centralised complex interact with a classical interstate conflict not characteristic of the European RSC at large. (For more on Turkey, see pp. 391–5.)

The Maghreb is a large southern periphery to the EU. The internal dynamics of this subregion, and its relations with the EU, are covered in chapter 7. The relationship to Europe is historically as strong as the link to the Middle East, and the weakening of inter-Arabic cohesion during the 1990s, plus a new dynamism in Europe, caused the Maghreb to drift towards Europe. Based on security reasoning about threats of immigration and of regional instability on Europe's doorstep, the South European members of the EU have tried to raise the Maghreb on the agenda. But although the Euro-Mediterranean Partnership launched in 1995 entangles the two regions in many ways, including security issues, unlike in the other concentric circles, the EU cannot use the promise of eventual membership to influence politics in the Maghreb. Whether it becomes a part of the European RSC, an overlaid neighbouring mini-complex, or yet another independent African complex like West Africa and the Horn of Africa is too early to judge. With increased tensions in the Levant and the global politicisation of Islamic radicalism after the 11 September attacks on the USA, the Maghreb's time as a Middle Eastern subcomplex has been prolonged, but the long-term prospect is likely to be closer to Europe (ch. 7).

Regional institutions and traditional security

In Europe, military security concerns do not unfold in the 'normal' way by each state fearing the other. However, traditional security issues do not die easily. The military sector has not disappeared from European security, and organisations for security in the narrow sense continue to be an important part of high politics in Europe, though not in the traditional sense. NATO, for instance, is in principle primarily about the classical collective defence against an attacker. In practice it is mainly preoccupied by enlargement, peacekeeping, and humanitarian interventions out of area. NATO is central not because it is about military security but because it is at the core of important political struggles. The controversy over the future roles for OSCE, NATO, and the EU has become an issue area in itself.

The continuation – and in some ways strengthening and enlargement – of NATO after the Cold War does not square easily with traditional alliance theory (Waltz 1993b; Walt 1998; Hellmann and Wolf 1993), nor actually with neoliberal institutionalism (Duffield 2001; Hellmann and Wolf 1993; Wallander and Keohane 1995, Haftendorn et al. 1999; Wallander 2000), because European security is not a field lacking institutions and cooperation. Europe is rather hyper-institutionalised and the evolutions of the different organisations are therefore not determined by the attempt to 'improve cooperation' but by the competition and accommodation between states to have given issues handled within one organisation or another.

This battle is not driven by 'security' in any direct sense. France does not resist American attempts to promote NATO as the supreme organisation due to concerns about French security, and similarly for the countries that fight for OSCE or NATO. The game rather reflects general foreign policy interests defined by grand visions for the structuring of Europe. As we have argued previously (Buzan et al. 1998: 49–70), one of the novelties of the 'new security agenda' is that not only is there 'non-military security'; one can also find much in the *military sector that is not security*. Much of the defence policies and the interventions by NATO countries are not now driven by existential concern for one's own security, but occur as foreign policy with military means, whether as policies for positioning of one's own country, or in response to the securitisation of humanitarian issues and human rights principles. Most clearly, Balkan politics was much shaped especially in the early 1990s by divergent visions for the future role of the EU and NATO and thereby the degrees and forms of American influence in Europe.

These institutions matter – contrast East Asia which is comparatively underinstitutionalised. They alleviate the German problem, and make it possible to intervene in conflicts on Europe's periphery. PfP and other NATO programmes socialise the East Central European states into creating post-national military professions and democratic civil–military relations.

A complex constellation of institutions has been carried over from the Cold War, and there is no reason to expect any easy rationalisation into a more 'logical' harmonic relationship than the current coexistence and partial cooperation between NATO, the OSCE, and the EU. The adjustment between the EU and NATO especially will be central to the future institutional set-up in Europe. Only in the very first post-Cold War years could one talk about a direct rivalry, as when NATO and the WEU had to divide the waters outside Yugoslavia because both wanted to patrol them during the Bosnian war. In principle, there has been a broad agreement since 1991 saying on the one hand that there should be no European duplication of NATO and on the other that there should be a greater European role including an ability by Europeans to act without the USA, possibly borrowing NATO assets. Year after year, summit after summit, this agreement was upgraded by spelling out more and more precisely the two sides of the compromise. However, the actual attempt to give the EU a substantial defence side was suddenly accelerated in 1999 in the wake of the Kosovo war (see Missiroli 2000). It is yet to be seen whether this can be realised according to the established formula, or whether it triggers American second thoughts, and/or whether the Europeans ultimately prove incapable of implementing plans.

NATO too has been strengthened. In Kosovo and in the alliance's new 'strategic concept' (NATO 1999), NATO has granted itself the freedom to act without a UN mandate. Defining the 2001 terrorist attacks on the USA as an attack according to article 5 extended the responsibility of NATO to combating terrorism. On the other hand, the United States' limited interest in actually channelling anything substantial through NATO triggered renewed speculation about the future of the alliance. Already during 'NATO's' Kosovo operation, US inclination to actually use parallel, national lines of command around NATO created a certain unease in Europe including importantly Britain. Julian

Lindley-French (2002: 54) puts this as harshly as an 'impression that whilst the United States might be *with* NATO it is hardly any longer *of* NATO'.

The OSCE in contrast has been only moderately developed as the main institutional expression of the supercomplex covering EU-Europe and the post-Soviet space. Its relative weakness indicates no strengthening of this supercomplex.

The ambiguities of the EU–NATO relationship are a reflection of the convoluted situation of the European RSC – with an American presence which is both welcomed and according to structural alliance theory surprising in relation to the larger power picture, and an emerging EU-centred order in Europe which is likely in the long run to make the EU, not the USA, the main source of stability in Europe. The American presence and the continuation of NATO are welcomed because they have numerous stabilising effects in Europe but, in the long run, there is a difference between an external power and a power of the region. US involvement will always be a choice, not a necessity, and this has already several times shown in the tendency for American policy to fluctuate between extremes: trying to stay out, or the need to demonise opponents because it is harder to convince the American public than the European of the necessity for intervention. This has generated sufficient irritations in European security establishments that it is likely that European countries will continue to strengthen their alternative to re-liance on the USA. A major question for European security due to the central position of an external power is whether the transformation of this dependence will be gradual and harmonious or eventually take the form of a rupture.

EU-Europe's global standing – self-securing? interregionally active? global power?

The interregional and global levels are particularly complicated for EU-Europe. It is penetrated by other powers, most notably the United States, but also Russia e.g. via the Contact Group on Balkan issues. The close-ness of Russia is less influential than one might imagine, whereas the participation of the USA, which is well established through three world wars, is a major factor. The EU is a great power, but a peculiar one. With most RSCs, one can take stock of the global power distribution first and treat it as condition for the complex. In the European case, the key regional development itself is part of the answer regarding the global status. The most important structuring force in the European case is this very ambivalence itself. The process of forming a global power out of discrete nation-states is the source of securitisation – both on its behalf and against it. And the process of shifting security focus from the purely intra-regional to thinking more globally or at least interregionally is ongoing.

Further complications stem from the continued role of individual states as regional and in some respects potentially great powers. France and the UK are likely to remain permanent members of the UN Security Council, and to take 'permanent' seriously, being unlikely ever to give up their position or accept radical reform of the UNSC. Also the nuclear deterrent is not easy to Europeanise and the nuclear question therefore continues to be fudged. The German role as global economic power is likely to become comparatively more Europeanised because, with EMU, the position of the Deutschmark is taken over by the euro; in the G8 the EU is present alongside the individual states, and a gradual shift towards a European voice is easier than in the UNSC.

Given this complicated situation, the global and interregional level questions are really three: is the EU able to take care of its own security without dependence on external powers? What are the interregional security dynamics between EU-Europe and its neighbouring complexes? And to what extent and in what ways does the EU appear at the global level as a power of sorts?

1. The Balkan wars have seemingly shown that EU-Europe is still *a partly penetrated region*. The United States is still a key actor and certain types of action – tough diplomacy and military action – materialise only when it so decides. Even the UN is involved in peacekeeping and quasi-trustee administration within EU-Europe. This conflicts strongly with the expectations of most Europeans only a few years back. Before one accepts the image of EU-Europe as greatly dependent on outside power, two qualifications are needed. One is that the wider concept of security shows that the EU is actually highly successful both in dealing with other non-war kinds of security problems in most of its periphery and in pre-empting many possible violent conflicts by non-military means (Wæver 1996b, 2000a). One should not suddenly on this specific issue narrow security down to the military question. The other is that the strong American role still does not amount to anything close to overlay. NATO increasingly operates as a dual-veto organisation – efficient when the USA and the (main) European powers agree, but easily blocked by either side.

2. *Interregionally*, EU-Europe interacts with the post-Soviet region and with the Middle East. The relation to the post-Soviet region – and Russia in particular – is important for three reasons. First, the Baltic states and potentially Ukraine (and Moldova) are boundary cases where the division between EU-Europe and the post-Soviet RSC is not final and uncontested. Second, the relationship to Russia is not very intense at the moment but is deemed important due to both positive and – especially – negative potentialities. Third, some nominally European organisations cover all (OSCE) or part (Council of Europe) of the CIS in addition to EU-Europe, and therefore some political processes are shared. None of this, however, amounts at present to intense security concerns either way. A crisis somewhere in the borderland between the two complexes could, however, strengthen this weak supercomplex.

The Europe–Middle East relationship has many dimensions including immigrant communities and continued immigration into Europe, and Middle Eastern concern about Western cultural hegemonism. But it has few classical strategic issues, of which the most important relate to the European stake in the Israeli–Palestinian conflict, and the situations of Turkey and the Maghreb (Wæver and Buzan 2000). More on this in chapter 12.

3. *At the global level*, defined by who or what are feared or drawn upon in alliances by other global level actors, the EU is clearly a great power, constituted as a part of the global power balance. One might even claim that a 'Global Troika' of the EU, Japan, and the USA manages global affairs in the post-Cold War system (Christensen 1999). But the global presence of Europe is inconsistent, stronger on issues like international trade, monetary matters, and the environment than on most high politics questions. An odd mix of the EU and some European powers act in the G8, and two member states are permanent members of the UNSC. The EU still does not take a general global attitude and act as a great power in relation to all issues. Some involvements are 'inherited' from single members (e.g. Spain and Portugal in Central and Latin America, France and Britain in Africa).

Conclusions

The full constellation of EU-Europe's security is as follows. At the domestic level in a narrow sense, there are few security problems. Most European states are relatively strong states, and domestic politics do not easily turn violent. However, given European post-sovereign trends, many security actors (such as ethnic minorities, environmental activists, and anti-EU groups) are located within the states and are thus 'domestic' in this respect. At the regional level, much action is concentrated, but again – due to post-sovereign forms – it is not mostly about state-to-state security but about unlike units. The primary example of this is the two interlocking security discourses about European integration threatening national identity, and renationalisation being a threat to 'Europe'. The interregional level is not very important, although an increasingly unified and capable EU must be expected to take more of an interest and shoulder more responsibility in dealing with the Maghreb, parts of the Middle East, and maybe the Caucasus and Central Asia if a constructive relationship with Turkey is finally established. The global level is important mostly because the pre-eminent global actor, the United States, is very active in European security and also because the motive of consolidating as a great power (potentially superpower) able to take care of one's own interest across sectors is a major motive behind European integration.

The levels scheme becomes awkward because the power structure is ambiguous in relation to the EU itself. It is a recent great power with even some superpower potential, but at the same time the 'old' powers remain regional powers in many contexts. The nature of the EU is hotly debated in both academia and politics, and the inclination is to avoid treating the EU as an emerging state. Thereby, despite much transformation in the nature of the states in the EU, the question of who the units are remains mostly uncontroversial. However, when asking the question of *powers* in a global context, things get difficult, because the EU is a great power, and thus one should in a sense adjust one's terminology about levels to this: domestic means then domestic vis-à-vis the EU, i.e., including much that is regional today. Such inescapable ambivalence certainly strengthens the case for treating the EU as postmodern.

Europe is a security community, which is rare in a global comparative perspective. The way Europe has become and remained a security community is even more intriguing. Whereas the classical security community theory (Deutsch) envisaged that states would become gradually more confident in each other and thus a regional state-based order would stabilise in a non-war mode, the actual development in Europe contains two surprises. One is that the states establish a peaceful order at the same time as they start to blur, merge, and fade, and numerous nonstate forms of securitisation enter. The other is that this security order does not take the form of a direct security system – like collective security – solving the security problems of the region. To a large extent the order is built on desecuritisation but it works only by mixing in a strong dose of resecuritisation in the form of a strong meta-narrative of the historical development of Europe, past, present, and future.

To this interpretation it will be objected that a Europe returning to its past is no longer a real possibility. It was in early EU history, but today it is only a myth invoked by elites to legitimise the project. Maybe – but this is very difficult to know for certain. Theories of democratic peace, interdependence, and trading states sometimes insist that war is irrevocably ruled out among the states of Western Europe irrespective of the degree of integration. But in the light of centuries of wars, any last doubt will be difficult to erase, and perhaps the fear itself might be the major force preventing war. The constitutive uncertainty about the possibility or not of a return to balance-of-power behaviour and possibly war is thus central to both European political reality and the present interpretation. This threat operates in a curious way as the replacement for the Cold War reasoning around nuclear deterrence whereby a breakdown of deterrence, and actual usage of the weapons, should be highly unlikely but could not be allowed to become totally impossible if deterrence was to function (Tunander 1989). As long as war is possible, it does not happen. If it becomes impossible, it might happen.

12 The Balkans and Turkey

The Balkan states (hereafter the Balkans) get a separate chapter because of the possibility during the 1990s that they would form a separate RSC. The outcome was not decided by internal Balkan dynamics but largely by the different securitisations external powers made of the Balkan situation. The Balkan case also serves to explore the nature of both subcomplexes and insulators, particularly Turkey. Europe is the best setting in which to study Turkey because of its special status in Turkish foreign policy.

In terms of interaction capacity and patterns of securitisation, the local actors in especially ex-Yugoslavia today mainly connect to each other, but the power of the surrounding actors is so overwhelming that the Balkans can easily be absorbed as a subregion within EU-Europe. Following the basic principle of RSCT whereby a constellation is produced bottom-up, by connecting actor to actor to actor, the conclusion should be that the Balkans is an RSC. This conclusion would be wrong. Due to the asymmetry of power between the actors in and around the Balkans, it is in the hands of the external powers to 'force' the Balkans into the European complex. However, it was also possible for them to try to fence the Balkans off, and decouple and contain it in order to keep its traditional security problems outside Europe. There was even an ideological basis for this in the availability of discourses of Balkan(isation). In 1991–2, the Balkan region was both relatively *separate* – interactions were clearly more intense within than across the boundary of ex-Yugoslavia – and also *distinct* in the sense that the kind of security dynamics here took a markedly different form (dehumanisation, war, ethnic cleansing) than in the rest of Europe. However, the outcome seems now almost certain: the Balkans will not be left to its own devices. The West has taken over the development. The commitments symbolised first by major military efforts and then by two de facto protectorates guarantee long-term economic and political efforts. Even promises of possible EU membership emerged in the context of a 'stability pact'. The wars came to underline the coherence of Europe: interventions were partly conducted in the name of Europe and European values, and afterwards the Balkans was reintegrated into the plans for EU and NATO enlargement.

It might be considered whether the Balkans should be defined as a subcomplex within the European RSC or as a case of overlay. The interpretation in terms of overlay would stress that the area's (then not a subregion, but a region external to Europe) internal dynamics are repressed by external powers – the Balkans is forced into peace against its will. If overlay was removed, the subregion would return to war. That is undoubtedly true at the moment. On the other hand, the Balkans seems to be on a track that will eventually transform it into an integral part of Europe – not a part without problems but with the more 'normal' East Central European problems. The medium-term position of the Balkans is therefore as a subcomplex, not overlaid. Long-term it might merge into Europe without 'sub'.

The concept of subcomplex becomes central in this chapter. It has neither been clearly defined previously in the literature on RSCT, nor been made the centre of any analysis. However, the concept is relatively straightforward (see pp. 51–2). The definition of an RSC is that security interdependence is relatively more intense inside it than across its boundaries. A subcomplex also has this feature of a relatively clear boundary, inside which most security interaction is inward-oriented, but, in contrast to a 'real' RSC, it forms part of a larger complex outside which it cannot be understood. In the Middle East, it is not possible to tell an undifferentiated story at the level of 'the Middle East', but the subcomplexes cannot be understood independently. The Balkan case is different from the Middle East (and more like the Caucasus, Central Asia, and Central America) in that its relationship to the other parts of the complex is highly asymmetric. In the Middle East, two of the subcomplexes (Levant and Gulf) are together constitutive of the Middle Eastern RSC as such, while the third (Maghreb) has been attached to the first two. Cases like the Balkans and Central Asia are peripheral and subordinate to another group of actors that make up the core of the RSC.

Regarding terminology and delineation, the chapter will use Balkans and (more acceptable to most members) Southeastern Europe synonymously. At specific points in time, more narrow subregions form, but in order to see these we should look at a quite inclusive list of countries associated with the Balkans: Croatia, Bosnia-Herzegovina, Yugoslavia (under reconstruction in 2002 as 'Serbia and Montenegro'), Macedonia, Albania, Bulgaria, Romania, Greece. Turkey and Cyprus are not Balkan but Southeastern Europe (Todorova 1997; Stoianovich 1967). Slovenia and Hungary are occasionally included. Since the mid-1990s, international attention has often been directed at subgroups like 'the neighbouring states affected by the Kosovo crisis': Albania, FYROM, Bosnia-Herzegovina, Croatia, Slovenia, Bulgaria, Romania, and Hungary (Friis and Murphy 2000: 111, n. 3), and the core of attention became in EU parlance 'the Western Balkans': former Yugoslavia minus Slovenia plus Albania, i.e., the most troubled countries (ICG 2001a).

Chapter 11 outlined a general EU-focused centre–periphery dynamic. It applies in varying degrees to most of the countries in the region – to all of the non-Yugoslav states and occasionally even Slovenia or others with a Yugo-history. Greece is already a member of the EU and NATO, and Turkey and Hungary are members of NATO. Against this background, the Balkan subcomplex exists to the extent that it differs from this general European pattern.

A central task of the chapter is to explain how the area got to the brink of becoming a separate RSC and how it came to its current position vis-à-vis the European RSC. A brief first section gives the historical background, notably the imprint of empires. The second section looks at the post-Cold War disintegration of Yugoslavia. This is the key to the constellation at the end of the 1990s and ahead. The third section maps the internal constellation of security fears in the region towards the end of the 1990s. Then a section looks at the Western policy towards the region and especially the dynamics that decided about integration or isolation of the Balkans. The fifth section looks specifically at Turkey as an insulator state.

Emergence of the main Balkan units

For most of European history, the Balkans was not a coherent region but was on the contrary divided (as was latter-day Yugoslavia) by many of the most important divisions in European history, some of which influence politics in the region today: the boundary of the Greek cultural sphere; the border between the East and West Roman Empires; the fact that the heartland as well as the limits of the Byzantine Empire fell in this area; the boundary of the push of the Slavic tribes; the limits of the empire of Charlemagne; the boundary between the Catholic and Orthodox churches; and not least 'the border between the Turkic and Habsburg empires was for centuries moved back and forth here' (Wiberg 1994: 8, our translation). 'Western' and 'East and Central' Europe differ by the latter being under empires much longer and notably so when nation-states formed in the west. The southeastern development is 'Eastern' in a special way because its empire was the Ottoman. The modern Balkans was formed by the disintegration of the Austrian and Ottoman Empires. Much of the variation among the successor states stems from differences between these two empires and the time and nature of their disintegration.

The Ottoman legacy is complex and diverse (Brown 1996). Among the more concrete traces is the Islamisation of large parts of the Albanians and of the population of Bosnia-Herzegovina. A series of revolts (and brutal repressions) shaped Serbian self-conception. Like Serbia, units such as Moldavia and Wallachia (later united as Romania), Bulgaria, East Rumelia, and Greece gradually emerged as modern states out of varying degrees of autonomy within the Ottoman Empire, and thus they had their 'state-building' shaped by the political and administrative traditions of the empire (even if they strongly deny this as they were born in a fight *against* the empire). The first two Balkan wars (1912–13) (where first Serbs, Greeks, and Bulgarians defeated the Ottomans, and then Bulgaria warred against its two former allies) led to a number of border changes and the birth of Albania. Except for Macedonia, the current states of the southeastern part of the Balkans were thus in place by then. Macedonia is a uniquely complicated issue where all neighbours have a stake in defining it. The Greeks insist on 'Macedonia' being the name of a Greek province; the Bulgarians see Macedonia as 'West Bulgaria', Serbs see it as a part of the Yugoslav project, Albanians have an interest due to the large Albanian minority, and finally Turkey gets involved when Greece does.

The decline of the Ottoman Empire coincided with nineteenth-century European nationalism, and revolts were readily supported by ('humanitarian') interventions by the other European powers. The main territorial beneficiary was the Austro-Hungarian Empire, although it too experienced internal pressure due to rising national aspirations. Bosnia, which Austria-Hungary took step-by-step, proved difficult to digest and, on one PR tour in the province, Archduke Franz Ferdinand was assassinated with well-known consequences. In contrast to the gradual retreat of the Ottoman Empire, the Austro-Hungarian fell at one stroke due to the First World War. The relationship between Hungary and all of its neighbours but Austria was troubled both because of resentment from the period of Hungarian rule among the Slavs, and because the peace imposed on Hungary meant the loss of not only borderlands with minorities to Serbia (Vojvodina), Slovakia, and Ukraine, but more dramatically Transylvania becoming part of Romania. To Romanians this was the missing third component of the kingdom already formed out of Moldavia and Wallachia, and the majority of the population was Romanian. However, to Hungarians, a consolidated part of Hungary was lost, and historians of the two countries have since struggled (even during the communist period) to project their national ties to Transylvania as far back in history as possible. Half as many Hungarians live outside Hungary as inside it. The Hungarian development explains many of the present-day tensions.

For RSCT, the first decades of the twentieth century are of special interest because in this period the Balkans looks most like a separate RSC, equipped with its own 'Balkan' wars. The newborn states formed a system of interdependent balances of power as witnessed by the shifting coalitions of the wars. In this respect it is similar to the many RSCs 'born fighting', clearly a conflict formation. But its separateness was in doubt from the start: the wars both of independence and among the states 'were never free of European politics. Their irredentist wars against Ottoman rule and the resultant borders were closely supervised by foreign patrons and regulated by the principles that governed European relations' (Veremis 2000: 22). The Balkan wars were sufficiently complicated that the region gained increasing independence for those years until this was reined in again during the First World War when Balkan and European dynamics merged. The interwar years exhibited much the same semi-independence as the post-Cold War period. A local balance-of-power system was in operation, but in the interwar period this connected to wider European dynamics.

The creation in 1918 of the first Yugoslavia stemmed from decisions among the great powers, but it was also the outcome of a complicated constellation of pan-ideologies and nationalism (Mørk 1991; Wachtel 1998). While nationalist histories project today's units far back in history, it has been open at several points what 'level' was to become the primary polity: Dalmatia, Croatia, Yugoslavia, or the Austro-Hungarian

Empire? The South Slav state paralleled pan-nationalisms elsewhere in Europe: pan-Germanism, pan-Scandinavianism, and the wider pan-Slavism. Tensions within the state were let loose during the Second World War, when a semi-independent Croatia emerged under German and Italian protection. The fascist Ustasa movement ruthlessly pursued a project of Greater Croatia by slaughtering hundreds of thousands of Serbs, Jews, Roma, and political opponents. After communist victory under Tito, Yugoslavia was recreated with largely the same boundaries – and the same internal tensions.

The *essential structure* of the subcomplex was much the same before and after the Cold War, while that during the Cold War differed. The disintegration of Yugoslavia should have meant the end of a pole in the subcomplex. This, however, makes less of a difference than expected. The same dynamics are present as either domestic or international (depending on the existence of Yugoslavia or not), and Belgrade is a power centre with or without Yugoslavia. The *boundary* of the subcomplex has remained ambiguous: the region has two cores. First the conflict constellation of Serbs, Croats, and Bosnians; second, one around Macedonia involving Albania, Serbia/Yugoslavia, Bulgaria, and Greece plus (thereby) Turkey. Partly due to the negative status of Balkanhood, marginal members want out. The outer boundary is unstable, with countries like Romania, Hungary, and Turkey being more or less involved at different points in time. The subcomplex has always been clearly *anarchic* – and not centred – but the exact *polarity* and *amity/enmity* pattern are often difficult to pin down. The more stable elements are located at the local level, but the subcomplex is not integrated just in the chain-like form seen in Africa, because the states (and other political actors) are keenly aware of the implication for them of the other conflicts. Continuity is made up of recurrent patterns at the local level and shifting patterns interconnecting these at the level of the subcomplex.

The effects of Cold War overlay and especially the Soviet dominance of Bulgaria, Romania, and Hungary follow the lines set out in chapter 11 (pp. 353–4, 364–8). Yugoslavia was special during the Cold War by being socialist but independent of the Soviet Union. (Albania took its own peculiar course of aligning itself with the Soviet Union, then China, and finally North Korea.) Yugoslavia acted as a buffer between East and West, and therefore it was widely feared that a winding down of the East–West conflict might get Yugoslavia into trouble: its external raison d'être and its domestic structure were sufficiently connected that its coherence could not be guaranteed.

We do not have space to tell the detailed story of the break-up of Yugoslavia, which has been covered in detail elsewhere (Glenny 1992; Wiberg 1993a, 1993b, 1994; Posen 1993; Malcolm 1994; Bringa 1995; Silber and Little 1995; Eide 1999; Roe 1999). The key point here is the influence of outside powers on the break-up. The external factor is in play already when the dynamics seem to be totally internally driven. During the period without decisive external action (from the breakdown of the first EC attempts at mediation in 1991 to NATO bombing and Dayton in 1995), the initiative was with local actors while the external powers, mostly represented by the UN, tried only to soften the consequences, but this does not mean that the development was uninfluenced by external powers. The key factor here is *expectations* by actors in the region about how the great powers would react. Thus, the area did not operate as an isolated one. The issues might have been settled sooner (although slightly differently) had the region been fully sealed off. Then classical military-political logic would have led the actors to calculate their chances – probably more realistically – and strive for compromise when they had no hopes of improving their situation on the battleground. But, because each of the main actors had powerful friends abroad, they kept hoping for support, and that made them less inclined to settle for less. The Croats heard supporting voices from Germany very early on and believed this would guarantee them EU and possibly NATO support; the Serbs hoped for the Russians; and the Muslims often had the impression that the USA was close to deciding to come to their assistance, and they therefore did not compromise even at their weakest time (see Brenner 1992; Wiberg 1993a; Maull and Stahl 2002). The Vance–Owen plan of 1993 probably failed primarily because voices in the United States – in Congress, as much as from the administration – gave the Muslims a motive to ditch the agreement (Stoltenberg and Eide 1996: 53–76). Also the Serbs often were given false hopes by listening to oppositional Russians rather than the official ones. Thus, differences among external powers never escalated into the competitive interventions feared at some point, but did still complicate solutions by being anticipated in the region.

Similarly, the uprising by the Kosovo-Albanian guerrilla movement UCK was aimed at drawing in external involvement – a strategy vindicated by NATO's 1999 air campaign against Yugoslavia and Western pressure for a settlement both before and afterwards.

Security dynamics in Southeastern Europe after the dissolution of Yugoslavia

After the 'dissolution wars', the question is what security issues are the main ones in Southeastern Europe at the beginning of the twenty-first century.

At the domestic level, the starting point is the nature of the state. 'Almost all state institutions in the Balkans are fragile, a large number are corrupt and a great many are discredited' (ICG 2001a: 15). Political, legal, and economic institutions are far from the modern normality they aspire to. They do not perform their main functions well, and are 'dominated by the expectation that public office and state-dominated assets should – and will – be exploited as a source of power and patronage' (ICG 2001a: 16). This underpins a number of the transnational security problems such as organised crime and corruption which increasingly become the main obstacle to economic development when military conflict diminishes; it was also involved in the original wars because this state-form made it both attractive (not to say mandatory) to old elites to hold on to power and easier to manipulate political and identity developments through 'conflict entrepreneurship' (Eide 1999). The state-form has some parallels with the African situation in that the states are more an arena for, than the agent of, power politics. Elites fight unscrupulously to stay in power irrespective of the ideological transformations necessary. Statist explanations are therefore insufficient, but the state is at the centre of most struggles.

The various sectors contain sources of securitisation. As already indicated, the societal sector is crucial, with questions of national identity often becoming the organising centre of struggle and fear. At the surface, religion is often the dividing line (Croat/Serb, the three Bosnian groups, Kosova-Albanians/Kosovo-Serbs, Slavic Macedonians/Albanians), but usually it is not religion that is securitised as such, but religion serves as the most convenient identity marker and thus defines *national* or ethnic identity.

The region contains a number of questions located at the intersection of societal and political, i.e., ethno-territorial conflicts: whether Bosnia-Herzegovina stays as one state or splits into two or three; Montenegro's fate as independent or as a member of the remaining Yugoslavia; whether Kosovo will in the future be independent, a part of Serbia/Yugoslavia or eventually part of greater Albania; the place of Albanians in southern Serbia; the relationship between the large Albanian

minority and the Slavic majority in Macedonia that caused open violence in early 2001; Cyprus; Hungarian minorities in all neighbouring
states; the large 'Turkic' minority in Bulgaria; the Turks in northeastern
Greece; mutual minority concerns between Albanians and Greeks; and
the competing interpretations of 'Macedonian' nationality and statehood among Serbs, Bulgarians, Greeks, Albanians, and the existing
'FYROM' state. These questions of potential secession blend into generally unstable situations in Albania and possibly within Serbia itself.

Albania is primarily a source of instability because, together with
Germany, Hungary, Russia, and increasingly Serbia, it is a major case of
a country pushed to much smaller size than its 'ethnic' span. There are
large Albanian minorities in Serbia (Kosovo and elsewhere), in Macedonia (close to 40 per cent of the population), and some in Greece. Albania
has special relations with Turkey and Italy. This points to the second
main regional security implication of Albania: its weak state structures
and strong clans allow particular space for the operation of transnational
networks of organised crime.

At the domestic level, most of the societies are marked by high degrees
of economic desperation which has been securitised so far most clearly –
and this time to positive use – in Serbia/Yugoslavia, where the economic
implications of the Milosevic regime and its wars were the main driving
factor behind the autumn 2000 'revelection' (Ash 2001). Another case of
economic security is Bosnia-Herzegovina, where the conflict has moved
through a trajectory of political-military-economic, and where now the
battle/competition among the groups is mainly conducted in terms of
who gains most from the international, Western assistance (Eide 2001).
The environmental situation, too, is dire in Serbia following the NATO
bombings, but so far this has not led to marked securitisation.

Increasingly both the international community and local actors securitise mainly transnational phenomena like illegal trafficking in drugs,
people (prostitution – often in slavery-like form – and organisation of
illegal immigration to the West), weapons, and organised crime generally. These challenges are both supported by and in turn amplify the
above-listed conflicts, weak state structures, and numerous cracks and
conflicts within societies. An important question for the future is how
the overall constellation will be influenced if these developments increasingly become the main object of securitisation either in the region
or – as with the USA in Latin America – from the outside.

These subregional, inter-unit level conflicts have roots in domestic
societal-political vulnerabilities. In addition, interstate conflicts lurk

between more stable states: Greece–Turkey, Hungary–Romania (linked via Hungarian minorities to Slovakia and Serbia), the international side of the Macedonian question, and – with rapidly decreasing likelihood – Moldovan reunification with Romania (Vukadinovic 2000: 40–55).

In terms of levels, the total constellation is thus one in which the domestic level is important especially in the ex-Yugoslav states and Albania, whereas the other Balkan states are more stable, although ethnic minorities are significant in several places, most importantly the Hungarians in Romania. The unit-to-unit level is strong in many places and most often conflicts are not bilateral but very often triangles: Slovenia, Croatia, Serbia; Croatia, Serbia, Bosnia; the three groups within Bosnia; etc. (Wiberg 1993a, 1993b, 1994). Since these triangles interlock, each conflict easily draws in a large number of countries. The fate of this constellation depends very much on external actors.

At the aggregate Balkan level, a pattern of formal and informal alliances often forms, although only a few elements are stable. An 'Islamic arc' links Turkey, Albania, Kosovo, and Bosnia-Herzegovina less as a religious alliance than as a pattern of Turkish obligations as protector (Lose 1995: 12; Kazan 2002). The counteralliance to this is primarily Greece, Bulgaria, Serbia (against Turkey, with an additional potential Serbian–Romanian link due to the joint issue of Hungarian minorities). However, the pattern of potential conflicts is too complicated and the number of players too high for any stable overarching pattern to form and, dependent on the driving issue at any given time, the pattern can be rearranged – as it was previously in the Balkan wars of the early twentieth century.

A particularly direct domestic–international link is the open question of the future of the (quite different) international protectorates in Bosnia-Herzegovina and Kosovo (and international involvement in Macedonia). How long can and will the international community stay and what happens if they leave?

Containment, intervention, and integration: the Balkans as Europe

As argued above, external actors were crucial for Balkan developments. Power differentials in combination with geography allow external actors to shape the development in the area. This defines the Balkans as potentially a part of the EU-Europe RSC. This potentiality is activated by the identity factor of the Balkans being seen as part of 'us' and therefore impossible to let descend into barbarism and cruelty to the degree which the West can accept in Africa. However, a case could certainly also be made for the West – the USA and the EU for slightly different reasons – trying to stay out. The United States originally wanted to stay out because it saw this as a European task (and a complete mess). The Europeans were interested only when they thought it could be handled relatively easily, thus boosting the EU foreign policy profile – as expressed in the infamous statement by Jacques Poos (the Luxembourg foreign minister) that 'the hour of Europe has come'.

The option of sealing off the (sub)region was tempting to some. This option meant constructing ('Balkanising') the Balkans as a separate RSC, but ultimately the other representation won out, whereby the Balkans is part of Europe (see box, pp. 388–90). However, in particular the nuanced analyses of Hansen (1998) and Frello (2002) correct the often quite dichotomous stories and show the complicated articulations and the contradictory policy possibilities within the different representations. Hansen further argues that the duality of Balkanisation and inclusion has been temporarily settled in favour of inclusion, but that the Balkan discourse has been reproduced enough to prepare a kind of exit option (Hansen 1999).

The strategy of containment and isolation was very difficult in practice, first because as argued above the external actors were 'counted in' by local actors and their likely involvement overestimated. Therefore, non-involvement would have had to be a much more active and consistent policy, which was unrealistic. The USA, the European states, and Russia *were* involved almost irrespective of their own choice. Even if they tried to opt out of the region, they would be influencing it. And non-involvement would have had to be coordinated not only in the RSC but in the supercomplex and at the global level, i.e., between the West European powers, the EU, Russia, and the USA.

Second, media and morality in the West did not allow for passivity. Politicians were pressured to 'do something', which in itself probably signified that the Balkans were seen as 'European' (compare the different reaction to tragedies in Africa). Nina Græger has used the securitisation approach and found human rights and other values to be the referent object (Græger 1999). It is hard to decide here the balance between 'universal' arguments and a 'European' factor. Most of the principles have been phrased in general terms, trying to avoid defining special European standards, but the fact that so much international action has actually taken place compared to elsewhere shows a European/white/Western factor in play.

Third, security interdependence might be too strong also in the Balkan-to-Europe direction. Even if the major powers had decided to try to define the Balkans as not (really) Europe, and the war as 'not our problem', this might not have been enough to disengage, because the war had spillovers in the form of issues that were securitised in other sectors, notably immigration.

Western securitisation of Balkan developments

Many discourse analyses have been made of Western politics on Bosnia in order to understand non-intervention and intervention (Hansen 1998; Ó Tuathail 1996: 128–224; Kuusisto 1998; Frello 2002; and many more). We can draw upon these to ask our specific question – not how the West constructed the conflict, blame, and responsibility, but who or what was securitised.

The most analysed discourse is the one of 'ancient hatred', of conflict and its particular cruelty being inherent to the Balkans. This discourse typically constructs 'equal parties' – not good against bad – and impossibility of a resolution. It points to the region as a threat against itself, but usually not a threat against the West. This is therefore a non-securitisation for the West itself. In order for a basically 'ancient hatred'-based construction to turn into securitisation, it needs one of two links.

One is the quagmire metaphor analysed by Ó Tuathail (1996), a securitisation of what happens to the United States if it does intervene. In the USA, the ancient-hatred discourse has therefore typically ended up as a non-intervention discourse.

The other argument is 'spillover' – more common in Europe. In this view, although the local parties neither deserve, nor are capable of, peace built on Western sacrifices, military action is needed in order to defend regional, European, or international 'stability' or strategic, national, or vital 'interests' (Hansen 1999).

The second discourse appropriately labelled by Lene Hansen 'Bosnia as Western self', is characteristic of American debate (and French intellectuals). Through this lens, Sarajevo epitomised the tolerance and multiculturalism we stand for. The attack and atrocities on Bosnians became a direct threat against us and we have to defend those principles because they are ours. This discourse has a clear aggressor (Serbia or Serbs) and therefore we also have to defend the principle of non-aggression in order to deter other future Milosevics in the world.

A third in-between version distributes blame relatively equally but does not present the Balkans as doomed. In a particularly European version of interventionism, continuity is constructed between the Balkans and the rest of Europe. Yes, currently Europe is on the path of integration and the Balkans mired in barbarism, but this duality is in them and us, two principles are competing – integration and civilisation against fascism and racism (Blair 1997, 2000a, 2000b; Cook 1999). A danger to the West follows from the fact that both principles exist in both places and thus we can be pulled in their direction if we do not pull them in ours. Similar to the 'Western self' discourse, a fatal choice is made that involves our principles, but the third discourse does not imply a true, untainted local hero of multiculturalism and a clear distribution of blame. It is possible to combine a general picture of Balkan cruelty with an interventionist argument about a fatal choice for us all by depicting a parallel duality deep in both EU-Europe and the Balkans. The root securitisation is here the one presented in chapter 11 about Europe's history (see box, pp. 361–4). Because of this threat to us, Balkan developments can be dangerous.

Compared to the later case of Kosovo, official policy constructed Milosevic as a unique threat only to a relatively limited extent. (In more independent and unofficial 'Bosnia as Western self' discourses, he is.) After all, the Bosnia process was about justifying an order *including* him. In Kosovo, it was a war *against* him, and the full repertoire of Hitler metaphors and 'absolute evil' unfolded (Frello 2002).

Intervention demands securitisation tied to Western actors. If only somebody purely local is threatened, intervention will rely on pure altruism, which implies that some principle is securitised (Buzan et al. 1998: 141–62) or the 'self' extended to include locals. Otherwise a more concrete chain is necessary whereby the conflict becomes connected to own security.

We follow Lene Hansen in concluding the analysis with President Clinton's November 1995 speech in which he justifies the Dayton agreement and American military involvement as 'the right thing to do' (Clinton 1995). As early as the first paragraph, a link to the American self is established: 'our values and interests as Americans require that we participate'. The link is made by historical analogy to the world wars and the classical contrast between interwar isolationism and Cold War involvement. The message is that 'leading the world' solves problems, whereas isolation is based on the illusion that problems will stay 'beyond our borders' while actually they 'can quickly become problems within them'. L. Hansen (1998: 354ff.) points out that the Clinton speech mixes elements of 'ancient hatred' and 'Bosnia as Western self'. It also combines in a curious way the two ways of creating chains. It is made an issue about principles and what America stands for, but it is not really spelt out what principles are threatened. Nor is it clear why this can become a general threat, implying that somehow problems in Bosnia can spread and become problems in the USA. The position is argued not by any very clear direct link, but by analogy and by a general argument about living in a globalised world. Ultimately, the strategy seems to be to avoid very strong securitisation but also to downplay the American action. Americans are not going to fight a war (then Clinton would have needed securitisation); they have helped the parties to reach an agreement, and American peacekeepers will help them implement it. Strikingly, the two strongest securitisations are indirect. One borrows the European argument that Bosnia can decide Europe's freedom and stability, which in turn is 'vital to our own national security'. The other is that American leadership and the credibility of NATO will be threatened if the United States fails to act.

This case demonstrates clearly the link between securitisation and action. To act, securitisation is needed. Those who wanted more perilous intervention earlier in the war had stronger securitisations; those against intervention made no such link. The key speech of the chosen approach downplayed the extraordinary (military) nature of the act and thus reduced the need for securitisation.

These factors brought the West from potential disengagement and containment to interventions, but a further step has been taken. After especially the Kosovo war, its costs on neighbouring states, and the bad experiences of trying to jumpstart development for Bosnia in isolation, the EU and other Western actors launched a subregional cooperative scheme.

The stability pact introduces an explicitly subregional approach. It has important effects in the direction of consolidating a Balkan region, because a country like Romania, which previously did everything to be considered 'not-the-Balkans' (as did Slovenia and Hungary), suddenly wants to establish its credentials as a leading, stabilising actor in South-eastern Europe, thus strengthening its position in the West by playing a constructive role.

The Balkans does not become a separate RSC but is it a lasting special case in Europe: is it a continuing subregion or likely to be fully absorbed? And is the integration necessarily irreversible? What if the Western powers get fed up with the Albanian mafia, Montenegrin corruption, and continued local violence in Kosovo? Could the decision be reversed and the Balkans after all left to itself? Hardly! In addition to the reasons given above, the West now has prestige involved in making the subregion successful.

A possible puzzle is that, if the Balkans is a subcomplex, it must be assumed that it is EU-Europe it is a subcomplex of, but at crucial points the most important external actor was the USA (and Russia mattered too). Thus, the question arises whether the subregion is, rather, overlaid by the regional great power *dynamics*, including external actors reaching into Europe. The period 1991–9 might be seen as demonstrating the latter interpretation. But as the military side becomes institutionalised and gradually pushed into the background, the stability pact takes over, and the whole civilian side comes to dominate, the EU becomes the central institution, and a European subcomplex interpretation is clearly justified.

This seeming anomaly is explained by Eide's analysis seeing the Balkans as Europe's security laboratory. All the major questions of European post-Cold War security have been tested – and sometimes settled in political competition – here, such as the EU–NATO relationship, the relationship of the West/NATO to Russia, the UN/regional division of labour on peacekeeping (Eide 1999). In this way, it is not the United States or Russia as such that has been present in the Balkans, it is their European projection, and thus it is still reasonable to see the Balkans as a subcomplex of the European RSC.

Turkey

The centrality of the Ottoman factor in Balkan history was argued above. After a long period (c. 1300–1800) of seeing its own society as superior to Europe – and regularly putting Europe under military pressure – Turkey's attempt to adapt to pressure from Europe and to learn from a modernising West/Europe has been a constant pattern for the last 200 years (Goodwin 1999; Lewis 1982; Kazan and Wæver 1994: 141). Total dismemberment at the beginning of the twentieth century was avoided only by its 1923 rebirth as the modern Turkish Republic. A Balkan subsystem was founded, largely composed of the Ottoman Empire's prior territories, and a Middle East formed out of its other possessions. Now Turkey was located between different RSCs, and it became important as an insulator.

Traditionally, an insulator state is expected to be relatively passive. Indirectly this was expressed in the key foreign policy doctrines of Kemalism: 'Peace at home, peace abroad [or peace in the world]' and 'Turkey does not desire an inch of foreign territory, but will not give up an inch of what she holds' (Mustafa Kemal quoted in Váli 1971: 25, 27).

Regions in the foreign policy of modern Turkey

The modern Turkish republic sought to imitate Europe (representing the modern/Western world), but the political relationship with the West was originally difficult. Turkey was neutral in the interwar period. During the Cold War, Turkey became a member of the west, expressed by membership in NATO, OECD, and the Council of Europe and an associated membership of the EU (since 1963). The Greece–Turkey relationship was problematic from the beginning (mutual expulsion of minorities), but became tense only after the Second World War.

The relationship to other regions was more passive. Towards Russia, the Turkish position was that of a NATO country with important US bases. The Turkic-speaking Central Asian republics were not part of policy. The policy towards the Middle East was also relatively passive, with Turkey avoiding being dragged into a general Islamic front against Israel. The relationship to the direct neighbours was much influenced by the Kurdish question, one of Turkey's main domestic security problems. It allowed, in principle, the possibility of cooperation for the countries with large Kurdish populations (Turkey, Iraq, Iran, Syria), but more often it gave them an instrument to undermine and trouble each other.

The general Turkish policy of not getting involved in the Middle East was also influenced by its ambition to become part of the West and therefore avoid being defined as 'Middle Eastern'. This was domestically controversial, because the Islamists viewed Turkey as part of the Muslim world. But since the westernising Kemalist line was always in charge, distance to the Middle East won out.

The insulator position was expressed in an attempt to avoid being drawn into conflicts on all sides (the risk facing an insulator state), and an attempt to get out of that position altogether by becoming more definitely 'West' and 'Europe'.

Turkey after the Cold War

The end of the Cold War raised worries in Turkey about a potential loss of importance. It was no longer needed as a frontline state against the Soviet Union, and it slipped down the rank of Europeanness as Europe started elevating its newfound brothers and sisters in East Central Europe, and perhaps even Russia. In Turkey as in many other countries, the end of the Cold War triggered a general identity crisis and a search for reorientation and redefinition. The Gulf War made it clear that Turkey was still strategically important, but the worry about Turkey's position remained.

A positive change for Turkey was the 'opening' of Central Asia. The sudden and surprising independence of a number of Turkic republics raised new perspectives – disturbing, demanding, and inspirational: disturbing because this direction was traditionally associated in Turkey with right-wing, pan-Turkic nationalism – would the other radical challenger to the Kemalist mainstream (in addition to Islamism) gain ground? It was demanding because Turkey would have to devise a much more activist policy in a dangerous area, but inspirational because of both the emotional appeal of reuniting with 'lost family' and the new grander mission for Turkey. High hopes faltered as Turkey lost out to Russia, and Central Asian republics rejected the idea of getting a new patron (ch. 13). However, Central Asia importantly became part of the Turkish self-conception as a larger nation consisting of many states. Especially during periods when relations to the EU sour, Turkey is not just the rejected applicant at the door to the EU: Central Asia is the main area where Turkey can project a new vision of itself, even if it is not to be immediately fulfilled. Also, the Caucasus has been upgraded and in the long drawn-out struggle over future pipelines Turkey is an important actor (ch. 13).

The second area where Turkey became more involved in the 1990s was the Balkan wars. Officially, Turkey's policy was that it could not be indifferent due to historic ties, but in practice it would go far to avoid any escalation. In identity terms it reinforced the picture in Turkey of being a power with interests beyond its borders, even if very little was actually done.

In the Middle East, Turkey has also become more active, both strengthening the 'strategic partnership' with Israel and (in 1998) confronting Syria (see ch. 7).

The relationship to the EU reached a low point in 1997 when Turkey was not even located alongside the second group of applicants from East Central Europe, but was given a special arrangement of its own, which it proudly refused. Turkey, which has been on some kind of applicant track since 1959, was overtaken by a number of new countries. However, by 1999 Turkey was granted a status that defines membership as the eventual aim but remains vague on how and when. This is a de facto return to the old situation of a 'process' and, to many actors in Turkey, such a process might well be the real aim, not membership, which would demand a lot of painful domestic adjustment. (The relationship to Greece and Cyprus is dealt with in chapter 11, pp. 368–9).

Towards the end of the 1990s, these diverse developments started to converge in a changing Turkish role vis-à-vis regions. Turkey does not officially accept that it is an insulator state. Officially, it defines the region in the most favourable way as 'Eurasia' (like many Russians). In a larger Eurasia, Turkey would be highly central and not an insulator at all but, as is the nature of an insulator, Turkey is unable itself to forge this reordering and it is not an accurate description of the current security patterns. In contrast to this more declaratory policy on security regions, Turkey's de facto policy increasingly changed to one that reflects the insulator state position. As argued by Işıl Kazan (2002), Turkey has in recent years taken an increasing interest in regions and regionalism and upgraded its involvement in the different regions. Increasingly, Turkey defines itself as an important regional power exactly because it is located at this intersection – as expressed in the metaphor of Turkey located in a 'Bermuda triangle' between the conflict regions of the Balkans, the Caucasus, and the Middle East (Kazan 2002). It believes it should naturally play a more important part in all regions and therefore also has a justification for demanding a higher standing internationally in general, not least as the main spokesman of 250 million Turkic speakers. This raises important questions as to the concept and nature of insulator states.

Turkey challenging the concept of insulator

Usually insulator states play their role by being relatively passive and thereby 'absorbing' energies from the separate complexes. Turkey seems to challenge this, by playing an increasingly active role from its insulator position. Is this compatible with being an insulator? Yes, Turkey is an insulator because it is not able to bring the different complexes together into one coherent strategic arena. What could challenge this interpretation of Turkey would be if too much more came of attempts by Greece, Russia, and Syria to coordinate (Kazan 2002). If actors from the different complexes can act strategically together, the boundary of the complexes has grown thin, and the general conceptualisation is challenged. If a much-strengthened Turkey actually becomes the regional great power it claims it is, it could trigger such a coalescence of its neighbours; it would then increasingly have to be analysed as a pole in some RSC, not only as insulator between RSCs. But for the foreseeable future Turkey will remain an insulator, but one that tries to handle its complicated situation through a more active policy than that traditionally adopted by insulators.

Conclusions

The main conclusion to this chapter is that the Balkans moved in the direction of becoming a separate RSC in the early 1990s, but from the middle of the 1990s and, decisively with the Kosovo war in 1999, the Balkans became a subcomplex within the European RSC.

Domestic vulnerability is dominant mainly in the ex-Yugoslavian states, although the incongruity of state and nation around Hungary is a potential source of security problems too. Ex-Yugoslavia's dense network of manifest and potential conflicts easily trigger each other. In contrast, the rest of the Balkans holds only a few and less mutually connected interstate risks. This conflict formation is not allowed to play itself out because of a decision by the West to bring the Balkans into Europe.

The Balkans neighbours an unusually strong and active insulator in Turkey which, as successor state to the Ottoman Empire, has historical interests in the region. This could have been a source of instability leading to competitive interventions rather than joint external 'management'. However, Turkey was very careful and cooperative throughout. It is difficult to judge how much this stems from Turkey being, after all, well integrated in the West through decades of NATO membership and how much is explained by structure, whereby an insulator has an interest in avoiding escalation around itself.

The overall pattern of regional security is decided outside the Balkans, in the EU-Europe core. To what extent the characteristic dynamics of the EU-Europe RSC – integration, enlargement, desecuritisation – expand to the Balkans will be decided in domestic politics in the various countries. Regime change in Croatia and Serbia in 2000 had strong elements of attempts to integrate into European 'normality' (K. S. Hansen 2000; Hansen and Güntelberg 2001).

The scenario feared at some point that a Europeanisation of the Balkans would be overtaken by a Balkanisation of Europe is not realistic anymore, except in the sense that the military factor in European politics has been generally strengthened with implications for both the nature of the EU and the continued influence of the USA in Europe via NATO (Simic 2001: 22). The main alternatives are whether the Balkans gradually blends into a general East Europeanness – still distinguishable from Western and Central Europe but part of the same overall process and differentiated multidimensional polity; or whether it remains a distinct subregion shaped by the tension between this European pull and indigenous developments that if left to themselves would restart the wars; or finally whether the West might eventually tire of the region and let it go its own way. The essential structure of the subcomplex itself has so far not been modified – the main change is the gradually shifting balance between the dynamics coming from this structure and from the larger EU-European RSC.

13 The post-Soviet space: a regional security complex around Russia

In most Western analyses of the area of the former Soviet Union, the situation is presented as anomalous due to the blatantly asymmetrical relations. The underlying agenda is how the weaker states around Russia can gain enough independence and equality to establish a more 'normal' relationship. However, as argued above, there is nothing historically (ch. 1) or theoretically (ch. 3) strange about regions with a dominant power at the centre. Analytically we should rather try to understand how this RSC operates and where it is placed and headed in the larger historical pattern. This particular region has historically been structured by two long-term patterns: (1) the waves of growth and contraction of the Russian Empire; (2) change in degrees of separateness and involvement with other regions, primarily Europe.

The chapter opens with a brief discussion of the historical trajectory of the Russian state as well as those of the new states that have significant state histories of their own. The main section examines security dynamics as they have evolved in the region from the dissolution of the Soviet Union to today, in terms of levels (domestic, regional, interregional, global). Within this it specifies the variation among four different subregions: the Baltic states, the western group of states, the Caucasus, and Central Asia. For most of the states, security concerns relate mainly to other states in the subcomplex plus Russia. What define the wider RSC, grouping them all together, are the unifying factors, first, of Russia and the Commonwealth of Independent States (CIS) and, second, that a coalition attempting to rein in Russia necessarily cuts across regions. The argument as to why the Russia-centred complex is separate was given in the introduction to part V. The major complicating factor in this division is the role of Europe in the identity struggles of Russia. However, it will be argued here that, although *Europe* historically played this role in Russian debates about themselves (Neumann 1996b, 1997a, 1997b), the *global* arena is today much more important than Europe for Russia's attempts both to secure a larger role outside its region and to legitimise its regional empire. The chapter will end with a discussion of the prospects regarding internal and external transformation, particularly three questions: the interplay of global, regional, and domestic dynamics in Russian policy and a possible redefinition of Russia's power status; the possibility that something like GUUAM evolves into a genuine counterweight to Russia; and finally the nature and location of the boundary with EU-Europe.

The RSC is clearly centred on a great power. Russia was until recently a superpower, and is still a great power. It neighbours two other RSCs containing great powers – EU-Europe centred on the EU, and the Asian great power complex with China and Japan – and one standard complex – the Middle East. In contrast to most other regions of the world, the one superpower, the USA, plays less of a role in this region, although a question mark has emerged in Central Asia and the Caucasus, mostly due to oil interests and, after September 2001, the war on terrorism.

Despite the centredness of the region, it is – unusually – also a conflict formation. This is less surprising when the end of the Soviet Union is seen as decolonisation suddenly producing whole neighbourhoods of newly independent states. Just as several RSCs were born fighting or at least dropped into immediate hostility, the level of conflict started out relatively high in Central Asia and especially the Caucasus, and traditional security concerns were intense in Baltic–Russian and Ukrainian–Russian relations.

History before 1991

Russian history conventionally is traced back to the beginnings of a Russian state in the ninth century. In 1238 Moscow fell as the Tatar Golden Horde swept over the Eurasian plain. After pulling back from Latin Europe, they established a more stable hold over a territory similar to the later Soviet Union's (Watson 1984b: 61). Muscovy developed under their suzerainty and took over techniques of war and administration (this in contrast to the self-image of Russians in which this period constitutes the dark Other). In 1480 Moscow freed itself fully and became the new Russian state, and soon reconquered much of the Tatar empire.

Russia was not closely connected to medieval and Latin Europe. With its identity centred on Slav Orthodox Christianity, it developed separately for a long time, although it gradually increased its involvement in European diplomacy and military engagements, and alliances in the Baltic Sea area (Kirby 1990: 51–5). Under the Romanov dynasty (from 1613), Russians began more systematically to connect – and fight. Russia was first part of the Northern European RSC, and only as this merged into an all-European RSC around 1700 did Russia begin to be drawn systematically into European politics. Famously, Peter the Great strengthened Russia by absorbing Western techniques, not least in the military field. He did this not to fight Europe, but in order to join it. Both culturally and in the equations of power, Russia was accepted during the first half of the eighteenth century. Through the divisions of Poland in 1772, 1793, and 1795, Russia expanded both its territory and its influence westwards. Its role culminated in the Napoleonic wars in which Russia became a key power. Russia had both French troops entering Moscow (1812) and their own ending up in Paris (1814).

Meanwhile Russia continued to expand into Siberia and Central Asia, meeting primarily tribal peoples. On its 'forest frontier', Russia expanded (as did the United States) first via the fur trade along the river system. Europeans became a majority in Siberia by about 1700 (Johnson 1991: 268ff.; cf. Kinder and Hilgemann 1999: 112–13; Gilbert 1993: 26–34, 46–8, 59–63; Baev 1996: 7; Kotkin 1997; Buzan and Little 2000: 257–63; Roy 2000: 25–34; Trenin 2001: 54–5). In contrast, on the 'steppe frontier', the Russians met much tougher opposition from the Turks on the Ukrainian steppes and nomadic tribes further east. The conquest of Central Asia took 300 years, and as noted by Johnson resembled the ousting of the Indians in North America. In 1828, Russian intervention against the Ottoman Empire meant expansion into both the Balkans and Turkish Transcaucasia. In Georgia, Christians sought the protection of Russia, but many Islamic peoples in the Caucasus were hard to break and their resistance continues to haunt Russia, as witnessed in Chechnya. Russian expansion eastwards even meant explorations down the west coast of North America, but eventually Russia limited its North American presence to Alaska, and that was sold to the USA in 1867. When the waterways of Siberia had been explored, fortified, and canalised, i.e., Eastern Europe linked to Russian Asia, the European population of Siberia started to grow rapidly. The nineteenth century also saw the so-called great game in Central Asia in which Russia pushed southwards through Central Asia as Britain came up from India through Afghanistan. The 1904–5 war with Japan was important both in exposing Russian weakness, thus paving the way for the revolution, and in settling the eastern border as well as to some extent Russia's relationship to East Asia. Since this humiliating defeat, Russia has not concentrated on Asia as a primary arena, and it is therefore not possible in RSCT terms to place Russia in East Asia.

The classical divide in Russian self-conceptions between Westernisers and Slavophiles took shape in the 1830s and continues to influence Russian domestic and foreign policy (Neumann 1996a, 1996b, 2002). Although the Russian Revolution was based on a European set of ideas, Marxism, it led to a limitation of contacts other than conflictual ones. In terms of security, the West and Russia became closely connected as archenemies. The enmity started right after the revolution and was interrupted by alliance during the Second World War, but came to structure the world for half a century during the Cold War. The extent of the Russian empire was temporarily reduced after the revolution and Russia pulling out of the First World War. All of the lost territory and much more was regained after the Second World War, when an informal outer empire was added in the form of the Warsaw Pact countries in Eastern Europe as well as leadership of the global communist movement including, for a while, China, but more consistently Cuba, Vietnam, and a number of African and Middle Eastern countries.

In RSC terminology, the Russian regional situation during the Cold War is difficult to characterise. Clearly, the Cold War took the Soviet Union out of Europe by elevating it to superpower rivalry with the United States. But did it sit in the middle of its own RSC consisting of its 'empire', or was this so tightly controlled as to be basically one political unit and thus really no region? Given that all of Europe – West and East – was overlaid (and Mongolia too), there were no independent, regional states left to constitute an RSC (see map 11, p. 349).

More important than this question about a possible regional level around the Soviet Union is the monumental fact of Moscow galvanising a tighter grip on both its formal (Soviet) and informal (East European) possessions than had ever been the case for the Russian Empire. Under communist rule society was penetrated by the state to a unique degree, and international and imperial relations to units within the Warsaw Pact and in the parts of the Soviet Union, which Russia had previously controlled only with difficulty (particularly the southern republics), became transformed to direct control. This happened in synergy with the Soviet rise to the global top two.

As outlined in chapter 11, Eastern Europe during 1945–8 became gradually integrated fully into the Soviet sphere of control. All states got a similar structure with a dominant communist party, military integration into the Warsaw Pact, and – with less success – economic integration and division of labour in COMECON. Yugoslavia and Albania took independent lines: they were still ruled by a communist party but not dependent on the Soviet Union. China joined the bloc after the civil war in 1949 and left in 1960. In global politics, the Cold War struggle with the USA took different forms in different parts of the world.

In some respects, the communist system was much less tight than it pretended (and was sometimes perceived to be by fearful Westerners). This was demonstrated by the inefficiencies of the command economy, and by widespread corruption and deception within this system. In other respects, it was nevertheless thoroughly organised and regulated. This meant a paradoxical combination of, on the one hand, 'law and order' in the sense of little (ordinary) crime and a high level of safety for the ordinary citizen and, on the other hand, insecurity for anybody who happened to come to crosspurposes with the system. In general, the whole region was characterised by an extremely high degree of predictability (which in the 1970s and early 1980s developed into gerontocratic stasis and decay under Brezhnev and his successors). This stability sharply contrasts with a post-Cold War situation of fluidity in overall relations and disorganisation and lawlessness at the micro-level.

This Cold War order unravelled with surprising speed and a relative absence of violence. From when Gorbachev took power as general secretary of the CPSU in 1985 and gradually introduced political and economic reforms, decentralising processes accelerated both within the Soviet Union and especially in Eastern Europe. During two years in 1989–91, communist rule ended in country after country, Germany was unified, and the Warsaw Pact officially dissolved. Within the Soviet Union, negotiations over a future union with increased independence for the republics were aborted by the August 1991 coup against Gorbachev. When the coup failed, the central figure was Russia's leader (since 1990) Boris Yeltsin; most of the republics declared independence and, in December 1991, the presidents of Ukraine, Belarus, and Russia dissolved the Soviet Union and proclaimed the CIS. At the end of the year, the Soviet Union ceased to exist, the Russian flag rose over the Kremlin and control of the nuclear arsenal was handed over to Yeltsin.

Thus, much of the history of the area is about the shifting tides of a Moscow-centred polity (Baev 1996: 3–19; Trenin 2001: 39–99; Lieven 2000: 201–411). However, some of the other now-independent states also have (or construct) separate state histories. Ukraine has a medieval history as well as a competitive claim on the original 'Rus'. Armenia and Georgia have histories of independence in the first century BC and again from the ninth century AD in the case of Armenia and from the eleventh and twelfth century in the case of Georgia. The Central Asian states could link back to the khanates of the fifteenth to eighteenth centuries – and ideologically more powerfully to the triumphant tribes and hordes who regularly threatened all neighbours for centuries, although they could hardly be seen as the constructors of stable states (Buzan and Little 2000: 188; Rashid 2002b: 20–3). The Baltic republics had an interwar experience of independent statehood, which in the case of Lithuania followed centuries of independence and even great power-hood (Polish–Lithuanian state).

The nationalities question was important and a continuing source of worry within the Soviet Union, but in the 1980s only the Baltic states and to some extent Ukraine and later Georgia, Armenia, and Azerbaijan had strong national(ist) movements aimed at a well-defined idea of statehood. Most of the others dropped inadvertently into independence and, although they have constructed national histories together with their states, the long story about the region is very much a unicentric one.

Paradoxically, the national identity of the new republics is to a large extent the result of Soviet nationalities policy. It both contributed to several of these groups forming a national identity and shaped it in some particular ways (Suny 1999–2000; Tkach 1999; Grannes 1993: 10–14). Soviet policy on nationalities was marked by the tension between on the one hand the communist assumption that eventually national particularism would be transcended and Soviet man emerge, and on the other a short-term policy of accommodating and even reinforcing national identity for purposes of divide-and-rule. The Soviet Union was structured by a four-layered system of ethnically based administrative political units, a system of 'matrioshka nationalism'. First there were the Union Republics (SSRs, Soviet Socialist Republics; officially with a right to secede), second, twenty Autonomous Soviet Socialist Republics located within the Union Republics. Then came eight Autonomous Regions (oblasti) and last ten Autonomous Areas (okruga). Each had a similar set of institutions, nested hierarchically within each other. Characteristic of Soviet policy was that each unit had a 'titular nationality' defined, the one after which the republic, region, or area was named. And, irrespective of the numerical balance in the unit, that nationality had various privileges. Nations were treated as real and primary, as almost something biological in the Soviet system and, with the idea of the titular nationality, the background for how to think about nation and state was predisposed towards ethnicised politics and a perception of the state as belonging not to the people on a territory but to the nation whose name it carried. Soviet drawing and redrawing of boundaries is at the root of many of the conflicts in present-day post-Soviet space.

Evolution of the RSC, 1991–2002

Domestic level

In most of the Central Asian and trans-Caucasian republics, domestic security is either high or top priority. Competing elites struggling for political power are willing to trade national autonomy for external support (Roeder 1997), and the state order is so weak that threats to the security of the regime can trigger a general crisis of political order and in some cases civil war. In Russia and the western republics (Ukraine, Moldova, and in its own odd way Belarus) the political order is more stable either because an autocratic ruler has taken control (Belarus) or because a democratic system is sufficiently well established that electoral outcomes will be respected and power transferred according to constitutional procedures (Russia, Ukraine, and Moldova). The democratic structures are even more mature in the three Baltic states. Internal tensions due to large (mainly Russian) minorities are in principle a problem in Estonia, Latvia, and Ukraine. In practice, the *domestic* dynamic has been contained in Estonia and Latvia, and thus the issue is really a question about Russian foreign policy. In Ukraine, an underlying tension exists, and domestic conflict remains a risk.

Politics in Central Asia are not only generally undemocratic – with unfair elections, a controlled press, and harsh persecution of especially Islamist but sometimes all opposition – they have increasingly turned personalistic (some say 'sultanistic') with power controlled in a tightly knit circle of family and friends. Lifetime powers and preparations for dynastic succession can be found within these orders, ingeniously labelled by Uzbekistan's President Karimov 'oriental democracy' (Parakhonsky n.d.). Having an individual at the centre of domestic level security often means volatile policies, as exemplified most clearly and importantly by the many abrupt changes in Uzbekistan's foreign policy. This also explains the repressive reaction to Islamism which many observers see as leading to a vicious circle actually generating more Islamists and eventually more terrorists (Rashid 2000, 2002a, 2002b, 2002c; Olcott 2001b;

403

Norton 2002). Whether caused by the repression or actually vindicating it, the strength and radicalism of Islamist movements seems actually to have increased in recent years (Peterson 2002; Rashid 2002b; Olcott 2001b; Gunaratna 2002: 167–72). The Islamic Movement of Uzbekistan (IMU) fought with the Taleban and al-Qaeda in Afghanistan in 2001, taking heavy losses, but the battle-hardened remains also picked up 'leftover' al-Qaeda Arabs. They are expected to shift from insurgency to terror and assassinations and to be regrouping in Tajikistan and Kyrgyzstan before hitting at Uzbekistan. The non-violent radicals in Hizb ut-Tahrir (HT) are accused of coordinating destabilisation efforts with IMU. The three factors of drugs trade, wide availability of arms in Afghanistan, and Islamic groups are mutually reinforcing (Olcott 2001b). Worsening socioeconomic conditions particularly among the large youth population in especially Uzbekistan make future recruitment for Islamic radicals likely.

Russia does not have domestic *security* problems to the same extent, but its domestic level is nevertheless important in order to understand the security of the region. In a centred region, the factors that drive the foreign policy of the dominant regional power are obviously of special importance. Russian policy changed after the first two to three post-Soviet years. A first period of clear Western orientation (Kozyrev's period as foreign minister, which has been called the 'diplomacy of smiles' and the 'policy of yes'; Mozaffari 1997: 28) led to increasing criticism for a lack of *Russian* foreign policy.

The failure of this policy had external as well as internal causes. Western policy did very little to give Russia a sense of a role (out of concern for NATO, the USA resisted Russian wishes for a strengthened OSCE, and the West Europeans were preoccupied with their own projects: '1992', Maastricht, and ex-Yugoslavia). As a result, it was impossible for the new Russian leadership to project itself into the world and the world into Russian domestic politics. Russia could not construct a vision of itself pointing towards a future world with itself in an attractive role and form (Wæver 1990b, 1995b; Christensen 2002). The policy of general participation in a Western, liberal order was therefore not viable. This foreign policy shift was closely connected with a partial backlash in domestic politics against the liberal reformers – both communists and nationalists gained ground and the president de facto accommodated much of their criticism regarding foreign policy.

The idea of the 'near abroad' as Russia's main priority started to emerge already in 1992 and became official policy from 1993 (Karaganov

1992; Lough 1993; Migranyan 1994; Lepingwell 1994; Shashenkov 1994; G. Simon 1994; Malcolm et al. 1996; Baev 1996, 1997a, 1997b; Smith et al. 1998: 11ff.; Matz 2001). The former Soviet republics were defined as a Russian sphere of interest, partly justified by the need to protect Russian minorities, partly in terms of joint interests, including economic ones. The very term, the 'near abroad', revealingly created an in-between category between domestic and truly 'foreign' affairs, thus suggesting a polity formed in concentric circles (à la Watson), a centred RSC. At the global level, Russian policy has consistently promoted multipolarity and resisted American unipolarity. Towards the end of the 1990s multipolarity gained force as a platform for cooperation with the Chinese and Iranians and flirtations with Amerisceptic West Europeans.

Thus, the primary Russian security problem at the domestic level is one that in curious ways connects to the regional and global levels: the threats to Russian state identity from a lack of recognition (Christensen 2002), a lack of a respectable international role. Another domestic security problem, still identity-related, involves the relationship between state and nation: 'What then is the "national" substance in the national interest, the national security and the national defence of the Russian Federation? Is it more properly Russian or multinational...?' (Rühl 1997: 22). It is ethno-Russian enough to take a special interest in Russians outside the borders, but open and inclusive enough in its conception of 'Russian' to keep the multinational federation together. We return to the Russian answer to this question in the box on pp. 406–8, but a similar question was posed in several of the other new states. It was in most cases resolved predominantly by the ethno-national answer. Even Ukraine, with its striking need to formulate an inclusive identity bringing the Russian minority on board (Lemaitre et al. 1993), started out with a narrowly conceived national identity (Poulsen-Hansen and Wæver 1996). Increasingly, this has been reversed and Russians have been included in the political process – and not as a separate group (Casanova 1998). Kazakhstan stands out because President Nazarbayev has handled the ever-looming threat of Russian-dominated Northern Kazakhstan seceding by an elegant balance between national protection and inclusive strategies in both foreign (CIS) policy and domestic policy regarding the relationship between Kazakhs and Russians (see e.g. Roy 2000: 191ff.; Suny 1999–2000). Most other states have been driven by the more straightforward nationalist conceptions of the 'titular' nations.

The increased attention to the 'near abroad' was mostly received as a national(ist) if not neo-imperial turn away from a liberal, Western policy. However, this reorientation also has a strong element of 'strategic retreat'. In one way, it is possible to draw a line from being mostly involved in European questions (still during the late and post-Soviet negotiations about German unification, troop withdrawal, etc.), through being interested in neighbouring states, to now being increasingly absorbed in domestic wars and fearing a disintegration of Russia itself (Baev 1999b). In a quasi-imperial structure like Russia's – and the EU's – one always has to give highest priority to the inner circles because their health is the precondition for that of the next circle outward. Still, the 'near abroad' should not be underestimated. In the series of 'doctrines' (foreign policy, national security, military doctrine) in 1999–2000 it is still the primary level that is allocated more long- or medium-term importance than both domestic and global security issues.

The main security importance of the political development in the other republics concerns statehood, i.e., economic and political viability. The only republic to directly seek a return to union and seemingly (try to) 'give up' independence was Belarus. All others managed in one way or another to continue as independent units. None of the ex-Soviet republics except the Baltic states has been terribly successful in terms of economic reform and growth, and all have experienced serious drops in GDP with ensuing social problems, crime, and disintegrative processes. However, economic decline has been halted in all the republics. In 1999 GDP grew in all except Ukraine and Moldova and in 2000 in all (IMF 2001). None of the republics seems on the verge of collapsing into the hands of Russia, but several are weak, vulnerable, or economically dependent enough to be easily manipulated and controlled from Moscow.

Nation, state, and security in Russian political thought

Russia shapes this region more than any of the other states. By examining the historical construction of Russian national and state identity what can we discover about the importance of the different levels and about specific constraints on how Russia can securitise or desecuritise?

Relatively less can be said about the basic Russian concept of state and nation than in other cases (such as Germany, France, or India), because Russian debates are polarised and politicised down to the deep questions about how to relate to Western traditions like *Rechtsstaat*, democracy, and individual rights. At least at first, it seems less can be found in the form of sedimented, taken-for-granted common basis

(Neumann 2002; Terpager 2001). Therefore, we should – in order to get at the necessary framework for almost all policy – begin not from the 'official' disagreements like the standard polarisation between Westernisers and Slavophiles but from the minimalist shared basis. It is: state or not. In the particular historical references by which this is repeatedly posed, familiar periods of state failure and chaos are constitutive for the idea of the state: mythic renditions in the Chronicle of Nestor about the ninth century, the 'Time of Troubles' at the beginning of the seventeenth century, and the turmoil and dismemberment after the revolution (Terpager 2001: 64; Trenin 2001: 87). The meaning of the state is defined in terms of order versus chaos. President Putin expressed this in his millennium speech:

> It will not happen soon, if it ever happens at all, that Russia will become the second edition of, say, the US or Britain in which liberal values have deep historic traditions. Our state and its institutions and structures have always played an exceptionally important role in the life of the country and its people. For Russians a strong state is not an anomaly, which should be got rid of. Quite the contrary, they see it as a source and guarantor of order and the initiator and main driving force of any change. Modern Russian society does not identify a strong and effective state with a totalitarian state.
>
> (Putin 1999)

The idea of Russia is further shaped by the absence of a political concept of nation. Although the concept of ethnic Russian clearly exists (see the debates on Russians outside Russia), it has not been constituted as a basis for statehood. Due to continuous expansion, Russia did not become a nation-state. Dmitri Trenin (2001: 74) points to 'Ivan the Terrible's fateful annexation of the two Muslim khanates on the middle and lower reaches of the Volga, Kazan and Astrakhan [1552, 1556], and the concomitant decision to grant the new arrivals a measure of ethnic and religious identity. Early on ethnicity in Russia became subordinated to the imperial state. If there was a "Russian Idea", it was that of a universal Eurasian empire. It was the state that formed the Russian mentality and way of life.'

From this followed the importance of the country's geographical extension. 'Generations of Russians have formed their conception of their country simply by looking at a map, which shows it to be the world's biggest by far. A tsarist-era school primer cites Russia's "bigness" as its natural defining quality' (Trenin 2001: 12; see also 20).

This explains the Russian fashion for geopolitics far beyond the *Realpolitik*-orientated quarters where it is found in other countries – for Russians it is a way to discuss identity. 'Russia *is* a geographical concept' (Trenin 2001: 22). If reduced to the original, ethnically Russian, European possessions, such a state would be *'Russian, but not Russia'* (Trenin 2001: 21).

A popular saying in Russia (which Putin quoted in the 2000 presidential campaign) is: 'He who does not regret the passing of the USSR has no heart; he who wants to restore it has no head' (Trenin 2001: 88).

There is near universal consensus that Russia must have a mission that transcends its confines, and must not be reduced to its ethnographic core (Prizel 1998: 178). The identity to which the state makes reference is therefore empire and civilisation rather than nation (Prizel 1998; Christensen 2002). The near abroad is the most obvious arena in which Russia might define a mission; it is also a means to an end, because having influence in a larger geographical area makes it easier for Russia to be recognised at the global level as a great power (Christensen 2002).

Security is not a 'first-order' question of dealing with actual challenges, nor only a 'second-order' question of defining what security is in order to handle issues in particular ways (securitisation theory); it is also a 'third-order' question of security being an arena for the state to obtain recognition (Christensen 2002; Ringmar 2002). If Russia does not gain recognition internationally, this would both have repercussions in terms of identity problems and raise questions about the ability of the state to guarantee order and society. The concept of a strong state connects international and domestic roles. Although concentric circle polities such as ancient empires, the EU, and Russia in some sense have to give priority to the inner circle in order for there to be an actor to deal with the next layer, in the case of Russia the inner circle is likely to be destabilised if the outer one fades. Therefore, it is unlikely that Russia even under pressure would retreat to a purely internal security agenda. The level of the 'near abroad' is a crucial arena and the ultimate measure is the global level.

Subregional and regional level

Most of the security dynamics operate at the regional – i.e., inter-unit – level although they are rarely of the traditional state-threatens-state form. Classical interstate war and rivalry have most strongly erupted between Armenia and Azerbaijan, and the Central Asian states watch each other wondering about questions of long-term dominance or hegemony in the subregion. Finally, the Russian–Chechen wars are almost interstate – at least according to one of the sides; whether they will be filed in the archives of history under civil war or interstate war depends as always on the outcome. Most other security problems are more unconventional. Their nature varies and, in particular, the aggregate formations differ between the four subregions. Therefore, this section first deals with general patterns and then discusses each subregion.

One characteristic form of conflict involving a package of interconnecting securitisations is the triangle: secessionist minority/ state/Russia. An example is Abkhazia, where a break-away minority threatened the territorial integrity of Georgia which at the time (1992–4) was defiant against Russian strengthening of CIS structures. Russia at first supported the rebels and then (as another mafioso offering 'protection') eventually assisted Georgia – but for a price. In this case the price was Georgian re-entry into the CIS and acceptance of military cooperation with Russia: CIS 'peacekeeping' and Russian bases. In other cases, the threats are not sponsored by Russia – such as the domestic and transnational Islamic rebels in Tajikistan – but Russian assistance is crucial both to the protection of the external borders of the CIS and to domestic control in various republics. When Russia enters as the 'solution', it is often accused of freezing rather than solving the conflict in order to continue to utilise it (Kuzio 2000; Baev 1996, 1997b).

These are the constellations that emerge out of local threats to states 'other' than Russia. In addition, most of the republics see Russia as a threat in itself although one that only few try directly to balance. The GUUAM cooperation among Georgia, Ukraine, Uzbekistan, Azerbaijan, and Moldova signals at least an exploration of the possibilities for such balancing. The main instrument of control by Russia is not direct military intervention but either manipulation of the domestic (or subregional) political scene in ways detrimental to obstinate leaders or simply exploitation of their dependence on Russia, not least economically.

In the opposite direction, seen from Russia, the 'near abroad' is important to security partly for specific reasons, partly for strategic ones. The specific reasons are (as with the USA in relation to Central America) externalities of various kinds (disorder, crime, environmental threats), the threat to infrastructure and thus often to production chains (because these were in Soviet days constructed across several republics), and the fate of the approximately 25 million ethnic Russians who landed out-side Russia when the Soviet Union dissolved. The bottom-line strategic threat is that, if Russia is to remain a great power able both to defend itself and to assert some influence globally, it needs to retain its sphere of influence in the CIS.

Under President Putin, Russian securitisation came to focus on terror-ism (Putin 2000). This was already the main Russian legitimisation of its Chechen operation, and Putin attempted to extend this rationale to the CIS. Transnational terrorism was to justify crossborder operations by Russian military and intelligence (*Monitor* 26 January, 13 March, 22 June 2000; McDermott 2002). Reluctantly, the other member states accepted this in a bargain that allowed some of them to securitise 'separatism and aggressive nationalism' (*Monitor* 26 January 2000). This is a major con-cern to countries such as Moldova, Ukraine, Georgia, and Azerbaijan. It is often directed against Russian policy and is a standard phrase from GUUAM documents. Dmitri Trenin (2001: 108, 130–1, 167, 171) argues that Russia after the first Chechen war moved from exploiting sepa-ratists towards a general anti-separatist, pro-(whichever) government policy.

Also in the context of the Shanghai Cooperation Organization (SCO), Russia put terrorism at the top of the agenda (Abbas 2000; Stratfor 2000a). (Russia, China, Kazakhstan, Kyrgyzstan, and Tajikistan formed the Shanghai Five in 1996; it was renamed in 2000 the Shanghai Forum and became the SCO in 2001 when Uzbekistan joined.) Russia and the Central Asian states try to construct religious extremism, separatism, in-ternational terrorism, and drugs trafficking as closely interlinked, and thus blame international, fundamentalist extremists for all major threats. 'The Shanghai-5's loud denunciations of these partially genuine but largely exaggerated threats are meant to justify their (present and future) oppressive policies against domestic political opponents' (Abbas 2000).

With terrorism in this prominent position, it was easy for President Putin to slot into the 'war on terrorism' started by the United States in 2001 – although Russians were often disappointed when their inter-pretation of the meaning of terrorism and of mutual support was not echoed by US policy especially in relation to Chechnya.

At the same time, the Duma upgraded securitisation in relation to eth-nic Russians in the neighbouring states. Chairman of the international affairs committee Dmitry Rogozin, says: 'Discrimination against and threats to the life, let alone taking the life, of Russian subjects amounts to a threat to the Russian state itself and its national security. We have

25 million compatriots in the near abroad. That problem is our number one problem, a national security problem' (*Monitor* 10 February 2000). The popularity in the West of 'non-military aspects of security has had the unintended side-effect of inspiring the Russian establishment to "securitize" several new issues and to propel a brand new body, the Security Council, into a position of power not unlike that accorded the old Politbureau' (Skak 2000: 16).

The prospects for Russian control of the near abroad are closely connected to the question about the consolidation of the CIS. As noted by Roeder (1997), the whole conception is too openly about Russian interests to become a successful international organisation. It does not include the necessary *quid pro quo* whereby the dominant power gains an empire by granting the peripheral states some influence over its policy (see Kupchan 1998). Russia is in the same situation as the USA is in the Americas, not wanting to give up its unilateralism and therefore finding it hard to sell 'multilateralism' to the others in the region. The CIS as of 2002 has twelve members, and it was shaped, especially around 2000–1, by a polarisation between the independence-oriented states (GUUAM and Turkmenistan) and the 'Russia plus five group' with Belarus, Armenia, Kazakhstan, Kyrgyzstan, and Tajikistan.

Plans for a free trade zone or an 'economic union' had little effect. Russia's own protectionism is among the major obstacles. The members of the Customs Union by mid-2002 were Russia, Belarus, Kazakhstan, Kyrgyzstan, and Tajikistan – the same as the Collective Security Treaty minus Armenia. In some cases, existing levels of integration threaten to unravel further as Turkmenistan in 1999 reintroduced visa requirements, and Russia threatens this move against obstinate neighbours who would often be severely hit due to the high number of their people working in Russia (Trenin 2001: 105, 286; *Economist* 17 August 2000). Generally, the economic part of the organisation has not been well developed, but by default many of the countries are drifting closer to each other as a result of post-Soviet dependence on infrastructure (including personal networks) and failure in alternative markets.

Something similar is happening in the military field where the collective security component of the CIS (the Tashkent Treaty, establishing the CSA) has had the problem of several countries not signing (Moldova, Ukraine, and Turkmenistan) and others leaving (Azerbaijan, Uzbekistan, and Georgia). (So Tashkent has left the Tashkent Treaty! Although Uzbekistan in 2000–1 moved back towards Russia, this was bilateral and did not include re-entry into the Treaty on Collective Security.) Most of the Central Asian republics have upgraded their bilateral ties with Russia so that today Russian troops are patrolling most of the external border of the CIS. Russian troops were deployed in Tajikistan as part of a CIS peacekeeping operation in March 1993. In April 1994, all Central Asian republics, Georgia, and Armenia allowed Russian participation in patrolling their borders (Roy 2000: 197; *Strategic Survey* 1999–2000: 12–13; Baev 1997a, 1997b; Trenin 2001: 118–19). Especially in the context of the Anti-terror Centre a new strategy seems to be to line up the intelligence services (*Monitor* 22 June 2000). Given the striking proportion of leaders in the CIS with a KGB background, this might be an ideal level for networking. After Russian insistence, the Collective Security Treaty was in 2002 transformed into the CIS Collective Security Organisation (CSO), but the implications thereof were unclear (Kuzio 2002a).

The lack of CIS development to some extent reflects obstruction by sceptics. But to Russia, the main role of the CIS is to project an image of Russia as a bloc-leader (*Monitor* 26 and 28 January, 22 June 2000). It is important to its global standing that Russia speaks on behalf of this larger region (as e.g. Turkey has tried to do on behalf of all Turkic-speaking peoples and as Brazil uses Mercosur without bothering to deepen it).

The second important organisation is GUUAM. It is even less organised than the CIS and its track record more problematic. Nevertheless, it is crucial both to an understanding of the present-day CIS and to estimates about the future. It is an indicator of the degree of dissatisfaction with Russian dominance and a measure of the possibilities for and constraints on independent organisation. If the members are able to consolidate their cooperation – and tie it to the Western powers as they intend – the result will be a region less dominated by Russia: if not exactly balanced, then at least one where Russia is not able to control everything by divide-and-rule. In October 1997, the presidents of Georgia, Ukraine, Azerbaijan, and Moldova formed GUAM. In April 1999, the primary policy statement as well as the inclusion of Uzbekistan (and a second U in the name) came symbolically in Washington at a meeting in the context of NATO's fiftieth anniversary summit. GUUAM aims to solve crises, conflicts, and the problems of terrorism on the basis of respect for 'sovereignty, territorial integrity, independence of states and inviolability of their internationally recognized borders' (GUUAM 1999). It is against 'dividing lines and spheres of influence', wants to develop the Europe-Caucasus-Asia transport corridor as a modern Silk

Route, and, finally, wants to strengthen cooperation with NATO (GUUAM 1999; Pashayev 2000).

Much of this is aimed at Russian dominance. The formulations reflect opposition to the fact that Russia, in conflicts in Moldova's Transdniestr, Nagorno-Karabakh, and Abkhazia and potentially in relation to Ukraine, supports solutions that imply either changing borders or a sharing of sovereignty between the (GUUAM) state and its rebelling minority. GUUAM has experienced difficulties since 2000 because of a rapprochement between Uzbekistan and Russia (RFE/RL 24 January 2000) and, despite Uzbekistan's turn to the USA with the US attack on Afghanistan in October 2001, Uzbekistan surprisingly left GUUAM in June 2002 – allegedly from dissatisfaction with its lack of action, possibly because Uzbekistan did not need GUUAM once it had direct access to the USA (Blua 2002; Kuzio 2002b). A Moldovan change of government in January 2000 made that country a little less anti-Russian.

GUUAM's long-term importance is the opening towards NATO with various degrees of ambition regarding hopes for membership. GUUAM can be the context for such cooperation. In the medium term, it has the effect of making opposition to Russian plans within the CIS easier. More and more often conflicts within the CIS line up with GUUAM (or now de facto GUAM, or even 'GUA') on the one side, against Russia and its closest allies on the other. It is thus not surprising that Russian leaders see GUUAM as a 'Trojan horse', 'anti-CIS', and 'anti-Russian' (*Central Asia Caucasus Analyst* 6 August 1999). Russian bilateralism is thwarted by a distinct coalition within the CIS. The members of GUUAM have tried to take specific steps to cooperate in the area of security, notably a joint peacekeeping unit and exchange of information on military and regional security issues.

Turning from organisations and alliance patterns to the actual conflicts, an emerging pattern in the ethnic conflicts is that the larger, more 'dangerous' conflicts are gradually cooling down, while possibly there are increasing numbers of more disorganised and not state-to-state conflicts notably in Central Asia and in Russia itself. The Ukrainian–Russian conflict – the most serious – has been gradually mollified, and also the Baltic–Russian controversies – with potentially significant impact on the relationship between Russia and the West – have come under control. The biggest military conflict, Nagorno-Karabakh, might finally be on a constructive development including plans for Armenia and Azerbaijan to swap territories to allow for access to the contested enclaves, constitutional creativity for the status of the enclave, and possibly a larger subregional 'stability pact'. Central Asia increasingly gets a subregional pattern of trans- and maybe interstate rivalry even with the potential to settle into a stable pattern of quasi-alliances. Internally in Russia, the big question is whether Chechnya is a forewarning about troubles to come elsewhere in the Federation. Generally, the CIS contains primarily the triangle struggles noted above, with secessionists and Russian interference – not classical interstate among 'the others' (except for Armenia–Azerbaijan and some mutual suspicions in Central Asia related mainly to the potential hegemony of Uzbekistan). Quantitative data on conflicts in the post-Soviet area indicate that since c. 1992, the number of *new* rebellions and protest movements started to decline dramatically (Rubin 1998: 165–70).

On the other hand, the whole RSC is shot through with geopolitical manoeuvring to a degree unseen at the present stage in any other part of the world. The combination of open decisions about alliance choices and therefore constantly shifting patterns, successful meddling in other countries' domestic politics to obtain the desired foreign policy orientation, and geopolitical struggles over natural resources and transportation routes makes both for more geopolitics than anywhere else and for an instability and difficulty of interpretation. In turn, this has effects on the nature of the sources for this chapter, which is, much more than others, based on news reporting and internet documents. The relative youth of the new states and the relative novelty and volatility of the basic situation goes some way towards explaining that there are rather few solid and thorough books, or even articles in major journals, on the subject (but many anthologies that date fast). Although we have not really seen the mooted 'new great game' with the powers *around* Central Asia competing for influence, the region – internal as well as external actors – plays a number of complicated and unstable strategic games that make it highly interesting but also very open.

While some trends can be concluded at the aggregate RSC level, especially in relation to Russian policy, the subregions differ sufficiently that they need to be looked at one by one.

The Baltic states have generally managed to move out of the post-Soviet sphere: not members of the CIS, but expected future members of the EU, and not in principle ruled out as members of NATO. Although in many ways 'lost for Russia' with little doubt as to where the states are ultimately heading, the area is important because it is currently the main locale where Russian and Western 'circles' overlap. In practice, the division between spheres is agreed, although Ukraine could in the future become a serious object of contention. Therefore, some of Moscow's rhetorical posturing around the Baltic states can be read as Russia defending a principle as a political 'forward defence' in relation to Ukraine.

Since analysts of European and ex-Soviet security assume that the Baltic states will make it to the West, there is a tendency already now to analyse them as part of the Western rather than the ex-Soviet system. A more exact picture demands that one look at the actual securitisations. Russian actors (in Russia more than in the Baltic countries) present the Russian minorities as threatened mostly by violations of their human rights. Conversely, Balts presented the minorities, especially in the early independence years, as a fifth column and thus a threat to the Baltic republics. Military security is a Baltic concern, because their situation is untenable in case of a military confrontation. Western aid has generally been cautious and indirect. Russian hardliners present Baltic independence as a security problem for Russia, because it interrupted the line of air defences towards the West, and reconstructing a system is costly. Finally, the entanglement of histories at the macro- (nation-state) and micro- (ownership of land) levels makes for numerous possible conflicts (Joenniemi and Prikulis 1994; Hansen and Heurlin 1998; Forsberg 1998; Sergounin 1998). The level of intensity in the securitisation has lowered compared to the first five years of independence. The Baltic states first securitised a Russian threat intensively both for domestic nation-building reasons and because this seemed to them a way to attract Western support and solidarity. However, they gradually learned that the West wants to be a postmodern polity, orientated towards a different agenda than this old-fashioned one, and therefore for the Balts to present a conflictual image of themselves is counterproductive to membership of the EU. The Balts have therefore gradually downscaled the intensity of securitisation (Joenniemi and Wæver 1997). From the Russian side, the level fluctuates as a reflection mostly of developments in domestic politics. In addition, Russia plays divide-and-rule in relation to the three states. Lithuania is most of the time presented in a positive light and Estonia and Latvia take turns at being criticised.

With de-escalation and even desecuritisation it is quite likely that the Baltic states will edge westwards and eventually join the EU-European RSC. However, a conflict scenario is a possibility and, at the opening of the twenty-first century, the Baltic states *are* in the Russia-centred RSC irrespective of how much they dislike this. A final complication in relation to the Baltic subregion is Kaliningrad, sometimes called the fourth Baltic republic, but a Russian enclave accessible from (the rest of) Russia only via Belarus and either Lithuania or Poland, and home to a large naval base in rapid deterioration. Very little has come of the optimistic scenarios from the first post-Cold War years for a free trade zone and possibly for more autonomy leading to a Hong Kong- or Singapore-like status (Joenniemi and Prawitz 1998). Nor has the complicated situation so far generated major conflicts with Lithuania, although it is obviously a source of continuing worry for both sides (see Jurgaitiené and Wæver 1996; Gricius 1998; Pavlovaite 2000; Trenin 2001: 155–7). Due to Kaliningrad, it will not be a fast and smooth process to 'move' the Baltic states to the West, because a bit of Russia comes along.

The western 'theatre' (Moldova and East Slavic Belarus, Ukraine, and Russia – or 'the new Eastern Europe', the old now being Central Europe) – is both the least and the most security-intense of the four subregions: least because states are more stable and conflicts fewer than in the Caucasus and Central Asia, and most because it is the subregion most important to Russia. Thus, even if security issues are fewer, they are vested with more significance. This is primarily because Ukraine and Belarus raise identity questions for Russia. In contrast to the newly independent states to the south, these states were seen as integral parts of Russia itself and hardly separate nations/nationalities. ('It is a strange Russia that includes Chechnya but excludes Crimea': Vitaly Tretyakov quoted in Trenin 2001: 180.) A second reason is that Europe is Russia's most valued interregional link, and therefore the western CIS states are strategically located. Politically, the subregion contains both the most pro-Russian republic, Belarus, and the leading counterbalancer, Ukraine.

Belarus is of high military strategic importance, located on the main East–West axis and crucial for air defence and connections to Kaliningrad (Trenin 2001: 160–1). In terms of political and societal security, Belarus is a curious case because at least the current leadership does not securitise identity or sovereignty as threatened; in fact, they attempt to give it partly up to a union with Russia. While narrow majorities support the idea of independent statehood and nationhood, the closeness to Russia(ns) is sufficiently deep in the identification that the idea of basing Belarus on close support from Russia is widely supported (Trenin 2001: 162–3; Hjortsø 2002). It is still an open question as to what comes of the plans for the 'Union State' between Belarus and Russia (one that even Yugoslavia tried to join during NATO's attack). Cooperation in defence (not least air defence) is proceeding, Belarus's military doctrine has been geared to the 'common defence space' with Russia (*Monitor* 31 May 2000), and neutrality has been conclusively abandoned. In the economic area, however, integration is much more complicated (at least as long as Belarus lags behind in reforms) because some of the economic schemes would be costly to Russia and allow Belarus to free ride, e.g., printing their own rubles or running a state deficit. By mid-2002, Putin seemed to be rejecting the union scenario, creating confusion in and renewed openness about the future orientation of Belarus (Hjortsø 2002). The relationship is little securitised and more about the joint handling of external security, i.e., cooperating in defence against NATO.

The Ukraine–Russia relationship holds much material for conflict (nuclear weapons, Black Sea navy, naval ports, Crimea, Russian minority, history). During the first years of independence, the situation was often tense and the conflict was seen as the most momentous of all post-Soviet conflicts. Generally, the relationship has stabilised during the mid- to late 1990s. Future conflicts cannot be ruled out because to Russia Ukraine is by far the most important of the ex-Soviet republics.

Future developments partly depend on to what extent the West (EU and/or the USA) becomes a credible alternative to Russia, economically and eventually militarily. With ultimate dependence on Russia, Ukraine can manoeuvre in relation to Russia, but must avoid a political showdown. Ukraine has moved up Western agendas in recent years and, with enlargement of NATO and the EU, the Western factor could begin to make a real difference and offer more of a choice to Ukraine. This, on the other hand, could trigger determined reactions from Russia, as seen e.g. in August 1997 when a NATO exercise in the Ukraine ('Sea Breeze 97') was modified after Russian protests. However, several further exercises have been held. In 1999, Ukraine began to express a clear preference for NATO and non-participation in CIS military structures. Yet, with a domestic political crisis in 2001, Russian–Ukrainian political alignment at the presidential level proved suddenly useful again.

The ultimate security problem is Ukraine's domestic vulnerability and many Russians' reluctance to accept Ukraine's independence. An independent national state exists for the first time since the Middle Ages and a short period after the 1917 revolution. The borders resulting from various more or less bizarre adjustments (such as the anniversary gift of Crimea to Ukraine in 1954) bring together territories with very different state histories and very different attitudes to the idea of an independent Ukraine, from nationalistic Galicia, to Crimea and the southeastern part of the country with a Russian majority (Poulsen-Hansen and Wæver 1996: 232, 239–44 and map on p. 241).

The most likely triggering issue is Crimea, both because it is seen as very Russian by many Russians and because of the important naval base in Sevastopol (Trenin 2001: 165–8). Regulated by agreements on borders and base rights in 1997, issues have been de-dramatised even if disagreements remain, and Ukraine therefore will continue to explore countervailing options like GUUAM and ultimately the West.

Moldova has had two crucial foreign policy issues. First was the wish for 'reunification' with Romania – a wish that faded rather fast. Second came the conflict over Transdniestr with a revolt of local Russians (and Ukrainians). Transdniestr is a textbook case of 'matrioshka nationalism', of nested ethnic identities. When Moldovans started to aim at independent statehood (or, worse, unification with Romania), the non-titular minorities (the previously privileged Russians and Ukrainians in Transdniestr and the Gagauz) reacted by putting forward their own claims for secession. The predominantly Slavic – and ideologically hardline communist – community on the left bank of the Dniestr River appropriated 15 per cent of Moldova's territory. During 1989–92 the conflict claimed hundreds of lives, and ended in non-resolution, whereby Moldova accepted Russia brokering an agreement despite Russia's lack of neutrality as well as a peacekeeping force composed of Russians, Moldovans, and local Transdniestr forces (Brzezinski and Sullivan 1997: 621–45; Tkach 1999). Moldova later protested against the continued presence of Russian troops. The Russian 14th Army drew its forces largely from the local population and often acted relatively independently of Moscow and seemed to be the army of the local Russians.

This illustrates Pavel Baev's general interpretation that 'peacekeeping' has become the new name for conquest – a necessary relabelling in a world (and especially Europe) that does not accept changes of borders by the use of force (Baev 1994, 1996, 1999a). A semi-permanent conquest could remain under the peacekeeping label for a long time. Moldova – in contrast to Azerbaijan and Georgia – has accepted the Russian concept of 'common state' as a solution to enclaves and secessionists, a model that grants much de facto autonomy to the insurgents (and continued Russian influence) (*Monitor* 10 February 2000; dpa 1 March 2002). Moldova seems to have become partially resigned to this fact, but it has simultaneously been party to the construction of the GUUAM group, which signals an intention to be on the countervailing side in the relationship to Russia within CIS.

This western 'theatre' has insufficient coherence to count as a subcomplex. There are few security connections among the three states. Partly, this is because they are at the core of the whole RSC. They are key players in central all-CIS politics: Belarus as Russia's closest ally, and Ukraine and Moldova as leading members of GUUAM and among the countries with closest connections to the West (together with Georgia and Azerbaijan). Generally, most issues have found a relatively stable existence even if they have not been solved. The main risk of major upsets probably stems from the chain effects of NATO enlargement.

The Caucasus, by contrast, does cohere as a subcomplex, and one having two parts. North Caucasus is in the Russian Federation including Chechnya, Dagestan, and five other units and dozens of ethnic groups. South Caucasus consists of Armenia, Azerbaijan, and Georgia and had violent conflicts in Nagorno-Karabakh, Abkhazia, and South Ossetia. The Caucasus is the object of external interest from Turkey, Iran, and the USA, primarily. The two parts of the Caucasus connect most clearly via border-straddling groups such as South Ossetia (in Georgia) and North Ossetia (in Russia).

Should the Caucasus and Central Asia be treated as one region? They share Turkic languages in most countries, Russian as a *lingua franca*, and a common Soviet past with legacies such as infrastructure. Among the differences are political developments, with ex-communists still in power in Central Asia whereas the Caucasus have seen often violent changes of elites (and sometimes back again). Most decisively for an RSC analysis, the two are relatively separate. The Caspian Sea unifies in relation to fish and hydrocarbons, but geopolitically it divides and not much securitisation happens across it (and when finally the dispute over territorial division of the Caspian is resolved, even less will tie the two sides together). The two are distinct subcomplexes (see also Mozaffari 1997).

North Caucasus is an ethnic mosaic with a certain religious radicalisation. 'The ethnic relations in Caucasus are so complicated that the Balkans and Afghanistan become simple and clear in comparison. The most complicated pattern in terms of different ethnic groups is in the republic of Dagestan' (Heradstveit 1993: 108 [our translation]). Should Dagestan – as just one illustration – be destabilised by the competition among ethnic elites or religious mobilisation and spillover from Chechnya (Pain 1999: 183), this would destabilise all of Northern Caucasus, interrupt crucial pipelines, and threaten spillover into Azerbaijan in the form of Lezgin irredentism. In the early 1990s, North Caucasus was interpreted by Russia in terms of a fear of general disintegration of the Federation, but once Yeltsin (who used regionalists as allies) was replaced by Putin (who tightened up) North Caucasus was approached more in its own terms.

Chechnya is in a sense simpler than most of the other conflicts in the area. The Chechens have always fought Russian control and, predictably, the disintegration of the Soviet Union renewed demands for independence. The 1994–5 Russian attempt to quell the uprising by force ended in military fiasco, humanitarian disaster, and an ambiguous compromise (the Khasaviurt Agreement of August 1996). In contrast, the 1999 military intervention was more successful as well as highly popular in Russia. Russian securitisation focused on the risk that Chechnya might become a haven of terrorism and the starting point for an Islamic 'mountainous confederacy' from the Caspian to the Black Sea. Therefore, the second intervention happened with reference to mysterious terror attacks in Russia and alleged instigation of revolt in Dagestan.

South Caucasus (Trans-Caucasus) is defined by a complicated interplay between on the one hand issues internal to the region such as secessionist conflicts especially in Georgia and the Armenia–Azerbaijan conflict over (primarily) Nagorno-Karabakh and on the other hand the issue of alignments out of the region, i.e., Russian involvement in Georgian conflicts and the ability of Armenia and Azerbaijan to obtain support from Russia, Iran, Turkey, or the USA – and at what cost. This ties into the question of energy and pipelines.

Georgia is threatened by both unresolved elements from its 1992–3 civil war, and secession in the three areas that had special status in the Soviet system: Abkhazia, South Ossetia, and Adzharia (Cornell 2002). Russia has exploited these conflicts to impose itself as guarantor of an inconclusive status quo. Abkhazia received support from the 'Confederation of the Mountain Peoples of the Caucasus'. Already in 1989, the smaller nations of North Caucasus tried to recreate a 'North Caucasian Mountain Republic' (as existed in 1921–4) which was to include the Abkhaz Republic with Checheno-Ingushetia, North Ossetia, Kabardino-Balkar, and Karachai-Cherkess all within the Russian Soviet Republic. By 2001, Georgia finally succeeded in achieving agreement in principle on closing down the main Russian bases but with incredibly slow implementation by Russia (Socor 2002) – and not on ending, or multi-lateralising, Russian 'peacekeeping'. In early 2002, US forces assisted

Georgia in fighting Islamic troops linked to both al-Qaeda and Chechen rebels in the Pankisi Gorge.

Nagorno-Karabakh is an area within Azerbaijan predominantly populated by Armenians to which Stalin – after considering joining it to Armenia – gave the status of Autonomous Region within Azerbaijan (Celac 2000; Brzezinski and Sullivan 1997: 597–8). Violent attempts to leave Azerbaijan and join Armenia began in 1987, and in 1994 Russia and Kyrgyzstan brokered a cease-fire which left the Karabakh Armenians in control of the enclave, and Armenia with control of 20 per cent of Azerbaijan including access to the enclave. The area is in a 'tension-filled lull' (Brzezinski and Sullivan 1997: 597). International efforts at resolution are in the hands of the OSCE-designated 'Minsk conference' (Celac 2000). An eventual resolution of the Karabakh conflict is likely to be part of a general 'stability pact' for the Caucasus, which would have to involve not only desecuritisation of economy (pipelines) and ethnicity, but also a settlement of the Nichitivan enclave, possibly by corridor swaps between Armenia and Azerbaijan. Initiatives were put forward by Turkey, Georgia, Armenia, Azerbaijan, the United States, the EU, and Russia around the same time (end of 1999, beginning of 2000; see Celac and Emerson et al. 2000; Coppieters 2000; *Monitor* 27 January, 4 April, 23 June 2000; RFE/RL Caucasus Report 2: 36, 10 September 1999; RFE/RL Extracts 18, 25 January 2000, 25 April, 15 May 2000; Interfax 22 February 2000). Importantly, a corridor swap would connect Turkey to its main ally Azerbaijan, but cut Armenia off from Iran.

In the general pattern of alignments, the most stable element has been the Russo-Armenian de facto alliance. It is traditional Armenian behaviour, as Christians, to seek Russian protection against Muslim neighbours. Changes of leadership in all three Caucasian states have been connected to (attempted) shifts in orientation towards the surrounding powers. Attempts to move Armenia closer to Turkey and thus balance the Russian link led to the fall of Armenia's first president, Petrosian; a similar process took place in Azerbaijan, where President Elchebey was replaced by President Aliev, supported by Russia, who proved disloyal to Russia and took the GUUAM route towards the West. As originally the only one of the Muslim republics to reject Russian frontier guards as well as military bases (Roy 2000: 194), Azerbaijan's problem has been that it did not get the 'usual' rewards from the West. Due to the power of the Armenian lobby in the USA, Azerbaijan has been blacklisted and barred from American support. In the new situation after 11 September, the US government and military have quietly been assisting

Azerbaijan, in order to counter the two challenges of Iranian threats and rising tensions in the Caspian Sea (Blank 2002). The relationship to Iran has traditionally been difficult due to Iranian fear of irredentism in its Azeri north but occasional overtures are made (Yeni Azerbaijan 14 January 2000, translated in RFE/RL 18 January 2000; *Monitor* 24 January 2000; Central Asian Caucasus Analyst 31 July 2002).

Russia has come to recognise the limits of its power and the independence of the existing states without giving up its paramount position in the area. Most important to Russia is probably to secure itself a role in the development and transport of oil and gas, especially Azerbaijan's offshore oil – and to prevent any other external power from gaining a strategic position.

In the longer run the EU could become an important player as enlargement rolls east, but so far the United States is most important and focused on pipelines too. Having cut itself off from Russia, Iran, and (until recently) Azerbaijan at one and the same time, the United States found it impossible to achieve wide-ranging strategic objectives in the region (Wiberg-Jørgensen 1999: 106; see also McKeeby 1999; *Strategic Survey* 1997–9: 27–8; Noreng 2000: 192; Rashid 2002b: 191).

The main prize in the geopolitics of Central Asia and the Caucasus is control of the transportation of oil and gas. For some this is about energy per se (China), for others mostly about the economic implications (the states in the region and to some extent Turkey and Iran, and the oil companies); to others again it is mainly a way to gain influence and/or prevent others from doing so (the USA and Russia, in particular). In Russia, the heads of the two energy monopolies were present at the signing of the new military doctrine in which 'Moscow now views the international battle for control over Caspian Sea oil and gas riches as a point of national security' (AFP 21 April 2000). The struggle is basically about the politics and economics of competing pipeline projects to connect Caspian basin hydrocarbon resources to world markets, whether via Russia and the Black Sea, via the Caucasus and Turkey, via Iran, via Afghanistan, or via Kazakhstan to China. This is a complicated story and, as we write, one far from resolution and too big to recount here (see Giragosian 2000; *Strategic Survey* 1997–8, 1999–2000: 12–15, and 2000–1; Oilonline 10 May 2000; Mann 2001; Rashid 2000, 2002b; Lysenko 2002).

Security in the Caucasus did not turn into a 'new great game'. The relative robustness of the new states has surprised many (*Strategic Survey* 1997–8: 23), and conflicts are now driven primarily by the regional actors themselves. The Caucasus is a complicated mini-complex and repeats its historical insulator functions. Still, Russian influence remains strong and CIS politics the primary arena, so the region continues to be a subcomplex within the post-Soviet RSC.

A peculiar feature, which underlines the current status as subcomplex, is that all of the four main dynamics that tie the Caucasus together have a strong Russian component, while none of them generate very active triangular politics among the three independent states of Southern Caucasus: (1) secessionists in Georgia, (2) the Armenia–Azerbaijan conflict over Karabakh, (3) spillover between North and South Caucasus through the micro-coalition patterns among small ethnic groups, and (4) energy and pipelines.

A possible future as a more fully insulating mini-complex outside the ex-Soviet RSC is signalled by a tentative bipolarised pattern involving both regional states (and secessionists) and external powers (Cornell 2002). Turkey and the USA jointly support Azerbaijan and Georgia, while Russia and Iran support Armenia (and separatist substates within Georgia).

Central Asia

Central Asia could be considered a candidate for a separate RSC (Peimani 1998). In some studies of security regions, it is given its own chapter (sometimes together with the Caucasus, e.g., Schulz et al. 2001). Others have had difficulty deciding as part of which region to treat Central Asia. Is it (as the name seems to indicate) a part of Asia, or a part of the Middle East, maybe a particular 'northern tier' with Turkey, Pakistan, Iran, and Afghanistan (Ragigh-Aghsan 2000)? We classify it as a weak subcomplex whose internal dynamics are still forming and in which the involvement of Russia is strong. After the dissolution of the Soviet Union, expectations were that it would become an arena for a 'new great game', this time with Russia, Turkey, Iran, and maybe China competing for influence. This has happened to a much lesser degree than expected, basically because the difficulties for all parties are bigger than expected and the potential gains smaller (despite oil and gas). Recently, the United States has entered as a main contender.

By Central Asia we refer to the four republics that made up Soviet Central Asia, Turkmenistan, Uzbekistan, Kyrgyzstan, and Tajikistan plus Kazakhstan. The security issues in the region are legion. All states are domestically vulnerable. The ethnic map points to both internal problems and transnational ties, but they have only occasionally been securitised. Real wars have been avoided (in contrast to the Caucasus) and the worst conflict has been Tajikistan's civil war. The amount of conflict is surprisingly low. As noted by Martha Brill Olcott: 'Central Asia has suffered virtually every social ill hyperinflation, rising unemployment, rising death rates, falling birth rates, deteriorating health care, government corruption and crumbling infrastructure which could be expected to increase social tension and so make inter-ethnic violence more likely, yet Central Asia has recorded no large-scale ethnic-based disturbances since 1991' (quoted by Goudie 1996). The main explanation is that Central Asia is a region of both weak states and weak powers. Interaction capacity is low, and the ability of states to engage in classical state-to-state rivalry is limited. Second, national and ethnic identities are weak and have to compete with other identities. This might well become a source of conflicts, but at first it makes the likelihood of straightforward ethnic conflict lower.

Conflicts over interstate boundaries are rare and threaten mostly in relation to the fertile Fergana Valley where a confusing border divides Tajikistan, Kyrgyzstan, and Uzbekistan. Another important boundary question is between Russia and Kazakhstan. 'Kazakhstan is obsessed with the risk that its northern Russian-majority territories might secede' (Roy 2000: 191). In that case, Uzbekistan might even try to grab the remnants (Noreng 2000: 189). To counter this risk, President Nazarbayev has consistently pursued a balanced policy, accommodating the Russians especially in CIS politics while pursuing Kazakhisation domestically. In Roy's summary, Nazarbayev 'wants to hitch the Kazakh wagon to the Russian train, but throw the Russians out of the first class compartment' (Roy 2000: 191). Kazakhstan's border with China is problematic both for boundary delineation and because of secessionism among the Uighurs in China's Xinjiang province (see pp. 431–2). China claims substantial territory in eastern Tajikistan containing gold and other minerals (Rashid 2002b: 87).

In this 'most Soviet' part of the Soviet Union, new boundaries and old infrastructure do not line up, and highways and railroads often cross international borders on domestic journeys. This could lead to cooperation or conflict. The states are Soviet creations and except for Kazakhstan the titular identities were not even related to previous nationalist movements (Roy 2000: 3). Names like 'Uzbeks', 'Kazakhs', and 'Tajiks' had referred to social or military categories or patterns of settlement (sedentary, nomadic, or oases) (Suny 1999–2000: 168–9). Clans are powerful and often cut across borders. Linguistically, the Central Asian peoples blend into each other. 'What distinguishes them most clearly from one another are the Soviet-constructed identities listed in their passports and the Soviet-made republics in which they live' (Suny 1999–2000: 166).

The most violent conflict has been in Tajikistan. A 1990–2 power struggle in the capital triggered a savage war in the south with all the elements familiar from the wars in ex-Yugoslavia (ethnic cleansing, massacres, rape, torture, looting, and summary executions; Roy 2000: 140; Grannes 1993: 47). The conflict was between political parties (neo-communist, Islamic, or democratic) but also among regionalist clans. After the ending of the civil war, Islamists were included in a coalition government, and Tajikistan became an experiment in power-sharing that strongly contrasts with neighbours like Uzbekistan and Kyrgyzstan. However, Islamist radicals in IMU and HT continue to be a source of unrest, and a pretext for both repression and international cooperation among Russia, Tajikistan, and increasingly Uzbekistan.

The region generally struggles with transnational problems such as drug trafficking and religious movements enabled by weak states. Especially Kyrgyzstan, Tajikistan, and Uzbekistan seek to cooperate (with each other, Russia, and increasingly China) to combat 'terrorism' and 'religious extremism'. They are criticised by Western observers for using the threat of 'Islamic fundamentalism' to legitimise anti-democratic procedures, but the foreign policy reorientation of Uzbekistan in 2000 was probably an indication that the worry was serious enough that leaders were willing to pay a price to ensure Russian support. Although not a serious military challenge to the state, both Kyrgyzstan and Uzbekistan are regularly involved in fights and lose many soldiers.

Dependence on Russia has increased to the point at which Tajikistan is de facto a Russian protectorate. The other possibility for dominance is internal: hegemony by Uzbekistan, the most populous country and the one that comes closest to a historical justification for leadership (Olcott 2001a). With Uzbeks in several of the other countries, Uzbekistan has the means for exerting some influence there. Its potential for becoming regional hegemon is hampered by the lack of economic reforms including a non-convertible currency (Olcott 2001; Cutler 2000). Politically, Uzbekistan sought distance from Russia and opted for GUUAM and the West. Dramatic change in mid-2000 led to new defence agreements with Russia. Allegedly this reorientation was due to 'the President's inordinate and indiscriminate fear of Islam and of the Afghan Talibs' (*Monitor* 29 June 2000). Also it was a disappointment that the Americans (who had been signalling a general commitment to balance Russia in the region) turned down an Uzbek request for modernising

Uzbek air defences. However, the Uzbeks might have concluded that achieving a subregional position of hegemony was most likely by co-operating with Russia, so that Russia gets a general presence in the region, while Uzbekistan plays the dominant role within it. The 2001 US re-engagement in Afghanistan might return Uzbekistan to a US orientation and a distancing from Russia. The fall of the Taleban removes some pressure on the regime in Uzbekistan from Islamist radicals, thus reducing the need for Russian assistance. The Americans are suddenly present militarily – in neighbouring Afghanistan; directly in Central Asia, with troops primarily in Uzbekistan and Kyrgyzstan, and with smaller numbers (together with French and Italian troops) in Tajikistan; and with an invitation from Kazakhstan – the first Western troops in Central Asia since Alexander the Great (Peterson 2002; Rashid 2002a: 2). However, the domestic drivers – including Karimov's repressive regime – might be strong enough to keep the Islamists going without the Taleban (*Economist* 10 November 2001: 60; Cutler 2001; ICG 2001b; Rashid 2002b; Olcott 2001b).

Security problems are generally more transnational than interstate in Central Asia. No pattern of amity and enmity has formed among the states, except a traditional suspicion and competition for regional leadership between Uzbekistan and Kazakhstan (potentially intensified by the US support for Uzbekistan). 'Nobody is looking to set up a system of alliances between the republics [of Central Asia]. Relations between them are relatively cool: there are few direct links, particularly as regards air transport; embassies have been slow in opening; and political summits are rare and tend to be a matter of form, despite the signature of technical agreements (customs, visa, etc.)' (Roy 2000: 191). Part of the explanation for the lack of regional security dynamics is the weak military forces possessed by the countries – except Uzbekistan. Thus, the region has elements of the unstructured type – the states are not very state-like, and therefore dynamics form at other levels and the region is relatively open to penetration by external powers.

Of the external powers, Turkey was originally seen as a strong candidate but had to lower its ambitions due to both its own economic difficulties and the lack of enthusiasm in the region for a new big brother (Winrow 2001; Jonson and Allison 2001: 17). However, Turkey, due to the role of Central Asia in domestic identity and politics, is not likely to give up (Kazan 1996; Kazan and Wæver 1994; Wæver 1996b; Kazan 2002). Platforms in language, culture, and the early victory in the 'alphabet war' make Turkey a long-term factor. So far, it is mainly felt in the states in the west of Central Asia, Turkmenistan and Kazakhstan, less in key country Uzbekistan (Jonson and Allison 2001: 17). Iran has not played the missionary role some expected, but religion has been powerful enough for the Sunni–Shi'a divide to prevent the full usage of the Persian language connector especially to Tajiks. As in the first Russian conquests of Caucasus and Central Asia, 'Russia's greatest ally...was the Sunni–Shia conflict' (Johnson 1991: 273). The predominantly Sunni Turks and the Shi'a Persians do not cooperate against the Russians but are more inclined to worry about each other's influence, because the competing Muslim faith is not only a geopolitical but also a religious threat.

Paradoxically, Iran, which many assume to be particularly ideological as an Islamic republic, has turned out to be the most pragmatic actor (Herzig 2001), and increasingly Iranian and Russian interests converge on opposing export of Taleban-like radicalism (IMU), on opposing US pipeline schemes, and, more generally on a quasi-alignment and arms trade because of the USA.

Russia generally has many assets including personal relations. Putin chose, against much criticism, not to protest against the US troops in Central Asia, but he reacted to the impression of a long-term US presence by taking steps towards increased Russian military presence. He has hinted that Russia should reassert a role in patrolling the CIS perimeter, which it gave up for all countries but Tajikistan (Blagov 2002; Najimova 2002). And, more importantly, the CSA substructure within the CIS has decided to set up 'Collective Forces of Rapid Deployment' to repel attacks – presumably by Islamist insurgents – against Central Asian states. The new airbase for this purpose was conspicuously placed in the one country among the CSA members which hosts a US airbase, Kyrgyzstan (Otorbaev 2002). The CIS anti-terrorist centre in Moscow and intelligence cooperation have also become increasingly useful as the Central Asian states prepare for attacks from IMU and related groups. Roeder (1997) argues that Russia wins first of all because it is the only power willing to be cynical enough to support those leaders able to gain power. Increasingly, however, it seems that the United States (re)learns this kind of practice, as witnessed by support for Turkmenistan's lifetime dictator Niyazov (Noreng 2000: 182) and the instrumental logic of the war on terrorism including alignment with Uzbekistan's Karimov. Russia's major weakness is economic and on this basis many experts predict long-term retreat (Jonson and Allison 2001; Jonson 2001; Allison 2001), but Russia's resources in terms of networks and geography should not be underestimated. China has so far mainly been driven defensively by concern for spillover into its Xinjiang province. Economy could make China a stronger factor in the future.

Finally, the position of the United States is the big question. NATO's PfP programme and the strong US promotion of the pipeline option of Baku–Ceyhan (i.e., from Azerbaijan's Caspian coast to Turkey's Mediterranean) were early signs of involvement. After September 2001, the USA moved in with bases in Uzbekistan and Kyrgyzstan and, although it had a quite limited presence with an unclear long-term outlook, this was sufficient to trigger yet another regional realignment centred on Uzbekistan. In the American media and political spheres many have already either pointed out the likelihood of the US bases becoming permanent or argued for this move at least for the medium term (Starr 2001; Hoagland 2002; Schmitt and Dao 2002). Similarly, the wisdom of Putin's acceptance of this US entrance into the region is hotly contested in Moscow. On the other hand, the seemingly certain victory for Baku–Ceyhan has become questioned by the post-Taleban reopening of the Afghanistan option as well as the permanent potential of the Iranian option which is much cheaper and kept out only by American obstruction. The USA immediately faced a difficult dilemma over the possibility that alignment with Central Asia would prop up repressive regimes like Karimov's and thus compromise the alleged opportunity to push for reforms (Olcott 2001b; Rashid 2002a, 2002b, 2002c; Eshanova 2002; Peterson 2002; Karatnycky 2002). The *possibility* of a long-term US role in the region has in itself redefined the terms of politics in the region, although it remains an open question how much the United States will eventually be able to shape the region. Since Central Asian foreign policies are mostly driven by concerns about regime security, it is far from clear that the United States will unequivocally be seen as a less dangerous ally than Russia.

At first sight, Central Asia could be a major problem for RSCT if powers otherwise located in three or four different RSCs were rushing in from all sides. This has not happened. The main external actors have shown surprisingly *low* interest despite oil and pipelines, and now the question is whether Central Asia is an RSC and/or a huge insulator zone, or a subcomplex in the Russia-centred RSC. Our interpretation is that Central Asia is a distinct subcomplex with a possibility of becoming an RSC. If the states in the region consolidate and gain an ability to threaten each other more directly, Russia is gradually weakened, and no other external power steps decisively in, then Central Asia might become an RSC in its own right. If the USA hangs on with a few small bases becoming semi-permanent, this is likely actually to stimulate the formation of an independent RSC because it weakens Russian hegemony while being insufficient to constitute an alternative source of external domination (see Starr 2001). Only in the unlikely case that the USA significantly upgraded its presence in Central Asia could an altogether different scenario open up whereby Central Asia became an arena for an odd mixture of interregional and global rivalry. Much more likely is a subcomplex gradually becoming a separate RSC. If Afghanistan were not already an insulator, this geographically large RSC could play an insulator function. In Central Asia, the geopolitical great game has materialised much less than expected, and less so than in the Caucasus because Turkey and Iran are less active. Instead the subregion has external involvement in more transnational ways including Islamic movements, drugs, and spillover to and from Afghanistan.

Inter-subcomplexes

What makes all of this one RSC? The organisation of CIS itself, but first of all the Russian fulcrum and the beginnings of a countercoalition (GUUAM) cutting across the subregions. Because of the dominance of Russia, whether a counterbalance will be established can be decided only at the level of the whole post-Soviet RSC.

Interregional level

A region located at the heart of the Eurasian landmass will have interregional links in several directions. Europe is the main interregional issue for Russia, although China is also important, and the rivalry to the south ties Russia to Middle Eastern politics. As argued above, Russia is no longer part of the EU-Europe RSC. During the Cold War, the United States became Russia's defining Other and to a large extent it has remained so after the end of the Cold War.

Between Russia and EU-Europe, the main issues have been NATO enlargement, Balkan wars, and the Baltic states.

NATO enlargement on the one hand showed clearly that Russia and the West do not run a shared security system for Europe: this issue was ultimately outside Russia's sphere and it had no veto. On the other hand, the issue became a burden on the relationship and thereby underlined connectivity (Lynch 1999; Dannreuther 1999–2000; Levitin 2000). Direct border-crossing relations between Central Europe and Russia are likely to decrease further with EU enlargement. As the Polish eastern border becomes the outer border of Schengenland, much tighter controls and regulations will be imposed meaning the end of grey businesses which have until now been in the mutual interest of at least the areas close to the border on both sides (Nyberg 1999: 20). The first round of eastern NATO enlargement (decided in 1997) produced a solid anti-Western opinion in Moscow that influences future questions. The improved atmosphere in US–Russian relations since September 2001 due to the war on terrorism weakened Russian reactions to the second round (decided autumn 2002) and led to a strengthening of the 1997 'Permanent Joint Council' which became the NATO–Russia Council in 2002. The Russian economic need for the West will probably be focused on the EU, both because it is Russia's main trading partner, and because its geographical closeness makes the long-term commitment of Europe stronger. The latter is partly based on security reasoning. Especially in Germany, worries about the long-term security effects of developments in Russia produce a deeper commitment to Russia than in the USA (Bahr 1998; Schmidt 1999; Thumann 1999). In Germany, it is often argued that Russia inevitably *is* European and that institutional developments must reflect this reality. Such reasoning implies a supercomplex for a larger Europe.

The controversies over Bosnia and Kosovo were often interpreted as Russian special interests in the Balkans based mostly on the idea of a Slavic Orthodox link. This is often overestimated, and Russians are not generally willing to sacrifice much for the Serbs. They saw support for Serbia as important to gaining acceptance of the principle that Russia should be heard both because it is a global great power (UN Security Council logic) and because it is a European great power (Lynch 1999; see also Levitin 2000; Antonenko 1999–2000; Terpager 2001). The Contact Group is a manifestation of a kind of concert logic that suits the Russians well (see Zelikow 1992; Wæver 1995b), and they still push for their OSCE-based vision of future European security. But increasingly the OSCE (just like the OAS) is a security organisation for two RSCs, EU-Europe and the CIS. These connections point to a weak supercomplex.

The Baltic republics are a very different case from the Balkans. They constitute the biggest problem for the two-separate-RSCs interpretation. They are not part of the CIS, and clearly aspire to the fullest possible membership of the West (EU, NATO, and any other organisation). However, an RSC is not defined by membership of organisations or by agreement on belonging together. On the contrary, the most common way of being tied together is by negative dynamics, i.e., by being each other's security problem. In this respect, the Baltic states do belong to the post-Soviet RSC. They are part of the West for most other purposes, but security-wise they are not. Their main security concern is Russia, and Russians often securitise the Baltic states, especially Baltic treatment of Russian minorities. Interregionally this is probably the most important link between the two RSCs. If the enlargement of the EU and/or NATO continues, it is possible that Ukraine in future will replace the Baltic states in this role.

In Asia, the relation to China has moved from threat to quasi-ally against American unipolarity. Improved Russian–US relations after September 2001 strengthened Russia's position in relation to China, which feared losing out in the triangle. Contrary to many Western expectations, Russia is unlikely to give up this comfortable position in favour of a full swing to the West. The global level recognition/identity question makes the war on terrorism ambiguous. While it improves Russian–US relations and gives some appearance of bilateral importance in the good old Cold War summitry sense, it also reinforces US unilateralism and thus confirms to Russia the need for a counter-unipolarity coalition in which China and Russia are the two leading members. One might expect Russia to be part of the (East) Asian power equation as in numerous considerations on the future relationship between China, Japan, the USA, and Russia as the 'regional great powers', but this has not happened. Russia is not strong enough at present to assert itself in Asia, and the eastern part of the country is so thinly populated and peripheral within Russia that its mere geographical position does not make Russia a major Asian actor. The China connection is on the one hand about local authorities cultivating crossborder cooperation and 'growth regions', Asian-style, and on the other hand a great power relationship oriented at the global level. Already in December 1992 Russia and China agreed to pull most of their troops back 100 kilometres along their common border, and in April 1997 (in addition to agreeing on criticising American world domination) they decided to further reduce troops along their shared border. The Far East is a source of Russian security concerns because of the stark contrast between population figures and growth rates in the Russian Far East and northeastern China, which arouses fears of ultimately losing Siberia (Trenin 2001: 214–20).

Russia and China act jointly in Central Asia. The SCO, originally formed to settle border questions, has now reorientated towards cooperation against terrorism, drugs trafficking, fundamentalism, and separatism. In practice, this is mainly about mutual support for repression of local revolts from Chechnya to Xinjiang. Islamic extremism is blamed for it all, and Afghanistan was singled out as a possible object for action (Abbas 2000). Uzbekistan started to move towards this group (and away from GUUAM) before the American war in Afghanistan changed all calculations. This cooperation is enabled by China's recognition of Russian leadership in Central Asia (Blank 2000; Trenin 2001: 130, 203–4), which China so far sees as the best strategy to ensure stability and thus handle its main concern, Uighur rebels in Xinjiang.

Mongolia has been more truly independent since the end of the Cold War than for several centuries. A nation of two million people on one million square kilometres, squeezed in between two of the world's great powers, China and Russia, Mongolia has notoriously been either occupied or under some form of suzerainty by one of them. China dominated for two centuries until 1921. From 1924 to 1992 it was overlaid by the Soviet Union including (1966–92) Soviet troops stationed in Mongolia (Pavliatenko 1999). Since the early 1990s, Mongolia has been an insulator, maintaining balanced relationships with the two great neighbours and diversifying relations beyond them especially towards the West. In regional terms, Mongolia strives to gain a position in Asia (e.g., to become a member of APEC) (Mongolia, Concept of Foreign Policy n.d.; Rossabi n.d.).

Due to the inadequate demarcation of the border and the movements of the nomadic people, there are routine violations of the borders with Russia and China. Mongolia makes territorial claims on the neighbouring Russian republics of Tuva and Buriatia where the titular nations are ethnically and culturally close to Mongols. This is, however, undramatic as long as transnational traffic can continue due to a lenient Russian border regime that makes the border less felt (Kunadze 1999). In the case of renewed conflict between Russia and China, Mongolia's position would become difficult.

The Russo-Japanese relationship remains deadlocked. Despite numerous attempts to move forward – and reap some of the potential economic benefits of cooperation (Supian and Nosov 1999; Sato et al. 1999) – it has proven impossible to unlock the question of the Kurile Islands. Not only has this relationship changed very little compared to the Cold War, even the Second World War has not formally been ended between the two (see *Monitor* 27 January 2000; Kunadze 1999; Kimura et al. 1999; Trenin 2001: 220–6).

The net Asian result is weak interregional connections.

In the Middle East, 'Russia's two and a half centuries of contiguity with the Middle East, initiated by Catherine the Great, has ended' (Halliday 2000: 218). Although Russia occasionally tries to play a role in the Middle East (e.g., in relation to the Israel–Palestinian peace process), the end of the Cold War basically meant an end to the system of Soviet allies in the region (see ch. 7). The main interregional link now goes via the newly independent republics in the Caucasus and Central Asia. Some of the republics have been strongly influenced by interregional dynamics, especially because of the Taleban in Afghanistan, but also more generally by Iranian and Turkish policy towards the subregions. But since the whole 'great game' has turned out much less intense than expected five to ten years ago, this has become a less powerful factor for Russia and, when external involvement in Central Asia began to be a serious concern for Russia in 2001, this was not for interregional but for global reasons, i.e., US power. The general pattern continues to be that, for Russia, the interregional level is not as important as the three other levels. This is surprising given the basic geopolitical location of Russia at the heart of the large Eurasian landmass.

The global level

The global level is more important than the interregional to Russia. It is a key aim of Russian policy to retain a position as global power, i.e., to secure its global say via the permanent seat in the Security Council and generally to cultivate concert-like (or, even better, bilateral) management patterns with the United States. Membership in the G8 (gradually achieved during 1994–8) was an important step in this direction. Directly, this is about fighting for Russia's place, but more structurally it is about whether the world is multipolar (because then Russia is most likely one of the powers) or it is unipolar. Thus, the overarching foreign policy aim for Russia is increasingly formulated as the need to secure a multipolar world. All the three major doctrine-like documents finalised during 2000 – 'Foreign Policy Concept', 'National Security Concept', and 'Military Doctrine' – refer to this struggle between 'two trends in the world', a unipolar project of domination, unilateralism, and use of military force ('humanitarian intervention') versus a multipolar world order based on international law.

Russia has to uphold an image of itself at the highest level of powerhood, call it superpower or great power. In our terminology, the country at least has to underline that it is a great power (not a regional power) and one with the potential for superpowerdom. This puts pressure on Russia to reproduce the defence appropriate for a superpower, notably the nuclear forces. In Russian defence debate, on one side stand those (like Head of the General Staff Anatoly Kvashnin) who prefer to

433

downgrade nuclear weapons and give priority to conventional forces since this is what Russia needs to deal with its immediate internal and regional needs. On the other side, Defence Minister Igor Sergeyev gives priority to upholding nuclear parity as the main basis for superpowerhood. 'The outcome of this debate will define not just policy, but how Russia views its place in the world. Nuclear weapons constitute less an instrument of war than a measure of Russia's self-image. The debate over them and the way that Moscow constitutes its forces in the coming years will reflect whether Russia intends only to be a great power or whether it aspires, again, to the status of superpower' (Stratfor 2000b).

A closely related choice concerns the American programme for missile defence (MD). The original Russian position was – not surprisingly – strong opposition to this programme that could in the long run question the Russian deterrent and thus nuclear parity. Furthermore, the issue worked well internationally as a campaign issue for those opposed to American 'unipolarity' (Russia, China, India, et al.). During 2001–2, Putin pursued a balanced policy in which de facto tolerance reaped 'rewards' such as a treaty on 'offensive weapons' that was more formalised than preferred by the US defence establishment. On the other hand, Russia did not literally endorse the US withdrawal from the ABM treaty. Russia had an interest in exploring potential cooperation on missile defence because 'rogue states', especially in the Middle East, were at least as much a concern to Russia as to the USA. However, simultaneously, widespread concern in Moscow over MD meant that US actions were closely tracked, particularly regarding the eventual choice of 'architecture' for the system, which will determine its exact military implications for Russia.

MD is one of three military-related areas where President Putin accepted 'retreat' with only modest compensation, the two other being NATO enlargement and American military presence in Central Asia. One scenario for Russia is therefore a repetition of ten years before, when a pro-Western policy failed to generate domestic support; then, when Western 'payment' – both economic and in terms of global position – failed to emerge, Russia shifted to a more critical line.

In general, Russian defence is in serious crisis and in many places literally falling apart. Defence reform is badly needed, but also very difficult to implement due to the interests it will violate. However, Russia is in any case sure to remain a very considerable military power and the West will likely treat Russia as a great power. Only in the case of dramatic disintegration of the country will Russia drop from being a great power

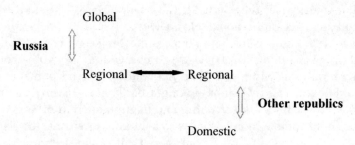

Figure 1. Post-Soviet constellation

to becoming only a regional power. To revive superpowerhood is even more unlikely.

General constellation

To Russia, the most important levels are the regional and the global (and the two are closely linked), whereas to most of the other states in the region the most important are the domestic and the regional. Surely, the domestic level counts for Russia too, but the key axes are those shown in figure 1.

Conclusions

The post-Soviet space is a centred region – around a great power – and part of a weak supercomplex with EU-Europe. Three transformations are possible: (1) a change in the global position of Russia, (2) internal transformation from centred to balanced, (3) external transformation most likely regarding the border to Europe.

(1) To assess a change in the global position of Russia it is necessary more generally to understand the interplay of global, regional, and domestic dynamics in Russian policy. At present, Russian policy is much driven by the aspiration to remain in the global rank, i.e., to avoid falling to regional power status. Thus, questions in the near abroad are defined as a problem in relation to global position. The top-down logic is: because we want to be a global power, we need to control our own region and especially our domestic space. Even more important is the domestic–global link. As shown in the box on pp. 406–8, domestic security in Russia cannot be self-contained but needs external definition either in the near abroad or globally, or probably both. Because of these internal links between the levels, it is unlikely that an intensification of security problems at the domestic or regional level will 'out-compete'

global security (see the South Africa box, pp. 235–8). Should Russia be forced out of its international role, the domestic effects will be dramatic. Conversely, Russia is likely to do the utmost to keep this position.

(2) For something like GUUAM to evolve into a genuine counter-weight to Russia within the CIS is not realistic in terms of material balance. However, coordination among a possibly increasing number of ex-Soviet republics makes control and manipulation from Russia more difficult. In combination with Russia's internal problems, Russian rule may become difficult. Post-Soviet space will remain a centred RSC, but with the centredness under degrees of challenge.

(3) The nature and location of the boundary between CIS and EU-Europe gradually consolidated during the 1990s, and it seemed to be favoured by both sides. However, new policy questions have arisen for Europe. So far it has been an advantage to have separate spheres, but now EU-Europe confronts two problems: (a) it is cut off from influence on Russian behaviour (see the critique of Western governments' inaction on Chechnya) and (b) the prospect of a future rift over the question of Ukraine and EU enlargement. Therefore, seen from EU-Europe it might be advisable to blur dividing lines by upgrading the OSCE and/or producing other all-European institutions.

Conclusions: scenarios for the European supercomplex

Europe consists of two centred RSCs, one centred on the EU, one on Russia. Both are centred on great powers. The EU-dominated one is a security community and its centredness holds high legitimacy in most of its periphery, which to a large extent tries to join the core as members. Russia in contrast dominates its area by more heavy-handed measures and its legitimacy is challenged, although at the elite level (especially in Central Asia) there is a certain voluntary participation in a Russian imperial order. The Balkans is a subcomplex in EU-Europe.

The Balkans is unlikely to change dramatically. More wars might be in store (e.g., in Montenegro, in Macedonia, in or around Albania), and the Balkans will remain a conflictual subcomplex within Europe. It is not likely that the EU can disengage and leave the Balkans as a separate RSC (though the USA is more likely to be able to do so). Nor will conflicts be overcome and political and economic transformations executed with such efficiency that the Balkans soon blends into European normality and stops being distinct.

For the whole European supercomplex, there are three primary questions.

(1) In the *EU-dominated RSC*, it is the general question of European integration. One can imagine a spectrum from the EU cohering further internally and becoming a much more efficient global actor, to something like the current contradictory status quo, or elements of disintegration. Complete fragmentation and renationalisation cannot be ruled out, but are increasingly unlikely. Thus, the complex basically stays centred, a security community, and a great power of (increasing) global relevance. This means continued avoidance of mutual state-to-state securitisation and most likely updated versions of the meta-securitisation about the threat that Europe's past poses to Europe's future.

(2) In the *Russia-centred complex*, the main open question concerns the relationship between Russia and the rest of the post-Soviet space. In pure power terms, the complex will undoubtedly remain unipolar, but it is undecided whether it will operate around a centre holding some general legitimacy or whether it will be a unipolar balance-of-power system. One possibility is that Russia manages to stabilise a truly imperial system with differentiated forms of control tailored to the different kinds of peripheral units. Most of the republics will stay formally independent, but Russia will generally be in control in the whole complex. The opposite scenario is that groups like GUUAM succeed in establishing some kind of counterweight to Russia. Technically, it is hard to see true 'balance', given the Russian ascendancy in terms of economic, military, and organisational power. But it might be possible to impede Russian dominance by a countercoalition. A third prospect is that a systematic countercoalition does not form, but resistance and friction are high enough that Russia does not 'run' the RSC.

(3) A merger *between the two complexes* can be imagined, either through increasing tension and thus (in)security interdependence, or by a strengthening of all-European security institutions and cooperation. The conflictual scenario is hard to imagine in the short term because Russia is both too weak and too preoccupied with problems internally in Russia and in its 'near abroad'. For the long term it cannot be excluded. The cooperative scenario can come about in three possible ways. One is driven by long-term security concerns, i.e., the EU wants to engage Russia more and create an overarching security order to avoid future problems – an argument that is heard most consistently in Germany. Second, popular pressure might make it intolerable to Western leaders to have so little influence on developments in the CIS area. The second war in Chechnya following on the heels of NATO's intervention in Kosovo created a sense in Western Europe of inability to act consistently on its humanitarian and human rights principles. This could create a rationale for a strengthening of pan-European political and security institutions that Russia wants for different reasons. Russia would be consulted more on matters like Kosovo, while higher demands are then put on Russia in cases like Chechnya. The third possibility is that the two grow together as EU enlargement reaches Ukraine and Moldova. Eventually, Russia will be either antagonised or drawn into the process – probably never as a member or serious applicant, but then some other way.

Thus, the current situation in Europe is likely to continue for quite a while – no external transformation, no internal transformation in EU-Europe, and in the CIS different possibilities on a spectrum of degrees of centredness and legitimacy. The primary long-term possibility for qualitative change is a gradual strengthening of the all-European supercomplex, though a full merger remains unlikely.

Part VI
Conclusions

Introduction

In the preceding chapters we have first set out our theory, and then applied it to all regions of the world. We have not been trying to 'test' some single formal relationship of cause and effect. Rather, we have been applying a systematic framework of concepts and expectations to a complicated period of world history. Our aim has been to see whether our concepts and expectations fit well enough into this world history to enable us (and others) to make a general interpretation of the structure of international security as well as specific and comparative interpretations of different regions.

Because we were constantly held in check by people with much deeper expertise than ours about the regions, the most important learning experience for us was in the tension between, on the one hand, our initial ideas about how the empirical material might be decanted into our theoretical containers and, on the other, our growing understanding of the specificity and uniqueness of each individual region. The result of this tension is a set of case studies that are all underpinned by the same set of questions, but whose main plots and themes often differ markedly. While we have tried to compare systematically on a number of dimensions, the individuality of each region demanded that the main synthesising plot(s) for each chapter be allowed to structure how the story was told. Thus the chapters have not proceeded as rigid checklists giving different answers to the same questions, but have focused on the particular points at which the dynamics and contradictions that decide the fate of each region congregate. We hope in this way to have preserved a balance between the presentation of an analytical framework systematic enough to allow for significant crossregional comparison, and the distinctiveness of each regional story.

443

Introduction

This final part of the book contains two chapters reflecting on the preceding analyses. Chapter 14 concludes our empirical enquiry by drawing together the regional and the global levels. It examines the interplay between regions and powers, and the potential for change in the overall structure of global security that emerged after the end of the Cold War. Chapter 15 draws the different regional studies together and explores the potential for comparative conclusions in RSCT. It also considers the validity of our starting assumptions about territoriality and regionality in security, and looks at some of the difficulties and advantages of pursuing this approach.

14 Regions and powers: summing up and looking ahead

Introduction: the structure of international security

In part I we differentiated global from regional level security dynamics, arguing that the best understanding of the structure of global security could be achieved by treating these levels as distinct, and seeing how they played into each other. Within the global level we established a distinction between superpowers and great powers, differentiating both from regional powers. On the basis of this scheme we then unfolded a story whose broad outlines were as follows:

- During the interwar period there was a 3 + 3 global power structure, with Britain, the USA, and the Soviet Union as superpowers, and Germany, Japan, and France as great powers. Africa, the Middle East, and most of Asia remained overlaid by the control of colonial powers, and RSCs were visible only in North and South America, Europe, and Northeast Asia – a total of four.
- During the Cold War/decolonisation period there was a 2 + 3 global power structure, with the USA and the Soviet Union as superpowers, and China, Japan, and the EU becoming great powers, albeit with the EU leaving room for questions about the standing of Britain, France, and Germany as independent players, perhaps only of regional status when taken individually. This period saw many new RSCs form (though the long-standing one in Europe disappeared under overlay) giving the following totals: three in Africa (counting the pre- and proto-complexes), three in Asia, one in South America, one in

North America, none in Europe, and one in the Middle East – a total of ten.

- During the first decade of the post-Cold War period the global power structure shifted to 1 + 4, with only the USA remaining as a superpower, and China, the EU, Japan, and Russia as great powers. There was some mobility in the pattern of RSCs. North and South America stayed much as before, but the meltdown of the Soviet Union meant that two (and for a while almost three) RSCs emerged in Europe. In Asia, the merger of the Northeast and Southeast Asian complexes reduced the total to two. In Africa, the Southern Africa complex expanded into Central Africa, and a Central African RSC emerged raising the number to four. In the Middle East, it was becoming a question as to whether the Maghreb was going to drift away from the core of the regional complex. If we still count the Middle East as one, then the global total in 2001 was eleven.

Thinking ahead we have argued that, at the global level, 1 + 4 remains the most likely structure for at least a couple of decades. A shift to 2 + x depends on either China or the EU being elevated to superpower status, and we share the widely held view that the emergence of a second superpower within the next two decades is unlikely (Kapstein 1999; B. Hansen 2000: 79). More possible is a shift to 0 + x. This could happen slowly if the USA undergoes a long-term relative decline in its material assets in relation to other powers, or quite quickly if the USA decided, as some within it advocate, to give up its superpower role and become a normal great power. Some writers, most notably Wohlforth (1999) and Krauthammer (2001a, 2001b; see also Spiro 2000), are strong advocates of a unipolarist strategy for the USA, and this tendency seems to have been strengthened both by the Bush administration and by the US response to 11 September. Others, most notably Layne (1993, 1997) and Kupchan (1998), and also Waltz (1993a: 61, 75–6; 2000b) and Huntington (1999: 37), have either advocated, or seen as inevitable, a multipolar world with the USA as one pole. This debate suggests that lone superpowers (especially ones favoured by geography as the United States is) are not compelled to securitise their status. If they try to maintain their status (as most of the participants in the debate believe the United States is trying to do), then they generate the necessary securitisation. If they seek to drop out, avoid the dangers of overstretch and free riding (Carpenter 1991; Layne 1997: 96–112), and configure themselves as one great power among several (as many of those just cited have advocated), then more things open up for desecuritisation. Quite a few commentators make the point that the United States is more likely to be driven out of its superpower status by the unwillingness of its citizens to support the role than by the rise of any external challenger (Calleo 1999; Kapstein 1999: 468, 484; Lake 1999: 78; Mastanduno and Kapstein 1999: 14–20; Spiro 2000). This interpretation has probably been weakened by the initial US response to 11 September. The main constraint on such a policy shift, aside from the deeply institutionalised and habituated commitment to being a superpower, is fear that a 0 + x world would not be benign for US interests, and might lead to some other power bidding for the slot of sole superpower.

Lacking our distinction between superpowers and great powers, much of this debate assumes that the USA dropping out of the superpower category would imply 'normal' multipolarity, i.e., a three-, or four-, or five-pole world. This ignores how different a 0 + x world is from such situations. The empty superpower level means first of all that these great powers do not share one homogeneous global arena. Because great powers are multiregional rather than global, probably none will be in contact with all, and most will be insulated from some of the others. Therefore, they do not follow global balance-of-power logic as in classical European multipolarity, where approximately five powers shared one geographical space. Instead, each would be mainly preoccupied by its role in its own and its adjacent RSCs. A second consequence of a 0 + x structure is the likely fear by all great powers that one of them could move into the vacant superpower slot. Working out the internal logic of these global level scenarios is beyond the scope of this book, and has been done elsewhere (Buzan forthcoming). Within either a continuation of 1 + 4, or a shift to 0 + x, the existing pattern and number of RSCs looks fairly stable. Possible changes in several places (Middle East, Africa, East Asia, South America) have been sketched, but the main prospect is for continuation of something fairly close in form to the eleven RSCs that existed at mid-2002.

Casting the international history of the twentieth and early twenty-first century in this way draws attention to two striking points. First is that the number of superpowers has been shrinking steadily. Second is that the number of RSCs rose sharply during the middle of the century and has remained stable. These events are broadly independent. Among the many lines of explanation for decolonisation, the idea that bipolarity as such (as opposed to the unit-level anti-imperialism of the USA and

447

the Soviet Union) was a main cause of decolonisation has not featured conspicuously. What these points suggest is that we have been living in a global security structure defined by regions and powers for more than half a century, and that this structure looks broadly durable. Global level polarity does not in itself cause the formation (or not) of RSCs but, as we have seen in parts II–V, the two levels do play into each other in a variety of significant ways. Bipolarity, for example, generated a particularly intense worldwide pattern of competitive intervention into RSCs. As demonstrated from Afghanistan to Angola, from Korea to Kuwait, and from Egypt to Ethiopia, it is the interplay between the regional and global levels that shapes much of the operational environment and politics of the global security structure.

In this chapter we reflect on the global and regional patterns of security, and the relationship between them, as they stand at the beginning of the twenty-first century. Are the patterns that emerged during the 1990s stable, or are changes underway at either or both levels that could reconfigure the post-Cold War global security order? The next section looks at the interplay of global and regional patterns: how stable are the existing eleven RSCs; and where, if anywhere, are the likely points of structural transformation? The third section considers the outlook for global power polarity, and the relationship between the USA and the great powers.

Regions and powers: the outlook for RSCs

Part of the rationale for this book was that a change in the global level from $2 + 3$ to $1 + 4$ had had a strong effect on the regional level by generally allowing more room for regional security dynamics to operate free from competitive superpower intervention. The effect varied quite a lot from region to region, and that was another rationale for the book: to use RSCT to highlight not only the role of the regional level in security generally, but also the particular distinctiveness of each RSC in its own right. Since we have devoted much space to the evolution and outlook for regions in parts II–V, a short summary will suffice here. The main theme is the diversity of regional security and how this diversity is captured by the framework of RSCT. For any given region, the key security structures and dynamics can be found at different levels and in different sectors, can be of different degrees of openness, and can analytically be more or less amenable to different theories or traditions. Some regions are sedimented into power-political patterns in which constructivist

448

and traditional analysis reach much the same conclusions, and others contain contested securitisations or post-sovereign dynamics that make a constructivist securitisation approach vital. Each of the main RSCs contains an open question or ongoing security dynamic that influences most significantly its future development.

South Asia's strong regional securitisation was reinforced but not much shaped by the Cold War, and was not much affected by the ending of the Cold War. Post-Cold War, South Asia was mainly affected by the '4' element of 1 + 4. Although China had also penetrated South Asia during the Cold War, with the withdrawal of Soviet power from the region and continued US indifference to it, the material position of China was strengthened. While this development increased the likelihood of the Asian supercomplex consolidating into a full Asian RSC, it was not completely matched by securitisation of China in India. In South Asia, the most important question is a potential change in essential structure made up of the synergy of an internal and an external transformation: Pakistan falling behind in its bipolar balancing of India while India moves up to the current interregional level, becoming a factor of importance to China and thereby beginning to play more of a role in the Asian supercomplex. The first round of the 'war against terrorism' pulled the United States strongly into South Asia, but it is too early to tell either whether the US engagement is likely to last, or whether its presence will accelerate South Asian trends (by heating up the internal crises of Pakistan, by solidifying a strategic partnership of democracies with India) or retard them (by bolstering Pakistan and by bringing China into the coalition against terrorism).

In East Asia we have already witnessed the merger of two previously independent RSCs, Southeast Asia and Northeast Asia. This process was mostly about the end of the Cold War and thereby the end of bipolarisation in Southeast Asia, and the rising power of China, which becomes increasingly the centre of a large Asian supercomplex. In East Asia, as in South Asia, the demise of the Soviet Union contributed strongly to the relative empowerment of China, and its move towards the centre of the US debate about possible 'peer competitors'. It also contributed to the emergence of a security regime in Southeast Asia and the merger of the Southeast and Northeast Asian RSCs. The continuation of the strong US link to Japan muted what would otherwise have been the impact of more regionally defined great power dynamic between Japan and China. The US position in the region worked to increase securitisation between it and China, while apparently dampening down securitisations of China elsewhere in the region. China is central but probably not in the near future strong enough to create a centred Asian RSC. Rather it is the main power in a regional balance-of-power system whose operation is strongly affected by the historical and present penetration of an external power, the USA, and by the question of how the US role will unfold in the future. China's centrality primarily works through the widespread expectation that the future of the supercomplex could be unipolar, though this way of thinking too easily discounts the role of Japan.

The Middle East is in some ways strikingly like Asia, a region where strong local conflict dynamics intersect with a powerful US presence and questions about the future of the US role. In this RSC, the effect of the ending of the Cold War was initially dramatic. The shift to a 1 + 4 structure produced a period of unipolar intervention by the USA aimed at a kind of coercive desecuritisation. This made a strong impact on the local distribution of power, boosting Israel, hammering Iraq, and putting all of the former clients of the Soviet Union into a weaker position. The Middle Eastern RSC has undergone some medium-sized changes due to the combined effect of the end of the Cold War, the peace process between Israel and the Palestinians, the Gulf War, and the reactivation of Turkey. These leave open a medium-sized question about whether the Maghreb remains as part of the wider complex, or drifts off to become a periphery of Europe. The pull of the EU and the economic dependence on it of the Maghreb are relatively constant. The pull of the Middle Eastern RSC on the Maghreb varies mainly with the intensity of the Israeli–Palestinian conflict, which at the time of writing looked set to inflict its inflammatory influence on Arab and Islamic politics for many years to come. Overall, there seems to be a huge weight of continuity built into the multiple conflict dynamics of the Middle Eastern RSC, and during the decade following the Second Gulf War the main open question was about the impact of the strong US unilateral presence in two directions – the peace process in the Levant and dual containment in the Gulf. By 2001, both strategies were coming unravelled in their own terms, and the US reaction to 11 September has both intensified its presence and sharpened the contradictions generated by that presence. The seeming failure of both the peace process and dual containment means that this transition period is probably now giving way to the strong internal dynamics of the region. The attacks of 11 September demonstrated starkly how much international security is generated by the specific interplays of regional and global security dynamics, and this cycle could easily enter another round if the United States again invades Iraq.

In Africa, the main impact of the ending of the Cold War was the reduction of external support for the postcolonial state structures – or in some views, accelerated undermining of those structures by the imposition of liberal economic standards and practices designed for strong states and having corrosive effects on weak ones. The ending of the Cold War meant a large withdrawal of superpower interest from Southern Africa and the Horn. Since sub-Saharan Africa, like South America, has no nearby great powers, it too was not much influenced by the '4' element of 1 + 4. Processes of securitisation were driven downward to the domestic level and upward to the global one. Much of the specific character of security in Africa is a product of the paradoxes of the postcolonial state (and more generally about substate issues). Africa is one of the two empirical chapters that do not correspond with a single RSC (the other is the Balkan chapter). Africa is likely to become the home of four RSCs. Southern Africa is the only part of Africa that qualifies without question as a longstanding RSC, and it has extended its boundaries to include a swath of Central Africa. Partly as a result of the same developments, Central Africa is also emerging as an RSC. West Africa and the Horn are proto-complexes. In Africa, the open question is about the formation and evolution of RSCs in a subcontinent dominated by state failure. The interesting condition is the lack of much interest or intervention on the part of the global powers, and the relatively strong roles of IGOs and transnational organisations.

In South America the ending of the Cold War did not have much impact. Since South America is geographically remote from any great powers, its processes of securitisation were very much influenced by the '1' element of 1 + 4, and not much by the '4'. South America has two important themes: the explanation for its low propensity for international war in the twentieth century, and how to understand the US role (and the latter is *not* the explanation for the former, irrespective of how benignly many American theorists are inclined to see the operation of American hegemony; see e.g. Mares 1997; Khalilzad and Lesser 1998; Bobrow 2001). South America is a case of a region that became an independent RSC comparatively early but is a very loosely connected one in which rising interaction capacity has only gradually been overcoming the problems posed by distance. This probably explains why there were so few twentieth-century wars, but increasingly the pressure of lurking conflicts became felt. In the northern part of the

451

continent, this intermingles with a host of transnational security problems focused on the production and transportation of drugs and the
US fight against these to produce a scenario of disintegrating states,
multilayered violence, and increasing US penetration. In the Southern
Cone, in (increasing) contrast, a security regime and regional integration
(Mercosur) formed with the help of joint securitisation of a threat from
economic globalisation and regional integration in other regions of the
world. In addition to the question about the stability of the positive process in the south and of the negative one in the north, an open question
is the future relationship between the two halves of South America. Will
they be held together by chains of securitisation or by overarching regionalism, or will the Andean North drift northwards into some form of
penetration or even overlay by the USA as a result of the war on drugs?
The two Americas have long been linked in a military-political sense by
the Monroe Doctrine and the Organization of American States, and the
proposed Free Trade Area of the Americas would be a way of consolidating this link. These developments do not, at present, look likely to
form a western hemisphere supercomplex, let alone a single RSC of the
Americas.

In North America, the main impact of the ending of the Cold War
was on the United States. The Cold War not only created an unprecedented durable foreign policy commitment of the United States to world
politics, it had also had a thoroughgoing effect on the USA in terms
of identity and political economy (stateness). The central question is,
therefore, how deep the change will be in the nature of the USA as an
international actor. US choices about (de)securitisation are a key factor
in whether a $1 + 4$ or $0 + x$ system will define the global structure of
international security. This raises the importance of the North American
region, usually absent from studies of regional security (because, seen
from the USA, regions just means 'the rest of the world'). If the USA
falls back into its own region, this will be a joint product of both its
regional and global policies. North America was previously interesting
as the main example of a global actor with a durably centred region. To
this is now added the increased salience of other referent objects (race,
local, hemispheric, etc.) and more generally, with the transformation of
the global role of the United States, a reweaving of the relationship between global, regional, and internal, including odd manifestations such
as the 'anti-globalisation' movements in the geographical heartland of
globalisation (Marchand 2001). Two possibly connected questions are
on the one hand the foreign policy question for the USA about grand

strategy, which determines $1 + 4$ versus $0 + x$, and on the other hand the potential for a fragmentation of the country as a security actor due to escalation of domestic and transnational securitisation. The outcome for the US global position is not determined only by a US policy choice, but also by domestic developments and by the *ability* to lead internationally. This will often be a question of the US ability to synchronise the securitisation elsewhere with that domestically, as seen on the issue of missile defence and, since the 11 September attacks, in the attempt to lead a coalition against terrorism. In the short term, this new agenda reduces the likelihood of a domestic revolt against statehood and foreign policy. But it might aggravate the instabilities of a $1 + 4$ world both because the United States attempts to lead but is not keen on doing this in an institutionalised form, and because there are larger gaps between US securitisations and those of its allies and followers.

In Europe, the end of overlay revealed both the centrality of the EU as the main security institution, and the raising of the stakes in the global great power status, or not, of the EU. It also showed the difference between the security community dynamics of Western Europe as compared with conflict formation dynamics in the former Soviet Union and its former empire. For the Central and Southeastern European countries caught in the middle, this contrast defined their whole foreign policy problematique. The demise of the Soviet Union not only removed one of the superpowers, but also created a new RSC. In both Europe and the post-Soviet region, the regional and global levels play strongly into each other because the regional dynamic is responsible for the emergence/reproduction (or not) of a great power.

Europe was the region most fully overlaid during the Cold War, and therefore the end of the Cold War had the most immediate and dramatic effects there. Despite the maintenance of the primary Cold War institutions linking the USA and Europe (NATO, OSCE), and the continued key US role in military-political developments in Europe (Bosnia, Serbia, Kosovo), the relationship is no longer one of overlay. Europe once again has its own distinctive regional security dynamics. For part of the 1990s, Europe had open questions about the number, boundaries, and structure of RSCs. Originally after the end of bipolarity, Russia seemed to be becoming part of a large all-European RSC. Not that the visions for OSCE as all-European collective security system were realistic, but a more informal concert held together a large region of mutual accommodation and partly overlapping organisations. However, from around 1993 a Russia-centred CIS complex and an EU-centred one parted ways, while the Balkans for a while held the potential of drifting off as a third RSC, but was eventually drawn into the EU-European one. The EU-dominated part of Europe is a uniquely interesting instance of a centred RSC being formed without a single power at the centre (much as North America was from the late eighteenth to the late nineteenth century). In the West, regional institutions have to work if the EU is to count as a great power. The formal construction of the EU is therefore a large part of the story; its ability to structure (dominate) the rest of the region (in a friendly way) as well as, to some extent, to emerge as a global actor is another part. The security agenda in post-Cold War Europe is exceedingly complicated and the pattern of different 'new' security issues is the key to the unfolding historical experiment. Central to this is the battle between a few overriding meta-securitisations about the history of Europe. The open question here is precisely about how the internal security dynamics of EU-Europe as an RSC, not least its absorption of the Balkan subcomplex, and the global dynamics about the formation (or not) of the EU as a great power play into each other.

The post-Soviet space is a centred RSC too, but of a partly imposed nature with Russia acting as a more traditional great power, not (like the EU) a post-sovereign formation gaining legitimacy for its central role from non-members. In the east, Russia has to create a centred complex, for if it fails to do so it ends up with the same problem as India, and risks sinking to regional power status. In the post-Soviet case, the open questions are thus on the one hand about the general development of/in Russia, and on the other about the different 'arenas' – Baltic states, western republics, the Caucasus, and Central Asia. The Baltic states are in a complicated situation moving from the post-Soviet RSC towards EU-Europe. The western republics contain both the Russia-leaning integrationist Belarus and the torn and indecisive Ukraine experimenting with counterbalancing and maybe eventually a 'Baltic' route towards the West. Towards the south, both the Caucasus and Central Asia are currently subcomplexes within the RSC with the potential for becoming an increasingly independent mini-complex in the case of Caucasus and an RSC in the case of Central Asia. Both are, on the one hand, in many ways integrated most closely into the CIS, especially in terms of military security. On the other hand, in some respects they play a role as insulator towards the Middle East, China, Turkey, and Afghanistan/South Asia. The main overarching question in the post-Soviet region is whether a countercoalition will form against Russia within the current regional boundaries, whether countries will drift off one by one, or whether

Russia will manage to integrate the region as a centred RSC. This will crucially influence the role Russia can play outside the region. In EU-Europe, the question is about the internal and external consequences of integration, in CIS-Europe about the internal and external consequences of disintegration.

Global level dynamics

In the short term $1 + x$ is likely to remain the security structure at the global level. For the reasons argued above, this makes the United States the most critical player, either in maintaining the $1 + x$ structure or pushing it towards $0 + x$. But it does not all lie in US hands. China is the most likely to challenge US authority, and its behaviour will have a major impact not only on whether $1 + 4$ or $0 + x$ wins out, but also on whether the operation of either structure will tend towards the benign or the malign. That, in turn, gives key elements of choice to Japan, Russia, and India. The nature of US superpowerdom in a $1 + 4$ structure and its strategy for maintaining a $1 + x$ structure hinge crucially on how it relates both to great powers and to regions. The basic pattern is already visible and is likely to remain the dominant one so long as the USA does not abandon, or lose, its superpower status. It might be called a *swing power* strategy, and it depends not only on US power, but also on a specific framework of institutionalisation.

What is remarkable about the US position in Europe, East Asia, and South America (though not the Middle East) is the degree to which its position has become institutionalised through the construction of superregional projects: Atlanticism, Asia-Pacific (or Pacific Rim), and pan-Americanism (Buzan 1998). These projects usually contain a strong mixture of superregional economic integration (or aspirations thereto), and mutual defence and security arrangements, the particular mix varying according to the local circumstances and history. Their attendant labels and rhetorics enable the USA to appear to be an actual member of these regions, rather than just the intervening outside power it is according to our theory, and thus help to desecuritise its role. Interestingly, the USA is not commonly thought of as a *member* of the Middle Eastern RSC (though it would be in Lake and Morgan's theory). But where superregional projects exist, it is quite common for the United States to be thought of, and perhaps to think of itself, as a member of those security regions. In this view, it is part of the Americas, part of the Atlantic community, and an Asia-Pacific power. By seeming to put the

USA *inside* these regions, superregional projects blur the crucial distinction between regional and global level security dynamics, and make them difficult to see from within the United States. This blurring becomes an important tool for the management of the USA's sole superpower position, not least in preventing the emergence of more independent regional integrations that might threaten its influence or its primacy. This is not to deny that these projects have substantial and sometimes positive political effects. But they can also hide the distinction between being a superpower and being a great or regional power.

In our theory, the US role in East Asia, South America, and Europe is comparable to its role in the Middle East – it is an outside global power penetrating into the affairs of a region. The key point in support of our theory is that there can be debates about an outside power withdrawing, or being expelled, from the region concerned. Germany cannot withdraw from Europe, nor Japan from East Asia, nor Brazil from South America. But the USA can remove itself (or be removed) from Europe, East Asia, and South America, and there are regular debates both in the USA and in those regions (and also the Middle East) about the desirability or not of such moves. US superpowerdom is expressed in its ability to act as a swing power, engaged in several regions other than its own but not permanently wedded to any of them, and in principle able to vary the degree and character of its engagement according to its own choice.

Because it has the option to delink from, or reduce the priority of its engagement in, any region except North America, the United States can use threats and inducements of increasing or decreasing its levels of engagement as a means of playing off one region against another. The United States is able to move its attention and favour among East Asia, Europe, and South America. This pattern of behaviour was visible during the Cold War, but was constrained by the overriding need to hold together a common front against the Soviet Union. Now that there is no superpower rival, the US swing strategy is the dominant pattern. Since East Asia and Europe contain all four great powers, the swing option between them is the key to US post-Cold War strategy. These superregions are designed to prevent the consolidation of East Asian and European regions that might shut the United States out, or even develop as global power rivals to it. As Wyatt-Walter (1995: 83–97) notes, this has been perhaps easiest to observe in the GATT/WTO negotiations, where the tactical quality of the United States' shift from globalism to regionalism (NAFTA, FTAA) was an attempt to gain more leverage over the EU and East Asia by playing them off against each other. It is no accident that the strongest US ties are to regions containing great powers. South America is an exception, being only a standard RSC, but qualifies as special because geography makes it the natural regional fallback for the USA. Russia/CIS is an exception in the other direction, containing a great power but *not* being closely tied to the USA. This explains much of the ambivalence and uncertainty in US–Russian relations. Since there is a strong interplay between Russia's fragile great power status and its control over its local region, any US penetration into the CIS is acutely sensitive.

The object of the swing strategy is not for the United States actually to choose one of these regions over the others, but to use the possibility of such a choice to maintain its leverage in all of them. Since each of these regions is dependent on the United States in important ways, it is not impossible to imagine a kind of bidding war among Europe, Latin America, and East Asia to engage US attention and commitment. Mahbubani's (1995) polemic in favour of a new and rising 'Pacific impulse', as against an old and declining Atlantic one, might be seen as an example of just this kind of wooing. Seen in this light, Sheldon W. Simon's (1994: 1063) argument that the United States is becoming a 'normal state' in the Asia-Pacific community, 'neither its hegemon nor its guarantor', is almost wholly wrong. While the United States may be becoming more normal in playing traditional foreign policy games of balance, its overall position is highly exceptional. It is the key partner for many other states both economically and military-politically, and it is the only successful purveyor of 'universal' values.

US engagements in other standard RSCs do not have this core quality and reflect more instrumental concerns. Although the USA is at the moment heavily engaged in the Middle East, that region is peripheral to the swing strategy. The US interest there hinges on its special relationship with Israel and its concerns about oil, and is unlikely to outlast them should those ties weaken. US interest in South Asia is similarly instrumental. The United States has never been heavily engaged in South Asia, and were it not for the issues of nuclear proliferation and international terrorism would have little durable interest there. That, however, could change should China come to be seen by the United States as a global challenger. In that case the latter might well look to India as a major ally, fellow democracy, and potential great power. Africa is almost out of this big picture, and likely to remain so, though even the marginal US engagement there has substantial impacts in the region.

In thinking about the interplay of regions and powers in a $1 + 4$ scenario, it is of course not only the superpower that is important. What the great powers do makes a difference to the political, economic, and strategic operation of the $1 + 4$ system, and even to its sustainability. And for some regions, neighbouring great powers also play leading outside roles. Africa is unique in having not much of either superpower or great power intervention. South America has only superpower intervention. The Middle East has been through a decade of almost exclusive superpower intervention (B. Hansen 2000), but the EU, Russia, and China have been players in the background, and any or all of them could increase their roles, and may well do so in response to, or as part of, the 'war' against terrorism. Everywhere else, great powers are embedded in regions, linking together the regional and global level security dynamics. As already noted, great powers have been prominent as drivers of both interregional level securitisations and boundary changes in RSCs. These regional–global links will be key shapers of both the character and sustainability of a $1 + 4$ system. In EU-Europe the success or not of the EU project determines both the character of the RSC and the viability or not of the EU as a great power. Now that the USA has no need of the EU as a bulwark against the Soviet Union, it is not clear that it is any longer in its interest to support the EU project. This explains the ambivalence in US (de)securitisations towards both the EU and Japan. In CIS-Europe, the success or otherwise of Russia in imposing itself on the successor states to the Soviet Union is crucial to its sustaining or losing its standing as a great power. Central and Southeast Europe, and probably the Baltic states, have escaped Russia's grip, but for the states in the Caucasus and Central Asia, not to mention Belarus and Ukraine, Russia is and will remain the dominant fact of life in security affairs. But neither Russia (because it is too weak) nor the EU (because it is too incoherent politically, and too tied to the USA in many ways) is likely to mount major challenges either within or to the $1 + 4$ order.

If challenges come, they will almost certainly come from Asia (Friedberg 1993–4), where, as noted, China is the great power most obviously placed to affect both its own region and US choices. What China will do depends heavily on how it evolves internally, and there are too many variables in play to allow any certainty of prediction. China could falter economically and politically, succumbing for a time to the many internal contradictions building up from its rapid development; it could therefore fail to fulfil its material aspirations to power. Just as plausibly, it could continue to gather strength. In the latter case, it could become more nationalistic, authoritarian, and assertive, or more liberal, democratic, and cooperative. A scenario of weakening, or one of strength accompanied by more compatibility with the dominant values of international society, would make the management and continuation of a 1 + 4 system easier, and relieve the neighbouring powers (Russia, Japan, and India) of some extremely difficult choices. A scenario of malign strengthening could disrupt the stability of the 1 + 4 structure. It would pose acute problems for Japan, which could hardly avoid either kowtowing to the new Chinese power or becoming the frontline against it. Japan has been capable in the past of making rapid and spectacular internal changes in response to serious outside pressures (middle of the nineteenth century, post-1945), and this talent makes it a more interesting and important variable among the '4' than turn-of-the-century gloom about its prospects might suggest.

If, for the reasons argued above, the USA failed to maintain a 1 + x system, either by giving up the game or by misplaying it, the shift to 0 + x would have several clear consequences for the relationship between the regional and global levels. First, it would intensify US engagement in South America as a now great power USA sought to consolidate 'its' superregion. Second, it would strengthen the possibility that the Asian supercomplex would evolve into a full Asian RSC, merging East and South Asian security dynamics. Much would then hinge on whether Japan sought to balance China or form a condominium with it. Third, and with less certainty, it would expand the engagement of the Eurasian great powers with the Middle East. All of them might get involved in the Gulf in pursuit of oil interests. The EU might also take a larger role in the Maghreb and the Levant to consolidate its sphere of influence. Here the open questions would be about whether the particular US commitments to Israel and to Gulf oil would survive its general retreat from great power roles, and that is difficult to predict. In a 0 + x world, sub-Saharan Africa would probably be even more neglected and be left more free, for better or worse, to evolve largely under the force of its own dynamics than is the case now. Russia seems likely to remain relatively marginal in either scenario though, like Japan, it could face a choice about bandwagoning with or balancing against a rising and assertive China. Russia faces a long struggle with both its internal redevelopment and its role in its immediate near abroad, and is unlikely to have either the resources or the standing

459

to exert much influence on the developments centred in Europe and Asia.

Whichever of these futures lies ahead, the structure of international security will be defined by the interplay of regions and powers. We hope we have demonstrated in this book that RSCT offers a significant tool for analysing and understanding not only the past and present structures of international security, but also, up to a point, the future one.

15 Reflections on conceptualising international security

This chapter reflects on a number of points about regional security complex theory (RSCT) and its application. The first section reconsiders the validity of the two starting assumptions about security that structured this study: territoriality and the regional level. The next section looks at the comparative element of RSCT, drawing together a series of questions that can be asked about all regions, and taking a first cut at some conclusions based on the present exercise. The third section sums up what we think are the advantages of the regionalist approach to security. Finally, the last section sets out some of the problems that arose for us in applying RSCT.

Starting assumptions: territoriality and the regional level of security analysis

When we began this project in 1998, the two starting assumptions that structured it were that territoriality still remained a central feature of international security dynamics, and that the regional level was both generally necessary to any coherent understanding of international security and increasingly important in the post-Cold War world. The logic linking these assumptions was that processes of securitisation would be strongly influenced by the fact that most types of threat travel more easily over short distances than long ones, and that this logic remained strong despite the numerous and well-rehearsed advances in technology that have been shrinking the planet for several centuries. How well have these assumptions stood up, both in general and under the specific challenge of international terrorism manifested since 11 September? Does our territorialist approach not block the view of various non-territorial dynamics that some globalists, and since 11 September much of the public at large, think are the wave of the future?

The theory of regional security complexes is organised around the relative importance of territorially coherent subsystems defined by interlocking patterns of securitisation, but non-territorial security constellations exist too. To get to these, the first step is a general mapping of security by 'levels'; the second is to look for security dynamics that the levels set-up has marginalised. This procedure is not generally problematic. Security dynamics of any sort, whether rhetorical or physical, are usually pretty conspicuous and not easily hidden. If something does not fit into the four-level scheme as global, interregional, regional, or domestic, it ought to show up, as international terrorism has now done. It might still be objected that the whole levels-of-analysis set-up is biased towards the territorial. The classical levels-of-analysis scheme locates things as domestic, state, or international, and thereby makes some transnational phenomena hard to slot in (Walker 1993; see also Buzan et al. 1998: 5–6). In our previous book, we used a category of 'non-territorial subsystemic' when we mapped securitisation (Buzan et al. 1998: 163–93). Therefore, it is reasonable in the present case both to use the general mapping to look out for non-territorial security and to ask separately after this whether there are transnational, global, or subsystemic non-territorial securitisations that have been ignored. One strength of the securitisation approach is that it will certainly pick up non-territorial securitisations.

Before we proceed to summarising the findings region by region, a caveat is called for: when we characterise securitisation as global, interregional, regional, or domestic, this is not a question of the ultimate causes or origins of a given security problem. Globalisation theorists (or neorealists) might very well have a case in many places if they want to argue that security problems that we treat as regional, interregional or domestic are really global in this respect. However, we map how things are securitised: who or what is defined as the (origin of) threats, and whom the actor targets in countermeasures. Thus, we try to track the chains of interaction generated by security action – not the ultimate causes of that which is securitised. When the root is global, the observer might well argue that a real solution can be found only at the global level. But action is always a matter of trying both to reach problems and to set a realistic target and, if it is more manageable to find partners regionally or to select an enemy to blame regionally, then the chains of interaction and interdependence become regional (see Buzan et al. 1998:

44–5). Very often, as we hope we have demonstrated, major processes of securitisation do target the regional level, though that does not make it always and everywhere the dominant level.

An attempt at summarising our region-by-region findings about the relative influence of levels during the 1990s necessarily involves quite high levels of aggregation. The domestic level, for example, might well be high in Pakistan, but only middle for South Asia as a whole. Similarly, in North America the regional level is low for the continental core, but high for Central America and the Caribbean. Ignoring this distortion, and speaking for the regional level as a whole, our argument has been as follows. The regional level takes top spot in South Asia and EU-Europe: in the first case followed by medium influence from the three other levels, whereas in Europe only the interregional is relatively strong and global and domestic are weak. The regional level is strong also in East Asia and the Middle East, where in both cases it has to share the top spot with the global level. In both cases medium strength is achieved by the domestic level as well as by the interregional level in the East Asian case, whereas it is weak in the Middle East. In South America too the regional level is strong, but here the domestic level is equally strong, whereas the combined global/interregional level is of some influence. The two regions where the regional level is clearly surpassed by another level are Africa and North America. In Africa, the domestic level is the most influential, the interregional is weak, and the regional and the global in-between. North America is most influenced by global level securitisation, whereas all the three other levels have some importance but with wide variation between the United States and the other two principal states. In the ex-Soviet region, the interregional level is – surprisingly – the weakest, but all the three others are strong, domestic, regional, and global. In sum, the regional level is commonly found at the high end followed most closely by the global, whereas the interregional seems the weakest, and the domestic in the middle and of most diverging importance.

RSCT demands not that the regional level is the only, or necessarily dominant, one, only that it is always part of the picture. This seems certainly to be the case. The regional level is often the most important, and overall ranks at least as high as the global and domestic levels. 'Global' here primarily means securitisations relating to the United States and/or the main great powers – and, when 'globalisation' is understood as 'Americanisation' or 'Westernisation', it links closely to this dynamic of powers. More surprising to us was that the interregional level shows up quite strongly. In the original theory this was not expected except where the boundaries between existing RSCs were on the brink of breaking down. The main explanation is the spillover effect of great powers, which we incorporated into the theory in part I, and which is sometimes strong enough to create supercomplexes. Securitisation of issues such as migration, drugs, and crime also brings in the interregional level.

Nevertheless, our *regions-and-powers* approach might have marginalised some non-territorial constellations – since 11 September, most obviously international terrorism. There are global issues (economic for instance) and there are security issues that create constellations of a non-territorial nature. How, for example, do globalisation, global warming, transnational crime, and 'international' terrorism fit into our scheme? In particular, how much of such issues can be understood within the levels scheme, as an interplay between the global and regional levels, and how much is genuinely transnational or non-territorial?

Globalisation – Globalisation is securitised as a threat by a wide variety of actors from states through to a range of activist groups and INGOs. As suggested in chapter 1, however, the threat from globalisation as defined by these actors often runs closely parallel with the threat from alleged unipolarity, and stimulates and intensifies a number of security problems that materialise as local or regional. As noted in part I it is widely accepted that resistance to globalisation often takes territorial forms, and therefore there is no contradiction in globalisation enhancing the territorial propensity in security dynamics. Related to this is the way in which identity politics are also often tied to territory. Deregulation and liberalisation enable easier trade in weapons and war-related resources, but this does not mean that actors target 'globalisation' or 'deregulation' as the threat – more likely they concentrate their worries on the actor who has come into possession of some threatening capability. Indeed, it might be argued that neoliberal globalisation is the source of a large part of especially (but not only) the non-traditional security problems, i.e., the spread of security to new sectors (Buzan and Wæver 1998). Thus, much of what we have already mapped in this book is linked to globalisation without globalisation as such appearing directly as the securitised threat.

However, there are also forms of deterritorialisation that become securitised precisely as a result of globalisation. Cha argues that the direct link is characterised by situations in which 'the basic transaction processes engendered by globalisation – instantaneous communication and transportation, exchanges of information and technology, flow of capital – catalyse certain dangerous phenomena or empower certain groups in ways unimagined previously' (Cha 2000: 394). He gives disease as an example of the link between globalisation and security: 'For example, the re-emergence of tuberculosis and malaria as health hazards has been related to the development of resistant strains in the South (because of black-market abuses of inoculation treatments), which then re-entered the developed North through human mobility' (Cha 2000: 394, n. 11). Turbulent flows of capital within the international financial system are another example. Some of these new threats are actually widely perceived as related to globalisation, and the relevant processes and actors are securitised in these terms – although most often with difficulty because when 'globalisation' as such is cast as the threat it does not so easily produce either a clear target or an obvious policy option. It is easier to securitise the United States than some amorphous set of global forces.

Global warming – It is an illusion (a nice sounding but ultimately false slogan) that environmental problems generally are global, that they show the limits of the nation-state because they respect no frontiers. Most environmental problems are heavily shaped by geography, and are often local (e.g., a polluted lake, river, or piece of land) or at most regional (air pollution drifting across borders – but not across the globe). A few – very high-profile – cases of securitised environmental issues are global or at least transregional: the depletion of the ozone layer and global warming (climate change). These are global in the sense that they are responded to by negotiations among all states where all become more or less dependent on each other. In another sense, global warming is interesting for producing distinct subgroups with shared interests and mutual dependence but along non-regional lines (yet shaped by geography): e.g., AOSIS, the Alliance of Small Island States, is a group of states with shared interests – they would more or less disappear with rising sea levels, but they are spread across the globe. As yet, however, and despite considerable help from Hollywood, global warming and other global environmental threats (such as asteroids and comets crashing into the earth) have not been successfully securitised. They are certainly on the political agenda, but are not yet widely seen as first-priority existential threats demanding emergency action.

Transnational organised crime – Although transnational drugs mafias have a long history, organised crime has in recent years taken increasingly international shape. Much of this is regional because it takes a network character, and much of its business is land-based, such as smuggling drugs, people, or arms across borders, and therefore distance matters – this is *ceteris paribus* easier over short than long distances. Accordingly, right after the fall of communism, the Russian mafia started challenging the Italian in much of Europe, only to be followed by Albanians stronger on the crucial capital in this business: ruthlessness. A decade later, however, the scene is gradually shifting from a regional set-up to an increasingly global one, where the Japanese and Chinese organisations penetrate Europe, and various kinds of smuggling (of drugs, migrants, women, guns) and money laundering take on a more global scale. Transnational crime is substantially deterritorialised but, although it has achieved standing as a political issue, it is not yet generally securitised (Shelley 1995; Viano 1999; Mandel 1999; Williams 2001) in this global respect. In analyses of particularly troubled (sub)regions like the Andean and the Balkans, it has become increasingly common to point to organised crime as a key security problem (Corpora 2002; Hansen 2002), but then again it is on a (sub)regional scale, not global.

International terrorism – Since 11 September 2001 international terrorism has vaulted high on to the security agenda. In many of its organisational aspects, such terrorism shares the transnational qualities of organised crime: network structures that penetrate through and around both state structures and the patterns of regional and global security. Its new and incredibly ruthless methods of suicide attacks seem, *inter alia*, purpose-designed to dissolve our key assumption that the transmission of threats (especially threats of force) is generally and closely linked to distance. Yet, also like organised criminals, 'international' terrorists often have territorial 'home' bases. Distinct from crime, the agenda of terrorists is often closely locked into both domestic (e.g., Irish, Basque/Spanish, Israeli, Afghan) and/or regional (e.g., Middle Eastern) politics, and the links between those levels and the global one. Despite the transnational quality of its methods and organisation, bin Laden's al-Qaeda network is intimately tied into the dynamics of the Middle Eastern RSC, and the interplay of those dynamics with the global level. Although there may well be a kind of globalist element in al-Qaeda's securitisation (a resistance of the worldwide faithful against the global cultural assault of capitalism), this does not seem to be the main motive. Much more prominent in their discourses of securitisation are the placement of US forces in the 'holy land' of Saudi Arabia and US backing for Israel (generally, as a 'crusader' invasion of Islamic territory; specifically, as the oppressor of the Palestinians). Thus while al-Qaeda manifests itself as a deterritorialised, transnational player, neither its existence, its operation, nor its motives can be understood without close reference to both the regional structures of security and the interplay of these with the global level, which have been the main feature of our analysis. International terrorism of the type, and on the scale, unleashed since 11 September does unquestionably strengthen the non-territorial aspect of security. But it is not separable from the main territorial dynamics, and it is nowhere close to replacing them as the prime structuring principle of international security. Its biggest impact may well be to change not only the security dynamics within the Middle Eastern and South Asian RSCs, but also the relationship of both of these to the United States, and the relationship of the United States to the other great powers. That would be no mean accomplishment, but it would amount to changes *within* the underlying territorial structure of international security, not a transformation *of* it.

In what is widely seen as an age of globalisation, it might be true that non-territorial security problems are of increasing importance. It might also be true that the perception of such an increase is more characteristic of postmodern regions (and thus part of what defines them as regions) than it is of many other parts of the world in which the more traditional security agenda remains dominant. We believe that our survey of world security dynamics has shown that, as of the early twenty-first century, any trend towards globalisation starts out from a situation in which territorial security dynamics are still greatly dominant. Thus, we are – even with a possible trend towards increased securitisation along non-territorial lines – firmly within a situation where a largely territorial (and in practice often regional) structuration shapes most security affairs. This is not a situation that can be assumed dogmatically or deductively. In the end it is an empirical question, and our basic set-up is open to the finding of primarily non-territorial security. Empirically, such a shift to a dominantly deterritorialised dynamic of security does not seem likely to happen for some decades, if ever. Analytically, although some things do not fit easily within the levels scheme, we believe that the matrix of sectors and levels plus the visibility of securitising processes ensures that nothing significant gets ignored (see arguments in Buzan and Little 2000: 68–89 on how putting sectors and levels together removes a lot of the objections of transnationalists and others to levels approaches). It will also be interesting to see whether many of the non-territorial security dynamics do crystallise out as a new conceptualisation of the global level, or whether they get largely subsumed into the still dominant territorial framework. Thus we remain confident that the assumptions in our theory about the importance of territory and region in the processes of securitisation remain broadly valid.

Comparing regions

A major purpose of RSCT is to enable comparative regional studies. This has proven difficult in the past. On the one hand area specialists, on whose work we have drawn heavily, tend to emphasise the uniqueness of their region, often taking a cultural view of what defines it, and being interested in many things other than security. They thus tend to reject or ignore the relevance of (strict) comparison or shared frameworks. On the other hand most theories with a global reach and systematising aspirations have been obsessed with the global level. Consequently the regional level in security has been neither adequately conceptualised nor sufficiently taken into account as a distinct element in the seamless web of global politics. B. Hansen (2000: 9), for example, approaches the Middle East as an international subsystem where 'Subsystem merely conceptualises a part of the international system which is selected for research purposes.' The attitude that regions are arbitrary constructions is reinforced by the media's creation of 'regions' ('arc of crisis' and suchlike) as a way of packaging any newsworthy conflict. With this perspective, the world has potentially hundreds of overlapping regions to compare – an impossible agenda. By our distinction between regional and global level, our focus on self-defining regional dynamics, and our concomitant insistence on mutually exclusive regions, we have produced a limited number of regions that can in principle be compared. And in relation to the first dichotomy between uniqueness and generalisation, we assume that, whatever their differences, regions are fundamentally comparable in terms of the elements of basic structure. They can thus be classified into types for purposes of comparison, and studied with the same theory across space and time. In this section, we take a first cut at sketching out the possibilities for comparison.

To understand regional security with comparative depth will be important to both theory and policy-making. To theory it is important because the regional level is little theorised and, if we are even half-right in our ideas, then this shortcoming seriously compromises security theory as a whole. For example, the domino theory which drove some Cold War interventions would have been much more difficult to sustain if something like RSCT had already raised awareness of how significant regional level factors can be. The possibility of systematic comparison across space and time should also act as a safeguard against hasty adoption of assumptions that ideas that work in one place (regional integration, domino theory) will necessarily work in another. These points are relevant for policy-makers as well. Comparisons between regions are in practice made, and often play a role, politically, but their basis is often problematic. For instance, growth in European integration both in the 1950s–60s and in the 1980s–90s stimulated efforts to emulate it in other regions but often without a clear understanding of where this would be possible or not. Similarly, regional security organisations like the OSCE have been an inspiration in several regions (Adler 1998). These examples relate to efforts at institution-building, but the negative side – i.e., experiences with escalation and disintegration – could be relevant in other regions. Domino theory, for example, might have implications in centred complexes that cannot be transferred to standard RSCs, and vice versa.

A third category of lessons has to do with the policy of external powers getting involved in a region. Several analyses (Lomperis 1996; Lowenthal 1979; Leffler 1992: 374–83) have shown how policy mistakes of the superpowers during the Cold War arose from an incorrect (or rather no) regional reading of the situation, e.g., the USA in Vietnam, the USSR in Afghanistan, and both in several African engagements. The superpowers tended to interpret the world as a seamless (global) web and thus ignored or discounted the existence of a distinct regional level. If the regional level is anything like as important as we argue it is, then actors neither outside nor inside a region can formulate soundly based policy without taking the specificities of the regional dynamics into account. This is true regardless of whether the policy aim is balance-of-power or building regional orders.

For any given comparison of RSCs, the following questions must be addressed:

1. Where should the regions be placed on a spectrum from conflict formation (balance-of-power system) through security regime to security community?
2. What type of regions is one comparing: overlaid, unstructured, pre- and proto-complexes, or RSCs? And if RSCs, then standard, centred, or great power?
3. What is/are the dominant unit(s) among which the dynamics of (de)securitisation occur?

4. What is/are the dominant sectors driving the dynamics of (de)securitisation?
5. What is/are the dominant level(s) on which the dynamics of (de)securitisation occur?
6. How stable are the essential structures (anarchy, polarity, amity–enmity, boundaries) and dynamics that define the RSCs, and what are the sources of these (in)stabilities? What do we learn about patterns of interregional interaction and the probability of it leading to external transformation?
7. What is the influence of history, particularly the legacy of state formation? Is there a historical pattern of development common to several RSCs: i.e., decolonisation to conflict formation to security regime?
8. What is the relationship between global and regional level dynamics (and, for contemporary cases, did we learn anything systematic about this from the ending of the Cold War)?

Questions 1–4, 6, and 7 are answered below. Question 5 was addressed in the previous section (p. 463), and question 8 was taken up in chapter 14.

We have already made many comparisons along the way to inform the case studies. For example, it has been useful to have Africa as a fairly extreme case of nonstate actors, because it heightens one's awareness of similar but less dominant cases elsewhere (e.g., Colombia, South Asia, Balkans, Middle East). And the consistent pattern of asymmetry between India and China has made visible the kind of relationship between an RSC with a great power and one with only regional powers, and made us attentive to it elsewhere (USA/South America; EU/Maghreb). Other structural comparisons have been possible between regions with strong penetration by the global level (Asia, Europe, Middle East), and the shift of that penetration from two superpowers to one. And we were able to think about one of Russia's future possibilities by reference to India as a regional power prevented from reaching great power standing because of its inability to transcend its regional conflicts. Along another dimension, the Middle East is the clearest illustration from recent history of a region shaped by the competition between nation-state logic and different pan-regional identities (Arabism and Islamism), and it has helped illustrate the emerging dynamics in Europe (with national and European identities) and attempts at pan-hemispheric identity in the

Americas. In the rest of this section we review the remaining questions of comparison more systematically.

Where should the regions be placed on a spectrum from conflict formation through security regime to security community?

Conflict formations are found in South Asia, the Middle East, most of Africa, and in some sense the CIS. East Asia is a conflict formation with elements of security regime mixed in. The two clear examples of security regimes are South America – and here only the Southern Cone, which might in turn be heading further towards security community – and ASEAN in Southeast Asia, though ASEAN's prospects have taken a severe knock since the economic crisis of 1997. The present security communities (where states of the region can no longer imagine war among themselves) are North America, EU-Europe, and increasingly the Southern Cone. The CIS is again complicated: an odd mix of security regime, conflict formation, and an attempt to install a hegemonic regime.

On this question there are some potentially useful synergies between Alex Wendt's constructivist scheme for looking at social structures and RSCT. In the light of our survey what can be said about Wendt's claim that his ideas also work for RSCs? Recall the two elements of Wendt's scheme: first, that anarchies will fall into one of three types of social structure (Hobbesian = enemy relations; Lockean = rivalry within some rules; and Kantian = friendly relations and strong restraints on war); and, second, that these social structures can vary in their depth and mode of internalisation from shallow (coerced) through middling (calculations of immediate self-interest) to deep (ideas accepted as legitimate). The degrees/modes of internalisation can be applied to any of the three social structures, and Wendt (1999: 247) assumes that any system (or subsystem) will have a dominant form of social structure. We broadly agree with him that this type of scheme can be applied to regional subsystems, including RSCs.

We could quibble about how Wendt defines his three types of social structure, but the interesting point is to see how the assumption that there is a clearly dominant social structure stands up. Such an assumption is also implicit in our spectrum of conflict formation, security regime, security community. The Middle East poses an immediate challenge to Wendt's formulation: some of its main relations are broadly Lockean, but others are clearly Hobbesian. Absolute hostility to Israel is easy to find in much of the region, and the attitude of Saddam Hussein toward Kuwait, and earlier Iran, is hard to distinguish from Hobbes, as, increasingly, is Israel's attitude towards the Palestinians. To classify this RSC as dominantly either Hobbesian *or* Lockean is quite problematic, whereas it is not problematic to label it a conflict formation. A similar problem arises in South Asia, where it is far from clear whether the India–Pakistan relationship is Hobbesian or Lockean; and also in Africa, where the social structures are so fragmented that it is hard to identify a dominant line. It would be misleading to call much of Africa either Hobbesian or Lockean – it contains both qualities mixed together. In other places, Wendt's scheme works fairly clearly: North America and EU-Europe are Kantian, the CIS, South America, and East Asia broadly Lockean.

Potentially more useful, though needing more space than we can give it here, is Wendt's insight into the depth and mode of internalisation of the social structure. A case could be made, for example, that many of the Hobbesian securitisations that centre around religious and/or ethnic divisions are deeply internalised and legitimate in the eyes of a majority of the people involved (Israel vs Arabs/Muslims, Tutsi vs Hutu, India vs Pakistan, north vs south in Sudan, Islamic extremists vs the USA, etc.). It also seems safe to say that the Kantian social structures in EU-Europe and the North American core are deeply internalised and legitimate. Questions can be asked, however, about how deeply internalised apparently Lockean social structures are in Asia, South America, the Middle East, and the CIS. It would be difficult to argue that internalisation is deep. At best it is probably instrumental and calculated, and at worst coerced by dominant Western power. If Lockean social structures in many places are, in effect, held in place by the dominant power of the West, then this has disturbing implications about the consequences of either a relative decline in Western power, or an abdication of US leadership of the type discussed in chapter 14.

What type of regions is one comparing: overlaid, unstructured, pre- and proto-complexes, or security complexes? And if RSCs, then standard, centred, or great power?

Overlay has been a prominent feature of the structure of international security for the last several centuries. But the ending of the Cold War removed the last overlaid regions from the international system, with only vestiges of heavy penetration remaining within some regions (North America, CIS, East Asia). Unstructured regions are also in retreat. In its pure form, this condition no longer exists, though parts of Africa and possibly Central Asia are pre- or proto-complexes. Thus, we are close to a situation in which all of the world is made up of RSCs. Of the eleven main RSCs (including pre- and proto-complexes) that currently comprise the regional structure of global security, three are clearly centred (North America, the CIS, and EU-Europe), one is a great power complex (East Asia), and seven are standard RSCs containing no global level powers (South America – with apologies to Brazil, Middle East, Horn, West Africa, Central Africa, Southern Africa, and South Asia – against Indian protests). Most great powers are at the centre of their own RSC where classical balance-of-power dynamics are therefore suppressed. The one exception to this pattern is East Asia, where two great powers are involved not only in regional power balancing and securitisation, but also at the global level. The link between global powers and centred RSCs is hardly surprising. It is easier to become a global power if one can draw on as much as possible of the resources of a region and avoid spending effort on handling regional security and power balancing. And, conversely, being involved in regional rivalry usually prevents a regional power from lifting itself to the global level.

In centred RSCs no classical balance-of-power dynamics are active. Within that rule, the three centred complexes display a range of possibilities. North America is centred on a superpower, EU-Europe on institutions, and CIS on a great power. North America and EU-Europe both have high levels of legitimacy and look stable. CIS is centred mostly by Russian power and the stationing of troops, and the question of legitimacy is still much more up in the air. It is not difficult to imagine the CIS shifting towards being a standard RSC should Russia's relative power decline sufficiently to bring its great power status into question. In East Asia, centring would require a Sino-Japanese condominium, of which there is so far little sign.

The seven standard RSCs also cover a range of variations. In terms of amity–enmity, it is revealing that none are (yet) security communities. Four are clearly conflict formations (Middle East, Horn, Central Africa, South Asia); one (South America) is a security regime showing possibilities (mainly in the Southern Cone) for becoming a security community; and the other two (West and Southern Africa) display elements of both conflict formation and security regime with no decisive development either way. In terms of polarity, four are clearly multipolar (Middle East, Horn, Central Africa, South America), but the other three are all unipolar or close to it. South Asia looks like the CIS in reverse gear: India seeming close to achieving unipolarity and Russia in some danger of losing it. South and West Africa are clearly unipolar in the sense that Nigeria and South Africa are hugely more powerful than any other regional actor, neither having a challenger of the weight that Pakistan poses to India. Despite being unipolar, none of these regions qualifies as centred, notwithstanding some efforts on the part of the leading power to make them so. India has pursued a typical great power model of centring, whereas South Africa and Nigeria have tried to operate more through institutions, but none has succeeded in overcoming balance-of-power dynamics within its RSC. Although we kept open in chapter 3 the theoretical possibility of an RSC centred on a regional power, we have no cases of it. Yet it does not seem ruled out. India could make South Asia centred, though if it did so the result would probably be to elevate India to great power standing. South Africa and Nigeria could at some future point centre their regions, though in neither case would this qualify them as global level great powers.

These general classifications are important for two reasons. First, the current picture is in itself interesting. The centred type is more relevant than usually imagined – and seemingly of increasing importance. Note how it is practically absent from the 'ladder' of security orders which is Lake and Morgan's (1997c) dependent variable. Morgan (1997: 33–4) makes an attempt to handle the centred situation in the post-Soviet region, but it is done through an odd variation on balance-of-power redefined as 'power restrains power', and does not really grasp the specificity of the situation. Nor does it explore the parallels and differences between centred formations with legitimacy (North America and the EU – seen as security communities) and unipolar ones with weak legitimacy such as the CIS. In most classical typologies of security orders, there is no room for 'centred regions' that hold legitimacy among the non-dominant units and/or are driven by global dynamics – at best there is a slot for pure power-based hegemony seen as imposed. This is a Eurocentric preference for sovereign equality systems (*anarchophilia*, Buzan and Little 2000: 21), and amounts to defining most of the world, most of the time, as anomalous. If we take a less moralistic, more empirical approach, centred orders should be taken more seriously (Watson 1992, 1997). They are often stable, they can be legitimate, and in an important way they connect the regional and the global level because becoming the centre of a region and becoming a global actor often go hand in hand (Wæver 1997c). The interpretation of the 'new world order' that flows from the current study will have to include such regional orders as of equal standing to the traditional security orders built on equality: collective security, alliance, concert, regime, or community (Wæver 2000a).

Second, the distribution of the different forms and their possible connection to other factors must be explored. On the face of it, achieving a security community looks difficult in an RSC that is not centred in some way. In some cases, the power factor (regional polarity) is obviously the starting point for any explanation: Russia, South Africa, Nigeria, and the USA are so dominant in their regions that a unipolar or centred development is most likely. However, the EU situation as well as the historical formation of the USA point to another possibility. No power was dominant in those cases, but the existing powers wanted a centred region and therefore they created a centre, which increasingly became in itself the power to play an extra-regional role. The latter situation points to the argument made by Watson (1992, 1997) that a degree of centredness in a region can carry significant legitimacy. It is a presumption of much IR theory that all states and nations strive equally for independence. But historically, and as we show currently, a more centred arrangement holds higher legitimacy in some important cases. In EU-Europe, this is an independent explanatory factor of strong standing. In the Middle East, on the other hand, the legitimacy of centredness is waning as pan-ideologies (Arabism and Islamism) decline relative to the legitimacy of the sovereign 'nation' state (Barnett 1998). Also in North America the variable of Watsonian legitimacy changes, and in this case it even varies regarding the degrees of centredness that carry legitimacy within an existing state. The Cold War had imposed a degree of stateness on the USA that had not traditionally been accepted in American political and popular thinking, and therefore there were indications after the Cold War – and until 11 September – of decreasing acceptance of centralisation.

Also worth noting under this heading is that many – increasingly many – RSCs have distinct subcomplexes within them. Europe has the Balkans. South America has the Andean North versus the Southern Cone. North America has Central America. East Asia has Southeast and Northeast Asia. The Middle East has the Levant, the Gulf, and the Maghreb. Often there is an element of core–periphery to this arrangement, with a major centre of gravity (EU, continental North America) and a relatively minor appendix (Balkans, Central America). The Middle East is at the opposite extreme, being constructed by two major and equal subcomplexes and a third minor one.

What is/are the dominant unit(s) among which the dynamics of (de)securitisation occur?

RSCT allows for units other than states, but states nevertheless remain de facto at the centre of much of the structure of global security. The strongly state-based regions are East Asia, South Asia, increasingly the Middle East, and (parts of) Latin America, while other actors and identities play a larger role in Africa, North America, and especially Europe, and did also for some decades in the Middle East. In the post-Soviet RSC, there are political formats competing at different levels, but the pan-regional one is undisguised imperial Russian policy, which does not invite most of the other states (except Belarus) to surrender themselves to it. Thus, the region comes closer to the state-based end. Does the degree of state-centrism correlate with conflictuality? No, it is possible to say neither that the more state-based, the more conflictual (as expected by some liberals and most critical approaches), nor that the state-based are the most stable (as expected by many realists). In the Middle East and Latin America, the growing concentration on stronger states is part of stabilisation while, in East Asia, the parallel with a nineteenth-century state-based balance-of-power dynamic is not comforting. By contrast, the state is being somewhat hollowed out both in relatively peaceful Europe and North America, and in a different way in much less stable Africa. Ironically, one of the most likely impacts of 11 September will be to strengthen the state in those areas where it was most under siege from the forces of postmodernity. Regional security is not a question of states versus other units, but of what kind of relations these units – states and/or others – form among themselves.

What is/are the dominant sector(s) driving the dynamics of (de)securitisation?

In terms of sectors, a rough summary says: South Asia – military-political with some recent impact from economic globalisation; East Asia – military-political although many in the region claim an economic interpretation; Middle East and post-Soviet – military-political; Africa – political and societal, with major arguments around the role of the economic sector; South America – Southern Cone, political and economic, and Andean North, military, political, economic, and societal; North America – political, societal, and economic, plus military dynamics for the USA as a global actor; Europe – political and societal. There is still a lot of the traditional military-political security agenda in the system, though there is also quite a bit of economic and societal, and some environmental. In the sense that there is a clear non-military core, the distribution broadly supports a 'two worlds' view of the global security structure, reinforced by a centre–periphery construction of much economic securitisation. But a closer look reveals too much variation in the non-core regions to support the idea of a homogeneous periphery. It is in capturing this variation that RSCT displays its strength. Generally (not surprisingly), there is a correlation between sector of securitisation and position on the spectrum from conflict formation to security community. Military and political and/or societal security dominate in most of the conflict formations, whereas economic and societal is usually prominent in the security communities. The causal arrow here points in both directions: political-military securitisation causes conflict and, when you have a conflict, you turn to the strongest instruments which often include the military one.

How stable are the essential structures (anarchy, polarity, amity–enmity, boundaries) and dynamics that define the RSCs, and what are the sources of these (in)stabilities? What do we learn about patterns of interregional interaction and the probability of its leading to external transformation?

There has been some emphasis in this book on questions of actual or potential transformations in the structure of global security, and this might have left the impression of RSCs as volatile. If RSCs were essentially unstable and transitory phenomena, that would question the usefulness of our theory – especially so given our commitment to exclusive, non-overlapping, and therefore comparable RSCs. Our original formulation described RSCs as durable but not permanent, and the empirical evidence seems to support that view. The overall picture in this book is one of a relatively limited number of transformations and thus the theory serves precisely to point out these particular, important developments against a background of continuity. In the period from the end of the Cold War to the immediately foreseeable future, internal or external transformation has occurred, or is in the making, in the following places:

- in East Asia, Southeast Asia shifted from being a conflict formation to a security regime, and then merged with Northeast Asia into a larger East Asian RSC potentially including in the future also South Asia in a huge Asian RSC;

477

- in the CIS, the various shock waves of the dissolution of the Soviet empire meant phases of merger and disjointing of EU-Europe and the CIS, and generally a drawn-out process of establishing the boundaries of the post-Soviet RSC, including the possibility that Europe evolves the Asian way as a supercomplex with sustained fairly strong linkage at the interregional level arising from the presence of great powers within the RSCs (although, so far, the level of security interdependence between EU-Europe and the CIS is surprisingly low);
- in the Middle East, the least important of the three subcomplexes, the Maghreb, could be splitting off from this RSC which had always been structured to an unusual degree by subcomplexes. For a time during the 1990s there seemed to be some possibility that the US-backed peace process might change the amity–enmity structure, but at the time of writing this process looks to have failed;
- in Africa, RSCs are still in the formation, but the best-formed one, Southern Africa, has expanded dramatically into the previously unstructured area of Central Africa, seemingly giving rise also to a Central African RSC;
- in South Asia, internal transformation is most importantly on the agenda where bipolarity might break down.

This list shows that changes have occurred, or are occurring, in all the key elements of essential structure: polarity, boundary, and amity–enmity. Changes in polarity are driven by well-understood forces and are a normal part of international life.

Changes in boundary respond to alterations in the processes of (de)securitisation, which need to be studied on a case-by-case basis. One might speculate whether there is a pattern, driven by increasing interaction capacity, whereby adjacent RSCs generate increasingly strong interregional dynamics, which leads to the formation of supercomplexes and eventually a merger of RSCs. This has been the pattern in Asia with first Northeast and Southeast Asia merging and potentially South Asia following suit. However, the pattern is not strong between EU-Europe and the post-Soviet region, where it might be expected. And in the Americas, there is currently a growing pressure from North America (the United States) on the Andean North of South America. But this is more likely part of a recurrent pattern of fluctuations in US involvement in South America rather than a trend, and it involves only the northern states (due to the drugs issue), not the Southern Cone which on the contrary organises on its own. There are pan-American plans for a free trade area, but this is unlikely to merge the two into one large RSC of the Americas. At the other meeting points of regions – Middle East/South Asia, Middle East/Europe, and Middle East/Africa – there are some challenges to insulators or emerging zones of interface (more on this in the next section), but the general picture is not one of a strong trend towards merger. The main factor in observed expansions of this sort is the influence of great powers. For standard complexes, increases in interaction capacity intensify internal dynamics as much as, or more than, interregional ones. The spread of weapons of mass destruction in the Middle East intensifies local securitisations more than it worries most outsiders.

Changes in amity–enmity should, according to Wendt (1999: 309), be difficult. The failure of the peace process in the Middle East supports this view, yet Southeast Asia and the Southern Cone in South America (and earlier Western Europe and North America) have made progress away from conflict formation towards security regime. The suggestion from these cases is that such transformations work best when developed from within the RSC rather than when imposed from outside, a conclusion with potentially disturbing implications for the current attempt to reform the Balkans.

What is the influence of history, particularly the legacy of state formation? Is there a historical pattern of development common to several RSCs?

There is no doubt that the legacy of history matters in the construction of RSCs. The type of state that dominates within a region seems to have a huge influence on the character of the RSC. It is not an accident that as a rule security communities are found in conjunction with clusters of the most advanced industrial and postmodern states, and conflict formations where modern states predominate (though the Southern Cone combines modern states and an attempt to move towards security community). Where clusters of premodern states exist, there is room for nonstate actors to play a large role in determining the dynamics of regional security. What might be called 'misplaced' states, the odd man out in their regions, either cause or face particularly difficult security policy problems (postmodern Japan in modernist East Asia, premodern Afghanistan between modernist South Asia and the Middle East, the modernist Central and Southeast European states in relation to the postmodern EU). The legacy of decolonisation plays a big role in all this. By and large, the former metropolitan states have evolved onwards towards postmodern status. The ex-colonies (whether formal or informal) have either made some sort of success out of the modernist state structure which was their legacy from the Western imperial era, or failed to do so. Where the modern state has taken root, as in much of Asia, the Middle East, and South America, it has generated standard RSCs almost always starting in conflict formation mode. Where the postcolonial state has either failed completely, or remained very weak, as in much of Africa, the conflict formation has taken on the distinctive form noted above. The former Soviet empire, constituting the last, and very recent, round of decolonisation, remains an exception. The former metropole has not achieved postmodern status, and some of the ex-colonies are attaching themselves to the postmodern core of the EU.

We have argued that one strong historical pattern has been the move from decolonisation to a standard RSC in conflict formation mode. Does this suggest some kind of expected evolution from decolonisation leading to a conflict formation that evolves into a security regime and possibly further to security community? That regions naturally travel some route from conflict formation to security regime to security community has been implied in a number of models for regional security (e.g., Haas 1958; Adler and Barnett 1998). In our view, it is difficult to see such a pattern. Many regions have stayed conflict formations and show little sign of moving beyond. The most peaceful regions are those that have become centred, either on a global power or through institutions. Centring on a global power is no guarantee of achieving deeply internalised regional peace, as shown by the experiences of the Soviet Union and South Asia and, in a different way, by West and Southern Africa. Centring via institutions is difficult, as the current struggles in Europe, Southeast Asia, and the Southern Cone of South America illustrate.

The advantages of the regionalist approach to security

Our view is that the main advantage of the regionalist approach is gained from differentiating global from regional security dynamics, and regional security dynamics from each other. Doing this reflects the territoriality inherent in many security dynamics (and still most of the main ones). It gives standing to the local dynamics of security, and forces evaluation of how global and local dynamics interplay with each other. This differentiation provides the basis for a distinctive and better-balanced interpretation of most security issues than ones that proceed either from the top (global level) down, or from the bottom (uniqueness of the local) up. In our view, it also gives a more relevant interpretation than those which proceed from an assumption of general and widespread deterritorialisation. Acknowledging the regional level as an independent, and frequently powerful, factor in the security equation is essential to both sound theory and sensible policy. And it is not just the fact of differentiating the regions both from each other and from the global level that is important, but also the way in which what counts as a security region is defined. In RSCT, regions are not given by geography or culture or patterns of current events, or the whims of analysts, or local discourses about regionalism. RSCs are socially constructed by their members, whether consciously or (more often) unconsciously by the ways in which their processes of (de)securitisation interlock with each other. They can therefore be changed by changes in those processes, though the scope for change may well be conditioned by the relative depth or shallowness of the way in which the social structure of security is internalised by the actors involved.

We have demonstrated that the regional level of security is active in all areas of the planet, and that it is the the most powerful level in many. Therefore both neorealists and globalists to some extent fail in the security realm when they try to explain mostly from the global level, be it great power global polarity in the case of neorealism or globalisation in the case of globalism. Both of the alternative approaches have their value and have to some extent been integrated into the regionalist perspective.

Reasons for the globalist approach have been given in the discussion above of non-territorial, globalisation-driven security issues. Because of a shared concern about global powers, there are significant opportunities for analytical synergy between RSCT and neorealism at the global level notwithstanding their different epistemological roots. But the weaknesses of the neorealist story compared to that of RSCT are at least three. First it lacks a clear conceptualisation of the specificity of the regional level and therefore both blurs regional and global and over-estimates the importance of global polarity. If a regional component is involved, it is typically seen as arbitrary and purely analytical, because only the global system is granted ontological status, not the regional. Second, in most regions it misses important dynamics because neorealism concentrates too narrowly on military security and on the state. To the extent that other referent objects and/or other sectors matter, something will be missing from the neorealist story. Third, the objectivist approach of traditional neorealism will in crucial instances make it overlook the dynamics related to the social construction of regions and security. B. Hansen's (2000) analysis of the Middle East, for example, quite nicely traces out the effects on the RSC of the global shift from bipolarity to unipolarity (in her terms), but overemphasises the dangers of US domineering and the influence of the unipolar agenda, while discounting or missing the possibility of US withdrawal or the prospect that the unipolar agenda will succumb to the regional dynamics of securitisation.

A specific theoretical argument that is likely to erupt between neorealists and RSCT is the question about the possible relationship between system and subsystem in a systemic theory. In neorealism it is assumed that global equals systemic and, if distinct and strong subsystems are allowed, the system cannot be enough of a system. As famously remarked by Waltz (1979: 58), 'a subsystem dominant system is no system at all'. Does RSCT claim that the system is subsystem-dominant? Not necessarily, but it does claim that systems contain emergent properties at several levels. The theory is systemic and structural in respect both to regions and to the global level. There is nothing in this that is incompatible with the basic structural aspirations of neorealism, but in practice realism (neo or not) has, as part of its (over)simplification, ignored the regional level, probably out of a fear that the result would not be systemic enough.

The paradox in relation to the realist tradition is that RSCT – at least in its pre-constructivist version – is a reinjection of something as realist as geopolitics into security analysis. Hans Mouritzen (1998) has usefully pointed to the basic factor of states being non-mobile units and therefore located spatially (and not just in an abstract 'system' without geographical coordinates). Mouritzen jumps to the opposite extreme in creating a foreign policy theory about each state's unique environment. We, in contrast, argue not only that geography is a concrete situation for each state, but, because of its influence on processes of (de)securitisation, that it also cuts the world into distinct chunks so that the actors in a given region share the properties of their region as a structural context.

If we ignore the more meta-theoretical differences between constructivist RSCT and materialist neorealism, it should, as noted in part I, in principle be possible for a neorealist to accept the importance of the regional level and its distinct shaping effects, parallel to those of the global system. In that case the RSCs would become the fourth tier of neorealism (Wæver 1997c). In each specific instance, one would have to move down the ladder of abstraction from anarchy (1st tier) to medieval/sovereign/post-sovereign principle of differentiation of units (2nd tier) and global polarity (3rd tier) to understanding the most immediate context for the main regional actors: the structure of the RSC (4th tier). We are not suggesting that RSCT is simply something to tack on to neorealism, and the epistemological differences would anyway complicate such a move. But we do think we have presented a powerful enough case to suggest that all those proceeding top-down in security analysis, whether neorealists or globalists, need to think hard about how they can bring the regional level into their frameworks. And they need to do so in a way that gives regions ontological status as independent factors, and not just as arenas in which events determined elsewhere take place.

Problems in applying regional security complex theory

In this section we pick up two issues that have recurred at various points along the way: how to deal with the insulators that exist at the boundaries of indifference between some RSCs, and how to apply securitisation theory when proceeding on the very high level of generality that this global survey has required. A third issue, being able to identify the boundary between the global and the regional levels, had in the past generated some not very satisfactory fudges, such as the distinction between higher- and lower-level complexes. In this book we think we have cracked that problem, and since the argument is fully laid out in part I we do not need to revisit it here.

Insulators and mini-complexes

When revising RSCT for this book we found it necessary to sharpen the distinction between two terms often used as synonyms: 'buffer' and 'insulator'. A buffer is internal to an RSC, where it keeps powers of the region apart. An insulator is located in the zone of indifference between RSCs, helping to keep separate from each other two or more sets of regional security dynamics.

The concept of insulator is both central and underexplored in RSCT. With the insistence on exclusivity of RSCs (and thus the impossibility of 'overlap'), the world in a sense consists of three things: RSCs, insulator states, and global level powers. All states can be located in one and only one RSC except for global level powers that engage in several regions and insulator states that seem to belong either to no region or to several. The basic category of insulator derives from the conceptualisation of RSCs in terms of 'relative indifference' (Buzan 1991b: 193): everything is connected to everything else but, relatively speaking, there are lines or zones with much less security interdependence than on either side. Here two RSCs stand back to back. Often (unless geography supplies enough water), one or more states occupy an insulating position. 'They define and occupy the boundaries of indifference between the self-contained dynamics on either side of them' (Buzan 1991b: 196). The classical examples are Burma between South and Southeast Asia during the Cold War; Turkey between Europe, the Middle East, and the CIS; Afghanistan between South Asia and the Middle East; Nepal between South Asia and Northeast Asia. Buzan (1991b: 196) originally added 'the belt of states stretching across the Sahara from Mauritania to Sudan between the Middle East and black Africa'.

When filling in the map we found that we needed to add another form of insulator not present in the original formulation: not a state (or a belt of largely passive or weak states as in Sahel), but a mini-complex. We want to say more about that here, and also to review briefly each of the classical cases of insulators to see whether they have changed and what can be learned about the possible ways an insulator can fill its difficult position. Turkey will be of special importance here.

Most insulator states face both ways while remaining unable to link the two complexes (Burma, Turkey, Afghanistan, and the Sahel states). A mini-complex can serve the same function because neighbours can get involved in the part of it which borders them, without this engagement 'coming out on the other side' and linking up with actors in another RSC. The Caucasus is an illustration, and Afghanistan also has been for some time more of a mini-complex than a state. Mini-complexes are usually relatively small in scale and low in power compared to the RSCs around them, and may well be areas in which weak states leave room for nonstate actors to play significant roles. Our interpretation of the current status of the Caucasus and Central Asia has been as parts of the CIS complex. But with a continued weakening of Russian power and/or consolidation of statehood (and local conflicts) within them, both are potential candidates for the role of large insulators with internal conflicts, but too weak to be independent complexes and actually with many links to several sides, sides that do not tie together across the region. Whereas Caucasus would then be a very clear illustration of the insulating mini-complex, Central Asia is too big to be a mini-complex; in addition, it could develop the internal dynamics needed to evolve down the road of proto-complex towards an RSC – but still with insulating functions. Central Asia has the interesting quality of being extremely low in power compared to all those around it (including several great powers whose spheres could in principle overlap, but which might allow Central Asia to exist because it would serve as an insulator among them, with none being able to dominate it without inciting the others to intervene). Currently, both the Caucasus and Central Asia are too much tied into the post-Soviet RSC for this scenario to have unfolded yet. The Caucasus is therefore a *sub*complex which functions as an insulating mini-complex; Central Asia too is a subcomplex, but with less of an insulator role because Afghanistan is already there to insulate, and because consistent and competitive external involvement has been limited. Still, the unwieldiness of the region has been sufficient for the often announced 'new great game' not to fully materialise. Given that Afghan and Central Asian developments have been closely linked through many historical periods and that many links exist today due to transnational ethnic ties and Islamist insurgents (Rashid 2000, 2002b; Hall 2001), a final possibility is that a larger insulator zone forms with Afghanistan merging into a larger Central Asia.

Insulators usually play their role by being relatively passive: either marking the zone of indifference, or absorbing peripheral energies from the separate RSCs. Turkey seems to challenge this, by increasingly playing an active role from its insulator position. Still, Turkey is not able to bring the different RSCs together, to make them form one coherent strategic arena, of which it is part. However, there are some indications that Turkey actually is enough of a 'regional power' to bring together Greece, Russia, and Syria from three different RSCs as quasi-allies against it. If those three started systematically to act strategically together, the boundaries separating the Balkans and the Middle East would have grown very thin, and the general conceptualisation of Turkey as an insulator would be challenged. Turkey is in many ways the best case to explore in detail in order better to understand the nature of an insulator state (the mini-complex type of insulator could be best studied in and around both Afghanistan and the Caucasus). One characteristic feature of Turkey is that it officially denies being an insulator state. Since the term insulator is not yet much used, in practice the Turks deny being a buffer – a more familiar, classical, geopolitical term of which Turkish policy-makers certainly are aware (and afraid). Even if they do not generally reason with reference to RSCT, it is evident that they do not see the role of buffer or insulator as attractive. They try instead to construct an understanding of a larger Eurasian region in which Turkey is centrally placed. Simultaneously, Turkey has started to explore 'regionalism' which is to a large extent a Turkish adaptation to the actuality that it is part of several 'regions' and needs to think of the inner dynamic of each of them separately (Kazan 2002).

Burma has traditionally been a case of a state existing in relative isolation from the security dynamics on either side, but this has begun to change somewhat, and there might no longer be any full illustrations of this form of insulator. During the 1990s, Burma became more problematic. Functionally, it remains an insulator between the South Asian RSC and the Southeast Asian subcomplex of the East Asian RSC. But Chinese penetration into Burma has made it increasingly a point of linkage between China and India, and consequently it has become a member of ASEAN. Burma's role as insulator looks increasingly like succumbing to the dynamics of the Asian supercomplex.

Nepal was originally classified (Buzan 1991b: 196) as an insulator between lower-level and higher-level complexes (together with Finland). We now have more clearly defined terms, which would label Cold War Finland as a classic buffer state within a confrontation. Nepal has always had a more complicated role because of its position in the Asian supercomplex. To the extent that South Asia and Northeast Asia are still distinct RSCs, then Nepal is an insulator. If Asia becomes a single RSC, Nepal becomes a buffer. In the Asian supercomplex that now prevails it is a bit of both.

Afghanistan is still an insulator, because South Asia and the Middle East – and now also the post-Soviet space – are separate RSCs. The war by the United States against the Taleban has not changed this. Afghanistan will either revert to its civil war or have an outside-sponsored coalition government. Either outcome would most probably preserve its insulator status. Afghanistan has not yet been absorbed more into one of the neighbouring RSCs than another, nor does such a development look likely. However, it has intense relations on all sides. More than Turkey, Afghanistan projects and connects into the RSCs around it, yet like Turkey it still separates its neighbouring RSCs rather than uniting them. Iran and Afghanistan have been on the brink of war; Pakistan and Afghanistan are linked by transnational politics (Pakistan supporting the Taleban, only to undergo a Talebanisation back at home, and then be forced into an anti-Taleban coalition by the United States); in addition, they are linked in relation to Central Asia, where there are strong links to Islamic and ethnic insurgency groups. Insurgents in Uzbekistan, Kyrgyzstan, and Tajikistan operated from Afghanistan, drugs traffic goes through Central Asia (especially Kyrgyzstan) and Iran, and the local actors increasingly unified against Afghanistan (even to the point of securitising the threat from Afghanistan as the main glue for forming new regional cooperation). Before 11 September Iran, Pakistan, and the states to the north of Afghanistan all meddled in the unsettled civil war in Afghanistan to avoid the total victory of the Taleban, and this consensus on keeping Afghanistan as an insulator seems likely to endure. Afghanistan is far from the passive zone that it has been for periods. Nor is it an active state trying to modify its own position, like Turkey. Most of the links are transnational, and related to the incoherent 'stateness' of Afghanistan. The links are from substate actors, guerrillas, or religious movements, and they confirm that Afghanistan plays its insulator role in a form close to a mini-complex. In any case, Afghanistan is clearly not strong or important enough to unify its neighbouring RSCs, and it seems keen to remain centred on itself. Even before 11 September there was some Iranian–Russian (and Chinese) cooperation which included hostile statements about Afghanistan, but this was not at all driven by the Afghan question – but by a mixture of global and regional level concerns of Russia, China, and Iran.

Insulator states are almost by definition always possible candidates for external transformation. They have links to several regions, and their continued insulator status depends on some balance being kept. If one side becomes gradually more intense while the other loses relative importance, the insulator could gradually be absorbed into one of its neighbouring RSCs. Surprisingly, this happens neither often nor easily. The key insulators have been quite durable and consistent. The insulator element in RSCT seems safe, and it would be interesting to have more detailed comparative and theoretical studies done on this role, and the policy complexities that it generates.

Applying securitisation theory

If seen as another step in the development of the general security approach of the Copenhagen School, what does the present book add? To some true fans, it may seem like de-cumulation, because it uses the methodology of securitisation less than one might have expected after our previous book (Buzan et al. 1998). The simple explanation for this, as set out in part I, is the very large scale of time and space that define this book. A detailed study of all of the (de)securitisation process covered here would mean that each threat and fear mentioned in this study would have required its own lengthy investigation of history and discourse. The ten-volume project this would require was beyond both our resources and the tolerance of any likely publisher. Our first priority has been to sketch out the general structure of global security, and accomplishing that required using sometimes crude indicators for processes of securitisation rather than investigating the discourses themselves. This compromise has (just about) kept the study to manageable length. The payoff, we hope, is a clear overview of the whole, and a wealth of suggestions about how to structure more focused securitisation studies.

Despite this compromise, the theory of securitisation is present in this study in two ways. One is as principled meta-theory which guides how to see and talk about security, i.e., avoiding objectivist assumptions, keeping open the constant possibility of constructions being something different from a reflection of some material development. The second is as an approach to be activated on a few crucial occasions. When a specific security issue is found to be crucial and it therefore needs to be understood in depth – such as the history argument in EU-Europe or the fear of globalisation in South America – the analysis zooms in and uses more of the tools of securitisation analysis. This is in the nature of the present exercise as macro-analysis, in contrast to various micro-studies of securitisation made by us and others.

The most obvious way to reunite the macro- and micro-strands of the Copenhagen School would be to do book-length studies (and/or dissertations) on single RSCs or insulators, in which it would be possible to operate something close to the full securitisation apparatus. The research agenda of securitisation studies as set out elsewhere (Wæver 2001a) contains a number of other ways to structure and delineate a study of securitisation, e.g., more detailed process tracing of a single instance of securitisation or desecuritisation, the study of failed securitisations, and many other tasks. All such studies can function as underpinnings of the study of specific RSCs, as could (as mentioned above) detailed studies of securitisation in an insulator state. This book can be seen as an overview, one of whose main purposes is to identify a range of subjects around which more detailed studies could be organised. In that sense, this book opens up a research programme rather than completing one.

Glossary

buffer
a state or mini-complex *within* a security complex and standing at the centre of a strong pattern of securitisation, whose role is to separate rival powers (see insulator)

centred security complex
a security complex that is either dominated by a single global level power, or sufficiently integrated by collective institutions to have actor quality at the global level

conflict formation
a pattern of security interdependence shaped by fear of war and expectations of the use of violence in political relations

desecuritisation
a process by which a political community downgrades or ceases to treat something as an existential threat to a valued referent object, and reduces or stops calling for urgent and exceptional measures to deal with the threat. The process can be directly discursive addressing the definition of the situation; more often it is indirect, where a shift of orientation towards other issues reduces the relative attention to the previously securitised issue

essential structure
the four constitutive elements of a regional security complex: deep structure (anarchy/hierarchy), polarity, pattern of amity/enmity, boundary (see full definition on p. 53)

external
transformation
: the outer boundary of a regional security complex expands or contracts, transforming either or both of polarity and amity/enmity (most probably as a result of two security complexes merging)

global level power
: either a great power or a superpower according to the definitions used in this book

great power
: for full definition, see pp. 35–7

great power
security complex
: a security complex whose polarity is defined by more than one global level power

insulator
: a state or mini-complex standing *between* regional security complexes and defining a location where larger regional security dynamics stand back to back (see buffer)

internal
transformation
: either the power polarity or the dominant patterns of amity/enmity change within the context of the existing outer boundary of a regional security complex

maintenance of the
status quo
: no changes to the essential structure of an RSC over time

mini-complex
: a formation with the characteristics of a security complex, but small in scale and usually composed at least in part of substate actors

overlay
: when the interests of external great powers transcend mere penetration, and come to dominate a region so heavily that the local dynamics of security interdependence virtually cease to operate. It usually results in the long-term stationing of great power armed forces in the region, and in the alignment of the local states according to the patterns of great power rivalry

pre-complex
: when a set of bilateral security relations seems to have the potential to bind together into an

RSC, but has not yet achieved sufficient
cross-linkage among the units to do so

proto-complex   when there is sufficient manifest security
inter-dependence to delineate a region and
differentiate it from its neighbours, but the
regional security dynamics are still too thin
and weak to think of the region as a fully
fledged RSC

regional power   an actor that counts in determining the
polarity structure of a regional security
complex (for full definition see p. 37)

*regional security
complex*   a set of units whose major processes of
securitisation, desecuritisation, or both are so
interlinked that their security problems cannot
reasonably be analysed or resolved apart from
one another

securitisation   the discursive process through which an
intersubjective understanding is constructed
within a political community to treat
something as an existential threat to a valued
referent object, and to enable a call for urgent
and exceptional measures to deal with the
threat

security community   a pattern of security interdependence in which
the units do not expect or prepare for the use
of force in their political relations with each
other

security constellation   the whole pattern formed by the interplay of
the four levels: domestic, regional,
interregional, global

security regime   a pattern of security interdependence still
shaped by fear of war and expectations of the
use of violence in political relations, but where
those fears and expectations are restrained by

	agreed sets of rules of conduct, and expectations that those rules will be observed
standard security complex	a security complex that does not contain a global level power, and whose local polarity is defined wholly by the regional powers within it
strong states	those having high levels of sociopolitical cohesion and low levels of internal political violence
subcomplex	essentially the same as an RSC, the difference being that a subcomplex is firmly embedded within a larger RSC
supercomplex	a set of RSCs within which the presence of one or more great powers generates relatively high and consistent levels of interregional security dynamics
superpower	For full definition, see pp. 34–5
unstructured security regions	where local states are so weak that their power does not project much, if at all, beyond their own boundaries, and so generate insufficient security interdependence to form the essential structures of a regional security complex
weak states	those having low levels of sociopolitical cohesion and generally high levels of internal political violence

References

Abbas, Najam (2000): *Behind the Breaking News: Shanghai Forum Calls for Institutionalized Efforts Against Terrorism, Extremism, and Crime*, Boston University: Institute for the Study of Conflict, Ideology, and Policy, http://www.bu.edu/iscip/

Abbink, J. (1998): 'Briefing: The Eritrean–Ethiopian Border Dispute', *African Affairs* 97 (389): 551–65

Abraham, Itty (1995): 'Towards a Reflexive South Asian Security Studies', in Weinbaum and Kumar 1995, 17–40

Acharya, Amitav (1992): 'Regionalism and Regime Security in the Third World: Comparing the Origins of the ASEAN and the GCC', in Job 1992, 143–66
  (1993): *A New Regional Order in South East Asia: ASEAN in the Post-Cold War Era*, London: International Institute for Security Studies, Adelphi Paper no. 279

Adams, Henry (1973 [1918]): *The Education of Henry Adams* (Ernest Samuels, ed.), Boston: Houghton Mifflin

Adams, Mark (2002): *Water and Security Policy: The Case of Turkey*, National Defense University, Washington, Near East South Asia Center for Strategic Studies, http://www.ndu.edu/nesa/docs/marksadams-water.pdf

Adler, Emanuel (1998): 'Seeds of Peaceful Change: The OSCE's Security Community-Building Model', in Adler and Barnett 1998, 119–60

Adler, Emanuel, and Michael N. Barnett (1998): *Security Communities*, Cambridge: Cambridge University Press

Ahmed, Samina (1998): 'Pakistan: The Crisis Within', in Alagappa 1998, 338–66

Ajami, Fouad (2001): 'The Uneasy Imperium: Pax Americana in the Middle East', in Hoge and Rose 2001, 15–30

Alagappa, Muthiah (1998) (ed.): *Asian Security Practice: Material and Ideational Influences*, Stanford, CA: Stanford University Press
  (forthcoming): *Asian Security Order: Instrumental and Normative Features*, Stanford: Stanford University Press

Albini, Joseph L. (2000): *Organized Crime: The National Security Dimension*, George C. Marshall European Center for Security Studies, Garmisch-Partenkirchen, Germany

Alexander, Yonah, and Michael S. Swetnam (2001) (eds.), *Usama bin Laden's al-Quaida: Profile of a Terrorist Network*, Ardsley, NY: Transnational Publishers

Allison, Roy (2001): 'Conclusion: Central Asian Security in the Regional and International Context', in Allison and Jonson 2001: 247–68

Allison, Roy, and Lena Jonson (2001) (eds.): *Central Asian Security: The New International Context*, New York: Brookings Institution Press/London: Royal Institute of International Affairs

Almond, Gabriel A., Emmanuel Sivan, and R. Scott Appleby (1995): 'Fundamentalisms Comprehended', in Marty and Appleby 1995, 399–504

Alvstam, Claes G. (2001): 'East Asia: Regionalization Still Waiting to Happen?', in Schulz, et al. 2001, 173–97

Andean Community (2002): *Declaration of the Ministers of Foreign Affairs and of Trade of the Andean Community Member States and of Mercosur, Guayaquil, July 26*, http://www.comunidadandina.org/ingles/document/dec26a-7-02.htm

Aning, Emmanuel Kwasi (1999): *Security in the West Africa Subregion: An Analysis of ECOWAS Policies in Liberia*, Copenhagen: University of Copenhagen, Ph.D dissertation

Antonenko, Oksana (1999–2000): 'Russia, NATO and European Security After Kosovo', *Survival* 4 (4): 124–44

Arblaster, Anthony (1984): *The Rise and Decline of Western Liberalism*, Oxford: Basil Blackwell

Arfi, Badredine (1998): 'Ethnic Fear: The Social Construction of Insecurity', *Security Studies* 8 (1): 151–203

Argentina, White Paper on National Defense (2000): *Part 1: The Strategic Scenario: An Argentine View*, http://www.defensenet.ser2000.org.ar/Archivo/libro-argentina-eng/arg-part1.htm

Armstrong, Karen (2001): 'Was It Inevitable?', in Hoge and Rose 2001, 53–70

Art, Robert J. (1998–9): 'Geopolitics Updated: The Strategy of Selective Engagement', *International Security* 23 (Winter): 79–113

Asaria, Iqbal, Ian Buruma, Fred Halliday, Abdelwahab El-Affendi, Merryl Wyn Davies, Roger Scruton, Mai Yamani, and Sami Zubadia (2001): 'Roundtable: Islam and the West', *Prospect* November: 16–21

Ash, Timothy Garton (2001): *History of the Present: Essays, Sketches, and Dispatches from Europe in the 1990s*, London: Vintage

Atkins, G. Pope (1999): *Latin America and the Caribbean in the International System*, 4th edn, Boulder, CO, and Oxford: Westview Press

Aves, Jonathan (1998): 'The Caucasus States: The Regional Security Complex', in Roy Allison and Christoph Bluth (eds.), *Security Dilemmas in Russia and Eurasia*, London: Royal Institute of International Affairs, 175–87

Aydınlı, Ersel (2002): *Securing the Transformation: Political Globalization vs Anarchy in the Modernizing World*, Ankara: Paper presented to ASAM conference on 'Globalization, Security and the Nation State', 15–16 June

Ayoob, Mohammed (1995): *The Third World Security Predicament: State Making, Regional Conflict, and the International System*, Boulder, CO: Lynne Rienner
(2002): 'South-West Asia After the Taliban', *Survival* 44 (1): 51–65

Bach, David (1995): *Frontiers Versus Boundary-Lines: Changing Patterns of State–Society Interaction in Sub-Saharan Africa*, Paris: Paper presented to Pan-European Conference of the ECPR Standing Group on International Relations

Baev, Pavel K. (1994): 'Russia's Experiments and Experience in Conflict Management and Peacemaking in the Near Abroad', *International Peacekeeping* 1 (3): 245–60
(1996): *The Russian Army in a Time of Troubles*, Oslo: International Peace Research Institute and London: Sage
(1997a): 'Russia's Departure from Empire: Self-Assertiveness and a New Retreat', in Tunander et al. 1997, 174–95
(1997b): *Russia's Policies in the Caucasus*, London: Royal Institute of International Affairs
(1999a): 'External Interventions in Secessionist Conflicts in Europe in the 1990s', *European Security* 8 (2): 22–51
(1999b): 'International Interventions in Secessionist Conflicts in Europe in the 1990s', in McDermott 1999, 87–116

Bahadur, Kalim (2000): 'Islamic Fundamentalism and International Terrorism', *AAKROSH: Asian Journal on Terrorism and International Conflicts* 3 (7): 27–39

Bahr, Egon (1998): *Deutsche Interessen: Streitschrift zu Macht, Sicherheit und Aussenpolitik*, Munich: Karl Blessing

Bailey, John, and Roy Godson (2001): *Public Security and Democratic Governance: Challenges to Mexico and the United States*, Washington, DC: Center for Latin American Studies, Georgetown University

Bailyn, Bernard (1992 [1967]): *The Ideological Origins of the American Revolution*, Cambridge: Belknap Press of Harvard University Press

Bajpai, Kanti (1998): 'India: Modified Structuralism', in Alagappa 1998, 157–97

Banega, Cyro, Björn Hettne, and Frederik Söderbaum (2001): 'The New Regionalism in South America', in Schulz et al. 2001, 234–49

Banerjee, Sanjoy (1997): 'The Cultural Logic of National Identity Formation: Contending Discourses in Late Colonial India', in Hudson 1997, 27–44

Barkawi, Tarak, and Mark Laffey (1999): 'The Imperial Peace: Democracy, Force, and Globalization', *European Journal of International Relations* 5 (4): 403–34

Barnett, Michael N. (1998): *Dialogues in Arab Politics: Negotiations in Regional Order*, New York: Columbia University Press

Baudrillard, Jean (1988): *America*, London and New York: Verso

Bayart, Jean-François, Stephen Ellis, and Beatrice Hibou (1999): *The Criminalization of the State in Africa*, London: James Currey

Behnke, Andreas (1999): *Inscriptions of Imperial Order: NATO's Mediterranean Initiative*, unpublished typescript, 30 pp.

495

Behrendt, Sven, and Christian-Peter Hanelt (1999) (eds.): *Security in the Middle East*, Munich, Guetersloh: Bertelsmann Foundation, unpublished working papers, Center for Applied Policy Research

Beltran, Virgilio R. (2000): *The Armed Forces of the Southern Cone of America on the Threshold of the Twenty-First Century: Some Alternatives for Change*, Strasburg: Paper for ISA Research Committee 01 Armed Forces and Conflict Resolution, Interim Conference, 13–15 October

Bemis, Samuel Flagg (1957 [1935]): *The Diplomacy of the American Revolution*, Bloomington and London: Indiana University Press

Bennett, David H. (1995): *The Party of Fear: The American Far Right from Nativism to the Militia Movement*, New York: Vintage

Bensel, Richard Franklin (1990): *Yankee Leviathan: The Origins of Central State Authority in America, 1859–1877*, Cambridge: Cambridge University Press

Bercovitch, Sacvan (1978): *The American Jeremiad*, Madison: University of Wisconsin Press

Berger, Samuel, and Mona Sutphen (2001): 'Commandeering the Palestinian Cause: Bin Laden's Belated Concern', in Hoge and Rose 2001, 123–8

Berger, Thomas U. (1993): 'From Sword to Chrysanthemum: Japan's Culture of Anti-Militarism', *International Security* 17 (4): 119–50

Bergsten, Fred (2000): 'East Asian Regionalism: Towards a Tripartite World', *Economist* July (15): 23–6

Berman, Bruce J. (1998): 'Ethnicity, Patronage and the African State: The Politics of Uncivil Nationalism', *African Affairs* 97 (388): 305–42

Bernier, Ivan, and Martin Roy (1999): 'NAFTA and MERCOSUR: Two Competing Models?', in Mace and Bélanger 1999, 69–91

Bigo, Didier (1996): *Polices en Réseaux: L'expérience européenne*, Paris: Presses de Sciences Po

bin Laden, Osama (1996a): *First Declaration of Holy War: Ladanese Epistle*, http://www.washingtonpost.com/ac2/wp-dyn?pagename=article &node=&contentId=A4342-2001Sep21&notFound=true. Reprinted as 'Declaration of War Against the Americans Occupying the Land of the Two Holy Places', in Alexander and Swetnam 2001, Appendix 1 A

   (1996b): 'The New Powder Keg in The Middle East', *Nida'ul Islam Magazine* 15 (http://www.islam.org.au). Reprinted as 'Mujahid Usamah Bin Laden Talks Exclusively to "NIDA'UL ISLAM" About the New Powder Keg in the Middle East', in Alexander and Swetnam 2001, Appendix 2

   (1998): Interview with al-Jazeera television channel, http://www.spaceship-earth.de/Letters/Editor/Interview_with_bin_Laden.htm

bin Laden, Osama, Ayman al-Zawahiri, Abu-Yasir Rifa'i Ahmad Taha, Shaykh Mir Hamzah, and Fazlur Rahman (1998): *Second Declaration of Holy War: Jihad Against Jews and Crusaders*, http://www.washingtonpost. com/ac2/wp-dyn?pagename=article&node=&contentId=A4993-2001Sep21&notFound=trueBemærk. Reprinted as 'Jihad Against Jews and Crusaders: World Islamic Front Statement', in Alexander and Swetnam 2001, Appendix 1 B

Blagov, Sergei (2002): 'Russia Mulls a New Unilateralism', *Eurasia Insight* July (16): http://www.eurasianet.org/departments/insight/articles/eav071602.shtml

Blair, Tony (1997): *Speech by the Prime Minister: The Rt. Hon. Tony Blair MP in Paris, May 27*, http://www.number-10.gov.uk/textonly/page840.asp

(2000a): *Speech by the Prime Minister, Tony Blair*, Warsaw: Polish Stock Exchange, 6 October

(2000b): *Speech by the Prime Minister, Tony Blair*, Zagreb: EU/Balkan Summit, 24 November

Blank, Stephen (2000): 'The New Russo-Chinese "Partnership" and Central Asia', *Central Asia and Caucasus Analyst* August (16): http://www.cacianalyst.org/Aug_16/RUSSO-CHINESE_PARTNERSHIP.htm

(2002): 'US Military in Azerbaijan, to Counter Iranian Threat', *Central Asia Caucasus Analyst* April (10): http://www.cacianalyst.org/2002-04-10/20020410_US_AZERBAIJAN_IRAN.htm

Blua, Antoine (2002): *Uzbekistan: Tashkent Withdraws from GUUAM, Remaining Members Forge Ahead*, Radio Free Europe/Radio Liberty, http://rferl.org/nca/features/2002/06/18062002164458.asp

Blum, William (1995): *Killing Hope: US Military and CIA Interventionism Since World War II*, Monroe, ME: Common Courage Press

Bøås, Morten (2000): 'Nigeria and West Africa: From a Regional Security Complex to a Regional Security Community', in Einar Braathen, Morten Bøås, and Gjermund Sæther (eds.), *Ethnicity Kills? The Politics of War, Peace, and Ethnicity in Sub-Saharan Africa*, Basingstoke: Macmillan, 141–62

Bobrow, Davis B. (2001): 'Visions of (In)Security and American Strategic Style', *International Studies Perspectives* 2 (1): 1–12

Bonde, Simon (2001): *USA og Slyngelstaterne – en konstruktivistisk analyse af amerikansk sikkerhedspolitik i 1990'erne*, Copenhagen: MA thesis, Institute for Political Science, University of Copenhagen

Boot, Max (2001): 'The Case for American Empire: The Most Realistic Response to Terrorism Is for America to Embrace Its Imperial Role', *Weekly Standard* 007(5): http://www.weeklystandard.com/Content/Public/Articles/000-000/000/318qpvmc.asp

Bourdieu, Pierre (1991): *Language and Symbolic Power*, Cambridge, MA: Harvard University Press

Bourne, Kenneth (1967): *Britain and the Balance of Power in North America*, London: Longman

Bracken, Paul (1994): 'The Military Crisis of the Nation State: Will Asia Be Different from Europe?', *Political Studies* 42 (Special Issue): 97–114

Braham, Mark, and Matthew Braham (2000): 'Romani Migrations and EU Enlargement', *Cambridge Review of International Affairs* 13 (2): 97–116

Brands, H. W. (1998): 'Exemplary America Versus Interventionist America', in Robert L. Hutchings (ed.), *At the End of the American Century*, Baltimore and London: Johns Hopkins Press

References

Bray, John (1997): 'Pakistan at 50: A State in Decline?', *International Affairs* 73 (2): 315–31

Bremer, Paul (2000): *Statement of Ambassador L. Paul Bremer, III, Chairman National Commission on Terrorism*, Senate Committee on the Judiciary, Subcommittee on Terrorism, Technology, and Government Information, 28 June

Brenner, Michael (1992): 'The EC in Yugoslavia: A Debut Performance', *Security Studies* 1 (4): 586–608

Bringa, Tone (1995): *Being Muslim the Bosnian Way: Identity and Community in a Central Bosnian Village*, Princeton: Princeton University Press

Brown, L. Carl (1996) (ed.): *Imperial Legacy: The Ottoman Imprint on the Balkans and the Middle East*, New York: Columbia University Press

Brzezinski, Zbigniew, and Paige Sullivan (1997) (eds.): *Russia and the Commonwealth of Independent States*, New York and London: M. E. Sharpe

Buchan, David (1993): *Europe: The Strange Superpower*, Aldershot: Dartmouth

Buchanan, Paul G. (1999): 'US Defense Policy for the Western Hemisphere: New Wine in Old Bottles, Old Wine in New Bottles, or Something Completely Different?', *Journal of Interamerican Studies and World Affairs* 38 (1): 1–31

Bull, Benedicte (1999): ' "New Regionalism" in Central America', *Third World Quarterly* 20 (5): 957–70

Bull, Hedley (1977): *The Anarchical Society: A Study of Order in World Politics*, London: Macmillan

  (1984a): 'The Emergence of a Universal International Society', in Bull and Watson 1984, 117–26

  (1984b): 'The Revolt Against the West', in Bull and Watson 1984, 217–28

Bull, Hedley, and Adam Watson (1984) (eds.): *The Expansion of International Society*, Oxford: Clarendon Press

Burnashev, Rustam (2002): 'Regional Security in Central Asia: Military Aspects', in Boris Rumer (ed.), *Central Asia: A Gathering Storm?*, Armonk, NY: M. E. Sharpe, 114–65

Bush, G. W. (2002): *Remarks by the President in Fayetteville, North Carolina, Cumberland County Complex, March 15*, http://usinfo.state.gov/topical/pol/terror/02031501.htm

Butler, Judith (1997): *Excitable Speech: A Politics of the Performative*, New York and London: Routledge

Buzan, Barry (1978): *A Sea of Troubles? Sources of Dispute in the New Ocean Regime*, London: International Institute for Security Studies Adelphi Paper no. 143

  (1983): *People, States, and Fear*, Brighton: Wheatsheaf

  (1988a): 'Japan's Future: Old History Versus New Roles', *International Affairs* 64 (4): 557–73

  (1988b): 'The Southeast Asian Security Complex', *Contemporary Southeast Asia* 10 (1): 1–16

  (1989): 'The Future of Western European Security', in Wæver et al. 1989, 16–45

  (1991a): 'New Patterns of Global Security in the Twenty-First Century', *International Affairs* 67 (3): 431–51

(1991b [1983]): *People, States and Fear: An Agenda for International Security Studies in the Post-Cold War Era*, 2nd edn, Hemel Hempstead: Harvester Wheatsheaf

(1994): 'The Post-Cold War Asia Pacific Security Order: Conflict or Cooperation', in Andrew Mack and John Ravenhill (eds.), *Pacific Cooperation: Building Economic and Security Regimes in the Asia-Pacific Region*, St Leonards: Allen and Unwin Australia; Boulder, CO: Westview Press, 130–51

(1996): 'International Security in East Asia in the 21st Century: Options for Japan', *Dokkyo International Review* 9: 281–314

(1998): 'The Asia-Pacific: What Sort of Region in What Sort of World?', in Anthony McGrew and Christopher Brook (eds.), *Asia-Pacific in the New World Order*, London: Routledge, 68–87

(forthcoming): *After Bipolarity What?*

Buzan, Barry, and Thomas Diez (1999): 'The European Union and Turkey', *Survival* 41 (1): 41–57

Buzan, Barry, Morten Kelstrup, Pierre Lemaitre, Elzbieta Tromer, and Ole Wæver (1990): *The European Security Order Recast: Scenarios for the Post-Cold War Era*, London: Pinter

Buzan, Barry, and Richard Little (2000): *International Systems in World History*, Oxford: Oxford University Press

Buzan, Barry, Richard Little, and Charles Jones (1993): *The Logic of Anarchy: Neorealism to Structural Realism*, New York: Columbia University Press

Buzan, Barry, Gowher Rizvi, et al. (1986): *South Asian Insecurity and the Great Powers*, London: Macmillan

Buzan, Barry, and Gerald Segal (1996): 'The Rise of the "Lite" Powers: A Strategy for Postmodern States', *World Policy Journal* 13 (3): 1–10

(1998): *Anticipating the Future: Twenty Millennia of Human Progress*, London: Simon & Schuster

Buzan, Barry, and Ole Wæver (1992): 'Framing Nordic Security: Scenarios for European Security in the 1990s and Beyond', in Jan Øberg (ed.), *Nordic Security in the 1990s: Options in the Changing Europe*, London: Pinter, 85–104

(1998): *Liberalism and Security: The Contradictions of the Liberal Leviathan*, Copenhagen: COPRI Working Paper 23

Buzan, Barry, Ole Wæver, and Jaap de Wilde (1998): *Security: A New Framework for Analysis*, Boulder, CO: Lynne Rienner

Cable, Vincent (1995): 'What Is International Economic Security?', *International Affairs* 71 (2): 305–24

Calderón, Ernesto Garcia (2001): 'Peru's Decade of Living Dangerously', *Journal of Democracy* 12 (2): 46–58

Calleo, David (1999): 'The United States and the Great Powers', *World Policy Journal* 16 (3): 11–19

Calvocoressi, Peter (1982): *World Politics Since 1945, 4th edn*, London: Longman

Cammett, Melanie (1999): 'Defensive Integration and Late Developers: The Gulf Cooperation Council and the Arab Maghreb Union', *Global Governance* 5 (3): 379–402

References

Campbell, David (1992): *Writing Security: United States Foreign Policy and the Politics of Identity*, Minneapolis: University of Minnesota Press

(1998): *National Deconstruction: Violence, Identity, and Justice in Bosnia*, Minneapolis and London: University of Minnesota Press

Cantori, Louis J., and Steven L. Spiegel (1970): *The International Politics of Regions: A Comparative Approach*, Englewood Cliffs: Prentice Hall

(1973): 'The Analysis of Regional International Politics: The Integration Versus the Empirical Systems Approach', *International Organization* 27 (4): 465–94

Caporoso, James (1996): 'The European Union and Forms of the State: West-phalian, Regulatory or Post-Modern?', *Journal of Common Market Studies* 34 (1): 29–52

Carpenter, Ted Galen (1991): 'The New World Disorder', *Foreign Policy* 84: 24–39

Carter, Ashton B. (1999–2000): 'Adapting US Defence to Future Needs', *Survival* 41 (4): 101–23

Casanova, José (1998): 'Ethno-Linguistic and Religious Pluralism and Democratic Construction in Ukraine', in Barnett R. Rubin and Jack Snyder, *Post-Soviet Political Order: Conflict and State Building*, London: Routledge, 81–103.

Castle, Allan (1997): *Transnational Organized Crime and International Security*, Institute of International Relations, University of British Columbia, Working Paper 19

Cawthra, Gavin (1997a): *Securing South Africa's Democracy: Defence, Development and Security in Transition*, Basingstoke: Macmillan

(1997b): *Sub-Regional Security Cooperation: The Southern African Development Community in Comparative Perspective*, University of the Western Cape, Southern African Perspective No. 63

(2000): *Reconceptualising Security for the Twenty-First Century: South Africa's Experience in Remaking Defence*, Buenos Aires: Paper prepared for the Workshop on 'The Traditional and the New Security Agenda: Inferences for the Third World', Universidad di Tella, Buenos Aires

Celac, Sergiu (2000): *The Nagorno-Karabakh Question: An Update*, Brussels: Centre for European Policy Studies, http://www.ceps.be/Pubs/2000/Caucasus/nkquestion.php

Celac, Sergiu, and Michael Emerson, et al. (2000) (eds.): 'A Stability Pact for the Caucasus', working document no. 145, May, CEPS Task Force for the Caucasus, Brussels: Centre for European Policy Studies, http://www.ceps.be/Pubs/2000/Caucasus/ndc/Newdeal.php#Contents

CFR (Council on Foreign Relations) (2000): *US–Cuban Relations in the Twenty-First Century, Independent Task Force Report*, http://www.cfr.org/public/resource.cgi?pub!3083

Cha, Victor D. (2000): 'Globalization and the Study of International Security', *Journal of Peace Research* 37 (3): 391–403

Chace, James (2000): 'The Next New Threat', *World Policy Journal* 17, 1 (Spring): 113–15

Chellaney, Brahma (1998–9): 'After the Tests: India's Options', *Survival* 40 (4): 93–111

Chirac, Jacques (1999): Intervention télévisée du président de la République M. Jacques Chirac à l'occasion de la Fête nationale, extraits, juilliet–août, 14 juli, 40

(2000): *Our Europe*, Berlin: Speech to the German Bundestag, 27 June

Christensen, Thomas (2002): *Russian Security Policy According to a Hegelianised Copenhagen School*, Copenhagen: MA thesis, Institute of Political Science, University of Copenhagen, http://thomas.dossier.dk/thesis/thesis.html

Christensen, Thomas J. (1999): 'China, the US–Japan Alliance, and the Security Dilemma in East Asia', *International Security* 23 (4): 49–81

(2001): 'Posing Problems Without Catching Up: China's Rise and Challenges for US Security Policy', *International Security* 25 (4): 5–40

Chubin, Shahram, and Charles Tripp (1996): *Iran–Saudi Arabia Relations and Regional Order*, London: International Institute for Security Studies, Adelphi Paper no. 304

Cilliers, Jakkie (1999): *An Emerging South African Foreign Policy Identity?*, Pretoria: Institute for Security Studies, Occasional Paper no. 39, http://www.iss.org.za/Pubs/Papers/39/Paper39.html

(2000): *African Security*, Abuja: Paper at the Ministerial Conference on Security, Stability, Development and Cooperation in Africa, 8–9 May

Clapham, Christopher (1995): 'The International Politics of African Guerilla Movements', *South African Journal of International Affairs* 3 (1): 81–91

(1996): *Africa and the International System: The Politics of State Survival*, Cambridge: Cambridge University Press

(1998a)(ed.): *African Guerrillas*, Oxford: James Currey

(1998b): 'Degrees of Statehood', *Review of International Studies* 24 (2): 143–57

(1998c): 'Discerning the New Africa', *International Affairs* 74 (2): 263–9

(1998d): *Westphalian Agendas in Tropical Africa*, Enschede: Paper for conference on '350th Anniversary of the Peace of Westphalia', July

Clark, Ian (1999): *Globalization and International Relations Theory*, Oxford: Oxford University Press

Clark, John F. (2001): 'Explaining Ugandan Intervention in Congo: Evidence and Interpretation', *Journal of Modern African Studies* 39 (2): 261–87

Claude, Innis L. (1984 [1956]): *Swords into Plowshares: The Problems and Progress of International Organization*, 4th edn, New York: Random House

Clermont, Jean (2002): *Regional Rivalries in Northeast Asia*, New Orleans: Paper presented to ISA Conference, 24–27 March

Clinton, William Jefferson (1995): 'Speech on Bosnia, November 27, 1995', http://www.cnn.com/US/9511/bosnia_speech/speech.html

Clissold, Gillian Gunn (1998): *Divergent International Perspectives on the Caribbean: The Interaction Between the Ongoing Caribbean, US, and European Adaptations to the New Global Economy*, Georgetown: Georgetown University Caribbean Project, Caribbean Briefing Paper

CNN.com/World (1999): 'China Lashes Taiwan over Lee's Rhetorical Change', 13 July: http://www.cnn.com/WORLD/asiapcf/9907/13/china.taiwan/

References

Cohen, Saul B. (1994): 'Geopolitics in the New World Era: A New Perspective on an Old Discipline', in George J. Demko and William B. Wood (eds.), *Reordering the World: Geopolitical Perspectives on the Twenty-First Century*, Boulder, CO: Westview, 15–48

Coleman, Max (1990): *State Violence: A Study in Repression*, Johannesburg: University of the Witwatersrand, Johannesburg, South Africa, Seminar No. 6

Conetta, Carl, and Charles Knight (1998): 'Inventing Threats', *Bulletin of the Atomic Scientists* 54 (2): 32–9

Connell, Dan, and Frank Smyth (1998): 'Africa's New Bloc', *Foreign Affairs* 77 (2): 80–94

Contreras Q., Carlos (1999): 'Interstate Relations in Latin America', *Security Dialogue* 30 (2): 239–46

Cook, Robin (1999): 'It Is Fascism That We Are Fighting "Ours is the Modern Europe of the Human Rights Convention"', *Guardian* May (5): 20

Cooper, Robert (1996): *The Postmodern State and the World Order*, London: Demos Paper no. 19

Coppetiers, Bruno (1996a): 'Conclusions: The Caucasus as a Security Complex', in Coppetiers 1996b

(1996b) (ed.): *Contested Borders in the Caucasus*, Brussels: VUB University Press, http://poli.vub.ac.be/publi/ContBorders/eng/

(1996c) 'Introduction', in Coppetiers 1996b

(2000): *A Regional Security System for the Caucasus*, http://poli.vub.ac.be/publi/crs/eng/vol5/coppetiers.htm

Corbridge, Stuart (1998): *The Militarisation of all Hindudom? The Bharatiya Janata Party, the Bomb and the Political Spaces of Hindu Nationalism*, Vienna: Paper presented to the Pan-European International Relations Conference, July

Cordesman, Anthony H. (1997): *Bahrain, Oman, Qatar, and the UAE: Challenges of Security*, Boulder, CO: Westview Press

Cornell, Svante E., (2002): 'Autonomy as a Source of Conflict: Caucasian Conflicts in Theoretical Perspective', *World Politics* 54: 245–76

Cornell, Svante E., and Maria Sultan (2000): 'Afghanistan as Center: Central Asia's New Geopolitics', *Central Asia Caucasus Analyst* November (22): http://www.cacianalyst.org/Nov_22_2000/Afghanistan_as_Center.htm

Corpora, Christopher A. (2002): *The Gas Station Blues in Three Parts: The Effects of Organized Crime on Stability and Development in Southeast Europe*, New Orleans: Powerpoint presentation at the annual meeting of ISA, 24–27 March

Corrêa, Luiz Felipe de Seixas (1999): *Brazilian Foreign Policy*, http://www.mre.gov.br/projeto/mreweb/ingles/discoursos/sgpale-i.htm

Cossa, Ralph A., and Jane Khanna (1997): 'East Asia: Economic Interdependence and Regional Security', *International Affairs* 73 (2): 219–34

Crawford, Beverly (1994): 'The New Security Dilemma Under International Economic Interdependence', *Millennium* 23 (1): 25–56

Crawford, Neta C. (1994): 'A Security Regime Among Democracies: Cooperation Among Iroquois Nations', *International Organization* 48 (3): 345–86

Croft, Stuart, John Redmond, G. Wyn Rees, and Mark Webber (1999): *The Enlargement of Europe*, Manchester and New York: Manchester University Press

Curry, W. Frick (1995): *Altered States: Post-Cold War US Security Interests in Central America*, www.us.net/cip/bibliogr/ca.htm

Cutler, Claire A. (1991): 'The "Grotian Tradition" in International Relations', *Review of International Studies* 17 (1): 41–65

Cutler, Robert M. (2000): 'Russia, Turkey and Iran: An Eternal Triangle', *Central Asia Caucasus Analyst* July (5): http://www.cacianalyst.org/July5/%C2%A0RUSSIA_TURKEY_AND_IRAN.htm

(2001): *US Intervention in Afghanistan: Implications for Central Asia*, Foreign Policy in Focus, http://www.fpif.org/pdf/gac/0111afghanint.pdf

da Costa, Thomaz Guedes (2000): *Brazil in the New Decade*, Washington, DC: Center for Strategic and International Studies

(2001): 'Strategies for Global Insertion: Brazil and Its Regional Partners', in Tulchin and Espach 2001a, 91–116

Daase, Christopher, Susanne Feske, Bernhard Moltmann, and Claudia Schmid (1993) (eds.): *Regionalisierung der Sicherheitspolitik*, Baden-Baden: Nomos Verlagsgesellschaft

Dannreuther, Roland (1999–2000): 'Escaping the Enlargement Trap in NATO–Russian Relations', *Survival* 4 (4): 145–64

Davies, Norman (1997): *Europe: A History*, London: Pimlico

Dawisha, Adeed (2000): 'Arab Nationalism and Islamism: Competitive Past, Uncertain Future', *International Studies Review* 2 (3): 79–90

Deegan, Heather (1996): *Third World: The Politics of the Middle East and Africa*, London: Routledge

Dehio, Ludwig (1963 [1948]): *Gleichgewicht oder Hegemonie: Betrachtungen über ein Grundproblem der neueren Staatengeschichte*, Krefeld: Scherpe Verlag

deLisle, Jacques (2000): 'The Chinese Puzzle of Taiwan's Status', *Orbis* 44 (1): 35–62

Delpech, Therese (1998–9): 'Nuclear Weapons and the New World Order: Early Warning from Asia', *Survival* 40 (4): 57–76

Deng, Francis M. (1995): *War of Visions: Conflicts of Identities in the Sudan*, Washington, DC: Brookings Institution

Derrida, Jacques (1977): 'Signature Event Context', *Glyph.* 1: 172–97

(1992 [1991]): *The Other Heading: Reflections on Today's Europe*, Bloomington: Indiana University Press

Dervis, Kermal, and Nemat Shafik (1998): 'The Middle East and North Africa: A Tale of Two Futures', *Middle East Journal* 52 (4): 505–16

Dessler, David (1989): 'What's at Stake in the Agent–Structure Debate', *International Organization* 43 (3): 441–73

Deudney, Daniel (1995): 'The Philadelphia System: Sovereignty, Arms Control, and Balance of Power in American States Union, circa 1789–1861', *International Organization* 49 (2): 191–229

References

Deudney, Daniel, and G. John Ikenberry (1999): 'The Nature and Source of Liberal International Order', *Review of International Studies* 25 (2): 179–96

Deutsch, Karl W., Sidney A. Burrell, Robert A. Kann, Maurice Lee jr, Martin Lichterman, Raymond E. Lindgren, Francis L. Loewenheim, and Richard W. van Wagenen (1957): *Political Community and the North Atlantic Area: International Organization in the Light of Historical Experience*, Princeton: Princeton University Press

Diamint, Rut (1999): *Control civil y las fuerzas armadas en las nuevas democracias latinoamericanas*, Buenos Aires: Universidad Torcuato di Tella, NuevoHacer GEL-Editores

—— (2000): *Demilitarization and the Security Agenda*, Buenos Aires: Workshop on 'The Traditional and the New Security Agenda: Inferences for the Third World', 11–12 September

—— (2001): *Security Assumptions in Argentine Security Policy*, Chicago: Paper presented at the 42nd ISA Annual Convention

Dibb, Paul (1995): *Towards a New Balance of Power in Asia*, London: International Institute for Strategic Studies: Adelphi Paper no. 295

Dibb, Paul, David D. Hale, and Peter Prince (1998): 'The Strategic Implications of East Asia's Economic Crisis', *Survival* 40 (2): 5–26

Diez, Thomas (2002): 'Last Exit to Paradise? The European Union, the Cyprus Conflict and the Problematic "Catalytic Effect" ', in Thomas Diez (ed.), *The European Union and the Cyprus Conflict: Modern Conflict, Postmodern Union*, Manchester: Manchester University Press, 139–62

Dominguez, Jorge I. (1999): 'US–Latin American Relations During the Cold War and Its Aftermath', *Weatherhead Center for International Affairs, Harvard University, Working Paper Series* 99 (01): 1–18

Doom, Ruddy, and Koen Vlassenroot (1999): 'Kony's Message: A New Koine? The Lord's Resistance Army in Northern Uganda', *African Affairs* 98 (390): 5–36

Dorrington, Rob, David Bourne, Debbie Bradshaw, Ria Laubscher, and Ian M. Timćus (2001): *The Impact of HIV/AIDS on Adult Mortality in South Africa: Technical Report*, South Africa: Burden of Disease Research Unit, Medical Research Council

Dreifuss, René Armand (1999): *Challenges and New Perspectives: Some Thoughts on the Future of the Brazilian Military*, Grenoble: Espace Europe, Observatoire des Relations Internationales dans l'Hémisphère Sud, Cahiers no. 5

Duffield, John S. (2001): 'Transatlantic Relations After the Cold War: Theory, Evidence, and the Future', *International Studies Perspectives* 2 (February): 93–115

Dunbabin, J. P. D. (1994): *The Post-Imperial Age: The Great Powers and the Wider World: International Relations Since 1945. A History in Two Volumes (The Postwar World)*, London and New York: Longman

Dunn, Timothy J. (1996): *The Militarization of the US–Mexico Border, 1978–1992: Low-Intensity Conflict Doctrine Comes Home*, Austin: University of Texas at Austin Center for Mexican American Studies

504

Eguizábal, Christina (1998): 'The United Nations and the Consolidation of Peace in Central America', in Pellicer 1998

Eickelman, Dale F., and James Piscatori (1996): *Muslim Politics*, Princeton: Princeton University Press

Eide, Espen Barth (1999): 'Regionalizing Intervention? The Case of Europe in the Balkans', in McDermott 1999, 61–86

(2001): *The International Security Challenge: Reforming Police, Judiciaries and Penal Systems in the Western Balkans*, Oslo: Western Balkans Stability Project, 2nd draft

Ekeh, Peter (1975): 'Colonialism and the Two Publics in Africa: A Theoretical Statement', *Comparative Studies in Society and History* 17 (1): 91–112

El-Affendi, Abdelwahab (2000): *The Perils of Regionalism: Regional Integration as a Source of Instability in the Horn of Africa*, London: CSD, unpublished typescript

(2001): 'The Impasse in the IGAD Peace Process for Sudan: The Limits of Regional Peacemaking?', *African Affairs* 100: 581–99

Engelbrekt, Kjell (1998): 'Östra Centraleuropa: Ett säkerhetskomplex?', *Kungliga Krigsvetenskapsakademiens Handlingar och Tidskrift* 200 (4): 123–35

Eshanova, Zamira (2002): 'Central Asia: Has New Alliance with West Helped Opposition Movements?', *EurasiaNet* July (11): http://www.eurasianet.org/departments/rights/articles/pp070502.shtml

Euben, Roxanne L. (1999): *Enemy in the Mirror: Islamic Fundamentalism and the Limits of Modern Rationalism*, Princeton and Chichester: Princeton University Press

Faiola, Anthony (2002): 'US Role in Coca War Draws Fire', *Washington Post* June (23): A1

Fairbank, John King (1968): *The Chinese World Order: Traditional China's Foreign Relations*, Cambridge, MA: Harvard University Press

Faulkner, Frank, and Lloyd Pettiford (1998): 'Complexity and Simplicity: Landmines, Peace and Security in Central America', *Third World Quarterly* 19 (1): 45–61

Fawcett, Louise, and Andrew Hurrell (1995) (eds.): *Regionalism in World Politics: Regional Organization and International Order*, Oxford: Oxford University Press

Filho, Joao R. Martins, and Daniel Zirker (2000): 'Nationalism, National Security, and Amazonia: Military Perceptions and Attitudes in Contemporary Brazil', *Armed Forces and Society* 27 (1): 105–29

(n.d.): *The Brazilian Armed Forces After the Cold War: Overcoming the Identity Crisis*, http://136.142.158.105/LASA98/MartinsFilho&Zirker.pdf

Finlayson, Jock A., and Mark W. Zacher (1983): 'The GATT and the Regulation of Trade Barriers: Regime Dynamics and Functions', in Krasner 1983, 273–314

Fischer, Joschka (2000): *From Confederacy to Federation: Thoughts on the Finality of European Integration*, Berlin: Speech given at University of Humboldt, 12 May

References

Fishel, Kimbra L. (1997): 'From Revolutionary Warfare to Criminalization: The Transformation of Violence in El Salvador', *Low Intensity Conflict and Law Enforcement* 6 (3): 48–63

Fitch, John Samuel (1998): *The Armed Forces and Democracy in Latin America*, Baltimore: Johns Hopkins University Press

Florini, Ann M., and P. J. Simmons (1998a): *The New Security Thinking: A Review of the North American Literature*, New York: Rockefeller Brothers Fund
   (1998b): 'North America', in Stares 1998, 23–66

Foot, Rosemary (1995): 'Pacific Asia: The Development of Regional Dialogue', in Fawcett and Hurrell 1995, 228–49
   (2001): 'Chinese Power and the Idea of a Responsible State', *China Journal* 45: 1–19

Forsberg, Tuomas (1998): 'Settled and Remaining Border Issues Around the Baltic Sea', in Lars Hedegaard and Bjarne Lindström (eds.), *The NEBI Yearbook 1998: North European and Baltic Sea Integration*, Berlin, Heidelberg, and New York: Springer-Verlag, 437–47

Frello, Birgitta (2002): *Identiteter på spil: Medierne og krigen i Kosovo* [Identities at stake: The media and the war in Kosovo], Aarhus: Centre for European Cultural Studies with Department of Gender Research, University of Aarhus, Ph.D dissertation

Friedberg, Aaron L. (1993–4): 'Ripe for Rivalry: Prospects for Peace in a Multipolar Asia', *International Security* 18 (3): 5–33
   (2000): *In the Shadow of the Garrison State: America's Anti-Statism and Its Cold War Grand Strategy*, Princeton: Princeton University Press

Friis, Lykke (1999): *An Ever Larger Union? EU Enlargement and the European Integration. An Anthology*, Copenhagen: Danish Institute of International Affairs

Friis, Lykke, and Anna Murphy (2000): ' "Turbo-Charged Negotiations": The EU and the Stability Pact for South Eastern Europe', *Journal of European Public Policy* 7 (5, Special Issue): 95–114

Galtung, Johan (1973): *European Community: A Superpower in the Making*, London: Allen and Unwin
   (1984): *There Are Alternatives: Four Roads to Peace and Security*, Nottingham: Spokesman

Gastrow, Peter (2001): *Organised Crime in the SADC Region: Police Perceptions*, Pretoria and Cape Town: Institute for Security Studies, Monographs no. 60

Gause, F. Frederick III (2001): 'The Kingdom in the Middle: Saudi Arabia's Double Game', in Hoge and Rose 2001, 109–22

Gause, R. Gregory III (1999): 'Systemic Approaches to Middle Eastern International Relations', *International Studies Review* 1 (1): 11–31

Gentleman, Judith A. (2001): *The Regional Security Crisis in the Andes: Patterns of State Response*, Carlisle, PA: US Army War College, Strategic Studies Institute

Gerges, Fawaz A. (1999): 'The Decline of Revolutionary Islam and Algeria and Egypt', *Survival* 41 (1): 113–25

Gholz, Eugene, Daryl G. Press, and Harvey M. Sapolsky (1997): 'Come Home, America: The Strategy of Restraint in the Face of Temptation', *International Security* 21 (4): 5–48

Giavarini, Dr Adalberto Rodríguez, Minister of Foreign Affairs, International Trade, and Worship (2000): 'Argentine Foreign Policy', speech, 30 May, http://www.mrecic.gov.ar/ministerio/canciller/disc12.html

Gilbert, Martin (1993): *The Dent Atlas of Russian History*, 2nd edn, London: Dent

Giragosian, Richard (2000): *Massive Kashagan Oil Strike Renews Geopolitical Offensive in Caspian*, Baltimore: Central Asia–Caucasus Institute, Johns Hopkins University, Paul H. Nitze School of Advanced International Studies

Girling, J. L. S. (1973): 'A Neutral Southeast Asia?', *Australian Outlook* 27 (2): 123–33

Glenny, Misha (1992): *The Fall of Yugoslavia: The Third Balkan War*, London: Penguin

Goldgeier, James M. (1999): *Not Whether but When: The US Decision to Enlarge NATO*, Washington, DC: Brookings Institution Press

Goldgeier, James M., and Michael McFaul (1992): 'A Tale of Two Worlds: Core and Periphery in the Post-Cold War Era', *International Organization* 46 (2): 467–91

Goldstein, Avery (2000): *Balance-of-Power Politics and Security Order in the Asia-Pacific*, Bali: Paper presented to the Workshop on Security Order in the Asia-Pacific, May–June

Goldston, James A. (2002): 'Roma Rights, Roma Wrongs', *Foreign Affairs* 81 (2): 146–62

Gong, Gerritt W. (1984): *The Standard of 'Civilization' in International Society*, Oxford: Clarendon Press

Gonzalez, Guadalupe, and Stephan Haggard (1998): 'The United States and Mexico: A Pluralistic Security Community?', in Adler and Barnett 1998, 295–332

Goodman, Sherri W. (1996): 'Ecosystem Management at the Department of Defense', *Ecological Applications* 6 (3): 706–7

Goodwin, Jason (1999): *Lords of the Horizons: A History of the Ottoman Empire*, London: Vintage

Gordon, Bernard K. (1986): 'The Third Indochina Conflict', *Foreign Affairs* 65 (1): 66–85

Goudie, Douglas (1996): 'An Overview of the Fergana Valley', *Perspectives on Central Asia* 1(1), http://www.eisenhowerinstitute.org/programs/globalpartnerships/securityandterrorism/coalition/regionalrelations/OtherPubs/Goudie.htm

Goulding, Marrack (1999): 'The United Nations and Conflict in Africa Since the Cold War', *African Affairs* 98 (391): 155–66

Græger, Nina (1999): 'Changing Security Concepts: The Human Rights Challenge', in McDermott 1999, 45–60

References

Grannes, Alf (1993): 'Mosaikk og konflikt i post-sovjetisk Sentral-Asia. Historie, etnisk, språklig, religiøs og annen bakgrunn for dagens konfliktbilde', in Grannes et al. 1993, 5–56

Grannes, Alf, et al. (1993) (eds.): *Etniske konflikter i Sentral-Asia og Kaukasus*, Oslo: Norwegian Institute of International Affairs

Greene, Jack P. (1993): *The Intellectual Construction of America: Exceptionalism and Identity from 1492 to 1800*, Chapel Hill and London: University of North Carolina Press

Grewe, Wilhelm G. (1988): *Epochen der Völkerrechtsgeschichte*, Baden-Baden: Nomos Verlag

Gricius, A. (1998): 'A Russian Enclave in the Baltic Region: Source of Stability or Tension?', in Joenniemi and Prawitz, 1998

Griffith, Ivelaw L. (1993a): 'Drugs and Security in the Commonwealth Caribbean', *Journal of Commonwealth and Comparative Politics* 31 (2): 70–102

(1993b): *The Quest for Security in the Caribbean: Problems and Promises in Subordinate States*, New York and London: M. E. Sharpe

(1995): 'Caribbean Security: Retrospect and Prospect', *Latin American Research Review* 30 (2): 3–32

(1997): *Drugs and Security in the Caribbean: Sovereignty Under Siege*, University Park: Penn State University Press

(1998a): 'Caribbean Geopolitics and Geonarcotics: New Dynamics, Same Old Dilemma', *Naval War College Review* 51 (2): 47–67

(1998b): 'The Geography of Drug Trafficking in the Carribbean', in Michael Desch, Jorge I. Dominguez, and Andrés Serbin (eds.), *From Pirates to Drug Lords: The Post-Cold War Caribbean Security Environment*, New York: State University of New York Press, 97–120

(2000): *The Political Economy of Drugs in the Caribbean*, Houndsmills, Basingstoke, and London: Macmillan

Guehenno, Jean-Marie (1998–9): 'The Impact of Globalization on Strategy', *Survival* 40 (4): 5–19

Gunaratna, Rohan (1995): 'The Burden of Ethnicity, Insurgency, and Insecurity in Sri Lanka', in Weinbaum and Kumar 1995, 79–101

(2002): *Inside Al Qaeda: Global Network Terror*, London: Hurst & Co

Gupta, Shekhar (1995): *India Redefines Its Role*, London: International Institute of Strategic Studies: Adelphi Paper no. 293

GUUAM (Alliance of Georgia, Ukraine, Uzbekistan, Azerbaijan, and Moldova) (1999): *Statement of the Presidents of the Republic of Azerbaijan, Georgia, the Republic of Moldova, Ukraine and the Republic of Uzbekistan*, Washington, DC

Guzzini, Stefano (1994): *Power Analysis as a Critique of Power Politics: Understanding Power and Governance in the Second Gulf War*, Florence: European University Institute, Ph.D thesis

Haas, Ernst B. (1958): *The Uniting of Europe: Political, Social, and Economic Forces 1950–1957*, Stanford, CA: Stanford University Press

Haas, Michael (1970): 'International Subsystems: Stability and Polarity', *American Political Science Review* 64 (1): 98–123

Habel, Janette (2002): 'Nouvelle architecture militaire dans les Amériques', *Le Monde Diplomatique* January: 18–19

Haddadi, Said (1999): '*The Western Mediterranean as a Security Complex: A Liaison Between the European Union and the Middle East?*', Jean Monnet Working Papers in Comparative and International Politics No. 24, http://www.fscpo.unict.it/EuroMed/jmwp24.htm

Haftendorn, Helga, Robert O. Keohane, and Celeste A. Wallander (1999) (eds.): *Imperfect Unions: Security Institutions over Time and Space*, Oxford: Oxford University Press

Hall, Michael A. (2001): 'Central Asia Takes Center Stage', *Perspective* 12 (2), Boston University, Institute for the Study of Conflict, Ideology and Policy, http://www.bu.edu/iscip/vol12/hall.html

Hall, Rodney Bruce (1999): *National Collective Identity: Social Constructs and International Systems*, New York: Columbia University Press

Halliday, Fred (2000): *Nation and Religion in the Middle East*, London: Saqi Books

Hamilton, Alexander, James Madison, and John Jay (1911 [1787–8]): *The Federalist Papers*, London and Toronto: J. M. Dent and Sons

Hansen, Birthe (2000): *Unipolarity and the Middle East*, Richmond, Surrey: Curzon Press

Hansen, Birthe, and Bertel Heurlin (1998) (eds.): *The Baltic States in World Politics*, Richmond, Surrey: Curzon

Hansen, Kenneth Schmidt (2000): *The Fall of Milosevic and the Kosovo Problem*, Copenhagen: Danish Institute for International Affairs, Working Paper 9/2000

   (2002): *Transnational organiseret kriminalitet: et sikkerhedspolitisk problem* [Transnational organized crime: a security political problem], Copenhagen: Danish Institute of International Affairs, Research Briefs, no. 5/2002

Hansen, Kenneth Schmidt, and Georg E. C. Güntelberg (2001): *Balkan Odysseen: Rejsen til Europa*, Copenhagen: Danish Institute of International Affairs, Fokus no. 5

Hansen, Lene (1995): 'NATO's New Discourse', in Birthe Hansen (ed.), *European Security – 2000*, Copenhagen: Copenhagen Political Studies Press, 117–35

   (1998): *Western Villains or Balkan Barbarism?*, Copenhagen: Institute of Political Science

   (1999): *NATO's Balkan Engagement: Institutional Reconstruction and the Representation of Bosnia and Kosovo*, UMIST/University of Manchester: Paper presented at the British International Studies Association's annual conference

   (2000): 'The Little Mermaid's Silent Security Dilemma and the Absence of Gender in the Copenhagen School', *Millennium* 29 (2): 285–306

Harrison, Mark (2001): 'The Politics of Inalienability: China's Claim for Taiwan', *La Trobe Forum* 19 (December): 3–5

Hassner, Pierre (1968a): *Change and Security in Europe. Part I: The Background*, London: International Institute for Security Studies. Adelphi Paper 45

   (1968b): *Change and Security in Europe. Part II: In Search of a System*, London: International Institute for Security Studies. Adelphi Paper 49

(1976): 'The Politics of Western Europe and East–West Relations', in Nils Andrén and Karl Birnbaum (eds.), *Beyond Détente: Prospects for East–West Cooperation and Security in Europe*, Leyden: A. W. Sijthoff, 15–37

(1993): 'Beyond Nationalism and Internationalism: Ethnicity and World Order', *Survival* 35 (2): 49–65

Heisbourg, Francois (1998–9): 'The Prospects for Nuclear Stability Between India and Pakistan', *Survival* 40 (4): 77–92

(2000): 'American Hegemony? Perceptions of the US Abroad', *Survival* 4 (4): 5–19

Held, David, Anthony McGrew, David Goldblatt, and Jonathan Perraton (1999): *Global Transformation: Politics, Economics and Culture*, Cambridge: Polity Press

Helleiner, Eric (1994): *Regionalization in the International Political Economy: A Comparative Perspective*, Toronto: University of Toronto and York University Joint Centre for Asia-Pacific Studies, Eastern Asia Policy Papers no. 3

Hellmann, Gunther, and Reinhard Wolf (1993): 'Neorealism, Neoliberal Institutionalism, and the Future of NATO', *Security Studies* 3 (1): 3–43

Hennop, Ettienne, Clara Jefferson, and Andrew McLean (2001): 'The Challenge to Control South Africa's Borders and Borderline', *Monograph* 57 (August): web edition 1–2

Heradstveit, Daniel (1993): 'Konflikter i Kaukasus', in Grannes et al. 1993, 95–110

Herz, Monica (2000): *Brazilian Perspectives on the Redefinition of the Concept of Security*, Universidad Tocruato di Tella, Instituto de Relacoes Internacionais PUC-Rio, Buenos Aires: Workshop on the Traditional and the New Security Agenda, 11–12 September

Herzig, Edmund (2001): 'Iran and Central Asia', in Allison and Jonson 2001, 171–98

Hettne, Björn (2002): *Communication and Non-Communication in a Regional System: The Pathological Cleavage Pattern of South Asia*, Lund: Paper for the SASNET Workshop on Global Networking in South Asian Studies, 27–28 August

Hey, Jeanne A. K., and Lynn M. Kuzma (1993): 'Anti-US Foreign Policy of Dependent States: Mexican and Costa Rican Participation in Central American Peace Plans', *Comparative Political Studies* 26 (1): 30–62

Higgott, Richard (1994): 'Ideas, Identity and Policy Coordination in the Asia-Pacific', *Pacific Review* 7 (4): 367–79

Hillen, John, and Lawrence J. Korb (1998): *Future Visions for US Defense Policy: Four Alternatives Presented as Presidential Speeches*, New York: Council on Foreign Relations

Hjortsø, Thomas (2002): 'Hvideruslands hersker gør tilnærmelser til NATO', *Orientering, Danish Radio, Channel 1* July (12): http://www.dr.dk/orientering/ark0228.htm

Hoagland, Jim (2002): 'Staying on in Central Asia', *Washington Post* January (20): B7

Hodge, Carl Cavanagh (1998–9): 'Europe as a Great Power: A Work in Progress?', *International Journal* 53 (3): 487–504

Hodgson, Marshall G. S. (1993): *Rethinking World History: Essays on Europe, Islam, and World History*, Cambridge: Cambridge University Press

Hoffman, Bruce (2001): *Combating Terrorism: In Search of a National Strategy*, Washington, DC: Testimony given before the Subcommittee on National Security, Veterans Affairs, and International Relations, House Committee on Government Reform, 27 March

Hoge, James F. jr, and Gideon Rose (2001) (eds.): *How Did This Happen? Terrorism and the New War*, Oxford: Public Affairs Ltd

Hollis, Rosemary (1997): 'Europe and the Middle East: Power by Stealth?', *International Affairs* 73 (1): 15–29

(1999): 'Barcelona's First Pillar: An Appropriate Concept for Security Relations?', in Behrendt and Hanelt 1999, 107–32

(2002): 'Two Dreams Dashed', *World Today* 58 (6): 4–6

Holm, Hans-Henrik, and Georg Sørensen (1995) (eds.): *Whose World Order? Uneven Globalization and the End of the Cold War*, Boulder, CO: Westview Press

Holm, Ulla (1992): *Det Franske Europa*, Aarhus: Aarhus Universitetsforlag

(2000): 'France: A European Civilizational Power', in Peter Burgess and Ola Tunander (eds.), *European Security Identities: Contested Understandings of EU and NATO*, Oslo: PRIO Report 2/2000, 173–91

Holsti, Kalevi J. (1996): *The State, War, and the State of War*, Cambridge: Cambridge University Press

Hoskin, Gary, and Gabriel Murillo (2001): 'Colombia's Perpetual Quest for Peace', *Journal of Democracy* 12 (2): 32–45

Howard, Michael (1976): *War in European History*, Oxford: Oxford University Press

Howe, Herbert M. (1998): 'Private Security Forces and African Stability: The Case of Executive Outcomes', *Journal of Modern African Studies* 36 (2): 307–31

Hoyt, Paul D. (2000): 'The "Rogue State" Image in American Foreign Policy', *Global Society* 14 (2): 297–310

Hudson, Valerie M. (1997) (ed.): *Culture and Foreign Policy*, Boulder, CO, and London: Lynne Rienner

Hughes, Christopher (1997): 'Globalisation and Nationalism: Squaring the Circle in Chinese International Relations Theory', *Millennium* 26 (1): 103–24

Hughes, Robert (1993): *Culture of Complaint: The Fraying of America*, Oxford: Oxford University Press

Huliaris, Asteris (2001): 'Qadafi's Comeback: Libya and Sub-Saharan Africa in the 1990s', *African Affairs* 99 (398): 5–25

Huntington, Samuel P. (1991): 'America's Changing Strategic Interests', *Survival* 33 (1): 3–17

(1993): 'The Clash of Civilizations?', *Foreign Affairs* 72 (3): 22–49

(1996): *The Clash of Civilizations and the Remaking of World Order*, New York: Simon and Schuster

(1999): 'The Lonely Superpower', *Foreign Affairs* 78 (2): 35–49

(1999–2000): 'Robust Nationalism', *National Interest* 58 (Winter): 31–40

Hurrell, Andrew (1992): 'Latin America in the New World Order: A Regional Bloc of the Americas', *International Affairs* 68 (1)

(1995a): 'Regionalism in the Americas', in Fawcett and Hurrell 1995, 250–82

(1995b): 'Regionalism in Theoretical Perspective', in Fawcett and Hurrell 1995, 37–73

(1998): 'An Emerging Security Community in South America?', in Adler and Barnett 1998, 228–64

Hurst, David (1999): 'Where Tyranny Spells Peace', *Guardian Weekly* March (28): 8

Hyden, Goran (1983): *No Shortcuts to Progress: African Development Management in Perspective*, Berkeley: University of California Press

ICG (International Crisis Group) (2001a): *After Milosevic: A Practical Agenda for Lasting Balkans Peace*, http://www.intl-crisis-group.org

(2001b): *Central Asian Perspectives on 11 September and the Afghan Crisis*, http://www.intl-crisis-group.org/projects/asia/centralasia/reports/Central_Asian_Perspectives_Afghan_Crisis.pdf

Ikenberry, G. John (2001): *After Victory: Institutions, Strategic Restraint, and the Rebuilding of Order After the Major Wars*, Princeton: Princeton University Press

Ikenberry, G. John, and Charles Kupchan (1990): 'Socialization and Hegemonic Power', *International Organization* 44 (3) (Summer): 283–315

Il Manifesto (ed.) (1979): *Power and Opposition in Post-Revolutionary Societies*, London: Ink Links (Italian original 1978)

IMF (International Monetary Fund) (2001): *The World Economic Outlook (WEO) Database October 2001*, http://www.imf.org/external/pubs/ft/weo/2001/02/data/index.htm

Inbar, Efraim (1995) (ed.): *Regional Security Regimes: Israel and Its Neighbors*, Albany: State University of New York Press

(2001): 'Regional Implications of the Israeli–Turkish Strategic Partnership', *Middle East Review of International Affairs* 5 (2): 48–65

Jachtenfuchs, Markus (1994): *International Policy-Making as a Learning Process: The European Community and the Greenhouse Effect*, Florence: Ph.D dissertation, European University Institute

Jachtenfuchs, Markus, and Michael Huber (1993): 'Institutional Learning in the European Community: The Response to the Greenhouse Effect', in J. D. Lifferink, P. D. Lowe, and A. P. J. Mold (eds.), *European Integration and Environmental Policy*, London: Belhaven, 36–58

Jackson, Robert H. (1990): *Quasi-States: Sovereignty, International Relations, and the Third World*, Cambridge: Cambridge University Press

(1992): 'The Security Dilemma in Africa', in Job 1992, 81–94

Jackson, Robert H., and Carl G. Rosberg (1982): 'Why Africa's Weak States Persist: The Empirical and the Juridical in Statehood', *World Politics* 35 (1): 1–24

(1984): 'Pax Africana and Its Problems', in Richard Bissell and Michael Radu (eds.), *Africa in the Post-Decolonization Era*, Rutgers, NJ: Transaction Books, 187–209

(1985): 'The Marginality of African States', in Gwendolen M. Carter and Patricia O'Meara (eds.), *Twenty-Five Years of African Independence*, Bloomington: Indiana University Press, 45–70

Jahn, Egbert (1981): 'Social Reform Policy and Detente Policy in Eastern and Western Europe', in Egbert Jahn and Yoshikazu Sakamoto (eds.), *Elements of World Instability: Proceedings of the International Peace Research Association. Eighth General Conference*, Frankfurt and New York: Campus Verlag, 323–35

(1982): 'Elemente eines friedenswissenschaftlichen Entspannungsbegriffes', in Peter Schlotter (ed.), *Europa zwischen Konfrontation und Kooperation: Entspannungspolitik für die achtzieger Jahre*, Frankfurt and New York: Campus Verlag, 15–36

Jansen, Johannes J. G. (1997): *The Dual Nature of Islamic Fundamentalism*, London: Hurst and Company

Jensen, Kurt Villads (2000): 'Temaer i Korstogshistorien – et historiografisk rids', *Den Jyske Historiker* 88: 8–29

Jensen, Steffen (2001): *Claiming Community – Negotiating Crime: State Formation, Neighborhood, and Gangs in a Capetonian Township*, Roskilde: Ph.D dissertation, International Developmental Studies, Roskilde University, Denmark

Jentleson, Bruce W., and Dalia Dassa Kaye (1998): 'Regional Security Cooperation and Its Limits in the Middle East', *Security Studies* 8 (1): 204–38

Jervis, Robert (1982): 'Security Regimes', *International Organization* 36 (2): 357–78

Jian, Chen (1996): 'Understanding the Logic of Beijing's Taiwan Policy', *Security Dialogue* 27 (4): 459–63

Job, Brian (1992) (ed.): *The Insecurity Dilemma: National Security of Third World States*, Boulder, CO: Lynne Rienner

Joeck, Neil (1997): *Maintaining Nuclear Stability in South Asia*, London: International Institute for Strategic Studies, Adelphi Paper no. 312

Joenniemi, Pertti and J. Prawitz (1998) (eds.): *Kaliningrad: The European Amber Region*, Aldershot: Ashgate

Joenniemi, Pertti, and Juris Prikulis (1994) (eds.): *The Foreign Policies of the Baltic Countries*, Riga: Centre of Baltic–Nordic History of Political Studies

Joenniemi, Pertti, and Ole Wæver (1997): 'Balternes "kolde krig" mod Rusland er ved at være slut', *Mandag Morgen* 12: 25–9

Joffe, George (2000): *Europe and the Mediterranean: The Barcelona Process Five Years On*, London: Royal Institute of International Affairs, Briefing Paper, n.s., 16 August

Joffe, Josef (2001): 'Clinton's World: Purpose, Policy and Weltanschauung', *Washington Quarterly* 24 (1): 141–54

Johnson, Paul (1991): *The Birth of the Modern: World Society, 1815–1830*, New York: Harper Perennial

Johnson, Stephen (2000): 'US–Mexico Relations: No More Business as Usual', *Heritage Foundation Executive Memorandum* 689 (July 20): 1–2

References

Jones, Howard (1992): *Union in Peril: The Crisis over British Intervention in the Civil War*, Chapel Hill and London: University of North Carolina Press

Jonson, Lena (2001): 'Russia and Central Asia', in Allison and Jonson 2001, 95–126

Jonson, Lena, and Roy Allison (2001): 'Central Asian Security: Internal and External Dynamics', in Allison and Jonson 2001, 1–23

Juergensmeyer, Mark (1993): *The New Cold War? Religious Nationalism Confronts the Secular State*, Berkeley, Los Angeles, and London: University of California Press

(2000): *Terror in the Mind of God: The Global Rise of Religious Violence*, Berkeley, Los Angeles, and London: University of California Press

Jung, Dietrich (1999): '"Die Rache der Janitscharen": Der türkische Modernisierungsprozess und seine Blockade', *Orient* 40 (2): 211–33

(2003) (ed.): *Shadow Globalization, Ethnic Conflicts, and New Wars: A Political Economy of Intra-State War*, London: Routledge

Jung, Dietrich, and Wolfgango Piccoli (2000): 'The Turkish–Israeli Alignment: Paranoia or Pragmatism?', *Security Dialogue* 31 (1): 91–104

Jurgaitiené, Kornelija (1993): 'Romantic Nationalism and the Challenge of Europeanization: A Case of Lithuania', in Pertti Joenniemi and Peter Vares (eds.), *New Actors on the International Arena: The Foreign Policies of the Baltic Countries*, Tampere: Tampere Peace Research Institute, 89–112

Jurgaitiené, Kornelija, and Ole Wæver (1996): 'Lithuania', in Mouritzen et al. 1996, 185–229

Kacowicz, Arie M. (1998): *Zones of Peace in the Third World: South America and West Africa in Comparative Perspective*, New York: State University of New York Press

(2000): 'Stable Peace in South America: The ABC Triangle 1979–1999', in Kacowicz et al. 2000, 200–19

Kacowicz, Arie M., Yaacov Bar-Siman-Tov, Ole Engström, and Magnus Jerneck (2000) (eds.): *Stable Peace Among Nations*, Lanham, MD: Rowman & Littlefield Publishers

Kadish, Ronald T. (2002): *Lt Gen. Kadish Special Briefing on Missile Defense*, United States Department of Defense, News transcript, June 25, http://defenselink.mil/news/Jun2002/t06252002_t0625kadish.html

Kaiser, Karl (1968–9): 'The Interaction of Regional Subsystems: Some Preliminary Notes on Recurrent Patterns and the Role of Superpowers', *World Politics* 21: 84–107

Kak, Kapil (1998): 'Management of India's Security and Higher Defence – 1', *Strategic Analysis* 22 (31): web edition 1–8

Kang, Dave (1995): *The Middle Road: Security and Cooperation in Northeast Asia*, Hanover, NH: Dartmouth College, unpublished typescript, 6 July

(2000): *Culture, Hierarchy, and Stability in Asian International Relations*, Hanover, NH: Dartmouth College, unpublished typescript

Kaplan, Morton A. (1957): *System and Process in International Politics*, New York: John Wiley

Kaplan, Robert D. (1994): 'The Coming Anarchy', *Atlantic Monthly* February: 44–76

(2002): *Warrior Politics: Why Leadership Demands a Pagan Ethos*, New York: Random House

Kapstein, Ethan B. (1999): 'Does Unipolarity Have a Future?', in Kapstein and Mastanduno 1999, 464–90

Kapstein, Ethan B., and Michael Mastanduno (1999) (eds.): *Unipolar Politics: Realism and State Strategies After the Cold War*, New York: Columbia University Press

Karaganov, Sergei (1992): 'Problems of Russia's Foreign Political Strategy Regarding the "Close Foreign Countries" ', *Diplomaticheski Vestnik* 22 December: (translation in *Baltic Independent*, 5–11 March 1993, p. 9)

Karakasidou, Anastasia (1995): 'Vestiges of the Ottoman Past: Muslims Under Siege in Greek Thrace', *Cultural Survival Quarterly* 19 (2): 71–5

Karatnycky, Adrian (2002): 'Bush's Uzbekistan Test', *Christian Science Monitor*, 13 March, http://www.csmonitor.com/2002/0313/p09s02–coop.html

Karawan, Ibrahim A. (1997): *The Islamist Impasse*, London: International Institute for Strategic Studies. Adelphi Paper no. 314

Kaski, Antti (2001): *The Security Complex: A Theoretical Analysis and the Baltic Case*, Turku: Ph.D dissertation, Turun Yliopisto

Katzenstein, Lawrence C. (1997): 'Change, Myth, and the Reunification of China', in Hudson 1997, 45–72

Katzenstein, Peter J. (1996a) (ed.): *The Culture of National Security: Norms and Identity in World Politics*, New York: Columbia University Press

(1996b): 'Regionalism in Comparative Perspective', *Cooperation and Conflict* 31 (2): 123–59

(2000): *Re-examining Norms of Interstate Relations in the New Millennium*, Kuala Lumpur: Paper for the 14th Asia-Pacific Roundtable

Katzenstein, Peter J., and Nobou Okawara (1993): 'Japan's National Security: Structures, Norms, Policies', *International Security* 17 (4): 84–118

Kazan, Işıl (1996): 'Tyrkiet mod det 21. Århundrede – tyrkiets nationale diskurser: osmannisme, islamisme, tyrkisme og kemalisme', *Den Jyske Historiker* 74 (December): 79–98

(2002): *Regionalisation of Security and Securitisation of a Region: Turkish Security Policy After the Cold War*, Copenhagen: Ph.D dissertation, COPRI

Kazan, Işıl, and Ole Wæver (1994): 'Tyrkiet mellem Europa og europæisering', *Internasjonal Politikk* 52 (2): 139–76

Kegley, Charles W., and Gregory Raymond (1994): *A Multipolar Peace? Great Power Politics in the Twenty-First Century*, New York: St Martin's Press

Keller, Edmond (1997): 'Rethinking Africa's Regional Security', in Lake and Morgan 1997c, 296–317

Kelly, Phillip (1997): *Checkerboards and Shatterbelts: The Geopolitics of South America*, Austin: University of Texas Press

Kemp, Geoffrey (1998–9): 'The Persian Gulf Remains the Strategic Prize', *Survival* 40 (4): 132–49

References

Kenworthy, Eldon (1995): *America/Américas: Myth in the Making of US Policy Toward Latin America*, University Park: Penn State University Press

Keohane, Robert O. (1990): 'Le Istituzioni internazionali del mondo nuovo', *Relazioni Internazionali* December: 3–17

Keohane, Robert O., and Joseph S. Nye (1977): *Power and Interdependence*, Boston: Little Brown

Kepel, Gilles (2002 [2000]): *Jihad: The Trail of Political Islam*, London and New York: I. B. Tauris

Keylor, William R. (1984): *The Twentieth-Century World*, New York: Oxford University Press

Khalilzad, Zalmay (1984): *Security in Southern Asia I: The Security of Southwest Asia*, Aldershot: Gower

Khalilzad, Zalmay, and Ian O. Lesser (1998) (eds.): *Sources of Conflict in the Twenty-First Century: Regional Futures and US Strategy*, Washington, DC: Rand

Khokhar, Camilla, and Poul Wiberg-Jørgensen (2000): *USAs interesser i Sydkaukasus* [U.S.'s interests in the South Caucasus], Copenhagen: Institute of Political Science, University of Copenhagen, MA thesis, http://www.kaukasus.dk/publikation21.htm

Khong, Yuen Foong (1997): 'ASEAN and the Southeast Asian Security Complex', in Lake and Morgan 1997c, 318–42

Kim, Shee Poon (1977): 'A Decade of ASEAN 1967–1977', *Asian Survey* 17 (8): 753–70

Kimura, Hiroshi Li Shaojun, and Il-Dong Koh (1999): ' "Frontiers Are the Razor's Edge": Russia's Borders with Its Eastern Neighbors', in Rozman et al. 1999, 150–71

Kinder, Hermann, and Werner Hilgemann (1999): *Atlas zur Weltgeschichte I. Von den Anfängen bis zur Französichen Revolution*, Munich: Deutsche Taschenbuch Verlag

Kinnes, Irvin (2000): 'Gang Warfare in the Western Cape: Background', *Monograph* 48 (June): web edition 1–4

Kinsella, David (1999): *Arms Transfers, Dependence, and Regional Stability: Isolated Effects or General Patterns?*, Washington, DC: Paper presented at the annual meeting of the International Studies Association, 15–16 February

Kirby, David (1990): *Northern Europe in the Early Modern Period: The Baltic World 1492–1772*, London and New York: Longman

Kissinger, Henry A. (1957): *A World Restored: Castlereagh, Metternich, and the Restoration of Peace, 1812–1822*, Boston: Houghton Mifflin

(1968): 'The White Revolutionary: Reflections on Bismarck', *Dædalus* 97 (Summer): 888–924

Klare, Michael (1995): *Rogue States and Nuclear Outlaws: America's Search for a New Foreign Policy*, New York: Hill and Wang

Kodama, Katsuya, and Unto Vesa (1990) (eds.): *Towards a Comparative Analysis of Peace Movements*, Worcester: Billing & Sons

Kotkin, Stephen (1997): *Defining Territories and Empires: From Mongol Ulus to Russian Siberia 1200–1800*, http://www.src-h.slav.hokudai.ac.jp/sympo/Proceed97/Kotkin1.html

Krasner, Stephen D. (1978): *Defending the National Interest*, Princeton: Princeton University Press

(1983) (ed.): *International Regimes*, International Organization 36 (2) (Special Issue) (Spring)

Kratochwil, Friedrich (1982): 'On the Notion of "Interest" in International Relations', *International Organization* 36 (1): 1–30

(1989): *Rules, Norms, and Decisions*, Cambridge: Cambridge University Press

Krause, Keith (1996): 'Insecurity and State Formation in the Global Military Order: The Middle Eastern Case', *European Journal of International Relations* 2 (3): 319–54

Krauthammer, Charles (1990–1): 'The Unipolar Moment', *Foreign Affairs* 70 (1): 23–33

(1999): 'A Second American Century', *Time* December (27): 186

(2001a): 'The New Unilateralism', *Washington Post* June (8): A29

(2001b): 'Unilateral? Yes, Indeed', http://www.washingtonpost.com/ac2/wp-dyn?pagename=article&node=opinion/columns/krauthammercharles&contentId=A41292–2001Dec13&notFound=true

Krepon, Michael, and Amit Sewak (1995) (eds.): *Crisis Prevention, Confidence Building, and Reconciliation in South Asia*, New York: St Martin's Press

Kumaraswamy, P. R. (1998): *India and Israel: Evolving Strategic Partnership*, Begin–Sadat Center for Strategic Studies, Bar-Ilan University, Security and Policy Studies no. 40

Kunadze, Georgi F. (1999): 'Border Problems Between Russia and Its Neighbors: Stable for Now, But Stubborn in the Long Run', in Rozman et al. 1999, 133–49

Kundera, Milan (1984): 'The Tragedy of Central Europe', *New York Review of Books* 26 April: 33–8

Kupchan, Charles A. (1998): 'After Pax Americana: Benign Power, Regional Integration, and the Sources of Stable Multipolarity', *International Security* 23 (2): 40–79

Kupchan, Charles A., and Clifford A. Kupchan (1991): 'Concerts, Collective Security, and the Future of Europe', *International Security* 16 (1): 114–161

Kuusisto, Riikka (1998): 'Framing the Wars in the Gulf and in Bosnia: The Rhetorical Definitions of the Western Power Leaders in Action', *Journal of Peace Research* 35 (5): 603–20

Kuzio, Taras (2000): 'Geopolitical Pluralism in the CIS: The Emergence of GUUAM', *European Security* 9 (2): 81–114

(2002a): 'CIS States Confront Questions Concerning Strategic Alignment', *Eurasia Insight* July (11): http://www.eurasianet.org/departments/insight/articles/eav070102.shtml

(2002b): 'GUUAM Reverts to GUAM as Uzbekistan Suspends Its Membership Prior to Yalta Summit', *Eurasia Insight* July (18): http://www.eurasianet.org/departments/insight/articles/eav071802.shtml

Ladd Hollist, W., and Daniel L. Nielson (1998): 'Taking Stock of Inter-American Bonds: Approaches to Explaining Cooperation in the Western Hemisphere', *Mershon International Studies Review* 42 (Supplement 2, November): 257–82

LaFeber, Walter (1989): *The American Age: United States Foreign Policy at Home and Abroad Since 1750*, New York and London: W. W. Norton

(1993): *The Cambridge History of American Foreign Relations, vol. II*, Cambridge: Cambridge University Press

LaFranchi, Howard (2002): 'US Poised to Take Terror War to Colombia', *Christian Science Monitor* May (31): 8

Lake, David A. (1992): 'Powerful Pacifists: Democratic States and War', *American Political Science Review* 86 (1): 24–37

(1997): 'Regional Security Complexes: A Systems Approach', in Lake and Morgan 1997c, 45–67

(1999): 'Ulysses's Triumph: American Power and the New World Order', *Security Studies* 8 (4): 44–78

Lake, David A., and Patrick M. Morgan (1997a): 'Building Security in the New World of Regional Orders', in Lake and Morgan 1997c, 343–53

(1997b): 'The New Regionalism in Security Affairs', in Lake and Morgan 1997c, 3–19

(1997c): *Regional Orders: Building Security in a New World*, University Park: Penn State University Press

Lakshmanan, Indira A. R. (2001): 'The Accidental Confidant: How bin Laden Chose His Biographer', *Boston Globe* 27 September: http://www.spicequest.com/clips/cult905.htm

Larsen, Henrik (1997): *Foreign Policy and Discourse Analysis: Britain, France and Europe*, London: Routledge

(2000): 'The Discourse on the EU's Role in the World', in Birthe Hansen and Bertel Heurlin (eds.), *The New World Order: Contrasting Theories*, Houndsmills, Basingstoke and London: Macmillan, 217–44

Lasswell, Harold D. (1950): *National Security and Individual Freedom*, New York, Toronto, and London: McGraw-Hill, Committee for Economic Development Research Study

Laustsen, Carsten Bagge, and Ole Wæver (2000): 'In Defence of Religion: Sacred Reference Objects for Securitization', *Millennium* 29 (3): 705–39

Layne, Christopher (1993): 'The Unipolar Illusion: Why New Great Powers Will Rise', *International Security* 17 (4): 5–51

(1997): 'From Preponderance to Offshore Balancing: America's Future Grand Strategy', *International Security* 22 (1): 86–124

Lee, Rensselaer, and Raphael Perl (2002): *'Terrorism, the Future, and US Foreign Policy'*: The Library of Congress, Congressional Research Service, Issue Brief for

Congress no. IB95112, Washington, DC: Foreign Affairs, Defense, and Trade Division

Leffler, Melvyn F. (1992): *A Preponderance of Power: National Security, the Truman Administration, and the Cold War*, Stanford, CA: Stanford University Press

Legrain, Jean-Francois (1991): 'A Defining Moment: Palestinian Islamic Fundamentalism', in Piscatori 1991a, 70–87

Leifer, Michael (1996): *The ASEAN Regional Forum*, London: International Institute for Strategic Studies Adelphi Paper no. 302

Lemaitre, Pierre, Kristian Gerner, and Torben Hansen (1993): 'The Crisis of Societal Security in the Former Soviet Union', in Wæver et al. 1993, 110–30

Lemke, Douglas (2002): *Regions of War and Peace*, Cambridge: Cambridge University Press

Lenin, V. I. (1961 [1917]): *Imperialism, the Highest Stage of Capitalism*, Moscow: Foreign Languages Publishing House

Lepingwell, John W. R. (1994): 'The Russian Military and Security in the "Near Abroad"', *Survival* 3 (23): 70–92

Levine, Barry B. (1989): 'A Return to Innocence? The Social Construction of the Geopolitical Climate of the Post-Invasion Caribbean', *Journal of Interamerican Studies and World Affairs* 31 (3): 183–204

Levitin, Oleg (2000): 'Inside Moscow's Kosovo Muddle', *Survival* 42 (1): 130–40

Lewis, Bernard (1982): *The Muslim Discovery of Europe*, London: Weidenfeld & Nicolson

Li, Nan (2001): *From Revolutionary Internationalism to Conservative Nationalism*, Washington, DC: United States Institute of Peace

Li, Rex (1996): 'The Taiwan Strait Crisis and the Future of China–Taiwan Relations', *Security Dialogue* 27 (4): 449–59

(1999): 'Partners or Rivals? Chinese Perceptions of Japan's Security Strategy in the Asia-Pacific Region', *Journal of Strategic Studies* 22 (4): 1–25

Li, Tzu-Ching (1997): 'CPC Thinks China and United States Will Eventually Go to War', *Cheng Ming* 235: 15–16

Lieven, Dominic (2000): *Empire: The Russian Empire and Its Rivals*, London: John Murray

Limaye, Sato P. (2001): 'Nuclear Weapons and Regional Security in East Asia', in Joachim Krause and Andreas Wenger (eds.), *Nuclear Weapons into the Twenty-First Century: Current Trends and Future Prospects*, Bern: Peter Lang, 177–93

Lindley-French, Julian (2002): 'Terms of Engagement: The Paradox of American Power and the Transatlantic Dilemma Post-11 September', *Chaillot Paper* 52 May: http://www.iss-eu.org/chaillot/chai52e.html

Lipschutz, Ronnie D. (1999): 'Terror in the Suites: Narratives of Fear and the Political Economy of Danger', *Global Society* 13 (4): 411–39

Little, Richard (1989): 'Deconstructing the Balance of Power: Two Traditions of Thought', *Review of International Studies* 15 (2): 87–101

References

Lobo-Guerrero Sanz, Luis Erneste (2000): *El Conflicto Armado Colombiano: ¿ Una Amenaza para la Seguridad Regional?*, Bogotá: Pontificia Universidad Javeriana, Monografía para optar al título de Politólogo con énfasis en Relaciones Internationales

Lomperis, Timothy J. (1996): *Flawed Realism. Hans Morgenthau and Kenneth Waltz on the Vietnam War: The Case for a Regional Level-of-Analysis*, San Francisco: Paper presented at the American Political Science Association meeting, 29 August–1 September

Lose, Lars Gert (1995): *Applying the Concept of Security Complexes to the Balkans Post-Cold War*, student paper, University of Warwick

Lough, John (1993): 'The Place of the "Near Abroad" in Russia's Foreign Policy', *RFE/RL Research Report* 2 (11): 21–39

Loveman, Brian, and Thomas M. Davies (1997) (eds.): *The Politics of Antipolitics: The Military in Latin America*, Lincoln: University of Nebraska Press

Lowenthal, Abraham F. (1979): 'Jimmy Carter and Latin America: A New Era or Small Change?', in Kenneth A. Oye, Donald Rotschild, and Robert J. Lieber (eds.), *Eagle Entangled: US Foreign Policy in a Complex World*, New York: Longman, 290–303

Lucero, Jose Antonio (2001): 'Crisis and Contention in Ecuador', *Journal of Democracy* 12 (2): 59–73

Lustick, Ian S. (1997): 'The Absence of Middle Eastern Great Powers: Political "Backwardness" in Historical Perspective', *International Organization* 51 (4): 653–83

Luttwak, Edward N. (1993): *The Endangered American Dream*, New York: Touchstone

Lynch, Dov (1999): ' "Walking the Tightrope": The Kosovo Conflict and Russia in European Security, 1998–August 1999', *European Security* 8 (4): 57–83

Lysenko, I. (2002): 'Caspian Pipeline Consortium', *International Affairs (Moscow)* 48 (2): 34–40

Mace, Gordon (1999): 'The Origins, Nature, and Scope of the Hemispheric Project', in Mace and Bélanger 1999, 19–36

Mace, Gordon, and Louis Bélanger (1999): *The Americas in Transition: The Contours of Regionalism*, Boulder, CO, and London: Lynne Rienner

Machon, Lotte (2000) (ed.): *Security and Peacebuilding in South Eastern Europe*, Copenhagen: Report from Danish Institute of International Affairs Conference, 1–2 December

Mackinder, Halford J. (1904): 'The Geographic Pivot of History', *Geographical Journal* 23 (4) (April): 421–42

Maduna, P. M. (1999): *Debate on the Directorate of Special Operations*, Cape Town: Address during the snap debate on the Directorate of Special Operations, 11 November

Mahbubani, Kishore (1995): 'The Pacific Impulse', *Survival* 37 (1): 105–20

Mahendra, K. L. (2002): 'Working-Class Struggles Against Globalisation', *New Age* 50 (12) (24 March): 5

520

Maier, Karl (2001): *This House Has Fallen: Midnight in Nigeria*, New York: Public Affairs

Malaquias, Assis (2001): 'Diamonds are a Guerilla's Best Friend: The Impact of Illicit Wealth on Insurgency Strategy', *Third World Quarterly* 22 (3): 225–311

Malcolm, Neil, Alex Pravda, Roy Allison, and Margot Light (1996) (eds.): *Internal Factors in Russian Foreign Policy*, New York: Oxford University Press

Malcolm, Noel (1994): *Bosnia: A Short History*, New York: New York University Press

Malmborg, Mikael af, and Bo Stråth (2002) (eds.): *The Meaning of Europe*, Oxford and New York: Berg

Mandel, Robert (1999): *Deadly Transfers and the Global Playground: Transnational Security Threats in a Disorderly World*, Westport, CT: Praeger

Mann, Steven R. (2001): *American Diplomat Sees Encouraging Signs on Baku–Ceyhan Pipeline*, http://www.eurasianet.org/departments/qanda/articles/eav110801.shtml

Manor, James, and Gerald Segal (1998): 'Taking India Seriously', *Survival* 40 (2): 53–70

Manwaring, Max G. (2002): *Nonstate Actors in Colombia: Threat and Response*, Carlisle, PA: US Army War College, Strategic Studies Institute

Maoz, Zeev (1997): 'Regional Security in the Middle East: Past Trends, Present Realities, and Future Challenges', *Journal of Strategic Studies* 20 (1): 1–45

Marcella, Gabriel, and Richard Downes (1999): *Security Cooperation in the Western Hemisphere: Resolving the Ecuador–Peru Conflict*, Miami: North–South Center Press

Marcella, Gabriel, and Donald E. Schulz (1999): 'War and Peace in Colombia', *Washington Quarterly* 22 (3): 213–28

Marchand, Marianne H. (2001): 'North American Regionalisms and Regionalization in the 1990s', in Schulz et al. 2001, 198–210

Marcussen, Martin, Thomas Risse, Daniela Engelmann-Martin, Hans Joachim Knopf, and Klaus Roscher (1999): 'Constructing European Identities? The Evolution of British, French and German Nation State Identities', *Journal of European Public Policy* 6 (4): 614–33

Mares, David R. (1997): 'Regional Conflict Management in Latin America: Power Complemented by Diplomacy', in Lake and Morgan 1997c, 195–218

(2001): *Violent Peace: Militarized Interstate Bargaining in Latin America*, New York: Columbia University Press

(n.d.): *Latin American Perspectives on the Causes, Prevention, and Resolution of Deadly Intra- and Interstate Conflicts, 1982–1996*, Carnegie Commission on Preventing Deadly Conflict, http://www.ccpdc.org/pubs/mares/mrfr.htm

Marty, Martin A., and R. Scott Appleby (1995) (eds.): *Fundamentalisms Comprehended*, Chicago: Chicago University Press

References

Mastanduno, Michael (1991): 'Do Relative Gains Matter? America's Response to Japanese Industrial Policy', *International Security* 16 (1): 73–113

(1997): 'Preserving the Unipolar Moment: Realist Theories and US Grand Strategy After the Cold War', *International Security* 21 (4): 49–88

Mastanduno, Michael, and Ethan B. Kapstein (1999): 'Realism and State Strategies After the Cold War', in Kapstein and Mastanduno 1999, 1–27

Matras, Yaon (2000): 'Romani Migrations in the Post-Communist Era: Their Historical and Political Significance', *Cambridge Review of International Affairs* 13 (2): 32–50

Matz, Johan (2001): *Constructing a Post-Soviet International Political Reality: Russian Foreign Policy Towards the Newly Independent States 1990–1995*, Ph.D dissertation, Uppsala University

Maull, Hanns W. (1990–1): 'Germany and Japan: The New Civilian Powers', *Foreign Affairs* 69 (5): 91–106

Maull, Hanns W., and Bernhard Stahl (2002): 'Durch den Balkan nach Europa? Deutschland und Frankreich in den Jugoslawienkriegen', *PVS: Politische Vierteljahresschrift* 43 (1): 82–111

Mazrui, Ali (1997): *Supra-National Ethnicity, Sub-National Religion and Vice-Versa: The Contradictions of Africa's Primordial Experience*, Stockholm: Paper for the International Symposium on Nationalism and Internationalism in the Post-Cold War Era, September

Mbeki, Thabo (1999a): *Opening Address at the Deputy President's Budget Debate, March 23*, Cape Town: http://www.anc.org.za/ancdocs/history/mbeki/1999/tm0323.html

(1999b): *Statement at the 35th Ordinary Session of the OAU Assembly of Heads of State and Government, July 13*, Algiers: http://www.anc.org.za/ancdocs/history/mbeki/1999/tm0713.html

(2001a): *Opening of Western Cape Municipal Police Service Training Facility*, Cape Town: Address at the opening of the Western Cape Municipal Police Service Training Facility, Phillipi, 12 September

(2001b): *Responses to Parliamentary Questions in the National Assembly, March 14*, Cape Town: http://www.anc.org.za/ancdocs/history/mbeki/2001/tm0314.html

(2001c): *State of the Nation Address of the President of South Africa at the Opening of Parliament, February 9*, Cape Town: http://www.anc.org.za/ancdocs/history/mbeki/2001/tm0209.html

McCann, Frank D. (1983): 'The Brazilian General Staff and Brazil's Military Situation, 1900–1945', *Journal of Interamerican Studies and World Affairs* 25 (3): 299–324

McDermott, Anthony (1999) (ed.): *Sovereign Intervention*, Oslo: PRIO Report 2/99

McDermott, Roger N. (2002): 'Looking for Trouble? Russia Steers Central Asian Antiterrorist Preparations', *Eurasia Insight* July (22): http://www.eurasianet.org/departments/insight/articles/eav072202a.shtml

McDougall, Walter A. (1997): *Promised Land, Crusader State: The American Encounter with the World Since 1776*, New York: Houghton Mifflin

McEvedy, Colin (1988): *The Penguin Atlas of North American History to 1870*, London: Penguin

McKeeby, David (1999): 'Caspian Dreams: A Case Study in Modern US Foreign Policy Making', *Young Leaders Forum* 3 (1): http://www.csis.org/intern/forum991h.html

McNeill, William H. (1963): *The Rise of the West: A History of the Human Community*, Chicago: University of Chicago Press

McNulty, Jennifer (2000): 'Guatemala's Peace Requires International Support, Says Author', *UC Santa Cruz Currents Online* February (28): 1–3

McNulty, Mel (1999): 'The Collapse of Zaire: Implosion, Revolution or External Sabotage?', *Journal of Modern African Studies* 37 (1): 53–82

Mearsheimer, John J. (1990): 'Back to the Future: Instability in Europe After the Cold War', *International Security* 15 (1): 5–56

Mendel, William W. (1999): 'The Brazilian Amazon: Controlling the Hydra', *Military Review* July–August: web edition 1–12

Metz, Steven (2000): *American Strategy: Issues and Alternatives for the Quadrennial Defense Review*, Carlisle, PA: US Army War College, Strategic Studies Institute

Migranyan, Andranik (1994): 'Russia and the Near Abroad: The Shaping of the New Foreign Policy Line of the Russian Federation', *Nesavisimaja gaseta* 12 and 18 January: Danish translation by Lars P. Poulsen-Hansen

Miller, Benjamin (2000): *Systemic Effects on the Transition of the Middle East and the Balkans from the Cold War to the Post-Cold War Era*, Los Angeles: Paper presented at ISA Convention, Los Angeles, March

Miniotaite, Grazina (2000): *The Security Policy of Lithuania and the 'Integration Dilemma'*, Copenhagen: COPRI Working Paper no. 5

Minnaar, Anthony (2001): 'Border Control and Regionalism. The Case of South Africa', *African Security Review* 10 (1): web edition 1–15

Missiroli, Antonio (2000): *CFSP, Defence and Flexibility*, Paris: Western European Union Institute for Security Studies

Moïsi, Dominique (2000): 'An Emperor with No Interest in His Empire', *Financial Times* May (8): http://www.ifri.org/F/Articles/Articles/dm_0005_emperor.htm

Møller, Bjørn (2000): *Security Cooperation in Southern Africa: Lessons from the European Experience*, Copenhagen: Southern African Regional Institute for Policy Studies (Annual Colloquium)

(2001): *Raising Armies in a Rough Neighbourhood: Soldiers, Guerillas, and Mercenaries in Southern Africa*, Copenhagen: SARIPS (Third Draft)

Mongolia, Concept of Foreign Policy (n.d.): http://www.indiana.edu/~mongsoc/mong/foreign.htm

Morgan, Patrick A. (1997): 'Regional Security Complexes and Regional Orders', in Lake and Morgan 1997c, 20–42

References

Morgenthau, Hans J. (1978 [1948]): *Politics Among Nations: The Struggle for Power and Peace*, New York: Alfred A. Knopf

Moriarty, Robert E. (1997): *Environmental Security: What Environmental Issues Impact Regional Stability and Affect United States Foreign Policy with Mexico?*, Research Paper presented to the Research Department, Air Command and Staff College

Mørk, Henning (1991): 'Jugoslaviskhed', *Den Jyske Historiker* (Hinsides Habsburg) 57: 90–111

Mouritzen, Hans (1998): *Theory and Reality of International Politics*, Aldershot: Ashgate

Mouritzen, Hans, Ole Wæver, and Håkan Wiberg, with Anjo Harrayvan et al. (1996) (eds.): *European Integration and National Adaptations*, Commack, NY: Nova Science Publishers

Mozaffari, Mehdi (1997): 'The CIS's Southern Belt: A New Security System', in Mehdi Mozaffari (ed.), *Security Politics in the Commonwealth of Independent States*, New York: St. Martin's Press, 3–34

(2002): 'Bin Laden and Islamist Terrorism', *Militært Tidsskrift* 131 (1): 23–35

Mufamadi, F. S. (1997): *Speech by Minister F. S. Mufamadi, Minister for Safety and Security on the National Assembly Budget Votes, April 18*, South Africa: Safety and Security Budget Speech, http://www.polity.org.za/govdocs/speeches/1997/secbudgt.html

Muller, Marie (1999): *South African Diplomacy and Security Complex Theory*, Leicester: Centre for the Study of Diplomacy, University of Leicester, Discussion Paper 53

Muñiz, Humberto García, and Jorge Rodríguez Beruff (1994): 'US Military Policy Toward the Caribbean in the 1990s', *Annals of the American Academy* 533: 112–24

Munro, Dana G. (1964): *Intervention and Dollar Diplomacy in the Caribbean 1900–1921*, Princeton: Princeton University Press

Nachmani, Amikam (1999): *Turkey and the Middle East*, Begin–Sadat Center for Strategic Studies, Bar-Ilan University, Security and Policy Studies No. 42, 29 May

Naím, Moisés (2001): 'The Real Story Behind Venezuela's Woes', *Journal of Democracy* 12 (2): 17–31

Najimova, Adolat (2002): *Russia: Moscow Seen as Moving to Increase Military Ties with Central Asia*, http://www.rferl.org/nca/features/2002/08/06082002141622.asp

NATO (North Atlantic Treaty Organization) (1999): *The Alliance's Strategic Concept*, Washington, DC: Approved by the Heads of State and Government participating in the meeting of the North Atlantic Council, 23–24 April

Neumann, Iver B. (1996a): 'Collective Identity Formation: Self and Other in International Relations', *European Journal of International Relations* 2 (2): 139–74

(1996b): *Russia and the Idea of Europe*, New York: Routledge

(1997a): 'Comments on Russia and Europe', in Ingmar Oldberg (ed.), *Priorities in Russian Foreign Policy: West, South or East?*, Stockholm: Swedish Defence Research Establishment, 43–64

(1997b): 'The Geopolitics of Delineating "Russia" and "Europe": The Creation of the "Other" in European and Russian Tradition', in Tunander et al. 1997, 147–73

(2002): 'From the USSR to Gorbachev to Putin: Perestroika as a Failed Excursion from "the West" to "Europe" in Russian Discourse', in Malmborg and Stråth 2002, 191–214

Neumann, Iver B., and Jennifer Welsh (1991): 'The Other in European Self-Definition: An Addendum to the Literature on International Society', *Review of International Studies* 17 (4): 327–48

Newton, Wesley P. (1991): 'Origins of United States–Latin American Relations', in T. Ray Shurbutt (ed.), *United States–Latin American Relations, 1800–1850*, Tuscaloosa and London: University of Alabama Press, 1–24

NIC (National Intelligence Council) (2000): *The Global Infectious Disease Threat and its Implications for the United States*, http://www.fas.org/irp/threat/nie99-17s.htm

Noreng, Øystein (2000): 'Rørledninger er storpolitik: det nye store spillet om oljen fra Kaukasus og Sentral-Asia', *Internasjonal Politikk* 52 (2): 161–94

Norton, James (2002): 'Islamic Militancy in Central Asia: The Causes Are Many, The Answers Complex', *Christian Science Monitor* February (28): 15

Nunez, Joseph R. (1999): 'A New United States Strategy for Mexico', *Low Intensity Conflict and Law Enforcement* 8 (2): 111–28

Nyberg, René (1999): 'Russia and Europe', *European Security* 8 (2): 15–21

O'Neill, Kathryn, and Barry Munslow (1995): 'Angola: Ending the Cold War in Southern Africa', in Oliver Furley (ed.), *Conflict in Africa*, London: I. B. Tauris, 183–97

Ó Tuathail, Gearóid (1996): *Critical Geopolitics: The Politics of Writing Global Space*, London: Routledge

Odén, Bertil (2001): 'Regionalisation in Southern Africa: The Role of the Dominant', in Schulz, et al. 2001, 82–99

Ohlson, Thomas (1998): *Power Politics and Peace Policies: Intra-State Conflict Resolution in Southern Africa*, Uppsala: Department of Peace and Conflict Research, Report no. 50

Okawara, Nobuo, and Peter J. Katzenstein (2001): 'Japan and Asia-Pacific Security: Regionalization, Entrenched Bilateralism, and Incipient Multilateralism', *Pacific Review* 14 (2): 165–94

Olcott, Martha Brill (2001a): 'Central Asia: Common Legacies and Conflicts', in Allison and Jonson 2001, 24–48

(2001b): 'Preventing New Afghanistans: A Regional Strategy for Reconstruction', *Carnegie Endowment Policy Brief* 11: http://www.ceip.org/files/Publications/Olcott_PrevNewAfghan.asp? from=pubtype

Oliver, Roland, and Anthony Atmore (1994): *Africa Since 1800*, Cambridge: Cambridge University Press

References

Otorbaev, Kubat (2002): 'Russia Backs Kyrgyz President', in 'Mail archive – uighur-1', 21 June 2002, http://www.mail-archive.com/uighur-l@takla-makan.org/msg03122.html

Pain, Emil A. (1999): 'Contagious Ethnic Conflicts and Border Disputes Along Russia's Southern Flank', in Rajan Menon, Yuri E. Fedorov, and Ghia Nodia (eds.), *Russia, the Caucasus, and Central Asia*, New York: M. E. Sharpe, 177–202

Papayoanou, Paul A. (1997): 'Great Powers and Regional Orders: Possibilities and Prospects After the Cold War', in Lake and Morgan 1997c, 125–39

Parakhonsky, Borys (n.d.): *Central Asia: Geostrategic Survey*, Luleå, Sweden: Central Asia and the Caucasus, Center for Social and Political Studies

Pashayev, Hafiz (2000): Ambassador Hafiz Pashayev's presentation at 'GUUAM and the Geopolitics of Eurasia' Seminar, 17 May, United States Senate, http://www.guuam.org/conf/amb_GUUAM_17 may 00.htm

Pavliatenko, Victor N. (1999): 'Russian Security in the Asia-Pacific Region: The Dangers of Isolation', in Rozman et al. 1999, 13–44

Pavlovaite, Inga (2000): *Paradise Regained: The Conceptualisation of Europe in the Lithuanian Debate*, Copenhagen: COPRI, Working Paper 24

Payne, Anthony (1999): 'The Remapping of the Americas', *Review of International Studies* 25 (3): 507–14

    (2000): 'Rethinking United States–Caribbean Relations: Towards a New Mode of Trans-Territorial Governance', *Review of International Studies* 26 (1): 69–82

Pearce, Jenny (1998): 'From Civil War to "Civil Society": Has the End of the Cold War Brought About Peace to Central America?', *International Affairs* 74 (3): 587–616

    (1999): 'Peace-Building in the Periphery: Lessons from Central America', *Third World Quarterly* 20 (1): 51–68

Pedersen, Thomas (1998): *Germany, France and the Integration of Europe: A Realist Interpretation*, London: Pinter

Peimani, Hooman (1998): *Regional Security and the Future of Central Asia*, Westport, CT: Praeger

Pellicer, Olga (1998) (ed.): *Regional Mechanisms and International Security in Latin America*, New York: United Nations University Press

Peña, Félix (1995): 'New Approaches to International Integration in the Southern Cone', *Washington Quarterly* 18 (3): 113–22

Perkins, Bradford (1993): *The Creation of a Republican Empire, 1776–1865: The Cambridge History of American Foreign Relations, vol. I*, Cambridge: Cambridge University Press

Perruci, Gamaliel (1999): ' "Green McWorld" Versus "Gold Jihad": The Clash of Ideas in the Brazilian Amazon', *Global Society* 13 (2), April: 163–80

Petersen, Ib Damgaard (2001): *The Invisible Continent: Political and Economic Integration in Latin America with Particular Emphasis on Mercosur*, Copenhagen: Copenhagen Political Studies Press

Peterson, Scott (2002): 'Central Asia: The Next Front in the Terror War?', *Christian Science Monitor* July (10): 7

Phillips, James, and James H. Anderson (2000): 'International Terrorism: Containing and Defeating Terrorist Threats', in Stuart M. Butler and Kim R. Holmes (eds.), *Issues 2000: The Candidate's Briefing Book*, Heritage Foundation, 831–42

Piccoli, Wolfgango (1999): *Alliance Theory: The Case of Turkey and Israel*, Copenhagen: COPRI Working Paper 20/1999

Pillsbury, Michael (2000): *China Debates the Future Security Environment*, Washington, DC: National Defense University Press

Pion-Berlin, David, and Craig Arceneaux (2000): 'Decision-Makers or Decision-Takers? Military Missions and Civilian Control in Democratic South America', *Armed Forces and Society* 26 (3): 413–36

Pipes, Daniel (2000): 'Islam and Islamism: Faith and Ideology', *National Interest* 59: 87–93

Piscatori, James (1991a) (ed.): *Islamic Fundamentalisms and the Gulf Crisis*, Chicago: American Academy of Arts and Sciences

(1991b): 'Religion and Realpolitik: Islamic Responses to the Gulf War', in Piscatori 1991a, 1–27

Plaut, Martin, and Patrick Gilkes (1999): *Conflict in the Horn: Why Eritrea and Ethiopia are at War*, London: Royal Institute of International Affairs: Briefing Paper, n.s. no. 1

Podeh, Elie (1998): 'The Emergence of the Arab State System Reconsidered', *Diplomacy and Statecraft* 19 (3): 50–82

Politi, Alessandro (1998): 'Western Europe', in Stares 1998, 115–25

Polomka, Peter (1986): *The Two Koreas: Catalyst for Conflict in East Asia?*, London: International Institute for Strategic Studies Adelphi Paper no. 208

Posen, Barry R. (1993): 'Nationalism, Mass Army, and Military Power', *International Security* 18 (2): 80–124

Posen, Barry R., and Ross, Andrew L. (1996–7): 'Competing Visions for US Grand Strategy', *International Security* 21 (3): 5–53

Poulsen-Hansen, Lars, and Ole Wæver (1996): 'Ukraine', in Mouritzen et al. 1996, 231–60

PPNN (Programme for Promoting Nuclear Non-Proliferation) (1998a): 'Programme for Promoting Nuclear Non-Proliferation', *News Briefs*, no. 42

(1998b): 'Programme for Promoting Nuclear Non-Proliferation', *News Briefs*, no. 43

Prescott, J. R. V. (1987): *Political Frontiers and Boundaries*, London: Unwin Hyman

Prizel, Ilya (1998): *National Identity and Foreign Policy: Nationalism and Leadership in Poland, Russia, and Ukraine*, Cambridge: Cambridge University Press

Putin, Vladimir (1999): *Russia at the Turn of the Millennium*, http://www.government.ru:8080/english/statVP_engl_1.html

(2000): *Address to the Federal Assembly (State of Nation)*, posted on Jonhson's Russia List and H-Diplo at H-net.msu.edu

Quinlan, Michael (2000–1): 'How Robust Is India–Pakistan Deterrence?', *Survival* 42 (4): 141–54

References

Rabasa, Angel, and Peter Chalk (2001): *Colombian Labyrinth: The Synergy of Drugs and Insurgency and Its Implications for Regional Stability*, Santa Monica, CA: RAND

Ragigh-Aghsan, Ali (2000): *The Dynamics and Inertia of the Northern Tier Cooperation: The Growing Role of Turkey and Iran and the Formation of a Cooperative Regional Hegemonic System in the Context of the ECO*, Copenhagen: Institute of Political Science, Ph.D dissertation series 2000/05

Rais, Rasul Bakhsh (1995): 'Security, State, and Democracy in Pakistan', in Weinbaum and Kumar 1995, 63–78

Rajmaira, Sheen (1997): 'Indo-Pakistani Relations: Reciprocity in Long-Term Perspective', *International Studies Quarterly* 41 (3): 547–60

Rashid, Ahmed (2000): *Taliban: Islam, Oil, and the New Great Game in Central Asia*, London: I. B. Tauris

(2002a): 'Central Asian Elites, Suddenly, Shift Into Revolt', *Global Affairs Commentary* May (2): Foreign Policy in Focus

(2002b): *Jihad: The Rise of Militant Islam in Central Asia*, New Haven: Yale University Press

(2002c): 'Russia, China Warily Watch for American Intrusions in Central Asia', *Global Affairs Commentary* May (3): Foreign Policy in Focus

Rees, Wyn (n.d.): *Organised Crime, Security and the European Union, Draft Paper for the ESRC Workshop, Grenoble*, http://www.essex.ac.uk/ecpr/jointsessions/grenoble/papers/w8/rees.pdf

Reich, Robert (1991): 'What Is a Nation?', *Political Science Quarterly* 106 (2): 193–209

Reno, William (1998): *Warlord Politics and African States*, Boulder, CO: Lynne Rienner

Richardson, James L. (1994): 'The Asia-Pacific: Geopolitical Cauldron or Regional Community', *National Interest* 38 (Winter): 2–13

Richter, Daniel K. (1983): 'War and Culture: The Iroquois Experiment', *William and Mary Quarterly* 40: 528–39

Riley-Smith, Jonathan (1997): *The First Crusaders 1095–1131*, Cambridge: Cambridge University Press

Ringmar, Erik (2002): 'The Recognition Game: Soviet Russia Against the West', *Cooperation and Conflict* 37 (2): 115–36

Rizvi, Hasan-Askari (1998): 'Civil–Military Relations in Contemporary Pakistan', *Survival* 40 (2): 96–113

Rochlin, James F. (1997): *Redefining Mexican 'Security': Society, State and Region Under NAFTA*, Boulder, CO: Lynne Rienner

Roe, Paul (1999): 'The Intrastate Security Dilemma: Ethnic Conflict as a "Tragedy" ', *Journal of Peace Research* 36 (2): 183–202

Roeder, Philip G. (1997): 'From Hierarchy to Hegemony: The Post-Soviet Security Complex', in Lake and Morgan 1997c, 219–44

Rohter, Larry (2002): 'Argentina and the US Grow Apart Over a Crisis', *New York Times* January (20): 4

528

Rondeli, Alexander (1998): 'Security Threats in the Caucasus: Georgia's View', *Journal of International Affairs* 3 (2): 43–53

(1999): 'TRACECA: A Tool For Regional Cooperation in the Caucasus', *Marco Polo Magazine* 1: 28–32

Rose, Gideon (1998): 'Neoclassical Realism and Theories of Foreign Policy', *World Politics* 51 (1): 144–72

Rosecrance, Richard (1986): *The Rise of the Trading State*, New York: Basic Books

Rosenau, James N. (1966): 'Pre-theories and Theories of Foreign Policy', in R. Barry Farrell (ed.), *Approaches to Comparative and International Politics*, Evanston: Northwestern University Press, 27–92

(1981 [1970]): 'The Adaptation of National Societies: A Theory of Political System Behavior and Transformation', in James N. Rosenau (ed.), *The Study of Political Adaptation*, London and New York: Pinter, 56–87

(1984): 'A Pre-Theory Revisited: World Politics in an Era of Cascading Interdependence', *International Studies Quarterly* 28: 245–305

(1990): *Turbulence in World Politics: A Theory of Change and Continuity*, New York: Harvester Wheatsheaf

Rosenfelder, Mark (1996): *US Interventions in Latin America*, http://www.zompist.com/latam.html

Ross, Dorothy (1991): *The Origins of American Social Science*, Cambridge: Cambridge University Press

Ross, Robert S. (1986): 'Indochina's Continuing Tragedy', *Problems of Communism* 25 (6): 86–96

(1999): 'The Geography of the Peace: East Asia in the Twenty-First Century', *International Security* 23 (4): 81–119

Rossabi, Morris (n.d.): *Mongolia in the 1990s: From Commissars to Capitalists*, http://www.eurasianet.org/resource/mongolia/links/rossabi.html

Roy, Denny (1994): 'Hegemon on the Horizon? China's Threat to East Asian Security', *International Security* 19 (1): 149–68

(1996): 'China's Threat Environment', *Security Dialogue* 27 (4): 437–49

Roy, Olivier (1998): 'Fundamentalists Without a Common Cause', *Le Monde Diplomatique (in the Guardian Weekly)* October: 2

(2000): *The New Central Asia: The Creation of Nations*, London and New York: I. B. Tauris Publishers

Rozman, Gilbert, Mikhail G. Nosor, and Koji Watanabe (1999) (eds.): *Russia and East Asia: The Twenty-First Century Security Environment*, London and New York: M. E. Sharpe

Rubin, Barnett (1998): 'Conclusion: Managing Normal Instability', in Barnett R. Rubin and Jack Snyder (eds.), *Post-Soviet Political Order*, London and New York: Routledge, 162–79

Ruggie, John G. (1979–80): 'On the Problems of the Global Problematique: What Roles for International Organizations?', *Alternatives* 5: 520–6

(1983): 'Continuity and Transformation in the World Polity: Toward a Neo-realist Synthesis', *World Politics* 35 (2): 261–85

References

(1993): 'Territoriality and Beyond: Problematizing Modernity in International Relations', *International Organization* 47 (1): 139–75

Rühl, Lothar (1997): 'The Historical Background of Russian Security Concepts and Requirements', in Vladimir Baranovski (ed.), *Russia and Europe: The Emerging Security Agenda*, Oxford: Oxford University Press, Stockholm International Peace Research Institute, 21–41

Rumsfeld, Donald H. (2001): 'Creative Coalition-Building for a New Kind of War', *New York Times* September (28)

Russett, Bruce M. (1967): *International Regions and the International System*, Chicago: Rand McNally

Ruthrauff, John (1998): *The Guatemala Peace Process and the Role of the World Bank and Interamerican Development Bank*, Guatemala: Conference paper at Universidad del Valle, March 26–28

Saikal, Amin (1998): 'Afghanistan's Ethnic Conflict', *Survival* 40 (2): 114–26

Samudavanija, Chai-Anan, and Sukhumbhand Paribatra (1987): 'Development for Security, Security for Development: Prospects for Durable Stability in Southeast Asia', in Kusuma Snitwongse and Sukhumbhand Paribatra (eds.), *Durable Stability in Southeast Asia*, Singapore: Institute of Southeast Asian Studies, 3–31

Sansoucy, Lisa J. (2002): *Japan's Regional Security Policy in Post-Cold War Asia*, New Orleans: Paper presented to ISA Conference, 24–27 March

Sato, Tsuneaki, Chun-Shen Tian, and Il-Dong Koh (1999): ' "Homemade Risks": The Economic Security of Russia in East Asia', in Rozman et al. 1999, 101–25

Sayigh, Yezid (2002): 'The Middle East in Comparative Perspective', in Christian-Peter Hanelt, Felix Neugart, and Matthias Peitz (eds.), *Europe's Emerging Foreign Policy and the Middle Eastern Challenge*, Munich: Guetersloh, 25–35

Schlaga, Rüdiger (1991): *Die Kommunisten in der Friedensbewegung – erfolglos?*, Hamburg: Münster

Schlesinger, Arthur M. jr (1992): *The Disuniting of America: Reflections on a Multicultural Society*, New York: W. W. Norton

Schlyter, Oscar (1997): *The South Asian Regional Security Complex: A Comparison of the Cold War and the Post-Cold War Period*, Stockholm: Department of Political Science, University of Stockholm, paper, 50 pp.

Schmidt, Helmut (1999): *Globalisierung: politische, ökonomische, und kulturelle Herausforderungen*, Stuttgart: Deutsche Verlags-Anstalt

Schmitt, Eric, and James Dao (2002): 'US Forces Dig in to Keep Presence in Central Asia for Years to Come', *International Herald Tribune* January (10)

Schoeman, Maxi (2000): 'South Africa as an Emerging Middle Power', *African Security Review* 9 (3): 47–58

Scholte, Jan Aart (2000): *Globalization: A Critical Introduction*, Basingstoke: Macmillan

Schoultz, Lars (1998): *Beneath the United States: A History of US Policy Towards Latin America*, Cambridge, MA: Harvard University Press

Schulz, Donald E. (1997): 'Between a Rock and a Hard Place: The United States, Mexico, and the Challenge of National Security', *Low Intensity Conflict and Law Enforcement* 6 (3): 1–40

(1998) (ed.): *The Role of the Armed Forces in the Americas: Civil–Military Relations for the Twenty-First Century*, Carlisle, PA: US Army War College, Strategic Studies Institute: http://carlisle-www.army.mil/usassi/

Schulz, Michael, Fredrik Söderbaum, and Joakim Öjendal (2001) (eds.): *Regionalization in a Globalizing World: A Comparative Perspective on Forms, Actors and Process*, London and New York: Zed Books

Schweller, Randall L. (1999): 'Realism and the Present Great Power System: Growth and Positional Conflict over Scarce Resources', in Kapstein and Mastanduno 1999, 28–57

Segal, Gerald (1988): 'As China Grows Strong', *International Affairs* 64 (2): 218–31

(1994): *China Changes Shape: Regionalism and Foreign Policy*, London: International Institute of Strategic Studies Adelphi Paper no. 287

(1997): 'How Insecure Is Pacific Asia?', *International Affairs* 73 (2): 235–50

(1999): 'Does China Matter?', *Foreign Affairs* 78 (5): 24–36

Sen Gupta, Bhabani (1997): 'India in the Twenty-First Century', *International Affairs* 73 (2): 297–314

Serafino, Nina M. (2002): *Colombia: The Uribe Administration and Congressional Concerns*, Washington, DC: Congressional Report Service, CRS Report for Congress, RS 21242

Serbin, Andrés (1998): 'New Trends in International Security in the Caribbean Basin', in Pellicer 1998

Sergounin, Alexander (1998): *Russia: A Long Way to the National Security Doctrine*, Copenhagen: COPRI Working Paper no. 10

Serrano, Mónica (1992): *Common Security in Latin America: The 1967 Treaty of Tlatelolco*, London: Institute for Latin American Studies, University of London, Research Paper 30

(1998): 'Latin America', in Stares 1998, 152–75

Sethi, Manpreet (2000): 'Novel Ways of Settling Border Disputes: The Peru–Ecuador Case', *Strategic Analysis: A Monthly Journal of the IDSA* 23 (10) (January): 1769–79

Shambaugh, David (1994): 'Growing Strong: China's Challenge to Asian Security', *Survival* 36 (2): 43–59

Shashenkov, Maxim (1994): 'Russian Peacekeeping in the "Near Abroad"', *Survival* 36 (3): 139–74

Shaw, Timothy (1998): *New Regionalisms in the Great Lakes at the Start of the Twenty-First Century*, unpublished typescript

Shearer, David (1999): 'Africa's Great War', *Survival* 41 (2): 89–105

Shelley, L. I. (1995): 'Transnational Organized Crime: An Imminent Threat to the Nation-State?', *Journal of International Affairs* 48 (2) (Winter): 463–89

Shelton, Henry H. (2000): *Statement of the Chairman of the Joint Chiefs of Staff*, Arlington, VA: Fletcher Conference

References

Shore, Sean M. (1998): 'No Fences Make Good Neighbors: The Development of the US–Canadian Security Community, 1871–1940', in Adler and Barnett 1998, 333–67

Shumway, Nicolas (1991): *The Invention of Argentina*, Berkeley: University of California Press

Sick, Gary (1998): 'Rethinking Dual Containment', *Survival* 40 (1): 5–32

Silber, Laura, and Allan Little (1995): *The Death of Yugoslavia*, New York: Penguin Books, BBC Books

Simic, Predrag (2001): 'Do the Balkans Exist?', *Chaillot Papers* 46 (April): 17–36

Simon, Gerhard (1994): 'Russland: Hegemon in Eurasien?', *Osteuropa* 44 (5): 411–29

Simon, Sheldon W. (1975): *Asian Neutralism and US Policy*, Washington, DC: American Enterprise Institute for Public Policy Research

(1983): 'Davids and Goliaths: Small Power–Great Power Security Relations in Southeast Asia', *Asian Survey* 23 (3): 302–15

(1984): 'The Two Southeast Asias and China's Security Perspectives', *Asian Survey* 24 (5): 519–33

(1994): 'East Asian Security: The Playing Field has Changed', *Asian Survey* 34 (12): 1047–63

Singer, Max, and Aaron Wildavsky (1993): *The Real World Order: Zones of Peace/Zones of Turmoil*, Chatham, NJ: Chatham House Publishers

Skak, Mette (2000): *Back in the USSR? Russia as an Actor in World Politics*, Copenhagen: Danish Institute of International Affairs, Working Paper 7

Skowronek, Stephen (1982): *Building a New American State*, Cambridge: Cambridge University Press

Sloth, Kristian (2001): 'Bristede illusioner i Afrikas mikrokosmos: Sudans mislykkede nationsdannelse' [Shattered illusions in Africa's microcosmos: Sudan's failed nation-building]', *Politica* 33 (4): 419–35

Smith, Gaddis (1994): *The Last Years of the Monroe Doctrine, 1945–1993*, New York: Hill and Wang

Smith, Graham, Vivien Law, Andrew Wilson, Anette Bohr, and Edward Allworth (1998): *Nation-Building in the Post-Soviet Borderlands*, Cambridge: Cambridge University Press

Smith, Peter H. (1996): *Talons of the Eagle: Dynamics of US–Latin American Relations*, New York and Oxford: Oxford University Press

Snyder, Glenn H. (1984): 'The Security Dilemma in Alliance Politics', *World Politics* 36 (4): 461–95

Socor, Vladimir (2002): 'The Russian Squeeze on Georgia', *Russia and Eurasia Review* 1 (2): http://russia.jamestown.org/pubs/view/rer_001_002_004.htm

Söderbaum, Fredrik (1998): 'The New Regionalism in Southern Africa', *Politeia* 17 (3): 75–90

(2001): 'Turbulent Regionalization in West Africa', in Schulz, et al. 2001, 61–81

Soeya, Yoshihide (1998): 'Japan: Normative Constraints Versus Structural Imperatives', in Alagappa 1998, 198–233

Solingen, Etel (1998): *Regional Orders at Century's Dawn*, Princeton: Princeton University Press

Spiro, Peter J. (2000): 'The New Sovereigntists: American Exceptionalism and Its False Prophets', *Foreign Affairs* 79 (6): 9–15

Spruyt, Hendrik (1998): 'A New Architecture for Peace? Reconfiguring Japan Among the Great Powers', *Pacific Review* 11 (3): 363–88

Stares, Paul B. (1998) (ed.): *The New Security Agenda: A Global Survey*, Tokyo: Japan Center for International Exchange

Starr, S. Frederick (2001): 'The War Against Terrorism and US Bilateral Relations with the Nations of Central Asia', *Testimony to the US Senate, Committee on Foreign Relations, Subcommittee on Central Asia and the Southern Caucasus* December (13): http://www.cacianalyst.org/Publications/Starr_Testimony.htm

Stein, Arthur A., and Steven E. Lobell (1997): 'The End of the Cold War and the Regionalization of International Security', in Lake and Morgan 1997c, 101–22

Stern, Eric (1995): 'Bringing the Environment In: The Case for Comprehensive Security', *Cooperation and Conflict* 30 (3): 211–37

Stern, Jessica (2000): 'Pakistan's Jihad Culture', *Foreign Affairs* 79 (6): 115–26

Stoianovich, Traian (1967): *A Study in Balkan Civilisation*, New York: Alfred Knopf

Stoltenberg, Thorvald, and Kai Eide (1996): *De Tusen Dagene – Fredsmeklere på Balkan*, Oslo: Gyldendal Norsk Forlag

Storrs, K. Larry, with J. F. Hornbeck, Nina M. Serafino, Mark P. Sullivan, and Maureen Taft-Morales (2002): *Latin America and the Caribbean: Legislative Issues in 2001–2002*, Washington, DC: Congressional Report Service, CRS Report for Congress, RL 30971

Storrs, K. Larry, and Nina M. Serafino (2002): *Andean Regional Initiative (ARI): FY 2002 Supplemental and FY 2003 Assistance for Colombia and Neighbors*, Washington, DC: Congressional Research Service, CRS Report for Congress, RL 31383

Strategic Survey (1991–2002): London: International Institute for Security Studies

Stratfor (2000a): *The Shanghai Six*, www.stratfor.com/asia/commentary/0007172332.htm

—— (2000b): *Superpower vs Great Power: Inside the Russian Defense Debate*, www.stratfor.com/SERVICES/giu2000/071700.asp

Stuart, Douglas T., and William T. Tow (1995): *A US Strategy for the Asia-Pacific*, London: International Institute for Strategic Studies Adelphi Paper no. 299

Suny, Ronald Grigor (1999–2000): 'Provisional Stabilities: The Politics of Identities in Post-Soviet Eurasia', *International Security* 24 (3): 139–78

Supian, Victor B., and Nosov, Michael G. (1999): 'Reintegration of an Abandoned Fortress: Economic Security of the Russian Far East', in Rozman et al. 1999, 69–100

Sutton, Paul (1993): 'The Politics of Small State Security in the Caribbean', *Journal of Commonwealth and Comparative Politics* 31 (2): 1–32

References

Tajima, Takashi (1981): *China and Southeast Asia: Strategic Interests and Policy Prospects*, London: International Institute for Strategic Studies Adelphi Paper no. 172

Takahashi, Sugio (2000): 'Redefinition of Cooperative Security and "Regional" Security in the Asia-Pacific', *NIDS Security Reports* no. 1: 101–15

Tanter, Raymond (1999): *Rogue Regimes: Terrorism and Proliferation*, London: Macmillan

Taylor, Charles (1992): *Multiculturalism and 'the Politics of Recognition'*, Princeton: Princeton University Press

Terpager Rasmussen, Pouline (2001): *Rusland og Kosovo: En diskursanalyse af den russiske Kosovo-politik 1999*, Copenhagen: MA thesis, Institute of Political Science, University of Copenhagen

Thatcher, Margaret (1996): *New Threats for Old*, Fulton, MO: The Rt Hon The Baroness Thatcher LG, OM, FRS, at Westminster College, 9 March

Thompson, E. P. (1982): *Beyond the Cold War: A New Approach to the Arms Race and Nuclear Annihilation*, New York: Pantheon

Thompson, Loren B. (1999): 'Military Supremacy and How We Keep It', *Policy Review* 97 (Oct.–Nov.): 19–37

Thompson, William R. (1973): 'The Regional Subsystem: A Conceptual Explication and a Propositional Inventory', *International Studies Quarterly* 17 (1): 89–117

Throup, David (1995): 'The Colonial Legacy', in Oliver Furley (ed.), *Conflict in Africa*, London: I. B. Tauris, 237–73

Thumann, Michael (1999): 'Moskau hört mich', *Die Zeit* April (8): 6

Tibi, Bassim (1993): *Conflict and War in the Middle East, 1967–1991: Regional Dynamics and the Superpowers*, London: Macmillan

Tickner, Arlene B., and Ann C. Mason (2003, forthcoming): 'Mapping Transregional Security Structures in the Andean Region', *Alternatives* 28 (3)

Tilly, Charles (1990): *Coercion, Capital, and European States AD 990–1990*, Oxford: Blackwell

Tkach, Vlada (1999): 'Moldova and Transdniestria: Painful Past, Deadlocked Present, Uncertain Future', *European Security* 8 (2): 130–59

To, Lee Lai (1997): 'East Asian Assessments of China's Security Policy', *International Affairs* 73 (2): 251–63

Todorova, Maria N. (1997): *Imagining the Balkans*, Oxford: Oxford University Press

Tökés, Rudolf L. (1979) (ed.): *Eurocommunism and Détente*, Oxford: Martin Robertson & Co

Trenin, Dmitri V. (2001): *The End of Eurasia*, Moscow: Carnegie Moscow Center

Tucker, Nancy Bernkopf (1998–9): 'China–Taiwan: US Debates and Policy Choices', *Survival* 40 (4): 150–67

Tulchin, Joseph S. (1994): 'The Formulation of US Foreign Policy in the Caribbean', *Annals of the American Academy* 533: 177–87

Tulchin, Joseph S., and Ralph H. Espach (2001a) (eds.): *Latin America in the New International System*, Boulder, CO: Lynne Rienner

(2001b): 'Latin America in the New International System: A Call for Strategic Thinking', in Tulchin and Espach 2001a, 1–33

Tunander, Ola (1989): *Cold Water Politics: The Maritime Strategy and Geopolitics of the Northern Front*, London: Sage

Tunander, Ola, Parel Baer, and Victoria Ingrid Einagel (1997)(eds.): *Geopolitics in Post-Wall Europe: Security, Territory, and Identity*, London: Sage

Turner, Frederick Jackson (1993 [1893]): 'The Significance of the Frontier in American History', in Frederick Jackson Turner (ed.), *History, Frontier, and Section: Three Essays by Frederick Jackson Turner*, Albuquerque: University of New Mexico Press, 59–91

Turner, John W. (1998): *Continent Ablaze: The Insurgency Wars in Africa 1960 to the Present*, London: Arms and Armour

Turton, Anthony R. (2001): *Hydropolitics and Security Complex Theory: An African Perspective*, Canterbury: Paper presented to the 4th Pan-European IR Conference, 8–10 September

Twomey, Christopher P. (2000): 'Japan: A Circumscribed Balancer', *Security Studies* 9 (4): 167–205

Ullman, Walter (1974): *Medieval Political Thought*, Harmondsworth: Penguin

United States, Department of Defense (2001): *Quadrennial Defense Review Report*, Washington, DC: Department of Defense

United States, Department of State (2000): *Patterns of Global Terrorism 1999: Washington, DC, Office of the Coordinator for Counterterrorism, April*, http://www.state.gov/s/ct/rls/pgtrpt/2000/

US Commission on National Security (2001): *Road Map for National Security: Imperative for Change: The Phase III Report of the US Commission on National Security/21st Century*, US Commission on National Security / 21st Century

US Government Interagency Working Group (2000): *International Crime Threat Assessment: Washington, DC, White House*, http://www.whitehouse.gov/textonl...ments/pub45270/pub45270index.html

USIS (1998): *Allied Relations and Negotiations with Argentina*, http://www.state.gov/www/regions/eur/rpt_9806_ng_argentina.pdf

Váli, Ferenc A. (1971): *Bridges Across the Bosporus: The Foreign Policy of Turkey*, Baltimore and London: Johns Hopkins University Press

Van Cott, Donna Lee (1996): 'Unity Through Diversity: Ethnic Politics and Democratic Deepening in Colombia', *Nationalism and Ethnic Politics* 2 (4): 523–29

Van Ness, Peter (2002): 'Hegemony Not Anarchy: Why China and Japan Are Not Balancing US Unipolar Power', *International Relations of the Asia-Pacific* 2 (1): 131–50

van Schalkwyk, Gina (n.d.): *Multilateral Cooperation Around Shared Watercourses in the Southern African Region: The Real Meaning of Positive Peace and Sustainable Development*, http://www.student-pugwash.org/uk/vanSchalkwyk.pdf

van Wolferen, Karel (1989): *The Enigma of Japanese Power*, London: Macmillan

van Wyk, Jo-Ansie (1998): 'Towards Water Security in Southern Africa', *African Security Review* 7 (2): 59–68

References

Väyrynen, Raimo (1988): 'Domestic Stability, State Terrorism, and Regional Integration in the ASEAN and the GCC', in Michael Stohl and George Lopez (eds.), *Terrible Beyond Endurance: The Foreign Policy of State Terrorism*, New York: Greenwood Press, 194–7

(1998): 'Towards a Pluralistic Security Community in the Baltic Sea Region?', in Georg Sørensen and Hans-Henrik Holm (eds.), *And Now What? International Politics After the Cold War: Essays in Honour of Nikolaj Petersen*, Aarhus: Forlaget Politica, 149–74

Veremis, Thanos (2000): 'Perspectives from the Region, South Eastern Europe: "The Predicament of the Western Balkans" ', in Machon 2000, 21–34

Viano, Emilio C. (1999) (ed.): *Global Organized Crime and International Security*, Aldershot: Ashgate

Vukadinovic, Radovan (2000): 'Challenges to Security in South East Europe', in Machon 2000, 35–60

Wachtel, Andrew Baruch (1998): *Making a Nation, Breaking a Nation*, Stanford, CA.: Stanford University Press

Wæver, Ole (1989): 'Conflicts of Vision – Visions of Conflict', in Wæver et al. 1989, 283–325

(1990a): 'The Interplay of Some Regional and Subregional Dynamics of Security: The Case of Europe, the Baltic Area and 'the North' in the 1980s', *Zeszyty Naukowe, Uniwersytet Szczecinski* 44 (Acta Politica, no. 2): 119–169

(1990b): 'Three Competing Europes: German, French, Russian', *International Affairs* 66 (3): 477–93

(1991): 'Danmarks Sikkerhedspolitiske Situation år 2000 (The Security Political Situation of Denmark, Year 2000)', *Militært Tidsskrift (published by the Danish Society of War Studies)* 120 (4, April): 96–129

(1993a): 'Europe: Stability and Responsibility', in *Internationales Umfeld, Sicherheitsinteressen und nationale Planung der Bundesrepublik. Teil C: Unterstützende Einzelanalysen. Band 5. II.A Europäische Sicherheitskultur. II.B Optionen für kollektive Verteidigung im Kontext sicherheitspolitischer Entwicklungen Dritter*, Ebenhausen: Stiftung Wissenschaft und Politik, SWP – S 383/5, 31–72

(1993b): 'Modelli e scenari futuri', *Politica Internazionale (Rome)* 21 (3, Jan.–Mar. 1993): 5–27

(1994): 'Resisting the Temptation of Post-Foreign Policy Analysis', in Walter Carlsnaes and Steve Smith (eds.), *European Foreign Policy Analysis: The EC and Changing Perspectives in Europe*, London: Sage, 238–73

(1995a): 'Identity, Integration, and Security: Solving the Sovereignty Puzzle in EU Studies', *Journal of International Affairs* 48 (2): 389–431

(1995b): 'Power, Principles and Perspectivism: Understanding Peaceful Change in Post-Cold War Europe', in Heikki Patomäki (ed.), *Peaceful Change in World Politics*, Tampere: TAPRI, 208–82

(1995c): 'Securitization and Desecuritization', in Ronnie D. Lipschutz (ed.), *On Security*, New York: Columbia University Press, 46–86

(1996a): 'European Security Identities', *Journal of Common Market Studies* 34 (1, March): 103–32

(1996b): 'Europe's Three Empires: A Watsonian Interpretation of Post-Wall European Security', in Rick Fawn and Jeremy Larkins (eds.), *International Society After the Cold War: Anarchy and Order Reconsidered*, London: Macmillan and Millennium, 220–60

(1997a): *Concepts of Security*, Copenhagen: Ph.D dissertation, Institute for Political Science, University of Copenhagen

(1997b): 'Imperial Metaphors: Emerging European Analogies to Pre-Nation State Imperial Systems', in Tunander et al. 1997, 59–93

(1997c): *Regional Realism: A Mildly Constructivist Interpretation of European Security with Implications for 'World Order'*, Copenhagen, Danish Institute of International Affairs: Paper presented to the 'New World Order: Contrasting Theories' Conference, 21–2 November

(1998a): 'Security, Insecurity, and Asecurity in the West European Non-War Community', in Adler and Barnett 1998, 69–118

(1998b): 'The Sociology of a Not So International Discipline: American and European Developments in International Relations', *International Organization* 52 (4, Autumn): 687–727

(2000a): 'The EU as a Security Actor: Reflections from a Pessimistic Constructivist on Post-Sovereign Security Orders', in Morten Kelstrup and Michael C. Williams (eds.), *International Relations Theory and the Politics of European Integration: Power, Security and Community*, London: Routledge, 250–94

(2000b): *Security Agendas Old and New – and How to Survive Them*, Buenos Aires: Paper presented for a Workshop on 'The Traditional and the New Security Agenda: Inferences for the Third World, Universidad Torcuato di Tella Buenos Aires, 11–12 September

(2001a): *Securitisation: The Copenhagen School and Its Research Agenda*, Unpublished draft

(2001b): 'Widening the Concept of Security – And Widening the Atlantic?', in Bo Huldt, Sven Rudberg, and Elisabeth Davidson (eds.), *The Transatlantic Link*, Department of Strategic Studies: Swedish National Defence College, 31–48

(2002): *Security: A Conceptual History for International Relations*, New Orleans: Paper presented to ISA Conference, 24–27 March

(in preparation): *The Politics of International Structure*, unpublished

Wæver, Ole, and Barry Buzan (1999): 'Europe and the Middle East – an Inter-Regional Analysis: NATO's New Strategic Concept and the Theory of Security Complexes', in Behrendt and Hanelt 1999, 73–110

(2000): 'An Inter-Regional Analysis: NATO's New Strategic Concept and the Theory of Security Complexes', in Sven Behrendt and Christian-Peter Hanelt (eds.), *Bound to Cooperate: Europe and the Middle East*, Gütersloh: Bertelsmann Foundation Publishers, 55–106

Wæver, Ole, Barry Buzan, Morten Kelstrup, Pierre Lemaitre, with David Carlton et al. (1993): *Identity, Migration and the New Security Agenda in Europe*, London: Pinter

References

Wæver, Ole, Henrik Larsen, and Ulla Holm (1990): 'Forestillingen om Europa: et studie i fransk og tysk tænkning efter revolutionerne i Øst' [The European Stage: A Study in French and German Thinking After the Revolutions in the East], *Vandkunsten: Konflikt, Politik og Historie* 3: 136–212

Wæver, Ole, Pierre Lemaitre, and Elzbieta Tromer (1989) (eds.): *European Polyphony: Beyond East–West Confrontation*, London: Macmillan

Walker, Martin (2000): 'Europe: Superstate or Superpower?', *World Policy Journal* 27 (4): 7–16

Walker, R. B. J. (1993): *Inside/Outside: International Relations as Political Theory*, Cambridge: Cambridge University Press

Walker, William (1998): 'International Nuclear Relations After the Indian and Pakistani Test Explosions', *International Affairs* 74 (3): 505–28

Wallander, Celeste (2000): 'Institutional Assets and Adaptability: NATO After the Cold War', *International Organization* 54 (4): 705–35

Wallander, Celeste A., and Robert Keohane (1995): *An Institutional Approach to Alliance Theory*, Cambridge: Center for International Affairs, Harvard University, Working Paper Series, 95: 2

Walt, Stephen M. (1987): *The Origins of Alliances*, Ithaca: Cornell University Press
   (1998): 'International Relations: One World, Many Theories', *Foreign Policy* 110: 29–46
   (2000): *Keeping the World 'Off-Balance': Self-Restraint and US Foreign Policy*, John F. Kennedy School of Government: Harvard University, Working Paper no. RWP00–013

Walton, C. Dale (1997): 'Europe United: The Rise of a Second Superpower and Its Effect on World Order', *European Security* 6 (4): 44–54

Waltz, Kenneth N. (1979): *Theory of International Politics*, New York: Random House
   (1993a): 'The Emerging Structure of International Politics', *International Security* 18 (2): 44–79
   (1993b): 'The New World Order', *Millennium* 22 (2): 187–95
   (2000a): 'Intimations of Multipolarity', in Birthe Hansen and Bertel Heurlin (eds.), *The New World Order: Contrasting Theories*, London: Macmillan, 1–17
   (2000b): 'Structural Realism After the Cold War', *International Security* 25 (1): 5–41
   (2002): 'The Continuity of International Politics', in Ken Booth and Tim Dunn (eds.), *Worlds in Collision*, New York: Palgrave Macmillan, 348–54

Ward, John (1997): *Latin America: Development and Conflict Since 1945*, London and New York: Routledge

Watson, Adam (1984a): 'European International Society and Its Expansion', in Bull and Watson 1984, 13–32
   (1984b): 'Russia and the European States System', in Bull and Watson 1984, 61–74
   (1987): 'Hedley Bull, State Systems and International Studies', *Review of International Studies* 13 (2): 147–53

(1990): 'Systems of States', *Review of International Studies* 16 (2): 99–109

(1992): *The Evolution of International Society*, London: Routledge

(1997): *The Limits of Independence: Relations Between States in the Modern World*, London: Routledge

Weatherbee, Donald E. (1978): 'US Policy and the Two Southeast Asias', *Asian Survey* 18 (4): 408–21

Weber, Cynthia (1995): *Simulating Sovereignty: Intervention, the State and Symbolic Exchange*, Cambridge: Cambridge University Press

Weinbaum, Marvin G., and Chetan Kumar (1995) (eds.): *South Asia Approaches the Millennium: Reexamining National Security*, Boulder, CO: Westview Press

Wendt, Alexander (1999): *Social Theory of International Politics*, Cambridge: Cambridge University Press

Whitehead, Laurence (2001): 'Bolivia and the Viability of Democracy', *Journal of Democracy* 12 (2): 6–16

Wiberg, Håkan (1993a): 'Jugoslavien som grekisk tragedi', *Internasjonal Politikk* 3: 291–308

    (1993b): 'Societal Security and the Explosion of Yugoslavia', in Wæver et al. 1993, 93–109

    (1994): 'Den lange historiske baggrund', in Erik A. Andersen and Håkan Wiberg (eds.), *Storm over Balkan: Fra Oldtidshistorie til Stormagtsspil*, Copenhagen: C. A. Reitzels Forlag, 8–21

Wiberg-Jørgensen, Paul (1999): 'America's Freedom to Act in the Caspian Area', *European Security* 8 (4): 100–8

Widfeldt, Åke (2001): 'The Caribbean: Legacy and Change', in Schulz et al. 2001, 211–33

Wilkinson, David (1999): 'Unipolarity Without Hegemony', *International Studies Review* 1 (2): 141–72

Williams, Michael C., and Iver B. Neumann (2001): 'From Alliance to Security Community: NATO, Russia and the Power of Identity', *Millennium* 29 (2): 357–87

Williams, Phil (2001): 'Transnational Criminal Networks', in John Arguilla and David Ronfeldt (eds.), *Networks and Netwars: The Future of Terror, Crime, and Militancy*, prepared for the Office of the Secretary of Defense, Santa Monica, CA: RAND, 61–97

Wills, Garry (1995): 'The New Revolutionaries', *New York Review of Books* 10 (August): 50–4

Winn, Peter (1999): *Americas: The Changing Face of Latin America and the Caribbean*, Berkeley: University of California Press

Winrow, Gareth M. (2001): 'Turkey and Central Asia', in Allison and Jonson 2001, 199–218

Wivel, Anders (2000): *The Integration Spiral: International Security and European Integration 1945–1999*, Copenhagen: Ph.D dissertation, Institute of Political Science, University of Copenhagen

Wohlforth, William C. (1999): 'The Stability of a Unipolar World', *International Security* 24 (1): 5–41

References

Wolfers, Arnold (1962): *Discord and Collaboration*, Baltimore: Johns Hopkins University Press

Wolfowitz, Paul D., US Deputy Secretary of Defense, with General Richard B. Myers (2001): 'Brief on QDR Update', Wednesday, 8 August 2001, http://www.defenselink.mil/news/Aug 2001/t08082001_t0808dsd.htm

Woods, Ngaire (2000): 'The Political Economy of Globalization', in Ngaire Woods (ed.), *The Political Economy of Globalization*, Basingstoke: Macmillan, 1–19

Wriggins, W. Howard (1992) (ed.): *Dynamics of Regional Politics: Four Systems on the Indian Ocean Rim*, New York: Columbia University Press

Wu, Xinbo (1998): 'China: Security Practice for a Modernizing and Ascending Power', in Alagappa 1998, 115–56

Wyatt-Walter, Andrew (1995): 'Regionalism, Globalism, and World Economic Order', in Fawcett and Hurrell 1995, 74–121

Yapp, M. E. (1991): *The Near East Since the First World War*, London: Longman

Yu, Chung-hsun (1996): 'Unification of the Asian Economics [sic] and Japan: With a Special Look at the Role by the Ethnic Chinese Economies', *Dokkyo International Review* 9: 217–37

Yu, Peter Kien-hong (1996): 'Chinese Re-unification: Opening a Window of Opportunity', *Security Dialogue* 27 (4): 475–84

Zagorski, Paul W. (1992): *Democracy vs. National Security: Civil–Military Relations in Latin America*, Boulder, CO, and London: Lynne Rienner

Zakaria, Fareed (1998): *From Wealth to Power: The Unusual Origins of America's World Role*, Princeton: Princeton University Press

Zanders, Jean Pascal (1997): *Evolving Global and Regional Approaches to Arms Control and Security Mechanisms*, Alexandria, VA: Draft Paper prepared for the SIPRI Middle East Security and Arms Control Project, 23–25 February (1999): *Security Through Universality. Some Fundamentals Underlying Article X of the Biological and Toxin Weapons Convention*, http://www.fas.org/ahead/zanders.htm

Zangl, B., and M. Zürn (1999): 'The Effects of Denationalisation on Security in the OECD World', *Global Society* 13 (2): 139–63

Zartman, I. William (1995) (ed.): *Collapsed States: The Disintegration and Restoration of Legitimate Authority*, Boulder, CO: Lynne Rienner

Zelikow, Philip (1992): 'The New Concert of Europe', *Survival* 34 (2): 12–30

Zha, Daojiong (2000): *Writing Security in the South China Sea*, Los Angeles: Paper presented at the International Studies Association Conference, March

Zhang, Yongjin (1998): *China in International Society Since 1949: Alienation and Beyond*, Basingstoke: Macmillan

Zhao, Suisheng (1999): 'China's Periphery Policy and Its Asian Neighbors', *Security Dialogue* 30 (2): 335–47

Žižek, Slavoj (2000): *The Fragile Absolute – or, Why Is the Christian Legacy Worth Fighting For?*, London and New York: Verso

Zysman, John, and Wayne Sandholtz (1989): '1992: Recasting the European Bargain', *World Politics* 42: 95–128

News media

Articles also from newspapers and internet news services have as far as possible been listed by their individual author, but anonymous articles from an agency are cited simply by reference to the publication, date, and page. Given the global coverage of the book, some of these news services are likely to be unfamiliar to some readers or ambiguous because there are several organs called, for example, *Monitor*. All news sources cited in this general way are therefore listed here with place of publication and a web address. This does not always mean that the articles can be accessed (for free) from the web page, but it is a way to locate the publication in question, even if only paper archives exist.

AFP. Paris, France. Available at: www.afp.com/english/home.
BBC. London, UK. Available at: www.bbc.co.uk.
BusinessWeek online. USA. Available at: www.businessweek.com.
Central Asia Caucasus Analyst. Washington, DC. Available at: http://www.cacianalyst.org/.
Central Asia Monitor. Benson, VT, USA. Available at: http://www.chalidze.com/cam.htm.
Christian Science Monitor. Boston, USA. Available at: www.csmonitor.com.
CNN. Atlanta, GA, USA. Available at: www.cnn.com.
dpa, Deutsche Presse-Agentur. Hamburg, Germany. Available at: http://www.dpa.de.
Economist. London, UK. Availabe at: www.economist.com.
Interfax Information Services. Prague, Czech Republic. Available at: www.interfax-news.com.
International Herald Tribune. New York and Washington, DC. Available at: www.iht.com.
Los Angeles Times. Los Angeles, CA. Available at: www.latimes.com.
Monitor. Jamestown Foundation, Washington, DC. http://www.jamestown.org.
Oilonline. Houston, TX, USA. Available at: www.oilonline.com.
RFE/RL, Radio Free Europe/Radio Liberty. Prague, Czech Republic. Available at: www.rferl.com.

News media

Stratfor, Strategic Forecasting. Austin, TX, New York, and Washington, DC. http://www.stratfor.com/.

Time. USA. Available at: www.time.com/time.

Washington Post. Washington, DC. Available at: www.washingtonpost.com.

Yeni Azerbaijan. Baku, Azerbaijan. Available at: www.yeniaz.com.

Index of names

General index

CAMBRIDGE STUDIES IN INTERNATIONAL RELATIONS